Iran and Islam

VLADIMIR MINORSKY

C. E. BOSWORTH, EDITOR

IRAN AND ISLAM

in memory of the late

VLADIMIR MINORSKY

EDINBURGH
University Press

22 George Square, Edinburgh

ISBN 0 85224 200 X

North America
Aldine Publishing Company
529 South Wabash Avenue, Chicago 60605

Library of Congress
Catalog Card Number 75-149846

Printed in Great Britain by
T. & A. Constable Ltd, Edinburgh

Preface

The fact that this is the second volume of essays in memory of the late Professor V.F. Minorsky to appear within five years of his death testifies to the fact that the dedicatee was no ordinary man and no run-of-the-mill scholar. Indeed, in both the range of his interests and the profundity of his knowledge he was the worthy successor of his compatriot, V.V. Bartold. Numerous obituaries of Minorsky have appeared in western European journals, in Russian ones and in Persian ones, of which those of Professor David M. Lang, Dr Ilya Gershevitch and the Georgian scholar O.V. Tskitishvili are especially detailed. Their existence makes it unnecessary to give more than a brief outline of Minorsky's remarkable life, which spanned almost ninety years.

He was born in the small town of Korcheva on the upper Volga near Moscow in 1877, a town which no longer exists, having been submerged beneath the Moscow Sea when the Volga was dammed to facilitate inland navigation. His studies in law and oriental languages were pursued in Moscow from 1896 to 1903. Hence although he missed the chance of studying under or with such luminaries of the St Petersburg orientalists as Baron Victor Rosen, the great Bartold and I.Kratchkovsky, he had the compensatory benefit of such teachers as A.E.Krimsky, Baron R.von Stackelberg and V.F.Miller. Moreover, his marriage in 1913 to Tatiana Shebunina, who is happily still with us in Cambridge as Mrs Minorsky, gave him a connection with another celebrated Russian family of scholars, for Mrs Minorsky is the granddaughter of the nineteenth-century orientalist and historian V.D.Smirnov.

It was service in the Russian Ministry of Foreign Affairs in Persia, Central Asia and Turkey which stimulated Minorsky's lifelong interest in the history and historical geography of the Islamic world, and in particular, of the Irano-Turkish parts of it. His work as a diplomatist, including a tour of duty in 1914 as a member of the commission delimiting the

Turco-Persian frontier, gave him a valuable practical experience of the problems of moving through a highly broken and mountainous region, from which so many conquering armies and nomadic hordes have debouched to the plains of the Fertile Crescent; it further excited his interest in a people who have not been over-noticed by orientalists and others, the Kurds. The topographical and linguistic knowledge gained from this and other travels throughout the Middle East went into a vast storehouse of information which he was able to draw upon later in life when he had embarked on the calmer waters of the scholar's life. Thus his article on 'The Turkish dialect of the Khalaj', which was published in 1940 and which connected the remnants of a Turkish-speaking people now living in northwestern Persia with a Turkish tribe known to have been nomadizing in eastern Afghanistan over a thousand years before, was based on field material gathered as far back as 1906 and 1917 and carefully conserved for use at an appropriate moment.

After the Russian Revolution, Minorsky settled in Paris, teaching at the École Nationale des Langues Vivantes Orientales and enlarging the reputation as a scholar and author which he had already acquired in pre-war days. Then in 1932 he was attracted to England by Sir E. Denison Ross, the Director of the School of Oriental Studies in London, and taught Persian studies at that School, succeeding to the Chair of Persian on Sir Denison's retirement in 1937. The evacuation of the School to Cambridge at the outbreak of the Second World War brought Professor and Mrs Minorsky to the last halting-place in their journey through life. After his retirement from the School in 1944 at the age of sixty-seven, they remained in Cambridge, residing at the house in Bateman Street so familiar to a succession of visiting scholars and students.

The thirty-odd years of his life spent in England saw Minorsky at the plenitude of his powers, his mind continuously absorbing fresh knowledge, his pen vigorous and searching till the end. As Dr Gershevitch has remarked 'Professor Minorsky's rich, long life conformed even at the last stage to a rule whose validity is all too often impaired long before death: that a creative and hard-working scholar's perceptive ability and speed of discovery progress in geometric proportion to the number of years he is given to accumulate knowledge and experience'. During the inter-war years he produced over a hundred articles for the first edition of the *Encyclopaedia of Islām*, and then a considerable number for the new edition begun after the Second World War; these, together with the stream of learned articles which he wrote for learned journals in western and eastern Europe in the three languages of English, French and Russian, and for journals in Iran in Persian also, would have sufficed to make a great reputation for any scholar.

Yet they were overshadowed in grandeur by Minorsky's full-length books and studies: by the *Ḥudud al-ʿālam* (1936), a Persian geographical text translated and accompanied by a commentary of a detail and complexity worthy of Minorsky's predecessor in these fields, Josef Markwart; by *Sharaf al-Zamān Ṭāhir Marvazi on China, the Turks and India* (1942), containing much historical and ethnographical information on the peoples of central, eastern and southern Asia; by the *Tadhkirat al-mulūk* (1943), a manual of Ṣafavid Persian administrative practice, again comprising a translation and detailed commentary; by two works on the history of the Caucasus region, one which interested Minorsky in particular, *Studies in Caucasian history* (1953) and *A history of Sharvān and Darband* (1958); by his edition and translation of a tenth-century Arab traveller, *Abū-Dulaf Misʿar ibn Muhalhil's travels in Iran (circa A.D.* 950) (1955); and by his abridged translation of Faḍlallāh b. Rūzbihān's *Ta'rīkh-i Amīnī*, a work dealing with the history of the Turkmen dynasties of the fifteenth century, a period which again had a special attraction for Minorsky. In all of these books he showed a felicitous knack of blending flashes of informed insight and well-grounded speculation with meticulously sound scholarly methods. One should certainly mention, too, as an illustration of Minorsky's deep aesthetic sensibilities (he was, amongst other interests, a great music lover and a pianist), his two books relating to Turkish and Persian art and book-production, *A catalogue of the Turkish manuscripts and miniatures in the Chester Beatty Library* (1958) and *Qāḍī Aḥmad's treatise on calligraphers and painters* (1959). Finally, there were the three volumes comprising *Four studies on the history of Central Asia*, translated by Professor and Mrs Minorsky from the Russian of V.V.Bartold (1956–8); one of these studies dates back to the end of the nineteenth century and demonstrates the enduring value of so much of Bartold's work, to which Minorsky time and time again acknowledged his debt.

Not surprisingly, honours came to Minorsky thick and fast, especially in the last two or three decades of his life. All who came into contact with him could not help becoming speedily aware of his intense love for Russia and his pride in the achievements of the Russian people. Hence the invitation from the Soviet Academy of Sciences to attend the Twenty-fifth International Congress of Orientalists held in Moscow in 1960 caused him great satisfaction. After an absence of over thirty years, he again stood on Russian soil, and was accorded a triumphant welcome in his homeland. In accordance with his wishes, the greater part of Minorsky's rich library went after his death to Leningrad, whose oriental holdings had suffered grievously during the siege of the city in the Second World War. Moreover, in the summer of 1969 Mrs Minorsky again visited Russia as guest of the Academy of Sciences and took her husband's ashes for interment in the cemetery of the historic Novodevichy monastery in Moscow, which is now exclusively reserved for outstanding scholars, artists, writers, soldiers and public servants.

Of Minorsky the man, generous appraisals have been made by his necrologists. It is a matter of regret to me personally that I only knew him during the last few years of his life, when, like so many others, I was a welcome guest in his study. He had a contempt for pretentious and inferior scholarship; but his personality was wholly genial and welcoming, and he was always ready to help others with advice and information from his rich store of information and from his prodigious memory. One feels that his death removed from us a last survivor from the heroic age of Islamic scholars.

Already within his own lifetime the University of Tehran published a volume containing a selection of the articles to which Minorsky attached special value, *Iranica, twenty articles* (1964). This also contains a valuable bibliography of his writings up to 1962, although Minorsky continued writing till his death at the age of eighty-nine, and at least two articles of his have appeared posthumously. Shortly after his death in March 1966, the University of Tehran invited contributions for a memorial volume, and this appeared, edited by two of Minorsky's Persian friends, Mujtaba Minovi and Iraj Afshar, in 1969 as the *Yād-nāme-ye Irāni-ye Minorsky* (Publications of Tehran University no. 1241). Nevertheless, the invitations to contribute to this volume had stipulated a maximum length of six pages only, and it seemed to myself and to another old friend and admirer of Professor Minorsky, M. Jean Aubin of the École Pratique des Hautes Études in Paris, that there was room for a second memorial volume in which there would be no restriction on space and in which contributors could accordingly spread themselves as much as their subject demanded. M. Aubin and I met in Paris to discuss the project, and it was agreed that I would look after the British and American side and he the continental one. At a subsequent stage, M. Aubin felt that the response which he had elicited from continental scholars did not honestly justify his further participation in the editorial work, and he insisted on withdrawing from the task. I am nevertheless very obliged to him for his preliminary work and, indeed, for his part in conceiving this book in the first place.

The Edinburgh University Press, whose interest in books dealing with the Middle East and Africa has been prominent over the last few years, offered to publish the volume. I have been deeply sensible of the help of the Secretary of the Press, Mr A.R.Turnbull, and of the Press Editor, Miss P.K.Duncan, in what has been a complicated piece of book production. At an early stage in publication, the kind intermediacy of Mr Peter Avery secured from the Board of Iranian Oil Participants Ltd a generous subvention towards the heavy cost of publishing a 600-page volume. I am most grateful to the Board for this enlightened act of patronage, a demonstration of their interest in the culture and history of Iran as a whole and not merely in its economic potentialities.

The passing of time between the ingathering of contributions and actual publication has removed from our midst two contributors, Professor Joseph Schacht and Dr S.M.Stern; Professor W.B. Henning unfortunately died before his promised contribution could be written; and a contribution submitted shortly before his death by Professor A.J. Arberry could regrettably not be used on technical printing grounds. Finally, it should be noted that difficulties arose at the page proof stage of publication owing to a postal strike in Britain. No proofs could be sent out to overseas contributors, and these proofs, together with those of some British ones, had to be read by myself and the Press Editor.

C.E.BOSWORTH
Manchester, 16 March 1971

List of Contents

Principal Abbreviations Employed

ABAW	Abhandlungen der bayrischen Akademie der Wissenschaften
AO, Acta Or.	Acta Orientalia
AHM	I. Gershevitch, *The Avestan hymn to Mithra*
AION-L	Annali dell' Istituto Universitario Orientale di Napoli, Sezione linguistica
APAW	Abhandlungen der preussischen Akademie der Wissenschaften
BGA	Bibliotheca Geographorum Arabicorum
BSL	Bulletin de la Société Linguistique de Paris
BSO[A]S	Bulletin of the School of Oriental [and African] Studies
CAJ	Central Asiatic Journal
CSCO	Corpus Scriptorum Christianorum Orientalium
EI^1	Encyclopaedia of Islām, 1st edition
EI^2	Encyclopaedia of Islām, 2nd edition
EVP	G. Morgenstierne, *An etymological vocabulary of Pashto*
GAL	C. Brockelmann, *Geschichte der arabischen Literatur*
GIP	Grundriss der iranische Philologie
GMS	Gibb Memorial Series
GOR	J. von Hammer, *Geschichte des osmanischen Reiches*
IF	Indo-germanische Forschungen
IIFL	G. Morgenstierne, *Indo-Iranian frontier languages*
JA	Journal Asiatique
JAOS	Journal of the American Oriental Society
JRAS	Journal of the Royal Asiatic Society
JRCAS	Journal of the Royal Central Asian Society
Mém. DAFA	Mémoires de la délégation archéologique française en Afghanistan
MSS	Münchener Studien für Sprachwissenschaft

NED	A new English dictionary on histori principles = The Oxford English dictionary
NTS	Norsk Tidsskrift for Sprogvidenska
ʿOM	Bursalı Meḥmet Ṭāhir, ʿ*Osmanlı mi lifleri*
RSO	Rivista degli studi orientali
TD	Tarih dergisi
TOEM	Tārīkh-i ʿos̱mānī enjümen mejmūʿ
TPS	Transactions of the Philological S iety
WZKM	Wiener Zeitschrift für die Kunde s Morgenlandes
ZDMG	Zeitschrift der deutschen morgen ndischen Gesellschaft
ZII	Zeitschrift für Iranistik und Indo gie

AZIZ AHMAD

The Formation of *Sabk-i Hindī*

The problem to be faced eventually in any determination of the characteristics and nature of the *Sabk-i Hindī* is one of its scope and extent. The question is: should the term be applied exclusively to the highly complex intellectualized style of verse, especially *ghazal* written in India from the sixteenth to the eighteenth century, from ʿUrfī to Bīdil, a definition of it attempted and a quest into its origins undertaken; or whether practically the entire corpus of Indo-Persian poetry be regarded as an indivisible unit, though of course, with diversity in its unity.

So far the former view has been generally held. It originates most probably with Wālih Dāghistānī who defines the *Sabk-i Hindī* as arising in the sixteenth century with ʿUrfī Shīrāzī under the influence of Fighānī Shīrāzī.[1] ʿAbd al-Bāqī Khān attributed a 'new style' to the Indian followers of Fighānī.[2] In India Ghālib accepted this view and traced the origin of the two streams of Persian verse written in India, one represented by Ẓuhūrī who wrote in the Deccan in the court of Bijāpūr, and the other by Ṣā'ib[3] who migrated to north India from Tabrīz in the seventeenth century, to the example and inspiration of Fighānī.[4] Shiblī does not commit himself definitely to this view, but follows it in the structure of the third volume of his *Shiʿr al-ʿAjam* which begins with Fighānī and ends with Kalīm Hamadānī, but also includes Fayḍī[5] who cannot be regarded as a follower of Fighānī.

Soviet and East European orientalism which is considerably attached to ʿAlī Shīr Nawā'ī, traces the 'Indian style' to his influence and that of Jāmī[6] and the poets of the court of Sulṭān Ḥusayn Bayqara at Harāt.[7] E.E. Bertels rejects the Fighānian theory and adds a sociological view that the 'Indian style' was conditioned by social and economic circumstances rather than national or geographical factors.[8]

Hardly any significant work has been done in the West on Indo-Persian poetry. Browne deals with individual Indo-Persian poets but not with Indo-Persian poetry as a whole. It is interesting to note that in treating ʿUrfī and Fayḍī together, Browne does no more than, in the wake of Shiblī, merely mention the Fighānian influence; and Browne, like Shiblī, sees little difference between the 'Fighānian' ʿUrfī[9] and the more indigenous Fayḍī.[10] Ḍiyā Pāsha whom Browne has quoted with approval regards ʿUrfī and Fayḍī as under the same rein or neck to neck (*ham-ʿinān*) and underlines the differences between them as individual characteristics of the content of their verse, rather than sharp stylistic features denoting separate ('Fighānian' or non-Fighānian) schools.[11] In his treatment of Naẓīrī, Ẓuhūrī, Ṭālib, Ṣā'ib and Kalīm,[12] Browne has very largely drawn upon Shiblī without any significant contribution by himself, with the exception of four pages dealing with the attraction of India during the Mughal period felt by the Safawid poets of Persia.[13] Rypka has only four pages dealing with Indo-Persian poets from ʿUrfī to Bīdil in his history of Persian literature.[14] Bausani is the only Western scholar who has made some special study of the 'Indian style', but instead of determining its frontiers, he concerns himself, on the basis of the conclusions of Mirzoev and Bertels, exclusively with an analytical definition of the 'Indian style'.[15] He has also written a brief and interesting survey of the entire range of Indo-Persian poetry.[16]

Persian scholars, on the other hand, generally regard the entire corpus of Indo-Persian poetry as representing a single school. This view is expressed by Luṭf ʿAlī Āzar who prefers a simple, regional classification.[17] Rashīd Yāsimī further simplifies the analysis by stating that 'the Persian verse twisted upon itself and became the Indian School'. In Pakistan Shaykh Muḥammad Ikrām, though he takes some cognizance of the 'Fighānian' theory, deals with the entire range of Persian verse written in India as a single unit.[18] The writer of this article has also argued that the term and definition *Sabk-i Hindī* is applicable to certain trends that distinguish almost the entire range of Indo-Persian poetry, and not specifically or exclusively to a group of poets whose work is tinged by 'Nawā'-ian' or 'Fighānian' influences.[19]

An analytical study of the formative trends of the Indo-Persian poetry would reveal it as a continuous unity in which elements that penetrated in the fifteenth century from the court of Sulṭān Ḥusayn Bayqara and in the sixteenth century received the intellectualizing stimulus of the example of Fighānī, constitute phases of deepening ingredients of a basis that was there almost from the beginning.

Indo-Persian poetry originated at the Ghaznawid court at Lahore with

Abū ʿAbdullāh Rūzbih ibn ʿAbdullāh al-Nakatī (or Nakhatī) al-Lāhawrī who was a court poet of Masʿūd (d. 1040).[20] Nakatī's verse continues the tradition of the earlier poets of the court of Ghazna Manūchihri, ʿAsjadī and ʿUnṣurī in the *ghazal*, but one sees in his work, occasionally, as in his description of a mangonel,[21] the beginning of a trend towards complicated and 'unexpected' imagery which was to develop later as one of the principal features of the *Sabk-i Hindī*.

Abu'l Faraj b. Masʿūd al-Rūnī (d. 1091?),[22] the court poet of Ibrāhīm b. Masʿūd (1059–99) at Lahore, the first of the Indo-Persian poets whose *dīwān* has survived, shows much more affinity with the later Khurāsānī school than the subsequent development of the Indian. It is not surprising that Anwarī imitated his style in his *qaṣīdas* and paid him tribute.[23] ʿUrfī considers Rūnī and Anwarī as poets of very nearly equal merit.[24]

Rūnī's rival and contemporary Masʿūd Saʿd Salmān, on the other hand, makes a significant contribution towards the beginning of the 'Indian' school. Though born at Hamadān, he was very attached to Lāhawr, and this attachment leads to the foundations of a regionalization of style.[25] ʿAwfī[26] and Amīr Khusraw[27] credit him also with a *dīwān* in *Hindawī* (pre-Urdu), a statement which has been contested by Rashīd Yāsimī.[28] Masʿūd Saʿd Salmān has two styles. One of these is the plain one on which the traditional, simpler stream of Indo-Persian poetry is based. Some of this plain verse is emotionally quite intense as in the poems protesting against his imprisonment during the reign of Ibrāhīm b. Masʿūd; while the greater part of it finds straightforward expression in his *qaṣīdas* and *ghazals*. But his second style is closer to the later intellectualized *Sabk-i Hindī* in its efforts to create difficulties of expression for itself. A remarkable piece of this later genre is, for instance, one of his *qaṣīdas*[29] which avoids the use of *bā* (ب) and *mīm* (م) in the alphabet with the aim and result that when reciting it the two lips never meet. The rhythm and vocabulary of its opening line forecast the future 'Indian style'.

A later Ghaznawid poet Abū Bakr b. Muḥammad b. ʿAlī al-Rūḥānī who wrote in the court of Bahrām Shāh (1118–54) has recourse to fanciful enigma in his description of a pen.[30] His contemporary Muḥammad b. ʿUthmān al-ʿUtbī al-Yamīnī uses intricate and fantastic imagery with closely similar words in quarter-lines to evolve a pattern of verbal music.[31] Other later Ghaznawid poets of Lāhawr like ʿAbharī, Masʿūd al-Nūkī and Ismāʿīl b. Ibrāhīm use a much simpler style.

The Ghaznawid court at Lāhawr can thus be viewed as a melting-pot of Persian verse in which on the one hand the comparatively straightforward stylistic tradition is maintained by Rūnī and a number of his minor successors; while on the other, difficult and complex experiments are made by Masʿūd Saʿd Salmān, Rūḥānī and others developing the more fanciful features of the *Sabk-i Hindī*.

Compared to the Ghaznawid Lāhawr a new trend develops under the Delhi Sultanate in the Persian spoken and written in India. It forges ties of greater affinity with the idiom and expression of Khurāsān; and is already distinguishable from Persian as spoken and written in Persia. By the time of Amīr Khusraw (1253–1324) this division is so marked that though he shows influences of Anwarī and Kamāl Iṣfahānī in his earlier, and of Niẓāmī in his later work, theoretically he rejects the Persian school of Persian poetry and commends the Khurāsānī. His views scattered in the *Dībācha-i Ghurrat al-kamāl*[32] have been succinctly summed up by Waḥīd Mīrzā:

> 'Similarly, the Persian language, although of course, its original home was Persia, had lost its purity of idiom everywhere except in Māwāraunnahr, the language of that poetry being like that of India. . . . But the Persian tongue in India from the river Sind to the sea-shore is one and invariable. When we possess such uniformity of idiom, it is but natural that our poetry is great. This Persian of ours is, moreover, the original and pure Persian. The Hindui tongue, no doubt, varies greatly in different parts of the country, but Persian is the same throughout its length and breadth, and it is pronounced as it is written.'[33]

It was most probably in this period that the use of *maʿrūf yā* (ی) and *wāw* (و) was standardized and the spoken Persian of India came to differ phonetically a great deal from the Persian of Persia.

Early poets of the Delhi Sultanate like Fakhr al-dīn ʿAmīd Sannāmī or Jamāl al-dīn Hānswī were journeymen in verse. Some of them were of indigenous origin; others came from Central Asia driven by the Mongol conquest from their homelands. No stylistic evolution took place until the advent of Amīr Khusraw, in whose verse the Indo-Persian poetry touched its highest qualitative, though by no means stylistic watermark.

There was a natural lyricism inherent in Khusraw's poetic genius which ignored the quaint, the complicated and the fanciful in his *ghazals*. Characteristics of the later highly intellectualized *Sabk-i Hindī* are therefore difficult to trace in Khusraw's *ghazals*, even in his *qaṣīdas*. But the 'cerebralism' (if one may borrow Bausani's expression), so characteristic of the Indian style is present structurally in some of Khusraw's *mathnawīs*, especially in the *Nuh Sipihr*.[34] There the content-arrangement, the mosaic of interspersed *ghazals*, the out-of-the-way imagery, the use of mathematical exactitudes to prove an argument, and the use of artifice in the construction of the narrative itself are charged with high, but forced, intellectuality.

The next landmark in the development of the *Sabk-i Hindī* is the work and style of Badr-i Chāch[35] who had migrated from Chāch or Shāsh (modern Tashkent) to the court of Muḥammad b. Tughluq (1325–51). In this court Badr-i Chāch found himself in his element. Muḥammad b. Tughluq's erudite curiosity, his promotion of rationalism in religion, his interest in other religions and philosophies of India had charged the atmosphere with an intellectual dynamism which is represented in Persian poetry by Badr-i Chāch who imported trends of Khurāsānian intellectualism in the Indian style, and by Ḍiyā al-dīn Nakhshabī who translated his *Ṭūṭī Nāma*[36] from Sanskrit, deepening the trend of regionalization in the Indo-Persian verse though contributing little to the development of its style. For this development Badr-i Chāch's was the key-figure. Most of the verbal complexities, coining of multiple expressions which are intellectual crossword puzzles, and other characteristics which are generally attributed to the post-Fighānian period are present in an intense and abstruse form in his *qaṣīdas*. With the exception of Bīdil, no other Indo-Persian poet subjected his work to such intellectual gymnastics.

Determination of the extent of Badr-i Chāch's influence on the Indo-Persian poetry is difficult. He was too difficult to be imitable. But his work was prescribed in the school curricula from the fifteenth century and continued to be prescribed until the twentieth. While interest in him can be traced in the post-Fighānian poets of the sixteenth century, in the later fourteenth and the fifteenth centuries the trends of simplification prevailed, owing to a number of causes. One of these was the Ṣūfī use of simpler expression for the sake of intelligibility and transmission of the ecstatic to the mind of the lesser élite. Another reason must have been a check in the flow of immigrants from Central Asia during the reigns of Tīmūr and Shāh Rukh when patronage was available at Samarqand, while northern India was passing through a phase of chaotic instability.

The principal poet of this period was Ḥāmid b. Faḍl-Allāh Jamālī (d. 1536)[37] who travelled extensively in the Dār al-Islām and met Jāmī and Wā'iẓ Kāshifī, though not Nawā'ī at Harāt. If here we turn again to the theories of Nawā'ī's influence on the *Sabk-i Hindī* propounded by Mirzoev and Bertels, we shall see that it could have reached India through two possible channels; either through Jamālī who was the only contact between the schools of Harāt and India, or later through Bābur and his entourage. The latter we shall examine presently; but in so far as Jamālī is concerned, there could hardly be anything more different than his own verse from that of the school of Harāt, and the possibility of any transmission of Nawā'ī's influence through him cannot be considered seriously. Jamālī's verse is plain, often verging on the prosaic, relying on comprehensive statement in the indigenous Ṣūfistic tradition, and shows no trace of the complex intellectuality which was in the process of evolution to form the Indian style.

While Jamālī was writing, the Persian language was going through another transformation in India. Under Sikandar Lodī (1489–1517) Persian had been made the language also of the lower administration replacing various Hindi dialects, with the result that Hindus had begun in large numbers to learn Persian and were fertilizing the Persian idiom with unfamiliar modes of expression. This new linguistic trend did not change the nature of Persian spoken and written in India as has been suggested[38]; but it certainly meant a step further in the direction of the regionalization of the Indo-Persian.

This was the situation when Bābur[39] brought to India a tradition of Turkish poetry which was modelled on Nawā'ī; while the Persian poets of his entourage had close affinities with the school of Harāt. In so far as the Turkish poetry of Bābur[40] and Bayrām Khān[41] is concerned, it is almost integrally in the tradition of the school of Harāt. The Persian poetry written by Bayrām Khān and Humāyūn[42] carries this stamp to a lesser degree. But during the age of Humāyūn (1530–56) and Akbar (1556–1605) Jāmī's verse was popular in India and his poetic expression made no less a mark on the Persian verse written during the Mughal period, than did his mystic illumination. All the same the example and inspiration of the school of Harāt was one of the several formative elements of the *Sabk-i Hindī*, and not the only or the principal one as Bertels and Mirzoev suggest.

During the reign of Akbar the Fighānian style was introduced in India by 'Urfī Shīrāzī. Compared to him Fayḍī represents the other traditional stream of the Indo-Persian poetry. Both these styles are highly intellectualized, both tend to be complex, ornate and difficult. Both were guided by a common critical stimulus traceable to Ḥakīm Abū-l-Fat'ḥ Gīlānī to raise poetry to the level of a difficult art. As the present writer has analyzed elsewhere 'the two streams jointly–and neither of them separately–constitute the "Indian style" of sixteenth and seventeenth centuries; concentrating on parallel statement, partly imagery, partly the imaged which is either atomistic experience or mere convention; on imagic argument (*mithāliyya*) as developed by Ghanī, Ṣā'ib and Kalīm,[43] on complex conceit . . . arising out of economy of expression and telescoping into a single image a variety of emotional states; on "cerebral" artifice in pushing familiar images to unfamiliar and unexpected lengths[44]; and on the creation of synthetic poetic diction in which a whole phrase constitutes a single image.'[45]

This complex Indian style was isolated from Persia but not from the Muslim world in general. As Gibb reminds us, after Jāmī, 'Urfī and Fayḍī were the chief Persian influences on the Ottoman Turkish poetry.[46] 'Urfī's influence is traceable in Nefi'ī, and there are quite a few 'Urfī manuscripts in the libraries of Istanbul and Ankara.[47]

Returning to the characteristics and the final emergence of the *Sabk-i Hindī* in Akbar's age, there are local undercurrents which cannot be ignored. Almost all the poets of Akbar's court including Qāsim Kāhī[48] and Wuqū'ī Nīshāpūrī were erudite scholars. Some like Nāmī and Tashbīhī held eclectic views which transpose the Ṣūfistic doctrine of 'peace with all' (*ṣulḥ-i kull*) on Akbar's heretical syncretism. This eclecticism essentially widened the intellectual horizon which in turn influenced the style. Ghazzālī Mashhadī had already been notorious for his heretical views before he migrated to India.[49] Ja'far Beg, a minor poet, was a member of Akbar's *Dīn-i Ilāhī* sect[50]; while Tashbīhī Kāshānī propagated the Emperor's heretical views.[51] Wuqū'ī Nīshāpūrī believed in the transmigration of souls.[52] Abtarī Badakhshānī adhered to Ibn al-'Arabī's pantheistic doctrines while Thānā'ī Harwī was inclined towards the Nuqṭawī sect.[53] Qāsim Kāhī lived in the company of Qalandars and had an active interest in esoteric Hinduism.[54] To him can be traced the beginnings of spiritual syncretism which led to the diffusion of Vedantic ideas in the poetry of Bīdil[55] in whom the *Sabk-i Hindī* reaches its culmination.

NOTES

1 Shiblī Nu'mānī, *Shi'r al-'Ajam* (Cawnpore 1920–3) III, 28.

2 Ibid., IV, 214.

3 Ṣā'ib Tabrīzī, *Kulliyyāt* (Tehran 1333 Shamsi).

4 Asad Allāh Khān Ghālib, *'Ūd-i Hindī* (Lucknow 1941) 65.

5 Fayḍī, *Kulliyyāt*. India Office Pers. MS. 269 (Ethé 1468).

6 Jāmī, *Dīwān*, ed. H. Pazhmān (Tehran n.d.).

7 Cf. A. M. Mirzoev, *Sajido Nasafi i ego mesto v istorii tadzikskoj literatury* (Stalinabad 1954) 34-56.

8 E. E. Bertels, 'K voprosu ob "indijskom stile" v persidskoj poezii', in *Charisteria Orientalia* (Prague 1956) 56-9.

9 'Urfī Shīrāzī, *Dīwān* (Lucknow 1915); *Qaṣā'id* (Lucknow 1944).

10 E. G. Browne, *A Literary History of Persia* (Cambridge 1953) IV, 241-8.

11 Quoted by Browne, IV, 242n.

12 Browne, IV, 252-65.

13 Ibid., IV, 165-8.

14 Jan Rypka, *Iranische Literaturgeschichte* (Leipzig 1959) 289-92. See also his *Dejiny perské a tádzicke literatury* (Prague 1956) 224-5.

15 Alessandro Bausani, 'Contributo a una definizione dello "stile indiano" della poesia persiana', *Annali dell' Istituto Universitario Orientale di Napoli*, N.S. VII (1958) 167-78.

16 Bausani, *Storia delle letterature del Pakistan* (Milan 1958) 65-97.

17 Luṭf ʿAlī Āzar, *Ātishkada*. India Office Persian MS. 2929 (Ethé 693).

18 S. M. Ikram, *Armaghān-i Pāk* (Karachi 1953); idem and Wahid Qureshi, *Darbār-i millī* (Lahore 1961).

19 Aziz Ahmad, *Islamic Culture in the Indian Environment* (Oxford 1964) 228-31.

20 Muḥammad ʿAwfī, *Lubāb al-albāb*, ed. Saʿīd Nafīsī (Tehran 1333 Shamsi) 290-91; Saʿīd Nafīsī's note on p. 678.

21 ʿAwfī, 291.

22 Ṣiddīq ʿAlī Khān, *Shams-i sukhan*, n.d., who does not mention his source for this date.

23 ʿAwfī, 419.

24 ʿUrfī, *Qaṣāʾid*, 8.

25 Masʿūd Saʿd Salmān, *Dīwān*, ed. Rashīd Yāsimī (Tehran 1318 Shamsi), passim; Ikram, *Armaghān-i Pāk*, 87-90.

26 ʿAwfī, 423.

27 Amīr Khusraw, *Dībachā-i Ghurrat al-kamāl* in BM Add. MS 25, 807, fo. 175a.

28 Rashīd Yāsimī, Introduction to his edition of Salmān's *Dīwān*.

29 ʿAwfī erroneously regards it as addressed to Sayf al-dawla Muḥammad b. Masʿūd (p. 426).

30 ʿAwfī, 446.

31 For instance, ʿAwfī, 450.

32 Amīr Khusraw, *Dībācha*, passim.

33 Wahid Mirza, *The Life and Works of Amīr Khusrau* (Calcutta 1935) 160-1.

34 Edited by Wahid Mirza (Calcutta 1950).

35 Badr-i Chāch, *Qaṣāʾid* (Lucknow 1884).

36 Ḍiyā al-dīn Nakhshabī, *Ṭūṭī Nāma*. India Office Persian MS. 3469 (Ethé 743).

37 Aziz Ahmad, 'Djamālī' in *EI*², II, 420-1.

38 M. J. Borah, 'The nature of the Persian language written and spoken in India during the 13th and 14th centuries', *Bulletin of the School of Oriental Studies*, VII (1933–5) 325.

39 Fuat Köprülü, 'Bābur' in *EI*², I, 847-50.

40 Bābur, *Dīwān*, ed. A. Samoilovich (*Sobranie stickotvoroney Imperatura Babura*) (Petrograd 1917); *Facsimile of Dīwān-i Babūr Bādishāh* (Calcutta 1910).

41 Bayrām Khān, *Persian and Tūrkī Dīwāns*, ed. E. Denison Ross (Calcutta 1910).

42 Hadī Hasan, 'The unique Dīwān of Humāyūn Bādshāh', *Islamic Culture*, XXV (1951) 212-76.

43 Shiblī Nuʿmānī, op. cit., III, 21, 196, 205.

44 Ibid., II, 24.

45 Aziz Ahmad, *Islamic Culture in the Indian Environment*, 230.

46 E. J. W. Gibb, *History of the Ottoman Poetry* (1900–6) I, 5, 127-9.

47 K. A. Nizami, 'Persian literature under Akbar', *Medieval India Quarterly* III/I (1957–8) 300-28.

48 Qāsim Kāhī, *Dīwān*, ed. Hadi Hasan (Aligarh n.d.).

49 ʿAbd al-Qādir Badāʾūnī, *Muntakhab al-tawārīkh*, Bibl. Ind. (Calcutta 1868–9) II, 170.

50 Abu'l Faḍl ʿAllāmī, *Āʾīn-i Akbarī* (Eng. tr. H. Bochmann) I, 636-7.

51 Badāʾūnī, III, 204.

52 Ibid., III, 378-9.

53 ʿAllāmī (Blochmann), I, 502-4, 531-2; Badāʾūnī, III, 188, 204-7.

54 Badāʾūnī, III, 173.

55 ʿAbd al-Qādir Bīdil, *Dīwān* (Cawnpore 1914); for studies of Bīdil see Khwāja ʿIbād-Allāh *Akhtar*, *Bīdil* (Lahore 1952); A. Bausani, 'Note su Mirza Bedil', *Annali dell'Istituto Universitario di Napoli*, N.S. VI (1957) 163-91.

JEAN AUBIN

Les Relations Diplomatiques entre les Aq-qoyunlu et les Bahmanides

En raison de l'importance de l'élément persan au Deccan, les Bahmanides ont entretenu des relations suivies avec les Etats iraniens, en particulier lorsque le célèbre marchand gīlānī Maḥmūd Gāwān eut accédé au vizirat. La correspondance que la cour bahmanide entretient alors avec la cour Aq-qoyunlu aide à saisir l'intensité des échanges indo-persans dans la seconde moitié du XVe siècle. Tant pour l'histoire sociale que pour l'histoire économique ces échanges sont un des traits majeurs de l'époque turkmène, dont Minorsky a montré quelles perspectives elle ouvrait aux historiens.

En février 1472 Maḥmūd Gāwān se félicitait, dans une lettre à un prince du Gīlān, de ce que Uzun Ḥasan soit en train de nettoyer les routes iraniennes pour permettre les déplacements des émissaires et l'envoi de présents.[1] En avril 1474 l'envoyé vénitien à Tabriz, Barbaro, assistait à la réception de deux ambassadeurs d'un prince musulman de l'Inde; entre autres richesses, ils apportaient au souverain Aq-qoyunlu deux éléphants, une girafe et trois perroquets.[2] A une date indéterminée, mais entre 1473 et 1477, deux envoyés bahmanides, Khwāja Shams al-Dīn Muḥammad Shīrwānī et Maulānā Muḥammad-i Aḥmad Khunjī, étaient dépêchés à Uzun Ḥasan.[3] Les identifier aux deux personnages qu'a rencontrés Barbaro n'est pas interdit. Toutefois, la vraisemblance enseigne que les contacts diplomatiques entre l'Inde et Uzun Ḥasan n'ont pas été limités à cette unique mission. Les deux envoyés bahmanides n' accompagnaient-ils pas un agent Aq-qoyunlu au Deccan, Khwāja Jalāl al-Dīn Luṭfullah Tarkhān, marchand lié avec les milieux gīlānīs, et dont nous savons par ailleurs qu'il était un ami du prince de Rasht[4]? Ce marchand semble s'être trouvé en Inde en 881/1476–7. Il demeure entendu qu'il a pu venir au Deccan antérieurement à la date où le hasard de la documentation nous fait connaître un de ses voyages. Il est communément appelé Khwāja Tarkhān,[5] ce qui indique qu'il était un 'marchand du roi', appartenant à cette catégorie de négociants exonérés de toutes taxes qui faisaient des affaires pour le compte de la cour, et qu'il devait donc beaucoup se déplacer. Le diplôme de 881 H. grâce auquel on peut inférer sa présence en Inde, exonère précisément de tous droits dans les provinces et les ports bahmanides Khwāja Ḥājī Shihāb al-Dīn Luṭfullah Tarkhān.[6] La différence de *laqab* constitue, à notre avis, un obstacle tout à fait mineur à son identité avec le Luṭfullah Tarkhān ci-dessus mentionné.

La politique fiscale de Khalīl Sulṭān b. Uzun Ḥasan, gouverneur du Fārs de 875/1470–1 à 882/1478, provoqua dans cette province un mécontentement sérieux. 'Lors du troisième hiver qu'il passa à Tabriz', Uzun Ḥasan, assailli de réclamations par les notables de Shiraz, leur expédia un personnage très influent à la cour Aq-qoyunlu, Ibrahīm Gülshenī. Gülshenī adressa d'énergiques remontrances à Khalīl Sulṭān.[7]

Les doléances des notables du Fārs ont trouvé écho dans une lettre de Maḥmūd Gāwān. A la demande d'un certain Maulānā Jalāl al-Dīn Fālī il écrit au souverain Aq-qoyunlu pour lui exposer la situation de ce notable:

> 'C'est un savant de mérite. Depuis des temps anciens les fonctions de *mudarris*, de *muftī*, de *ḥāfiẓ* et la charge de *qāḍī* ont été illustrées dans sa famille avec le soutien des sultans passés qui furent gouverneurs de cette province et de ses territoires. Dans le temps présent, à cause de l'abondance des impositions et du *kharāj* et des impôts sur les biens, tels que . . .,[8] taxe sur le bétail (*mawāshi*), taxe sur les palmiers (*nakhīlāt*), dont le revenu assure ses moyens d'existence, les bureaux du vizirat de Shīrāz l'accablent. (...) Depuis l'époque des Turkmènes [*sic*] jusqu'à maintenant la situation dudit Maulānā et des autres *mawālī* ne vous a pas été rapportée. Je vous prie d'abolir la tyrannie qui pèse sur lui et sur sa famille (*aqārib*), et même que ce qui est porté à son nom sur le rôle du fisc (*daftar-i dīwān*), tel que *kharāj* et choses semblables, soit abrogé (*ba minqasha-yi ʿafw maḥw gardad*) ou que le fardeau du *ẓiyādatī* soit écarté de son cou, et que le susdit Maulānā Jalāl al-Dīn soit distingué entre les gens de sa qualité par un accroissement de bienveillance et de ses moyens d'existence (*wajh-i mashīʿatī*), de sorte que cela procure la solidité à votre pouvoir (*tā maujib-i thabāt-i khilāfat-i abad-paywand gardad*).'

Le document, que nous connaissons par une copie figurant dans un recueil épistolaire,[9] ne comporte ni date ni adresse. Le destinataire peut donc être soit Uzun Ḥasan soit son fils Khalīl Sulṭān, soit même Yaʿqūb Beg.

Il faut peut-être voir une autre trace de l'insatisfaction persistante qu'entretenait l'administration Aq-qoyunlu en Fārs dans la célérité avec laquelle Yaʿqūb Beg confirma les privilèges fiscaux des *shaikh* Abū Najmī de Khunj, en septembre 1478, six semaines seulement après son triomphe sur Khalīl Sulṭān.[10] On remarquera que Yaʿqūb Beg ne confirmera qu'en juin 1479 les privilèges des *naqīb* Ḥusainī d'Ispahan, et en novembre 1479 ceux des *naqīb* Riḍawī de Qum,[11] deux familles dont l'influence sociale était grande en Iran central. Il est vrai que le renouvellement des diplômes dépendait de l'initiative du demandeur. La date du firman en faveur de Khunj montre du moins que Yaʿqūb Beg ne fit pas attendre sa décision.

Le Fārs méridional, qui entretenait des liens au moins aussi étroits avec le Deccan bahmanide qu'avec l'Iran intérieur, souffrit des projets du gouverneur nommé en Fārs par Yaʿqūb Beg, Ṣūfī Khalīl Mauṣillu. Du Garmsīr et de Jarūn les plaintes contre ses exactions affluaient à la cour.[12] Si l'on en croit Faḍlullah b. Rūzbihān, tel que l'a traduit Minorsky, il ne visait pas moins qu' à la conquête de l'Inde: 'Khalil even intended to conquer India (Hind) and, to this effect, now prepared ships and now built strongholds on the coast of Fars'. La traduction littérale est un peu différente: 'Il se fixa comme but la conquête des ports de l'Inde (*furaḍ al-Hind*); tantôt il construisait des bateaux pour mener des troupes et faire passer des armées (*junūd*) au pays des Indiens (*bilād-i Hunūd*), tantôt il élevait de puissants châteaux-forts sur les côtes du Fārs pour y établir des garnisons'. Cette phrase, bien que recherchée, est sans équivoque. Elle ne signifie pas que Ṣūfī Khalīl ait eu le projet démesuré de traverser la mer d'Arabie pour débarquer en Inde, et le 'even' ajouté par Minorsky dans sa traduction abrégée est trompeur. L'expression 'port de l'Inde' s'entend, non pas des ports qui se trouvent sur la côte de l'Inde, mais des ports qui trafiquent avec l'Inde, et dans ce sens-là elle est souvent appliquée à Ormuz. C'est Jarūn et les ports du royaume d'Ormuz qu'elle désigne ici, comme le contexte porte d'ailleurs à le comprendre. Faḍlullah, il est vrai, ajoute que Ṣūfī Khalīl voulait débarquer des troupes au *bilād-i Hunūd*; mais le terme vient ici en allitération de *junūd*, ce qui motive en partie sa présence, l'intention sarcastique de l'auteur suffisant au reste à l'expliquer.

La tentative de Ṣūfī Khalīl d'envahir le royaume d'Ormuz échoua. Faute d'embarcations, il ne put franchir le bras de mer séparant Jarūn du continent.[13] Son action contre Ormuz lui avait valu d'abord une lettre de félicitation de Yaʿqūb Beg, que nous transmet le recueil épistolaire de Idrīs Bidlīsī, secrétaire du divan Aq-qoyunlu avant son émigration en Turquie, et dans laquelle les opérations sont qualifiées emphatiquement de 'conquête, victoire et capture des territoires de Jarūn' (*fatḥ wa ẓafar wa taskhīr-i bilād-i Jarūn*).[14] La pression des notables du Fārs fut cependant assez forte pour obtenir peu après, en 1486 ou 1487, son rappel en Azerbaydjan.[15] Il fut remplacé en Fars par Manṣūr Beg Pornak,[16] qui avait déjà administré la province sous Khalīl Sulṭān.[17] En 1490 un ambassadeur du roi de Jarūn et des régions maritimes (*baḥriyāt*) est signalé à la cour Aq-qoyunlu.[18]

Les relations diplomatiques de Yaʿqūb Beg avec l'Inde furent suivies. En juillet 1485 un ambassadeur 'de l'Inde' était reçu à Qazwīn.[19] Les *Munshaʾāt* de Idrīs Bidlīsī renferment deux lettres non datées, que j'attribue sous réserve à Yaʿqūb Beg, adressées au souverain du Deccan. L'une est portée par un certain Shaikh Aḥmad-i Ḥamza à Sulṭān Shams al-Dīn Muḥammad [III Bahmanī], en réponse à une mission effectuée par Khwāja Ikhtiyār al-Dīn Farīdūn,[20] personnage qu'on sait d'autre part avoir fréquenté la cour de Ghiyāth al-Dīn Muḥammad Khaljī de Mandu.[21] L'autre, destinée au '*sulṭān-i Hindūstān-i Dakan*', est confiée à Khwāja Burhān al-Dīn Khalīlullah,[22] connu par ailleurs comme émissaire de Maḥmūd Gāwān auprès du prince gīlānī Amīr Dībāj.[23]

NOTES

1 Maḥmūd Gāwān, *Riyāḍ al-inshā*, éd. Haydarabad du Deccan 1948, p. 164 (date calculée par référence à la prise de Goa).

2 Barbaro, *Travels*, trad. Hakluyt Society (1873) 53-6.

3 *Riyāḍ al-inshā*, pp. 375 et 380. Le shaikh khunjī, qui, contrairement à son compagnon de voyage shīrwānī, ne semble pas être un marchand professionnel, est appelé Muḥammad-i Aḥmad p. 375, et Aḥmad p. 380. Les lettres qui les accréditent ne sauraient avoir été rédigées qu'entre 1473 et 1477, année d'achèvement du *Riyāḍ al-inshā*.

4 *Persia in A.D. 1478–1490. An abridged translation of Faḍlullāh b. Rūzbihān Khunjī's Tārīkh-i ʿĀlam-ārā-yi Amīnī by V. Minorsky*, Royal Asiatic Society Monographs XXVI (Londres 1957) 57.

5 Cf. *Tārīkh-i ʿĀlam-ārā-yi Amīnī*, MS. B.N. Paris, Ancien fonds Persan 101, fol. 111b, lignes 20 et 23.

6 Nīmdihī, *Kanz al-maʿānī*, MS. Aşir Efendi 884, fol. 12b-14a. Sur cet ouvrage, cf. J. Aubin, dans *Revue des Etudes islamiques*, XXXIV (1966) 64-5.

7 *Menāqib-i Sheykh Ibrahīm Gülshenī*, MS. obligeamment prêté par M. Tahsin Yazıcı, fol. 12b-13b, 22a. Pour la biographie de Gülshenī, cf. *EI*², art. 'Gulshanī' (Yazıcı).

8 Mot non lu.

9 Nīmdihī, *Kanz al-maʿānī*, fol. 18a-19a.

10 Sur ce document et sur les Abū Najmī, cf. J. Aubin, dans *Iran*, VII (1969) 31.

11 Cf. *Mélanges Massignon*, I (Damas 1956), 129 et 137.

12 Faḍlullāh b. Rūzbihān, trad. Minorsky, 54.

13 Pedro Teixeira, *Relaciones d'el origen, descendencia y succession de los reyes de Persia, y de Harmuz* (Anvers 1610) *11, 43; trad. Sinclair-Ferguson, *The Travels of Pedro Teixeira*, éd. Hakluyt Society (Londres 1902) 189. Le vers persan cité par Teixeira a été restitué par ʿAbbās Eghbal, *Muṭālaʿātī dar bāb-i Bahrain wa jazāyir wa sawāhil-i khalīj-i Fārs* (Téhéran 1327 s.) 48 (ainsi que par A. Faroughy, *Histoire du royaume de Hormuz*, 50). Tate a nié sans aucun argument, dans le *JRAS* de 1903, 817-20, le bien-fondé de l'information de Teixeira, en avançant qu'elle se rapportait à l'attaque du prince timouride Muḥammad Sulṭān contre Ormuz en 1396.

14 Le *tarbiyat-nāma ba Ṣūfī Khalīl dar ḥain-i fatḥ-i qilāʿ-i Jarūn* est conservé dans les *Munshaʾāt* de Idrīs Bidlīsī, MS. Ayasofya 3986, fol. 48a, et dans les *Munshaʾāt* de son fils Abu'l-Faḍl Muḥammad Daftarī, MS. Istanbul Üniversite Kütüphanesi F 906, fol. 10a-10b.

15 Sur la date, cf. *Persia in A.D. 1478–1490*, 53 note 3, 54, 89, 122. Idrīs Bidlīsī reproduit le texte d'un *istimālat-nāma ba Ṣūfī Khalīl* qui, bien que non daté et dépourvu d'allusions précises, doit concerner le rappel de Ṣufī Khalīl, de qui on ne sait pas qu'il ait encouru d'autre révocation sous le règne de Yaʿqūb Beg. Cette 'lettre de réconfort' lui notifie que son rapport (*ʿarḍa-dāsht*) est parvenu au souverain et que la vérité a été connue; qu'il se rassure (*khāṭir jamʿ dārad*), il sera toujours le plus sûr appui (du souverain) (*hamwāra ḥuṣn-i ḥaṣīn wa ḥabl-i matīn ū khwāhad būd*). Le rappel du gouverneur n'est pas énoncé dans le document (*Munshaʾāt* de Idrīs Bidlīsī, MS. cité, fol. 41b, et *Munshaʾāt* de Daftarī, MS. cité, fol. 29b-30a). Il est toutefois patent que Bidlīsī nous transmet les principales pièces d'un même dossier (cf. note suivante), dont fait partie le *istimālat-nāma*.

16 Le début du diplôme de nomination de Manṣūr Beg Pornak au gouvernement du Fārs est reproduit par Idrīs Bidlīsī, *Munshaʾāt*, fol. 52a (formules stéréotypées; les instructions particulières et la date ne sont pas transcrites).

17 Nīmdihī, *Ṭabaqāt-i Maḥmūd-shāhī*, année 875.

18 *Persia in A.D. 1478–1490*, 101. Les *Menāqib-i Sheykh Ibrahīm Gülshenī*, MS. cité, fol. 40b, mentionnent à une date indéterminée l'envoi d' 'une caisse de présents et de produits rares (*tafāriq*) en provenance de Shīrāz et de Lār'.

19 G. Berchet, *La repubblica di Venezia e la Persia* (Turin 1865) pp. 151, 152.

20 Bidlīsī, *Munshaʾāt*, fol. 51b mukarrar.

21 Ḥusain Maybudī, *Munshaʾāt*, MS. Istanbul Üniversite Kütüphanesi F 584, fol. 5a-7b.

22 Bidlīsī, *Munshaʾāt*, fol. 45a-45b; Daftarī, *Munshaʾāt*, fol. 37b-41b. Cf. d'autre part une réponse de Yaʿqūb Beg au 'roi de Hind', Daftarī, fol. 32a-33a.

23 Nīmdihī, *Kanz al-maʿānī*, fol. 122a.

P. W. AVERY

An Enquiry into the Outbreak of the Second Russo-Persian War, 1826-28

Russia and Persia were again at war thirteen years after they had concluded the Treaty of Gulistan. The war ended in Persia's defeat and under the Treaty of Turkomanchai she not only had to pay a heavy indemnity, but was left in a disadvantageous position in relation to Russia until at least the year 1921.[1] A cursory view of the history of the second Perso-Russian War's outbreak leaves the blame for it mainly on Fatḥ ʿAlī Shāh (1797–1834) and his son, the Crown Prince ʿAbbās. ʿAbbās Mīrzā was the governor of Āzarbāījān. Also in command of an army there, his appointment to Tabrīz made him the guardian of Iran's north-western frontier with the Ottoman Empire and with Russia's recent acquisitions in the Caucasus and beyond the River Aras. Article 3 of the Treaty of Gulistan acknowledged Russian dominion over Georgia, Qarabāgh, Dāghistān and part of Tālish.[2]

A demand for war against Russia couched in religious terms and promulgated by Āghā Sayyid Muḥammad Iṣfahānī expressed resentment at Russia's treatment of Muslims and encroachment on Muslim Persian territory, but though this demand remains an important factor in ʿAbbās Mīrzā's decision to fight in 1826, his policy cannot be dissociated entirely from exclusively secular motives. His procrastination over agreement on the final definition of a new frontier envisaged in the treaty requires explanation. It is also possible that he was influenced less by religious pressures than by those of the military element in Fatḥ ʿAlī Shāh's court, led by his brother-in-law, Allāh Yār Khān, who was his agent with the Shāh in Tehran, besides being Prime Minister.

In 1812 at Aslandūz ʿAbbās Mīrzā had been defeated by the Russians and lost his artillery. This defeat was serious enough for observers at the time to consider any desire on his part again to try arms with such an enemy imprudent. Commentators since have found the ascription of imprudence, impetuosity even, to ʿAbbās Mīrzā incongruous, because he has been regarded by many as the hero who, had he not predeceased his father in October 1833, might have lived to become one of Iran's greatest rulers. As it is, he is still praised as one of Iran's first reformers.[3] Thus his part in leading Iran into a war which proved so disastrous to it poses a problem. It is partly the problem of the Prince's personality; his relations with his father; and his relations with his elder brother, Muḥammad 'Alī Mīrzā, who had not been named heir apparent because his mother was a concubine. The large number of Fatḥ 'Alī Shāh's male offspring[4] and the struggle for the succession to the throne anticipated on his death, were factors which influenced 'Abbas Mīrzā and were also taken into account by the Russians and the British. Several of his brothers were governors of provinces, each with his own military establishment or field of recruitment, and friends at court.

It was important for the heir apparent to expunge the shame of past military defeat; to give evidence of ability to defend Islam; and to have money, both to equip and maintain an army and to possess that visible manifestation of power which treasure confers, besides being useful in purchasing support where loyalty generally had its price. The Treaty of Gulistan by Article 4 engaged the Emperor of Russia, out of a wish that 'the Sovereign of Persia always . . . be firmly established on the throne', to assist 'the Prince who shall be nominated heir-apparent' against any opposition. This provision, however, could embarrass 'Abbās Mīrzā if Russian conduct towards Muslims in the Caucasus or the threat of further Russian encroachments on Iran rendered Russian protection odious in the eyes of those whose support he wished to enjoy in his own country, and whom he looked upon as his future subjects. The proffer of Russian assistance could be prevented from entailing complete subservience to them by recourse to the English who, though not by treaty explicitly bound to support the heir-apparent, were interested in him as Iran's future Shāh and, moreover, were bound in certain circumstances to provide money, while they did provide officers and N.C.O.s to train 'Abbās Mīrzā's new and European-style army, the *Niẓām-i-Jadīd*. It should be added that 'Abbās Mīrzā's relations with the Russians were complicated by antipathy between him and the Russian Commander-in-Chief and Governor-General in the Caucasus from 1817, General Yermolov.[5]

British involvement in Persian affairs was due to fears of an overland invasion of India. It began in 1798 with Napoleon I's correspondence with Tippu Sultan, his invasion of Egypt and being party to rumours of a projected attack on India across Central Asia in collusion with Tsar Paul. Malcolm went to Tehran in 1800 and demonstrated with gifts and specie that the British authorities in India were willing to pay danegeld, to keep Persia empty of European agents and forces inimical to India, and ultimately to support it as a bulwark in India's defence. Malcolm's treaty of 1801 became practically a dead letter after Napoleon left Egypt, and Zamān Shāh of Afghanistan's death in 1801 removed a threat to India from that quarter. The fears of Russia entertained by Iran's Qājār ruler died harder than British fears of Bonaparte in the East: neglected by the British, Fatḥ ʿAlī Shāh concluded the Treaty of Finkenstein with Napoleon in May 1807. In December, to re-awaken British concern, General Gardane reached Tehran with a military Mission, from which grew the then twenty-year-old ʿAbbās Mīrzā's desire for a modern army on the European model.[6]

In the meantime, though Gardane was secretly instructed that France would recognize the Shāh's dominion over Georgia, which was then being invaded by Russia, at Tilsit in July 1807 Napoleon allied himself with Tsar Alexander I. Persia's hopes of aid against Russia were disappointed. Fatḥ ʿAlī Shāh determined not now to treat with the 'subordinate government' of the British in India but with the sovereign government in England. The former's envoy, Malcolm, was rejected and Sir Harford Jones, from London, received in Tehran in 1808, Gardane having been dismissed.

On 12 March 1809 Sir Harford Jones concluded a Preliminary Treaty with Persia. Article 4 offered, in case any European power invaded or 'shall invade' Persia, a force or a subsidy and military stores with officers in place of it. This treaty underwent two revisions, when Sir Gore Ouseley concluded the Definitive Treaty on 14 March 1812, and James Morier and Henry Ellis a final recension on 25 November 1814–the version which governed action based on the treaty for Morier's successor, Henry Willock, who remained British Chargé d'Affaires in Iran from 1814 until the end of 1826. The 'shall invade', which implied arms or money for Persia against possibility of attack as well as in the event of it, was dropped in the Ouseley and Morier revisions. The financial alternative of a subsidy, defined as 200,000 tumans (approximately £110,000 sterling, in the value of the time)[7] annually, became, on the other hand, a prominent feature of these Anglo-Persian arrangements. The East India Company had no intention of supplying an army to protect Persia. It was readier with money, to be supplied from England.[8] A form of wording crept in which endowed the subsidy with less the character of an extraordinary payment in the event of invasion by 'any European power', and more that of a recurrent dole: it was to be paid in early 'instalments', to be accommodated to 'the Persian custom' of paying the army six months in advance.

This accommodation is interesting because it indicates 'Abbās Mīrzā's attempt to establish not only a European type of army, but one to be paid by the government as a standing force. This was an innovation; it is referred to 'Abbās Mīrzā because only he had the new army, that in view when the drafters of the treaties spoke of provision of training officers, muskets and other military stores.[9] Also interesting is the fact that by introducing the principle of payment by instalments, the British could retain an initiative and, if it was useful to do so for their purposes, tantalizingly render the subsidy to the Persians piecemeal, thus to hold them in a state of anticipation. Though the arrangement was ostensibly to ensure early payments, the instalment principle resulted in arrears, some of which were withheld.

The war with Russia ended in 1813. Payments on the subsidy were stopped only in 1821. Their cessation caused a quarrel between Fatḥ 'Alī Shāh and Henry Willock, who as a result left suddenly for England in 1822, not to return to his post till the next summer. Paradoxically it was in the autumn of 1821 that Willock had, 'anticipating the views of His Majesty's Government', attempted to purchase 'Abbās Mīrzā's acquiescence not to respond to prompting by the Russian representative, Mazarovich, at Tabrīz, to go to war with the Ottoman Empire.[10] This recourse to arrears on the subsidy was an abuse of it, because the Morier treaty had, in addition to emphasis on the treaty's 'defensive nature', explicitly repeated Ouseley's provision that the subsidy was solely for the purpose of equipping and disciplining an army.[11] Willock was in a difficult position in relation to the subsidy because a third point of interest about admitting the principle of payment by instalments was that the onus for so far as possible arranging this to coincide with the seasons of Persian army payments was placed on the British minister resident at the Shāh's court. Willock's refusal to pay more made the Shāh bully him, and send Mīrzā Ṣāliḥ Shīrāzī[12] to England with Willock, as his own envoy to the British Government.

The Morier treaty differed from its predecessors in one very important particular. While its Article 4 invested the subsidy with the nature of 'an annual subsidy' to be 'two hundred thousand (200,000) tomans annually', it for the first time made the point that it 'shall not be paid in case the war with such European nation shall have been produced by an aggression on the part of Persia'. As if to make assurance doubly sure, Article 3 defined 'the purport of the word aggression in this Treaty' as attack on another State's territories. Nevertheless, the subsidy was defined as annual not as extraordinary; and was offered by Willock to obtain 'Abbās Mīrzā's acquiescence to 'pacifick measures'.[13]

Given their notorious desire for money, Fatḥ ʿAlī Shāh and ʿAbbās Mīrzā can hardly be blamed for reading into the treaties' articles on the subsidy an invitation to make demands. They might also have decided that the British readiness to pay was proportionate to British anxiety about the Persian frontier with Russia. ʿAbbās Mīrzā, aware of this as he certainly was, and aware too that his father's parsimony was such that if Āzarbāījān were not the seat of danger, taxes and accounts from it would be required of his government, saw the possibility of his interests being served, his coffers lined and army maintained, if the situation on his frontier remained perilous.

Owing to the Morier provision about aggression, however, he had to attempt maintenance of a state of crisis without incurring an open breach with Russia in which he was the aggressor. In procrastinating over the determination of the frontier he attempted to continue the crisis. He also advertised the Russian occupation of the northern shore of Lake Gokcha as what Willock also believed it was,[14] an act of aggression. He used Russian violation, or alleged violation, of Muslim privacy and conventions as evidence of Russian aggressive tendencies towards Islam. In doing both these things, he brought about a popular excitement which in the end left him with no alternative but war, especially after rebels in Tālish against the Russians had sought his aid.[15] He needed crisis conditions to extract money from his father and from the British.[16] In connection with the latter, he must even have hoped for Russian aggression; it is difficult to agree with Willock that he incited a stirring of religious feeling with a view to forcing Fatḥ ʿAlī Shāh into war.[17] He tried to keep a precarious balance between peace and war, but nearer war than peace. Circumstances went beyond his control and he lost this balance.

This is perhaps to endue ʿAbbās Mīrzā's actions with a greater degree of consistency than they deserve. Shortly before the outbreak of war in 1826, but also before he reached the Shāh's summer camp at Sultānieh, to be influenced by Allāh Yār Khān, to encounter face to face a suspicious father, and to experience at first hand the protests of Sayyid Muḥammad Iṣfahānī and his followers, he was reported as 'dreading war'.[18] This fact should not be discounted, but there is also the, albeit retrospective, testimony of both Reza Qulī Khān Hedāyat and Muḥammad Taqī Lisānu'l-Mulk Sipihr that at the time of the conclusion of the Treaty of Gulistan, ʿAbbās Mīrzā wanted, not peace, but that the war with Russia should continue, to give him the opportunity to retrieve his defeats of 1812.[19] It seems possible, therefore, that while the Powers saw in the Treaty what its first Article declared it to be, the establishment of peace 'between the respective sovereigns and their allies for ever', ʿAbbās Mīrzā only regarded it as a temporary armistice.

The Treaty of Gulistan's Article 2 about the demarcation of new frontiers between Iran and Russia's Caucasian conquests was not, however, a very strong earnest of perpetual peace, especially in an area where religious differences and wandering tribes were possible irritants. It was the Russians who, though the victors, sued for peace,[20] and there is evidence that their then representative in the Caucasus, de Rtischeff, approached the matter in a conciliatory spirit with promise of a concessive attitude over frontier alignments left by the treaty to be settled later.[21] A reason not given by the authorities cited, for this Russian desire for conciliation, may well have been the wish to end a state of affairs in which payment of the British subsidy was justified. Impoverishment of the ruling house of Iran might make the Shāh, and his successor, more amenable.

Here it will be useful, before discussing Article 2 of the Treaty of Gulistan, to view the subsidy as it would appear to Fatḥ ʿAlī Shāh simply in terms of revenue, gained without the vexation of collection. Fraser admits that it was difficult to arrive at a precise figure for Iran's revenue in the year 1821, the year he took, but based on his estimate of a total of 2,489,000 tomans,[22] the British subsidy can be reckoned as approximately equivalent to 8 per cent of the total. It is also significant that in 1821 and 1822 Iran was suffering from a severe epidemic of cholera. This epidemic gradually spread from city to city, resulting in heavy mortality in mercantile centres. Production and provincial seats of government were thus seriously affected, with consequent dislocation of revenue collection. In any case, the subsidy was not negligible. Viewed in terms of the revenue of a productive province like Fārs, it exceeded this in its annual total by 50,000 tomans, if Fraser's estimate for Fārs, of 150,000 tomans to the Treasury after deduction of 150,000 tomans for the expenses of the provincial government, is accepted. In terms of receipts accounted a bonus offsetting provinces non-productive of revenue, the Shāh might have calculated the British payments as a substitute for revenue failures in Kirmānshāh, Khurāsān or Āzarbāījān. According to Fraser, none of these rendered anything to the Central Treasury, while Khurāsān and Āzarbāījān cost it money.[23] The last point is pertinent because for both Āzarbāījān and Khurāsān money was needed for defence. The Shāh had been taught to perceive that this defence was not only a Persian or Qājār concern; it also appeared requisite in connection with the defence of India. Particularly was this so in Āzarbāījān; but Khurāsān also was assuming a significance related to the defence of India[24]; and there is no reason to suppose that the Shāh could not draw his own conclusions from Fraser's journey to Khurāsān in 1821–2. As will be seen, mention of Gurgān and Khurāsān had not been entirely absent from Fatḥ ʿAlī Shāh's discussions with General Yermolov, when the latter visited him as an ambassador in 1817.

Article 2 of the Treaty of Gulistan based agreement on existing frontiers, and future demarcations of these and decisions on borders not yet determined, on the *status quo ad presentem*. Commissioners were to be appointed by the two sides to settle the undelineated border in the Tālish area, part of which the Russians had gained and part of which Persia still held. To this piece of unfinished business was added provision of a kind far more dangerous to peace: that 'If the possessions of either of the High Contracting Parties shall have been infringed by the above-mentioned boundaries', i.e. those which the Article did lay down, 'the Commissioners shall rectify it on the basis of the *status quo ad presentem*'. In effect this Article left the whole frontier question fluid. Reza Qulī Khān Hedāyat says that any reluctance on the Persians' part to conclude the Treaty was dispelled by news of Turkoman raids in Māzandarān and Gurgān[25]; but it seems likely that anyway, especially if ʿAbbās Mīrzā remained intent on continuing the war, it suited the Persian Government not at once to have the frontier question removed from the sphere of future discussion and compromise.

If Baddeley's account of Yermolov's 'central idea', with the Aras as Russia's ultimate boundary, is acceptable,[26] it seems probable that the undetermined frontier situation also suited the Russians. The frontier was a gambit to be played if other schemes, whose purpose was to gain greater control over ʿAbbās Mīrzā as future Shāh, failed; such schemes were tried between 1817 and 1825.

Yermolov's Embassy of 1817, apart from exchanging ratified copies of the Treaty of Gulistan, seems to have been intended as little more than a ceremonial expression of friendship and a somewhat ostentatious demonstration of desire for peace. It was an imposing Embassy, but Yermolov, who was recalcitrant over certain requirements of etiquette, though he made a better impression on the Shāh than on the Crown Prince, was only a provisional ambassador for the occasion. Certain issues were raised, but not apparently pressed. Accounts of the Shāh's response to them indicate his determination to stand on the letter of the treaty; to prevent Russian penetration into Gīlān; to limit foreign officers in his or the Crown Prince's service to the British; to obviate Russia's establishing a base in Astārābād or penetrating Khurāsān; and to postpone final tariff and transit arrangements over the as yet not fully determined Russo-Persian boundaries.

The last point adds credence to the supposition that he, in common with 'Abbās Mīrzā, desired no immediate crystallization of the Āzarbāījān-Qarabāgh frontier, and the whole tenor of his answers showed his intention that this and kindred matters should be left to future negotiations when an Iranian envoy went to Tiflis. Not an envoy from the Shāh, however, but one from the Crown Prince, for the Shāh insisted that Yermolov's representative, Mazarovich, was not to be posted to Tehran and the Shāh's court, but to Tabrīz and 'Abbās Mīrzā's court. Thus was another Russian demand not complied with though the British representative was accredited to Tehran.

Fatḥ 'Alī Shāh would not hear of a Russian Consulate being established at Rasht, though Vatsenko remained several years in Tehran in the hopes of being able to go to Gīlān. As for tariffs and transit affairs, he said commerce was not the business of great monarchs.[27] Asked by the Russians if, because the Khivans harassed Russian merchants there, he would either restore Persian paramountcy in Central Asia, or permit the Russians to embark on operations in that region and use Astārābād as a base, Fatḥ 'Alī Shāh replied that no provision for the latter existed in the treaty, and to accomplish the former proposal, for a campaign in Central Asia he would have to follow Nādir Shāh's (1736–47) example and first be recognized as suzerain of the keys to Central Asia, Herāt, Balkh and Bukhārā.[28] Asked to prove his friendship for Russia by assisting in hostilities against the Turks, he said that the treaty did not envisage this; according to one source, he sent a warning message to Sultan Maḥmūd II.[29] In answer to the suggestion that Russian troops be supplied for the Persian army, he simply stated that they were not required. Willock seems uncertain about this last Russian proposal, but, if it is to be seen in the context of an attempt to strengthen the patronage of 'Abbās Mīrzā already implied by the Article in the treaty promising the heir apparent assistance, Willock's report of a later Russian attempt, through Mazarovich, to provide the Crown Prince with a special guard is significant.[30] Also significant is the fact already mentioned that Mazarovich did encourage the Prince to go to war with the Turks in 1821; though at the same time his brother, Muḥammad 'Alī Mīrzā, was achieving success against the Pashalik of Baghdad, in the campaign during which he died of cholera–indeed, evidence shows that 'Abbās Mīrzā might have been the more easily encouraged because he did not want to be outshone. Mazarovich acted in accordance with what he took to be Yermolov's wishes[31]; his action, however, gained the Tsar's disapproval.[32]

ʿAbbās Mīrzā not only saw Muḥammad ʿAlī Mīrzā as the jealous because passed-over elder brother, deprived of nomination as Crown Prince; he was also in command of a formidable army which, though of the traditional pattern, had one or two French officers for its artillery[33]; and he was regarded as one of the Crown Prince's principal opponents in his efforts to establish a modern army–efforts which have won him praise as one of Iran's first 'modernizers'. ʿAbbās Mīrzā complained that Muḥammad ʿAlī Mīrzā tried to make his *Niẓām-i-Jadid* 'odious to the Persians, by attempting to show that in adopting the customs of infidels he was subverting the religion of Islam'.[34] It may be said that this affront to ʿAbbās Mīrzā's pride and threat to his hopes of gaining popularity as future Shāh was removed by Muḥammad ʿAlī Mīrzā's demise in 1821. It may also be gathered that in this rivalry lay part at least of the explanation for his acquiescence in some degree of Russian patronage; in the provisions of the Treaty of Gulistan for example and his relations until 1821 with Mazarovich, which later deteriorated, while he had never ingratiated himself with Yermolov.[35] On the other hand it seems clear that the removal of Muḥammad ʿAlī's competition resulted in a greater lack of restraint in ʿAbbās Mīrzā's behaviour, but at the same time came too late to enable him to recover from the psychological effects of it. Willock's view that the rival's death also accounted for his neglect of his army seems too simple[36]; it is more likely that he deliberately neglected the army after 1821 in order to keep the British anxious.[37]

The psychological effects went deeper because of an attitude on Fatḥ ʿAlī Shāh's part towards his two eldest sons which seems to have been designed to promote the sense of insecurity of the younger, the Crown Prince. Sir Harford Jones describes Fatḥ ʿAlī Shāh's review of both the Princes' armies at his spring camp in 1809. The Crown Prince's was like 'the awkward squad of a newly raised regiment of infantry'. Muḥammad ʿAlī Mīrzā's traditional force was, by contrast, that 'finest of spectacles . . . the assemblage of an irregular body of horse'.[38] At such a review the father could pit one son against the other; Monteith reports that the Shāh 'addressed his two sons, . . . as rival candidates to the throne, and said he expected to see which of them could prove himself worthy of it'.[39] If weakness in ʿAbbās Mīrzā's personality had anything to do with his renewal of the war with Russia, here is evidence of his father's culpability in this regard, if in no other. The mutual suspicion between father and son became manifest on the very eve of the war.[40] On 15 July 1826 Willock reported how most regrettably 'the Shāh and the Prince do not avow to each other their real sentiments. The Shāh is most peacably disposed, the latter lately declared himself so, yet by alternate blustering they contrive to keep up a continual clamour, and the Prince from having been accused of pacifist views is more afraid of losing popularity with the Military, than of the disasters which must attend both his fortune and fame in the course of a contest with Russia.'[41]

In 1822 the Prince lost Mīrzā Buzurg, the first Qā'im Maqām, also taken off by the cholera epidemic. Mīrzā Buzurg was an implacable enemy of the Russians,[42] at least in so far as he saw peace with them inimical to the possibility of 'the aggrandizement of Abbas Mirza'. Willock reports that he placed this and 'the preservation of his own power and authority' above the country's other interests. 'He foresaw that if the Shāh felt himself at perfect security on the northern frontier, both the consequence of The Prince, and of those employed under him must at once sink, and that in lieu of receiving annual supplies from the Tehran treasury for the support of the guardians of the frontier, he might be called upon to render an account of the income and expenses of the Āzerbāījān Government, and to pay a part of the surplus revenue to His Majesty. H.E. at all times had opposed the conclusion of peace with Russia, and having been deceived by the promises of General de Ritischeff [*sic*], he cherished the hope, that by the procrastination of a definitive settlement of the frontier, circumstances might afford an occasion to renew hostilities under the appearance of aggression on the part of Russia, which would once more oblige Great Britain to defray a great part of the expenses of the war.' The Mīrzā had hoped for outbreaks among Asiatic tribes recently made subject to Russia, and had fostered the climate of procrastination over final determination of the frontier.[43] Though ʿAbbās Mīrzā's proneness to debauchery had increased on the removal of Mīrzā Buzurg's restraining hand,[44] the Mīrzā's political attitudes remained one of the Prince's chief influences. Meanwhile according to Willock ʿAbbās Mīrzā neglected 'the only man of talent about his Court', Mīrzā Buzurg's son, Abul Qāsim, the second Qā'im Maqām.[45] In view of this disregard for Abul Qāsim Khān, whom ʿAbbās Mīrzā, though he was allowed the title of Qā'im Maqām on Mīrzā Buzurg's death, did not immediately make his vazir,[46] it is strange that Ambourger, a Russian diplomatist, should have urged that he be made the channel for a last, and British-inspired, peace overture. The neglect of Abul Qāsim Khān as revealed by Willock's papers is of interest, because he, like his master, has subsequently been praised as a great man and early modernizer of Iran. He died tragically, the victim of despotism, at the hands of ʿAbbās Mīrzā's son, Muḥammad Shāh, on 26 June 1835. He was to some extent a literary innovator. He was also the patron of another of the men looked upon by later reformers as a precursor, Mīrzā Taqī Khān, who, like his mentor, was in 1852 executed, this time the autocrat being Nāṣiru'd-Dīn Shāh (1848–1896), Muḥammad Shāh's successor. If it is true that Abul Qāsim had slight influence over ʿAbbās Mīrzā, then the paradox of a man regarded by later generations as one of sagacity and high aspirations for Iran having helped to precipitate a war disastrous to it is removed.

After his return to Tehran in 1823 Willock's own influence over both the Shāh and the Crown Prince, and thus over the course of events in general, was handicapped by the duty imposed upon him of persuading the Persians to accept a change in British diplomatic representation to Persia, from that of London to representation from the East India Company's Government in Calcutta. The Shāh was reluctant to accede to the change. He feared that acceptance of a representative from a 'subordinate government' of the English would entail the risk of the Russians pressing upon him acceptance of men accredited from Tiflis, precluding his having recourse directly to the Tsar.[47] Thus Willock had to struggle to extract agreement on a point which entailed, though the principle might be eventually conceded, minutiae of etiquette required for the reception of an envoy from a non-sovereign government. These minutiae gave the Shāh ample scope for protracting the negotiation. Willock was also hampered in being forthright with ʿAbbās Mīrzā, in years the event proved so crucial, because to gain a lever with the Shāh, the Crown Prince's agreement had also to be sought and won. To do this meant at least the insinuation that representation from the Governor General in India bore with it good promise of arms and a renewed supply of officers for the Prince's army; in such a connection, the subsidy could not be far from the Prince's mind. It is, therefore, arguable that Willock's additional duty indirectly involved flattering any optimism, in the sphere of military strength and additions to his treasury, which the Prince might have entertained. Willock was left in a state of suspense over his replacement from India until after the war began. He had been sent out 'in the meantime' in 1823, 'a Mission from India on a scale somewhat higher' relieving him 'after a few months'.[48]

In spite of Fatḥ ʿAlī Shāh's insistence during Yermolov's embassy in 1817 that outstanding questions relating to the frontier and trade could be settled on a lower level by an emissary from Tabrīz to Tiflis, it was not until 1825 that such an emissary, in the person of Fatḥ ʿAlī Khān the Beglerbeg, went. When he did go, it was presumed that arrangements already discussed at Tabrīz between the Prince and Mazarovich or Ambourger only required Yermolov's agreement to be final. Willock used the verb 'ratified' to describe Yermolov's acceptance of all Mazarovich's proposals.[49] It was 'supposed that The Prince Royal would have closed with a settlement decidedly favourable to Russia', but he 'demurred on the cession of some lands on the north side of the Lake of Gokcha he was formerly willing to relinquish'. He wanted to return the Treaty of Gulistan to Yermolov, but the Shāh refused to entrust a document brought him by an Emperor's Ambassador to the Prince's courier.[50]

The idea that ʿAbbās Mīrzā had earlier been willing to concede the Gokcha lands arose from an arrangement proposed by Yermolov that he could have in exchange for these empty lands an area between 'Chikrondar and Kepenek, well peopled, from which Your Royal Highness derives a considerable revenue . . .'.[51] His Royal Highness did not regard this as a fair exchange, because he believed the Russians had improperly occupied Kapanak in the first place.[52] Nevertheless it appears that at least ʿAbbās Mīrzā had once, as early as 1819, been formally asked to permit Yermolov to occupy the Gokcha lands, for Willock in his diary for 21 July 1826 reports 'finding amongst the records the copy of a letter written in the year 1819 by General Yermoloff to ʿAbbās Mīrzā' allowing that the lands north of Lake Gokcha 'belonged to Persia, and requesting permission to occupy them'.[53]

Yermolov refused to countenance Fatḥ ʿAlī Khān's return to Tiflis with fresh proposals and stood upon the suggested exchange, of the Gokcha area for that of Kapanak. Whatever may have been ʿAbbās Mīrzā's earlier attitude, by 1825, and no doubt urged to it by the Sirdar of Erivan,[54] his attitude was uncompromising. Occupation of the northern and north-western shores of the Lake gave the Russians passage from Tiflis, between the Alagez range and the waters of the lake, directly on to Erivan. Erivan would be of strategic advantage to them in any future attack on the Ottoman Empire's north-eastern borders. Likewise it was of interest to Iran as a base in operations against the Turks. It was also potentially a rich revenue producer. There was also a history, to be associated with a place such as Erivan, of Muslim-Christian competitiveness and jealousy over holding important Christian religious centres. This history was particularly relevant to Islamic relations with the Tsar. Tsar Alexander I had in July 1816 informed Yermolov of his reply to Abul Ḥasan Khān, Fatḥ ʿAlī Shāh's

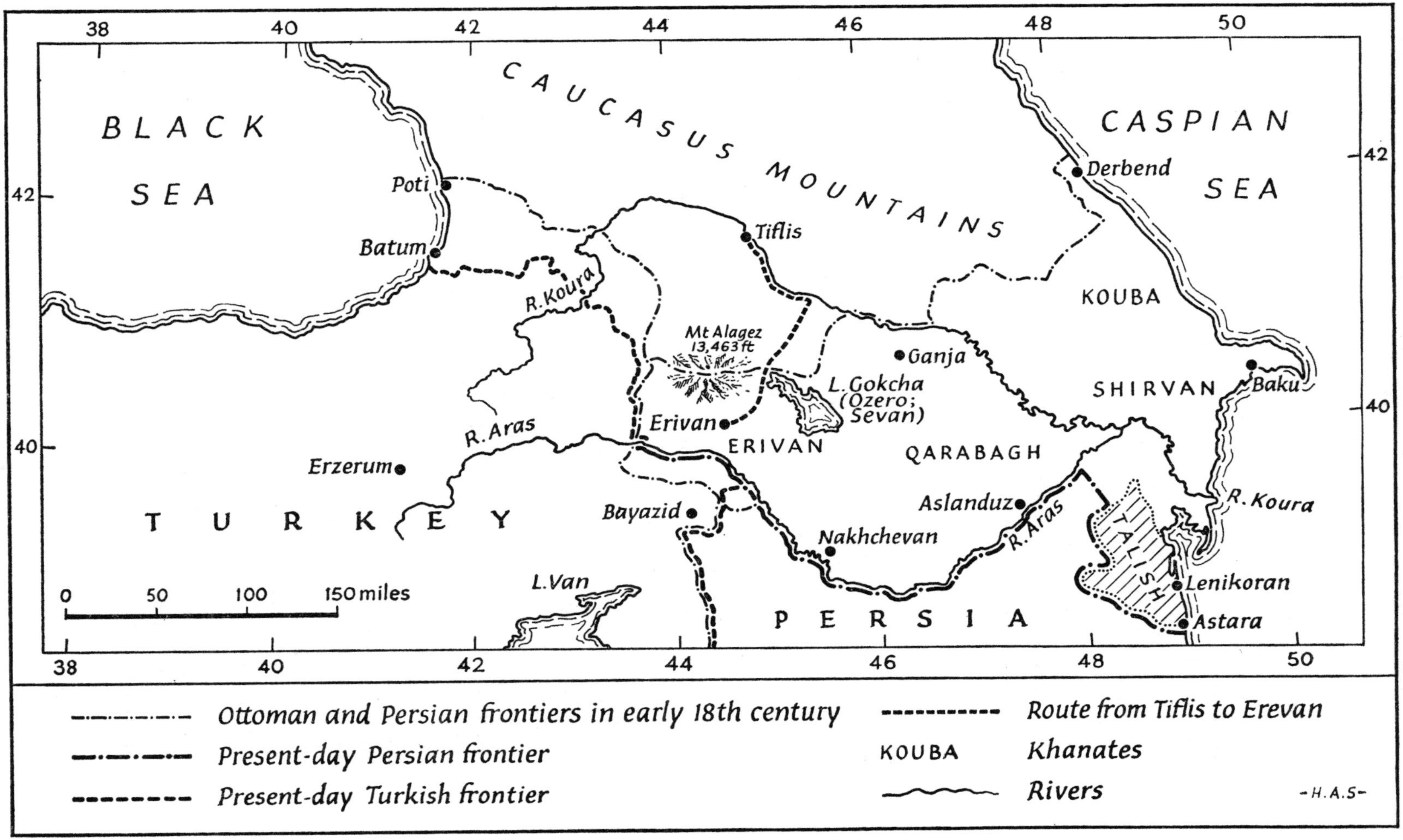

BLACK SEA
CASPIAN SEA
CAUCASUS MOUNTAINS
Poti
Batum
Derbend
Tiflis
KOUBA
SHIRVAN
Baku
R. Koura
Mt Alagez 13,463 ft
Ganja
L. Gokcha (Ozero; Sevan)
Erivan
ERIVAN
QARABAGH
R. Aras
Erzerum
TURKEY
Bayazid
Nakhchevan
Aslanduz
TALISH
Lenikoran
Astara
L. Van
PERSIA
0 50 100 150 miles
38 40 42 44 46 48 50
42 40
Ottoman and Persian frontiers in early 18th century
Present-day Persian frontier
Present-day Turkish frontier
Route from Tiflis to Erevan
KOUBA Khanates
Rivers
-H.A.S-

envoy to him, that there was no hope of Iran recovering any of the territory ceded by the Treaty of Gulistan,[55] which was intransigent enough; but in respect of Erivan, not ceded by the treaty, when the geo-political significance of Yermolov's occupation of the Gokcha lands is realized, Alexander's self-appointed rôle as the protector of Christians and Christian Holy Places also becomes involved. Erivan was near the seat of the Armenian Catholicos at Etchmiadzin, 'The Three Churches' so important in Armenian ecclesiastical history. Etchmiadzin had interested Alexander I from as early as 1801, when he had interfered in a Catholicate succession dispute.[56]

Tsar Alexander's death in December 1825 stiffened the Persian refusal to accept the Russian contention that the exchange of Gokcha for Kapanak ought to be ratified. Indeed, when the Crown Prince's obduracy was clear to him, Yermolov wrote to Mīrzā Abul Ḥasan Khān Shīrāzī, the Shāh's foreign Minister, in March 1825, and more than contended: he had 'to solicit the good offices of Your Excellency in concluding this arrangement so beneficial to Persia'.[57] Willock continues by reporting that on this occasion 'Abbās Mīrzā's views prevailed and 'the Shāh did not ratify Futteh Alī Khān's arrangements. Directly this became known in Georgia, General Yermoloff chose to consider as binding on Persia the unsealed and unratified articles of Futteh Alī Khān's Negotiation, and maintained in opposition to the will of Persia possession of lands ceded to Russia by that compact.'

Willock wrote this in March 1826 and could therefore also discuss the disturbances in Russia following Alexander I's assassination, and the brief interlude of Constantine's Tsardom pending the accession of Yermolov's enemy, Nicholas I.[58] The expectancy that the disturbances might increase had induced Fatḥ 'Alī Shāh to postpone sending an embassy to St Petersburg. As usual when a deadlock seemed to have been reached at the local level, the Shāh desired to place matters on the level of communication between sovereigns. Similarly the Prince had wanted to send an envoy to England, but Willock, saddled with instructions to prevent this in view of the negotiations to win acceptance of representation for the British from India, had 'strongly urged that British mediation could not be effective'. He had also brought up the recent agreement for 'relations of the two Empires (to) be superintended by the Supreme Government of India', and induced the Prince 'to give up the mission to England'.[59]

Willock was informed that the Russian disturbances had, according to the Crown Prince, 'given hopes to the disaffected in Georgia, Shakee, Sheerivan and Carabagh; and His Royal Highness informs this court' (the

Shāh's) 'that overtures have been made to the Chiefs of those Provinces now residing under the protection of H.R.H.' (in Tabrīz) 'by the people they formerly governed'. Willock says that he cannot ascertain the exact extent of the disturbances in Russia, but that it suits 'Abbās Mīrzā's 'purpose' to represent them as grave 'to the Shāh, and unless I can persuade His Majesty to send an Ambassador to St Petersburgh, the Prince having' – in the Gokcha occupation – 'a plausible case of aggression on the part of Russia will endeavour to hurry the Shāh into war. With this intent he has now sent a confidential person to Court, and since his arrival, His Majesty has again spoken of proceeding to Āzerbāījān, and of expelling by force the Russian troops from his Territory.'[60]

Meanwhile Abul Ḥasan Khān, who with Minūchihr Khān the Chief Eunuch and 'Abdul Wahhāb the Mu'tamidu'd-Dauleh, was for peace, emphasized that Yermolov had conceded, in his letter to him, that 'the ratification of the respective sovereigns must be obtained' for his occupation of 'the trifling and unprofitable strip of land on the borders of... Gokcha', which he required 'for the purpose of strengthening our frontier, and of putting an end to the disputes which continually arise between our Eecliaats'. Abul Ḥasan Khān brought the point about the necessity for ratification 'particularly' to the attention of the British; like Fatḥ 'Alī Shāh, he expected that, if nothing could be negotiated locally, the matter might be settled at St Petersburg, but with the help of pressure from London. London, anxious to gain recognition that its affairs with Persia be in future handled from India, was unresponsive.

In believing that London could and should act to ameliorate the situation, the Persian Court's views were not dissimilar to those of Lord Amherst, the Governor General in India from 1823 to 1828, a period almost coinciding with Canning's career as Foreign Secretary, 1822 to 1827. Amherst wrote to Canning from Barrackpore on 23 March 1825 to say that Willock and the Government of India's envoy designate to Persia, Kinneir Macdonald, who was waiting at Bombay, 'have both a great deal to say upon the subject of the encroachments of the Russians', but he concluded that 'if it be expedient to check any further advances of the Russians towards the Persian provinces, this object is to be effected by remonstrances from the authorities in England, rather than by any proceeding on the part of the Bengal Government'.[61] Macdonald was rebuked for having suggested[62] that strong language be held to St Petersburg, and told that to give the Persians any hope of such action 'could not fail', in Lord Amherst's opinion, 'to produce the most embarrassing consequences'.[63]

It therefore appears demonstrable that while Amherst was certainly not of the 'forward' school of Governors General in India, he also knew Canning's views well enough to understand that it was not intended in Europe to jeopardize Anglo-Russian relations for Persia's sake. The business of the change in the order of England's diplomatic relations was useful to Canning as the pretext for not receiving pleas directly from Fatḥ 'Alī Shāh, thus to be forced at least to acknowledge Persia's case against Russia. In retrospect it becomes clear that, though Willock might have felt himself in a most trying position because of it, suspense – promoted by the Shāh – over the arrival of an envoy from India served Canning in a more important respect. In using the proposed change in British representation at the Court of Persia as the reason why approaches from that Court to London could not be accepted, Canning was able to forestall a Persian attempt to play off Britain against Russia.

The Russians meanwhile made it clear to Willock that, in any event, his mediation was not acceptable, although in the Morier Treaty's third Article it was stated that the limits of Russia's and Persia's territories should 'be determined according to the admission of Great Britain, Persia, and Russia'. The British might claim that this provision merely awarded them the right to have surveying officers attached to the frontier commissions provided for by the Treaty of Gulistan. Fatḥ 'Alī Shāh, seeking protection from the Russians and hoping to make the British the counterpoise against their Russian allies, no doubt read more into it.

Willock recognized that the Russian retention of the Gokcha lands was not just – it depended on power rather than 'the law of reason and justice' – but his alarm was contingent upon the necessity of removing a 'cause of contention', not upon the sense of Persia's victimization. He pleaded with Canning to bring pressure on the Russians, because the danger of the 'cause of contention' lay in the 'Prince Royal's desire to effect a rupture with Russia with the hope of again exacting a subsidy from England'. This hope 'will not be checked' while the possibility' remains of proving a case of aggression on the part of Russia, to which an ill-defined frontier is particularly favourable'.[64] It was not until the last moment that Willock expressed the opinion that 'the sincerity of the conciliatory professions of Russia' was 'questionable'.[65] Imbued with 'Abbās Mīrzā's anxiety to promote a renewal of the war in such a way that he could again 'exact' the subsidy, Willock does not seem to have thought that the Russians might have been awaiting developments and themselves, by for example the occupation of Gokcha, occasionally giving them a pattern, until the Prince, ensnared in his desire for the subsidy, hoist with the petard of anti-Russian propaganda Willock says he deliberately incited,[66] and unable to refuse help to rebellious chiefs whose hopes he had encouraged, would be forced to make the fatal move.

Willock's doubts about Russian sincerity arose after his peace effort, made when Prince Menchikov, the envoy sent to announce his accession by Tsar Nicholas I, was at the Shāh's camp at Sultānieh in July 1826. Willock's assistant McNeill had proposed to Ambourger that war be averted by permitting Russian and Persian pickets to remain in the positions on Lake Gokcha which they had assumed, while reference was made to St Petersburg for the Tsar's ruling; the Russians said that they could not withdraw unless ordered to do so by the Tsar. Menchikov accepted this proposal and the Qā'im Maqām was suggested by Ambourger as the man on the Persian side whom McNeill should approach, though McNeill had shortly before considered Abul Qāsim Khān 'so much deranged, and so much to have fallen into the war faction' that he had stopped calling upon him.[67] Abul Qāsim Khān had proposed modifications to the plan whereby, pending a reply from St Petersburg, both sides should evacuate Gokcha. Menchikov had seemed also to agree to this proposal, but with one condition 'that no hostilities should be caused by Persia'. The proposal broke down over this condition because the Shāh said he could not undertake that hostilities 'might not already have commenced on the frontier, and to enter into any such arrangements under such circumstances was delicate'. It is probable, however, that the Shāh already knew what came in an addition to Willock's despatch on this stage of the proceedings: that the insurrection in Tālish against the Russians, of which he had just heard, afforded 'circumstances ... which in some measure account for the rejection of Prince Menchikoff's proposal'. He had heard that a hundred decapitated Russian heads were on their way to the Shāh's camp from Tālish. 'The inhabitants (of Tālish) have called to their aid the Persian troops in their neighbourhood.... The Prince Royal was to have left Tabrīz ten days since for Carabagh by way of Ordoobad', i.e. on 20 July 1826.[68]

Willock's suspicions of a Russian policy of *reculer pour mieux sauter* were certainly neither emphatic nor early expressed; though his letters to Calcutta subtly emphasize the Russian danger to Persia and ultimately India more than any of his communications with London do.[69] When home in 1822, Canning, with his 'I know a Mr Willock in Tehran but not in London' on Willock's sudden appearance in the latter place, had not been encouraging, though he had given him 'a patient and attentive' hearing when Willock pleaded for a rapid decision over the appointment, whether from London or India, of the English Minister to Persia.[70] It was perhaps in order not to offend Canning that Willock (who was later knighted) so heartily blamed ʿAbbās Mīrzā, and had so little to say in criticism of the Russians, save to state that they used power rather than 'the force of justice'.

He might, for instance, have been suspicious of the slowness with which Menchikov proceeded to the Shāh once the contact with the Russian Court which the Shāh desired had been occasioned by the new Tsar's accession. It was not quite the kind of contact Fatḥ ʿAlī Shāh looked for after his second mission to Yermolov, under Muḥammad Ṣādiq the Court Annalist, had been rebuffed. For though Yermolov had refused to countenance the return of Fatḥ ʿAlī Khān, Muḥammad Ṣādiq had gone to Tiflis, only to receive no recognition other than that of a 'courier', and an abusive letter to ʿAbbās Mīrzā, and letters about him which contrary to normal diplomatic usage referred to him without his titles.

Menchikov refused to be drawn into conversations at Tabrīz and in any event the Shāh had instructed the Prince not to negotiate; but there he showed some signs of a conciliatory attitude, and there, too, he lingered. In his diary for 21 June 1826 Willock noted that Prince Menchikov did not like 'quick travelling', but added that 'he was evidently gaining time to know the result of the negotiation at the Porte and if the Turks yielded to the desires of Russia he might not talk so smoothly'.

This delay was serious because it gave time for passions to be aroused in the Shāh's camp and further afield before which forces in favour of peace crumbled. Already in May 1826 Willock had reported that the Shāh had been persuaded by ʿAbbās Mīrzā's 'agents' in Tehran to disburse the sum of 45,000 tomans for distribution among 'the disaffected in Georgia'. His own desire, that by promoting rebellion against the Russian Government ʿAbbās Mīrzā should not succeed in bringing about a situation in which the Russians would be prompted to punitive measures against the Prince's protégés, and his constant concern with ʿAbbās Mīrzā's cupidity, are revealed when he adds that he has 'the satisfaction to think that the whole of this sum will be placed in the Treasury of The Prince Royal . . . not applied . . . to disseminate disaffection amongst the subjects of Russia'.[71]

The knowledge, however, that a scheme so to spread disaffection was being mooted in Persian court circles perhaps coloured Willock's twice-repeated view that the Russians had not mistreated their Muslim subjects or insulted the conventions of Islam in a manner which warranted the 'clamour' against them he first mentions in June 1826. This view is in marked contrast to that expressed by a seemingly well-informed writer in *Blackwood's Magazine* for February 1827. The writer states that it was known how Russian misrule in Georgia and 'wanton interference' with Muhammadans' 'religious prejudices' had produced serious discontent. 'Proposals had even been made to Persia by the heads of the tribes, and chiefs of districts, to co-operate with her in a war against Russia. Letters had been written by the Mahomedan population of all the Russian provinces bordering on Persia, to the head of their religion, imploring his interference on their behalf; and he had come from the sanctuary of Kerbelaee [*sic*], expressly to urge the Shāh to take up arms in defence of his insulted religion'.[72]

The person here referred to is Āghā Sayyid Muḥammad Iṣfāhanī, who resided at Kāzimain near Baghdad (not Kerbela).[73] Willock accused ʿAbbās Mīrzā of deliberately inciting Georgian and Qarabāgh pilgrims on their way through Tabrīz to the Shīʿite Holy Places in Mesopotamia, to carry tales to this important religious authority against the Russians. He says the Crown Prince did this with a view to incite the Shāh 'indirectly' to war.[74] His account of the Sayyid's reaction and Fatḥ ʿAlī Shāh's response differs from that given in *Nāsikhu't-Tavārīkh* and *Rauzatu'ṣ-Ṣafā*. Muḥammad ʿAlī Tabrīzī in the *Raiḥānatu'l-Adab* says the Sayyid lived in Kāzimain until Fatḥ ʿAlī Shāh, having decided to counter Russian evils against Islam, sought his spiritual aid and desired his presence in the royal entourage.[75] According to the other accounts, as a result of the pilgrims' tales, the Sayyid wrote to the Shāh, but doubting the sincerity of his reply, himself came to Iran, where he reached Tehran on 25 May 1826.

Willock says that the Sayyid 'addressed the Shāh saying that he had heard the Russians had taken possession of part of His Majesty's territory, had not observed their engagements with His Majesty, had shown themselves disposed to overturn the Mahomedan faith, and that it was incumbent on His Majesty, both as sovereign of Persia, and as the head of the Mahomadan faith to rise in protection of his rights, and of the faithful'. The Shāh had responded by inviting the Sayyid 'to come and head his troops', 'probably in the expectation that Said Mahomad would discontinue this language if called upon to take part in the measures he proposed'. 'Contrary to His Majesty's expectation', the Sayyid came.[76]

The Shāh reached his summer camping-ground at Sultānieh on 12 June and on 9 July Willock was urging him to hasten Menchikov's arrival there and to halt the progress thither of Sayyid Muḥammad and his followers, who by that time included all the most eminent divines in Iran.[77] Willock said that their arrival 'might much embarrass H.M. and unnecessarily irritate the Russians', who, he reiterated, had done nothing to warrant such a demonstration of religious feeling as by then was agitating Persia.[78] The Shāh sent messages to Qazvīn to stop the Sayyid's progress, but the Sayyid reached the camp amid tumultuous scenes of welcome, and lamentation for the state of Islam under the Russians, on 11 July 1826.

'Abbās Mīrzā was already there and Menchikov had just arrived. Before he left Tabrīz, according to McNeill the Prince had been dismayed on hearing of the large number of troops and amount of treasure assembled by the Shāh at Sultānieh, so that he was 'alarmed at the threatening aspect of affairs which his own Counsels have produced, and has fairly stated his incapacity to engage in so unequal a contest with a Power evidently anxious to break the peace if a commencement of hostilities on the part of Persia should justify her in the eyes of Europe'.[79] Meanwhile, the Shāh was reported by Willock not to want war, though he had thought it 'necessary to establish the belief that he is determined on war if the Russians do not comply with his demand'.[80]

The demand was for the evacuation of Gokcha, and the scandal of the Russians occupation of that area had grown to such an extent that Willock perceived that the Shāh and the Prince could not risk a concession on this issue. Gokcha was on everybody's lips.

In the excitement at the royal camp, the Prince's fear of war was converted into a more belligerent emotion. In addition to the religious passion, the influence of the military element in the camp, whose chief exponent was Allāh Yār Khān, prevailed over him. Allāh Yār Khān, besides marriage relations with 'Abbās Mīrzā through his sister, had marriage ties with the Shāh. He was moreover a Qājār, significantly of the Davalu branch of the Qājār tribe, a branch with which Fatḥ 'Ali Shāh's ancestors had been in conflict.[81] He seems to have been the evil genius of the situation at Sultānieh; every time Fatḥ 'Alī Shāh showed signs of being impressed by proposals tending towards peace, he was ready with dissuasive arguments.

The prime example of this type of conduct occurred when the Willock-McNeill peace proposals already referred to seemed to be making some headway. Mīrzā Abul Ḥasan Khān, the Foreign Minister, reported the arrangements thrashed out by McNeill, Ambourger and the Qā'im Maqām, and it will be recalled that the Shāh had replied that he could not accede because he feared hostilities might already have begun. At first, however, he had seemed gratified by the proposals, but Allāh Yār Khān had hastened to him and reminded him of the way in which his emissary to Yermolov, Muḥammad Ṣādiq, had been insulted. The Shāh had then decided that 'we should all proceed to the frontier, and there determine what was to be done'. The lengths to which Allāh Yār Khān was prepared to go in countering any peaceful views which the Shāh might be ready to hear is further illustrated by his assertion to the Shāh that Menchikov would not be listened to by Yermolov, and that his object was to gain time; and by his alleged perversion of Menchikov's statement to him about Russian negotiations at Constantinople.

After Allāh Yār Khān's attempt to counteract the pacific influence of Abul Ḥasan Khān, the door to further parleys at Sultānieh was not quite closed: the Shāh had later instructed Mīrzā Ḥasan Khān 'to keep negotiations open'. Then on the afternoon of 20 July Willock was summoned. The Shāh asked him how he was and he replied that he was perplexed over the threatening situation. The Shāh replied that he ought, on the contrary, to be happy: 'You will witness such doings, such galloping, such flying of heads, such destruction of life – My troops will rush to death as they would to marriage'. Still Willock knew that, if the Gokcha matter could be settled, Fatḥ 'Alī Shāh did not want war.[82] His Majesty asked him what news he thought a recent courier had brought Menchikov from Constantinople. The Āsafu'd Dauleh, Allāh Yār Khān, had told him that Menchikov had learnt that his government's negotiations with the Porte 'bore no promise of favourable conclusion'. The reference was to negotiations to which, as Willock had reported, Menchikov's delays might have been attributable, as he waited in Tabrīz to hear how they progressed. On 6 April 1826 the Anglo-Russian Protocol of St Petersburg had been concluded, by which, with the subsequent adhesion of France, the two powers had agreed to mediate between the Sultan and the Greeks. In March Tsar Nicholas had already demanded of the Porte that Turkish troops be withdrawn from Roumania and that Serbian autonomy be confirmed. Awed by the Protocol of April, in May the Sultan accepted these demands. The Convention of Akkerman was ultimately signed in October, but nevertheless following Prince Menchikov's arrival at Sultānieh on 10 July 1826, there was every reason for his news from Constantinople to be encouraging.

Willock told the Shāh that in what Allāh Yār Khān had reported there must be 'some mistake, as I had the authority of H.B.M. Ambassador at Constantinople for the demands of Russia being complied with'. That night Willock visited Menchikov. The latter confirmed that the Porte had agreed to Russian demands and that arrangements were to be made to settle the revised frontiers. His surprise over what Allāh Yār Khān had told the Shāh was the greater 'because in giving this information he had added a wish that Persia would follow the example of Turkey, and send negotiators to the frontier'.

Menchikov left the Shāh's camp on 24 July 1826, the day upon which the Shāh departed for Ardebil, which he reached on 1 August. By 10 August Willock reported that sixteen days had elapsed since the outbreak of war. The whole of this period had been marked by Persian successes, a fact which Canning, in a rare reply to Willock in terms more than that his despatches had been 'laid before His Majesty and met with approval', acknowledged with satisfaction. The crystal couch sent for the Shāh by Tsar Nicholas was, in the meantime, to be sent to Tehran under British auspices.

According to the *Raiḥānatu' l-Adab*, though he had at first been enthusiastically received by them, the royal circles had in the end deviated from Sayyid Muḥammad Iṣfahānī's 'holy intention'. The sincerity they had entertained towards him had languished and, full of weariness, he had returned to Qazvīn where in the autumn of 1826 he died. He had, nevertheless, been able at Sultānieh seriously to embarrass Mīrzā Abul Ḥasan Khān Shīrāzī and Mīrzā ʿAbdul Wahhāb, who steadfastly opposed the war when the Sayyid proclaimed that failure to fight *jihād* meant *kufr*, unbelief, and *ẓalālat*, error. In the end the '*ulamā*' sent 'these two intelligent ones' threatening messages, and 'they too submitted out of fear'.[83] The principal influence of the religious agitation on events seems to have lain in the fact that it precluded any concession over the Russians' hold on Gokcha on the Shāh's or ʿAbbās Mīrzā's part. The Russians on their side would not make any concession, so that diplomacy reached a deadlock.

Thus the religious agitation did not make it easier to preserve peace, but the war embarked upon was not the holy war which the Sayyid and his supporters had wanted; it was of the more secular nature which Allāh Yār Khān, who had been Fatḥ ʿAlī Shāh's chief minister since the spring of 1825, seems to have desired. He can be put at the head of the court military party; 'the great nobles', Willock says, 'whose consequence has declined during the tranquillity so long established' and who 'wish for war'.[84] Though ʿAbbās Mīrzā addressed him as *arjmandi*, i.e. his most precious friend, the way in which he fell under Allāh Yār Khān's influence so fatally has a tragic appearance not diminished by the suspicion that Allāh Yār Khān might have been the Crown Prince's most treacherous associate. He might have secretly longed for his undoing. ʿAbbās Mīrzā was the expected future Shāh out of a rival group in the Qājār family. As it was, Allāh Yār Khān fought bitterly against Fatḥ ʿAlī Shāh's successor, Muḥammad Shāh.

Willock seems to have known and understood Allāh Yār Khān less than was expedient for a diplomatist in his position. At first in the summer of 1826 he thought him averse to war, because he had been nominated to a command and did not relish having to leave the court. Having, however, as 'agent of the Prince Royal', 'in pursuance with his instructions from Āzerbāījān instigated the Shāh to war', he was 'afraid at once to communicate to the Shāh his own pacific views, and in all his conversations with me has held out the advantage of war'. Willock concludes, 'As he has not honoured me with his confidence, I have not taken much pains to combat his opinions delivered for the publick ear'. Ironically enough it was upon those 'great nobles' that ʿAbbās Mīrzā would think of relying when the succession struggle began, whatever foreign support he may have been promised or have hoped for – or have wished ultimately to be able to discard.

In 1838 Lord Auckland, the Governor General in India, took the step of advancing an army beyond India for its defence. The extensive preparations made for this 'service across the Indus'[85] prove how exceptional such a step was. They provide the measure of the East India Company's preoccupation up to that time with defending India without having to mount an army for expeditions outside it. This policy was epitomized in the subsidy to Persia; and in 1826 there was neither a 'forward policy' in Lord Amherst's head, nor the desire in Canning's for a breach of the peace with Russia.

One difficulty was how to keep on friendly terms, against future contingencies, with Persia, if the latter went to war with Russia; and how not in such an event to quarrel with Russia for the sake of Persia's friendship. This difficulty was resolved by sacrificing Persia, whose 'friendship' could in the end be maintained by Britain's good offices when the Treaty of Turkomanchai was concluded in 1828. Then the subsidy was paid for the last time. It was 'presented as an aid to Persia in consideration of the losses she has sustained in the war with Russia'[86]; or 'towards the liquidation of the indemnity due by us to Russia', when Articles 3 and 4 of the Morier-Ellis treaty of 1814 were annulled.[87]

Another, and perhaps ultimately the chief, diplomatic problem occurring to the authorities in London has already been alluded to in connection with prolongation of negotiations, especially in regard to etiquette, for the reception of the British Envoy Designate from India. There is no evidence in Willock's papers that he himself was aware of this problem, but it seems legitimate to postulate that Canning was determined to avoid giving Fatḥ ʿAlī Shāh and ʿAbbās Mīrzā scope, further to that afforded them by Anglo-Persian treaties concluded before he was Foreign Secretary, to save Iran by balancing Great Britain and Russia against each other. It has often been said that Persia was successful throughout the nineteenth century in doing just this, so that it was able to maintain its independence. Perhaps, caught between Russia and Great Britain, successive Shāhs were left with no alternative but to endeavour to maintain this balance; but the history of nineteenth-century Iran does not point to any high degree of success in this context, though it must be admitted that a measure of independence and territorial integrity was maintained. The initiative, however, was not Iran's: the situation was always governed by the diplomatic requirements on the European stage, and the European Powers' manœuvres in relation to the Ottoman Empire.

NOTES

1 The Irano-Soviet Treaty of 26 February 1921, Article 1, declared 'null and void' 'the whole body of treaties and conventions concluded with Persia by the Tsarist Government'. (Text in Nasrollah Saifpour Fatemi, *Diplomatic History of Persia 1917–1923* (New York 1925) Appendix E, 317-24.)

2 C. U. Aitchison, *A Collection of Treaties, Engagements and Sanads Relating to India and Neighbouring Countries*, vol. XIII (Calcutta 1933) Appendix No. V, pp. xv-xviii. All citations from treaties are taken from this compilation.

3 See for example William R. Polk and Richard L. Chambers (Editors), *Beginnings of Modernization in the Middle East* (Chicago 1968); Hafez Farman Farmayan, *The Forces of Modernization in Nineteenth Century Iran: A Historical Survey*, 119-20.

4 Accounts vary, but James B. Fraser, *Narrative of a Journey into Khorasan, in the Years 1821 and 1822* (London 1825) 203, states that Fatḥ ʿAlī Shāh had 'about fifty sons, and at least an hundred daughters'. He lists fourteen governorates in the hands of sons of the Shāh, and four possessed by grandsons.

5 John F. Baddeley, *The Russian Conquest of the Caucasus* (London 1908) 103-4. Yermolov's 'high-handed, not to say insolent treatment of' ʿAbbās Mīrzā (during his passage through Tabriz in 1817 as the Tsar's envoy) 'confirmed the latter in his hostility to Russia, and made him Yermoloff's bitterest enemy, a fact that had no little influence on coming events'.

6 According to R. G. Watson, *A History of Persia 1800–1858* (London 1866) 269, on his death in 1833, ʿAbbās Mīrzā was 46.

7 According to the reckoning of Fraser, op. cit.

8 Texts in Aitchison, Harford Jones treaty, Article 4; Ouseley's Article 2; Morier-Ellis's, Article 4.

9 As mentioned in the Articles of the treaties cited above.

10 FO 60/25 Willock to Canning, 13 February 1825.

11 Ouseley, Article 2; Morier-Ellis, Article 4.

12 Mīrzā Sāliḥ Shīrāzī had been sent in the first group of five despatched to England by ʿAbbās Mīrzā for European education in 1815, to return to Tabrīz in 1819. On his return to Persia after his diplomatic mission to Britain, Willock reported to Canning on 5 February 1825 that he was ill-received by the Prince. The muskets he brought back with him were faulty and his accounts not straight. He left Tabrīz for Gīlān and thence escaped to Russia, whence very friendly but quite domestic letters are in FO 60/25 from him to Canning. It seems possible that in reality his 'escape' to Astrakhan was contrived and that he had been assigned duties while in Russia by ʿAbbās Mīrzā. L. P. Elwell-Sutton deals with a later aspect of his career in *JRCAS*, XLIX, 183-7, *Parleying with the Russians in 1827*.

13 See note 10 above.

14 Willock's Despatch No. 2 of 17 February 1826 to Canning (FO 60/26).

15 FO 60/27. Willock to Canning, 23 July 1826.

16 The Shāh was the recipient of the Subsidy in theory, and would only release it to the Crown Prince if his frontier situation seemed to require it.

17 FO 60/26. Willock to Canning, 27 June 1826.

18 Willock's diary for 25 June 1826, forwarded under his despatch No. 13 to Canning of 27 June 1826, recording the arrival at Sultānieh from Tabriz on 25th of Dr McNeill with the report that the Prince was 'weak in body and mind – That he dreads war... confesses he has not the means to conduct it and is anxious to lull the storm he has aroused'. When McNeill (ibid.) told the Shāh that the Prince had made no warlike preparations and was averse to war, 'he laughed heartily and asked whether the Prince had not collected his Troops.... Persia... wished for war.... The Prince had done wrong in making no show at least of preparation... this was a time when H.R.H. ought to be drilling as many troops as he could collect'.

19 Rezā Qulī Khān Hedāyat, *Rauẓatu'ṣ-Ṣafā-ye-Nāṣirī* (Tehran 1960) IX, 493, and Sipihr, *Nāsikhu't Tavārikh* (Tehran n.d.) folio 78.

20 James Morier, *A Second Journey Through Persia etc.* (London 1818) 217, and *Rauẓatu'ṣ-Ṣafā*, ibid.

21 See Willock's comment on the policy of Mīrzā Buzurg, whom he describes as 'having been deceived by the promises of General

Ritischeff [*sic*]'; FO 60/25, Willock to Canning, 4 September 1825. (Cf. note 43 below.)

22 Fraser, op. cit., 214-22, and the same author's *An Historical and Descriptive Account of Persia* (Edinburgh 1834) 257.

23 Ibid.

24 FO 60/25; Willock wrote at length to Lord Amherst, the Governor General in India, with a copy to Canning, on 7 April 1825, about the significance of the manner in which the Treaty of Gulistan's Article 5, permitting only Russian ships-of-war on the Caspian, made that sea into 'part of Russia', across which troops could be ferried to Central Asia and supplied once there. It was only twelve days' march from Astārābād to Mashhad, he pointed out, and thence to Herat only fifteen days. He described how weak was the Qājār rule in Khurāsān, effective only in Mashhad and its environs and on the route thither from Tehran. The Khurasanians were antagonistic to the 'Persians', and might regard the Persians' enemy, Russia, as their friend.

25 *Rauẓatu'ṣ-Ṣafā*, op. cit., 493.

26 Baddeley, op. cit., 99-105. 'Russia's improvised Ambassador... fully satisfied with the immediate success of his mission, and caring not a jot for ʿAbbas Mirza or his feelings, hastened to Tiflis, already determined in his own mind to reduce the khanates to Russian provinces...'.

27 FO 60/25. Willock to Canning, 13 February 1825. *Rauẓatu'ṣ-Ṣafā*, op. cit., 550-1. On the Embassy, cf. *Nāsikhu't-Tavārīkh*, op. cit., folio 79.

28 Willock, *Rauẓatu'ṣ-Ṣafā* and *Nāsikhu't-Tavārīkh*, ibid.

29 *Nāsikhu't-Tavārīkh* only mentions the message to the Sultan. In other respects the accounts are remarkably similar.

30 Letter to Lord Amherst dated 23 July 1825, copied to London as enclosure to Despatch No. 17, in which Willock proposed that the expected envoy from India, Macdonald, came 'accompanied by officers to save having to negotiate for them on his arrival' – then expected 'in the beginning of summer 1826'. 'We urged' on ʿAbbās Mīrzā, 'the necessity of redisciplining his Army'. ʿAbbās Mīrzā had reported Mazarovich's (the Russian representative) offer of an Infantry Brigade to be called The Emperor's and guard the Prince. This looks like an early germ of the idea of the Cossack Brigade. Willock states at this stage that it was known that in 1817 Russia offered officers 'and also to restore the Aslanduz guns'. He speaks of a possible Russian scheme 'to possess the person of the Prince'. He wrote to Calcutta with more freedom on Russia's 'designs', and military aid for ʿAbbās Mīrzā, than to Canning, though his letters to the Governor General in India were copied for London's perusal.

31, 32 Baddeley, op. cit., 141. Yermolov was at the time absent from Tiflis.

33 *Rauẓatu'ṣ-Ṣafā*, op. cit., 598.

34 James Morier, op. cit., 213.

35 See note 26 above.

36 Willock to Canning, 13 February 1825. Willock also refers to the withdrawal of British officers, with the exception of Hart and Lindsay (Bethune) in 1815, and the cessation of the British subsidy, which reduced the Shah's payments for the upkeep of the army, which 'is now seldom assembled for more than forty days during the year. But Abbas Mirza was still dear to the Nation; he conciliated all Ranks and he divided with Mahomed Ali Mirza popular favour. His rival brother died. He no longer saw any impediment to succession, and he ceased to court the people in authority at the capital and the chiefs of the powerful Tribes.'

37 Such an anxiety is reflected in paragraph 23 of the long review of Russo-Persian affairs the British Envoy Designate, Col. Macdonald, addressed to the Government of India from Bombay on 22 February 1825, where he states with an interesting reference to 'secret' arrangements between ʿAbbās Mīrzā and the Russians, that 'we should... use our utmost endeavours to open the eyes of The Prince Royal to the dangers that menace him. We should show him that the fulfilment of his secret engagements with Russia can only end in his becoming an empty Pageant, the tool of the hereditary enemies of his country. We should exhort him to restore the number, efficiency, and discipline of his regular Infantry, for which purpose a few steady and experienced officers paid by ourselves might be spared him.'

38 Sir Harford Jones Brydges: *An Account of the Transactions of His Majesty's Mission to the Court of Persia in the Years 1807–11* (London 1834) 255-6.

39 W. Monteith, *Kars and Erzerum* (London 1856) 58.

40 Fatḥ ʿAlī Shāh's laughter on hearing that ʿAbbās Mīrzā was not preparing for war – see note 18 above – is startling revelation of a sense of scorn and contempt in the father, but the report by Willock of a note from the Shāh to the Crown Prince reveals more. In its final sentence, it betrays suspicion that the Prince might have planned treachery against the Shāh. As given in Willock's diary for 9 July 1826, enclosed to Canning under despatch No. 14 of 15 July 1826, it reads: 'In everything I have done your counsel has been followed. You recommended that Aga Seyud Mahomed [*sic*] should be brought forward with the heads of the religion (see note 73 below) – Here they are – You told me to come to Sultanieh – Here I am – Your required money – Money you have had – If you want more I have brought it – You know the state of the frontier and aspect of affairs – If you think peace advisable, conclude it – If you are for war commence it and take the responsibility. *But having brought me so far forward do not pretend to say that I have receded.*' (Italics inserted.)

41 Willock to Canning, 15 July 1826.

42 Baddeley, op. cit., 101.

43 See note 21 above.

44 Willock to Canning 13 February 1825, and 1 April 1825, where he reports ʿAbbās Mīrzā's 'violent inflamation of the liver which endangered his life', due to indulgence in 'spirituous liquors'.

45 Willock to Canning, 13 February 1825.

46 *Rauzatu'ṣ-Ṣafā*, op. cit., 613.

47 Willock to Canning, 5 February 1825.

48 *Memoir of the Right Hon. Sir John McNeill, G.C.B.*, by his Granddaughter (London 1910) 45.

49 Willock to Canning, 5 February 1825.

50 Ibid.

51 FO 60/25. Translation of a letter from Yermolov to ʿAbbās Mīrzā. Enclosure No. 1 with Willock to Canning, 1 April 1825.

52 Willock to Canning, 15 June 1825.

53 FO 60/27. Enclosed under No. 16 of July 23 1826 to Canning.

54 The Sirdar of Erivan was a brave warrior. Under his despatch to Canning of 13 January 1826, Willock forwarded the translation of a letter from Yermolov's deputy, General Wilhelmenov, who said, 'If the Sirdar of Erivan and other Persian authorities attempt to molest our pickets or exceed the line of frontier now in their hands I shall be obliged to protect the possessions and property of the Emperor and oppose those who wish to disturb the friendship between the States'.

55 Baddeley, op. cit., 100, citing the Tsar's instructions to Yermolov of 29 July 1816.

56 See Leon Arpee, *A History of Armenian Christianity* (New York 1946) 245.

57 FO 60/27. Willock to Canning, 31 March 1826.

58 Baddeley, op. cit., 153.

59 Willock to Canning, 28 November 1825.

60 FO 60/27. Willock to Canning, 31 March 1826.

61 FO 60/25. Amherst to Canning, 23 March 1825.

62 In paragraph 22 of his long letter cited in note 37 above.

63 Letter from George Swinton, Secretary to the Government of India, to Macdonald dated 18 March 1825 and enclosed under Willock's despatch No. 14 to Canning of 3 July 1825.

64 Willock to Canning, 17 February 1826.

65 Willock to Canning, 18 July 1826.

66 FO 60/27. Willock to Canning, 27 June 1826.

67 Willock's diary for 22 July 1826.

68 FO 60/27. Willock to Canning, 23 July 1826.

69 See note 30 above.

70 *Memoir of Sir John McNeill*, op. cit., 41.

71 Willock to Canning, 20 May 1826.

72 *Blackwood's Edinburgh Magazine*, XXX, No. CXXII (February 1827) 158-68.

73 Muḥammad 'Alī Tabrīzī Mudarris, *Raiḥānatu'l-Adab* (Tehran 1949) vol. II, 447.

74 Willock to Canning, 27 June 1826. (See note 66 above.)

75 *Raiḥānatu'l-Adab*, op. cit., 447.

76 Willock to Canning, 27 June 1826.

77 *Raiḥānatu'l-Adab*, ibid.

78 Willock to Canning, 27 June 1826.

79 Ibid.

80 Ibid.

81 'Abdullah Mustawfi in the *Sharḥ-i-Zindagānī-ye-Man* (Tehran n.d.) 2nd Edition, vol. I, 66-7, describes how Allāh Yār Khān's father refused nomination instead of Āgha Muḥammad Khān Qājār in the bid for sovereignty of Iran, when the latter had asked the people of Astārābād to support him, and some had suggested Muḥammad Khān Davalu, Allāh Yār Khān's father, as more suitable. He, unlike Āghā Muḥammad Khān Qājār, was not a eunuch. Without his 'self-sacrifice and withdrawal, Āghā Muḥammad Khān's régime may never have been established'–Fatḥ 'Alī Shāh was its second ruler.

82 Willock's diary for 20 July 1826.

83 *Rauẓatu'ṣ-Ṣafā*, op. cit., 645-6.

84 Willock also states, in his despatch No. 14 of 15 July 1826, following a report given him by an informant on 30 June 1826, that 'It appears that many of the Courtiers headed by the Chief Eunuch Muntchehr Khan [*sic*] had prepared a paper for the Shah showing the large amount of presents lately received by the Prime Minister, who, threatened by this danger, and alarmed at the increasing influence of Mirza Abdul Wahab, and of Mirza Abul Hasan Khan, pressed the attendance of the Prince Royal' – the latter came 'express' and for some days 'with the Premier seemed to engross the whole of the Shah's confidence, and succeeded in keeping from access to His Majesty those who do not entertain sentiments congenital with their own'.

85 John William Kaye, *History of the War in Afghanistan* (London 1878) vol. I, 369, from 'The Simlah Manifesto'.

86, 87 'Ruckum of His Royal Highness the Heir-Apparent, ratifying the Abrogation of the Articles 3 and 4 of the Treaty with England, and Translation of a Bond granted by Abbas Mirza, Prince Royal of Persia, to Lieutenant-Colonel Macdonald, British Envoy'–1828, in Aitchison, op. cit., 65 and 64 respectively.

F. R. C. BAGLEY

The Iranian Family Protection Law of 1967. A Milestone in the Advance of Women's Rights

The 17th Dey/7th January of every year is commemorated in Iran as Women's Emancipation Day[1]; it is the anniversary of the date in 1937 on which Rezá Sháh announced at a Girls' High School prize-giving that Iranian women would be forbidden to wear the veil. Another anniversary deserving commemoration will be the 23rd Tir/15th July, date of the entry into force of the Family Protection Law of 1346/1967, which virtually prevents polygamy and restricts divorce to cases of proved irreconcilability. The initiative for these reforms came from the Iranian Women's organizations and from the pro-government New Iran party. Dr Amir ʿAbbás Hoveydá's cabinet submitted the bill in February 1967, and the 21st Majles and the Senate approved it without substantial modification. The text of the bill was kindly sent to me by Mrs Badr ol-Moluk Bámdád, a feminist leader and headmistress whose valued friendship I owe to Mr L. P. Elwell-Sutton.[2] My attempted translation forms the appendix to this article, which sketches the historical and legal backgrounds.

The compulsory unveiling in 1937 was a royal move to force the pace of social evolution. At that time the great majority of the people, and even many of the intelligentsia, were not ready for such a change. Poor women possessing no suitable outer garment other than the *chádor* (veil) suffered severely. The police enforced this law with unbending sternness. The law of 1967, on the other hand, was overdue in the contemporary Iranian social context, and has followed rather than anticipated the trend of public opinion. Nor has there been any sign of significant opposition. A sudden rush of divorces was indeed observed, as husbands made haste to repudiate unwanted wives while they could still do so under the old law; the government responded by closing the divorce registers a few days before 15 July. One reason for the lack of opposition may be that the new law has been carefully drafted so as to ensure compatibility with Islamic principles and law (*shari'at*). In the past, moves to improve women's legal status had encountered bitter clerical opposition.

Although the Iranian Constitution had been won primarily by the joint efforts of patriotic *ákhunds* (*'olamá*) and modernizing Democrats, many women also had in the course of the struggle given proof of ardent patriotism; during the defence of Tabriz by Sattár Khán and Báqer Khán (June 1908 to April 1909), some had actually fought alongside the men. Yet scarcely a voice had been raised to speak from an Islamic viewpoint on behalf of women: to point out, for instance, as the Azharite Qásem Amin had done in Egypt in 1900, that the Qor'án (XXIV, 31; XXXIII, 53, 55, 59) enjoins decency in dress but does not enjoin veiling (except for the Prophet's wives). One of the very few such voices was that of the Esfaháni *mojtahed* (most learned religious scholar) Hájji Mirzá Hádi Dowlatábádi, who stressed the need for girls' education on the basis of a Prophetic saying that all Moslem men and women have a duty to seek knowledge. His daughter Sadiqeh, the pioneer of Iranian feminism, founded at Esfahán in 1918 a women's educational weekly, *Zabán-e Zanán*, the first Iranian publication ever edited by a woman. Having been forced to leave Esfahán, and having been unable to keep the paper going at Tehrán, she went to Paris where she became the first Iranian woman graduate of a foreign university. There have probably been three main reasons why most *ákhunds*, not excluding strong patriots and constitutionalists, have shown hostility to any sort of women's emancipation: (i) they have regarded it as contrary to the *shari'at* and have been unwilling to exercise the right of reinterpretation (*ejtehád*) allowed by Shī'ite Islamic doctrine; (ii) they have regarded it as a move towards the Europeanization of manners (long in evidence among the intelligentsia) and have been opposed to European influence on Iranian manners no less than on Iranian politics; (iii) they have regarded it with suspicion because it was preached by the Bábis and Bahá'is and by Christian missionaries, and was advocated by sceptics such as the poet Iraj (1874–1925) and also by communists. In point of fact, the clerical attitude to women was an important factor in pushing some of the intelligentsia towards scepticism and even towards communism. Other members of the intelligentsia remained believers while sharing the conviction of the poetess Parvin (1906–41): 'The eyes, and the heart, need a covering – but one of decency. The flimsy veil is no foundation for being Moslem.'

Not only the ideological, but also the social, environment was long unfavourable for women's emancipation. When Rezá Sháh came to the throne in 1925, only four State High Schools and a number of American,

British, and French Christian missionary schools provided secondary education for girls. Except in agriculture, domestic service, and the textile and carpet industries, no work outside the home was available for women apart from a handful of teachers. While the popular literature of the period was focused on women and their romances and tragedies, it often represented them as either silly or wily, which no doubt some of them were or had to be in their then uneducated state. Rezá Sháh's attitude to the problem was practical rather than ideological. He desired to enlist 'half the nation' in the nation's service, and saw female seclusion and ignorance as impediments to the nation's health and efficiency. With such considerations in mind, he gave a great impetus to education and public health services for both sexes, and took many other steps, such as founding the Girl Guides as well as the Boy Scouts (both of which were revived after twenty years' abeyance in 1962). At the same time he opened the professions and the civil service (but not the judiciary) to women. Early in his reign he caused Sadiqeh Dowlatábádi, who after returning from Paris would not wear the veil, to be appointed a schools inspector. In 1937 she became head of the Ladies' Centre (*Kánun-e Bánuván*),[3] and in that capacity devoted herself mainly to adult education for women until her death in 1961. Another lady who would not wear the veil, Sárá Khánom (the Iranian widow of a Russian citizen killed by the Bolsheviks), managed to become the first woman typist in the civil service, thanks to support given by the then Prime Minister Mohammad ʿAli Forughi in the face of strong opposition. In the same year 1926, Mrs Bámdád, who then wore the veil, wrote the first Persian textbook of domestic science, and could not get the Ministry of Education to publish it because it was by a woman; she was finally able to carry the matter to the Shah, who ordered the Army press to print the work. In 1936 Mrs Bámdád and ten other ladies[4] managed to gain admission to the recently founded Tehran University as its first women students, again with royal support.

While the groundwork for educational and vocational advance was being laid in these ways, only a quite small fraction of Iranian women had been affected when the unveiling edict struck. Before 1937 only a minority of wives and daughters of officers and officials were following the example of the royal ladies, who had begun to appear in public without the veil (even in the shrine at Qom, where an incident occurred). By 1941, however, a foreign observer could write:

'The announcement (of Rezá Sháh's abdication) was received with gloom by the governing class and the younger generation, who feared

> a return to the medieval, mulla-ridden Persia they thought they had left behind for good and all. This fear received some confirmation from the fact that very soon, for the first time for years, women appeared in the streets of Meshed in the *chadur* enjoined by religion but forbidden by the late Shah'.[5]

(Needless to say, the younger generation would not have agreed that Islam enjoins the *chádor*.)

During Rezá Sháh's reign, the laws of civil status were secularized and the *ákhunds* were deprived of their legal functions. Registration of marriages and divorces, and of births and deaths, in State registries (where existent) was made compulsory by a law of 1931 and again by Book III of Vol. 2 of the Civil Code. The religious (*shar'i*) courts were abolished in all but name. The Judiciary Law of 1936 made future promotion and appointment of judges conditional upon secular qualifications, and a law of 1940 transferred administration of deceased persons' estates and appointment of guardians to the civil courts. In practice, since there was a shortage of lay-trained judges and registrars, clerical personnel continued to be employed, but in a civil capacity. The Civil Code (*Qánun-e Madani*), enacted in 1930 and 1935 and revised and completed in 1939, incorporates much of the *shari'at* into an Iranian civil statute. The laws of wills and successions (Vol. 1, Book II, Part 4, articles 825-949), marriage and divorce (Vol. 2, Book VII, articles 1034-1157), legitimacy, and custody and maintenance of children (Book VIII, articles 1158-1194), guardianship (Book X, articles 1207-1256), and a number of other provisions, follow the Twelver Shī'ite Islamic laws with very few deviations. Among these are article 1041, which lays down minimum marriageable ages of 18 for men and 15 for women, whereas the *shari'at* has nothing to say on the matter. Articles 1121-1132 contain somewhat broader provisions whereby the wife may obtain dissolution of the marriage for medical reasons, non-maintenance, or 'conduct of the husband towards her such that continuation of conjugal life becomes impossible'. The Penal Code, enacted in 1940, is almost wholly European (Italian) in inspiration, but contains a provision (article 189) taken from the *shari'at* whereby a man's killing of his wife, daughter, or sister caught in the act of adultery is not counted as murder[6]; apart from other possible considerations, this is open to the objection that the law contains no provision exempting a woman who kills her husband, son, or brother in the same circumstances.

One of the features of the Iranian scene after Rezá Sháh's abdication was a revival of clerical influence, which reached its peak during the premiership of Dr Mohammad Mosaddeq (1951–3). In general the *ákhunds* spoke in defence of the Constitution, which besides being the charter of national liberties establishes Twelver Shīʿite Islam as the state religion in perpetuity, and contains in the never-implemented article 2 of the Supplementary Fundamental Law a provision whereby the Islamicity of proposed legislation ought to be assessed by a committee of five most learned *mojtaheds*. As defenders of the Constitution, the *ákhunds* were natural allies of those Iranians who, like Dr Mosaddeq and other leaders of the National Front, feared possible external domination and internal dictatorship. Although Iranian women were second to none in nationalist fervour, sermons broadcast from loudspeakers in mosque-minarets not infrequently denounced foreign manners, and many well-educated Iranian ladies resumed the veil—not the black *chádor-namáz*, but the grey or blue *chádor* which leaves the eyes uncovered. (It should be mentioned that since 1941 the compulsory unveiling law has not been enforced.) There was no halt, however, in the advance of girls' education and women's entry into employment. The process has continued with growing rapidity, especially between 1957 and 1960 and since 1963. Even more striking than the emergence of distinguished women surgeons, lawyers, professors, and officials is the increasingly large-scale employment of women as factory-workers, shop-assistants and secretaries, and as teachers and now also as hospital-nurses. This has gone hand in hand with growing urbanization. The census of November 1966 showed a total population of 25,781,000 of whom 9,280,000 are 'urban', including 2,695,000 in Tehran and something over 3,500,000 in other cities and large towns. In most towns the great majority of children, girls as well as boys, now go to primary school. In the countryside, the position is very different; but the Literacy Corps, established in 1963, is attacking the vast problem of rural illiteracy and meeting with an eager response. Between 1941 and 1966, primary school pupils increased in number from 286,000 to 2,033,000, and secondary school pupils from 26,000 to 413,000. Among the 24,344 university students in 1964, 4,183 were women.

The years 1960–63 were a time of renewed tension in Iran, and from May 1961 to September 1963 parliament was suspended. The principal issues were land reform and electoral reform. At the same time, leading Iranian women showed great activity in organizations formed not only for social and charitable purposes but also to demand political rights and legal reforms. With royal encouragement, many of them in 1959 joined in a High Council of Women's Organizations. The electoral laws dating from

1911, besides being unsuited for the increasingly literate population, withheld the suffrage from minors, lunatics, convicts and women (and also from the military and police). Women were debarred from the Majles and Senate and from cabinet office. Their legal status under various provisions of the Civil Code (some of which will later be mentioned) was out of keeping with modern urban conditions, in which the old patriarchal 'extended' family relationships have largely disappeared. Some of the most forceful advocacy of reform came from the Women's United Nations Association founded in 1959 by Mrs Bámdád to demand full application of the UN Charter of Human Rights in Iran with particular reference to women's rights, and from the Women Lawyers' Union led by Dr (later Senator) Mrs Mehrangiz Menuchehrián, Mrs Safiniá, and Mrs Sufi. In 1962, when municipal elections were held at Esfahán, Mrs Hakami, wife of a locally well-known doctor of medicine, stood as a candidate but was forced to withdraw, even though the Municipal Elections law contained no clause debarring women. The Shah's sisters, and later Queen Farah and her mother, added strength to the feminist cause by their outspoken sympathy. At the same time, substance accrued to it from research, e.g. from the studies of Iranian rural women by Dr Ázar Rahnomá (daughter of the modern biographer of the Prophet Mohammad and of the Emám Hoseyn, Mr Zeyn ol-ʿÁbedin Ráhnomá).

Mention must also be made of the poetess Forugh Farrokhzád (b. 1934), whose passionate verses have won immense popularity.[7] Her life was cut short by a car crash in Tehran on 13 February 1967. In a poem 'To my Sister' she has written:

How much longer, for a scrap of bread
  have you to become a centenarian Hájji's temporary wife,
to put up with rivals, a second, a third,
  to suffer injustice and oppression . . . my Sister?

This angry sob must surely
  become a roar and a shout;
you must smash these heavy fetters
  so that life may be made free for you.

Arise from your abode, pluck out the root of injustice,
  give relief to your grief-stricken heart,
strive, strive for your freedom's sake
  to change the Law!

Dr ʿAli Amini, Prime Minister from May 1961 to July 1962, was unsympathetic to the women's cause; he urged them to devote themselves to charity instead of demanding the vote, and accused them of selfishness. It appears that on account of disproportion between the numbers of well-educated young men and well-educated young women, parents of the latter have sometimes been able to stipulate excessive dowries in marriage contracts, and that the young women themselves have sometimes through their demands for modern luxuries imposed heavy financial and mental strains on their husbands. This problem was partly linked with the insecurity of wives under the divorce laws before the reform of 1967. Such 'spoiltness' was confined to a small fraction of the upper classes, and will be further remedied if the government, having established the Literacy Corps, the Health Corps (1964), and the Extension and Development Corps (1965) for male graduates of secondary schools and universities, proceeds to set up a similar social service corps for women.

Clerical attitudes during the years 1960 to 1963 appear to have been influenced mainly by the land reform and the suspension of parliament. Even when it was made clear that *vaqf* (religiously endowed) lands would be leased by the Land Reform Organization for ninety-nine years and not expropriated, and that the *vaqf* revenues would actually be increased, many *ákhunds* feared – in the event incorrectly – that they might lose their financial and therewith spiritual independence. They also objected to the enactment of such measures by decree while parliament was in abeyance; and the revived National Front, while favouring land reform, was in agreement with them on this point. The same situation was seen when Dr Amini's successor, Mr Asadolláh ʿAlam, and the Shah himself, indicated the government's intention to grant women's suffrage. Another question which arose was whether women would have the same rights as men to acquire ownership of lands being distributed under the land reform, or whether they would only be able to acquire half shares or would be debarred altogether. Women were allowed to vote 'unofficially' in the referendum of 26 January 1963, when the nation approved land reform and electoral reform and other points of the Shah's Six-Point programme, and 271,000 women voted in this way. In March the Women Lawyers' Union secured the government's pledge of equal rights for women in the land reform. In August an electoral reform law, providing *inter alia* for full women's suffrage, was promulgated by decree; together with the land reform and other measures, it was retrospectively ratified by the 21st Majles. In the meantime, religious riots had taken place at Qom in March and at Tehrán and Shiráz in June. The rioters had demanded release of two arrested *mojtaheds*, Áyatolláh Khomeyni and Áyatolláh Khunsari, and restoration of parliamentary government. Government sources spoke of a foreign (Egyptian) hand in the disorders. Another factor was the denunciation of women's suffrage by certain *ákhunds* who believed it to be un-Islamic. The Shah, on the other hand, emphasized his conviction that Iran's 'White' revolution (in which women's suffrage formed an important item) was 'sacred because it is based on the principles and spirit of Islamic teachings, namely on the principles of equality and justice, which are the most modern principles and the wishes of the modern civilized society'.

Women voted officially for the first time in the general election of 17 September 1963, which returned six women deputies to the 21st Majles. Two women Senators were appointed, and in June 1965 Iran's first woman minister, Dr Farrokhru Parsáy, joined Dr Hoveydá's cabinet as Vice-Minister of Education. In the civil service, Mrs Varzi became head of the State Factories Department, and Mrs Qaraghozlu became head of the Tribal Affairs Department. More recently Iranian recognition of the political equality of men and women has been reasserted by the constitutional amendment of May 1967. This requires the Majles and Senate to elect a Regent, who will exercise the royal powers in the event of the Shah's demise before the heir to the throne reaches majority (which is fixed at 20). The two Houses chose as the Regent-Designate H.I.M. Queen Farah.[8] (The monarch must still constitutionally be male.) At the Coronation on 26 October 1967, for the first time in Iranian history the Queen also was crowned. Queen Farah's dignity and beauty on this occasion symbolized for Iran and the world the new standing of Iranian women.

It was noteworthy that for a long time the 21st Majles and the Senate with their women members did not debate the question of reform of the Civil Code. A probable explanation is that after the riots of 1963 the government wished to allow time for cooling of tempers and continuance of the evolution in public opinion. Royal visits to the principal shrines indicated the government's desire to accord respect to the *ákhunds*. The Women's Organizations, however, began to criticize the silence on legal reform. After a national conference in 1965, the High Council of Women's Organizations enlarged its scope in 1966 to include more provincial and other groups, and changed its name to All-Iran Women's Organization; and the 7,000 delegates at its first assembly in October of the same year insisted that the need for reform was urgent. The New Iran party was sympathetic, and in response to the women's and the party's demands, the Family Protection Bill of 1967 was drafted by the Ministry of Justice.

Women's disabilities under the Civil Code form a subject of vast extent and complexity. In regard to the inheritance provisions whereby a woman receives half the comparable share allotted to a man, it will suffice to say that in modern conditions the law can be particularly hard on widows. A widow who was the only wife receives one eighth of the estate, or one-quarter if childless (articles 913, 927 and 938); co-wives receive proportionately less. Children, however, are legally obliged to maintain indigent parents and grandparents (articles 1197 and 1200) if they are able to do so (article 1198). The Law of 1967 does not touch on inheritance.

Polygamy is rare in Iran, particularly among the educated younger generation, though the late Hasan ʿAli Mansur, Prime Minister from March 1964 to January 1965, took a second wife. The number of 'co-wives' in 1964 was given as 74,000. Among the upper classes, it is common practice to put a clause into the marriage contract stipulating that the wife may obtain a divorce if the husband takes a second wife; article 1119 empowers the courts to enforce such stipulations. The majority of co-wives today appear to have the status of temporary wife (*sigheh*).

Temporary marriage (*motʿeh*), sanctioned by articles 1075, 1076 and 1077 (cf. Q. IV, 28), is not uncommon. Although the husband cannot divorce his temporary wife, he may renounce the unexpired period of the marriage (article 1139), while she cannot do likewise. She is entitled, like the full wife, to a dowry (*mahr*) which becomes her permanent property, and like the divorced wife to maintenance during the *ʿeddeh* (waiting period before possible remarriage); the *ʿeddeh* is three menses for the divorced wife, two menses for the temporary wife, and four months and ten days for the widow in both types of marriage (articles 1150-1157). Unlike the full wife, the temporary wife cannot inherit from her husband, nor he from her (article 940); but children of temporary and full marriages have equal inheritance rights. In the past, temporary marriage was often a form of prostitution, and this may still sometimes be the case. In modern times, temporary wives are more often domestic servants, whose presence and labour the proprietor desires to keep for life or for a quite long time. Members of the lower classes sometimes also prefer temporary marriage so as to save the expense of marriage celebrations. The status of the *sigheh* (temporary wife) can lead to severe hardship when the marriage expires or the husband dies, and is inconsistent with the dignity of the modern female citizen of Iran.

Although article 1062 requires that both parties to a marriage shall clearly give their consent, articles 1042 and 1043 require the woman to obtain her father's or grandfather's permission before contracting a first marriage, though if over eighteen she may appeal to the court against refusal. Furthermore, either party may appoint a proxy to conclude the marriage contract (articles 1071-1074). Under the *shari'at* the prospective wife in a first marriage had to be represented by her father or other guardian as proxy, and this custom is still widespread. The Civil Code does not adequately protect daughters from thus being 'given away' against their wish by parents, and the new law does not tackle this problem.

Article 1059 follows the *shari'at* in forbidding the Moslem woman to marry a non-Moslem man but not *vice versa*, and article 1060 requires the Iranian woman to obtain official permission before marrying a foreigner but not *vice versa*. All Iranians, including Bábis and Bahá'is, are assumed to be Moslems unless they are members of the Zoroastrian, Jewish, Armenian, Assyrian or other Christian communities, whose religious courts possess statutorily recognized jurisdiction over their family legal matters. In recent years, marriages between Iranian Moslem women and Iranian or European and American non-Moslem men have become more frequent. The man must make a profession of Islam before the registrar and an *ákhund*, and take an additional Moslem first name; he and the children will be classified as Moslems. Some of these husbands take the view that they have made the profession under legal duress. An Iranian woman's marriage to a foreigner abroad under foreign law is not recognized in Iran, and she runs a risk of losing her inheritance rights. These provisions, which lie beyond the scope of the new law, are criticized by secularists and by those who think that the problem should be regulated on a reciprocal basis.

Much the most serious problem is divorce, not only because it is widespread in Iran (as elsewhere), but also because the wife's insecurity under the old law could undermine conjugal happiness. Under articles 1133 and 1134, the husband could divorce his (full) wife whenever he pleased, by pronouncing the verb *talaq* in the presence of two witnesses (Q. LXV, 2), who were supposed to urge caution and reconciliation; but in practice the legal requirement of their presence was not enforced. The husband could, if he wished, revoke the divorce before the expiry of the waiting period (*'eddeh*); but after pronouncing the verb three times, in principle before the two witnesses, he could not remarry the wife unless she had meanwhile been married and divorced by another man, the *mohallel* (whose role figures prominently in modern Persian fiction). In point of fact, it is stated that 42½ per cent of the dissolutions of marriages registered before the new law were obtained on the initiative of the wife. This could be done *inter alia* by virtue of the non-maintenance and ill-treatment clauses (articles 1129 and 1130), and by the provisions called *khol'* and *mobára'at* whereby the wife could buy a divorce by making a gift or ceding her dowry to the husband (articles 1146 and 1147). Among the upper classes, the wife's insecurity was commonly mitigated by the practice of stipulating a large dowry, sufficient to deter the husband from thought of divorce; but this practice, as already mentioned, could itself be a source of unhappiness. Among the mass of the people, the dowry is inevitably too small to make much difference to the divorced wife's financial position. The divorce provisions of the Civil Code presupposed a patriarchal society in which the divorced or temporary wife would be readmitted and maintained by her own clan. Modern urban Iranian society is not of such a character. Public opinion could no longer tolerate the position in which a man might at any moment throw his wife (and children) out of the house, often in order to take a younger wife.

The custody of children of divorced parents belongs to the mother while the son is under two and the daughter is under seven, and thereafter reverts to the father (article 1169); but the legal guardianship of children (from continuing and dissolved marriages alike), and the financial responsibility for their maintenance and upbringing, fall upon the father and paternal grandfather, or if they are deceased on a male guardian appointed by them (articles 1180-1194). These provisions often cause friction and unhappiness, and may or may not in a given situation be in the children's best interest.

The Law of 1967 does not expressly repeal any articles of the Civil Code, but prevails where the two statutes are in conflict.

The restriction of polygamy in Article 15 of the new Law follows the Qor'án, IV, 3 ('if you fear you will not be equitable, then only one'). A man may not now marry an additional wife without Court permission, which will only be given when the Court finds after enquiry that he is financially and otherwise able to do justice to both or all. Cases in which Courts will be satisfied as to such ability are expected to be very rare. Plural marriage without Court permission now becomes a penal offence. Previously a man could legally marry four full wives and any number of temporary wives. The new law makes no mention of temporary marriage, but allows only one wife by either form of marriage unless Court permission for the taking of a co-wife is granted. Existing plural marriages are of course respected.

As the law now stands, a presently unmarried man may still marry one temporary wife for a specified term, and may still (if he so wishes) renounce his rights over her before the expiry of the term.

Repudiation of the wife by the husband is no longer permitted. Divorce can now only be effected with the permission of a Court, which must first satisfy itself that the husband and wife cannot be reconciled. The wife has the same right as the husband to apply to the Court for a Certificate of Irreconcilability; if there is mutual consent they may jointly apply (articles 6, 8, and 9).

The Court's duty to try to reconcile the estranged spouses (articles 7 and 8) accords with the spirit of the Qor'án, IV, 39 ('if you fear a breach between the two, bring forth an arbiter from his people and an arbiter from her people'), and of the Twelver Shī'ite *sharī'at*, which imposes this duty on the two required witnesses of a divorce. Since divorce under the new Law can only be granted after proof of irreconcilability, it is now always final (article 18), and the provisions of the Civil Code concerning revocable divorce are superseded.

Articles 13, 14, and 9 greatly improve the position of children of divorced parents. The Court may now decide that a child is to stay with the mother or another person (instead of the father). Besides determining the children's manner of upbringing and expenses of maintenance, the Court may now fix the sums to be paid by the father or mother or both; previously only the father was financially liable, though the mother might voluntarily accept a liability. Divorced mothers who are well off may thus be required to contribute. The Court is also to prescribe arrangements whereby each parent may see the children. A breakdown of the upbringing and maintenance arrangements may be brought by a parent or relative, or by the Public Prosecutor, to the attention of the Court, which must then if necessary prescribe new arrangements.

The legal aid provision in article 4 should enable all classes to take advantage of the new Law.

Article 16 deserves criticism for its non-reciprocity, because it empowers the husband to restrain the wife from engaging in a disreputable activity but gives the wife no similar legal power over the husband.

It remains to be seen how the courts will cope with the burden of the new Law. Court business of all kinds (including matrimonial business) was already increasing very rapidly, and delays were getting worse on account of less rapid increase in the supply of judges and lawyers. Under article 3, expert assessors and social workers will also be required. On the other hand, procedure is to be simplified (article 1), and many of the complications of the Civil Code are superseded. There are obvious risks of intimidation and corruption; but in recent years, the Iranian law courts, though overworked, have maintained high standards of integrity. It may be some time before the Law can be enforced in rural Iran. These matters do not come within the jurisdiction of the Houses of Justice (courts of village elders), which the government has been setting up since 1963 in order to make legal facilities available in the villages, especially for land reform cases.

Mrs Bámdád in her letter made the following comment:

'Of course not all the Women's demands have been fulfilled in this Law. At the same time it is going to be very useful. One of the matters which will have to be pursued is that of the wife's subsistence after divorce, which has not yet been provided for. If this problem is to be properly solved, thought will have to be given to the matter of (more) substantial dowries.

The Moslem woman has always enjoyed financial independence, provided of course that she owns some assets. Moreover she can accumulate assets. But the great number whose only work is house-keeping and child-rearing do not possess or acquire anything, and after divorce are left hungry.

I once made a speech on this subject at a gathering. "Do you feel sure", I asked, "that a divorced woman after her three months and ten days of legal maintenance can straight away find another husband?" A gentleman in the audience said jokingly, "Not unless the Court takes on the job of finding one!"'

The Family Protection Law [*Qánun-e Ḥemáyat-e Khánvádeh*] Brought into Force on 23rd Tir 1346/15th July 1967

ARTICLE 1. All civil cases arising over matrimonial matters, and all family disputes, will be examined in the District [*Shahrestán*] Courts or, in places where no District Court exists, in the Sub-District [*Bakhsh*] Courts, without observance of the formalities of the Code of Civil Procedure.

ARTICLE 2. Family disputes mean disputes which have arisen between any of the following – wife, husband, children, paternal grandfather, executor [*vaṣi*], or guardian [*qayyem*] – over rights and duties laid down in Books VII (Marriage and Divorce), VIII (Children), IX (The Family), and X

(Legal Incapacity [*Ḥajr*] and Guardianship), of the Civil Code, and Articles 1005, 1007,[9] 1028, 1029 and 1030[10] of the said Code, and also in the relevant Articles of the Uncontested [*Ḥasbi*] Cases Law.

ARTICLE 3. The Court may carry out any sort of investigation or action needed to clarify disputed matters and verify facts – e.g. inquiry from witnesses and informants, utilization of social workers, etc. – in whatever manner may be appropriate.

ARTICLE 4. The Court, if it finds either party to be indigent, may exempt [him and / or her] from payment of the cost of the proceedings, professional fees, court fees, etc., and may appoint an advocate free of charge. If the award is in favour of the indigent party, the other party may, at the Court's discretion, be compelled to pay the said costs.

ARTICLE 5. The advocates and professional experts mentioned in the previous Article are required to carry out the Court's instructions.

ARTICLE 6. On application by either party, the Court is required to refer disputed matters, except examination of the authenticity [*rasidegi be-aṣl*] of a marriage or divorce, to one or not more than three Judges. Determination of the delay pending announcement of the Judges' opinion rests with the Court. If the Court finds that the said application has been made for purposes of avoiding examination or of procrastination, it will refrain from accepting the application. Judgements under this Law will not be subject to the regulations on judgements contained in the Code of Civil Procedure.

ARTICLE 7. The Judge or Judges will endeavour to reconcile the parties. If they do not succeed in establishing concord, they will express their opinion on the substance of the case and transmit it to the Court. The Judges' opinion will be notified by the Court to the parties, and will within a period of ten days from the date of notification be open to appeal [*eʿteráẕ*]. If the parties accept the Judge's opinion, or make no appeal within the prescribed period, the judgement will be made binding. In the event of an appeal, the Court will in special session study the grounds of the appeal and pass judgement. This judgement is final.

ARTICLE 8. Execution of a divorce will take place after examination of the case by the Court and issue of a Certificate of Irreconcilability. The applicant for a Certificate of Irreconcilability must submit an application-form to the Court. On the said application-form the reasons for the application must be stated explicitly and in detail. After receipt of the application-form, the Court will endeavour, directly or if it thinks fit through the Judge or Judges, to establish concord between the husband and wife and to prevent the occurrence of divorce. If the Court's efforts to obtain reconciliation achieve no result, the Court will issue a Certificate of Irreconcilability. After receipt of the said certificate, the Divorce Registry will take steps to execute and register the divorce-deed [*ṣigheh-ye ṭaláq*].

ARTICLE 9. In cases in which mutual agreement on execution of the divorce has been reached between the husband and wife, the parties must declare their agreement to the Court, and the Court will issue the Certificate of Irreconcilability. When the two spouses, in the declaration which they make to the Court, do not give grounds to expect [*pishbini*] satisfactory arrangements for maintenance and payment of the expenses of the children, the Court will take action in accordance with Article 13 of the present Law. If the arrangements made by the two spouses for maintenance of the children break down after the occurrence of the divorce, action will be taken by the Court on the basis of a declaration from one of the child's parents or relatives, or by the public Prosecutor of the District [*Shahrestán*], in accordance with Article 14 of the present Law.

ARTICLE 10. In a situation arising under Article 4 of the Marriage Law,[11] if the wife wishes to divorce herself by proxy through the agency of the husband, she also must obtain a Certificate of Irreconcilability from the Court in accordance with Article 8 [of the present Law].

ARTICLE 11. In addition to the situations mentioned in the Civil Code, the wife or husband may also in the following situations apply to the Court for a Certificate of Irreconcilability:

(i) If the wife or husband is sentenced finally and definitely to a penalty of five or more years' imprisonment, or to a fine involving five years' imprisonment as the consequence of inability to pay, or to imprisonment and a fine which together might result in five or more years' imprisonment, and if the prison-sentence or fine is in the course of execution.

(ii) Affliction with any sort of pernicious habit [*e'teyád*] which in the judgement of the Court is capable of making the husband's and wife's life impossible and of imparting damage to the foundation of the family life.

(iii) When the husband takes another consort, without the wife's consent, even if with Court sanction.

(iv) When one of the spouses abandons the family life.

ARTICLE 12. When either of the spouses is finally and definitely convicted in Court following commission of a crime which detracts from the family's respectability and the other spouse's repute, the wife or husband may apply to the Court for issue of a Certificate of Irreconcilability. The decision whether a crime detracts from family respectability and repute rests with the Court [and is to be made] with due regard to the circumstances of the two parties and to customary usage [*'orf*] and other criteria.

ARTICLE 13. In all situations in which a matrimonial case leads to the issue of a Certificate of Irreconcilability, the Court will determine and fix the manner of maintenance of the children, and the scale of subsistence [*nafaqeh*] for the woman in the waiting period before possible re-marriage [*'eddeh*], having due regard to the moral and financial position of the two parties and the welfare of the children. The Court in issuing the Certificate of Irreconcilability is required to determine how the children shall be maintained after the divorce, and if it is decided that the children shall stay with the mother or with another person, to specify the arrangements for their maintenance and the scale of their expenses. The subsistence of the dependent woman [*'eyál*] will be provided from the income and assets of the man and the subsistence of the children from the income and assets of the man or the woman or both, including retirement-pension payments. The Court will determine what sum must be provided out of the husband's or the two spouses' income and assets for each child, and will fix a satisfactory method for payment of it. The Court will also prescribe arrangements for the two parties to see [*moláqát*] the children. In the event of absence or decease of the father or mother, the right to see the children will be transferred to the absent or deceased parent's first-degree relatives. Children whose parents have separated before the passage of the present Law will come under the provisions of this Article, unless arrangements for the cost of their maintenance and upbringing [*ḥeẓánat*] have been made in a satisfactory manner.

ARTICLE 14. In every situation in which the Court, acting upon the declaration of a parent or relative of the child or upon that of the District Public Prosecutor, finds that reconsideration of the [provision for] upbringing is necessary, it will reconsider its previous decision. In such situations the Court may transfer the upbringing to any person whom it deems appropriate; but in any event the expenses of the upbringing are chargeable to the person who is made responsible for their payment by virtue of the present Law.

ARTICLE 15. When a man wishes, while keeping one wife, to take another wife, he must obtain permission from the Court. The Court will give permission to take a new consort at the time when it will have obtained, by means of inquiry from the actual wife and by taking other necessary steps, evidence of the man's financial capacity and of his ability to do justice [*ejrá-ye' adálat*] to his consorts. When a man proceeds to marry in disregard of the provisions of this Article, he will be prosecuted and punished in accordance with Article 5 of the Marriage Law approved in 1310/1931–1316/1937.[12]

ARTICLE 16. The husband may, with the Court's sanction, restrain his wife from engaging in any sort of employment [*shoghl*] which will be incompatible with the family's best interests or his own or the wife's respectability.

ARTICLE 17. The Court's decision is final in the following fields and only open to appeal [*pozhuhesh-pazir*] in other fields:

(i) Issue of Certificates of Irreconcilability.

(ii) Determination of subsistence in the waiting period before possible remarriage and of children's maintenance expenses.

(iii) Children's rights to see the father or mother or the first-degree relatives of an absent or deceased [parent].

(iv) Grant of the permission prescribed in Article 15.

ARTICLE 18. Divorces which take place in accordance with this law are irrevocable [*qábel-e roju' nist*].

ARTICLE 19. The provisions of Articles 11, 12, 15, and 18 will be inserted in marriage contract documents as part of the terms of the contract. In these contexts a woman's authorization of a proxy to apply [on her behalf] for execution of the said provisions will be clearly and explicitly stated.

ARTICLE 20. One or both spouses may apply to the Court demanding that before the Court goes into the substance of the dispute it shall urgently examine problems of the children's upbringing or actual circumstances or maintenance expenses and issue an injunction [*qarár*]. The Court when it receives such an application is required to examine the problem. The Court's provisional injunction in the matter of the children's upbringing or expenses is binding [*qat'i*] and will be put into execution forthwith.

ARTICLE 21. After the implementation of the present Law, Divorce Registries may not proceed with the execution and registration of a divorce-deed unless the Certificate of Irreconcilability has been produced. Persons who contravene [this provision] will incur disciplinary penalties from grade 4 upwards.

ARTICLE 22. Examination of family matters in the Courts will be performed without the presence of spectators.

ARTICLE 23. Execution of sentences passed by the Courts is subject to the General Regulations.

ARTICLE 24. Rules for the implementation of the present Law will be drawn up by the Ministry of Justice within one month from the date of its enactment and will be put into execution after approval by the Council of

Ministers. Implementation of the Law is contingent on approval of the said rule-book.

NOTES

1 Since this was written, Mrs Bámdád (see below) has told me that the celebration is now held on the 8th Esfand/27th February, anniversary of H.I.M. the Shah's speech to the Senate in 1963 announcing that women's legal disabilities would be removed and in particular that women would receive the right to vote.

2 I am also indebted to Mr Elwell-Sutton for the loan of vol. 2 of the Civil Code and other material.

3 This Centre had been founded at Rezá Shah's request by twenty ladies in April 1936. Their task was initially to make propaganda for unveiling, and after the decree of 7 January 1937, to facilitate its enforcement. The Centre afterwards established a school for adult women.

4 Among them were Senator Dr Mrs Mehrangiz Menuchehrián, President of the Women Lawyers' Union and authoress of the most important Persian book on women's legal rights; and Mrs Shams ol-Moluk Javáher al-Kalám, teacher and authoress, wife of the journalist and author Mr ʿAli Javáher ol-Kalám. The University authorities had at first refused to matriculate them on the grounds that the genderless Persian language refers to men only unless women are specified. On the same grounds in 1962, women were disqualified from election to municipal office (see below).

5 Sir Clarmont Skrine, *World War in Iran* (London 1962) 109.

6 In English law, such killing is 'manslaughter', not 'murder'.

7 See article by Girdhari Tikku in *Studia Islamica*, XXVI (1967) 149-73.

8 Iranian history records three reigning queens: Purándokht (629–30) and Ázarmidokht (631) of the Sásánid dynasty, and Ábesh Khátun (1264–84) of the Salghorid Atábek dynasty of Fárs.

9 Articles 1005 and 1006 concern Domicile.

10 Articles 1028, 1029 and 1030 concern Absence.

11 I.e. the Marriage and Divorce Law of 1st Mehr 1310/4th October 1931. Article 4 states that the parties 'may insert in the marriage contract or in any other contract any stipulation which is not in contradiction with the marriage itself'.

12 Article 5 of the 1931 Law imposes a penalty of 6 months to 2 years' imprisonment on a husband or wife who before the marriage contract practises a fraud on the other party without which the marriage would not have taken place. The 1937 Law amends the 1931 Law in regard to penalties for marriage outside the official Registry Office where one exists, and for marriage below the minimum age (18 for men and 15 for women).

H. W. BAILEY

Ancient Kamboja

The Kamboja problem of ancient Afghanistan touches a field which it was always a pleasure to discuss with my old friend Professor Vladimir Minorsky. That land played a large part in his book, the Ḥudūd al-ʿĀlam, and he had an insistent interest in names.

An ethnic name *Kamboja-* has been transmitted in ancient Indian books. A statement in the Nirukta of Yāska,[1] about 300 B.C., whether before or after Pāṇini, has often been quoted: *śavatir gati-karmā kambojeṣv eva bhāṣyate* 'the word *śavati* as a verb of motion is spoken only among the Kambojas'.

If, as seems now agreed,[2] *śavati* 'he goes' is Iranian, it corresponds to OPers. *šiyav-* (=*šyav-*), Av. *šyav-*, *šav-*, Sogd. *šw-*, NPers. *šav-*, *šud*, Pašto *šwəl*, beside which the more archaic form is kept in Saka (of Khotan) *tsv-*, *tsuta-*, 2nd sing. imperative *tso* (*ts*=*tsy*), Saka (of Tumšuq) *ccha-*, Ossetic Digoron *cäu-*, *cud*, 2nd sing. *co* (*c*=*ts*). The oldest Indo-Iranian form is OInd. *cyávate*, *cyutá-*, *cyautná-*.

The *Kă̆mboja-* are frequently named in OIndian texts. The earliest dated reference is in the Aśoka inscriptions,[3] Rock Edict 3, *yona-kaṃboja-gaṃdhāra-* with variants *kaṃboca-* and *kamboya-*. There is also the compound *yona-kaṃbojeṣu* (variant *-oyeṣu*).[4]

The Kāmboja are frequent in the Mahābhārata (listed in S. Sörensen's *An index to the names in the Mahābhārata*). The associations are *kāmboja-vara-bāhlikāḥ*; *yavana-kāmbojāḥ*; *śaka-kāmboja-bāhlikāḥ*; *yauna-kāmboja-gāndhārāḥ*. The *kāmboja-rāja-* is named. Their horses are particularly celebrated (*aśva-*, *vājin-*, *haya-*, *turaga-*); the *javana- haya-* 'swift horses' indicate the famous horses of Farghānah breed.

Later the Bhāratavarṣa[5] of the Purāṇas cites the *kāmbojā daradāś caiva*. The name occurs in a long geographical list of Rājaśekhara's Kāvyamīmāṃsā[6] naming people in the Uttarāpatha 'northern lands': *śaka-kekaya-vokkāṇa-hūṇa-vāṇāyuja-kāmboja-vāhlika-vahlava-limpāka-*. Here we note *Vokkāṇa-* 'Wakhān', *Vāhlika-* 'Bactria', *Limpāka-*, *Lampāka-* 'Lamghān'.

Bāṇa[7] (seventh century) refers to the horses: *āskandat-kāmboja-vāji-śata-* 'a hundred prancing Kāmboja horses'. Here the Commentator remarks: *kāmbojāḥ, bāhlika-deśajāḥ* 'the Kāmbojas originate in Bactria'.

A Buddhist Sanskrit Vinaya text[8] has the *śataṃ kāmbojikānāṃ kanyānām* 'a hundred girls of Kamboja', rendered by Tibetan *thog-gar* (Derge ed.: *tho-gar*) *yul-gyi bu-mo brgya*, Mongol *togar ulus-un yagun ükin*.

The tenth-century Formulary[9] (Sanskrit-Tibetan) has *kamodza-radza* (with *-m-* from *-mb-*). The Tibetan Chronicle Dpag-bsam-ljon-bzaṅ (The Excellent Kalpa-vṛkṣa)[10] has a long list of peoples including *tho-gar yul daṅ yobana daṅ kambodze daṅ khaśa daṅ ḫuna daṅ darta daṅ*.

Sten Konow[11] saw *kambojika* in the *kamuia* of the Mathurā Lion capital in Kharoṣṭhī script.

Identifications of the Kamboja- country have varied. The Commentator on Bāṇa said *Bāhlika-deśa-*; the Tibetan Vinaya rendered *Tho-gar*; J. Marquart, *Untersuchungen zur Geschichte von Eran*, II, 140, put it in south-west Chitral, land of the Kāfirs; Sylvain Lévi, *JA* (1918, part 1) 128 proposed Kafiristan, but in *JA* (1923, part 2) 52 thought *Kapiśa*, in Tibetan *Ka-bu-śa* was a form of the word Kamboja; B. Liebich, *Zur Einführung in die indische einheimische Sprachwissenschaft*, I, 26, suggested the Kābul valley; J. Bloch for Aśoka offered the Kōhistān north-east of Kābul. Helmut Hoffmann, 'Literarhistorische Bemerkungen zur Sekoddeśaṭīkā des Naḍapāda' in the *Festschrift Schubring*, 142, identified Nūristān with Udyāna. More recently E. Benveniste, *JA* (1958) 45-8, proposed to see in the Graeco-Aramaic inscription from Qandahār with its Iranian words an address to the closely associated *Yona-* and *Kamboja-* of that region.

The Pali Jātaka Book (6,208) refers to the Kambojas' *anariya-* 'non-Aryan' practice of killing many kinds of insect, in which a Zoroastrian Mazdean custom has been detected.

If then the Kamboja language is attested as Iranian by Yāska's *śav ati* and by the Iranian words in the Graeco-Aramaic inscription of Qandahār, their name may also be Iranian. Assuming this Iranian origin it is suggested here that a connexion can be found in the Iranian vocabulary. The interpretation here offered receives some support from the fact that it provides solutions to two outstanding problems.

First as to the form of the word *kamboja-*: this will be in Iranian orthography **kambauǰa-*. It may contain a triple suffix *-au-ǰ-a-*, as a (different) triple suffix *-au-t-a-* is found in OPers. *kapautaka-*, OInd. *kapota-*, Saka *kavūta-*, Balōčī *kapōt*,[12] added to a word *kamba-*. Or it may be a compound. Then *kamba-* (in Av. *kambišta-* 'least' to *kamna-* 'little') with *auǰa-* 'force' (Av. *aoǰah-*, ZorPahl *ōž*, OInd. *ójas-*) would give 'having little force', unsuitable for an ethnic name; something more laudatory or arrogant will be desired. A third analysis seems to be more promising: **kam-bauǰa-* or **kan-bauǰa-*, with the following justification.

The second component **bauǰa-* (*-boja*)- derives from a base Iranian *baug-*. Three bases *baug-* can be posited in Iranian.

(1) *baug-* 'to bend' in Saka *haṃbujs-* 'to bow down', pres. 3rd sing. *haṃbuśdä*, participle in pret. *haṃbujsyāṃdä* 'they bowed', and from **buxta-* the participle *haṃphve*, and 1st sing. pret. *haṃphutemä* 'I bowed down', with adjective *haṃbujsai* 'bowed'. With *ni-* 'down' Saka has *nihujs-*, pres. 3rd sing. *nihuśdä*, participle *nihuta-* 'to sink, set'; *nihujsandä* 'occident, west'.[13] Here Indo-Iranian *bh-* has had three treatments: after *-m-* by *b-* and *ph-*, and intervocalically by *-h-*. probably replacing *-f-* from *bh-*. Balōčī *bōg*, *bōγ* 'limb' as the 'bending part' is from **bauga-*.

(2) *baug-* 'to open, free, loose, deliver, save' in Av. *baog-*, ZorPahl. *bōž-*, *bōxtan*, *bōxt*, *bōxtak*, Armen. lw *boyž*, *boužem*, Balōčī *bōǰag*, *bōhta*, *bōtka*, *bōžay*, *bōxta*, *buxta*, Ossetic Digoron *buγdäg* 'open'.

(3*a*) *baug-* 'to enjoy, experience pleasure or pain; cause to enjoy, satisfy, supply food' in Av. *baog-*, *baoxšna-*, OPers. *σαθραβουζανης*, Mid-Iranian names *-bōžan*, *-bōxt*, Armen. lw *bošxnem*, *əmbošxnem* 'to enjoy', Saka *haṃbuśdä* 'he enjoys, possesses',[14] *būka-* 'food', *būkaja* 'steward' (if not from **baxtaka-*) corresponding to Pali *bhattakāraka-* 'preparer of food', *bǖjsana* 'feast' (from the contexts).[15]

(3*b*) *baug-* 'possess, be lord, rule' deriving from 'enjoy', in Saka *bǖjsaṃjā-* fem., a title used of a queen and a *devī* goddess, hence 'lady, madame' from 'female ruler'. It is a title of the *devī* Sthānavatī.[16]

A similar series can be cited from OIndian.[17]

(1) *bhogá-s* 'bend', *bhúja-s* 'arm', *bhujáti*, *bhugná-* 'to bend'.

(2*a*) *bhog-* 'to enjoy, make to enjoy', *bhóga-s* 'enjoyment', *bhójana-m* 'food', *bhunákti*, *bhuktá-* 'to enjoy, possess', Pali *bhogga-m* 'property'.

(2*b*) Vedic Aitareya-brāhmaṇa *bhojá-* 'royal title', *bhaujya-m* 'status of a bhojá- prince'; Pali *bhoja-* 'dependent, freed slave, villager', *bhoja-rāja-* 'head of village, subordinate king', as in *khattiyā bhoja-rājāno* 'warrior-nobles, *bhoja*-kings', *bhojaka-* 'possessor', *gāma-bhojaka-* = *gāma-pati-* 'head of a *gāma-* village'.

It seems unlikely that Pali *bhoja-* 'freed slave', *bhujissa-* 'freedman', Vedic *bhujiṣyà-* 'servant, independent' require an OIndian base *bhog-* 'to set free'.[18] Here then we have the Vedic *bhojá-* (Ait.br. 8, 12, 14, 17) as a royal title 'ruler' derived secondarily from 'possessor, one who enjoys'. There is also in the Aśoka inscription[19] and the Mahābhārata a people called *Bhoja-* in western India. Thus Mahābh. 1, 3533 *druhyoḥ sutās tu bhojāḥ* 'the Bhojas are descendants of the Druhyu- tribe'. There is reference to *Bhojā* 'the princess of the Bhoja', and in the Harivaṃśa, 5016, *bhojādhipati-* 'overlord of the Bhojas'; Kālidāsa refers to the *bhoja-pati-*.

The assumption is now made that the *-boja-* of *Kamboja-* is the Iranian word for 'possessor' cognate with OInd. *bhojá-*, to which Saka *bǖjsaṃjā-* is a feminine formed by fem. suffix *-jā-* from *bǖjsana-* (older **baujana-* or **bujana-*).

The first component remains to be examined. Note that OIranian *vasasə-*, *vasō* 'will, at will' occurs as first component with Av. *xšaθra-* 'ruling'. Thus we find Yasna 9, 17 *yaθa gaēθāhva vasō.xšaθrō fračarāne* 'that I may fare forth among the households ruling at will'; and Yasna 43, 8 *vasasə̄.xšaθrahyā* 'rule at will, independent dominion'. A similar concept is expressed by Av. *ušta-* as in the Parthian name of the Auramān document υστοβωγου (gen. sing. to a nominative in -ης or -ος)[20] from **ušta-bauga-*. OIndian has *kāma-* 'desire' in this meaning in such compounds as *kāma-kṛ́t-*, *kāma-cara-*, *kāma-vṛ́tti-* 'acting at will'.

The type of first component (monosyllabic suffixless base) so assumed in *kamboja-* (from **kam-bauja-* or **kan-bauja-*) is similar to that found in OInd. *śam-bhū́-* 'producing good', the proper name *śáṃ-tanu-*, and *sam-rā́j-* 'universal director'.

The Indo-Iranian base *kan-* 'desire' occurs in Av. H 2, 12 *čakana*, Yasna 44, 13 *čaxnarə̄*, in *čanah*, *činah-*, *činman-*, participle *činvat-*, *čanvat-*, and in OIndian *akāniṣam*, *cākana*, *caniṣṭám*, *cánas-*. This *kan-* is the archaic type of basic noun like *śám-* 'welfare', *dám-* 'house', beside the developed OInd. *dáma-s*, Greek δόμος, Lat. *domu-s*, Av. *dəmāna-*, Saka *damäna-*. The *k-* is kept (contrasting with *čanah-*) as in Av. *gar-*, OInd. *gir-* 'utterance' beside OInd. *jaritár-* 'celebrator'. These two bases Avestan and OIndian *kan-* represent *kan-* beside *kā-*, as OInd. *bhánati* 'he speaks' beside Greek φᾱ in φᾱ́μᾱ 'speech' contains *bhan-* beside *bhā-* (Pok. 515,105). OIndian also developed *cakamé*, *kamitar-*, and *kamiṣyate* beside *kāma-*. Similar is Saka *ātama-* 'desire', verbal *ātīm-* from **ā-kamya-*, and pret. base *ātaunda-* from **ākām-*.

A noun *kan-* can occur beside *čanah-* as OInd. RV *tán-* 'lineage', in instr. sing. *tánā* and dat. sing. *táne*, beside the unique RV 5, 70, 4 *tánasā* from *tánas-*, formed like *mánas-* 'thought'.

An ethnic name, self-adopted or not, meaning 'lords' recalls the German-OE ethnic name *Eorlas*, in Latin *Heruli*, which is in Runic Norse *erilaz* 'earls, princes'. Similarly the OIndian ethnic name cited above *Bhoja-* is likely to be another use of the same word occurring as *bhojá-* 'royal title'.

Such a name as *kamboja-* interpreted as **kan-bauǰa-* 'lord' (beside Saka fem. *bŭjsaṃjā-*) could serve also as a personal name whether taken by the chieftain from the ethnic name, or given by parents as a programmatic name for a child, or used as a throne-name, or adopted by personal choice of an adult. Greek similarly had *Κρέων* 'ruler, lord', with fem. *Κρέουσα*. The female name *Gauśurya* 'princess' as interpreted earlier will be of the same kind.[21] For title and proper name note also OPers. *bagabuxša-* 'serving the baga-distributor', in Greek *μεγάβυξος* explained as *νεωκόρος* 'temple-servant', but used also as a personal name.[22]

The problem of the OPersian personal name *k.b.u.ǰi.i.y* *Καμβύσης* therefore becomes once more urgent.

A connexion of the ethnic name *kamboja-* in Indian sources used of ancient Afghanistan and OPers. *k.b.u.ǰi.i.y* was proposed by J. Charpentier. It was rejected by E. Benveniste, but has again once more been asserted by W. Eilers.[23] The Achaemenid empire was a world with close contacts both west and east; it was therefore possible that *Καμβύσης* could be connected with the word *Kamboja* in the east.

The name *Καμβύσης* is attested in various spellings, the Iranian form being most satisfactorily shown in OPersian. Thus we have OPers. *k.b.u.ǰi.i.y* **kambauǰiya* or **kambuǰiya* (or with *-n-* in place of *-m-*); Elamite *kán-bu-ṣi-ya*; Akkad. *kam-bu-zi-ya* and *ka-am-bu-zi-ya*; Aram. *knbwzy*[24]; Greek *Καμβύσης*.

Note that Elamite besides *kán* could write a syllable *kam* (which in *kam-bar-wa* was for *gau-* of OPers. *gaubaruva-*), and *qa-um-* for *kam* in *qa-um-pan-taš*, OPers. *k.p.d.* Hence here *kán* may be intended to mark *-n-*, not *-m-*. The Aramaic also has *-n-* before the *-b-*. Akkadian wrote *-mb-*; Greek regularly knew only *-μβ-* in indigenous words; OPersian left nasal sounds unmarked before consonants. Buddhist Sanskrit had *-mb-* in *Kamboja-*, but knew *-ṇp-* in the plant name *caṇpaka-*, usually written *campaka-*, Saka *caṃbai*.[25]

For the second vowel note that Akkad. *-u-* is frequent for OPers. *-au-*. Elamite *-u-* is ambiguous: in *u-ra-maš-da* the initial is in OPersian *a-u*, *ahuramazdā*, Akkadian wrote *ú-* and *aḫu-*. Similarly Elamite *u-mu-mar-qa* is OPers. *haumavarga-*. But Elamite had *a-u-* in *ya-u-na*, OPers. *yauna*, and *ḫa-u-ti-ya-ru-iš*, OPers. *autiyāra*. In Elamite names *awu* and *u* alternate:

bawukšamira, *bukšira*, *irtabawukša*, *irdapukša*.[26] Greek has *-u-* for *-ava-* in Ἀμύργιοι, OPers. *haumavarga*, but usually for OPers. *-au-*, later *-ō-*, Greek used ου or ω as in the second component -βουζανης and υστοβωγου (above).

The other diphthong *-ai-* of Akkad. *nabū-na'id* is Elamite *nabu-nida*, OPers. *nabunaita* (OPers. *na*, *nu*, *ni* are distinct), where Greek had Λαβύνητος.

As an ordinary, non-royal, proper name Elamite *kanbuziya* is quoted from Persepolis.[27]

For the suffix *-ya-* in OPers. *kambaujiya*, note Av. *xšaθra-* and *xšaθrya-*, and OInd. *kṣatrá-*, *kṣatríya-*.

NOTES

1 Nirukta 2, 2; ed. L. Sarup, 45; transl. 22.

2 E. Benveniste, *JA* (1958) 46, quoting J. Wackernagel, *Zeitschr. f. vgl. Sprachforschung* LXI (1934) 198.

3 Ed. J. Bloch, 103; there identified with *Kōhistān*, the 'arrière-pays montagneux de Kābul', with reference to 'ces mystérieux Kambōjas'.

4 Ed. J. Bloch, 130-1.

5 W. Kirfel, 44.

6 Ed. Gaekwad's Oriental Series, I (1916) cap. 17; introd., xxvi. Rājaśekhara is dated *c.* 880–920.

7 *Harṣa-carita*, ed. Nirṇaya-sāgara Press (1918) 207.

8 N. Dutt, *Gilgit Manuscripts*, III, 3, 136, quoted earlier in *BSOAS*, XIII, 404.

9 Ed. J. Hackin, *Formulaire sanscrit-tibétain du xe siècle*, 59, 1. 16.

10 Sarat Chandra Das, *Pag-sam-jon-zang* (1908), 1. 9.

11 *Kharoshṭhī Inscriptions*, no. 15, A 3; 'Notes on Indo-Scythian chronology', *Journal of Indian History*, XII, 21.

12 See *BSOAS*, XX, 52-3.

13 *Khotanese Texts* (= *KT*), VI, 393, 395.

14 *KT*, VI, 395. Avestan and Armenian recognised by E. Benveniste.

15 *KT*, VI, 255-6; *BSOAS*, XXIX, 524.

16 *Saka Documents*, text volume to Portfolio IV on Ch. ii, 001, a2; *KT*, II, 57.

17 Pok. (= J. Pokorny, *Indogermanisches etymologisches Wörterbuch*) 152-3.

18 *bhujiṣyà-* is explained by E. Benveniste, *Titres et noms en iranien ancien* 112 (= *Titres* below) as 'serviceable to' from *bhog-* 'be useful to'.

19 Ed. J. Bloch, 130-1.

20 E. Benveniste, *Titres*, 113.

21 *BSOAS*, XIII, 391-3.

22 E. Benveniste, *Titres*, 109.

23 J. Charpentier, *Zeitschr. f. Indologie und Iranistik*, II (1923) 144 et seq.; E. Benveniste, *JA* (1958) 28; W. Eilers, 'Kyros', *Beiträge zur Namenforschung*, II (1964) 210.

24 A. Cowley, *Aramaic papyri of the fifth century B.C.*, 112-13.

25 *KT*, VI, 81.

26 The cuneiform syllables are not cited beside these interpreted spellings in E. Benveniste, *Titres*, 113.

27 E. Benveniste, *Titres*, 86.

C.F.BECKINGHAM

Ibn Ḥauqal's Map of Italy

Several allusions in the text prove that Ibn Ḥauqal intended that his geographical treatise should be accompanied by maps. His work has been preserved in two recensions, the first represented by MSS at Leiden (Arab. 314) and Oxford (Bodl. Arab. 963), which have no maps though spaces have been left for them in the latter, and the second represented by a MS in the Topkapı Saray (Arab. 3346), in which there are twenty-three maps. Kramers used both recensions for his edition and included the maps from the Istanbul MS.[1] They are also reproduced in the French translation by Kramers and Wiet published in the UNESCO collection of representative works in 1964.

Italy appears on three of the maps, I, which is a map of the world, where the scale is naturally very small, IV, a map of the Maghrib and Balad al-Rūm, and VIII, which is a map of the Mediterranean. Map IV provides the representation of Italy on the largest scale; Maps I and VIII supply no additional place names or other legends.

Twenty place names and three other legends are written on the mainland of Italy on Map IV. Kramers and Wiet did not identify many of them and seem to me to have identified one incorrectly.[2]

Moving from east to west round the coast of the Italian peninsula the first place marked is بذرنت at the tip of a peninsula at the southern end of the Adriatic, opposite a similar peninsula on the Balkan side where اذرنت is marked. These two places appear on all three maps which include Italy. On Map VIII they are as on Map IV. On Map I, the world map, however, their positions are reversed; اذرنت is on the Italian, and بذرنت on the Balkan side of the strait. In the French translation there is a note suggesting that بذرنت is perhaps Brindisi, although this note is appended to the map which locates it in the Balkans. Surely بذرنت is Butrinto and اذرنت Otranto and they have been transposed in error on Maps IV and VIII. These are the forms of the names used by Idrīsī.

The next place قسانه must be Cassano, which Idrīsī does not mention. Then comes رسيانه, Rossano, which is Idrīsī's form. Next is قطرونيه, Cotrone, Idrīsī's قطرونه. Next is سبرينه, which is Santa Severina, which is Idrīsī's شنت سميرى. Then comes استلوا, which is Stilo, Idrīsī's استيلو. This may have been the scene of the celebrated Muslim victory over Otto II in 982 in which the Prince of Capua and the Abbot of Fulda lost their lives; the Emperor escaped with difficulty to Rossano, where he had left his Empress and his treasure, and thence to Cassano and Salerno. The site of the battle is disputed. In the first edition of his great work Amari accepted that it was fought at Stilo, but in the second he located it at Cape Colonna, beyond the eastern end of the Gulf of Squillace, south of Cotrone. Ibn Ḥauqal's استلوا cannot be Cape Colonna, which, if Amari and Schiaparelli are correct, is Idrīsī's افلوميه, a corruption of اقلومنه.

Next is جراجيه, Gerace, Idrīsī's جراجى, which is often mentioned in the chronicles of the wars of the second half of the tenth century and was occupied by the Muslims in 986.

The next place marked, قسطرقوقه, is a more difficult problem. There is a place called Castrocucco on the opposite coast of the Calabrian peninsula, south of Maratea, but its location makes it very improbable that this is the place meant. I would suggest that Ibn Ḥauqal means the place sacked by the Muslims in 952, the name of which Amari restored as Petracucca. It occurs as بطرقوقه in a quotation from Ibn Ḥauqal in Yāqūt s.v. قِلَّوْرِيَة, a quotation which is not found in any surviving recension of Ibn Ḥauqal's text (see below). Amari commented on this passage: 'la menzione fattane in suo breve cenno prova che nel x secolo fosse importante per popolazione e commercio'. He cites the طرفوقه of the Cambridge Chronicle and Ibn al-Athīr's بطرقوقه. Idrīsī mentions a perennial stream three miles from Cape Zefirio and six from Bruzzano called وادى بطرقوقه. Elsewhere he calls what is obviously the same wādī بطرقونه. Amari remarked that *cocca*, *cucco* are words that survive in the dialects of Calabria and Sicily with the meaning 'civetta, coccoveggia' (i.e. the Little Owl, *Athene noctua*).

Next is بوّه, obviously Bova. Idrīsī's form is uncertain. Amari and Schiaparelli print توجش, of which there are several variants; they suggest reading بوبس. The next name, ابن ذقتل is evidently Pentedáttilo. Idrīsī's forms are not less confused here; he has بنتد قطله, variants بلد, بلتد and بليد, and elsewhere بنتو قطله. Next is ريّو, identified by Kramers as Reggio, for which Idrīsī has the same form. Next is منتيه, Amantea, which is Idrīsī's form. Then comes قسنشه for which I suggest Cosenza. This place is not mentioned by Idrīsī but it was well known to Muslim commanders of the tenth century and was besieged by Ibrāhīm b. Aḥmad in 902 on his last campaign. Next is مسنيان for which I would propose Bisignano, Idrīsī's بسنيان. There follows an unnamed enclosure on the map and in the mountains behind it is written شلورى. De Goeje incorporated in his edition of Ibn Ḥauqal a suggestion of Amari's that this should be identified as Salerno, Idrīsī's سلرنو. In his text Ibn Ḥauqal refers to ارض شلورى as the first part of Lombardy that one reaches after leaving Calabria. The allusion is evidently to the duchy of Salerno. Next comes ملف, obviously Amalfi, its position on the coast precluding Melfi. Idrīsī uses the same form for both names but distinguishes Melfi as ملف البرّيه. Next is نابل already identified by Kramers and Wiet as Naples. Next is غيطه as in Idrīsī, identified in the French translation as Gaeta, but transliterated Ghita, though in the Arabic text a *fatḥa* is clearly marked above the first letter. Then comes بيش, Pisa, for which Idrīsī uses the same form, and then قرره, identified in the French translation as Carrara, which is not mentioned by Idrīsī. Genoa is called جنوه and is marked as an island.

The places marked on the map of Italy thus extend from Otranto to Genoa and include a few like Bisignano which lie inland. The position of Rome is odd. It is marked as روميه, some distance inland on the east bank of a large river flowing into the Mediterranean through southern France and evidently meant for the Rhône, but given no name. If Ibn Ḥauqal had been writing a few centuries later one might have been tempted to think he had confused Rome and Avignon. A possible explanation is that being aware of the significance of Rome for the Empire and knowing that the Emperors were crowned there and were nevertheless rulers of the Franks he concluded not unreasonably that Rome must be in the country of the Franks.

There are three other legends on the map of Italy. To the east of the mountains, between them and the head of the Adriatic, is written مضيق سكن rendered by Kramers and Wiet 'défilé de Sakan'. This can be identified with the help of Idrīsī, who mentions a rock of S.K.N. صخرة سكن and a Wādī S.K.NA in the itinerary from Reggio to Taranto. They can be identified with some precision. He says that the rock lies six miles from the wādī and twelve from Roseto, and that it marks the boundary between the Franks and the Lombards.[3] By the Franks must be meant the Normans of Sicily and the rock must be at or near Rocca Imperiale, the S.K.NA being the Sinni.

Venice as a town is not marked but the following legend is written at the head of the Adriatic:

هذا جون البناديق وفيه جزائر كثيره مسكونه واهل كالشاغره والسنه مختلفه من افرنجيين ونمتين وصقالبه وبرجان وغير ذلك

This is translated by Kramers and Wiet as follows: 'C'est le golfe de Venise, dans lequel se trouvent de nombreuses îles habitées et des peuplades comme celle des Shaghira; les langues y sont variées, français, autrichien, slave, bulgare, etc.'

The name Shaghira has not been identified. It would seem at least conceivable that the Hungarians are meant, for their raids had penetrated deeply into Italy and the Balkans. If so, I would suggest, very tentatively, that شاغره may be a corruption of a form مجاغره.

The translation of برجان as Bulgarian is open to objection. It is true that the word can have this meaning and it is also true that at its height the first Bulgarian empire did extend as far as the southern Adriatic. But though Ibn Ḥauqal refers to the Bulgars over a dozen times in his text and marks them on Map I they are always called بلغار. برجان occurs only on Maps IV and VIII. I would suggest that it means, not the Bulgars, but the Burgundians. The word had been used in this sense about a century earlier, by Hārūn b. Yaḥyā, as was remarked by Minorsky.[4] When Ibn Ḥauqal was writing the dominion of the Burgundian kings reached to the Gulf of Lyons, for it included the old Kingdom of Arles, and for a short time beginning in 922 Rudolf II was recognised as King of Italy.

The only other legend is the name written down the centre of the peninsula. On Maps IV and VIII this is ارض قلوريه; on Map I it is قلوريه. The term Calabria must be understood in accordance with Byzantine usage. Jules Gay remarked that before acquiring its restricted modern sense 'le mot de Calabre commence par désigner indifféremment les deux péninsules; il désigne proprement l'ensemble des possessions byzantines autour du golfe de Tarente'.[5] The three maps are not at all consistent, however, in representing the shape of Italy or the relation of the towns marked to the curvature of the peninsular coast. On Map IV the western side of the peninsula commences near Salerno where the mountains are shown coming down to the sea. The other places named from Amalfi to Carrara are on the northern coast of the Gulf which extends to the base of the Iberian peninsula. On Map VIII, on the other hand, the head of this gulf is not a flat coast line but a sharp point. Bisignano (if my suggested identification is correct) lies at the head of this gulf and the places from Salerno to Genoa inclusive disappear

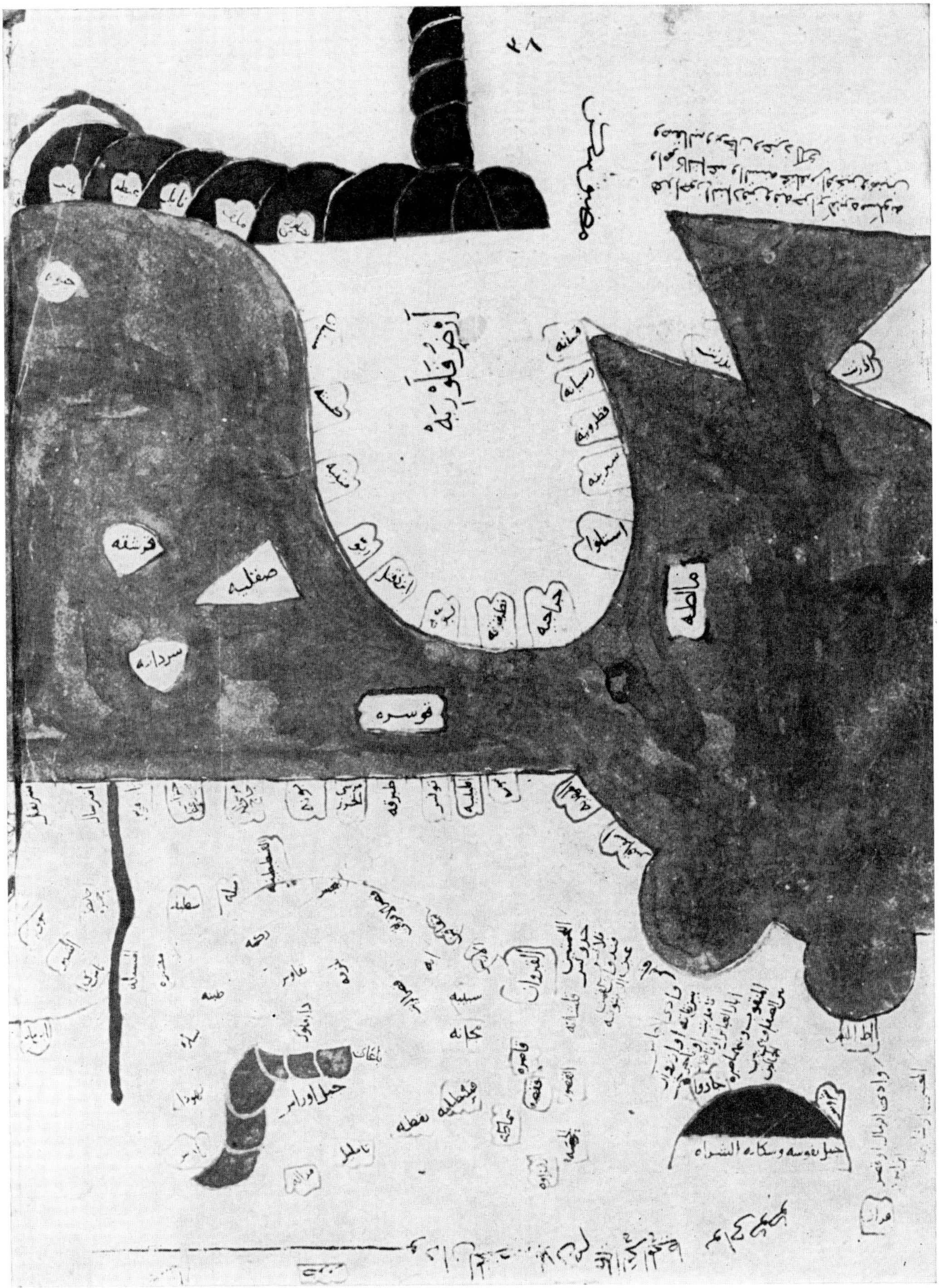

Plate 1. Italy on Ibn Ḥauqal's map of the Maghrib.

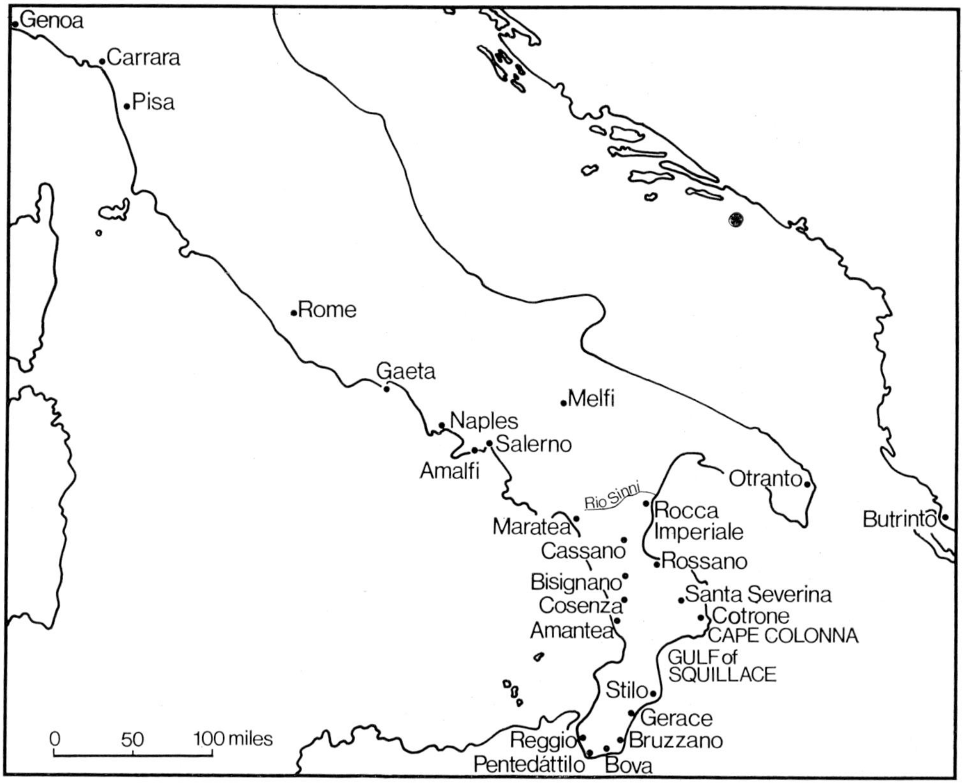

Map showing actual location of places marked on Ibn Ḥauqal's map (Plate 1).

altogether. On Map I Calabria protrudes from a coast which extends in a line to the western extremity of Europe.

These inconsistencies suggest the possibility that the maps may not, or at least may not all, represent correctly Ibn Ḥauqal's own conceptions. It is notable that no less than fifteen of the twenty place names marked on Map IV are nowhere mentioned in the text, although some of them occur also on Map VIII. This is not so to anything like the same extent with the other maps in the treatise. Ibn Ḥauqal completed his book about 378/988. The copyist of the Istanbul MS finished his work in Rajab 479/October 1086. However accurately he may have transmitted the text we cannot be sure that he or whoever drew the maps copied the originals exactly and did not add further names. One or two of the places marked on the map of Italy would be much more likely to be known to a Muslim cartographer of the eleventh than the late tenth century. Pisa, for example, after the attacks of 1004 and 1011, and Bisignano after 1020 must have become more familiar names among the Arabs of Sicily and southern Italy.

It has long been realised that Yāqūt made extensive use of Ibn Ḥauqal. Over twenty explicit quotations from his work occur in the *Muʿjam al-buldān* and one of the most important of these concerns Calabria. In at least three instances, of which this is one, the statements which Yāqūt attributes to Ibn Ḥauqal are not to be found in any version of his work which has survived. It has usually been assumed that they were quoted from a recension that has been lost. If, however, these passages are compared with the relevant parts of Map IV it becomes obvious that Yāqūt is not quoting Ibn Ḥauqal's words but describing what was marked on his maps.

The passage about Calabria (قِلَّوْرِية) is as follows:

قال ابن حوقل وهى جزيرة مستطيلة اولها طرف جبل الجلالقة وبلادها التى على الساحل فسانه وستانه وقطرونيه وسبرسه واسلو حراحه وبطرقوقه وبوه ثم بعد ذاك على الساحل جون البناديقيين وفيه جزائر كثيرة مسكونة كالشاعرة والسنة مختلفة بين الافرنجيين ويمانيين وصقالبة وبرجان وغير ذاك ثم ارض بلبوس

The names are much more corrupt than those in our text of Ibn Ḥauqal but Yāqūt must refer to Cassano, Rossano, Cotrone, Sta Severina, Stilo, Gerace, Petracucca, and Bova.

The other two instances concern N.W. Africa. In the entry for Arzila (أَزِيلَى) we read:

قال ابن حوقل الطريق من برقة الى ازيلى على ساحل بحر الخليج الى فم البحر المحيط ثم تعطف على البحر المحيط يسارا

Again, this statement does not occur in the text but it is an accurate description of the relevant portion of Map IV where the African coast is made to turn southwards just west of Arzila.

The last instance is perhaps the most convincing. In the entry for the Rio Barbate (بَرْباط) Yāqūt says:

قال ابن حوقل وفى المغرب فى اقصاه اذا عطفت على البحر المحيط مدن كثيرة منها مدينة يقال لها برباط على شاطى نهر شُبَّة من شماليه

This is unintelligible until we look at Map IV where a river is shown that has two mouths, one in the Mediterranean at Ceuta (سبتة) and the other on the Atlantic coast between Rabat and Sale. Yāqūt's شُبَّة is a corruption of سبتة.

It is evident that the names on at least one of the maps that Yāqūt used were more corrupt than those in the Istanbul MS known to us. It is obvious also that when Yāqūt writes *qāla 'bn Ḥauqal* he may mean no more than 'Ibn Ḥauqal's map shows'. Yāqūt must in fact have regarded the maps as an integral part of the book, as indeed they are.

NOTES

1 This was the first time they had been published. The MS was not known to scholars when Konrad Miller compiled his *Mappae arabicae*. I am much indebted to the Director of the Topkapı Saray Müzesi for permission to reproduce in this article Ibn Ḥauqal's map of Italy. I also wish to offer cordial thanks to my friend Nuri H. Arlasez for the trouble he took to obtain a photograph for me, and to Miss E. A. Lowcock of the Drawing Office, School of Geography, University of Manchester, for drawing a map to show the actual location of the places marked by Ibn Ḥauqal.

2 I made some of the following suggestions in a review of the French translation in the *Journal of Semitic Studies*, XI, no. 2 (Autumn 1966).

3 Jules Gay remarks that under Leo VI, a contemporary of Ibn Ḥauqal, 'le domaine byzantin, dans l'Italie méridionale, se divise en deux thèmes: *Longobardie* et *Calabre*' (*L'Italie méridionale et l'empire byzantin* (1904) 167).

4 *Ḥudūd al-ʿĀlam* (London 1937) 423.

5 op. cit., 6.

A. D. H. BIVAR

Petroglyphs and Buddhist Remains of Jāghūrī District, Afghanistan

During a brief visit to Kabul in August-September 1962 in the course of study leave from the School of Oriental and African Studies, the writer chanced to hear from Dr Aḥmad ʿAlī Khān Kohzād, the well-known authority on Afghan antiquities, reports of monuments and inscriptions existing in the district of Jāghūrī. This is a district situated in the upper valley of the Arghandāb, some thirty-five miles west of the Ghazni-Kandahar road, and to the south-west of Ghazni. The modern administrative centre is at Sang-i Mashā, accessible by two recently constructed motor roads, diverging from the main road at Qarabāgh and at Mukur respectively. These two roads join before reaching Sang-i Mashā, at a point some five miles east of Lomān, which last spot proved after investigation to be the source of the reports. Although a visit to the district showed that the account given by Dr Kohzād's local informants in some ways exaggerated the antiquity of the monuments, the remains found to exist are not without interest for various aspects of Afghan archaeology and anthropology, in particular for the history of the curious rock-drawings known as petroglyphs, and merit description. The district is moreover not well known to travellers, and of some interest in itself, and there appear to be further monuments at points not visited on the occasion described here, which would justify further investigation. The present note is offered as a tribute to the memory of Professor Minorsky, whose interest in the exploration of Afghanistan the writer remembers with gratitude.

A few preliminary remarks on the name of the district seem desirable. To the visitor it is not entirely clear whether in present usage the name Jāghūrī is regarded as the designation of a tribe, or of the district which they inhabit. It seems to be used impartially of both. At any event, its occurrence is not exclusively modern, for a connexion between the modern Jāghūrī and the Sanskrit Jāguḍa was suggested by Foucher.[1] Foucher in turn cited an article of S. Lévi,[2] who sought to derive from Jāguḍa the geographical or tribal name Zābul. The latter seems originally to have been the name of a sept of the Hepthalite (or perhaps the Chionite) Huns, and of a district which they ruled, and it achieved some celebrity in Islamic history.[3] Yet it may be that Jāguḍa was a Sanskritization of Zābul rather than its antecedent, and the matter is still not clear. Another authority who had reason to refer to Jāguḍa was Watters, who identified it with the 'Tsu-ku-cha' of Hsüan-tsang.[4] Of this country it was said: 'There are several hundred sangharamas with 1,000 or so priests', and 'There are some ten *stûpas* built by Aśôka-râja, and several tens of Dêva-temples, in which sectaries of various denominations dwell together'.[5] If a significant group of Buddhist monuments should come to light in Jāghūrī District, this would therefore tend to support the identification with Jāguḍa (Tsu-ku-Cha). At the same time, Buddhist remains are so numerous in every part of Afghanistan that such evidence would not in itself be conclusive for the identification. As for the connexion of the name Jāguḍa with the Hūṇa tribes, it seems true that it is not firmly attested before their advent in the fourth century A.D. It is true that the name appears in the *Mahābhārata*,[6] but this is presumably to be taken as an interpolation, since the same context contains a reference to the Hārahūṇa, who are obviously to be regarded as a Hunnic group. Therefore if the names of Jāguḍa and the Jāghūrī are in fact related, a Hunnic element in the composition of the latter is certainly a possibility.[7]

In recent times the Jāghūrī people have not been closely studied.[8] Earlier authorities spoke of them as a tribe of Hazāras,[9] but individuals encountered during the visit described here strongly asserted their claim to be regarded as a distinct community. An obvious distinction was the practice amongst the young men of wearing the *tsūṇrai*: that is to say, long hair bobbed at the neckline in the fashion of such Pashtu-speaking tribes as the Khattaks and Mahsuds. This fashion seemed the more unusual since they were in the main of stocky physique like their neighbours the Hazāras. As amongst the Hazāras too, Persian was spoken, and in their conversation with outsiders no pronounced dialect features were noted, though there seemed a propensity for the use of certain Mongol words. The traditional account of their origin, everywhere repeated, was a claim to descent from Chinggis Khān, which is, of course, familiar too amongst the Hazāras, to whom a Mongol origin is usually ascribed. During the visit, parties of nomadic Afghans were encountered travelling through the area cultivated by the Jāghūrī (who themselves practised a degree of short-range transhumance), and some of these claimed membership of the Ahmadzai, Achakzai and Kharawt sub-sections. Evidently the exchange of pastoral products for cereals between the nomads and the villagers was a regular factor in local economic life.

The route chosen for the journey was that from Qarabāgh.[10] There the track branched off to the west from the main road; this track sloped gently uphill across the plain towards the line of hills, which it entered along the course of a river-bed. After some 30 miles the road reached the settlement of Zardālū, at the foot of an impressive pass over the first high watershed, that dividing the basin of the Tarnak from that of the Arghandāb. About 24 miles beyond the pass, and just short of Lomān village, a group of recently built shops stands by the road, and here cloth and simple groceries are sold. This was said to be the closest point to the inscriptions, and from it the journey was to be continued on foot. The most prominent landmark in this region, and a decidedly striking one, is the mountain known as Kūh-i Ūd. It is an isolated pinnacle of rock lying due north of the settlement mentioned, and overtopping the lines of hills which enclose the plain of Lomān. There was general agreement among the bystanders that the inscriptions best-known locally, and presumably those which had been reported, lay close to Kūh-i Ūd on its western side, in a sandy defile known as Rīg Gardūn. A guide, one of the local Sayyids, was soon forthcoming, and the last stage of the journey began on foot across the cultivated plain in the direction of the Kūh-i Ūd.

A two-hour march led to the village of Bīdsay, close to the northern extremity of the plain. Just short of the village, and not far to the left of the track, there was pointed out the first of the reputed epigraphs (Plate 1). It was a large rectangular stone, the southern face of which was covered with incised drawings of animal figures. Informants, both in Kabul and locally, had described the monument as an inscription in Syriac (*sūriyānī*) or Greek (*yūnānī*), but other instances are known in which the schematized Afghan petroglyphs have been reported by villagers as inscriptions, and this contradiction need not imply that the monument visited was other than the one intended. The engravings on the rock at Bīdsay are mostly figures of ibex, but that at the upper right-hand corner may represent two men in combat with swords. Animal petroglyphs of generally similar style have been widely reported in Afghanistan and neighbouring lands. The questions of their date, context, and purpose are largely unanswered. To judge from the patina covering the incised portion of the stone, the example at Bīdsay seems not to be very recent. It may be grouped tentatively with the older series of petroglyphs, of which the best-known example is that of the Ghorband Valley, situated at the 100th kilometre from Kabul.[11] Recently a rumour has been current that the petroglyph of the Ghorband was accidentally destroyed during road-making operations several years ago. Some purpose may therefore be served by reproducing here (Plate 2) a photograph taken in 1953, as a supplement to the small photograph reproduced by Foucher.

Examples of generally comparable petroglyphs to those of Ghorband and Bīdsay have been reported on several occasions in recent years. The present writer observed, but was not able to record, similar petroglyphs some five miles north of Kāfir Qalʿa on the road between Tirīn and Uruzgān in Kandahar Province.[12] More recently specimens were reported by Dessau in Persian Baluchistan.[13] The latest, and most comprehensive survey of the petroglyphs is by William Trousdale in the context of his discovery of ibex figures at Tang-i Tīzāo near the valley of the Harī Rūd.[14] He distinguishes between what we may call the 'ibex group', and another group further to the south and east represented by examples found by Beatrice de Cardi at Siāh-āb between Dilarām and Farāh,[15] and by D. H. Gordon near Attock in West Pakistan.[16] He shows also that a closer analogy with our 'ibex group' is offered by numerous examples reported from Soviet territory, in particular from the notable site of Saimaly-Tash in Kirgiziya,[17] Kazakstan,[18] Tadzhikistan,[19] and in great profusion from Mongolia.[20] Rock-drawings of ibex in Uzbekistan closely resembling those of Bīdsay were reproduced in the London *Times* accompanied by a claim that they dated from about 1000 B.C.[21] It appears that a close chronology of the Soviet examples has still to be worked out on the basis of a comprehensive survey. For our present purposes more dependence can perhaps be placed on the observation of Mizuno, noted by Trousdale, that a petroglyph of this style is found on the interior walls of Cave 6 at Haibak.[22] Since in general terms it may be maintained that the caves at Haibak were excavated during the Kushan period, *c.* second century A.D., it follows that any petroglyphs engraved in their interiors must be more recent. It is therefore tempting to ascribe the Afghan petroglyphs of the 'ibex group' to some body of invaders who entered Afghanistan from Mongolia and Kirgiziya at a date later than the second century A.D. Two ethnic groups appear to meet this requirement. that of the Hūṇas (Chionites and Hephthalites) during the fourth century A.D., and that of the Mongols during the thirteenth century. Either, and indeed both of these groups could well have influenced the culture of present-day Jāghūrī.

It was soon to become clear that petroglyphs were decidedly numerous in the district of Jāghūrī, and indeed were still occasionally being carved at

Plate I. Petroglyphs at Bīdsay village.

Plate 2 (above). Old petroglyph at km 100 in the Ghorband Valley.
Plate 3 (below). Rīg Gardūn: petroglyphs and *graffiti* on second rock.

the present day. It was hardly to be doubted that they possessed some traditional significance for the Jāghūrī people. In front of the petroglyphs, both at Bīdsay and later at Lomān itself, heaps of pebbles were seen to have been piled up, sometimes in a crescent formation. That they had been brought, and heaped up, by the inhabitants, possibly in the past, was sufficiently evident. Inquiry as to the origin and purpose of the petroglyphs and stones from various bystanders elicited rather indefinite replies, but one informant explained them as hunting talismans, the animals being drawn either to commemorate success in killing an ibex, or to ensure the success of future hunts. That this may indeed have been part of their purpose appears likely, but their wide distribution would suggest some more general significance.

The village of Bīdsay was of interest not only for its petroglyphs. A short way to the east of the village a limestone knob about 15 feet in height projected above the level of the plain. Both in this feature, and in the limestone face of the hills lying further to the east were the openings of numerous caves. These were obviously artificial, the whole system constituting a Buddhist cave-monastery, similar on a small scale to the celebrated complex at Bāmiyān. However, so far as could be seen, or ascertained by inquiry, there were no examples of architectural decoration at Bīdsay, nor any surviving frescoes. The caves were described as uninhabited – surprisingly, perhaps, since cave habitations are usually the most comfortable in the climate of the Afghan plateau – but some were in use as storerooms, and others as shelters for the village livestock.

Passing on from Bīdsay, still in the direction of the Kūh-i Ūd, the track passed the village pond and left the Lomān plain through a low col which crossed the encircling line of hills; thence down past a spring into the adjoining plain. There the track branched; the left-hand fork, which seemed to represent the principal route, led directly across the plain towards a large, upstanding limestone bluff, over a hundred feet high, which stood in its centre. In this feature too, a system of caves was to be seen. But since the immediate objective of the journey lay to the right, and the afternoon was well advanced, there was no opportunity to inspect them. The right-hand track swung back towards the north-east, heading for the village of Lāla Khel, which was the nearest settlement to the defile of Rīg Gardūn. Just beyond the village, the Kūh-i Ūd came into full view for the first time, since previously only the summit had been visible above the encircling hills. Now the base of the pinnacle was little over a mile away, and its sheer sides obviously represented a dangerous proposition to climb. Yet the summit had none the less been once inhabited. Remains of buildings could easily be distinguished from below, though the distance was too great to form any opinion of their probable age. Villagers claimed that the feature had been climbed in living memory by local youths, but supplies for former garrisons must have been drawn up by rope. It is not easy to guess what authority occupied this remote stronghold, or for what purpose, if it were not for a watch-tower. The view from the summit was said to be extensive, but the claim that it extended as far as the 'Arachosian' plain, round Ghazni and Qarabāgh seems very doubtful.

The Kūh-i Ūd was now left on the right, up a converging wādī bed, and the trail entered the Rīg Gardūn. Large rocks became numerous on either side of the track, and to judge by the footprints and droppings it was much frequented by caravans, though their destination was not evident. Finally, about five hundred yards beyond the junction of the wādīs, the first of the inscriptions came in sight (Plate 4). These were on a large rock to the right of the track, which bore, in addition to petroglyphs, numerous *graffiti* in Persian script. The style of this further group of rock pictures was manifestly more perfunctory than those of Bīdsay, and at the same time less strictly schematized. It was fairly clear that they were considerably more recent, and this impression was to some extent confirmed by inscribed dates visible here and there, though it seemed probable that the dates and the *graffiti* were more modern than the accompanying drawings. In the left centre of this first boulder were the words سید احمد 'Sayyid Aḥmad', with the Hijrī date 1326/1908–9. Though the drawings may be older, one of the human figures in this group, not shown in the photograph, unmistakably points a firearm at an ibex, so none can be of any great age. Further down the defile, there are quite a number of other rocks with drawings and *graffiti*, all generally similar. About a hundred yards beyond the first engraved stone, and to the left of the track are a group with claims to a rather earlier date (Plate 3). The *graffito* at the right-hand side of the photograph reads ١١٧٥ سنة *sannata* 1175 (= A.D. 1761–2), and here one of the two sketchy figures of hunters is shown thrusting at the standing ibex with a long spear. It is difficult to establish when the possession of firearms became general in this part of Central Afghanistan, but they are not likely to have been in extensive use before the eastern campaign of Nādir Shāh of Iran in A.D. 1738. The date and the picture may thus be roughly contemporary.

The petroglyphs at Rīg Gardūn provide evidence that whatever the origins and purpose of such engravings, they have continued to be made in very recent times, and have played a part in the culture of the Jāghūrī within living memory. Further evidence of this presented itself during the return

Plate 4. Rīg Gardūn: petroglyphs and *graffiti* on first rock.

Plate 5 (above). Lomān village: upper cave with decoration in the form of a blind arcade.
Plate 6 (below). Lomān village: recess in wall of cave, apparently intended to accommodate Buddha figure.

journey to Lomān. A young man, engaged as a guide for the march back, hearing that an interest was being taken in the petroglyphs, remarked that he had himself, as a boy, made a drawing of this kind. He described its form as the outline of a human hand, engraved upon a rock beside a stream-bed not far from the path. When the spot was reached he pointed out the rock-drawing, and since its appearance was not inconsistent with a recent origin, there seemed no cause to doubt the guide's claim that he had drawn it himself. His manner gave no indication that he regarded the undertaking as in any sense a magical or religious operation, but more of a schoolboy's exercise in sketching. Thus the tradition of rock drawings seems to have flourished extensively amongst the Jāghūrī down to very recent times. At Lomān another minor group will be briefly mentioned. That some of the specimens, exhibiting a distinct style, which we have christened the 'ibex group', are of definitely earlier date, seems fairly clear. In view of the fact that there are numerous analogies for the earlier petroglyphs in Mongolia, Kirgiziya, and elsewhere in Soviet Asia, and also that a Mongolian element in all probability exists in the ethnic composition of the Jāghūrī, the hypothesis is certainly worth considering that these enigmatic monuments may be characteristic of the Mongols, and introduced by them into Southern Asia during their celebrated invasions in and after A.D. 1220. At the same time, the possibility that they are characteristic of the Hephthalites, who performed a rather similar migration in the fourth century A.D., cannot on present evidence be wholly ruled out.

The journey on foot from the main road near Lomān to the defile of Rīg Gardūn, and back to Lomān occupied the time from 9 a.m. until about 11 p.m. the same evening (13 September 1962). When allowance is made for various halts, for photography, refreshments and conversation, the distance may be reckoned, as has already been noted, at a little over ten miles in each direction. At Lomān itself, however, antiquities were reported to exist, and the following day was devoted to their examination.

At the approach to the village of Lomān (several hundred yards west of the shops which had formed the starting-point of the previous day's journey) the road makes a sharp turn to the left in front of a conspicuous limestone dome some 25 feet in height. Inspection showed that it had been cut off from the ridge of high ground lying to the north by an artificial fosse. It was evident that this dome, though weathered and deteriorated in places, was a monument of the rock-cut stupa type, with the fosse providing a path for circumambulation. The limestone of the dome is honeycombed with caves, and the main group of these are inhabited by villagers, who have walled up unwanted openings with mud-brick, and fitted doors. In the bitter cold of winter on the plateau, these caves must afford a very comfortable shelter. Above the inhabited caves may be seen another group now used for the stabling of animals. One of these (Plate 5) shows an architectural decoration, in the form of a blind arcade of three, approximately parabolic, arches.[23] Their form suggests a date fairly early in the Sasanian period, perhaps about the fourth century A.D. The walls of this cave have also a number of significant recesses. One, which is rectangular, gives no obvious indication of its purpose, but the shape of another (Plate 6) suggests that a Buddha figure was affixed here, its head occupying the circular indentation, and attached by a wooden peg driven into the hole indicated by the pointing finger.

The kindness of the residents of the lower caves made it possible also to examine their homes. Inside, the light was not sufficient for photography, but it was interesting that the roof of one of the chambers was provided with plain squinches, similar to those in the monastery at Haibak,[24] and in several of the caves at Bāmiyān.[25] The more complicated architectural features, for example lantern vaults, found in some of the later caves at Bāmiyān were not present here. Some general deductions are therefore possible as to the date of these caves. First, they appear to have been excavated and occupied originally, as on so many sites of Afghanistan, by a Buddhist monastic community. Second, their fairly simple architectural decoration suggests a date towards the end of the Kushan period, or early in the epoch of the Sasanians; that is to say, in the third century A.D., or early in the fourth. The inhabited caves seem to be earlier in date than those now occupied by the animals.

Inquiries made from the occupants as to the possible existence of painted frescoes, further architectural decoration, inscriptions, or fragmentary documents from the débris of cave-floors produced negative replies. Indeed if major antiquities of such a nature had been present anywhere in this complex, it is difficult to believe that they would not have attracted attention previously. It is worth noting that the débris of the cave-floors, more particularly of the stables, are fairly deep, and seem not to have been very recently disturbed. That they could contain documents, as have been found on several occasions at Bāmiyān, is therefore not out of the question. But the real interest of the visit is to call attention to the fact that the whole mountain area of the Upper Arghandab, and no doubt also further west about the Upper Helmand, is likely to be no less rich than the vicinity of Lomān in Buddhist cave-monuments. Although rich artistic finds, comparable with those of Bāmiyān, are hardly to be expected, these more humble cave-dwellings, scattered along the caravan-routes, are also worthy of some attention. Not only are they valuable as indicating the extent of Buddhism in this little-known area. The conditions here, in cave-dwellings at an altitude of some 8000 feet, are exceptionally favourable for the preservation of manuscripts; and in the hundreds of obscure caves, not all inhabited, that are likely to exist, here or there one is likely to be found that would reward exploration, if experience of the Judaean and Samarian caves is anything to go by. Moreover, the history of this area of Zābulistān, its Buddhist culture and gradual penetration by Islam, is little known. Any evidence from its caves would be of the greatest value.

A few final remarks on further petroglyphs are necessary. To the North of the Lomān cave-monastery, on the ridge of higher ground, were a number of rocks bearing the now familiar animal drawings. In front of several, stones had been piled in various configurations, including the crescent formation already mentioned. It seemed hardly probable that they had been arranged for the wind-breaks of nomad tents, but no better explanation was forthcoming. In style this group resembled that of Rīg Gardūn, and there seemed little doubt that they were modern. Yet not one of several passers-by claimed any acquaintance with these petroglyphs, or offered any explanation of their purpose. Once again, yet a fourth group were seen on the way back to Qarabāgh, at a point just short of the junction of the Qarabāgh and Mukur roads, at the eastern end of the Lomān plain. Once more, heaps of stones were piled in front of the petroglyphs. Obviously, the Lomān area has a surprising concentration of these rock-drawings, which seem to have played an important role in the cultural life of the Jāghūrī during the not far distant past, and may form some part of their Altaic heritage.

Postscript. Though the excursion described here was not successful in locating a new Greek-letter inscription, subsequent news has shown that the reports which inspired it were not without foundation. In 1968 Dr Paul Bernard of the Délégation Archéologique Française en Afghanistan announced in a press release the discovery of a bilingual inscription, the 'Rosetta stone of Afghan archaeology', at high altitude in the mountains of Central Afghanistan.[26] In the following year Professor ʿAbd ul-Ḥayy Ḥabībī described the site of the discovery, close to the Dasht-i Navār, in his pamphlet entitled *Haft Katība-yi qadīm* (Kabul 1348/1969), p. 49, and printed a small photograph of the version in Greek characters. The Dasht-i

Navār lies less than twenty miles north of Rīg Gardūn, and may well have been the source of the rumours of a Greek inscription. Detailed publication of the new inscriptions is now keenly awaited.

NOTES

1 A. Foucher, *La vieille route de l'Inde*, II, 231.

2 'Le catalogue géographique des Yakṣa dans le Mahāmayūrī', *Journal Asiatique* (Jan.-Fév. 1914) 84.

3 Zābulistān appears to have been the district of which Ghaznī was the capital, but extended also considerably towards the west. Muslim tales of the Kings of Zābulistān (cf. M. Niẓ ámu'd-dín, *Introduction to the Jawámi' u'l-ḥikáyát*, 163) may represent some memory of the Hūṇa kings of the house of Mihirakula, though the anecdote cited is also narrated of Kanishka.

4 Thomas Watters, *On Yuan Chwang's travels in India*, II, 266.

5 S. Beal, *Buddhist records of the Western World*, II, 284.

6 Calcutta ed., 3, 1991, cf. Lévi, loc. cit.; H. W. Bailey, 'Hārahūṇa' in *Asiatica: Festschrift Friedrich Weller* (Leipzig 1954) 15-21.

7 Cf. Klaus Ferdinand, *Preliminary notes on Hazara culture* (Hist. Filos. Medd. Dan. Vid. Selsk. XXXVII, 5) (Copenhagen 1959) 18; 'In the cases of the Jāghōrī and Shahristan we must think of other possibilities, such as an intermixture with a *pre-Hazara* population, or influx of larger groups of foreigners'.

8 Some recent notes appear in H. F. Schurmann, *The Mongols of Afghanistan* (The Hague 1962).

9 E.g. Mounstuart Elphinstone, *Caubul* (1839) 211.

10 As interpreter I was accompanied by Mr Gul Muhammad, of the Afghan Tourist Bureau, who has since become well known to visitors in Afghanistan as Manager of the Bamiyan Hotel. His cheerful response to the exigencies of travel contributed greatly to the success of the excursion.

11 A. Foucher, *La vieille route de l'Inde de Bactres à Taxila* (Mém. D.A.F.A. I) II, 390; Pl. XXXIX, c; cf. W. A. Fairservis, 'Exploring the Desert of Death', *Natural History*, LIX (1950) 248.

12 'The inscriptions of Uruzgan', *JRAS* (1954) 117.

13 G. Dessau, 'Rock engravings (graffiti) from Iranian Baluchistan', *East and West*, XI (1960) 258-66.

14 'Rock engravings from the Tang-i Tizao in Central Afghanistan', *East and West*, XV (1965) 201-10.

15 Beatrice de Cardi, 'On the borders of Pakistan: recent exploration', *Art and Letters*, XXIV (1950) 52-7 and Pl. III.

16 D. H. Gordon, *The prehistoric background of Indian culture* (Bombay 1958) 112.

17 A. N. Bernshtam, *Po sledam drevnikh kultur* (Moscow 1954) 270; idem, 'Naskal'nye izobrazheniya Saimaly Tash', *Sovetskaya etnografiya*, (1952) ii, 50-68. As summarized by G. Frumkin, *Central Asian Review* XII (1964) 26, there are over 100,000 petroglyphs at this site, but the chronology of styles is not yet fully ascertained. The examples illustrated in Bernshtam's earlier publication, e.g. p. 59, are freer and less schematic than the 'ibex group 'in Afghanistan.

18 Reports of petroglyphs at eight sites in Kazakstan are listed by Frumkin, 'Archaeology in Soviet Central Asia: II, Kazakstan', *Central Asian Review*, XI (1963) 29.

19 See recently V. A. Ranov and A. V. Gurskiy, 'Kratkie obzor naskal'nikh risunkov Gorno-Badakhshanskoi avtonomnoi oblasti Tadzhikskoi SSR' *Sovetskaya etnografiya* (1966) 110-19.

20 Besides the article of D. Dorzh, 'K istorii izucheniya naskal'nikh izobrazhenii Mongolii', *Mongol'skii arkheologicheskii sbornik* (Moskva 1962), 48, noted by Trousdale, E. Tryjarski, 'The Turks in distant Asia', *Illustrated London News* (6 July 1968), 34 (= Archaeology 2292) reports the discovery of tens of thousands of petroglyphs in Mongolia by Okladnikov, Rinchen and Namkhaïdagva. These great concentrations of finds must be historically significant.

21 *The Times*, Thursday, 11 November 1965.

22 Mizuno Seiichi and others, *Haibak and Kashmir Smast: Buddhist Cave temples in Afghanistan and Pakistan surveyed in 1960* (Kyoto 1962) 12.

23 For arches of this form, cf. André Godard, Y. Godard and J. Hackin, *Les antiquités Bouddhiques de Bamiyan*, Pl. XXXII, a.

24 A. Foucher, *La vieille route de l'Inde* I, Pl. XXVII, e.

25 André Godard *et al.*, *Les antiquités Bouddhiques de Bamiyan*, Pl. XXXI; J. Hackin and J. Carl, *Nouvelles recherches archéologiques à Bamiyan*, Pl. I; Pl. XLV, 55.

26 *The Chicago Tribune*, 20 July 1968.

The Place and Date of Birth of Fużūlī

As I was entrusted by UNESCO to write a preface to the English translation of the poem *Leylā and Mejnūn* by Fużūlī, I have been involved in the study of the life of this man, who 'may be considered as the greatest Turkish poet'.[1] The first problem which confronted me was that of the place and date of birth of Fużūlī. In this field I formed an opinion based especially on the Persian *Dīvān* of Fużūlī, the whole of which was published in Ankara in 1962 by Hasibe Mazıoğlu.[2] I introduced my opinion in the above-mentioned preface, but it was not possible to discuss there the still unsettled problem at sufficient length. I propose to do so here. An article on Fużūlī, who, though at different levels, was a master of Arabic, Persian and Turkish literature, will not be out of place in a volume dedicated to V. Minorsky, a scholar who supremely dominated the fields of Arabic, Turkish and Persian philology.

The earlier biographers are unanimous in maintaining that Fużūlī was from Baghdad.[3] This is the information given by the Ottoman Laṭīfī[4] and by the Ṣafavid Sām Mīrzā,[5] who completed their works while Fużūlī was still alive, the former in 953/1546 and the latter in 957/1550; by ʿAhdī, an authoritative informant because he was Fużūlī's fellow-countryman, but who wrote in 971/1563, when Fużūlī was already dead (he had died in 1556)[6]; and by the Ottoman ʿĀshiq Chelebī, whose work dates from many years after the death of the poet, because it was presented to Selīm II in 976/1568.[7] The Ottoman historian ʿĀlī, who wrote towards the end of the century,[8] states precisely that Baghdad was the place of birth of Fużūlī, while the other writers merely say that Fużūlī was 'from Baghdad' (*Baghdādī* or *az Baghdād*).

Abdülkadir Karahan, the author of an extensive and worthy monograph on Fużūlī published in 1949, does not agree that Fużūlī was born in Baghdad. He first observed that the words of the biographer Ṣadīqī, librarian of Shāh ʿAbbās (whose book is dated 1007/1598), *Ibrāhīm Khān khidmätidä*

Baghdādgha barub, 'he went to Baghdad in the service of Ibrāhīm Khān'[9] show that Fużūlī did not originate from Baghdad; then he points out, and this is a stronger argument, that Fużūlī in poems written in Baghdad speaks of his condition as a stranger (*ghurbet*). Karahan quotes as evidence only two *qaṣīdas* from the Turkish *Dīvān*.[10] It is true that in these *qaṣīdas* there is no mention of Baghdad, but the poet refers to the presence (*dīdār*, *viṣāl*) of the Pashas (Ayās and Meḥmed) to whom the *qaṣīdas* were addressed and whose residence was Baghdad (but it is not excluded that both Meḥmed Pasha, 'who intended to bring water to Karbalā'', and the poet, with whose sojourn in Karbalā' I shall deal later, were in Karbalā'). If we accept the opinion of Karahan, which seems to be reasonable, we must think that the nisba *Baghdādī* adopted by the earlier sources was applied to Fużūlī because he acquired fame as a poet while he was in Baghdad. We may also suppose that the expression *az Dār as-Salām-i Baghdād* 'from Baghdad, the Abode of Peace', used by Sām Mīrzā, does not refer to the town itself, but generally to its country. The same may be thought of a couplet of the Persian *Dīvān*, which Karahan did not consider, where the poet speaks of himself as *az Baghdād* 'from Baghdad', in contrast to a friend who was *Vāsiṭī* 'from Vāsiṭ'.[11]

Some later sources connect Fużūlī with another town in Iraq, that is, Ḥilla. The Ottoman biographer Ḥasan Chelebī Qïnalïzāde, who wrote in 994/1586, says that Fużūlī was from Ḥilla (*Ḥilleden*)[12] and the already-mentioned Ṣafavid librarian Ṣadīqī says that Fużūlī was established (*mutavaṭṭin*) in Ḥilla when Süleymān the Magnificent entered Baghdad (1535).[13] The modern Turkish writer Süleymān Naẓīf (d. 1927), in a monograph on Fużūlī published in Istanbul in 1926, quotes from the well-known scholar 'Alī Emīrī, a quatrain which is a satire of Fażlī, son of Fużūlī and himself a poet, from which both appear as resident in Ḥilla

در حلّه دو شاعر اند فضلی پسر و پدر فضولی
عکس اند جمیع کار عالم فضلی پدر و پسر فضولی

> 'In Ḥilla there are two poets: Fażlī the son and Fużūlī the father. Every thing in this world is upside-down: the father is excellent and the son is a silly fellow.'[14]

It is probable that Rieu, the author of the catalogue of Turkish manuscripts of the British Museum, follows the evidence of Qïnalïzāde when he states that Fużūlī 'was born in Ḥillah'.[15] E. J. W. Gibb, in the third volume of his classic *A History of Ottoman Poetry* (edited posthumously in London in 1904) recalls Rieu, saying that the birthplace of Fużūlī was 'probably either

Ḥilla, as the British Museum Catalogue says, or, as is suggested, though)t distinctly stated, by the early biographers, the city of Baghdad'.[16]

The opinion that Fużūlī was born in Ḥilla was expressed in more rece times by K. Edib[17] and was supported by such an authoritative scholar, ä F. Köprülü. Köprülü invokes not only what Ṣadīqī says and 'the expres sions of other sources', but also, as does K. Edip, a line that occurs in an Arabic poem by Fużūlī, who says:

لسانك حلوٌ لحظ طرفك ساحر كأنّك حلّي وأرضك بابل

'Your tongue is sweet and the glance of your eyes is enchanting, as if you were from Ḥilla and your country were Babel' (as is known the location of ancient Babel, which was, according to Moslems, a country of magicians, is near Ḥilla; note the *jinās*: *ḥalw–Ḥilla*).[18]

The same view is adopted by C. Özulus mainly on the basis of an expression of Fużūlī in the poem *Leylā and Mejnūn* (*men sāḥir-i Bābilī-niẓhādem* 'I am a magician of Babylonian race').[19]

Karahan is against this theory. He calls attention to the fact that the word *mutavaṭṭin*, employed by Ṣadīqī, excludes the idea that Fużūlī was born in Ḥilla, because it properly refers to a person who moves from one place to another, in order to establish himself there, as if in a second home.[20] As far as the Arabic line quoted by Köprülü is concerned, it proves nothing about the native country of the poet, because the poet does not speak of himself, but addresses his speech to a friend who was 'as a native of Ḥilla'.[21] The expression *Bābilī-niẓhād* is merely a literary device.

Karahan concludes that such evidence, as afforded by Köprülü or Özulus, cannot prove that Fużūlī was born in Ḥilla and can only indicate that the poet spent some time in Ḥilla.[22] The same may be thought of the statement of Qïnalïzāde, which Karahan does not discuss. As a matter of fact, in the writings of Fużūlī there is not any explicit mention of a sojourn in Ḥilla, unless we suppose that Fużūlī was in Ḥilla when he wrote two Persian *qaṣīdas* addressed to friends who were leaving Ḥilla respectively for Asia Minor and Arabia.[23] As we shall see, there was a doubtful tradition that Fużūlī was the son of the *muftī* of Ḥilla and that he was buried there.[24]

Karahan, leaving aside Baghdad and Ḥilla, proposes a third town in Iraq as the birthplace of Fużūlī, that is Karbalā'. For Karbalā' also, there is early evidence, but it is later than the death of the poet. One piece of evidence belongs to an Ottoman biographer, Riyāżī, whose work was finished in 1018/1609.[25] Riyāżī bases his statement that Fużūlī was born in Karbalā' exclusively on a quatrain of the Persian *Dīvān*, which I shall quote later, when I am dealing with Karahan's theory, which is itself also based on this quatrain. There is also a short notice on the life of Fużūlī introduced in the edition of 1328/1910 of the *Külliyyāt*, at the end of the poem *Leylā and Mejnūn*, according to which Fużūlī was born in Karbalā' in 910/1504, was the son of the *muftī* of Ḥilla, started writing verses because he was in love with the daughter of his teacher Khōja Raḥmatullāh, died in 975/1567, and had his tomb in Ḥilla, a tomb visited by pilgrims (*ziyāretgāh*).[26] Karahan assumes that this information goes back to the famous book *Nümūne-i edebiyyāt-i ʿOṣmāniyye* by Ebūzziyā Tevfīq, published in 1879,[27] where no evidence is given, but the origin from a scholium in some manuscript is not excluded. However, the dates of birth and death indicated are erroneous. Karahan considers the information as not reliable. He bases his theory rather on the prefaces to the Turkish and to the Persian *Dīvāns* of Fużūlī. The latter is chronologically precedent, because Fużūlī speaks in the former of his Persian poems as already collected. Karahan calls attention to the following passage:

از من سودا زده توقع این فن عجب است که مولد ومقامم عراق عرب است زیرا که بقعهٔ ایست از سایهٔ سلاطین دور وبواسطهٔ سکان بیشعور نامعمور بوستانیست سروهای خرامانش کرد باد های صرصر سموم وغنجه های ناشکفته اش قبهای مزار شهیدان مظلوم بزمکاهیست شرابش خون جکرهای پاره ونغمه‌اش نالهای غریبان آواره نه نسیم راحتی‌را بصحرای محنت فزایش کذاری و نه بیابان پر بلایش‌را از سحاب رأفت امید تسکین غباری . درچنین ریاض ریاضت غنجهٔ دل چکونه کشاید و بلبل زبان چه سراید

'It is a wonder to expect such an art that is [of poetry] from me, who am afflicted with an intense passion, because my place of birth and residence is Arabian Iraq. This is a country far from the protecting shadow of the Sultans, and not flourishing on account of its heedless inhabitants; it is a garden whose graceful cypresses are the whirlpools of the violent poisonous wind of the desert and its not yet opened rose-buds are the domes of the tombs of the innocent martyrs; it is a banqueting-place whose wine is the blood of torn livers and whose music is the moans of the vagrant strangers; a breeze of tranquillity does not pass through its troublesome desert and the dust of its wilderness full of calamities does not hope to be calmed by the cloud of benignity. In such gardens of austerity, how does the rose-bud of the heart open and what does the nightingale of the tongue sing?'[28]

In conclusion, says Karahan, 'this passage lets Karbalā' clearly live under our eyes and provokes the image of the tombs of the innocent martyrs. The country of "grief and torment" (*karb u balā*, that is Karbalā' !) can be presented only in such a lively and imaginative manner.'[29] In other words the term Arabian Iraq, indicated as the 'place of birth and sojourn' can be no other than Karbalā'.

But the words following in the preface do not justify such a conclusion:

بدانکه اکثر اولیا وصلحا ومشایخ وعلما که سرمستان بادهٔ شوق الٓهی و عاشقان
جمال محبوب حقیقی بوده اند و همیشه ترك لذات دنیا و مخالفت هوا می نموده اند،
چون به تیغ محبت هلاك شده اند، همه درین دیار خاك شده اند. حالا خاك این
دیار بخاك آن مظلومان آمیخته است و خون آن شهیدان برین خاك ریخته است

'Know that most of the saints, pious men, shaykhs, doctors drunk with the wine of the aching desire for God and the lovers of the beauty of the True Beloved, who have always abandoned the pleasures of the world and have fought against the passions, when they perished through the sword of love, have all become earth in this country; and now the earth of this country is mingled with the earth of these victims and the blood of these martyrs has been poured on this earth!'[30]

It is evident that the phrase 'the domes of the tombs of the innocent martyrs' occurring in the first passage, is explained by these words and, therefore, it does not refer only to the tombs of the martyrs of Karbalā', but to a larger group of holy and pious men, of shaykhs, doctors and mystics immersed in divine love and suffering martyrdom for its sake. Accordingly, the country which Fużūlī indicates as his native country is Iraq in general and not Karbalā' in particular.

A. Karahan gives also the following passage from the same preface:

واین نورسیدکان روزکار ندیده واین یتیمان غربت نشنیده که از خاك نجف
وخطهٔ کربلا سر بر آورده اند ودر آب وهوای برج أولیا پرورده اند

He translates this passage as follows: 'my poems, similar to youngsters who have no experience of the world, and to orphans who have not suffered separation from their country, were born in the region of Karbalā', in the territory of Najaf (*Kerbelâ sahasında Necef toprağında*) and grew up in the atmosphere of Baghdad'.[31]

According to such a translation Karbalā' would be the country where the poems of Fużūlī were first born. But, I think that the words *dar khāk-i Najaf va khiṭṭa-i Karbalā'* should be translated 'in the territory of Najaf and in the region of Karbalā' ', because of the conjunction *va* between the two terms. Therefore Karbalā' follows and does not precede Najaf.

Further, always in the same preface, the following quatrain occurs:

چون خاك كربلاست فضولی مقام من
نظمم بهر كجا كه رسد حرمتش رواست
زر نیست سیم نیست گهر نیست لعل نیست
خاكست شعر بنده ولی خاك كربلاست

'Because the earth of Karbalā', O Fużūlī, is my residence, my verse wherever it arrives ought to be held in honour. My poetry is not gold, is not pearl, is not ruby; it is earth, but it is the earth of Karbalā'.'[32]

Riyāżī, as I said, on the basis of this quatrain states that Fużūlī was born in Karbalā' and A. Karahan employs it with the same intention. But it is evident that from this quatrain we can only infer that Karbalā' was a 'place of sojourn' (*maqām*) of Fużūlī, a fact to which we shall return later.[33]

More inconclusive for the Karbalā' theory is another quatrain, which is quoted in several sources, but also appears in the Persian *Dīvān*:

آسودهٔ كربلا بهر حال كه هست
گر خاك شود نمیشود قدرش پست
بر میدارند و سبحه‌اش میسازند
میگردانندش از شرف دست بدست

'One who is at rest (Karahan translates: *oturan* "dwelling") in Karbalā', whatever his condition is, if he becomes earth, his value does not diminish. The people take it up (sc. the earth), make chaplets of it, hand it around from hand to hand with honour.'[34]

It seems to be beyond doubt that the quatrain refers to the well-known practice of the Shī'ites, and not only those of Iran, of letting themselves be buried in Karbalā'. The word *āsūdā* in such a case does not mean 'dwelling' (certainly not 'native'), but has the meaning of 'lying peacefully', as referred to a dead person, as in other lines of the *Dīvān*.

A. Karahan also recalls the preface to the Turkish *Dīvān*, and precisely the following two passages, connected by some lines of verse and prose:

امیددر كه اصحاب فصاحت و ارباب بلاغت مشاهده و مطالعه قلدقده منشأ و مولدم عراق عرب اولوب تمامیء عمرمده غیر مملكتلره سیاحت قلمدیغمه و اقف اولدقده بو علتی موجب سقوط اعتبار بیلمیه‌لر. و محل و مقامه كوره رتبهٔ استعدادمه حقارتله

نظر قیلمیه‌لر. زیرا اعتبار وطن استعداد ذاته تأثیر ایتمز. وطپراقده یاتمغله طلادن جلا کیتمز.

لله الحمد و المنه که خاك کربلا سائر ممالك اکسیرندن اشرف اولدیغی معلومدر. و رتبهٔ شعرمی هریرده بلند ایدن حقیقتده بو مفهومدر.

'I hope that people speaking clearly and eloquently in observing and reading [my ghazals], being aware that my origin and place of birth is Arabian Iraq and that in all my life I did not travel in other countries, will not consider this as a reason for diminishing their esteem, and will not look with contempt upon the degree of my capacity, out of regard for my place and residence, because consideration of the native country does not affect the capacity of the person, and brightness does not leave gold if it lies in the earth.' [34a]

'Praise and thank God that it is known that the earth of Karbalā' is more noble than the elixir of other countries. It is this concept that in truth exalts the degree of my poetry everywhere.'[35]

Karahan points out that 'if we put aside the short passages in verse and prose occurring between the two quoted passages, according to the requirements of the old style, we have no difficulty in stating that the expression "earth of Karbalā'" corresponds perfectly to the expression "my place of origin and birth"'.[36]

The preface to the Turkish *Dīvān*, written, as we said, after the preface to the Persian one, reproduces the ideas of the latter. The specific appeal to Karbalā' may be intended as related to the prerogatives of Iraq in general. However, the connection which occurs between 'the poetry of Fużūlī' and 'the earth of Karbalā'' means only that at the time when Fużūlī wrote the preface he lived in Karbalā', that is that Karbalā' was his 'place of sojourn' (*maqām*) as is said in the above-mentioned Persian quatrain.

As a matter of fact, several *qaṣīdas* in honour of Imām Ḥusain and of Karbalā' were written in Karbalā'.[37] One couplet in particular indicates a long sojourn (*rūzgāri*).[38] We are able to make a suggestion about the epoch when the two prefaces were written and consequently of the sojourn of Fużūlī in Karbalā'. In several lines of the Persian and Turkish *Dīvāns* the poet hints at his advanced age; the prefaces to the two *Dīvāns* where such hints occur must therefore belong to a late period of Fużūlī's life. Moreover, Fużūlī in the preface to the Turkish *Dīvān* declares that he has no time to compose new *ghazals* because 'the banker of his intellect was spending the money of time on important books (*taṣānīf-i mu'tebere*) and the falcon of his natural disposition was looking after bigger prey (*mu'azzam ṣaydlar*)'.[39] It is tempting to think that by using such expressions Fużūlī hinted at the free translation of the *Ḥadīqatu 's-su'adā* of Ḥusain Vā'iẓ Kāshifī, which certainly was a big work (if the *Maṭla' al-i'tiqād*, the dogmatic treatise by Fużūlī recently edited, was not intended, or also intended).[40] Now, the above-mentioned translation was written by Fużūlī in the last years of his life, as appears from the mention of Meḥmed Pasha, the ruler of Baghdad at that time. It is an obvious conclusion that the work, being a glorification of the martyrs of Karbalā', was written while the author was staying in Karbalā'.[41]

No valid argument compels us to suppose that Karbalā' was the birthplace of Fużūlī. On the contrary, there is an argument *ex silentio* against this view. In none of the *qaṣīdas* dedicated to Imām Ḥusain, the martyr of Karbalā', and to Karbalā' itself, does Fużūlī hint at the fact that he was born in that much-glorified holy place, as one might expect. On the contrary, in one of them, certainly written in Karbalā', he alludes to his condition as a stranger (*gharībi*)[42] and in another he defines Karbalā' as a 'place of shelter' (*ma'vā*).[43]

Hemid Arasly, a scholar of Soviet Azerbaijan and himself the author of a good monograph on Fużūlī published in Baku in 1958, is of the same opinion as Karahan. He gives particular importance to the above-mentioned words of the Persian *Dīvān*.[44]

Karahan himself is, however, not completely convinced of having attained certainty, because in the excellent article on Fużūlī written by him for the second edition of the *Encyclopedia of Islam*, he cautiously says that Fużūlī 'was born in 'Irāḳ, at the time of the Aḳ-Ḳoyunlu (White Sheep Dynasty) domination, probably at Karbalā' although Baghdād, Ḥilla, Nadjaf, Kirkūk, Manzil and Hīt are also mentioned as his birthplace'.[45]

Two scholars, who dealt with Fużūlī in the second volume of the *Philologiae Turcicae Fundamenta*, published in 1964, do not mention the place of birth of the poet. W. Björkman says only that 'Sein Leben verbrachte er zumeist in Hille, Kerbela und Neğef'[46] and A. Caferoğlu that he 'verbracht sein Leben in Baghdad'.[47]

In my opinion, a better case than for either Ḥilla or Karbalā', as places of Fużūlī's birth, may be made out for another town in Iraq, I mean Najaf. A couplet in the Persian *Dīvān* offers convincing evidence which as yet has not been brought forward for this purpose. The couplet occurs in a *qaṣīda* dedicated to 'Alī and refers to his tomb in Najaf:

شکر للّه ز ابتدای عمر تا غایت مرا
روضهٔ خاك در شاه ولایت منزل است

'Thanks be to God! From the beginning of life to the end, the garden of the earth of the Gate of the King of Holiness (the shrine of ʿAlī in Najaf) has been my dwelling place.'[48]

As a matter of fact, this couplet did not escape the attention of Karahan, but he quotes it, together with others, in order to demonstrate only that Fużūlī 'during many years stayed in Najaf among the guardians of the tomb of ʿAlī'.[49] It is not to be excluded that Fużūlī with the word *ibtidā'* 'beginning' intended to denote the first period of his existence, not necessarily including the moment of his birth, but it is more obvious to think that his birth is included, while arguments to the contrary are lacking. The word *ghāyat*, if it does not indicate the 'climax' of life (which is possible, but unlikely, since the poem was apparently written in his old age), indicates the extreme end of his life. The poet, who has passed the threshold of senility, imagines that he will die in Najaf. While *ghāyat* seems to denote the moment of his death, the corresponding term *ibtidā'* should denote the moment of his birth. In other words, Fużūlī is pleased, and therefore thanks God that the holy land of Najaf has seen both the initial and final events of his life.

There is another piece of evidence in favour of Najaf rather than Karbalā'. I mean the passage of the preface to the Persian *Dīvān*, whose terms, as seen before, Karahan inverted in his translation. The translation I propose is: 'My poems, similar to youngsters who have no experience of the world and to orphans who have not suffered separation from their country, were born in the territory of Najaf and in the region of Karbalā' and have grown up in the atmosphere of Baghdad'. In other words, Fużūlī enumerates the halting places of his poetical production, which did not go beyond the limits of Iraq. His poetical activity started in Najaf, continued in Karbalā' and reached maturity in Baghdad.

Moreover, the circumstances themselves of the life of the poet lead us to assume that he was a native of Najaf.[50] It is likely that this was the reason why as a young man he entered the service of the shrine of ʿAlī in Najaf,[51] why he implores not to be transferred to another place,[52] why we find him repeatedly in Najaf: when Ibrāhīm Khān, Ṣafavid ruler of Baghdad from 1514, arrived there[53]; again, after thirty-odd years, in 1546, at the time of the Ottoman governor Ayās Pasha[54]; when a mission of the Shīʿite Sultan of the Deccan arrived at the shrine of ʿAlī[55]; when Fużūlī declares that he is willing to dedicate himself to the service of the shrine, in his old age, as he did before in his youth.[56]

We do not have at our disposal definite starting points for establishing the date of birth of Fużūlī. The scholars who have dealt with the question arrived at vague conclusions and I also am unable to suggest anything new. I only wished to discuss some of the arguments put forward. A. Karahan bases his theory mainly on the fact that a *qaṣīda* by Fużūlī was dedicated to one Elvend Bey, whom he identifies with a member of the Aqqoyunlu dynasty, who shared the reign with his cousin Murād, was defeated in 1502 by Shāh Ismāʿīl, retired to the region of Diyārbakr and died in 1504. If we suppose, says the Turkish scholar, that Fużūlī presented this poem in the year 1500, and if we consider that Fużūlī was then at least twenty years old in order to be able to write in such an elaborate style as the poem shows, we arrive at the conclusion that Fużūlī was born about the year 1480. He adds that we can reach the same conclusion in another way. In another poem Fużūlī says that 'for fifty years' he has been inspired to sing the glory of ʿAlī.[57] If we assume that Fużūlī was twenty years old when he began to write poetry, and that he was seventy years old when he wrote this poem (he died in 1556 and it is likely that the poem is some years earlier than his death), we also arrive approximately at the year 1480 as the date of his birth.[58]

The arguments of Karahan have been the object of criticism by the already-mentioned H. Arasly. He asserts first that the Elvend Bey of Fużūlī's poem cannot be the Aqqoyunlu Alvand Mīrzā, because the title of the latter was 'Mīrzā' and not 'Bey' and because this person was not in Baghdad in 1500. Arasly maintains as the *terminus ad quem* of the poetical activity of Fużūlī the date of the poem *Bang u bāda*, which was certainly written between the years 1510 – because a line refers to an event of this year (the use of the skull of the Uzbek sovereign Shaybānī as a cup by Shāh Ismāʿīl) – and 1524, date of the death of Shāh Ismāʿīl, who is mentioned as the ruling king. Arasly chooses a date closer to 1524 and assigns to Fużūlī an age of between twenty and twenty-five years at the moment of the composition of the poem; he is therefore inclined to calculate the year 1498 as the year of the poet's birth. The Soviet scholar quotes another couplet by Fużūlī saying that he had sung the glory of ʿAlī for fifty years,[59] but he is of the opinion that the expression 'fifty years' in this couplet, and in the other quoted by Karahan, is not to be taken literally, but merely denotes 'for a long time'. Arasly arrives at this opinion from the theory that if one accepts Karahan's view, Fużūlī should have written the poem *Leylā and Mejnūn* at the age of fifty-five years, and this does not agree with the spirit of the poem. Arasly further feels that this age does not accord with the fact that the poet speaks of a son who is still a boy, and therefore he could not have been very advanced in life at that time.[60]

Arasly's criticism may be accepted only in part. As far as the *qaṣīda* addressed to Elvend Bey is concerned, the argument of the title is not valid because Alvand Mīrzā appears in the sources also with the title of 'Bey', but there are other arguments against the identification of Elvend Bey with Alvand Mīrzā. Not only was the latter not in Baghdad in the year in which Karahan supposes that the poem was written, but he never had power in that town, and therefore it is unlikely that Fużūlī addressed a *qaṣīda* to him. On the other hand a closer examination of the poem reveals that it is addressed to a person from whom Fużūlī had received 'a thousand gifts' (*hazār ʿaṭā*) and who is returning from a journey, which, from a couplet, seems to have taken place in Egypt and the Holy Cities of Islam.[61] Not only is there no evidence that Alvand Mīrzā made such a journey, but such a journey is unlikely to have taken place in the troubled existence of the Aqqoyunlu prince. The same may be said for a *qaṣīda* in Turkish dedicated by Fużūlī also to Elvend Bey, who, according to this poem, had carried out irrigation work and increased the prosperity of the country.[62] It is questionable who this Elvend Bey was. According to Arasly's book, the manuscript of Fużūlī's works preserved in Leningrad (written in 1589) indicates this person as a 'son of ʿAlī Pasha'[63]; according to the edition of Fużūlī's *qaṣīdas*, published in Baku in 1961 (edited by the same Arasly), Elvend Bey is shown in the above-mentioned Leningrad manuscript as 'the father of ʿAlī Pasha'.[64] It is not excluded that he was the father or the son of Temerrüd ʿAlī Pasha, who was first *serdār* then governor of Baghdad until 1552.[65] But more probably he was the father of ʿAlī Pasha b. Elvend, a governor of Baghdad, who in the year 991/1585 repaired the shrine of Ḥusain in Karbalāʾ.[66] The opinion expressed by Ata Terzibaşı that Elvend Bey was the *sanjaq-begi* of Ḥamīd-eli mentioned in a report by Süleymān Pasha to the Sultan on the campaign in ʿIrāq has been criticized by A. Karahan.[66a]

Arasly's argument against the possibility that Fużūlī wrote his poem *Leylā and Mejnūn* at the age of fifty-seven years appears too vague. However, Fużūlī's lines where he speaks of a young son do not necessarily have an autobiographical character because they are inspired by analogous lines of the poem *Laylā and Majnūn* by the Persian poet Hātifī, whom Fużūlī follows in this part of his poem.[67]

The starting-points for determining the date of birth of Fużūlī remain those indicated by Karahan: the period between the years 1510 and 1524, to be considered as the period in which Fużūlī had already attained poetical skill, and the fact that Fużūlī for fifty years eulogized ʿAlī. The period 1510 to 1524 may be reduced. It is certain that Fużūlī was already a skilful poet in 1514, the year to which a *qaṣīda* apparently welcoming Ibrāhīm Khān on his arrival in Baghdad belongs.[68] For writing such a stylistically precious poem and for addressing a governor as he does here, Fużūlī must have been at least twenty years old. On the other hand, one of the two couplets in which Fużūlī speaks of his fifty years spent in eulogizing ʿAlī belongs to a *qaṣīda* written in Najaf,[69] that is presumably before the supposed long sojourn of Fużūlī in Karbalāʾ, and therefore several years before the death of the poet, in 1556. To sum up, it may be said that the poet's birth lies between the years 1480 and 1490.

NOTES

1 M. Fuad Köprülü, art. *Fuzûlî* in *Islâm Ansiklopedisi*, 37 cüz (Istanbul 1947) 686 b.

2 *Fuzûlî. Farsça Divan. Edisyon Kritik, yayınlayan* Professor Dr Hasibe Mazıoğlu (Ankara 1962) (Ankara Üniversitesi Dil ve Tarih-Coğrafya Fakültesi yayınları No. 135. Türk Dili ve edebiyatı serisi No. 20). On previous partial editions see ibid., p. v.

3 The references have been collected, by consulting unedited manuscripts, by A. Karahan, *Fuzulî. Muhiti, hayatı ve şahsiyeti* (Istanbul 1949) 221 ff.

4 Ed. Istanbul 1314/1896, 265; A. Karahan, op. cit., 221.

5 Ed. V. Dastgirdī (Teheran 1314 *shamsī*/1936), 136.

6 Inedited. A. Karahan, op. cit., 224.

7 Inedited. A. Karahan, op. cit., 228.

8 Inedited part of the *Künh al-akhbār*. A. Karahan, op. cit., 240.

9 A. Karahan, op. cit., 243 (after manuscripts).

10 A. Karahan, op. cit., 68; *Külliyyāt* of Fuẓūlī (Istanbul 1328/1910) (hereafter *Külliyyāt*) 53 and 63.

11 Persian *Dīvān*, 73, couplet 16.

12 Inedited. A. Karahan, op. cit., 231.

13 A. Karahan, op. cit., 243.

14 Süleymān Naẓīf, *Fuẓūlī* (Istanbul 1926) 16.

15 Ch. Rieu, *Catalogue of the Turkish manuscripts of the British Museum* (London 1888) 39b.

16 E. J. W. Gibb, *A History of Ottoman Poetry*, III (London 1904) 71.

17 K. Edip, *Fuzulî' nin bilinmeyen bir farsça kasidesi*, Ankara Üniversitesi Dil ve Tarih-Coğrafya Fakültesi Dergisi, IV (1946) 315 n. 1.

18 M. F. Köprülü, op. cit., 687a. Köprülü quotes only the second hemistich; the entire line is in E. E. Bertel's, *Arabskie stili Fuzuli*, in Zapiski Kollegii Vostokovedov, V (1930), cf. *Izbrannyj trudy. Nizami i Fuzuli* (Moscow 1962) 515.

19 *Külliyyāt*, 241; ed. N. H. Onan (Istanbul 1956) 38. Cf. Özulus, *Fuzulî* (Niğde 1948) 18-23.

20 Op. cit., 69. This observation had already been expressed by A. N. Tarlan, cf. ibid.

21 Ibid., 271-2. The same criticism of K. Edib and Köprülü was raised by A. Gölpinarlı, *Fuzulî Divanı* (Istanbul 1948), CXLI and ff.

22 Op. cit., 272.

23 Persian *Dīvān*, 72-6 and 185-90.

24 See below, n. 26.

25 Inedited. A. Karahan, op. cit., 247.

26 *Külliyyāt*, 348.

27 Op. cit., 76, n. 2.

28 Ibid., 70. The same passage, with slight variants, in Mazıoğlu's edition of the Persian *Dīvān*, 7.

29 Op. cit., 71.

30 Persian *Dīvān*, 8.

31 Op. cit., 71; Persian *Dīvān*, 15.

32 A. Karahan, op. cit., 71; Persian *Dīvān*, 15.

33 This observation is already in Süleymān Nazīf, op. cit., 17:

هر مقام مولد دكل در، و حتى مولد مدلولنه ايراث ضعف ايدر

'every *maqām* is not *mevlid* (place of birth), moreover (the word *maqām*) makes difficult the meaning of place of birth'.

34 A. Karahan, op. cit., 71; Persian *Dīvān*, 648, where *fi'l* takes the place of *ḥāl*.

34a *Külliyyāt*, p. 6.

35 Ibid., 7.

36 Op. cit., 70.

37 Persian *Dīvān*, 191-3, 200-3, 204-6, 241-3. Only in the second *qaṣīda* the presence of Fużūlī in Karbalā' is not clearly indicated.

38 Ibid., 206, couplet 21.

39 *Külliyyāt*, 6.

40 Ed. Ankara 1965.

41 I suggested above that a *qaṣīda* addressed to Meḥmed Pasha (*Külliyyāt*, 63-2) was written in Karbalā'.

42 Persian *Dīvān*, 193, couplet 27.

43 Ibid., 206, couplet 21.

44 H. Arasly, *Böyük Azerbaizan šairi Füzuli* (Baku 1958) 92-3.

45 *Encyclopédie de l'Islam*², Tome II, Livraison 37 (Leiden–Paris 1964) 957a. Whether Fużūlī was born in Najaf is discussed in the latter part of this article. The opinion that Kirkūk was his birthplace, as has been put forward by Ata Terzibaşı in *Türk Yurdu* (1955) has been convincingly criticized by Karahan, *Fuzulî'nin doğum yeri problemi*, Türk Yurdu (1956) 494-8, and does not require further discussion. Where, and upon what basis, Manzil has been proposed as Fużūlī's brithplace is unknown to me. The statement that he was born in Hīt is stated in a *menāqib-nāme* of very doubtful value, cf. C. Öztelli, *Fuzulî menakıbı uydurma mıdır?* Türk Dili, VII (1958) 396-9.

46 *Philologiae Turcicae Fundamenta*, Tomus secundus, Aquis Mattiacis (Wiesbaden) MCMLXIV, 434.

47 Ibid., 644.

48 Persian *Dīvān*, 153, couplet 27.

49 Op. cit., 276.

50 More about these circumstances is to be found in the above-mentioned preface I prepared for the poem *Leylā and Mejnūn.*

51 At least, this is distinctly stated by the above-quoted couplet. See also Persian *Dīvān*, 120, couplet 59.

52 See Persian *Dīvān*, 214-15.

53 *Külliyyāt*, 44.

54 Ibid., 35.

55 Persian *Dīvān*, 210, couplet 23.

56 Ibid., 120, couplets 59-60.

57 The verse is to be found in the Persian *Dīvān*, 145-6, couplet 32.

58 Karahan develops his arguments in pp. 272-5 of his book.

59 The couplet is to be found in the Persian *Dīvān*, 209.

60 Op. cit., 88-92.

61 Persian *Dīvān*, 87, couplet 23.

62 *Mehemmed Füzuli. Eserleri. IV zild* (Baku 1961), 90. (This *qaṣīda* is not to be found in *Külliyyāt*; it appears also dedicated to Üveys Bey, cf. ibid., 349).

63 Op. cit., 89.

64 *Mehemmed Füzuli*, 362.

65 Cf. A. Karahan, op. cit., 29.

66 Cf. *Encyclopédie de l'Islam*¹, Tome III, 453 b (Leiden–Paris 1932), s.v. Meshhed Ḥusain (E. Honigmann).

66*a* Cf. the article cited in n. 45. No further information is available on this personage. I do not share Karahan's view that the poems dedicated to

Elvend Bey are addressed to a sovereign. The fact that one of these poems is in Persian does not exclude that he was an Ottoman dignitary; many such poems are dedicated to Ottoman governors in Baghdad.

67 On the relationship Hātifī-Fużūlī, cf. the above-mentioned preface to the poem *Leylā and Mejnūn*.

68 *Külliyyāt*, 43-4.

69 Persian *Dīvān*, 145, couplet 32.

C. E. BOSWORTH

The Banū Ilyās of Kirmān (320–57/932–68)

Kirmān is a somewhat isolated corner of the Iranian plateau, with its mountainous configuration and with the protective zone on the east of the Dasht-i Lūṭ. The main access routes from the west to Kirmān are by land through Fārs, and the province has accordingly tended to be politically dependent on Fārs and the ruling power in south-western Persia.[1] However, at certain times it has enjoyed a measure of political independence. This was most notable during the Seljuq and Mongol periods; for 150 years Kirmān was ruled by a separate branch of the Seljuq family, the descendants of Qāwurd b. Chaghrī Beg Dā'ūd (sc. from 433/1041 to 582/1186), and then in the thirteenth century was under the rule of scions of the Qara Khiṭai, the Qutlugh-Khanids (sc. from 619/1222 to 703/1304). But in the tenth century also, Kirmān, poised between the empire of the Sāmānids in Khurāsān and the possessions in western and southern Persia of various Dailamī adventurers, was virtually independent under the Banū Ilyās or Ilyāsids, even though these last were nominally tributary to the Sāmānids.

The Ilyāsids have left little mark in the historiography of mediaeval Persia. The prime source is the Būyid official and chronicler Miskawaih, who refers to events in Kirmān when they impinge on the history of the Būyid dynasty; thus he gives detailed accounts of the expeditions against Kirmān by Mu'izz ad-Daula in 324/936 and by 'Aḍud ad-Daula in 357/968 and the succeeding years. This material was utilized, in a slightly condensed form, by Ibn al-Athīr, who also has additional information about the origins of Muḥammad b. Ilyās's power in Kirmān, doubtless derived from the unspecified sources for Khurāsānian history upon which he drew for the history of Sāmānid and Dailamī activity in Persia at this time. The Ghaznavid historian 'Utbī describes 'Aḍud ad-Daula's conquest of Kirmān and the deposition of Ilyasa' b. Muḥammad b. Ilyās, but only as background to the story of Maḥmūd of Ghazna's entente with Bahā' ad-Daula Fīrūz b. 'Aḍud ad-Daula after the Ghaznavid conquest of Sīstān in 393/1003. There is a fair amount of *inshā'* literature, collections of official correspondence, surviving from the early Būyid period, and letters from the collections of 'Aḍud ad-Daula's secretary 'Abd al-'Azīz b. Yūsuf ash-Shīrāzī (d. 388/998) and of Abū Isḥāq Ibrāhīm b. Hilāl aṣ-Ṣābi' (d. 384/994) make reference to the Būyid expeditions of 360/970 and 364/975 against Kirmān (see below, p. 118, n. 40). Apart from one or two mentions of the Banū Ilyās in the Arabic geographers of the tenth century, this exhausts the contemporary or near-contemporary sources on the family; when the later general historians, such as Ḥamdallāh Mustaufī, Mīrkhwānd and Khwāndamīr, touch on the Ilyāsids, they reproduce information from the above historical sources.[2]

However, the local histories of towns and provinces often throw light on the wider historical scene. A rich genre of local historical writing, at first dealing with the *faḍā'il*, excellences, of the place in question and with the prominent scholars and religious leaders who adorned it, and then dealing with the historical events affecting the place, has flourished in Persia down to the present day (the works of Sayyid Aḥmad Kasravī on his native province of Azerbaijan and on Khūzistān can clearly be attached to this ancient tradition).[3] Historians of the eastern Islamic world have long recognized the richness of such sources as Narshakhī's *Ta'rīkh-i Bukhārā*, the anonymous *Ta'rīkh-i Sīstān* or Mu'īn ad-Dīn Isfizārī's *Rauḍāt al-jannāt fī auṣāf madīnat Harāt*, which fill out by their intimate but significant details the barer bones of the general histories. Kirmān, culturally a region of second rank in the earlier Islamic centuries, did not apparently produce any local histories at that time; but in the twelfth century we find the commanding figure of Afḍal ad-Dīn Aḥmad b. Ḥāmid Kirmānī (died before 615/1218), called by Bāstānī-yi Pārīzī (see below) 'the Baihaqī of Kirmān'. Amongst his three works on the history of Kirmān is the *'Iqd al-'ulā li'l-mauqif al-a'lā*, written for the Ghuzz chieftain Malik Dīnār, who in 582/1186 seized control of the province from its last Saljuq Amīr. As well as containing a history of the Ghuzz conquest, the third *qism* or section of the book has historical material on the earlier rulers of Kirmān and on the special merits and characteristics of the province. In this section there occurs information on the Ilyāsids not found elsewhere, e.g. on Muḥammad b. Ilyās's building activities in various towns of Kirmān (see below). The *'Iqd al-'ulā* was used by the nineteenth-century historian of Kirmān, Aḥmad 'Alī Khān Vazīrī, in his *Ta'rīkh-i Kirmān*, known as the *Ta'rīkh-i Sālāriyya* (thus named after the author's patron, the Sālār-i Lashkar Mīrzā Farmān-Farmā, governor of Kirmān). In his excellent edition of this text (Publications of the Farmān-Farmāyān Memorial Library No. 1, Tehran 1340/1961), Muḥammad Ibrāhīm Bāstānī-yi Pārīzī adds further citations from the *'Iqd al-'ulā* to his extensive commentary on Aḥmad 'Alī Khān Vazīrī's text.[4]

Numismatic evidence can often fill the lacunae of the literary sources, for coins are uniquely valuable in that they provide a direct, tangible link with the past. Unfortunately, no coins of the Ilyāsids are known to be extant, although this does not preclude the possibility that Ilyāsid coins might yet turn up.[5]

In the second half of the ninth century, Kirmān, together with the neighbouring province of Fārs, was incorporated in the vast if transient military empire built up by the brothers Ya'qūb and 'Amr b. Laith. In the opening years of the tenth century, Kirmān and Fārs passed from the Ṣaffārid Amīr Ṭāhir b. Muḥammad b. 'Amr into the hands of the Ṣaffārids' slave commander Subkarī (? Sebük-eri[6]), who made himself independent there until defeated by Caliphal troops in 298/911 or 299/912. Abbasid rule was thus re-established in southern Persia, with 'Abdallāh b. Ibrāhīm al-Misma'ī as governor.[7] For the brief period between 301/914 and 304/917, when the Ṣaffārids had been temporarily crushed and the Sāmānid suzerains of Sīstān were distracted by dynastic troubles in Transoxania and Khurāsān,[8] the Abbasids were even able to re-assert their authority in Sīstān for a time. The then governor of Fārs, the slave general Badr b. 'Abdallāh al-Ḥammāmī, sent to Sīstān al-Faḍl b. Ḥāmid and the deputy governor of Kirmān, Abū Zaid Khālid b. Muḥammad; the latter in 304/917 rebelled against Badr but was defeated and killed at Dārābjird in Fārs.[9] The governorship of Fārs and Kirmān subsequently passed to 'Abdallāh al-Misma'ī's son Ibrāhīm; during Ibrāhīm's tenure of power, an expedition was sent against the Kufichīs or Qufṣ in Kirmān, and 5,000 of that predatory race were deported to Fārs. When Ibrāhīm died in 315/927, al-Muqtadir appointed as governor of Fārs the slave general Yāqūt, with Abū Ṭāhir Muḥammad b. 'Abd aṣ-Ṣamad as his deputy in Kirmān.[10] In 318/930 the Caliph appointed his son Hārūn as honorary governor of Fārs, Kirmān, Sīstān and Makrān, but in the next year Yāqūt again became executive governor of Fārs, with his son Abū Bakr Muḥammad appointed to Sīstān. However, there is no record that any representative of the Abbasids was ever able actually to establish himself in Sīstān at this time. The province was by now firmly in the control of a member of the Ṣaffārid family, the Amīr Abū Ja'far Aḥmad b. Muḥammad b. Khalaf b. Laith; in 317/929 Abū Ja'far Aḥmad had been able to send an army into Kirmān with impunity, and had collected a million dirhams there.[11]

It is in 317/929 that Abū ʿAlī Muḥammad b. Ilyās is first mentioned. In that year, the Sāmānid Amīr Naṣr b. Aḥmad was faced with the revolt in Bukhārā of his three brothers Yaḥyā, Manṣūr and Ibrāhīm, whom he had until then kept imprisoned there. Discontented and turbulent elements in the capital (according to Gardīzī, *fuḍūliyān* 'trouble-seekers and meddlers', and members of the army; according to Ibn al-Athīr, 'Dailamīs, ʿAlids and *ʿayyārs*', i.e. volunteers and ghāzīs) proclaimed Yaḥyā as Amīr. Muḥammad b. Ilyās was one of Amīr Naṣr's commanders, and apparently of Iranian Soghdian origin (*az maḥall-i Ṣughd-i Samarqand*, according to Aḥmad ʿAlī Khān Vazīrī); the family seems to have retained property and interests in Ṣughd whilst its members ruled in Kirmān. Muḥammad b. Ilyās had incurred the Amīr's displeasure and had been imprisoned, but through the intercession of the famous Vizier Abū'l-Faḍl Muḥammad b. ʿUbaidallāh Balʿamī, had been released and sent on an expedition to Gurgān. He now joined the rebel Yaḥyā's side. As the rebellion lost its momentum and began to collapse, Yaḥyā went to Nīshāpūr, but was barred from that city by its governor, the Dailamī Mākān b. Kākī, at that time in the Sāmānid service. Muḥammad b. Ilyās went over to Mākān's side, and took over the city when Mākān left for Gurgān, but he then admitted his former master Yaḥyā to Nīshāpūr and made the *khuṭba* there for him. Naṣr b. Aḥmad regained control of his kingdom and marched on Nīshāpūr in 320/932. A general scattering of Yaḥyā's former partisans ensued. The general Qaratigin Isfījābī withdrew to Bust and ar-Rukhkhaj in southern Afghanistan; Muḥammad b. Ilyās went to Kirmān and there established his authority.[12]

The uncertainty prevailing in Kirmān and in southern Persia in general gave Muḥammad b. Ilyās a useful opportunity. This was a time when the remnants of Caliphal authority in Persia were crumbling under the upsurge of Dailamī expansionism. In the years after 316/928 Mardāvīj b. Ziyār and Asfār b. Shīrūya extended their power southwards through Jibāl towards Iṣfahān and the borders of Khūzistān. In Khūzistān and Lower Iraq, Abbasid control was only exercised through such powerful and independent-minded figures as Abū ʿAbdallāh Aḥmad al-Barīdī and the *Amīr al-Umarā'* Muḥammad b. Rā'iq. Yāqūt remained governor of Fārs, but was under increasing pressure from Mardāvīj and his associates, the three Būyid brothers. In 322/934 Yāqūt was defeated by ʿAlī b. Būya, the later ʿImād ad-Daula, and his capital Shīrāz fell into Būyid hands; two years later he was killed in battle with Abū ʿAbdallāh Aḥmad al-Barīdī.[13]

In 322/934 the Sāmānid Naṣr b. Aḥmad took steps fully to restore his authority in outlying parts of his dominions, and he unleashed against Muḥammad b. Ilyās the Dailamī Mākān b. Kākī. Muḥammad b. Ilyās went to Iṣṭakhr to seek help from Yāqūt, but failed to get it, and on returning to Kirmān was defeated by Mākān and driven out to Dīnawar in western Persia. Mākān then took over Kirmān on behalf of the Commander-in-Chief of Khurāsān, Muḥammad b. al-Muẓaffar b. Muḥtāj. In the latter part of 323/935 and the earlier part of 324/935–6, Mākān was summoned to join Muḥammad b. al-Muẓaffar b. Muḥtāj for operations in Qūmis and Gurgān against Mardāvīj's brother Vushumgīr; this departure allowed Muḥammad b. Ilyās to return, and after prolonged fighting with the Sāmānid garrisons in Kirmān, his authority was restored there.[14]

But before the eventual triumph of Muḥammad b. Ilyās, a new factor had appeared in Kirmānī affairs in the shape of the dynamic and aggressive Būyids. ʿAlī b. Būya had seized Fārs from Yāqūt (see above), and al-Ḥasan b. Būya, the later Rukn ad-Daula, controlled Iṣfahān and much of Jibāl. The youngest brother Aḥmad, the later Muʿizz ad-Daula, was in 324/936 diverted by ʿAlī towards Kirmān, at that time racked by strife between Muḥammad b. Ilyās and the Sāmānid commander Abū ʿAlī Ibrāhīm b. Sīmjūr ad-Dawātī, who had been left in Kirmān when Mākān had departed. An army of 1,500 of the best Dailamī troops and 5,000 Turks was sent with Muʿizz ad-Daula,[15] with Aḥmad b. Muḥammad ar-Rāzī, called Kūr-Dabīr, as his secretary and lieutenant. The Būyid forces reached Sīrajān in western Kirmān, where Muḥammad b. Ilyās was at that moment being besieged by Ibrāhīm b. Sīmjūr. The latter returned to Khurāsān, and Muḥammad b. Ilyās also fell back to Bam, which being on the edge of the Great Desert was strategically well situated for a swift withdrawal to Qūhistān or Sīstān. Muḥammad b. Ilyās did, in fact, flee to Sīstān without a fight. Muʿizz ad-Daula was already in firm possession of Sīrajān, from whose population he exacted a large financial subvention for his army. He now placed one of his officers in Bam and turned to Jīruft in the southern part of the province. Muʿizz ad-Daula's entry of Jīruft had to be preceded by negotiations with ʿAlī b. az-Zanjī, called ʿAlī K.lūya (? Gulūya), leader of the local Kufīchīs and Balūch. These dwellers in the mountains of southern and eastern Kirmān, the Jabal al-Qufṣ and the Jabal Bāriz of the geographers, had customarily paid some tribute to the ruler of Kirmān but had otherwise enjoyed virtual independence.[16] ʿAlī Gulūya agreed to pay an annual tribute to the Būyids of a million dirhams, and an immediate, non-recurring payment of 100,000 dirhams, and to provide a hostage for good behaviour.

According to Miskawaih, the secretary Kūr-Dabīr advised Muʿizz ad-Daula to make peace and wait for a favourable opportunity to catch ʿAlī unawares and then dispose of him. So Muʿizz ad-Daula tried to surprise and overcome the rival leader, but ʿAlī's spies alerted him, and in the ensuing fighting, the Būyid was severely wounded in the head and trunk, losing also his left hand and several fingers of his other one. ʿImād ad-Daula had to send a new force from Fārs of 2,000 men in order to secure the withdrawal to Sīrajān of the remnants of Muʿizz ad-Daula's army. However, ʿAlī Gulūya recognized the superior might of the Būyids; he tended the wounded Muʿizz ad-Daula in Jīruft and made peace with ʿImād ad-Daula. Muḥammad b. Ilyās, then in Sīstān, heard about Muʿizz ad-Daula's difficulties, and returned to Khannāb (on the road between Bam and Sīrajān), but after several days' fighting, was defeated and forced to flee. With this victory behind him, Muʿizz ad-Daula was able to wreak his vengeance on ʿAlī Gulūya, whom he now defeated in battle. ʿImād ad-Daula apparently decided that Būyid resources could not at that point be diverted for the pacification of Kirmān and its unruly mountaineer and tribal elements; he recalled Muʿizz ad-Daula, who reluctantly returned to Iṣṭakhr, and ʿImād ad-Daula later sent his brother for operations against Khūzistān in 326/937–8.[17]

A much less detailed, but varying and anecdotal, account of Muʿizz ad-Daula's attempt to conquer Kirmān is given by Aḥmad ʿAlī Khān Vazīrī, for which the only authority quoted is the late source of Khwāndamīr's *Ḥabīb as-siyar*. He relates that Ibrāhīm b. Sīmjūr was sent by the Sāmānid Amīr in 320/932 to recover Kirmān, but when Ibrāhīm reached Rāvar, to the north of Bardasīr, he heard of Muʿizz ad-Daula's expedition from Fārs to Kirmān, and returned to Khurāsān. Muḥammad b. Ilyās's son Sulaimān, governor of Sīrajān, abandoned that town to Muʿizz ad-Daula and fled to Bardasīr. Sulaimān and Muḥammad b. Ilyās were both besieged there, but in the end, Muʿizz ad-Daula agreed to make peace, accepting tribute and the mention of the Būyids in the *khuṭba* before Muḥammad's own name. He then returned to Shīrāz.[18] The vagueness of the account, and the impossibly early date of 320/932 (ʿImād ad-Daula did not conquer Fārs till two years after this, see above, p. 110), make it of dubious reliability; the mention of Sulaimān as governor of Sīrajān suggests a conflation with the events leading up to ʿAdud ad-Daula's conquest. The only other possibility is that we have here the recollection of a Būyid expedition against Kirmān later in Muḥammad b. Ilyās's reign, unnoted by Miskawaih, and which led the Ilyāsids temporarily to acknowledge Būyid suzerainty (as is pointed out just below, ʿUtbī and Maqdisī say that Muḥammad b. Ilyās normally acknowledged the Sāmānids). Can this have any connection with the coin of ʿAḍud ad-Daula apparently minted at Bardasīr in 348/959–60, mentioned above, n. 5? Muʿizz ad-Daula did not die till 356/967, but after 334/945 he was established in Baghdad as *Amīr al-Umarāʾ* and can have had no connection with affairs in Kirmān. ʿAḍud ad-Daula, on the other hand, was ruler of Fārs from 338/949 onwards. Could Muʿizz ad-Daula's name, already connected with Kirmān through the events which took place at the outset of Muḥammad b. Ilyās's reign there, have been confused with that of ʿAḍud ad-Daula, when it was a question of events which took place much later?

Finally, we may note in connection with Muʿizz ad-Daula's attempt to conquer Kirmān that the *ʿIqd al-ʿulā* speaks of his clashes with the Kufīchīs,[19] but the only fresh detail is that his battle with ʿAlī Gulūya is said to have taken place at the head of the defile of Dar-i Fārid or Dilfārid[20] in the district of Sardūya (i.e. to the south-west of the Kūh-i Hazār, the highest point of the mountains of Kirmān).

For the next thirty years or so, the chroniclers record virtually nothing of affairs in Kirmān. It seems that Muḥammad b. Ilyās returned after the Būyid withdrawal and made firm his rule there for the greater part of this period. He acknowledged the Sāmānids in the *khuṭba*, but was regarded as *de facto* independent, and in 348/959–60 the Caliph al-Muṭīʿ sent him a banner and robe of honour, two of the insignia of independent political sovereignty.[21] Afḍal ad-Dīn Kirmānī calls Muḥammad b. Ilyās an *ʿayyār* and brigand, and says that he derived a steady income from despoiling caravans travelling from Fārs to Kirmān.[22] Information in the accounts of ʿAḍud ad-Daula's final conquest of Kirmān certainly implies that he was in the habit of receiving a proportion of the profits from the Kufīchīs' predatory activities (see below), and it is very likely that a *modus vivendi* with these tribespeople was a prerequisite for the stability of Muḥammad b. Ilyās's rule in Kirmān.

On the credit side, the Arab geographers and Afḍal ad-Dīn Kirmānī mention considerable activity by Muḥammad b. Ilyās in the way of buildings and charitable works. In Bardasīr or Guvāshīr, the town where he kept his treasury and accumulated riches,[23] he built a mosque; he rebuilt the old citadel and laid out gardens there, with a deep well; and he built two new strong-points and a protective trench. There was one stronghold in the town on the summit of a hill, up to which Muḥammad b. Ilyās used to ride each night and sleep there in the coolness. Someone is supposed to have inscribed on the doorway of one of his two new fortresses, the 'castle on the hill' (*qal'a-yi kūh*) the lines

> 'Ibn Ilyās built you, and then someone else came along and occupied you. But that is the way of Time: it sweeps onward and then it brings things back.
>
> You were built by a man who, if we had said to him "You have been given eternal life", would have objected and claimed that he had been granted a further eternity after the first eternity.'

Afḍal ad-Dīn Kirmānī says that he searched for the inscription, but could find no trace of it. At Zarand, two stages to the north-west of Bardasīr, Muḥammad b. Ilyās also built a castle. At the small town of Ghubairā, to the south of Bardasīr, he built a market just outside the walls. Again, between the small settlements of Avārik and Mihrgird, to the north-west of Bam, he built a castle. At Khabīṣ, too, on the edge of the Great Desert, he was active, and had his own name inscribed on the gates of the town; Afḍal ad-Dīn Kirmānī mentions this inscription as still existing in his own time two centuries later. Muḥammad b. Ilyās's son Ilyasa' is described as the builder of the government headquarters, the *Dār al-Imāra*, in Bardasīr.[24] Muḥammad b. Ilyās also achieved some favourable mention in the 'Mirrors for Princes' literature; thus Niẓām al-Mulk speaks of his nobility and merit.[25]

The events leading up to the end of Ilyāsid rule in Kirmān are given by the chroniclers under 356/967 and 357/968, the latter year being that of 'Aḍud ad-Daula's conquest of Kirmān. The preliminary events to this must, however, clearly be placed at least two or three years before these dates. There had already been some ill-feeling between Muḥammad b. Ilyās and his son Ilyasa', and Ilyasa' had taken refuge with 'Aḍud ad-Daula, ruler of Fārs since his uncle 'Imād ad-Daula's death in 338/949, until the breach had been healed.[26] According to Miskawaih, Muḥammad b. Ilyās had over the years amassed a great quantity of wealth in his various castles scattered over Kirmān, above all at Bardasīr, this wealth being the fruits of his predatory activities; he had 'behaved just like a brigand' (*jarā majrā ba'ḍ al-mutaṣa'-likīn*), and had allied with the Kufīchī and Balūch bandits, dividing with them the proceeds of their depredations. Muḥammad b. Ilyās was on his way to the districts of the Kufīchīs to pocket his share of the wealth from a plundered caravan, when he was afflicted by a paralytic stroke. He was therefore compelled to make arrangements for the succession to the amīrate. Of his three sons, Ilyasaʿ was made commander of the army and *walī al-ʿahd* or heir, with Ilyās next in line. The third son, Sulaimān, was on bad terms with Ilyasaʿ. Muḥammad b. Ilyās therefore decided that Sulaimān should go to their native province of Ṣughd, and he gave him a document listing his buried treasures and deposits there. Yet Sulaimān refused to have his rights within Kirmān set aside. He set off ostensibly for Ṣughd, but then turned aside to the Kufīchīs and claimed from them the plunder which his father had been in the course of collecting when the stroke had afflicted him. Having secured this, he raised a force from the Kufīchīs and marched on Sīrajān, the town where he had previously been governor. Muḥammad b. Ilyās sent against him his army, under the command of Ilyasaʿ, with instructions either to let Sulaimān depart for Ṣughd or, failing that, to bring him back a captive. After stiff fighting, Sulaimān fled to Khurāsān, and Ilyasaʿ seized Sīrajān, plundering the town extensively until the chief Qāḍī and notables asked for pardon.[27]

Ilyasaʿ should now have been in a strong position in Kirmān, but his relations with his father were poisoned by a conspiracy of a trio of enemies at court, comprising ʿAbdallāh b. Mahdī, called Busūya; the [? Jewish] physician Isrāʾīl; and an architect called al-Marzubān. Muḥammad b. Ilyās's old suspicions of his son were re-aroused. He dismissed Ilyasaʿ from command of the army and gave the office to one of his personal ghulāms, Turmush Ḥājib; and by means of a ruse, he lured Ilyasaʿ unaccompanied into one of his fortresses, where Ilyasaʿ was seized and fettered. The mothers of Ilyasaʿ and Ilyās agreed that Muḥammad b. Ilyās's judgement was impaired by his illness and by the maleficent influence of his three evil counsellors. During one of the periods of unconsciousness which periodically came over Muḥammad b. Ilyās, they released Ilyasaʿ, who was welcomed back by the army, by now weary of Muḥammad b. Ilyās's capriciousness and despotic behaviour. Muḥammad b. Ilyās had to accept this reversal of affairs, and agree to abdicate in Ilyasaʿ's favour and depart for Khurāsān. Ilyasaʿ allowed him to take with him all his wealth and possessions, which included 100 loads of treasure, jewels and clothing, and to be accompanied by 300 of his ghulāms. The castle passed to Ilyasaʿ; the three conspirators were captured and handed over to Ilyasaʿ's secretary and Vizier, Abū Naṣr Muḥammad al-Bammī. Their wealth was extracted from them by torture and then they were put to death.[28]

Muḥammad b. Ilyās travelled through Khabīṣ and Qāʾin and eventually reached the court of Manṣūr b. Nūḥ at Bukhārā, where his son Sulaimān also was. He recovered somewhat from his affliction and became one of the Sāmānid Amīr's boon-companions. He is said to have been active in urging Manṣūr to launch an offensive against the Ziyārids and Būyids in northern Persia. His death is then placed by ʿUtbī and Ibn al-Athīr in Shawwāl 356/September-October 967, and by Miskawaih soon after Ramaḍān 357/August 968.[29]

The young and inexperienced Ilyasaʿ was not long able to hold out against the overwhelming might of the ambitious and aggressive ʿAḍud ad-Daula, fresh from his conquest of ʿUmān in 356/967. According to ʿUtbī, Ilyasaʿ was foolish enough to dispute with the Būyid over some territory on the border of Fārs and Kirmān; ʿUtbī here quotes a saying, 'The wild ass sought a pair of horns, but lost its ears in the process', referring to the dangerous situation in which Ilyasaʿ had now placed himself. Ilyasaʿ also gave refuge to certain of ʿAḍud ad-Daula's followers who had deserted their master, but he then maltreated them, believing their coming to have been a Būyid ruse. For his part, ʿAḍud ad-Daula assiduously bought over members of Ilyasaʿ's army and retinue, so that a thousand of his Dailamī troops and many of his Turkish ones deserted to Fārs. He then invaded Kirmān, occupying the capital Bardasīr and seizing the several strong points within that town (Ramaḍān 357/August 968). Ilyasaʿ, abandoned by much of his army, could only flee without a fight to the Sāmānid territories, his arrival coinciding (according to the chronology of Miskawaih) with his father's death in Bukhārā. ʿAḍud ad-Daula made firm his power in Kirmān, which was now exhausted from all the troubles and warfare of the preceding years; according to Ibn Ḥauqal (wrote *c.* 366/976), the revenues of Kirmān had become reduced and scattered because of these calamities.[30] ʿAḍud ad-Daula also received a deputation from the Ṣaffārid Amīr of Sīstān, Walī ad-Daula Khalaf b. Aḥmad, who agreed to make the *khuṭba* in his territories for the Būyids instead of for the Sāmānids, as had hitherto been the practice in Sīstān; and he received from the Caliph al-Muṭīʿ the formal investitute of Kirmān. He appointed his son Abū'l-Fawāris Shīrzīl (the later Sharaf ad-Daula) nominal governor of Kirmān, with executive power in the hands of his general Kūrkīr[31] b. Jastān, and returned to his capital Shīrāz. According to Aḥmad ʿAlī Khān Vazīrī (with the ultimate source unspecified), the Shīʿī Abū'l-Fawāris Shīrzīl made the *khaṭībs* of Kirmān introduce the cursing from their pulpits of the Umayyad Caliph Muʿāwiya. Ilyasaʿ was well received in Bukhārā, but he later began to criticize the Sāmānids for not helping him regain his principality. He was therefore expelled to

Khwārazm, and at the same time Abū'l-Ḥasan Muḥammad b. Ibrāhīm b. Sīmjūr seized the possessions and the ghulāms which Ilyasaʿ had left at Khūst in Qūhistān before going on to the Sāmānid capital. In Khwārazm, Ilyasaʿ was stricken with ophthalmia and died there; according to Ibn al-Athīr, this was divine retribution for his rebellion against his father.[32]

This really marks the end of Ilyāsid rule in Kirmān, although other members of the family continued to watch from beyond the borders of the province, hoping for a convenient opportunity to return. In 359/969–70 Sulaimān b. Muḥammad b. Ilyās persuaded the Sāmānid Manṣūr b. Nūḥ to give him an army so that he could raise the Kufīchīs and Balūch and other elements in Kirmān unreconciled to Būyid rule. A large force was assembled, but in a battle between Jīruft and Bam against ʿAḍud ad-Daula's viceroy Kūrkīr, the invaders were defeated. Sulaimān, two of his brother Ilyasaʿ's sons, Bakr and al-Ḥusain, and a large number of the Khurāsānian troops, were killed.[32a] The resistance of the Kufīchīs and Balūch continued, however, into the next year; this persistent opposition was the cause in the next years of a determined Būyid onslaught on their territories and into the later Persian Makrān and Baluchistan, where Būyid authority had never been recognized and where Islam itself was not universally prevalent. The Būyid generals Kūrkīr and ʿĀbid b. ʿAlī marched to Jīruft, and then defeated a large concentration of the Kufīchīs and Balūch and the 'Manūjāniyya', i.e. the inhabitants of Manūjān between Jīruft and Hurmuz on the Persian Gulf coast (Ṣafar 360/December 970)[33]; they then proceeded eastwards into Tīz and Makrān, and imposed the prescriptions of Islam there. Finally, ʿĀbid b. ʿAlī turned against the the Jurūmiyya (i.e. the people of the *garmsīr*, the hot regions of Kirmān bordering the Gulf)[34] and against an associated group, the Jāsakiyya, inhabitants of the island of Kīsh or Kishm;[35] these groups were notorious for banditry and piracy and had also given aid to Sulaimān b. Muḥammad b. Ilyās. From all these campaigns, large numbers of slaves were collected and sent to the markets of Shīrāz.[36]

Despite these draconian measures, the Balūch soon returned to their old activities and were terrorizing the caravan traffic across Kirmān to Khurāsān and Sīstān. Hence in Dhū'l-Qaʿda 360/September 971 ʿAḍud ad-Daula came himself to Sīrajān to direct operations against them. ʿĀbid b. ʿAlī was sent with an army of 'Dailamīs, Jīlīs, Turks, Arabs, Kurds, Zuṭṭ and sword-bearing infantrymen'[37] into the Jabal Bāriz region, where the Balūch believed that the rugged terrain made the access of a hostile army impossible. ʿĀbid nevertheless forced his way through, and in Rabīʿ I 361/January 972 decisively defeated them, slaughtering the fighting men and enslaving the women and children. ʿAḍud ad-Daula then deported the remnants of the Balūch from the Jabal Bāriz and settled there peasants and cultivators.[38] An expedition against the Jurūmiyya, the inhabitants of the territories beyond the Jabal Qufṣ towards the Tīz and Makrān coast, was led by ʿĀbid's brother. Supplies for this expedition were sent both by sea in ships from Sīrāf to Hurmuz and the coastland and by land on dromedaries, and a successful campaign mounted.[39]

It must be these series of operations which are referred to by Ibn Ḥauqal, for this information is not in Iṣṭakhrī and must, accordingly, relate to contemporary events. Ibn Ḥauqal says of the Balūch: 'The ruler has extirpated this running sore and broken their power. He searched out their dwelling-places, destroyed their lands and scattered them; then he took them into his own service and resettled them in various parts of his kingdom.' Some twenty years later, Maqdisī wrote that the Būyid campaigns against the Kufīchīs and Balūch, and the requiring of hostages from them, had had some effect, in that caravans across the Great Desert, which had long been terrorised by Kufīchī and Balūch marauders, were tolerably safe if they had an escort from the Būyid Amīr of Fārs.[40]

The last appearance of a scion of the Ilyāsids was in 364/974–5. Whilst ʿAḍud ad-Daula was occupied with events in Iraq and ʿUmān, and Fārs was largely denuded of troops, one Ṭāhir b. aṣ-Ṣimma led a rebellion in Kirmān of the Jurūmiyya. Ṭāhir was in communication with Yuz-Temür, a Turkish commander of the Sāmānids who had fallen foul of Abū'l-Ḥasan Sīmjūrī in Khurāsān; the two joined forces, although Yuz-Temür was soon able to set aside Ṭāhir as leader of the rebels. News of these events came to the Ilyāsid al-Ḥusain b. (?) Muḥammad b. Ilyās,[41] then in Khurāsān, and he came to Kirmān and placed himself at the head of the Jurūmiyya and other malcontents. But by now, ʿAḍud ad-Daula's Vizier Abū'l-Qāsim al-Muṭahhar b. ʿAbdallāh had completed his operations in ʿUmān and had returned to Fārs. He was instructed by the Amīr to deal with the Kirmān outbreak, and left Shīrāz in Rajab 364/April 975. Yuz-Temür was caught unawares and defeated, and forced to flee to the citadel of Bam. He was besieged there by Abū'l-Qāsim al-Muṭahhar, and eventually persuaded to surrender. The Ilyāsid al-Ḥusain had meanwhile assembled 10,000 men under his command, but he was defeated at Jīruft and captured by the Būyid Vizier. Nothing was subsequently heard of him, and with his presumed death, Ilyāsid attempts to recover Kirmān ended.[42]

Thus after the capture of al-Ḥusain, the Ilyāsids disappear from history. For the next eighty years, Kirmān remained an integral part of the Būyid dominions, at times coveted by the Ghaznavids, but not finally relinquished by the Būyids until the Oghuz nomads under the Seljuq Qāwurd b. Chaghrī Beg Da'ūd overran the province.

ADDENDA

In his *Lubāb al-albāb*, the thirteenth-century literary biographer ʿAufī has a section on the poetry of kings and great men. This includes an entry on al-Amīr Abū 'l-Ḥasan ʿAlī b. Ilyās al-Āghāchī al-Bukhārī, described as a contemporary of Daqīqī and as being the *mamdūḥ* of many eulogists, as well as being an able poet himself. The editor Nafīsī surmised that this ʿAlī b. Ilyās was the brother of Muḥammad b. Ilyās and that the *nisba* of 'al-Āghāchī' implied that he was head of the Sāmānid palace ghulāms (in fact, from the time of Ismāʿīl b. Aḥmad onwards, this office seems usually to have been held by Turks). Nafīsī further surmised that ʿAlī (and therefore Muḥammad b. Ilyās) was a scion of the Sāmānid royal family, Ilyās being a grandson of the Sāmān-Khudā Aḥmad b. Asad; it is certainly true that the name 'Ilyās' was found in the Sāmānid family, and is rare elsewhere.[43]

A source of the later eleventh century, the Qāḍī Ibn az-Zubair's *Kitāb adh-dhakhā'ir wa't-tuḥaf*, has an interesting passage referring to the abdication of Muḥammad b. Ilyās and the assumption of power by his son Abū'l-Muẓaffar Ilyasaʿ. The author seems to have written under the Fāṭimid Caliph al-Mustanṣir (427–87/1036–94), but to have had a background of earlier service under the Būyids of southern Persia, and may thus have had access to Būyid traditions concerning the Ilyāsids whom they had supplanted in Kirmān.[44] In the fifth chapter of the *Kitāb adh-dhakhā'ir wa't-tuḥaf*, that dealing with celebrated treasure hoards, is given an account of the treasures which Muḥammad b. Ilyās had amassed in the citadel of Kirmān. According to this, the deposed Amīr took away with him to Khurāsān a princely escort of 300 ghulāms, 30 personal slaves or perhaps eunuchs and 200 slave girls, and he still had, in addition to this, much property in Soghdia and treasure deposited there. Ilyasaʿ fell heir to a hoard of immense richness; specifically mentioned are chests full of gold and silver objets d'art, a gilded dais and a bejewelled throne. These two last were stripped of their precious metals and jewels and burnt, together with the former Amīr's store of clothing, symbolic no doubt of Ilyasaʿ's renunciation of everything connected with the old régime.[45]

Genealogical Table of the Ilyāsids

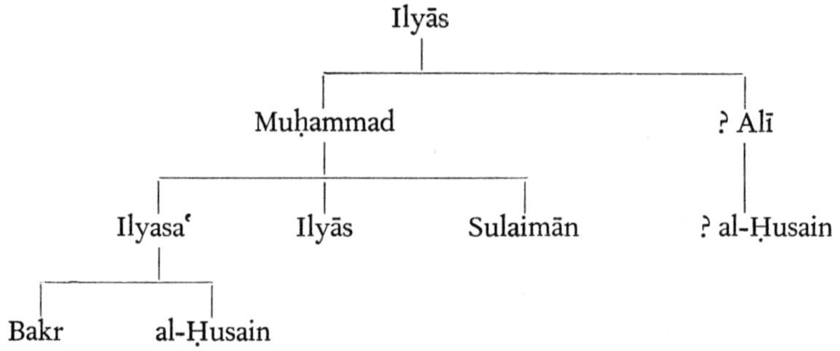

NOTES

1 On the province in general and its rôle in history, see J. H. Kramers, *EI*[1] s.v., and on the geography, ecology and demography of the region round the town of Kirmān, see P. W. English, *City and village in Iran: settlement and economy in the Kirmān basin* (Madison, Wisc. 1966).

2 The only relevant article in the *Encyclopaedia of Islam* is that of Cl. Huart in *EI*[1] s.v. 'Abū ʿAlī Muḥammad b. Ilyās', brief and uninformative.

3 See the remarks of Cl. Cahen, *Mouvements populaires et autonomisme urbain dans l'Asie musulmane du Moyen Âge* (Leiden 1959) 76-7 (originally in *Arabica*, VI [1959] 250-1), who sees in the lively genre of local histories in the Islamic world a sign of the towns' vitality and independent life.

4 The *ʿIqd al-ʿulā*, known in several MSS (see Storey, *Persian literature*, Vol. 1, Part 1, 357, and Part 2, 1297), has been published at least three times in Tehran; the edition cited in this present article is that of ʿAlī Muḥammad ʿĀmirī Nā'inī (Tehran 1311/1932).

5 This absence of coins has been confirmed for me by Miss Helen Mitchell and Dr George C. Miles. Miss Mitchell, has, however, drawn my attention to an interesting Būyid coin in the Ashmolean Museum, Oxford, dated 348/959–60 and minted by ʿAḍud ad-Daula, apparently at Bardasīr. If the mint has been correctly read (the coin has in it a hole which partly obscures the mint name), we have what can only be interpreted as a momentary extension in that year of Būyid authority over

Kirmān, possibly the result of a Būyid raid or invasion unmentioned in the historical and literary sources (see also below, pp. 112-13).

6 On this name, see Bosworth, 'The armies of the Ṣaffārids', *BSOAS*, XXXI (1968) 545-6.

7 *Ta'rīkh-i Sīstān*, ed. Bahār, 295-6; Ibn al-Athīr, *Chronicon*, ed. Tornberg, VIII, 44-6; 'Arīb, *Tabari continuatus*, ed. de Goeje, 34-5, 69; Ibn Khallikān, *Biographical dictionary*, tr. de Slane, IV, 333.

8 Cf. Barthold, *EI*[1] Art. 'Ismā'īl b. Aḥmad'.

9 *Ta'rīkh-i Sīstān*, 302-6; Ibn al-Athīr, VIII, 59-60, 77.

10 Ibid., VIII, 117, 131.

11 Ibid., VIII, 164-5; *Ta'rīkh-i Sīstān*, 313.

12 Gardīzī, *Zain al-akhbār*, ed. Nāẓim, 29-30; Narshakhī, tr. Frye, *The history of Bukhara*, 95-6, 155; Ibn al-Athīr, VIII, 154-7, 207-8; Aḥmad 'Alī Khān Vazīrī, *Ta'rīkh-i Kirmān*, 59-60; Barthold, *Turkestan down to the Mongol invasion*, 242; Spuler, *Iran in früh-islamischer Zeit*, 90.

13 Miskawaih, *Tajārib al-umam*, ed. and tr. Amedroz and Margoliouth, *The eclipse of the 'Abbasid Caliphate*, I, 282-4, 295-303, 339-50, tr. IV, 320-2, 333-43; 380-94; Ibn al-Athīr, VIII, 204-7, 235-40.

14 Ibid., VIII, 207-8, 227-8; cf. Nāzim, *EI*[1] Art. 'Mākān b. Kākī'.

15 For convenience, the three Būyid brothers are henceforth referred to by their honorifics, although these *alqāb* were not actually bestowed by the Caliph until the Būyids entered Baghdad in 334/946 (Miskawaih, II, 85, tr. V, 88-9; Ibn al-Athīr, VIII, 337).

16 On the Kufīchīs and Balūch, whose fighting qualities are attested by more than one reference in Firdausī's *Shāh-nāma*, see Le Strange, *The lands of the eastern Caliphate*, 316-17, 323-4, and *Ḥudūd al-'ālam*, tr. Minorsky, 65, 124, 374-5. Minorsky surmised that the Kufīchīs might possibly be of Brahui stock. It was some decades after this – apparently about the time of the Seljuq invasion of Kirmān in the mid-eleventh century – that the Balūch moved eastwards into their present home of Persian and Pakistani Baluchistan; cf. Frye, *EI*[2] Art. 'Balūčistan. A. Geography and history', and idem, 'Remarks on Baluchi history', *Central Asiatic Journal*, VI (1961) 44 ff.

17 Miskawaih, I, 352-6, tr. IV, 396-401; Ibn al-Athīr, VIII, 242-4; Ibn Khallikān, tr. I, 155-6 (biography of Mu'izz ad-Daula); Mafizullah Kabir, *The Buwayhid dynasty of Baghdad* (Calcutta 1964) 42-3.

18 *Ta'rīkh-i Kirmān*, 61-3.

19 *'Iqd al-'ulā*, 66; *Ta'rīkh-i Kirmān*, 65-6.

20 There are varying spellings of this name, detailed in Iṣṭakhrī, ed. de Goeje[2], 165 note *d*.

21 Maqdisī, ed. de Goeje, 472; Ibn al-Athīr, VIII, 393; 'Utbī-Manīnī, *at-Ta'rīkh al-Yamīnī*, II, 116; Jurbādhqānī, *Tarjuma-yi Ta'rīkh-i Yamīnī*, ed. 'Alī Qavīm (Tehran 1334/1955), 195.

22 *'Iqd al-'ulā*, 67; *Ta'rīkh-i Kirmān*, 60. It is also stated in Ḥamdallāh

Mustaufī, *Ta'rīkh-i guzīda*, ed. ʿAbd al-Ḥusain Navā'ī (Tehran 1339/1960), 380, that Muḥammad b. Ilyās was originally an *ʿayyār*, and that his tyranny eventually led the people of Kirmān to overthrow him.

23 Miskawaih, II, 249, tr. V, 265-6, cf. *Ḥudūd al-ʿālam*, 374. In Maqdisī's time (*c.* 375/985), Bardasīr was the administrative capital of Būyid Kirmān and the place where the army of Kirmān was quartered (Maqdisī, 461); it remained the capital under the Seljuqs, acquiring, by an obvious process of identification, the additional name of '[the city of] Kirmān', which it bears at the present day (cf. *ʿIqd al-ʿulā*, 72-4; Le Strange, *The lands of the eastern Caliphate*, 302 ff.). Bāstānī-yi Pārīzī plausibly surmises that Muḥammad b. Ilyās's transfer of the capital from Sīrajān, the chief city in the early Arab period, to the newer city of Bardasīr, had the aim of removing his wealth as far away as possible from the Būyid territories (*Ta'rīkh-i Kirmān*, 62 n. 2).

24 Maqdisī, 461-2, 466; *ʿIqd al-ʿulā*, 66-7; *Ta'rīkh-i Kirmān*, 60-1; cf. Le Strange, op. cit., 305, 308, 313.

25 *Siyāsat-nāma*, ch. vii, ed. H. Darke (Tehran 1340/1962), 60, tr. idem, *The book of government or rules for kings* (London 1960), 49-50. However, the anecdote on Maḥmūd of Ghazna's punitive expedition against the Kufīchīs and Balūch (ch. x, ed. Darke, 80 ff, tr. 67 ff.) is clearly anachronistic in making the great Sultan and Muḥammad b. Ilyās contemporaries, as is noted by Darke.

26 Miskawaih, II, 250, tr. V, 266; Ibn al-Athīr, VIII, 432; cf. H. Bowen, *EI*[2] Art. 'ʿAḍud al-Dawla', and Kabir, *The Buwayhid dynasty of Baghdad*, 43.

27 Miskawaih, II, 249-50, tr. V, 266-7; *ʿIqd al-ʿulā*, 67-8; Ibn al-Athīr, VIII, 432. ʿUtbī-Manīnī, II, 117, and Jurbādhqānī, 195, place Sulaiman's revolt in Sīrajān *after* Ilyasaʿ's replacement of his father as ruler of Kirmān.

28 Miskawaih, II, 251-3, tr. V, 267-70; ʿUtbī-Manīnī, II, 116-17; Jurbadhqānī, 195; *ʿIqd al-ʿulā*, 67-8; Ibn al-Athīr, VIII, loc. cit. According to ʿUtbī, Turmush or Tuzmush and Bishr b. al-Mahdī (? the brother of ʿAbdallāh) became the young and inexperienced Ilyasaʿ's advisers.

29 Miskawaih, II, 232-3, 253, tr. V, 246, 270; ʿUtbī-Manīnī, II, loc. cit.; Jurbādhqānī, loc. cit.; Ibn al-Athīr, VIII, 429, 433; cf. Huart, 'Les Ziyârides', *Méms. de l'Acad. des Inscrs. et Belles-Lettres*, XLII (1922) 400-1.

30 Ibn Ḥauqal[2], ed. J. H. Kramers 315, tr. Kramers and G. Wiet, *Configuration de la terre* (Paris 1964) II, 309. He adds that some of the local officials in Kirmān had told him that for several years, the Sāmānid Naṣr b. Aḥmad had drawn half a million dīnārs annually from Kirmān (as tribute from the Ilyāsids?).

31 Read by Spuler, *Iran in früh-islamischer Zeit*, 100, as Körgöz, but the combination of this Turkish name with the Iranian one of Jastān makes this unlikely.

32 Miskawaih, II, 253, tr. V, 270; ʿUtbī-Manīnī, II, 117-19; Jurbādhqānī, 195-6; *ʿIqd al-ʿulā*, 68; Ibn al-Athīr, VIII, 433-4; *Taʾrīkh-i Kirmān*, 66-7; Spuler, loc. cit.; Kabir, op. cit., 43-4. Amongst the epistles of ʿAbd al-ʿAzīz b. Yūsuf is one in which ʿAḍud ad-Daula acknowledges Khalaf b. Aḥmad's letter, and in turn sends a delegation to Sīstān with presents (J. C. Bürgel, *Die Hofkorrespondenz ʿAḍud ad-Daulas und ihr Verhältnis zu anderen historischen Quellen der frühen Būyiden* [Wiesbaden 1965], 52 n. 1). [I now find that Muḥammad b. ʿAbd al-Malik al-Hamadhānī, *Takmilat taʾrīkh aṭ-Ṭabarī*, ed. A. Y. Kanʿān (Beirut 1961), I, 200, gives Shawwāl 357/September 968 as the date of the coming of ʿAḍud ad-Daula's general Abū Aḥmad ash-Shīrāzī from Shīrāz.]

32*a* According to Hilāl b. al-Muḥassin as-Ṣābi', citing one ʿAbdallah al-Fasawī, ʿIzz ad-Daula Bakhtiyār's son Nūr ad-Daula Shāhfīrūz was in 390/1000 buried under the same cupola (*qubba*) as Sulaimān b. Muḥammad b. Ilyās was buried (*Taʾrīkh*, in *The eclipse of the ʿAbbasid Caliphate*, III, 360, tr. VI, 387).

33 Cf. Le Strange, *The lands of the eastern Caliphate*, 317. These Manūjāniyya were probably the people of the mountainous region called the Kūhistān-i Abū Ghānim, cf. ibid., 318, and *Ḥudūd al-ʿālam*, 65, 124, 374-5.

34 According to Iṣṭakhrī, 165, Ibn Ḥauqal, II, 311, tr. II, 305, three-quarters of the province of Kirmān was *garmsīr*, only the mountainous region around Sīrajān being *sardsīr*. *Jurūmiyya* is ludicrously misread and misinterpreted by Margoliouth, *Eclipse of the ʿAbbasid Caliphate*, II, 299, tr. V, 321, as *Khurramiyya*, but correctly read in ibid., II, 359, tr. V, 392.

35 Thus according to Le Strange, op. cit., 261; unless, perhaps, the Jāsakiyya are the inhabitants of the hinterland of the modern port of Jask on the Makrān coast of the Gulf of Oman, cf. *Admiralty handbook, Persia* (1945) 507-8.

36 Miskawaih, II, 298, tr. V, 320-1; Ibn al-Athīr, VIII, 448-9, 451-2; *Taʾrīkh-i Kirmān*, 68, citing the *Takmilat al-akhbār* of the Ṣafavid historian ʿAlī Zain al-ʿĀbidīn Shīrāzī (cf. Storey, Vol. 1, Part 2, 1239); Kabir, op. cit., 44-5, who also cites the congratulatory letters received by ʿAḍud ad-Daula on his conquest of Kirmān and given in the *Rasāʾil* of Ibrāhīm b. Hilāl aṣ-Ṣābi'.

37 *Ar-rijāl as-saifiyya*. Margoliouth, V, 322, translates this phrase as 'veterans of Saif al-Daulah', and it could conceivably refer to troops who had passed from Ḥamdānid to Būyid service.

38 Iṣṭakhrī, 104-5, and Ibn Ḥauqal, II, 310, tr. II, 305, explain that the Jabal Bāriz had fertile soil and was well-forested. The region has, however, continued to be a haunt of brigands and robbers down to the present century; cf. P. M. Sykes, 'A fifth journey in Persia', *Geographical Journal*, XXVIII (July-Dec. 1906) 433.

39 Miskawaih, II, 299-301, tr. V, 321-3; Ibn al-Athīr, VIII, loc. cit.; Spuler, *Iran in früh-islamischer Zeit*, 100-1; Kabir, op. cit., 45.

40 Ibn Ḥauqal, II, 310, tr. II, 304; Maqdisī, 489. The Būyid military operations of 360–1/970–2 are referred to in a letter of ʿAbd al-ʿAzīz b. Yūsuf; and in letters of Abū Isḥāq Ibrāhīm aṣ-Ṣābi' there is mention of Būyid activities in Kirmān and the extension of suzerainty over the ruler of Tīz and Makrān. See Cl. Cahen, 'Une correspondance būyide inédite', *Studi orientalistici in onore di Giorgio Levi della Vida* (Rome 1956) I, 88, citing Shakīb Arslān's edition of Abū Isḥāq Ibrāhīm's letters and also two unpublished letters; and Bürgel, *Die Hofkorrespondenz ʿAḍud ad-Daulas*, 84-7, with a detailed account of ʿAḍud ad-Daula's conquest of Kirmān from the Ilyāsids.

41 Thus in Miskawaih, but Zambaur, *Manuel*, 216 (apparently following Sachau, 'Ein Verzeichnis Muhammedanische Dynastien', *APAW*, Phil.-Hist. Kl. [1923], No. 1, pp. 10-11, No. 14), makes al-Ḥusain a nephew of Muḥammad b. Ilyās. Since al-Ḥusain is nowhere else mentioned as one of Muḥammad b. Ilyās's sons, Zambaur is probably correct here.

42 Miskawaih, II, 359-61, tr. V, 392-4; Ibn al-Athīr, VIII, 482-3.

43 *Lubāb al-albāb*, ed. Saʿīd Nafīsī (Tehran 1333/1954), 32-3, 623-4.

44 See on the author and his work, Bosworth, 'An embassy to Maḥmūd of Ghazna recorded in Qāḍī Ibn az-Zubayr's *Kitāb adh-dhakhā'ir wa't-tuḥaf*', *JAOS*, LXXXV (1965) 404.

45 *Kitāb adh-dhakhā'ir wa't-tuḥaf*, ed. Muḥ. Ḥamīdullāh (Kuwait 1959) 187-8.

The Zoroastrian Houses of Yazd

It has been said that 'in Persia old houses are bad houses',[1] and that 'houses that are not very new are always more or less tumble-down'[2]; but this is plainly somewhat exaggerated. The traditional materials of domestic architecture, mud-brick and wood, deteriorate quickly without good maintenance; but if houses built with them are well-cared-for, they can last for centuries.[3] Individual houses are usually difficult to date, however; the more so since it is probable that the standard house of the Persian plateau has changed very little over hundreds of years.

There are of course local variations in the basic design. For Yazd a detailed description of its Muslim houses at the beginning of the present century was provided by the English missionary Napier Malcolm, who spent several years in that city.[4] The essential features of better-class houses were then an enclosed courtyard or courtyards, usually paved, containing each an open tank and flower-beds. On the south side of the courtyard, facing north for coolness, was a big open portico, the *tālār* or *ṣuffe*, used in summer. At the back of this portico was the *bādgīr*, a tall airshaft with long slits in its sides to catch any movement of air and carry it down to the space below. The *tālār* was raised some 3 ft above the courtyard, and in the wall thus created was a grated opening giving light and air to the *zīr-zamīn*, the underground room beneath, which was used in the hottest months. The other rooms opened round the courtyard, each with direct access to it. There might be many rooms; but the open space of the courtyards occupied a greater area than all of them.

This basic plan still prevails; but now the houses of the well-to-do are built, not with the traditional mud-brick (*xešt*), laid in clay (*gel*), but with baked bricks (*ājor*), which in the Yazdī area are pale yellow in colour, laid in white layers of powdered gypsum (*gač*), mined locally. The flat roofs are still generally plastered with *xāgel* (mud and chopped straw), which in humbler houses is also used as a finish for the mud-brick walls.

In the houses of the poor (not described by Malcolm) the wide courtyard contracts to a small space of trodden earth, with a little *tālār* on its south side, a low *bādgir* and no *zir-zamin*. The few rooms also often open on the south side of the tiny yard. None has windows, 'all light and air reaching them through the rickety and warped wooden doors'.[5]

The traditional Zoroastrian houses of Yazd and its villages, which have never been described, are strikingly different in design, though made of the same materials (mud-brick, mud-plaster, and a little wood for doors).[6] Like those of the Muslim poor, they are small and cramped in their proportions, for the Zoroastrians were held down in poverty, and restricted moreover in the scope of their building. There are two standard types of old Zoroastrian house, built until the last decades of the nineteenth century. These are called in their own speech *dō-pesgamī* and *čōr-pesgamī*, that is, houses with two or four *pesgams*, the 'Darī' word for *tālār*.[7] The *čōr-pesgam* plan is common, and is regarded as typical; but there are reasons to think the *dō-pesgamī* one the older.[8] It is impossible, however, to establish this with certainty, as one cannot arrive at exact dates for any house built before the present century.

Through the kindness of Aγa Khodarahm Rashidi of Sharīfābād[9] I was able to examine in detail, in 1964, his *dō-pesgamī* house, which dates back at least to the time of his great-great-grandfather, he himself being now in his late sixties or seventies. The Zoroastrians are usually long-lived, and the family home passes by custom to the youngest son; so that one may assume the house to be at least 150 years old, probably much more. It thus antedates by a number of years the arrival in Iran of the Parsi agent, Manekji Hataria,[10] and so belongs to the dark time of oppression for the Zoroastrians, when they lived both in poverty and precariousness of life. (See fig. 1.)

Perhaps the most salient feature of the Rashidi house is its defensibility. There is only one entrance, by the *bar-i kīča* or lane-door, opening to the north-east on one of the narrow village-lanes. The doorway is wide enough to admit a donkey with laden panniers. The door itself, a heavy wooden one, consists of a single leaf or *lange* (the Zoroastrians were forbidden doors with two *lange*, which were lighter and easier to handle).[11] It is of strong irregular planks, the curved and bent pieces of wood being fitted together with considerable skill to form its rectangle.[12] They are reinforced by two thick crossbars nailed across the back, formed from half-sections of young trees. (See Plate 4.) The walls in which the door is set are of solid *xešt*, some 2½ ft thick. One passes through it into a dark passage-way, the *kīča-yi kδa* or 'house-lane',[13] which is barrel-vaulted and unlit. The first

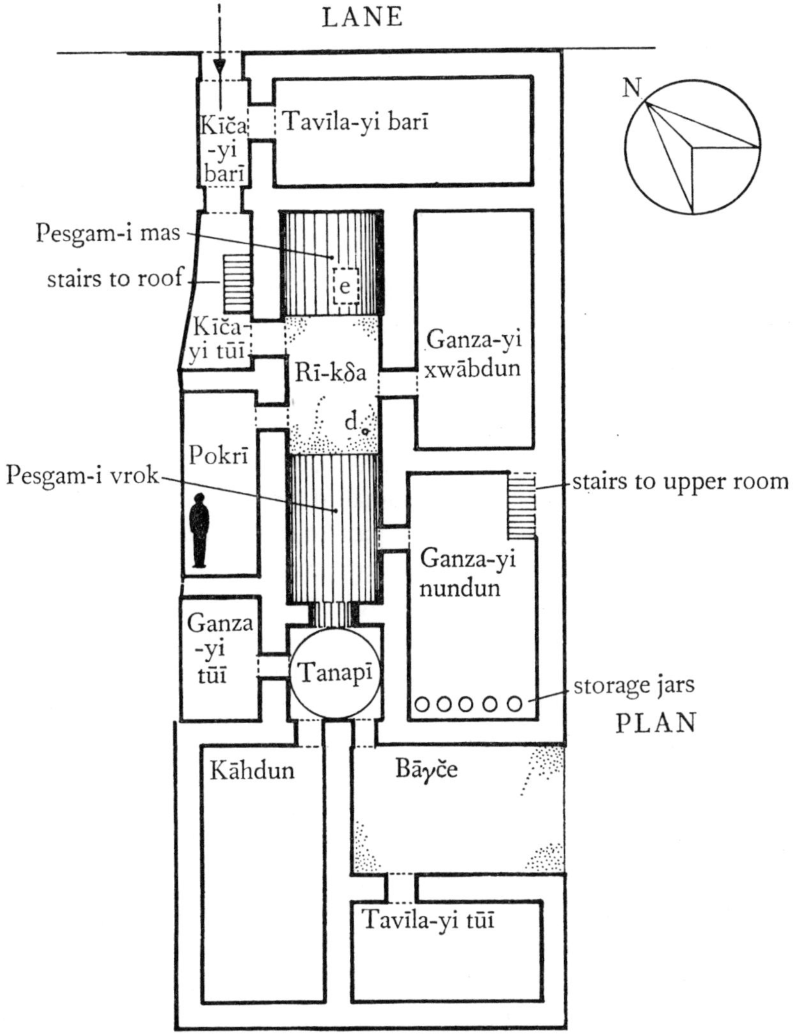

Figure 1. *Dō-pesgamī* house of Khodarahm Rashidi, Sharīfābād. Key: a. corn-store; b. hiding-place; c. door to *šīw-ẓwīn*; d. drainage hole; e. weaving-well; f. *šīrōk*; g. *ganẓa-yi pūnidun*; h. privy; i. wood-store; j. *taxt*. [Note: This key is designed for all three figures, and not all the letters given appear on each.]

part of this passage, the *kīča-yi barī* 'lane of the door' is 18 ft long by 4 ft 4 in. wide. On the left as one goes in is another wide door, leading into a big stable and wood-store, the *tavīla-yi barī*[14] or *ganza-hizvun*, just over 21 ft long by 10 ft 10 in. wide. This again is barrel-vaulted, and lit only by a small hole in the roof.

Formerly there was another heavy door, the *miyun bar*, across the passage-way beyond the stable. After this the *kīča-yi tūī*, 'inner corridor' narrows to 3 ft 10 in. On the left-hand side again there is a flight of mud-brick stairs, the *račūne-yi būm*,[15] leading up to the roof, with a small wooden door at the head, fastened on the inside. Beyond these stairs, at right angles to the corridor, is the third heavy door, the *bar-i piš*, which opens into a tiny courtyard, the *rī-kδa* or 'open space of the house', 11 ft 10 in. long by 7 ft 3 in. wide. The surface of this is trodden earth, and to one side is a tiny drainage hole, edged with stones.[16]

On one's left hand as one enters the *rī-kδa* is the *pesgam-i mas*, the 'great *pesgam*' facing south-west. This is so-called, not from any question of size or stateliness, but because it is that part of the house which is used for religious observances.[17] Certain rules govern its construction. Firstly, it is never built to face north, the direction of hell. In this respect it is unlike the Muslim *tālārs*, which always face in this direction. Then it is never directly opposite the doorway, so that, even if a *juddīn* were admitted as far as the threshold of the *bar-i piš*, his eyes would not fall upon it. The *pesgam-i mas* is kept pure (*pāk*), though it may be freely used in the ordinary course of daily life, for the Zoroastrians hold most normal things to be 'clean'. But no one in a state of ritual uncleanness (such as a woman in menses) may set foot upon it. Annually a fresh layer of clean earth is spread on its floor for the great *Farvardagān* festival, to welcome back the spirits of the dead. Thus in an old house the floor of the *pesgam-i mas* is always higher than that of the other *pesgams*. In the Rashidi house the difference is a good 6 inches. In some houses there is a low step up from the *rī-kδa* to the *pesgam*, but here there is no clear-cut sill – the earth floor of the *pesgam* simply slopes up from the courtyard. The *pesgam* itself is very small, 8 ft 4 in. long by 7 ft 8 in. wide, and barrel-vaulted. The height of the open arch is 13 ft at its apex. On one side of the *pesgam* is the *čala-yi kārbāfī*, the 'weaving well'.[18] This is a rectangular pit sunk in the floor, with an earthen bench on one side, just big enough to allow a woman to sit there and work a treadle-loom. The warp-threads of the loom are carried across the little courtyard and fastened to a wooden hook set in a wall of the opposite *pesgam*, just above head-height (see Plate 3). This is standard practice in all old Zoroastrian houses; and the steady clack of the loom is a characteristic sound to be heard in them.

There is no door opening out of the *pesgam-i mas* in the Rashidi house; but on the further side of the courtyard, opposite the *bar-i piš*, there is a narrow door opening into the *ganza-yi xwābdun*, the 'sleeping-room', which runs along part of the side of the courtyard, and along the *pesgam-i mas*. Here clothes and bedding are kept, and the family sleeps during the winter months. (In summer they sleep on the roof, a positive pleasure to many of the villagers, who have a deep enjoyment of the cool starlit nights.) The *ganza-yi xwābdun*, 19 ft long by 9 ft 3 in. wide, is barrel-vaulted, and lit only from the door. The darkness in such a room on a winter's night is total; but warmth is then much more important than light or air, for there is no means of heating any room but the kitchen.[19] Bedding and spare clothing are kept in the *ganza-yi xwābdun*, wrapped in homespun cotton cloths. Cupboards are rare in old houses, and where they exist are very small, perhaps 2 ft by 1 ft, hollowed out of a wall. But all walls, whether of living-room, passage-way or stable, have arched recesses or *tāqčes*, sometimes quite deep, which serve as shelves. The finish of the mud-brick walls is of *xāgel*; and traditionally among the Zoroastrians the first division of the day, the *Hāvan Gāh*, begins when it is light enough to distinguish the tiny bits of chopped straw in the surface of the clay.

On the opposite side of the courtyard there is a small door, 4 ft high and 2 ft 9 in. wide, with a clay sill 8 in. high. (All the inner doorways have high sills, as a barrier to rain-water and a slight discouragement to hens.) This door leads into the *pokrī* (kitchen),[20] whose earthen floor is worn down well below the level of the courtyard. The *pokrī* is 15 ft long, but only 5 ft 8 in. wide. At the south-west end is the big clay oven (*trīn*),[21] and the open hearths, where the household fire is kept ever-burning. This room again is barrel-vaulted, with two small openings in the roof, one in the centre, one over the oven and hearths. At the north-east end there is a small opening (*rōzanī*), with thick mud-brick lattice-work, into the dimly-lit *kīča-yi tūī*. The kitchen is nevertheless dark, with its walls black from wood-smoke.

On the south-west side of the courtyard is the *pesgam-i vrok* (or *v*^{u}*rok*), the 'little *pesgam*'.[22] The adjective again has nothing to do with relative dimensions, but simply distinguishes it from the religiously important *pesgam-i mas*. In the Rashidi house this *pesgam* is in fact the larger of the two, 11 ft 10 in. long by 7 ft 3 in. wide, with the apex of its arch 16 ft from the ground, so that it casts a shadow over the courtyard during much of the hot summer day. (There is the corresponding drawback that in the depth of winter the sun's warming rays never reach the interior of the house; but the Yazdī builds for the long summers rather than for the shorter, though bitterly cold, winter season[23]). The floor of the *pesgam-i vrok* is a little higher than the level of the courtyard, and has a sill of narrow unbaked bricks, set on edge.

On the southerly side of the *pesgam-i vrok* is a door opening into the *ganza-yi nundun*, the 'bread-store', 15 ft long by 9 ft 3 in. wide, which is in fact a general store-room for flour, blocks of salt, sugar-loaves, herbs and other foodstuffs. At the south-west end is a row of fine earthen storage-jars (*xūm*), each some 4 ft high. At the other end is a flight of stairs leading up to a *bālā-xuna*, a fine big room, 42 ft long by 13 ft 6 in. wide, running the entire length of the *ganza-yi nundun* and the *ganza-yi xwābdun*, and over part of the *tavila-yi bari*,[24] and taking in, too, part of the thickness of the lower walls. This long room is faintly lit by a small latticed *rōzanī* at each end, making it a little less dark than the rooms below. It too is barrel-roofed, about 6 ft 6 in. high at the highest point inside the room. This big *bālā-xuna* must be an addition to the original house, for up to the late nineteenth century Zoroastrians were not permitted to build on a second storey.[25] It is now used as a general store-place.

At the back of the *pesgam-i vrok* is an arched opening leading into the *tanapī*.[26] This is a squarish area, 8 ft wide by 7 ft 3 in. long, covered by a fairly high-vaulted dome, which has a small aperture at its apex to admit air. (In winter such apertures, in room and stable, are thatched over with straw or haulm; so that from a distance a village looks then as if a flock of storks had built nests all over it.) On the further side of the *tanapī* are two doors. One opens into a straw- and hay-store, the *kāhdun*, 22 ft by 12 ft; the other into an inner yard, the *bāyče*, 17 ft by 10 ft 8 in., with a second stable, the *tavila-yi tūi* (18 ft by 13 ft) on its further side. The *tanapī* is the coolest place in the house in summer, with its high roof, and some movement of air from *bāyče* and *ri-kδa*. (It was one of the harsh restrictions imposed on Zoroastrians that they were forbidden to build *bādgīrs*. This restriction remained in force until the beginning of the present century.[27]) For further movement of air there is a rough lattice of small squarish holes cut in the *tanapī*-wall above the arch from the *pesgam-i vrok* (see Plate 3).

The *tanapī* is fairly dark as well as cool. On the northerly side is a small inconspicuous doorway with a very high sill (1 ft 10 in.). This leads into a little room, which, having no other opening, is very dark indeed. This, the *ganza-yi tūi*, the 'inner room', only 10 ft 4 in. by 6 ft 3 in., is piled high with a household clutter of spinning-wheels, carding-combs, raw cotton, etc.;

and through this workaday tangle, and the deep gloom, it takes sharp eyes indeed to distinguish a hole in the ceiling over the corner farthest from the door. Through this hole one can clamber up into a tiny, totally dark loft, a *panāhgāh* or place of hiding, where the householder could conceal a few valuables, a jar or two of wine (much sought after by Muslim *lūtis* or roughs), and, at times of real trouble, his wife and daughters.

The privy (*hlā*) is in the outer stable; and major ablutions are performed either in the *bāyče* or in the back stable. The stabling is for donkey, cow and sheep, the two former being bought, the latter bred as a staple of the household economy. The pretty little hens and their strutting cock have the run of the *bāyče* and *rī-kδa*. Despite the narrow dimensions of the house, and the proximity of man and beast, all is kept neat and orderly, as is to be expected in a Zoroastrian household, although the work required to have it so is considerable. At harvest-time especially much sweeping is needed, as the loads of straw (carried in a great cloth on the back of donkey or cow) are taken right through the house to be stored in the *kāhdun* at the rear.

It is plain that this *dō-pesgamī* house, with its thick walls, and the three heavy doors, one after another, across the entry-passage, was not easy to break into. Its vulnerable point was the roof. The stairs to this are protected by the first two doors; but the Zoroastrians were forced to keep their buildings low, and so the flat areas of the roof itself are only about 10 ft from the ground.[28] It was not difficult, therefore, for robbers to get up on the roof and from there to drop down into the courtyard, from which they commanded the house. The Zoroastrian farmers were mighty men,[29] and in a straight fight could doubtless have defended themselves well; but the dice were loaded against them. Even apart from the question of numbers, a Muslim could kill a Zoroastrian without more penalty than a small money-fine, seldom, apparently, exacted; whereas for a Zoroastrian to kill a Muslim was certain death for himself and probably others. The Zoroastrians were thus largely helpless. The family of Mihr, the first Yazdī Zoroastrians to acquire wealth and influence, preserve the memory of the struggles of their founder, Mihraban.[30] He worked prodigiously hard as a weaver; but each time when by toil and thrift he had collected a little money, his house in Yazd was broken into and stripped of its possessions, and he was reduced to poverty again – a pattern which must have prevailed for Zoroastrians over centuries. On one occasion, when Mihraban had warning of a raid, and fled with his family to the village of Taft, he returned to find the house stripped bare, and even the stones of the courtyard removed. Only a little money hidden under the earth floor of one of the rooms had escaped the plunderers. (It was presumably such measures by Zoroastrians to baffle their oppressors which led to the local Muslim conviction that every old Zoroastrian house contains buried treasure.) It was contact with the Parsis in British India which enabled Mihraban's sons at last to break free from oppression and to establish the family fortunes.

If one compares the Rashidi house with those of local Muslim villagers, what is remarkable is the smallness of the open space in relation to the area of rooms, and the fact that this open space is at the centre of the house, instead of being merely flanked by dwelling-quarters. This difference in layout appears to have been forced on the Zoroastrians through the need to protect their lives and property, and also through the desire to shield their religious observances from mockery and desecration. The great drawbacks to such a house are that it is hot in summer through lack of adequate currents of air, and cold in winter through absence of sunshine.

There are many other *dō-pesgamī* houses in Sharīfābād, of much the same basic dimensions. Some have been radically altered to suit later conditions, others have been adapted in minor ways. Thus in the so-called Dastūr's House a small *bādgīr* has been built at the back of the *pesgam-i vrok*. This *dō-pesgamī* house is fortunate in having its own water-supply within its walls. In the inner *bāyče*, behind the *pesgam-i mas*, there is a flight of stone steps leading down to where a *qanāt* stream flows between broad slabs of stone. Here water is drawn for household use and clothes are washed. Halfway down the steps there is a room hollowed out of the ground, once a *panāhgāh*, now a cool store-room for melons and cucumbers. A pair of pied wagtails nests regularly at the bottom of the dark, damp steps, and there are fish in the stream, whose water is cold even in midsummer. In most houses water has to be fetched from the public watering-places by the village *qanāts*, where utensils and clothes are washed, vegetables scrubbed, animals watered, sheep dipped, straw steeped and much talk exchanged. All Sharīfābādī households fetch their drinking-water from the village *āb-ambārs*, most of the *qanāt* water being brackish.

The *čōr-pesgamī* house appears to be a development from the *dō-pesgamī*, designed to provide more living-space without loss of security. That this is in fact the order of evolution cannot be proved; but it seems, architecturally, the logical sequence. It is also perhaps significant that only two *pesgams*, the *mas* and *vrok*, have unvarying, fixed names. The others, held according to this theory to be secondary developments, have a variety of designations. Because, presumably, of its greater convenience the *čōr-pesgamī* plan became the standard one. This type of house has a central cruciform design, with the four *pesgams* forming the arms of a cross.[31] The *čōr-pesgamī* house whose plan is given here[32] (see fig. 2) belongs to Aγa Shahriyar Zohrabi, in the village of Mazra' Kalāntar, some 3 km across the desert from Sharīfābād. This house has been empty for about 30 years, since Shahriyar's father built a new one near by, on a more open plan; but although deserted, the old house stands sturdily. It shares with the neighbouring *čōr-pesgamī* a broad entry-passage or *darvāze*, entered by the usual heavy single-*lange* door from the village street. The house-door proper opens from the *darvāze* directly into the back of one of the *pesgams*. This is called either the *pesgam-i dam-i bar* 'the *pesgam* by the door' or the *pesgam-i rārōg*, 'the passage *pesgam*'. This *pesgam* runs north and south, with the house-door in its south-wall. The north side is open to the *rī-kδa*, which is 10 ft square. On the east side of the *pesgam-i rārōg* (which is itself 12 ft long by 9 ft wide) is a door into a store-room, set in one of the arms of the *pesgam*-cross. Beyond this is another room, a stable and wood-store, entered by a door from the *darvāze*.

On the opposite side of the courtyard is another *pesgam* of the same dimensions, barrel-vaulted like the first, with a door in each of its three walls. Those on the east and west sides lead into rooms set, like the store-room, in the space between two *pesgams*, and covered, like it, by a domed roof. The door at the back of the *pesgam* opens into a long barrel-vaulted room, which runs across the *pesgam* itself and the other two rooms. This big room is lit only by the doorway at the dark end of the *pesgam*, and (formerly) by a small opening in the roof. These three rooms were at one time the living-rooms (*ganza-yi xwābdun*) of three brothers and their families.

On the west side of the courtyard is the *pesgam-i vrok*, at the back of which is the weaving-pit. On its south side is a door into the *pokrī*, with its oven and hearths. One corner of the *pokrī* is enclosed by a low retaining wall to form a place for keeping wood, the *hīδmadun*.[33]

The barrel-vault of the *pesgam-i vrok* is lower than that of the other *pesgams*, which are all about 13 ft from the ground at the apex of the arch. It and the other two *pesgams* already described are floored with *sangrīž* (or *sangrīze*), small rounded cobble-stones, as is the *rī-kδa*.

The fourth *pesgam*, facing west, is the *pesgam-i mas*, which (like all the rooms) has a floor of trodden earth, several inches higher than the level of the courtyard and the other *pesgams*. In the south-west corner of this *pesgam* is a *šīrōk* for holding ritual vessels, i.e. the *āfrīnagān* used in household ceremonies,[34] and the bowls, spoons, etc., consecrated in the names of

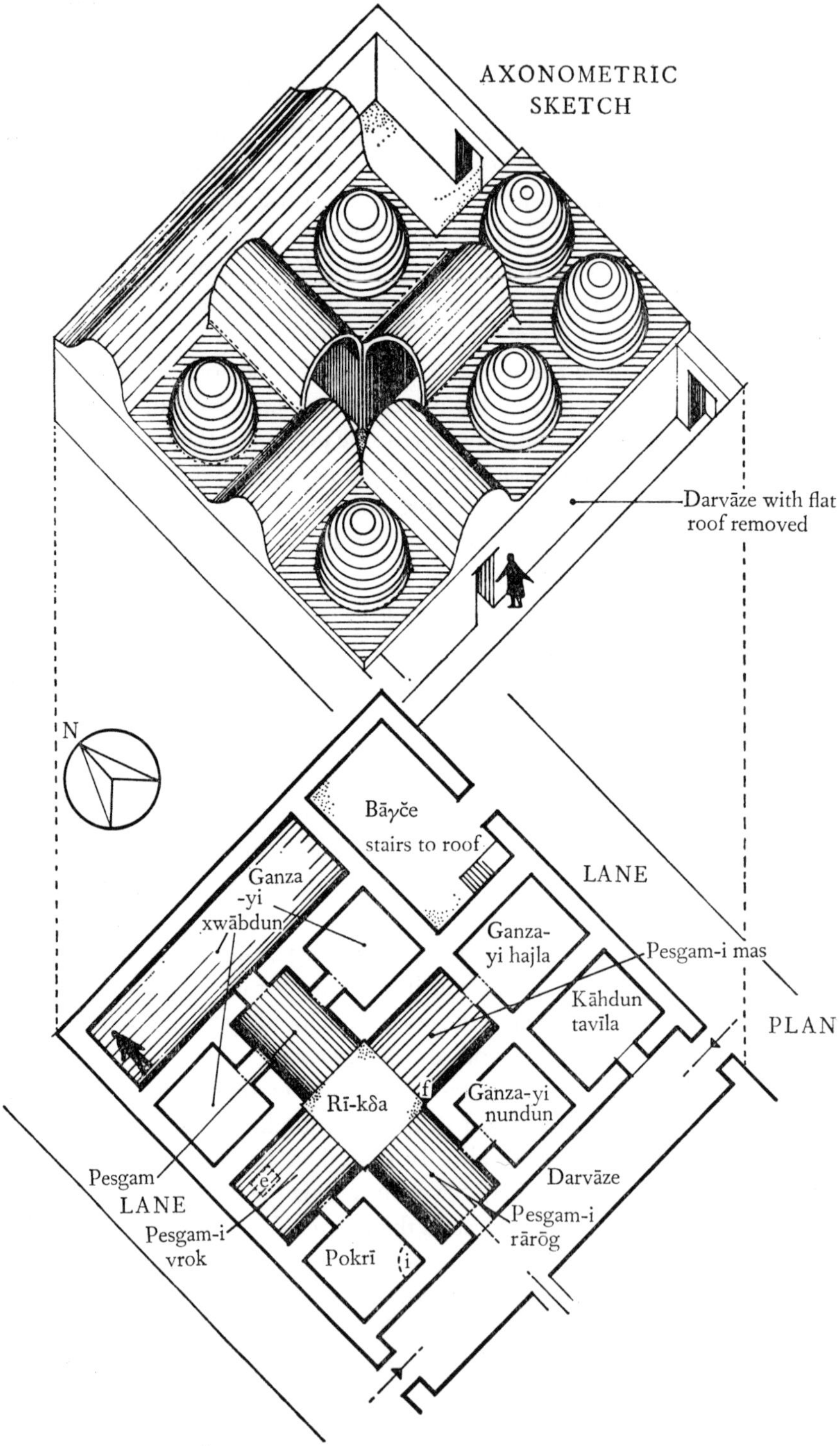

Figure 2. *Čōr-pesgamī* house of the family of Shahriyar Zohrabi, Mazraʿ Kalāntar. Key, see Figure 1.

Plate 1 (above). The arch of the *pesgam-i vrok* of an old *dō-pesgamī* house in Sharīfābād, with modern *bādgīr* and garden in the background.
Plate 2 (below). A young kinsman of the Zohrabi family by the mark of the *Penje* fire on the roof of a *čōr-pesgamī* house in Mazraʿ Kalāntar.

Plate 3 (left). Khodarahm Rashidi in the *pesgam-i vrok* of his house in Sharīfābād. On the left is the door of the *ganza-yi nundun*, and behind him, through the *tanapī*, the door into the *bāyče*. The warp-threads of the loom pass just over his head.
Plate 4 (right). Gushtasp, son of Rustam Belivani, by the *bar-i pīš* of the Dastūr's House, Sharīfābād.

used his own and his inherited money to make impressive extensions to the *čōr-pesgamī* house. The house, thus added to, has been unoccupied since 1928; but like the Zohrabi one, it shows few signs of decay. Through the kindness of Dastur Shahriyar's grandson, Dastur Khodadad Neryosangi of Sharīfābād, I was able to go over it with the family when they celebrated a *gahāmbār* there in 1964 (see fig. 3). The measurements taken then were, however, necessarily rough and incomplete.

The basic plan of the house is a familiar one. One enters by the heavy street-door into a long *kiča-yi kδa*, which leads to the *miyun bar*. This second door opens directly into a *kelyās*, which the Muslim Yazdīs term a *hašte*. This is an eight-sided, domed space, often just inside the front door (like the square space in the Yazdanpanah house). Several of the eight sides have narrow mud-brick benches against them, topped with stone, this being a favourite cool place to sit and talk; but the main purpose of the *kelyās* is to provide a place for loading and unloading donkeys, since most household goods arrived, and still arrive, in this way. On one of the eight sides of the *kelyās* is a door opening on to the *račūne-yi būm*. Yet another door opens into the yard, where are the earth-closet and roomy stables. On one side of the yard is a tiny free-standing mud-brick hut with earthen floor. Its doorway is only 4 ft by 2 ft, and inside it is about 5 ft high, but only 4 ft square. Dastur Khodadad's daughter, Parizad, was puzzled by this hut, and suggested that it must have been a hen-house; but later her mother, Khanom Piruza Belivani, explained that this was the old *ganza-yi pūnidun*,[40] the place where a woman sat apart during the first days of menses. (The rules of purity are still generally observed, but nowadays a corner of passage or room serves for withdrawal.)

The fourth door in the *kelyas* opens into the back of the *pesgam-i rārōg*, which faces south. Opposite is the *pesgam-i pokrī*, with a largish kitchen opening off its east side, with two ovens in a mud-brick bench along one side, and open hearths along the other, with the *hiδmadun* at the further end. On one's right hand as one enters is the *pesgam-i mas*, facing east. The whole of the old part of the house is floored with *sangriz*. The *pesgam-i rārōg* is some 6 in. higher than the level of the *rī-kδa*, the *pesgam-i mas* some 3 in. higher, both being edged with dressed stones; but the *pesgam-i pokrī* is almost flush with the courtyard, so that there could be coming and going from the kitchen without the awkwardness of a step.

On the left, as one enters the *pesgam-i mas*, is a door into the *ganza-yi nundun*, or *ganza-yi vījū*. (The *vījū*[41] is a hanging larder, consisting of a square of wood suspended by ropes at its corners from a bar laid across

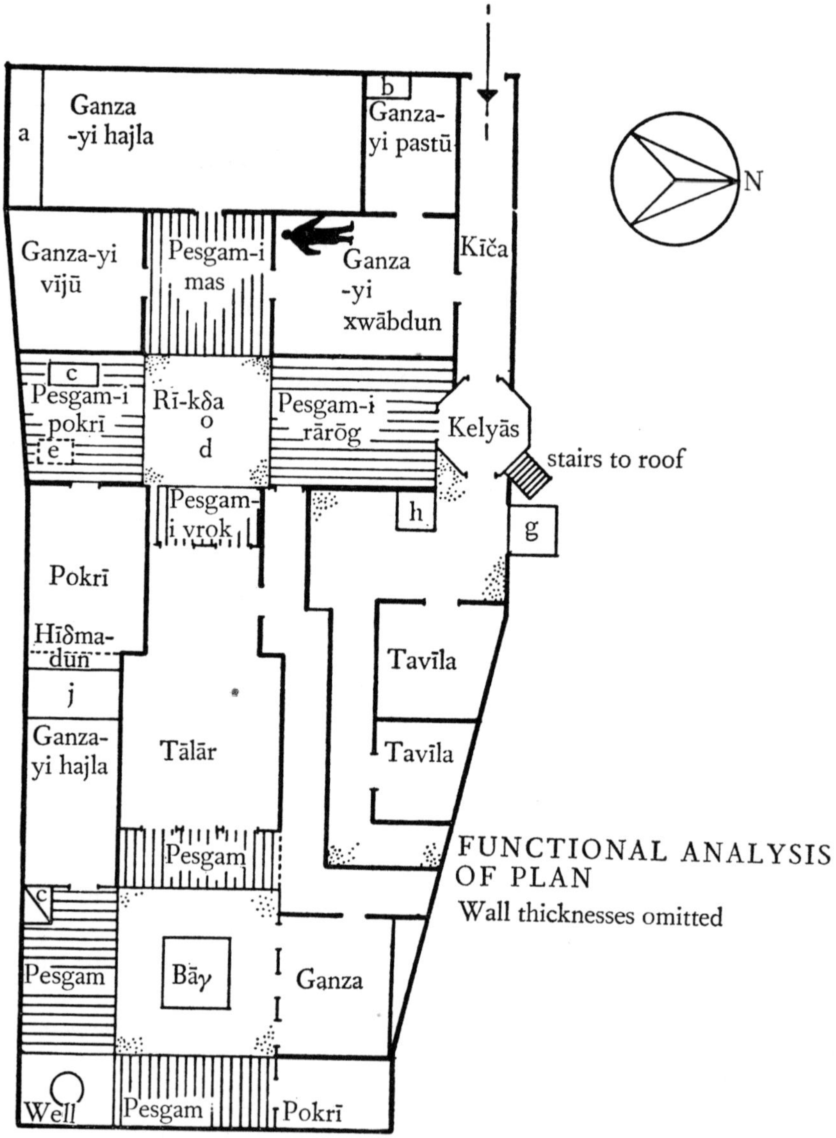

Figure 3. House of Dastūr Shahriyar Namdar, Yazd. Key, see Figure 1.

the hole at the apex of the dome. Food is placed there out of reach of cats, mice, ants, etc.). From the *ganza-yi nundun* steps lead up to the main *bālā-xuna*, called the *bālā-xuna-yi gannomdun*, or corn-store, which runs above the relatively big *hajla* at the back of the *pesgam-i mas*. The *bālā-xuna* is lit by a small window in the west wall of the *pesgam*, above the door into the *hajla*. This window is filled, not with the usual heavy lattice-work of *xešt*, but with an elegant tracery of white plaster, characteristic of old houses of Muslim Yazd. It, like the *bālā-xuna* itself, is evidently a later addition to the *čōr-pesgamī* house.

Under the *bālā-xuna*, at the south end of the *ganza-yi hajla*, is a kind of broad mud-brick bench, hollow, with some half a dozen holes in its side – a corn-store for immediate household use. Near by are several fine old storage-jars.

On the north side of the *pesgam-i mas* is a *ganza-yi xwābdun*. This can also be entered directly by a door from the outer passage, cut evidently when the need for defensiveness was past. By the door from the *pesgam* a heavy glass bottle has been let into the wall, forming a tiny crude glass window. On the north wall is a small door into a narrow slip-room, the *ganza-yi pastū* 'the back room',[42] which is very dark. At the back of it is a tiny *panāhgāh*, little more than a 3 ft wide mud-brick shelf, some 8 ft from the ground, which in the darkness might pass unnoticed when the room was filled with household goods.

There is a *šīw-zwīn* under the three *pesgams* already described, with the *bar-i šīw-zwīn* in the floor of the *pesgam-i pokrī*, and its *lok* in the floor of the *pesgam-i mas*.

Opposite the *pesgam-i mas* is what remains of the *pesgam-i vrok*, which is where the modernized part of the house begins. The floor of this *pesgam* has been raised to form a platform of baked brick,[43] about $3\frac{1}{2}$ ft high, with a metal grating in the front to give light and air to a lofty *šīw-zwīn* running under the new part of the house – a cool twilight place contrasting most agreeably with the blackly-dark, cellar-like old one, where one can only guess at the presence or not of tarantulas, snakes and scorpions. This brick platform runs back under two arches, and is continued as the floor of a long *tālār*, with solid walls on north and south, in whose upper *tāqčes* are elegantly moulded designs in white gypsum. At the further, eastern, end are glass doors opening on to a sunken paved courtyard, reached by steps, in the centre of which is a small square garden where pomegranates grew. (The withered trees are still standing, victims of the Yazdī drought.) On the south and east sides of this courtyard are shallow open pavilions, or *pesgams*, their brick floors on a level with the *tālār*. In the south-east corner is a well, from which water was raised by treadle-wheel; and in the south-west corner is a small second kitchen. (When Yazdī Zoroastrians acquired wealth, a second kitchen was often installed, and kept solely for preparing ritual foods in purity.) The north side of the courtyard is taken up by a pleasant room with three French windows opening on to the courtyard, an agreeably warm and sunny place for the winter months. This room can be reached either across the courtyard or by an enclosed passage-way running along the north side of the *tālār*. In this passage-way is still propped a big man-sized loom for weaving the *kustī* or sacred girdle; for this, now woven by women, was formerly woven by the priests themselves.

The south side of the *tālār* is taken up, partly by the old *pokrī* (which runs the length of the former *pesgam-i vrok*), partly by a new *ganza-yi hajla*. One goes up three steps to this long narrow room, at the further end of which is a raised brick platform (*taxt*), some 3 ft high by 4 ft across, where bride and groom sat to receive their guests. The room is lit by its door, and by a slit window into the southern pavilion of the courtyard. In it there still stands the bridal chest of Dastur Shahriyar's wife, wooden, and raised on wooden blocks, with the front covered with silk, embroidered in a pleasant design of birds and flowers; and in a corner of the *taxt* are still lying some leaves of her manuscript Avesta, beautifully written, though not old. Over the other end of the *taxt* is a small hole in the ceiling, through which one can climb up into a *panāhgāh* above. It is interesting to find that such places of concealment were still thought necessary at the time when the extensions were made (that is, during the last decades of the Qājār dynasty).

The *račūne-yi būm* has a feature evidently introduced at the time of the extensions, for it is not found in old houses. Each mud-brick step (*taxtō*) has a small stone slab let into the middle of it; and on the roof itself there are square stones set like stepping-stones in the *xāgel*, leading to a secluded corner. In some houses in the priestly quarter these stepping-stones branch, one set leading to a little pavilion on the roof, floored with *sangrīž*, the other to a screened corner where ablutions can be performed. These stone steps are all for use by women in menses, as a more tolerable alternative to the tiny hot *ganza-yi pūnīdun*, so that they might withdraw instead to the roof. This is not strictly orthodox, and appears to be a development of urban and suburban Yazd in the late nineteenth or early twentieth century. Similar stepping-stones can be found also in the houses of prosperous *behdīns* of that period.

Outside the city the Zoroastrian population has not been wholly static down the centuries. A number of the villages are very old, and contain predominantly *dō-* and *čōr-pesgamī* houses. Others are comparatively recent settlements, which do not contain a single example of this old type of building. One can thus say with confidence that *čōr-pesgamī* houses were not built after about 1880 (though the 'covered' houses may have been modified after this time). For example, Nusratābād, just to the north of Yazd, was developed by Zoroastrians about that time, and has only open houses with large courtyards, laid out along wide, tree-shaded streets, very different from the narrow dusty lanes of the old villages. But though Nusratābād was developed in comparatively prosperous times, still the Zoroastrians there suffered from their nearness to Yazd, and raids by the city *lūtis*. Some of them therefore moved on to the most recent of the Zoroastrian villages, Hasanābād-i Turkābād, in the neighbourhood of kindly Maybod. This Hasanābād was developed about sixty years ago from a tiny Muslim hamlet, through improvement to its water-supplies by enterprising Zoroastrian landlords. It forms a single *hūšt* or parish with Sharīfābād and Mazra' Kalāntar, and forms a complete contrast with these two ancient villages. Hasanābād would be a pleasant place in any setting, and in the arid Yazdī plain it seems a demi-Paradise. The soil is fertile, the water sweet, and the trees planted by the first settlers have matured, so that the place is full of greenness and fragrance and the sound of running streams. The village has impressive walls and watch-towers, put up to protect it from brigands coming up from Fars through the notorious Aγda gap; but this was a 'foreign' hostile element, threatening Muslim and Zoroastrian alike. Within the walls the houses are all more or less the same, with big garden-courtyards, full of pomegranate and myrtle, honeysuckle and rose. There is usually only the one *pesgam*, brick-floored, and raised above the level of the courtyard; but off this is the *ganza-yi pāk*, floored with stone, and with white-washed walls, where ceremonies are performed. Behind the courtyard there is often a stream flowing between the house and an orchard, with sometimes a grape-arbour, and fine mulberry- and apricot-trees, and more thickets of roses. Hasanābād serves to remind one that Persia, with its love of gardens and flowers, was Zoroastrian before it was Muslim; and that it was poverty and oppression that forced the Yazdī Zoroastrians into their small bare fortress-homes, without a blade of greenness to relieve the monotony. As soon as pressure on them slackened, they created houses with gardens again.

NOTES

1 *Persia, Geographical Handbook, Naval Intelligence Division* (London 1945) 349.

2 Napier Malcolm, *Five Years in a Persian Town* (London 1905) 27.

3 The old English cob house, built of clay mixed with straw and grit, is very similar. It too will stand for centuries, but only if well looked after.

4 Op. cit., 13-30.

5 Ella C. Sykes, *Persia and its people* (London 1910) 217 (on the Persian village-house in general).

6 The information given here concerning these houses was gathered during a 9-months' stay in the Yazdī area, 1963–64. Professor Minorsky, with his great interest in all things Persian, questioned me eagerly on my return to England, and urged publication of the materials which I had collected. It is with gratitude as well as deep respect that the present short article is dedicated to his memory.

7 See Jamshid Sorushian, *Farhang i behdīnān* (Tehran 1956) 32, who gives *peskem* (as the pronunciation of Yazd and Kermān). The 'Darī' words given in the present article are all in the pronunciation of Sharīfābād, some 60 km to the north of Yazd; whereas those given by Sorushian belong to the speech of Kermān and Yazd, as do those listed by W. Ivanow in 'The Gabri Dialect spoken by the Zoroastrians of Persia IV', *RSO*, XVIII (1939) 1-58. Pronunciation and even occasionally vocabulary differ slightly locally, as Ivanow notes in *RSO*, XVI, 55; and the Zoroastrians themselves claim to be able to tell each man's village by his speech.

The *dō-* and *čōr-pesgamī* houses appear to have been unknown in Kermān; at least no tradition of such houses survives there. The old *Mahalle-yi Gabrān* of the city of Kermān was totally destroyed in the eighteenth century.

9 I am much indebted to Aγa Khodarahm, his wife and daughter for their kindness and tolerance in giving me the freedom of their house, in the summer of 1964, to measure all its rooms; and also to my young friend Piruza, daughter of my Sharīfābādī host, Aγa Rustam Belivani, who patiently took the other end of a tape-measure. The resulting sketches and measurements were necessarily rough; and my thanks are further due to Mr Martin Weaver, A.A.Dipl., Visiting Ford Foundation Lecturer in the Conservation of Historic Monuments, Orta Doğu Teknik Universitesi, Ankara, for generously using his professional skill to prepare from them, and from other even less exact data, the accompanying plans of three typical Zoroastrian houses. These plans are only approximately to scale, the scale being given by a human figure drawn in each house, to be taken as exactly 6 ft tall, with the other measurements in proportion.

10 See Boyce, 'Manekji Limji Hataria in Iran' in the *K.R. Cama Oriental Institute Golden Jubilee Volume* (Bombay 1969), 19-31.

11 See Malcolm, op. cit., 46.

12 The Yazdī carpenter works with wood from orchard- rather than from timber-trees.

13 Ivanow, 44 and Sorushian, 68 agree on *xda* as the Yazdī form of the word for 'house' (with variants apud Ivanow).

14 The only other term I heard for stable was *ganza-haivān*. The word for 'room' is given by Ivanow, 13, as *genza*. Sorushian, 140, gives *genza* as the Yazdī form, *ganza* as the Kermānī one. The *iḍāfat* is quite often omitted between two words where there is vowel-consonant, or consonant-vowel.

15 Sorushian, 86, gives *raačūna* as the Yazdī form, *raačīna* as the Kermānī, both in the meaning of *pallagān* or 'stairs'. Ivanow, 30, gives only *račina* in the sense of *palle* 'step (in staircase)'. But 'step', in Sharīfābādī Darī, is *taxtō*. *Račūne* (or *raačūne*) is there the general word for 'stairs'. In Yazd itself there is a very old fire-temple with a flight of steps in it, which is called the *Bar-i mihr-i račūne'ī*.

16 These little drainage-holes are quite inadequate when there is heavy rain. I was in the neighbouring village of Mazraʿ Kalāntar in January 1964, when it rained hard for 6 hours. In the old houses the little courtyards were swiftly flooded, and stepping-stones were put down by which one could pick one's way through the mud and water from one *pesgam* to another.

17 The equivalent in a Parsi home is the *muktad-nō ordō*, the room set apart for the *Farvardagān* festival.

18 Cloth being woven is referred to simply as *kār*.

19 Even the Muslims of Yazd use the *kursī* less than their co-religionists in other Persian cities (see Malcolm, op. cit., 22). The Zoroastrians never use this means of heating.

20 Ivanow 27 (*pukrī*), Sorushian 33 (*pokrī*, as the Yazdī word).

21 Sorushian, 44 (as the Yazdī word).

22 *Vrok* is given neither by Ivanow nor by Sorushian; but is standard Sharīfābādī, in antithesis to *mas*.

23 A fact ruefully commented on by Malcolm, op. cit., 29-30.

24 The barrel-vaulted *tavīla-yi barī* has a flat external roof. Barrel-vaults are often built up in this way to provide a flat place for drying clothes, sitting, sleeping, etc.

25 Malcolm, op. cit., 49, records that in about 1883 a Zoroastrian was killed by Muslims because an upper room was built on a Zoroastrian house in the village of Kūče Biyūk.

26 See Sorushian, 48, who gives the Kermānī pronunciation as *tinabī*, the Yazdī as *tanabī*, with the meaning of 'a large room'.

27 Malcolm, op. cit., 46, mentions that 'in 1900 one of the bigger Parsi

merchants gave a large present to the Governor and to the chief *mujtahid* . . . to be allowed to build one'. This merchant was Arbab Khusrau i Shah-Jehan. His daughter, Khanom Simindukht, still recalls the terror she experienced as a small child at the howls of the mob in the street outside, clamouring for the *bādgīr's* destruction; but the present had been large enough, and it was allowed to stand.

28 The prescribed height is said to have been the reach of a man's hand extended above his head (Malcolm, op. cit., 46); but this seems generally to have been a little exceeded.

29 Aγa Sohrab Lohrasp, formerly headmaster of the Marker School in Yazd, told me that when he travelled from Tehran to Yazd to take up his appointment, just after the First World War, he halted at Sharīf-ābād, and was amazed at the size and bulk of his fellow-Zoroastrians who met him there, feeling that he had come among giants.

30 Information from Aγa Gudarz Mihr, a great-grandson of Mihraban (who still has a tiny diary kept by his redoubtable forebear), and from Aγa Bahman Amanat, son of Mihraban's son Ardashir, who was host to Edward Browne during his stay in Yazd in 1888. Mihraban's seven sons all became prosperous merchants, and leaders of the Yazdī Zoroastrian community. On the founding of a fire-temple in Yazd by one of them, Rashid, see *BSOAS*, XXXI, i (1968), p. 58.

31 Such a ground-plan is not, of course, peculiar to this region. For example, Mr Weaver has drawn my attention to the somewhat similar ground-plan of certain Turkish houses. In the hotter zones of S.E. Anatolia there exist 'courtyard' houses with three and four *īwāns*, e.g. in the Diyarbakir region. For the Yazdī area the striking fact is that houses of this type were built only by Zoroastrians.

32 The measurements for this house are rougher than for the Rashidi *do-pesgamī*, since they were merely paced out.

33 Ivanow, 16, gives the form *hiʒma* for 'firewood'; Sorushian, 187, has *hīʒma* as the form for Yazd and Kermān.

34 Nowadays most Zoroastrian households have a metal *āfrīnagān*; but *āfrīnagāns* made of clay (such as were presumably general in the times of oppression) are still to be found at the smaller shrines, which are exposed to pillaging.

35 < Arabic *ḥajla*. In Yazd I also heard the term *ganʒa-yi dō-bā-ham*.

36 See further *BSOAS*, XXXI, iii (1968), p. 272.

37 The Zoroastrians sometimes compensated for having to keep their roofs low by digging down below the level of the street, see Malcolm, op. cit., 46.

38 Or *šīw-ʒəwīn*; see Ivanow, 36 (*šiv*), 48 (*ʒwin, ʒewin, wʒin*); Sorushian, 115 (Kermānī *šīw-ʒamīn*, Yazdī *šīv-ʒvīn*).

39 See above, p. 125.

40 Ivanow 27, Sorushian 37 (for *pūnī* 'menstruation', the general 'Darī' term).

41 Sorushian, 178, gives *vījū* as the Yazdī form, the Kermānī word, 114, being *šīrovīz*.

42 Ivanow, 29, Sorushian, 32.

43 Brick is not considered suitable flooring for the *pāk* part of a Zoroastrian house, which must be of earth or stone.

CLAUDE CAHEN

ʿAbdallaṭīf al-Baghdādī et les Khwārizmiens

Joseph de Somogyi a fait connaître jadis[1] les passages empruntés par Dhahabī à ʿAbdallaṭīf al-Baghdādī sur les premiers temps de l'invasion mongole en pays musulman d'Asie Centrale et d'Iran. Ces textes, très remarquables par leur tenue intellectuelle et littéraire, et par la lumière qu'ils jettent sur l'impression produite par la catastrophe sans précédent que constituait cette invasion pour l'Islam,[2] n'ont cependant retenu beaucoup l'attention ni des historiens de ces évènements ni des spécialistes qui depuis quelque temps se sont intéressés de nouveau à la personnalité exceptionnelle de ʿAbdallaṭīf.[3] J'ai suggéré incidemment en 1940[4] qu'ils étaient tirés de l'ouvrage usuellement nommé l'*Autobiographie* de ʿAbdallaṭīf, en raison du caractère des extraits reproduits ou analysés par Ibn abī Uṣaybiʿa[5] au travers desquels seuls on le connaissait jusqu'alors, mais qui devait constituer plutôt des sortes de 'Mémoires pour servir à l'histoire de son temps'. Quoi qu'il en soit, je l'avais signalé aussi, Dhahabī nous en conservait également d'autres passages d'un intérêt équivalent sur les Khwārizmiens, le Calife al-Nāṣir et les Ayyūbides. Je les avais relevés chez Dhahabī dans le manuscrit autographe de son *Taʾrīkh al-Islām* aujourd'hui conservé à Aya Sofya (le manuscrit de ʿAbdallaṭīf utilisé par lui se trouvait apparemment à Damas, puisque c'est là qu'il travaillait et qu'avait auparavant travaillé Ibn abī Uṣaybiʿa: s'y retrouvera-t-il un jour?) Je ne m' en étais cependant plus occupé, parce que l'on pouvait croire que l'édition alors entreprise du *Taʾrīkh al-Islām* mettrait rapidement les textes de ʿAbdallaṭīf à la disposition du public savant; malheureusement elle a été interrompue. Comme je l'ai réalisé il y a déjà un certain temps pour un ouvrage parallèle,[6] je crois donc être utile en publiant prochainement ceux qui concernent al-Nāṣir et les Ayyūbides dans le Bulletin d'Etudes Orientales de l'Institut Français de Damas; et en faisant connaître ici aujourd'hui ceux qui concernent les Khwārizmiens, en hommage à la mémoire de notre grand ami Vl. Minorsky qui s'était tant occupé, sinon d'eux-mêmes, du moins des territoires et des peuples au milieu desquels se déroulent leurs exploits.

Les 'Mémoires' de ʿAbdallaṭīf ne prétendaient certainement pas à être une histoire générale de son temps. Sur les gens et les choses qu'il a connus, il donne des témoignages reçus, des impressions vécues, des réflexions, en un style souvent coloré qui en augmente le prix. Sur les Khwārizmiens, ses connaissances proviennent du vizir d'Alep, mais aussi d'informations recueillies de marchands et du fait, sur lequel les extraits conservés de ses Mémoires ne nous renseignent malheureusement pas, qu'il avait séjourné de longues années à la cour du sultan mangudjaqide d'Erzindjān Bahrāmshāh[7] puis en d'autres lieux d'Asie Mineure orientale, et apparemment s'y trouvait au moment de l'invasion de l'Anatolie par le Khwārizmshāh Djalāl ad-dīn Manguberti[7a] et de la défaite consécutive de celui-ci près d'Erzindjān même. Cette bataille nous a été rapportée par divers historiens, parce que du côté des adversaires de Djalāl ad-dīn elle réunissait une coalition des Seldjuqides de Rūm (avec leurs vassaux et mercenaires étrangers) et des Ayyūbides de Syrie-Egypte-Mésopotamie supérieure[8]; et récemment encore un nouveau récit particulièrement circonstancié en a été traduit et commenté savamment par H. Gottschalk.[9] Ce dernier lui-même a cependant ignoré les renseignements que procurent également les extraits de ʿAbdallaṭīf, et qui même maintenant gardent leur prix à côté des autres. Pour le reste, ce que nous apprend ʿAbdallaṭīf sur les Khwārizmiens pèse assez peu à côté de ce que nous trouvons dans ses historiens classiques[10]; il est tout de même intéressant de voir comment était campée la silhouette des Khwārizmshāhs et de leurs bandes dans la conscience d'un homme cultivé et perspicace de leur propre temps.

Comme l'on sait, l'exposé du *Ta'rikh al-Islām* est ordonné année par année, chaque année comprenant d'une part le récit des évènements qui s'y sont produits, puis les biographies des notables qui y sont morts. Les citations de ʿAbdallaṭīf qui nous importent ici sont introduites d'une part à l'occasion de la mort du Khwārizmshāh Muḥammad b. Takash dans le nécrologue de 617 et de celle de Djalāl ad-dīn Manguberti en 629, d'autre-part au milieu des évènements de 627 H.

Biographie du Khwārizmshāh Muḥammad b. Takash[11]

Takash était borgne, chétif, fervent de musique. Il fut appelé par le Dīwān Sublime pour écarter la malfaisance de Tughril le Seldjuqide, seigneur de Hamadhān; il tua Tughril, envoya sa tête, et se mit en marche pour réclamer les droits du Sultanat; mais il se produisit un mouvement du peuple des Khiṭā, qui le contragnit à retourner défendre son pays.[11a] Il eut pour successeurs ses deux fils. L'un, Muḥammad, était valeureux, énergique, batailleur, entreprenant, heureux dans ses projets, amateur de *ghazwa*; jamais il ne laissait disparaître le feutre (de selle de sa monture), il franchissait les plus grandes distances en un temps dont l'ennemi n'aurait pu soupçonner que le double eût pu lui suffire; il était aussi violent, perfide, traître: pour commencer il fit tuer son frère dont il se fit apporter la tête alors qu'il était en train de manger, sans y faire attention. Il dormait peu, veillait beaucoup, longtemps debout, rarement au repos. Dans ses expéditions il servait ses hommes: dormaient-ils, il veillait sur eux. Ses vêtements et l'équipement de son cheval n'atteignaient pas (la valeur) d'un dinar. Son plaisir était dans sa peine, son repos dans sa fatigue. Il ramassait force butin, mais était prompt à le dépenser. Il avait des connaissances, et fréquentait les savants; avant son avènement il avait été assidu auprès de Fakhr ad-dīn Rāzī,[12] mais il cessa lorsqu'il fut au pouvoir, car alors le monde s'ouvrit devant lui, il y étendit la main, et ce pouvoir lui gâta le jugement, le rendant orgueilleux, arrogant, confiant dans le salut. Cela le fit nécessairement se conduire sans prendre d'avis et se détourner du souvenir des fins, il sousestima les adversaires et oublia la fin des temps. 'Muḥammad, disait-il, fera triompher la foi de Muḥammad'.[13] Puis il suspendit la khuṭba abbaside dans ses Etats, et cessa de combattre les infidèles; il se mit à entreprendre de combattre le midi (la *qibla*) de l'Islam, le cœur de la Loi, Baghdad.[14] Il décida d'attaquer Tiflis afin d'en faire sa capitale et de gouverner de là le pays de Rūm, l'Arménie, le Qipdjaq, et tous les pays de l'est et de l'ouest.[15] Mais il gâta ses affaires par son mauvais gouvernement et se tua lui-même avant son heure par la dureté de son avidité et de ses désordres. Il voulait ressembler à Alexandre; où y at-il plus aveugle à l'évidence, où l'associé (en sottise) d'un Turc? car Alexandre, avec toutes ses qualités, sa justice, sa foi monothéiste, avait autour de lui trois cents sages qu'il écoutait et dont il suivait les avis, c'était son maître Aristote qui était son lieutenant sur ses Etats, et il ne liait ni ne déliait sans l'avoir consulté ou avoir envoyé chercher son opinion.[16] On sait bien par expérience que tout prince dont le but n'est pas de maintenir le Droit, de faire régner la justice et d'assurer la prospérité hâte sa fin.

La première épreuve en fut son alliance scellée par mariage avec les Khiṭā. Après quoi il les mit aux prises avec le people des Tatars, qui les extirpa, et il ne lui resta que ceux qui entrèrent dans son obéissance et s'agrégèrent à son armée. Il engagea sept émirs de ses oncles maternels et en fit le cœur de son armée et ses intimes (*khawāṣṣ*). Après quoi il se tourna vers le peuple des Tatars, et détruisit les Khiṭā par le glaive, ne laissant subsister que ceux qui se rangèrent sous sa bannière. Le pays du Māwarān-nahr obéissait aux Khiṭā, auxquels les princes de Bukhārā, de Samarqand et autres payaient tribut, et qui répendaient sur eux la justice.[17] Ces peuples fermaient le passage aux Turcs de Chine, et voilà que notre prince, dans l'exiguité de son savoir, ouvrit cette fermeture de sûreté. Alors tout fut gâté dans ces pays et ces villes, on en arriva à la dévastation du pays et à l'aliénation des cœurs, où furent déposé toutes sortes de haines et d'oppositions.[18] Pensant qu'il ne restait cependant parmi ses sujets personne de nature à lui résister, il se tourna vers le Khurāsān, le Sidjistān, le Kirmān, puis l'Iraq et l'Adharbaydjān, et aspira même à la conquête de la Syrie et de l'Egypte,[19] s'entretenant en lui-même de tous les royaumes de la Terre. Chose qui eût été bien simple avec l'aide divine si celle-ci lui avait été accordée pour ses qualités de gouvernement, la fermeté de son jugement, la bonté, l'anéantissement de l'injustice.

Il faisait venir les marchands et les interrogeait sur les pays éloignés. Ibn abī Yaʿlā, vizir d'al-Malik al-Ẓāhir Ghāzī,[20] m'a raconté une nuit que le Sultan cette nuit était soucieux des nouvelles reçues du Khwārizmshāh qui, disait-on, voulait conquérir la Syrie. 'C'est un bonheur pour le Sultan, pour toi et pour moi, lui dis-je. – Comment cela? – Ce prince aux vastes horizons ne pourra pas rester en Syrie. Son désir est de vaincre et de soumettre: que notre Sultan le flatte, lui prodigue les marques d'amitié et les caresses. S'il approche, qu'il l'accueille avec des marques de déférence et des cadeaux, et, lorsqu'il nommera un lieutenant pour la Syrie, il n'en trouvera pas d'autre que lui. – D'où sais-tu cela? – Des marchands.' Le matin le vizir raconta au Sultan cette conversation, et les soucis de ce dernier furent dissipés. Il ordonna de vérifier ces dires, et fit venir un marchand expérimenté de Bagdad, avec lequel il parla. Le marchand assura qu'il s'était rendu auprès du Khwārizmshāh, auquel il avait vendu des objets. De son caractère il rapporta que ce souverain restait quatre jours à cheval sans en descendre, et encore n'était-ce que pour passer d'un cheval à un autre. Il avait le visage tanné, et parcourait le pays. Il arrivait parfois à la ville qui était son objectif avec peu de monde, mais ne l'en assaillait pas moins; le lendemain matin il était rejoint par dix mille hommes de ses troupes, le soir par vingt mille autres, mais bien souvent au moment où arrivait ce renfort le besoin même en avait cessé. Bien souvent il envoyait des armées et elles arrivaient les dernières, le besoin en avait cessé, il avait parfois assailli la ville avec cent hommes, et le besoin avait cessé, parfois il avait tué le prince de la ville ou l'avait capturé, et alors seulement affluaient les troupes. Sa selle, dit toujours le marchand, et les brides ne valaient pas un dâniq, ni ses vêtements deux dâniqs. Au cours d'un de ses raids, racontait le même, il s'arrêta à la fin de la nuit avec ses compagnons, environ soixante-dix cavaliers, qu'il fit dormir; il prit leurs chevaux, pour les renvoyer après qu'il eussent bû à un puits, et les abreuva tous; puis, constatant que ses hommes avaient pris leur part de sommeil, il en réveilla quelques-uns, et leur enjoignit de veiller avec attention, il dormit un peu, puis se leva, ils se levèrent comme les scorpions et donnèrent l'assaut à la ville: il tua le roi.[21]

Le vizir m'interrogea une autre fois sur les Khwārizmiens. Je lui dis qu'il ne pourrait pas occuper la Syrie, car ou bien il viendrait avec peu d'hommes, et il n'obtiendrait rien de ce qu'il voulait devant la vaillance des Syriens, ou bien il viendrait avec une grande armée, et la Syrie ne la supporterait pas, parce que les chevaux khwārizmiens mangeaient du chanvre dont il n'y a pas en Syrie; quant à l'orge, il n'y en avait dans chaque ville que juste de quoi entretenir les bêtes qui s'y trouvaient. Je me mis alors à compter combien il y avait de bêtes à Alep, et nous arrivâmes à un total de l'ordre de 53 000. Supposons, dis-je, qu'il arrive 700 000 chevaux [sic], ils prendront la ration d'un mois en un ou deux jours, et il ne leur restera plus d'aptitude à d'autre genre de guerre qu'aux coups de main; car leurs conquêtes reposent sur la crainte et la frayeur, et non la justice et l'amour; de telles condition ne valent pas contre la vaillance des Syriens.[22]

Au lendemain de la mort d'al-Malik al-Ẓāhir Ghāzī arriva à Alep un envoyé du Khwārizmshāh. Les gens accoururent et les autorités sortirent à sa rencontre. On vit que c'était un soufi, derrière lequel était un autre soufi qui tenait levé un bâton sur sa tête; avec lui il y avait deux membres de l'armée khwārizmienne et un envoyé du seigneur d'Irbil. Il monta à la citadelle, et dit en présence des émirs: 'Le Sultan des Sultans vous salue. Il est mécontent de ce que vous ne l'ayez pas félicité de sa conquête de l'Iraq et de l'Adharbaydjān. Son armée compte 700 000 hommes. 'Ils firent de bonnes excuses, en disant qu'ils étaient dans le deuil de la mort de leur roi et la dépression de leurs âmes.' Mais quand nous serons remis, ajoutaient-ils, nous sommes les esclaves (du Shāh).' Les paroles de cet homme et son extérieur témoignaient du peu de sens de celui qui l'avait envoyé. Il alla ensuite trouver al-Malik al-'Ādil et lui dit: 'Le Sultan des Sultans te salue et te dit de venir à son service, car il t'a distingué et choisi pour être le chef de son étrier (son *rikābdār?*). – Entendu et obéi; cependant nous avons un shaykh qui est notre chef et que nous consultons: quand il m'ordonnera d'y aller j'irai. – Qui est-ce? – Le Prince des Croyants.' Puis l'envoyé s'en alla, tandis qu'on se moquait de lui.[23]

Le même Ibn abī Ya'lā raconte encore avoir entendu dire que le Khwārizmshāh avait fait 'Izz ad-dīn Kaykāūs, prince de Rūm, son porte-étendard (*amīr-'alam*) et le Calife son predicateur *khaṭīb*. A chaque roi il donnait ainsi une fonction; mais les rois qui étaient auprès de lui, il les méprisait et les traitait avec toutes sortes de dédain. Lorsqu'on frappait pour lui la *nauba*, il mettait des tambours d'or au cou des rois qui debout frappaient. Cela montre son orgeuil en ce monde où il était, et son peu de confiance dans le Très-Haut.[24]

Puis il alla à Ispahān et Hamadhān, et expédia ses armées en sens divers sur Ḥulwān et les confins d'Irbil; Muẓaffar ad-dīn l'accueillit avec des approvisionnements et des vivres.[25] Les habitants de Bagdad s'inquiétèrent et rassemblèrent des troupes, se préparant à la fois à un siège et à une bataille rangée. Puis Dieu leur envoya son usuelle bonté en l'écartant d'eux (le danger). Car le pays du Māwarānnahr se troubla, et il se retira sur les talons, fuyant lamentablement, sans savoir ce qu'il laissait de ce qu'il avait sous la main. De plus, lorsqu'il était arrivé à Ḥulwān, il était survenu de grandes tempêtes de neige, et certains de ses intimes avaient dit que cela était un des prodiges attachés à la Maison de la Prophétie.[26]

Lorsqu'il eut détruit les Khiṭā et les Tatars qui étaient maîtres de Jand, du Turkestan et de Tankut, il apparut d'autres peuples, encore appelés Tatars. Ceux-ci étaient divisés en deux parties, les uns habitant Tamghādj et les environs et nommés Iwāiya, les autres habitant les confins de l'Inde et les pays contigus à la Chine dans la montagne appelée Sank-Sulākh, où se trouve une brèche qui conduit en Inde (c'est par là que le Sultan Muḥammad pénétra en Inde et survint par où on ne l'attendait pas). Il y eut bataille entre les deux groupes de Tatars, et les Iwāiya furent battus par les Tamghādjiya au point que ceux-ci vinrent troubler les environs de Bukhārā et de Samarqand.[27] Ils apprirent alors que le Sultan Muḥammad se trouvait dans la région de Bagdad, et que c'était à une grande distance. Cela leur donna le désir de profiter de son absence pour s'emparer du pays. Il l'apprit alors qu'il se trouvait à Hamadhān, il revint à toute vitesse, arriva à Bukhārā, réunit les troupes et marcha sur l'ennemi. Il envoya son fils Djalāl ad-dīn en embuscade à la tête de 15 000 cavaliers, mais la nouvelle fut colportée aux Tamghādjiya, dont le chef était Djinghiz-Khān, ils tombèrent sur l'embuscade et la pulvérisèrent. Djalāl ad-dīn, après des efforts acharnés, s'enfuit jusqu' auprès de son père. Celui-ci convint de livrer bataille; mais l'ennemi tint ferme dans la bataille le premier jour, et le Sultan en fut surpris, car il n'avait pas l'habitude qu'un ennemi tînt devant lui. Puis les Mongols tinrent ferme un second et un troisième jour. Alors Muḥammad se démoralisa, et ses compagnons de même, leurs esprits s'altérèrent, ils donnèrent des signes de frayeur et de faiblesse. Là-dessus arrivèrent (cependant) des espions, qui rapportèrent que l'armée des Mongols était moitié moins nombreuse que celle des Khwārizmiens. Mais la perte de la Fortune fit penser à Muḥammad que les émirs complotaient contre lui, il fit arrêter leurs chefs, et l'altération des esprits ne fit que s'aggraver. Il s'imagina que son armée était maintenant pure, et livra une autre bataille. Il fut détruit et arriva à Bukhārā en fuyard. Il fit proclamer dans la population qu'on eût à se préparér à un siège de trois ans, ce qui éloigna les esprits de lui.[28] Alors il fut d'avis de se retirer à Nīshāpūr et d'y opérer une concentration de troupes. Il ne pensait pas que les Tamghādjiya allaient traverser le Djayhūn, ils prirent Bukhārā en huit jours et exterminèrent les habitants, puis ils foncèrent sur le Khurāsān.[29] Le vizir de Muḥammad, 'Imād al-Mulk, lui conseilla de gagner Hamadhān, et s'engagea à lui réunir là des troupes et des resources autant qu'il lui en fallait. Mais le Khwārizmshāh n'était pas arrivé à Rayy que les escadrons des Tatars étaient déjà sur sa tête. Il se sauva à la forteresse de Baradjīn : épuisé, il y resta deux jours, et voilà que les Mongols étaient là. Il se traina à Derbend Qārūn, localité des confins du Fārs, avec trois cents cavaliers dépourvus de tout, sans même un souffle de vie. La faim les torturant ils demandèrent à manger à des Kurdes du pays, qui ne se soucièrent pas d'eux. Ils dirent qu'ils avaient avec eux le Sultan : 'Nous ne connaissons pas le Sultan', fut la réponse. A force de supplications ils obtinrent deux brebis et deux grandes écuelles de lait, qu'ils se partagèrent. Par la suite Muḥammad repartit pour Nahāvand, et passa par les régions frontalières du pays jusqu' à Hamadhān, puis au Māzandarān, avec le cliquetis des lances et des sabres ennemis qui remplissaient ses oreilles et ses yeux. Il s'arrêta dans un petit lac au lieu dit Av-Germ, il fut saisi d'une diarrhée rapide, et demanda un médicament, car il manquait même de pain. C'est là qu'il mourut. Il fut, dit-on, porté par mer au Dihistān. Selon d'autres lorsqu'il s'était trouvé dans le bateau, il n'avait cessé de se battre la tête sur le bord, si bien qu'il en mourut.[30] Quant à son fils les pays se le renvoyaient comme balle de fronde : le premier le jeta en Inde, et l'Inde le rejeta au Kirmān (comme il sera exposé dans sa biographie, si Dieu le veut).[31]

An 627, la Bataille d'Erzindjān[32]

... Quelques émirs ouvrirent aux Khwārizmiens une porte de Khilāṭ par l'autre côté, sans garder fermes leur foi ni leur serment, mais sous l'impression de la mort dont la menaçait la croissante disette. (Les Khwārizmiens) entrèrent donc et tuèrent, capturèrent, violèrent tous les harems, depuis leur entrée au milieu de la nuit jusqu'à la fin de la matinée suivante; après quoi ils levèrent le glaive et se mirent à extorquer de l'argent par la torture, promettant la mort et les tourments plus qu'à tous autres, aux fuqahā', et aux hommes de bien.[33]

Al-Kāmil, cependant, retournait en Egypte, irrité, et les gens, désemparés, ne doutaient pas que, si les Khwārizmiens s'emparaient de la Syrie et du pays de Rūm, il n'en resterait plus trace et c'en serait fait des habitants.[34] Mais al-Ashraf et 'Alā' al-dīn conclurent une paix aussi totale qu'avait été obstinée leur hostilité, ils levèrent leurs armées malgré la peur toujours maîtresse des cœurs, et cette frayeur exagérée dura après la jonction de leurs armées, jusqu'au jour où Dieu fixa le désastre des Khwārizmiens dans la facilité de son renfort.[35]

J'ai lu dans la lettre d'un soldat ce qui suit: 'Nous quittâmes Siwas et gagnâmes le campement de Yasi-Djuman,[36] aux limites de la province d'Erzindjān. Il s'y trouvait de l'herbe et de l'eau. Apprenant l'approche des armées, l'ennemi, par une marche dissimulée de trois jours, atteignit les pâturages susdits, et surprit un détachement de l'armée au matin du 24 ramadhân. Al-Ashraf engagea la bataille avec les Khwārizmiens, et la mêlée dura sans interruption jusqu'à près de midi; puis Dieu (lui) donna la victoire, et l'ennemi subit une méchante défaite le 29 ramadhân. Alors on vit se succéder les gens amenant des prisonniers et un butin d'esclaves, de bêtes et d'armes, le tout en mauvais état, si bien qu'on vendait la cuirasse 3 dirhams, l'arc là, 5 et 20 à Alep, voire 30, malgré leur extrême détérioration; ainsi pour les arcs et leurs autres armes. Et il arriva ceux qui avaient été faits prisonniers, et parmi eux un individu qui raconta aux fuqahā' persans entrés en conversation avec lui que leur maître avait été stupéfait et désorienté à la vue de l'armée syrienne, et qu'alors leur moral était tombé; mais, n'eût été l'armée syrienne, nous aurions anéanti l'armée de Rūm: à moi seul j'en ai tué cinquante cavaliers.'[37]

Un soldat de mes parents raconte ce qui suit: 'Nous arrivâmes aux pâturages de Yasi-Djuman, nous dirigeant vers Khilāṭ où nous pensions qu'était l'ennemi, lorsque celui-ci nous entoura et attaqua un détachement de l'armée de Rūm auquel il tua quelque deux cents hommes et prit du butin et des gens. Le lendemain l'armée khwārizmienne attaqua l'armée de Rūm, et lui tua beaucoup de monde, lui fit beaucoup de prisonniers: sept mille tués, raconte-t-on, d'entre leurs meilleurs combattants, d'autres disent plus ou moins; et un homme d'Erzindjān qui était dans l'armée de Rūm m'a dit qu'elle comptait en tout douze mille hommes, et que nul n'en réchappa que blessé ou fuyard, en gravissant les montagnes. Le seigneur de Rūm resta avec un faible contingent des siens, environ cinq mille hommes. Quant aux nôtres le jeudi ils se rangèrent en bataille, il y eut des escarmouches où les nôtres combattant sans cesse à cheval, apprirent à connaître le mode de combat (des Khwārizmiens), leurs flèches, la faiblesse de leurs chevaux, la médiocrité de leur adresse équestre, si bien que notre peur se changea en courage et en mépris, et que nous nous demandâmes comment ces hommes avaient pu vaincre tant de peuples. Nous passâmes la nuit du vendredi en ordre de bataille; si un homme voulait fuir, deux esclaves s'élançaient sur lui et le réconfortaient. Au matin on reçut deux transfuges, qu'al-Ashraf interrogea sur le nombre des Khwārizmiens: trente mille, dirent-ils. Al-Ashraf parcourut longuement les rangs, exhortant tout le monde, dépréciant l'ennemi. Le samedi matin on fut en parfait ordre. Al-Ashraf demanda aux deux esclaves où était le Khwārizmshāh: sur cette colline, dirent-ils, et ses cheveux sont dans une enveloppe noire, et au-dessus des omoplates (?) un petit (b.r.dj.m.?) cousu à son *qabā'*.

Un corps de Khwārizmiens chargea alors contre l'armée de Rūm, qui soutint le choc; al-Ashraf, avec cinq mille cavaliers de l'armée égyptienne s'avança vers Sābiq al-dīn et les armées de Ḥoms, d'Alep et de Ḥamāh, et en tira mille cavaliers; il entraina également des émirs arabes[38] à la tête de mille cavaliers des leurs; et tous chargèrent sur la colline où se trouvait le Khwārizmshāh. Quand ce dernier aperçut la mort sanglante toute proche, il s'enfuit, et son armée, le voyant faire, le suivit. Quant à ceux qui avaient chargé contre l'armée de Rūm, ils résistèrent au milieu, et nul n'en échappa. Les autres Khwārizmiens, trop effrayés pour fuir et trouver un chemin, descendirent la plupart de cheval et se tapirent dans les fonds d'oueds et les maisons en ruine, où leur sort fut réglé par les paysans et les jeunes esclaves, dont les plus faibles pouvaient encore les tuer. Trois mille cependant filèrent vers le pays de Djānīt[39]; mais là aussi les paysans de Rūm et les chrétiens les massacrèrent jusqu'au dernier.[40]

Pour le Khwārizmshāh il creva dans sa fuite quelque deux cents étalons. Il entra à Khilāṭ avec sept compagnons, prit sa famille et les affaires qu'il put, coupa vers Manāzgird qu'assiégeait son vizir, et y arriva affamé; son vizir lui donna à manger.[41] Il rentra en Adharbaydjan dans l'humiliation et la confusion, et extorqua de l'argent aux habitants de Khuway dont plusieurs moururent sous les tortures.

Al-Ashraf, lui, s'il avait poussé son armée à leur poursuite, aurait achevé de les tuer et de les capturer. Il occupa Erzerum, qu'il remit à 'Alā' al-dīn Kayqubādh, non sans recevoir force biens de tout le royaume de celui-ci. Le prince de la ville, Ibn Mughīth al-dīn, cousin de 'Alā' al-dīn, accusé de défection, se réfugia dans une caverne, où une femme le prit.[42] Al-Ashraf assiégea Manāzgird, où il se proposait d'entrer derrière les Khwārizmiens, mais, après y être resté quelques mois, il accepta des négociations de paix. L'accord fut conclu à condition qu'al-Ashraf se retirât. Il licencia l'armée.[43] L'aman fut accordé à Khilāṭ, que l'on entreprit de restaurer.[44]

Un émir raconte: 'Nous chargeâmes contre les Khwārizmiens, qui subirent une déroute dans un oued, et y périrent; nous les poussâmes au pied d'une montagne plongeant dans un oued profond, ils s'y entassèrent avec leurs chevaux et furent taillés en pièce. Le lendemain nous regardâmes de dessus l'oued, et nous le vîmes rempli de morts; le seul vivant que nous y trouvâmes était un esclave khwārizmien qui avait le pied brisé. Nous restâmes quelques jours à retourner les cadavres, pour rechercher si le Khwārizmshāh ne se trouvait pas parmi eux. On captura beaucoup de ses familiers, ses insignes et ses drapeaux. Et l'on raconte que les Arabes prirent dans sa tente une jarre d'or de vingt-cinq *raṭls*, qu'al-Ashraf leur pesa. Ce qu'il y eut de remarquable dans cette bataille est qu'il n'y fut pas tué un seul homme de l'armée syrienne, ni blessé un seul cheval; seul fut blessé, d'une flèche, un homme de Ḥomṣ. Et la frayeur causée par les Khwārizmiens cessa, comme cessa aussi leur chance.[45]

Biographie du Khwārizmshāh Djalāl al-dīn Manguberti

Il était d'une jaune tirant sur le brun, et maigre, laid, parce que sa mère était une Hindoue. Il portait le *ṭarṭūr* avec des crins de cheval et teint en plusieurs couleurs. Son frère Ghiyāth (ou Rukn) al-dīn était par contre un des plus beaux hommes et des plus délicieux à voir, malheureusement brutal et violent; sa mère à lui était turque.[46]

Chez les Khwārizmiens l'adultère est répandu et la sodomie n'est ni grandement ni petitement condamnée ni blâmée.[47] La perfidie est un trait de caractère qui ne les abandonne pas: ils prirent par l'aman une forteresse près de Tiflis: lorsque les habitants en furent descendus, les Khwārizmiens, après s'être un peu éloignés, revinrent et tuèrent ceux auxquels ils avaient promis une paix sans tuerie, firent prisonniers ceux auxquels ils avaient promis une paix sans prisonniers.[48] Un habitant de Tiflis qui était venu me trouver pour prendre avec moi des leçons de médecine me raconta tout cela. Il avait séjourné six ans à Tiflis, où il avait réalisé par la médecine une jolie fortune. Lorsque les Khwārizmiens approchèrent, un envoyé vint de leur part avec de douces paroles: il était encore dans la séance qu'un messager arriva annonçant que ces gens faisaient des ravages aux frontières. Alors la reine dit à l'envoyé: 'Est-ce ainsi que les rois agissent, envoyant un ambassadeur dire une chose et en faisant une autre?' Et elle le fit expulser. Quinze jours plus tard ils arrivèrent, et l'armée géorgienne sortit les combattre. Iwānī dit: 'Constituons l'armée avec un centre, une aile droite et une aile gauche.' Mais Shalūh: 'Ils ne valent pas tant de précautions: je m'en charge.' Il descendit avec une force de sept mille cavaliers la plupart turcomans, impudent comme un ivrogne: il avança, et se trouva au milieu d'eux; ils l'entourèrent, et son drapeau tomba. Alors Iwānī dit: 'Voilà que Shalūh est battu, occupons-nous de nous-mêmes.' Il prit par un défilé, suivi par les fuyards, et ils se brisèrent dans un défilé profond à tel point que la plupart y moururent. Iwānī avec les siens se retrancha dans une forteresse, tandis que les Khwârizmiens continuaient à piller et ravager tout ce qu'ils trouvaient. Et la reine de son côté se réfugia dans les forteresses des défilés. Puis Ibn al-Sadīd al-Tiflīsī sortit négocier la paix, croyant qu'ils étaient comme tout le monde et avaient parole et loyauté. Il alla donc demander l'aman pour tous les habitants, musulmans, géorgiens et juifs, et il reçut la signature de Djalāl al-dīn et de son frère Ghiyāth al-dīn, avec sa *ḥamya*[49] et son sceau, ainsi qu'une tablette d'argent avec inscription d'or qu'on appelait *pāïẓa*.[50] Avec cela il se crut garanti. Une heure plus tard les Khwārizmiens entraient, pillaient les esclaves d'Ibn al-Sadīd et ses biens, et il se repentit; et ils firent de même avec tout le monde. Appelant les Musulmans pénitents, ils s'attribuèrent le droit à leurs biens et à leurs harems, ne laissant ni femme jolie ni joli enfant. Et n'importe lequel d'entre eux sautait sur les gens, on l'invitait à manger et boire, il recherchait la femme du maître de maison et la demandait sur la natte en disant: 'c'est notre sœur'. Et au matin, trouvait-il un enfant qui lui plaisait, il l'emmenait. S'il y avait chez quelqu'un une marchandise qu'il avait envie d'acheter, et dont on lui demandait cinquante dinars, il la prenait pour cinq, et si l'autre essayait de parler, il le frappait d'un fouet à bout de métal qu'il portait, ce dont il advenait que l'homme mourait ou perdait connaissance.[51] Le nombre des Khwārizmiens n'atteignait pas cent mille, peut-être soixante mille, tous affamés, dépourvus de tout. Ils portaient des *qabā'* de coton, et leurs armes consistaient en flèches rudimentaires lancées avec des arcs faibles et ne faisant aucune marque sur les cuirasses. Ils n'ont ni *dīwān* (militaire) ni solde: rien que le pillage de ce qu'ils trouvent, sans qu'il soit possible à (Djalāl al-dīn) de les retenir de rien.[52] Et, ajoutait cet homme de Tiflis, quiconque a combattu les Tatars atteste que leur conduite est encore meilleure que celle des Khwārizmiens.[53]

Lorsque Djalāl al-dīn se dirigea vers Ghazna et l'Inde, fuyant devant Djinghiz-Khān, pour demander secours au roi de ces pays, ce-lui-ci lui envoya une armée, et pendant quelques jours ils combattirent les Tatars; puis il s'enfuit, égaré, solitaire, et gagna le Kirmān.[54] Il y avait là deux grands princes qui l'accueillirent généreusement, et lorsqu'il eut repris quelque force il trompa leur confiance et en tua un. Il s'enfuit de nouveau et arriva à Shīrāz avec boeufs et ânes,[55] et la plupart de ses compagnons à pied. Le prince du pays l'emmena vers Bagdad, et Djalāl al-dīn fit quelques ravages à Shahrabādh et dans cette région.[56] Cependant son frère Ghiyāth al-dīn s'était enfui de son côté avec seulement trente hommes et un soufi qui lui faisait la prière. Lorsqu'il fut endormi ses gens s'entendirent pour le tuer et porter sa tête aux Tatars afin d'entrer en grâce auprès d'eux. Le soufi approuva et les laissa s'endormir; alors il réveilla le prince, le mit au courant, et lui, les devançant, en égorgea un certain nombre, n'en laissant que quelques-uns pour témoigner de leur dessein.[57] Il atteignit alors Ispahan, pauvre et solitaire, et y fut bien reçu; il se groupa autour de lui des éléments dispersés de l'armée de son père, et il reçut des vêtements d'honneur de Bagdad, un diplôme et promesse du Sultanat. Il apprit alors l'approche de son frère, et dit qu'il n'entrerait que sur l'ordre du Dīwān; la permission fut demandée et obtenue. Djalāl al-dīn arrivé eut peur de son frère et le fit enfermer et enchaîner quelque temps; puis, renforcé et victorieux, il le libéra.[58]

A la fin de son règne[59] Djalāl al-dīn s'affaiblit et se fit détester par sa mauvaise conduite. Aucun prince ne lui garda son amitié, et il se fit au contraire des ennemis de tous. Puis son armée même se détacha de lui, à cause des extravagances auxquelles il se livrait pour montrer son amour des princes: l'un d'eux mourait-il, il menait un deuil énorme, ordonnait aux habitants de Tauriz de pleurer et de se frapper, et ne l'enterrait pas, mais manifestait le désir de l'accompagner, et poussait des cris; et malheur à qui disait que le prince était mort. Les émirs ne ressentirent plus pour lui que mépris et honte.[60] Les Tatars apprirent (?) sa défaite par al-Ashraf, et conquirent sur lui Marāgha et autres lieux.[61]

NOTES

1 Dans *Der Islam*, XXIV (1937) 105-30; cf. *JRAS* (1936) 595-604.

2 Il est remarquable que presque tous les historiens contemporains de ces évènements, Ibn al-Athīr, Sibt b. al-Djawzī, al-Makīn b. al-ʿAmīd etc. interrompent vers le même moment la suite de leur narration pour donner un exposé général et des impressions sur les Mongols. Le texte de ʿAbdallaṭīf s'inscrit dans ce même ensemble.

3 Surtout S.M. Stern, *A collection of treatises by ʿAbdallatif*, in *Islamic Studies*, 1/1 (1962) 53-70.

4 *La Syrie du Nord à l'époque des Croisades*, 61-2. Voir aussi *Bulletin de la Faculté des Lettres de Strasbourg* (1950) 320 sq.

5 *Ta'rīkh al-Aṭibbā'*, éd. Aug. Müller, II, 15 sq.; cf. Brockelmann, *GAL*, I, 481.

6 Voir le *Bulletin* signalé n. 4. Il s'agit des *Mémoires*, de même époque, de Saʿd ad-dīn b. Ḥamawiya Djuwaynī.

7 Voir en dernier lieu sur celui-ci ma *Pre-ottoman Turkey* (1968), 108, 252. Sur la dynastie, cf. surtout Van Berchem et Halil Edhem, *Corpus Inscriptionum arabicarum*, *Asie Mineure*, I, 510 sq.

7*a* Je garde cette forme généralement usitée mais très douteuse (cf. *EI*/2 *sub* Djalāl al-dīn); ʿAbdallaṭīf se contente d'ailleurs de dire Djalāl al-dīn sans plus.

8 Voir infra n. 35.

9 Dans *Festschrift H. Duda*, *WZKM*, LVI (1960), sous le titre *Der Bericht des Ibn Nazif über die Schlacht von Yasycimen.*

10 Ibn al-Athīr, Nasawī, Djuwaynī, etc. Sur les Khwārizmiens en général, voir encore surtout W. Barthold, *Turkestan down to the Mongol invasion* chap. III (nouvelle édition revue par C. E. Bosworth); aussi Ibr. Kafesoğlu, *Harezmşahlar Devleti Tarihi* (1958).

11 Je garde cette forme peu compromettante, comme il est fait dans l'*EI*, mais la vraie lecture serait probablement Töküsh ou Tekish.

11*a* Cf. *EI*/1, art. Ṭughril b. Arslan; sur l'affaire des Khiṭā, Barthold, *Turkestan*, 344-6.

12 Sur Fakhr al-dīn Rāzī, voir l'article d'Anawati dans *EI*/2.

13 Ce portrait, en gros analogue à ce que suggèrent les autres sources, n'a cependant pas d'exact homologue; on ne trouve pas ailleurs la rumeur sur le meurtre du frère.

14 En 614/1218 Muḥammad attaqua le territoire califal et fit la khuṭba au nom d'un Alide, Barthold, 373.

15 Je ne connais pas d'autre témoignage de ce projet, que plus tard Djalāl al-dīn réalisera partiellement dans des conditions nouvelles.

16 Ces idées sont exprimées dans les prétendues lettres d'Alexandre et d'Aristote si volontiers utilisées dans la littérature arabe, où l'on n'en discutait pas l'authenticité (déjà dans le *Kitāb al-Kharāj* de Qudāma); voir A. Abel, *Le Roman d'Alexandre* (1955); et G. Richter, *Studien zur ... arabischen Fürstenspiegel* (1932).

17 Cf. très en gros Barthold, passim 349-80.

18 Il y a là un écho des griefs des Musulmans contre Muḥammad (Barthold, 375-80), qui contribuèrent a briser sa capacité de résistance lors de l'assaut mongol.

19 La conquête de l'Iran oriental et méridional a eu lieu en 611/1214 (le Khurāsān avait été trouvé, malgré quelques troubles, dans l'héritage

paternel), celle de l'Iran occidental, Adharbaydjān compris, en 614/1217. Le mot Iraq désigne ici l'Iraq ʿadjamī au sens que lui donnaient les chancelleries orientales, c'est-à-dire le Plateau iranien occidental. Nous n'avons pas d'autre témoignage d'ambitions de Muḥammad sur les pays ayyubides; il ne peut guère s'agir, s'il y a quelque chose de vrai, que d'une prétention à la suzeraineté, en liaison avec le conflit que Muḥammad avait avec le Calife sur la question du Sultanat général qu'il réclamait comme un héritage seldjuqide, et comme l'avait déja réclamé son père. Voir supra n. 14. Nous savons seulement qu'en 615/1218 une ambassade khwārizmienne atteignit al-ʿĀdil, le chef de la famille ayyubide, à la veille de sa mort (Sibṭ b. al-Djawzī, *Mirʾāt al-Zamān*, sub anno); voir infra n. 23.

20 Il est difficile de taxer d'anachronisme un auteur aussi contemporain des faits que ʿAbdallaṭīf, mais il est difficile de penser que le Khwārizmshāh, dont les premières conquêtes en Iran occidental sont postérieures à la mort d'al-Ẓāhir Ghāzī (613/1216) ait pu paraître réellement menaçant a celui-ci. – Sur Ibn abī Yaʿlā, voir Kamāl al-dīn b. al-ʿAdīm, *Zubda* (Histoire d'Alep), éd. Sāmī Dahān 111 (1968), sub anno 613; ce vizir peut avoir antidaté son récit à ʿAbdallaṭīf.

21 Voir n. 13 et 19. Il est impossible d'identifier le dernier épisode, même s'il est exact.

22 On retrouvera des traces de cet orgueil syrien, voir infra n. 37.

23 Cette ambassade ne peut être que juste postérieure à la conquête de l'Iran Occidental, donc de la fin de 614/1217, un certain temps après la mort d'al-Ẓāhir, et on peut supposer que la continuation, qui en atteint al-ʿĀdil, est identique à l'ambassade reçue par celui-ci en 615/1218 (voir supra n. 19). Le seigneur d'Irbil en question est le fameux Muẓaffar al-dīn Gökburī, alors vieux (il devait mourir en 630/1233 à 81 ans lunaires), sur lequel et les jeux diplomatiques duquel voir l'article *Begteginides* dans *EI*/2.

24 Sur cette *nauba*, voir Nasawī, trad. Houdas 37 (il s'agit évidemment des 'rois' des territoires effectifs de l'Empire khwārizmien proprement dit). Il se peut – mais nous n'en avons pas d'autre témoignage – qu'à la fin de son règne Muḥammad ait accompagné sa prétention au Sultanat universel d'ouvertures aux souverains comme celle dont il est ici question à ʿIzz al-dīn Kaykāūs de Rūm (607/1211–615/1218), mais, en ce qui concerne le Calife, il ne peut s'agir ici que d'un bruit moqueur puisqu'il y avait eu rupture entre le Calife al-Nāṣir et le Khwārizmshāh, qui avait découvert un anticalife alide (voir Barthold, 374).

25 Voir n. 23.

26 La tempête de neige est attestée aussi bien par Nasawī, Ibn al-Athīr etc.; et naturellement les nouvelles d'Asie Centrale, prodromes à l'invasion mongole.

27 Ce résumé d'histoire est assez difficile à interprêter en tous ses points. Le nom d'Iwāiya, qui est celui d'une tribu turcomane puissante à cette

époque en Adharbaydjān, ne peut provenir que d'une confusion de ʿAbdallaṭīf ou de Dhahabī, mais sans qu'on puisse assurer avec quoi, car il n'en parle pas, du moins en donnant de nom, dans sa section mongole, et l'on ne voit pas, dans les noms connus par ailleurs parmi les Mongols et apparentés de cette époque, qu'il y en ait de bien proche de celui-ci, graphiquement s'entend. Les Tankut (Tangut), pris ici comme nom géographique, sont un peuple connu des confins tibétains (?), mais je ne vois pas à quel groupe ethnique se rapporte, l'appellation de 'Tatars de Djand' (la région de Djand relevait de l'Etat khwārizmien). La géographie impliquée dans la suite du passage est obscure, on voit mal ce qui distingue Tamghādj, nom ordinaire de la Chine chez les peuples d'Asie Centrale, de la Chine appelée de ce nom; je ne sais quelle montagne se dissimule sous le nom de Sank-Sulākh, qui d'une part doit être contigüe à la Chine et d'autre part communiquer avec 'l'Inde' par le passage qu'avait emprunté Muḥammad b. Takash dans sa campagne de 1206 (Barthold 350-3;). Puisqu'il nous est dit plus bas que les Tamghādjiya sont les Tatars de Djinghiz-Khān, ceux qu'il avait battus auparavant et qui sont appelés ici Iwāiya devraient être les Naïmans, ou plutôt les Mergits (Barthold, *Turkestan*, 370-2).

28 Nous ne pouvons évidemment suivre ʿAbdallaṭīf dans le détail de sa chronologie. Si les Mongols avaient eu vent de la campagne de Muḥammad en Iran en 1217–18, cela se situe bien avant leur arrivée dans les Etats du Khwārizmshāh, et ce n'est pas au lendemain de son retour de Hamadhān que celui-ci eut à faire face à l'invasion, bien que le mouvement de peuples et de troupes en Asie Centrale ait dû être pour quelque chose déjà dans son retour. Quant au récit de la campagne de Muḥammad contre les Mongols, il est presque sans aucun rapport avec ce que disent nos autres sources, et paraît reposer sur des confusions entre évènements divers. Le récit des premières hostilités, au cours desquelle se distingue Djalāl al-dīn, paraît se référer plutôt à la bataille qui avait eu lieu entre Muḥammad et une armée mongole aux confins de leurs Etats en 613/1216. Le climat de suspicion dans l'armée khwārizmienne en 1220 est abondamment illustré par toutes les sources (voir Barthold, *Turkestan* p. 405), mais il n'y a eut pas de bataille, et Muḥammad évacua Bukhārā dans l'idée de l'impossibilité de défendre le pays au-delà du Djayhān (Amou-Darya); il encourageait, il est vrai, avec plus ou moins d'espoir, les grosses villes à soutenir le siège mongol.

29 Il est probable qu'au contraire, comme le pense Barthold, Muḥammad ne croyait pas à la possibilité de défendre le Djayhān, sans quoi il ne serait pas parti si loin. D'après les sources principales, les habitants furent dépouillés et expulsés mais non massacrés (à la différence d'autres villes); mais la ville, exprès ou non, fut détruite par le feu.

30 Le récit haletant rend bien là l'impression que firent sur les contemporains les dernières aventures du Khwārizmshāh, mais le détail en est sans doute un peu romancé et difficile à accorder exactement avec

l'exposé des sources usuelles. Il est exact que Muḥammad, en quittant Nīshāpūr, eut l'appui de ʿImād al-Mulk, ancien lieutenant du vizirat et maintenant vizir du fils de Muḥammad, Rukn al-dīn Gūrshānshāh, à Hérat. L'épisode de Barādjīn est inconnu, et je n'identifie pas le nom, peut-être déformé, de la forteresse. Le lieu-dit Av-Germ n'est pas autrement attesté, et de toute façon la suite même du récit implique que c'était sur la Mer Caspienne. Le détail de la mort du Khwārizmshāh varie d'auteur à auteur, et ressortit évidemment aux racontars populaires.

31 Infra, 111.

32 Après la mort de Muḥammad, son fils Djalāl al-dīn Manguberti avait fini, avec les bandes 'khwārizmiennes' ralliées autour de lui, par se tailler une espèce de nouvel empire dans la moitié occidentale de l'Iran, l'Adharbaydjan et la Géorgie. Néanmoins cela ne lui suffisait pas encore, en partie en raison de son tempérament guerrier, en partie parce qu'il fallait nourrir ses troupes dont la guerre était la seule ressource, et surtout enfin peut-être parce que la pression mongole lui donnait le désir d'un refuge éventuel au-delà de l'Iran. En 627/1230 il forçait, par la prise d'Akhlāṭ/Khilāṭ, sur le Lac de Van, l'une des deux grandes routes traditionnelles de pénétration de l'Adharbaydjān vers l'Arménie occidentale et l'Anatolie. La puissance khwārizmienne commençait à se faire sentir dans le jeu complexe des querelles entre princes de Mésopotamie, de Syrie et d'Asie Mineure. Pendant assez longtemps ʿAlāʾ al-dīn Kayqubādh, le prestigieux Seldjuqide d'Anatolie, avait entretenu avec le Khwārizmshāh des rapports cordiaux, son alliance lui ayant paru utile contre les petits Etats intermédiaires et en particulier la principauté d'Erzerum tenue par un cousin mal disposé envers lui. De leur côté les Ayyubides se jalousaient les uns les autres, et al-Muʿaẓẓam de Damas intriguait avec les Khwārizmiens contre al-Ashraf, le maître des possessions de la famille en haute Mésopotamie, jusqu'à Akhlāṭ comprise. L'arrivée de Frédéric II, dont il pouvait craindre que ses frères al-Muʿaẓẓam et, en Egypte, al-Kāmil ne tirassent parti contre lui, empêcha al-Ashraf d'assurer personnellement la défense de la valeureuse cité, dont la résistance fut dirigée par son lieutenant le ḥādjib Ḥusām al-dīn ʿAlī. Elle devait être vaine, et c'est à ce moment que se situe le début de l'extrait conservé par Dhahabī de ʿAbdallaṭīf. Bien qu'Akhlāṭ appartînt à un Ayyubide, la chute en était au moins aussi dangereuse pour l'Etat seldjuqide que pour la haute Mésopotamie ayyubide. Le prince d'Erzerum venait de retourner le Khwārizmshāh en sa faveur. Dès lors il n'y avait plus d'autre solution pour Kayqubādh que de se préparer à repousser une invasion. L'intérêt le rapprochait, malgré de récentes querelles, des Ayyubides, et d'abord d'al-Ashraf, maintenant libre, et qui put entrainer à sa suite ses frères ou cousins de Syrie septentrionale. Les armées coalisées se réunirent à Siwas en ramadhân/début d'août. La suite est racontée infra dans la version de ʿAbdallaṭīf.

33 Sources et récit de ces faits dans H. L. Gottschalk, *Al-Malik al-Kāmil*, 185-6.

34 Des affaires intérieures rappelaient en Egypte al-Kāmil, le suzerain de la famille, qui venait de se réconcilier avec al-Ashraf; c'est en accord avec lui qu' al-Ashraf put répondre favorablement aux appels de Kayqubādh.

35 Les principaux autres récits de la campagne sont ceux d'Ibn Bībī, qui donne le point de vue seldjuqide, de Nasawī, qui donne le point de vue khwārizmien, et, indépendants les uns des autres, d'Ibn al-Athīr, Ibn Wāṣil, Sibṭ b. al-Djawzī et Ibn Naẓīf. Voir supra n. 8 et 9, et Gottschalk, *Der Bericht*, 57 n. 2. Encore *Kyrakos de Kantzag*, trad. Brosset, 113.

36 Yāsī-Čemén, la vaste prairie (turco-persan), est le nom connu de tous les chroniqueurs, à l'exception de Sibṭ b. al-Djawzī, qui parle d'al-Waʿra; le sens (sol raboteux) de ce dernier mot n'a rien d'impossible, mais il est douteux qu'un mot arabe ait en cette région servi de nom de lieu. Le site est proche de celui du Köseh Dagh où, treize ans plus tard, les Mongols devaient forcer l'entrée de l'Etat seldjuqide.

37 Nous trouvons là, et encore infra, l'expression de l'orgueil syrien et du mépris envers les gens de Rūm qui devait une fois le danger khwārizmien passé, entrainer pour son malheur al-Kāmil, avec les autres Ayyubides, dans une tentative de conquête de l'Asie Mineure.

38 Bédouins, utiles contre d'autres cavaliers légers. Cf. *Bericht*, 62.

39 La zône montagneuse de l'Etat grec de Trébizonde.

40 ʿAbdallaṭīf nous donne donc de la bataille trois récits. On peut faire abstraction du premier, bref et peu précis. Au deuxième, qui précède, il faut ajouter le troisième, qu'on va lire un peu plus loin, et qui le complète en partie, sans le contredire. Toutes les sources s'accordent sur le premier combat, à l'exception d'Ibn Bībī qui évidemment le présente sous des couleurs plus satisfaisantes pour l'amour-propre des gens de Rūm. Elles le sont aussi sur l'intervalle qui le sépare de la bataille décisive et, en gros, sur le déroulement de celle-ci: d'abord attaque victorieuse des Syriens sur ce qui était resté en arrière de l'armée khwārizmienne et fuite du Khwārizmshāh, entassement des vaincus dans les gorges et fuite de beaucoup vers Trébizonde.

41 Il faut intervertir l'ordre des deux places dans l'itinéraire de Djalāl al-dīn, Manāzgird se trouvant à l'ouest d'Akhlāṭ.

42 La principauté fut annexée et le prince exécuté.

43 Pas de recoupement; al-Ashraf ne resta pas longtemps en Orient.

44 Chez les Seldjuqides, on eut l'impression bientôt, au contraire, qu'al-Ashraf se désintéressait de la ville ruinée, et on l'occupa, sans qu'il parût s'en soucier beaucoup. C'est sous l'administration seldjuqide que des efforts plus précis, à notre connaissance, furent faits pour le relèvement de la ville.

45 Voir note 40.

46 Nasawī 217 le dit brun et petit, mais d'air turc. La correction de Ghiyāth en Rukn peut-être de Dhahabī; c'est de Rukn al-dīn que Nasawī 26 vante la beauté.

47 Ce trait, s'il a quelque réalité, s'applique sans doute uniquement aux bandes errant à la suite de Djalāl al-dīn dans des conditions de vie anormales; en tous cas pas à la population du Khwārizm proprement dit.

48 Je ne peux recouper l'épisode.

49 L'usage de ce terme m'est inconnu; il s'agit évidemment d'un signe de garantie.

50 Y a-t-il erreur de copie, ou Djalāl al-dīn aurait-il adopté la *pāīẓa*, toujours considérée comme propre aux Mongols?

51 Nasawī, 112-13 et 121-2 met à juste titre quelqu' intervalle entre la bataille où fut capturé Sheluh (1225) et la prise de Tiflis (1227). Il est impossible d'identifier sûrement celles des forteresses géorgiennes auxquelles se rapportent les récits recueillis par ʿAbdallaṭīf; je ne connais pas non plus Ibn al-Sadīd; sur l'ensemble voir surtout M. F. Brosset, *Histoire de la Géorgie*, trad. française, I, 497-507, qui confirme, bien que d'autre manière, le désaccord ou le malentendu entre le vieil 'atabek' géorgien Ivane et le chef militaire Shilwa (Shilūh); voir aussi la discussion, dans les notes pp. 498-99, d'autres sources (Ibn al-Athīr, Giragos, Orbélian).

52 Que les Khwārizmiens n'ont pas de *dīwān* signifie qu'ils n'ont pas de régistre d'enrôlement des troupes ni par conséquent de soldes; cela ne se conçoit que trop bien dans les conditions de leurs équipées et ne s'applique bien entendu pas au régime khwārizmien proprement dit au Khwārizm avant les Mongols. Cf. un alinéa parallèle dans Somogyi, art. cit., 129-30.

53 C'est l'impression transmise par toutes les sources, ou peu s'en faut.

54 Le roi dont ʿAbdallaṭīf ignore le nom est sans doute le Sultan mamluk de Delhi Iltutmish. Le départ d'Inde de Djalāl al-dīn est en réalité de trois ans postérieur à sa défaite sur l'Indus par Djinghiz-Khān.

55 Ce détail dans Nasawī, 95.

56 Rien dans Nasawī sur ces deux rois. Djalāl al-dīn s'entendit en fait avec le Qarakhitaï Burāq Ḥādjib qui s'était rendu maître du pays, et poussa vers le Fārs, où l'atabek Saʿd aussi lui fit hommage, et l'emmena combattre sinon Bagdad du moins la province califale du Khūzistān (mais je ne peux rien trouver sur Shahrābād, nom peut-être corrompu).

57 Pas d'autre source.

58 Cf. Nasawī 72 sq. et 105 sq., qui ignore cependant les relations à ce sujet avec le Califat.

Rien ne s'oppose à ce que la suite de cet alinéa soit encore bien de ʿAbdallaṭīf; elle est cependant une addition marginale dans l'autographe de Dhahabī.

60 Un exemple dans Nasawī-Houdas, 200.

61 Sur ces faits, toutes références dans B. Spuler, *Die Mongolen in Iran*, 3e éd. (1968) 33.

SIR GERARD CLAUSON

A Late Uyğur Family Archive

The invitation to contribute to a volume in memory of my old friend Vladimir Minorsky gave me great pleasure. He was a living example of the close ties between Orientalists in the country of his birth and that of his adoption. No one who was privileged to be present on that historic occasion will ever forget the friendly warmth of his reunion with his old friends in the great hall of Moscow University at the International Congress of Orientalists in 1960. To his memory I dedicate, as a British scholar, this study of one of the treasures of the Leningrad branch of the Institute of the Peoples of Asia.

The document transcribed below (where the correct transcription of a word is uncertain it is preceded by (P U), i.e. 'pronunciation uncertain') was acquired by N. N. Krotkov, the Russian Consul General in Urumchi, Chinese Turkestan, in the first decade of this century, and has been preserved ever since in the manuscript collection of what is now the Leningrad branch of the Institute of the Peoples of Asia under the catalogue number SJ$\frac{\text{Kr.4}}{638}$ Packet 8. Krotkov was a keen collector of Uyğur manuscripts and sent several collections (judging by the catalogue numbers at least four) to Leningrad. Several of these documents were published by Professor V. V. Radlov (hereafter called R.) in *Uigurische Sprachdenkmäler*, edited by S. Ye. Malov (Leningrad 1928) (hereafter called *USp.*). In particular *USp. 107-127* are business documents from his third collection, in which two of the persons mentioned in this document also appear. The person most often mentioned is Inançu (R. spelt this *Inetschi*, which Malov in his Uyğur texts spelt *Inençi*, but Inançu is the normal spelling). *USp. 114* is a contract for the purchase of a slave by him; he is also mentioned in *115-121*; and *USp. 125* refers to a payment by Basa Toğrıl.

The present document is a roll of coated paper 289 cm (nearly 10 ft) long, but the text ends 22 cm before the end and the rest is blank. It is incomplete at the beginning, and is different in character from the documents published in *USp.* since those are original contracts and the like, while this roll contains copies of seven separate but interconnected documents, hereafter referred to as I to VII (the last perhaps an appendix to VI and not a separate document), of the first of which only a few damaged lines have survived.

In its present state the roll contains the whole or part of 200 lines; the first eight are more or less fragmentary and some letters are missing from the beginnings of nearly all the lines from 9 to 53 and some lines from 57 to 100. The remainder are complete.

The roll is made up of five sheets of paper of unequal length gummed together. The joins occur between lines 66/67; 94/95; 136/137 and 184/185. The individual documents begin: I before line 1; II line 11; III line 80; IV line 104; V line 125; VI line 137; VII line 187. It will be seen that the documents too are of unequal length but that only VI begins on a new sheet. Some time may have elapsed between the completion of the copying of V and the attachment of a new sheet, but the roll seems to be in the same hand throughout. Lines 185 to the end are in a rather larger hand than the rest, which suggests that the scribe had to stop at the end of the fourth sheet to attach a new one and continued to copy VI in a slightly larger hand.

As long ago as 1920 R. published a transcription and translation of the first 40 lines in *Aziatskiy Musey Rossiskoy Akademii Nauk, 1818–1918, Kratkaya Pamyatka* ('The Asiatic Museum of the Russian Academy of Sciences, 1818–1918, a Short Historical Note') (Petrograd 1920) 37, and quoted some other passages from it in his manuscript dictionary of Uyğur, still preserved in the Institute. It is clear that at that time some words which have since disappeared owing to the flaking off of the coated surface were still legible. In the transcription below words which were read by R. but are no longer legible are entered in square brackets with (R.) in the margin; other words in square brackets are conjectural reconstructions of the text. A facsimile of the MS. about half the size of the original was published as an appendix (pp. 241ff.) to D.I. Tikhonov's *Khozyaystvo i Obshchestvenniy Stroy Uygurskogo Gosudarstva X-XIV vv.* ('The Economy and Social Structure of the Uyğur Kingdom of the 10th to 14th centuries') (Leningrad 1966) and a slightly smaller facsimile was republished with transcription (including R.'s readings), translation, notes and vocabulary by E. R. Tenishev (hereafter referred to as T.) in an article entitled *Khozaystvenniye Zapisi na Drevneuygurskom Yazyke* ('Economic Documents in the Old Uyğur Language') in *Issledovaniya po Grammatike i Leksike Tyurkskikh Yazykov* ('Researches in the Grammar and Lexicon of the Turkish Languages') (Tashkent 1966) 37ff. My excuse for republishing this text so soon is that it is of great interest from several points of view, that it is difficult even for Soviet scholars, and almost impossible for Western scholars, to get hold of a book published in Tashkent in a limited edition of 650 copies (I owe my own copy to the generosity of my friend, S. G. Klyashtornyi of the Leningrad Institute) and that I think that I have found better readings than T. for some of the more difficult words and phrases.

Without particulars, which are unlikely to be available, of the circumstances in which the MS. was found, it is impossible to date it closely, but there is no reason to disagree with R.'s opinion that it belongs to the fourteenth century, and, for the reasons stated below, is some decades later than the connected business documents published in *USp.* It contains a number of late forms like *kardaş* (for *karındas*), *kapu* (for *kapuğ*) and *yetgür-* (for *yétür-*) which are unusual in Uyğur. It is appallingly difficult to read. The late Uyğur cursive script is one of the most imperfect media for representing language that has ever been devised, and although contemporaries whose personal vocabulary was the same as that of the compiler, and who knew more or less what the roll might be expected to contain, may have read it without too much difficulty, modern scholars can read it only by a series of subjective judgements in the light of the context. To take one simple example, T. reads the fourth word in line 10 *kış* 'winter'; to me the context requires *kız* 'girl', both words would be written in exactly the same way. There are particular difficulties about reading Proper Names (P.N.) which are not at the same time common nouns like *Toğrıl* and *Sevinç*. It would be uncivil of me to point out in every case where I have chosen a different reading from T., but I must record the fact that I should have been completely baffled by some words if he had not already divined the right reading.

Most of the persons mentioned in this roll belong to at least one generation later than those mentioned in *USp. 107-127*. When it was compiled Inançu was already dead; indeed he must have been dead for some time since the debts incurred to pay for the weddings of his children had already assumed massive proportions (see VI). Wherever he is mentioned he is described as *apam. Apa:* originally meant rather vaguely 'ancestor' or more precisely 'grandfather'; in the mediaeval period it came to mean 'elder sister' (which had originally been *eke:*); but Inançu was obviously a man, and almost certainly the grandfather of the compiler of the roll, who speaks of himself in the 1st Person. It is possible that the compiler was also the scribe who wrote the roll, but there are obvious signs of careless copying, see in particular the preliminary note to VI, of which the actual compiler is unlikely to have been guilty.

Two of the documents relate to funerals, IV to that of Inançu himself, and V to that of three relatives of the compiler; the financial summary in V aggregates the cost of the two funerals, and the postscript to VI also recapitulates the expenditure on a funeral which may or may not be that referred to in V.

Four of the other documents, I, II, III, and VI, relate to expenditure on weddings. It appears from lines 171ff. that, apart from two daughters who are specifically excluded, Inançu had two sons and three daughters, all of whom got married, but it is not clear that any of the documents relate to expenditure on these weddings, though some very well may. III seems to relate to expenditure on the wedding of the daughter of a man called Toğrıl 23 years previously, but there is nothing to show what relation, if any, she was to Inançu. The four documents fall into two classes, there are resemblances between I and II and close resemblances between III and VI, but not many between the two groups.

Four of the documents contain dates. III is described as a report for the Pig (12th) Year and refers to a marriage which took place 23 years earlier and a funeral which took place 13 years earlier. I records a wedding in the 9th month of the Hare (4th) Year. IV refers to a funeral which took place on the 1st of the 3rd month of the Snake (6th) Year. The financial debts arising from this funeral were liquidated, respectively, 20 months later (in the Sheep Year), 3 years and 4 months later (in the Ape Year) and four years later (in the Hen Year). V refers to deaths which took place on the 11th of the 10th month of the Sheep (8th) Year. The debts incurred in respect of the funeral were met a good deal later, but no precise date can be calculated. VI refers to a wedding which took place in the 8th month of the Sheep Year.

There is no means of determining precisely how many 12-year cycles these events cover; what is certain is that the wedding and funeral mentioned in III occurred in the preceding cycle; and as III was copied after I it is likely that the dates of both belong to the same cycle. If the order of copying is significant, Inançu's funeral (IV) must have occurred in the following cycle, and as the debts in respect of that funeral and the funeral referred to in V were dealt with in a single document both funerals must have taken place in the same cycle, but the debt in grain mentioned in V had grown to such dimensions by the time the document was written that it cannot have been written until some date in the next cycle. There is no good reason for supposing that the wedding referred to in VI did not occur in the same cycle as the funeral in V, but here too the volume of debts suggests that the actual document was written sometime in the next cycle. The dates can therefore tentatively be tabulated as follows:

Year	*1st Cycle*	*2nd Cycle*	*3rd Cycle*	*4th Cycle*
Mouse	wedding of Toğrıl's daughter (III)			earliest possible date of V (and VI?)
Ox				
Tiger				
Hare		wedding in I		
Dragon				
Snake			funeral of Inançu (IV)	
Horse				
Sheep			part debt repaid (IV) death of three (V) wedding (VI)	
Ape			part debt repaid (IV)	
Hen			part debt repaid (IV)	
Dog	funeral in III			
Pig		date of III		

The innumerable financial transactions recorded in these documents are all stated in a currency of three denominations *yastuk*, *sıtır* and *bakır*, the words *kümüş* or *tartma kümüş* being occasionally appended. There can be little doubt that *bakır* was the Chinese copper cash; traditionally in China this was the only coin in circulation, the next denomination above it being the *tael* (Chinese ounce) of silver, which was not a coin but an ingot. In the T'ang Dynasty it was laid down that the cash should be one-tenth of a tael's weight of copper and that the tael of silver should be worth 1,000 cash, making silver worth exactly 100 times as much as copper (in London today, 1 September 1967, it is about 57 times, but both prices vary so widely that it is impossible to state a 'normal' modern relationship). In fact these weights and rate of exchange were by no means constant, in particular some Sung and Yüan dynasty copper coins were heavier, 'double cash' and the like. The documents never show sums in *bakır* of more than single figures, so it can safely be assumed that ten went to the *sıtır*. This word, invariably spelt *stir*, is a Sogdian loan word, ultimately derived from the Greek word *statēr*; there can be little doubt that it was merely a currency unit and not an actual coin. The highest number of *sıtır* mentioned is 42, so it is reasonable to assume that 50 went to the *yastuk*, literally 'pillow', but here metaphorically 'a pillow-shaped ingot', no doubt a silver tael. This rate of exchange is confirmed by the calculation of interest in III; it gives 500 *bakır* to the silver tael, a plausible rate of exchange for the Yüan dynasty, during the rule of which the roll must have been written. *Kümüş*, literally 'silver', in this context seems to mean 'in coin' as opposed to 'in paper money' and *tartma kümüş* 'coin by weight' or 'minted coin'.

The prices quoted show that this currency had a very high purchasing power by modern standards. So far as foodstuffs are concerned sheep cost 2 *sıtır* (*l. 95*), 10½ *bakır* (*ll. 150-1*) or 11 *bakır* (*l. 161*); the price in *l. 5* was probably 12½ *bakır* and in *l. 68* over 2 *sıtır* but these passages are damaged. The price of an ox for slaughter was 4 *sıtır*, 6 *bakır* (*l. 162*, with the sheep for 11 *bakır* in the same sentence) and of a horse 2 *sıtır* (*l. 70*); this must have been a horse for slaughter; a riding or pack horse could hardly have been as cheap. The price of grain (or wheat, *tarığ*) was 2 *sıtır*, 5 *bakır* (*ll. 72-3*) for a *shih*, conventionally in China 2½ bushels. Wine cost 8 *sıtır* for a *küp*, presumably 'a skin' (*l. 114*), but in *l. 71* a purchase of wine for 1½ *sıtır* is mentioned. These prices give a rough basis of comparison for the cost of other articles.

In some documents there are references to *asığ* 'interest', but when what has been borrowed is grain the word used is *tüş*. The phrase *asığı bını* (*ll. 101, 123*) obviously means 'interest and principal', the latter clearly a loan word from Chinese *pên* (Giles, *Chinese-English Dictionary*, No. 8846) which has precisely this meaning, among others. The rates of interest were not quite uniform, Sevinç (*l. 107*) lent half a *yastuk* at 20 per cent per annum, and the debt referred to in *ll. 97ff.* carried that rate, but Tokuz and Ögrünç (*ll. 108-11*) lent smaller sums at 2½ per cent a month, 30 per cent per annum. These were loans at simple interest, but the phrase in *ll. 134-5* seems to mean 'at compound interest'.

Before dealing with the actual texts in detail it will be useful to discuss certain words which occur more or less frequently, and fix their precise meanings. II and III are headed *ötüş* and IV and V *yuŋlağ ötüş*; *ötüş* also occurs elsewhere. The context shows that *ötüş* by itself means 'report', 'statement', and *yuŋlağ ötüş* 'statement of expenditure'. This is a common meaning of *ötük*, but *ötüş* does not seem to be noted elsewhere in this meaning; it is however impossible, except perhaps in *l. 127* to read the word otherwise than as *ötüş*.

Kabın occurs in all the documents relating to weddings. T. takes it as a word which occurs several times in *USp.*, 14, 13; 21, 13, etc., and is tentatively taken to be some kind of tax. That cannot possibly be the meaning here. The context shows clearly that it means 'a sum of money provided to meet the expenses of a wedding' or perhaps, more briefly, 'dowry'. It is no doubt a loan word from Chinese *chia* (Middle Chinese *ka*; Giles No. 1141) 'bride' and *pên* (see above). This word occurs in Iranian Xwarazmian as *kābīna* and in Persian as *kabīn*, *kābin*, *kābīn*, see G. Doerfer, *Türkische und Mongolische Elemente im Neupersischen*, III, 579 (Wiesbaden 1967).

The word *törülük* (and *törülüg*?) occurs equally frequently in the documents relating to funerals. *Törü*: (originally *törö*:) meant 'customary, traditional, or unwritten law', and so *törülük* must mean something like 'a ceremony prescribed by tradition (for funerals)' and *törülüg*, if it occurs, 'connected with such a ceremony'.

A good many of the purchases recorded are textiles and articles made of textiles. There is a wide range of such words in Kāşğarī's *Diwān Lugāti'l-Turk* (hereafter referred to as *Kaş.* followed by the volume and page in Atalay's translation), most of which are, as might be expected, loan words. Some of the words in these documents are easily recognized; *torku*: 'silk fabric, brocade' (*Kaş.*, I, 427); *çikin* 'silk; embroidered brocade embellished with gold' (*Kaş.*, I, 414); *böz* 'cotton cloth' (*Kaş.*, III, 122); *eşük* 'blanket, coverlet' (*Kaş.*, I, 72). Some words are less common, but still identifiable. *Altunluk* (*ll. 25, 31, 41*) qualified by 'scarlet, purple, or red' is given in the Chinese-Uyğur Dictionary of the fourteenth century as the Uyğur equivalent of 'gold embroidered brocade', see L. Ligeti, *Un Vocabulaire Sino-ouigour des Ming* (Budapest 1966) 129. *Éşgirti*, which occurs several times with slightly different spellings, is translated 'embroidered Chinese silk brocade' in *Kaş.*, I, 145; it is obviously a loan word and occurs, with various spellings in the Orkhon inscriptions (*IS3*, *IIN3*) and in other Uyğur texts. (PU) *ületü*: is otherwise noted only in *Kaş.*, I, 135 where it is translated 'a piece of silk which a man carries in his pocket to wipe his nose with'. The word which occurs in *ll. 60* and *167* preceded by (PU) *çuğ* and in *l. 92* preceded by a word which might be *tavar* is puzzling. The obvious reading is *örmen*, but this is a word, noted only in Uyğur, meaning 'a swelling, tumour' and such a meaning cannot be right here. One possible alternative is *örmek* which means 'a woven garment' in Çağatay and occurs in *USp. 31, 18*, probably in this sense: *örmen* is a possible Secondary form of this word and could perhaps mean 'woven fabric'. Another word which is fairly common and is qualified by 'purple, yellow, white, or red' is transcribed *çok* by T. and translated 'tassel, plume (for the hat), tuft' with a reference to Budagov's *Comparative Dictionary of the Turco-Tatar Dialects* (in Russian) (St Petersburg 1869) 495, where it is ascribed to the Tobolsk dialect and Kazan Tatar. This word also exists in Kırğız. This is a possible explanation but there is no early occurrence of such a word. A preferable reading seems to me to be *çuğ* which occurs in the Uyğur translation of the *Suvarṇaprabhāsasūtra* (*Suv.* 165, 20-1) and is translated 'a bag for merchandise' in *Kaş.*, III, 128; it also occurs in this meaning in several mediaeval authorities and some modern Siberian dialects. This meaning seems to me to suit the contexts better. Another difficult word is (PU) *çımatu* in *ll. 2* (?), *48-50*. T. connects it with the Türkmen word *çabıt*, 'a woman's silk robe'. It is qualified by three different words. T. reads the first *tama* and translates it 'cotton material', with a reference to Malov's notes on the *Codex Cumanicus* (not accessible to me) and R.'s *Wörterbuch*, III, 993, where a Sagai word with this meaning is quoted. This is not very plausible; no such word occurs in the *Codex Cumanicus*, where *tama* is the Arabic word *tamaʿ* 'envy'. It looks to me much more like *temen* 'a large (packing) needle' (*Kaş.*, I, 402). There is no difficulty about the second word *törtgil* 'rectangular'. T. reads the third as *üsgük* (*üzgük*) 'combed material' derived from *üz-* 'to tear apart'. If *temen* is right, the obvious reading is *üşgük* 'an awl'; this word is not noted elsewhere (nor is *üzgük*), but is a perfectly regular derived noun from *üş-* 'to pierce'. If these readings are right (PU) *çımatu* cannot be a kind of garment, but must be something like 'box, case, or packet' and is probably a Chinese loan word; the prices quoted, 1 *sıtır* for 'two packets of large needles' and 1 *sıtır* for 'two packets of awls and one rectangular packet of large needles' are reasonable, if these conjectures are correct.

The phrases *evdin ün-* (and *evdin ündür-*), literally 'to rise (and to raise) from the house', which occur several times, clearly mean 'to be provided (and to provide) from the family resources', as opposed to 'to borrow from someone else'.

Quantities of grain are expressed in *şık*. This is the Chinese word *shih* (Giles, No. 9,964), literally 'a stone', and, as a measure of capacity, 'an amount equal to 10 *küri*: (in Chinese *tou* (Giles, 11,427), conventionally 'a peck'), that is conventionally $2\frac{1}{2}$ bushels, but the actual quantity probably varied from time to time.

In concluding this introduction, might I remind my readers of the Xākānī proverb *yazma:s atım yağmur, yaŋılma:s bilge: yaŋku*: 'the only shot that never misses is the rain, the only scholar that never makes a mistake is the echo'. *Kaş.*, III, 379, 19?

I

line 1] *sıtır altı* [*bakırka*]
[*al*]*dı. bir sıtırka* (PU) *temen çım*[*atu*. . . .
(R) [*bak*]*ırka aldı. üç yastuk* [. . . . .
[. . . . . . .] (PU) *nuŋ yetgekni* [. . . . .
[?*toy*]*dakı tört koynka* (PU) *béş sıtır bérdi*
[. . . . . . .] *sıtırka kolup bérmeyük Kutluğ*
[. . . . . . .] (PU) *körgeni* (PU) *sab bérdi. bir yastuk*
(PU) *el*(*l*)*ig sıtır kabın adırıp bir*
yastuk yéti yegirmi sıtır tört bakır
evdin ündi. bu kız [*nı*?] *tavışgan* [*yıl*]
(R) [*tokuzunç ay*] *küdegüke bérdim.*

This text is clearly the end of a document relating to the marriage of a girl (see *ll. 10-11*) and must have been very like II; there are direct parallels between *ll. 2* and *49*; *4* and *70*; *8* and *74*. *Line 5* can perhaps be restored by a comparison with *l. 68*. *Lines 6* and *7* are most obscure and the readings are uncertain; *Kutluğ* is probably here a Proper Name; *körge* means 'a wooden dish' (*Kaş.*, I, 430), but the word is not recorded in Uyğur and does not fit the context; for *sab* see the note on *l. 174*. *Yetgek* (*l. 4*) means 'a sack, or bale' (*Kaş.*, III, 70).

(1-2) he bought . . . for . . . *sıtır*, six (*bakır*). (2-3) He bought a needle-case (?) for one *sıtır* and (something else) for . . . *bakır*. (4) For 3 *yastuk* . . . a sack for . . . . (5) He gave 5 (?) *sıtır* for four sheep for the [wedding feast?] . . . asking for . . . at . . . *sıtır*, he did not give (it) . . . . (7ff.) Analysing the dowry of 1 *yastuk* 40 (?) *sıtır*, 1 *yastuk*, 17 *sıtır*, 4 *bakır* came from the family resources. I gave this girl to the bridegroom in the 9th month of the Hare (4th) year.

II

line 12 [ ]*niŋ* (PU) *sab ötüşi. kabın iki*
(R) [*yastu*]*k b*[*éş*] *kırk sıtır kümüş aldım*

(R) [yét]i otuz sıtır kümüşke (PU) şırağ aldım. iki
(R) [yegirm]i sıtırka Koçodın ürüŋ yinçü alıp
(R) [......] (PU) tuşağlığ yinçü tokuz sıtır béş b[akır]
(R) -ka]... dbalığ toyındın bir sıtır iki
(R) bakırka yérlig (PU) sırağka yetgek aldım
[...] sıtır üç bakırka sekiz şişir
(R) [aldı]m. (PU) kodıkni bir sıtırka aldım.
(R) [bir] sıtır yéti bakırka tört monçuk
(R) [ald]ım. iki bakır (PU) al... nı iki sıtır [altı]
(R) [bakı]rka aldım. uluğ közüŋü üç sıtır
(R) [sekiz] bakırka aldım. kiçig közüŋü bir
(R) [sıtır]ka aldım. al altunluk yéti sıtır-
[-ka] aldım. béş sıtır béş bakırka
[.....]bim aldım. iki sıtır üç bakırka
[.....]lik (?) aldım. altı sıtırka
[.....]çuğ kögüzlük aldım. iki yegirmi
[sıtır]ka yalmalığ könni aldım.
[.....] tonluğ yipgin altunluk tört
(R) [sıtır]ka aldım. iki (PU) sunma tonka
[.....]gülük torkunı üç sıtırka aldım
[.....] yalmaka bir yarım sıtırka (PU) kökülüg
[?torku] aldım. altı sıtırka urumluğ
[.....] aldım. (PU) samsıka (PU) kökülüg torku
[bir ya]rım sıtırka aldım. tavar eşük
[.....] sıtırka aldım (PU) evlig eşükke
[.....]ünçüglüg yipgin çuğnı iki sıtır
(R) [...bakır]ka aldım. yastukluğ kızıl
(R) [altun]luk bir sıtırka aldım. bir
[?sıtır]ka çikin kirlik aldım. bir yarım
[?sıtır]ka iki kula sağri, üç sıtırka
[.....] kulaç yolak eşükke béş yinçge
[.....] tört sıtırka aldim. iki
[.....] (PU) ükmen tört sıtırka aldım
iki pulad biçek altı bakırka aldım
iki (PU) temen (PU) çimatu bir sıtırka aldım
iki (PU) üşgek (PU) çimatu bir törtgil
(PU) temen (PU) çımatu bir sıtırka aldım.
yastukka (PU) turğu bir teŋ (PU) yük
[.....] üç bakırka aldım. başğakka

[. . . . .]*luk yarılğuka* (PU) *yağırlık iki*
bürgelüg kenzini yéti bakırka aldim.
(PU) *yeŋ* (PU) *ağızlığ yakalığ bir ületü*
yipgin çuğ tört bakırka aldım.
[PU *yét*]*i bakırka yarık aldım. béş bakır*
[*-k*]*a kav aldım. béş bakırka bir kiş*
[*al*]*dım. sekiz bakırka sağrı etük bir*
[PU *sıt*]*ırka kızıl cuğ* (PU) *örmek aldım. tört*
bakırka iki bilek (PU) *batu aldım. tört*
[*bi*]*lek sata iki bakırka aldım. yürüŋ*
(PU) *sata üç bakırka aldım. iki çikin*
(PU)*-ni* (PU) *altı sıtır kümüşke tört*
büküm (PU) *karın töşek iki sıtır*
[*küm*]*üşke* (PU) *tartbın* (PU) *karın töşek*
[*al*]*dım. toydakı koynka* (PU) *alı*
(PU) *etçi oğlı* (PU) *Tamandın üç koynnı*
[*?al*]*tı sıtır béş bakırka aldım.*
M. . . . rdın iki sıtırka at aldım.
bir yarım sıtırka bor aldım. bir
(R) [*şık*] *tarığnı iki yarım sıtırka aldım*
iki yastuk béş kırk sitır kabın
adırıp evdin ünmişi bir kırk
sıtır boldı. mundın taş sevdi atlığ
béş otuz yaşlığ (PU) *yigit* (PU) *urum*
böz tokır ked bözci kulnı
inim (PU) *içinde meni tokıp kızka*
b[*é*]*rdi.*

This is a fairly detailed report on financial transactions in connexion with the wedding of a girl. The parallels to the fragment of I suggest that it was something like a standard form. It starts (*ll. 12-13*) with a statement of the amount of the dowry, 2 *yastuk*, 35 *sıtır*, which is restated in *l. 73*, and is identical with the dowry stated in VI (*l. 138*). This is followed by a roughly classified list of goods bought for the bride: (1) personal ornaments (*ll. 14-22*); (2) mirrors, textiles, clothing and the like (*ll. 22-45*; some unidentifiable owing to lacunae in the text); (3) household equipment and the like (*ll. 45-67*). Next follows a list of the provisions bought for the wedding feast (*ll. 67-72*). The amount of the dowry is then restated, together with the amount provided from the family resources. The rest was presumably borrowed. Finally a wedding present in kind, an expert weaver, is mentioned. There is one obvious difficulty about the present transcription. If the expenditure is added up it comes to 143 *sıtır*, 124 *bakır*, that is 3 *yastuk*, 5 *sıtır*, 4 *bakır* not including the missing figures in *ll. 19, 38*, and *40*, that is at least 20 *sıtır*, 4 *bakır* more than the dowry. The error probably occurred in the two very high figures in *ll. 14, 15*, where we are dependent on R.'s readings of words no longer legible. If *iki* were read in both places the total would be 23 *sıtır* less; other misreadings too are possible.

l. 12 R. read the missing word as *ay* and translated it 'month'; this is not plausible. A P.N. seems to be required. For *sab* see the note on *l. 174*.

l. 14 The fourth word represents an object bought for a large sum, 27 *sıtır*, the price of say 25 sheep or 6 oxen for slaughter. The word occurs both here and in *l. 18*; here there are two dots, implying *ş*-, under the first letter; the rest of the word is ambiguous, *-a-*/*-i-*, *-n-*/*-r-*, *-k-*/*-ğ*. T. reads *şırağ* and takes it to be a secondary form of Persian *çirāg* 'a lamp'. He is right to the extent that if it begins with *ş*- it is almost certainly a loan word, but it is almost incredible that a lamp should be given pride of place at such a high price, and it seems likelier that it is some article of personal adornment which cannot now be identified.

ll. 15-23 There are close parallels between the objects listed here and a list of precious objects in *Suv.* 515, 16ff.: gold, silver, beryl (*vayduri*, Sanskrit *vaidūrya*), (PU) *sababır*, *sisir* (or *şişir?*), (PU) *batu*, coral (*sata*, *Kaş.*, III, 218), (PU) *kopık*, turquoise (*çaş*, in *Kaş.*, I, 330 *çaş*), jade (*kaş*), pearls (*yinçu*), beads (*monçuk*).

l. 16 The first missing word probably qualified the second. The likeliest transcription of the latter is *tuşağliğ*. *Tuşağ* (*Kaş.*, I, 411) properly means 'a horse's hobble', but in this context might mean 'a string, or chain' for pearls, qualified by some such word as 'gold' or 'silver'.

l. 17 *Toyın* means 'a Buddhist monk'; the preceding word, which has a Tibetan look, might describe either the place from which he came or the sect to which he belonged. T. reads it *Şardpalığ*, but the first letter does not look like *S* or *Ş*, it might, for example, be *T* and the *-r-* is not obvious, and in a Tibetan word would be embarrassing; some spelling like *Tadpalığ* seems likelier.

l. 18 *Yérlig* 'local, native' is the likeliest reading of the word before (PU) *sırağ*.

l. 19 *Şişir* (with the *ş*'s marked) is translated *ma nao* 'cornelian' (Giles, *Chinese-English Dictionary* Nos. 7682, 8160) in the *Chinese-Uyğur Dictionary of the 14th Century*, Ligeti, op. cit., 198.

l. 20 (PU) *kodık* is an error for the word spelt (PU) *kopık* in *Suv.* and that Dictionary, where it is translated *ma p'o*, 'amber' (Giles Nos. 7682, 9018), Ligeti, 167.
l. 22 T. reads the fourth word as *altun* and takes the third, *bakır*, to mean 'the weight of a copper cash', but it is inconceivable that gold should have been bought for thirteen times its weight in copper. The rest of the word after *al* is hard to read, but does not look very like *-tun*; probably we have here the name of some (copper) implement or vessel.
l. 27, l. 28 The mutilated names of the articles mentioned at the beginning of these lines cannot be restored.
l. 29 *Kögüzlük*, though not recorded elsewhere must mean 'something worn on the chest'; the preceding word is lost except for the end; if *-cuğ* it was probably an Adjective qualifying *kögüzlük*, if *-çuk* probably some other article of apparel.
l. 30 *Yalma*: (see also *l. 34*) was a quilted or padded coat worn either as body armour (see Orkhon inscription *IE* 33) or as a protection against rain and cold (see *Kaş.*, III, 34); 'leather' (*kön*) would be an appropriate component of it.
l. 31 *Yipgin* is translated 'purple' in *Kaş.*, III, 37; it is a rather common word. The first, lost, word must have qualified *tonluğ* (purple gold-shot brocade) 'for a . . . garment'.
l. 32 The fourth word is completely ambiguous. T. transcribes *surma*, and translates it 'quilted', quoting a word *sırma* with this meaning in Malov's observations on the *Codex Cumanicus*, but so far as I am aware no such word exists either in that text or elsewhere. *Sun-* means 'to stretch out', hence 'to offer, present', so the word might be *sunma* (garments) 'for presentation as gifts', but this is not very convincing.
l. 33 The first word might be something like *tikgülük* or *tikilgülük* 'to be sewn into' (garments).
l. 34 (PU) *kökülüg* also occurs in *ll. 36* and *90* followed by *torku* 'brocade'. T. plausibly suggests that (PU) *kökü* is a Chinese loan word; there is in fact no evidence of the existence of a native Turkish word of this form. He also suggests that it means 'domestic, home-produced' as opposed to 'imported', but this is a mere conjecture.
l. 35 [*Torku*] can be restored with confidence. T. is no doubt right in taking *urumluğ* as meaning 'belonging to Rome', i.e. Byzantine; whatever it was, perhaps a fabric or garment, it was rather costly, 6 *sıtır*, the price of 5 or 6 sheep.
l. 36 *Samsı/samzı* is a Chinese loan word surviving in Sarığ Yuğur with

the meaning 'fabric, material'; it must here mean 'a silk garment' of some kind.

l. 37 *Eşük* means 'a blanket, or coverlet' (*Kaş.*, I, 72). The antithesis between *tavar* here and (PU) *evlig* in *l. 38* suggests that *tavar*, a word with several meanings, here means 'horse' and *evlig* 'for use in the home'.

l. 39 Two or three letters are missing at the beginning of the line and the first surviving letters are probably the end of a word. T.'s reading *öçüklüg*, and translation 'faded', are unconvincing. *Öçük*, if it existed, would be an Adjective meaning 'extinguished' and could hardly take the Suffix *-lüg*.

l. 40 *Yastukluğ* here has its literal meaning 'for a pillow', and has no connexion with *yastuk* as a currency unit.

l. 42 *Kirlik* is a Concrete Noun in *-lik* from *kir* 'dirt', not recorded elsewhere, which must mean something like 'duster' or 'dust cover'.

l. 43 *Sağrı*, which later acquired other meanings, originally meant 'raw hide' (*Kaş.*, I, 421). See also *l. 59*.

ll. 43-5 The grammar becomes rugged after *sağrı*; *eşükke* is perhaps an error for *eşük aldım*, otherwise there seem to be two sums of money for one set of articles. R. read *sekiz* 'eight' at the beginning of *l. 44*, but as *kulaç* is 'a fathom', about two yards, this is improbable unless *eşük* here means 'blanketing material'; but 3 *sıtır* seems a low price for sixteen yards of blanketing, as the price of one horse blanket was at least one *sıtır*, if not more. *Yolak* is 'striped' (*Kaş.*, III, 17). R. read *tavar* at the beginning of *l. 45*, which T. translated 'silk', but this is an unlikely meaning for *tavar* here (compare *ll. 37* and *193*), and the word may well have been *torku*, of which the *-u* still seems to survive in the facsimile.

l. 46 The first word is missing, the sum involved, 4 *sıtır* is fairly high, and it might be *yegirmi*, converting 'two' to 'twelve'; alternatively it might be a word qualifying the next one, which T. translates 'harvest' quoting *Budagov*, I, 148, where the word is described as 'Çağatay'. It also occurs in Pavet de Courteille, but no earlier Çag. authority. 'Harvest' is obviously inappropriate, but the word might be a Nomen Instrumenti in *-men* from *ük-* meaning 'an instrument for heaping up', perhaps a rake or the like.

l. 47 The second word is the Persian word *pulād* 'steel'. Six *bakır* seems a modest price for two steel knives.

ll. 48-50 See the preliminary note on the goods mentioned in this sentence.

ll. 51-2 This sentence is puzzling. In the mediaeval period *bir teŋ yük* came to mean 'half a load', i.e. one of two equal parts of a load put across a pack animal; if that is the meaning here, the missing word at the beginning of *l. 53* might have been something like 'wool', *turğu* should be read rather than *torku* and the whole might mean something like 'half a load of (wool?) for stuffing pillows'.

ll. 52-4 T. is probably right in taking *kenẓi* as the Chinese loan word spelt *kenẓi*: and translated 'a Chinese woven fabric of mixed colours' in *Kaş.*, I, 422, the two pieces of this material being particularized in the preceding phrases. T. fell into the trap of translating *başğak* 'thigh', quoting *Kaş.*, I, 470, but that word is a scribal error for *sapğak* which had a slightly different meaning. *Başğak* here seems to be a noun in *-ğak* derived from *ba:ş* 'a wound' (*Kaş.*, III, 151) not noted elsewhere and meaning something like 'injury'; the word parallel to it is *yarılğu*, also not noted elsewhere but a Deverbal Noun in *-ğu* from *yarıl-* meaning 'a split, or tear'. *Yağırlık* is a Concrete Noun in *-lık* from *yagır* 'a saddle gall' (*Kaş.*, III, 9) and must mean something like 'a dressing for a saddle gall', of the word parallel to it only *-luk* is legible. *Bürgelüg*, also not noted elsewhere, is ultimately derived from *bür-* 'to twist, wind' (*Kaş.*, II, 6) and must mean something like 'for use as a bandage'.

l. 55-6 The grammar is obscure, but the small sum involved, 4 *bakır*, suggests that only two objects are mentioned, a purple bag and a silk handkerchief, qualified by the preceding words, the reading of which is doubtful. If correctly read they could mean 'to be put in the mouth of the sleeve' and 'with a border', but this is rather dubious.

l. 57 *Yarık* is a generic term for 'chain mail' and 'plate armour' (*Kaş.*, III, 15); it might here mean 'breast plate', but 7 *bakır* is a small sum, and it may have some other meaning which has not survived.

l. 58 *Kav* is 'tinder' (*Kaş.*, III, 155) and *kiş* 'a sable skin' (*Kaş.*, III, 126).

ll. 60-3 Both (PU) *batu* and *sata* ('coral') appear in the list of precious things in *Suv.* (see the note on *l. 15*). *Bilek* means 'wrist', a common word; T. takes the two phrases to mean 'a *batu* bracelet' and 'a coral bracelet', but this is grammatically difficult, and I am inclined to think that it is here used metaphorically for 'a branch' (of *batu*, and coral).

l. 64 The first word is not clear; T. takes it to be the Accusative Suffix *-ni*, but it looks longer than that and might be a Noun qualified by 'silk'. The text of this sentence seems to be corrupt, two sums of money and three sets of goods being mentioned, the price of the third seems to have been omitted. *Töşek* is 'a mattress' (*Kaş.*, I, 387); *büküm* 'a fold, or roll' might properly be associated with it. The word preceding *töşek* twice is very difficult; T. reads *kırığ* and translates it 'piece, edge, border' quoting R.'s

Wörterbüch, II, 270, but there are several errors here; the last letter is *-n*, marked with a superscript dot in *l. 66*, not *-ğ*; *kıruk* (so to be read) is an Adjective, 'broken, crippled', not a Noun; the meaning 'edge, border' belongs to *kıḏığ* for which *kırığ* in the Çagatay dictionaries is a scribal error, and finally the 'alternative form' *kırağ*, which he quotes, is a corruption of the Arabic word *qaraq* and means 'a waterless desert', as stated in *Sanglax*, 295, v. 7. The first vowel might be either *-a-* or *-i-*, and the second consonant *-ç-*, *-n-* or *-r-*; neither *kaçın* nor *kanın* are known, or even probable, words; *karın* 'belly' is difficult to fit into the context. The second word in *l. 66* is completely obscure; no possible readings produce a word which looks Turkish.

ll. 67ff The second word in *l. 68* must be *oğlı* 'son of', which implies that the following word is a P.N. perhaps *Taman*, cf. *l. 199*. T. reads the preceding words as *Ali etçi* "Alī (Arabic P.N.) the butcher'; this is not entirely satisfactory, but I cannot offer any better suggestion.

l. 70 T. reads the first word *Masar*; with initial *M-* it cannot be a Turkish P.N., so is presumably a foreign one.

l. 76 The last two words are most obscure. T.'s explanation, 'wild hemp' (a modern meaning of a word which properly means 'string' and is derived from *çig-* 'to tie') and 'grass' (the suggested meaning of *oru* as a derivative from *or-* 'to reap') is not plausible. I am inclined to think that they are *yigit Urum* (cf. *l. 35*) 'a young man' (*böz tokır*, 'who weaves cloth') in the Byzantine (style), but this is purely conjectural.

l. 78 *içinde meni tokıp* might mean 'including me in the transaction', but this is rather dubious.

(*12*) Periodical (?) report of .... I received 2 *yastuk*, 35 *sıtır* (in cash) (to spend) as a dowry. I bought a .... for 27 *sıtır* in cash. (*15*) I bought white pearls from Koço for 12 *sıtır*, pearls on a .... chain(?) for 9 *sıtır*, 5 *bakır*, and a local sack for the .... from the Buddhist monk of .... for 1 *sıtır*, 2 *bakır*. For .... *sıtır*, 3 *bakır* I bought eight (pieces of) cornelian. (*20*) I bought amber for 1 *sıtır*, I bought four beads for 1 *sıtır*, 7 *bakır*. I bought two copper .... for 2 *sıtır*, 6 *bakır*. I bought a big mirror for 3 *sıtır*, 8 *bakır*. I bought a small mirror for 1 *sıtır*. (*25*) I bought scarlet gold-shot brocade for 7 *sıtır*. For 5 *sıtır*, 5 *bakır* I bought a .... For 2 *sıtır*, 3 *bakır* I bought a .... For 6 *sıtır* I bought a .... breastplate (or chest protector?). (*30*) for 12 *sıtır* I bought leather for a padded coat. I bought purple gold-shot brocade for a .... garment for 4 *sıtır*. I bought brocade (to be made in to?) a presentation (?) garment for 3 *sıtır*. I bought home-produced

(?) brocade for a .... padded coat for 1½ *sıtır.* For 6 *sıtır* I bought a Byzantine .... I bought home produced (?) brocade for a silk garment (?) for 1½ *sıtır.* I bought a horse blanket for .... *sıtır.* I bought a .... purple bag for the household blanket(s) for 2 *sıtır* .... *bakır.* I bought red gold-shot brocade (to cover) a pillow for 1 *sıtır.* For 1 *sıtır* I bought a silk dust cover (?). I bought for 1½ *sıtır* two (pieces of) brown raw hide (and?) for 3 *sıtır* a striped blanket of .... fathom's length. I bought five thin (pieces of brocade?) for 4 *sıtır* I bought two (or twelve?) .... rakes (?) for 4 *sıtır.* I bought two steel knives for 6 *bakır.* I bought two packets (?) of packing needles (?) for 1 *sıtır.* I bought two packets (?) of awls (?) and one rectangular packet (?) of packing needles (?) for 1 *sıtır.* I bought one half load of .... for stuffing (?) pillows for 3 *bakır.* I bought two (lengths of) coloured silk fabric for bandages (?) of which one was a .... for injuries (?) and the other a saddle-gall dressing for open wounds. I bought one silk handkerchief with a border (?) to be carried up the sleeve (?) and a purple bag for 4 *bakır.* I bought for 7 *bakır* a breastplate (?). For 5 *bakır* I bought tinder. For 5 *bakır* I bought a sable skin. For 8 *bakır* I bought (a pair of) leather boots, and for 1 *sıtır* a red bag in woven material (?). For 4 *bakır* I bought two branches (?) of *batu* (?). I bought four branches (?) of coral for 2 *bakır.* I bought white coral for 3 *bakır.* I bought two silk .... for 6 (?) *sıtır* in cash, four rolls (?) of mattresses for the stomach (?) for 2 *sıtır* in cash, and a .... mattress for the stomach for .... For sheep for the wedding feast, I bought three sheep from Taman (?) the son of ʿAli the butcher (?) for 6 *sıtır*, 5 *bakır.* I bought a horse for 2 *sıtır* from M.... For 1½ *sıtır* I bought wine. I bought 1 *shih* (2½ bushels?) of grain for 2½ *sıtır.* Analysing the dowry of 2 *yastuk*, 35 *sıtır*, the amount provided by the family was 31 *sıtır.* In addition to this my younger brother, including me in the transaction (?), gave the girl a slave, an excellent weaver, able to weave Byzantine (?) cotton cloth, a young man (?) aged 25 called Sevdi.

III

line 80 *toŋuz yılkı ötüş. Toğrılnıŋ*
kızka kabın yastuk (PU) *özge-*
[*din*] *iki yastuk asığ aldı. bir*
yastuk evindin ündürüp üç yas-
-tuknı bérdi. baş kabındın (PU) *urğu*

yürüŋ éşigirtini tört sıtır-
-ka aldı. bir yarım sıtır kümüş bile
aḏnağu (PU) *ḏiḏim* (PU) *şaş kaş* (PU) *étingü kıldı.*
(PU) *uluğ kiçig* (PU) *eŋlik bir sıtırka aldı.*
[*k*]*üḏegü turmış takı* (PU) *tonluğ tavarka*
bir yegirmi sıtır (PU) *kökülüg torkuka*
iki sıtır (PU) *balka üç yegırmı sıtır*
[PU *ta*]*var* (PU) *örmekke üç sıtır bérdi.*
[*k*]*ız tegürü kelgüçi terimlerke iki*
yipgin çuğ altı sıtır bérdi.
[?*toy*]*dakı on koynnuŋ satığı yegirmi*
[*sıt*]*ır bérdi. eşek başlap kelgüçike*
[PU *ik*]*i yipgin çuğ alıp bérdim. kabın bérmiş*
iki yastuknuŋ asığın üç otuz yıl
bérdim. törülük almış yastuk-
[PU-*nu*]*ŋ asığın üç yegirmi yıl bérdim.*
bu üç yastuknuŋ asığı bını bile
tört yegirmi yastuk iki el(*l*)*ig sıtır*
kümüş boldi.

This document, headed 'Report for the Pig (12th) Year', relates mainly to expenditure in connexion with the wedding, 23 years earlier, of the daughter of a man called Toğrıl, who is presumably the subject of the verbs in the 3rd Person in *ll. 82* to *95*. The change to the 1st Person in *96* is presumably a scribal error, but the verbs in the 1st Person in *ll. 99* and *100* presumably relate to the compiler of the document and the assumption is that by that time Toğrıl was dead. The general shape of the document is very different from that of II, and probably I, but very close to that of VI. Almost every sentence in it reappears in the same or a similar form in that document; compare (1) *ll. 81-4* and *138-9*; (2) *84-6* and *139-140*; (3) *86-7* and *141-2*; (4) *88* and *143*; (5) *89* and *163-4*; (6) *93-4* and *154-6*; (7) *96-7* and *156-7*, but both documents contain one or two sentences which are not paralleled in the other. This document begins (*ll. 81-4*) with a statement of the amount of the dowry and the sources from which it was derived. It continues (*ll. 84-92*) with a brief list of certain purchases and (*ll. 93-7*) with payments in connexion with the transport of the bride, presumably to the bridegroom's house, and the wedding feast. The total amount of expenses recorded is only 62 *sıtır*, 5 *bakır* plus the cost of the gift in *l. 97* which cannot have been large, but obviously substantially the whole of the dowry must have been spent since the whole amount borrowed was repaid much later. The document ends with the statement that the amount borrowed was repaid with interest 23 years later and that 1 *yastuk* borrowed in connexion with a funeral was repaid with interest 13 years later. The total amount of principal and interest paid over was 14 *yastuk*, 32 *sıtır*. Deducting the 3 *yastuk* of principal repaid and assuming, as seems reasonable, that only simple interest was paid and that the rate was the same for both loans, we can deduce that the amount of interest paid was 11 *yastuk*, 32 *sıtır*, that is 582 *sıtır*, representing 59 years' interest on 1 *yastuk*. If the rate had been 20 per cent, the total for 59 complete years would have been 590 *sıtır*, so it can be assumed that one period or the other was a few months short of the round figure stated.

l. 81 *Kabın yastuk* is rather clumsy but could perhaps mean 'the dowry in cash'; alternatively *yastuk* might qualify the following word, which is not clear. The likeliest reading is, however, *özge*[*din*] 'from someone else, a third party'; if so *yastuk* seems to be superfluous and a scribal error.

l. 82 *Baş kabındın* reappears, without *urğu*, in *ll. 139-140* and *148*; it is completely obscure, but no other reading seems possible. *Baş* might be an unusual way of saying 'in the first place', but this hardly suits the context in *l. 148*, and *baş kabın* might have some special meaning like 'the dowry proper', as opposed to additional expenditure (see *ll. 170-1*). *Urğu* seems meaningless, and is perhaps a miscopying, which should have been deleted, of the following word *ürüŋ*.

l. 87 which is repeated in a slightly different order in *ll. 141-2* is a major problem. The amount mentioned is small, $1\frac{1}{2}$ *sıtır* here and 1 *sıtır* in *l. 141*, and this is the only sentence in which that sum is not in the Dative but is followed by *bile* here, and *üze* in *l. 141*, and the verb is *kıldı* 'he made', not *aldı* 'he bought'. This suggests that it refers to work done, not goods purchased. Most of the other words are ambiguous. If *kaş* is 'jade', then PU *şaş* might be a secondary form of *çaç/çaş* 'turquoise' (see the note on *l. 15*) and the preceding word, although the last letter looks more like *-k* or *-ğ*, might be *ḏiḏim* a loan word from Greek *diadēma*, through Sogdian, translated 'the crown which a bride wears on her wedding night' in *Kaş.*, I, 397. The likeliest reading of the first word is *aḏnağu*, 'various', and that of the fifth word, which could be read in several ways (it looks most like *evüsgü* 'a winnowing fan', which is obviously absurd) *étingü* which might be a Noun 'ornament' or a Participle. The least improbable explanation seems to be that the sentence refers to the remodelling or resetting of family jewels for the use of the bride, but this rests on one or two rather bold assumptions.

l. 88 The first word is damaged but can be restored by comparison with *l. 143* as *uluğ*. The third word is ambiguous; T. reads *erneklik* and translates it 'setting, rim'. To me it looks more like *eŋlik* 'red cosmetic', and this is to some extent confirmed by its association with *opu* 'white cosmetic' in *l. 145*, but this is by no means certain.

l. 89 This presents another problem; in the parallel passage, *ll. 163-4*, the words (PU) *tonluğ tavarka* do not appear; this suggests that *takı* is a noun and not *takı* 'and' or the suffix *-takı*, but its meaning, and that of the preceding word *turmış* is most obscure, and the difference in the amount paid, 11 *sıtır* here, 1 *sıtır*, 7 *bakır* in *l. 164* presents a further difficulty. *Tak* is a rare word; in Buddhist Uyğur it occurs only in the phrase *muŋ tak*, which seems to mean 'distress and need', but in Old Osmanli (see *Tanıklariyle Tarama Sözlügü*, I, 670) there is a phrase 'he has no need (*tak*) of gifts', and that is probably the meaning here. The phrase can therefore perhaps be taken to mean 'the personal requirements of the bridegroom' and the difference between the two prices is perhaps explained by the fact that here they included (PU) *tonluğ tavar* 'a horse with saddlery' (?), while in *ll. 163-4* they were more modest.

l. 91 T. reads *balka* 'for honey' and I cannot make any better suggestion, but it is an odd commodity to buy for a wedding and 13 *sıtır*, the price of six or seven sheep (see *l. 95*), seems surprisingly high. There is no corresponding entry in VI.

l. 93 *Terim*, probably an abbreviation of *teŋrim* is well attested; *Kaş.*, I, 396 says that it was used only of royal ladies, but here it means no more than 'a lady commanding respect'.

l. 99 *Törülük almış* seems to mean 'borrowed (to finance) a funeral.'

(*80*) Report of the Pig Year. Toğril borrowed for his daughter a dowry 2 *yastuk* from someone else(?). He raised 1 *yastuk* from the family resources and gave the 3 *yastuk*. He bought (*85*) white embroidered brocade for 4 *sıtır* from the dowry proper (?). With 1½ *sıtır* he had various bridal crowns, turquoise and jade made into ornaments(?). He bought a large and a small (packet of) red cosmetic(?) for 1 *sıtır*. He gave 11 *sıtır* for a horse with saddlery(?) required(?) by the bridegroom, (*90*) 2 *sıtır* for home-produced (?) brocade, 13 *sıtır* for honey(?), and 3 *sıtır* for a woven cloth(?) for the horse(?). He gave the ladies who brought the girl two purple bags (costing?) 6 *sıtır*. He paid 20 *sıtır* as the price of ten sheep for the wedding feast. He (MS 'I') gave two(?) purple bags to the man (or men?) who came leading the donkey(s). I paid interest for 23 years on the two *yastuk* given as a dowry. I paid 13 years' interest on one *yastuk* borrowed (to finance) the funeral. The interest on these 3 *yastuk*, together with the principal came to 14 *yastuk*, 32 *sıtır* in cash.

IV

line 104 *yılan yıl üçünç ay bir yaŋıka*
Inançu apamnıŋ ölüg kötürmiş
yuŋlag ötüşi. Alp turmış tört oğlı
Sevinçtin yarım yastuk béşer sıtır-
-ka asığka aldım. (PU) *Tokuzdın iki yegirmi*
sıtır kümüş bir ayda üçer bakır-
-ka asığka aldım. Ögrünçtin sekiz
sıtır ikirer bakır asığka aldım.
(PU) *Çınuudın yéti sıtır* (PU) *altı törülük*
sekiz şık tarığ tüşke aldım. bir
küp bornı sekiz sıtır kümüş bérgüke
atadın aldım. Sevinçniŋ yarım
yastukka yegirmi sıtır asığı bile
bérdim. (PU) *Tokuzka iki yegirmi sıtır kümüş-*
-nün asığı altı sıtır kümüş bile
bérdim. Ögrünçnün sekiz sıtır kümüş-
-nüŋ asığı sekiz sıtır bile bérdim.
(PU) *Çınuu tuka yéti sıtır bérdim*
Inançu apamka (*sic*? read *-nuŋ*) *ölüg kötürmiş men*
almış kümüşlerniŋ bını asığı bile
bir yastuk iki el(l)ig sıtır bérdim.

This document, relating to expenses incurred in respect of the funeral of 'my grandfather(?) Inançu', is very similar to V and must be read in conjunction with that document. It must have been compiled at least four years after the funeral. The transaction with (PU) Çınuu (*ll. 112, 129*) or (PU) Çınuu tu (*l. 121*) (an odd name, possibly Chinese) is obscure; the loan in cash was perhaps paid off quickly; the loan in grain is dealt with in V. The loans from (PU) Tokuz and Ögrünç were at the higher rate of $2\frac{1}{2}$ per cent a month, or 30 per cent a year, and these were paid off first, the first in 20 months, the second in 3 years 4 months. The loan from Sevinç at the more usual rate of 20 per cent was paid off in 4 years. The sum of 1 *yastuk*, 42 *sıtır* in *l. 124* exceeds the total of the repayments listed in *ll. 115-120* by 6 *sıtır*;

there is no obvious explanation of the discrepancy, unless the interest paid to Çınuu was overlooked.

l. 106 The word *tört* was written in above the line.

l. 112 The fourth word, which is fairly clearly *altı* (or *aldı*) makes no sense and is perhaps a miscopying of *bile* 'together with'. Alternatively *bakır* may have fallen out of the text.

l. 114 *Bérgüke* seems to mean 'at a price of', and to be used instead of the more usual Dative suffix.

l. 115 The first word is difficult to read (T. read *Erük* and took it to be a P.N.) but *ata* 'father', perhaps referring to *Alp turmış* (*l. 106*), seems the likeliest reading.

(*104-6*) Financial report on the funeral of my grandfather(?) Inançu on the 1st of the 3rd month of the Snake Year. (*106*) Of the four sons of Alp turmıs I borrowed $\frac{1}{2}$ *yastuk* from Sevinç at a rate of 5 *sıtır* (per annum). I borrowed 12 *sıtır* in cash from (PU) Tokuz at a rate of 3 *bakır* a month. (*110*) I borrowed 8 *sıtır* from Ögrünç at a rate of 2 *bakır* (a month). I borrowed 7 *sıtır* together with(?) 8 *shih* of grain (or wheat?) at interest from (PU) Çınuu. I bought one skin of wine at a price of 8 *sıtır* in cash from the father(?). (*115*) I repaid Sevinc's $\frac{1}{2}$ *yastuk* with 20 *sıtır* in interest. I repaid the 12 *sıtır* in cash to (PU) Tokuz together with 6 *sıtır* in cash as interest. I repaid Ögrünç's 8 *sıtır* in cash (*120*) with 8 *sıtır* in interest. I repaid 7 *sıtır* to Çınuu tu. I repaid the principal of the money which I borrowed for the funeral of my grandfather(?) Inançu with interest, (to an amount of) 1 *yastuk*, 42 *sıtır*.

V

Koyn yil onunc ay bir yegirmike oğul
kardaş yengeçim öldi. ölüg
kötürmiş yuŋlag ötüşı. bir yastuk
(PU) *Bakınçtın alıp yuŋladım. törülük*
tarığ on şık Çınuudın tüşke
aldım ötüş. Toğrılka törülük
tarığ (PU) *ançulamış* (PU) *Sıladın on şık tüş-*
-ke aldım. Inançu apamka (? read *-nıŋ*) *törülük*
bu üçegünüŋ törülük tüşke almış
tarığlarının tüş tüşi asığ
asığı kavışıp yüz şık tarığ
bolmış.

This document, which is very similar to IV, relates primarily to expenditure incurred in respect of the funeral of three persons (*üçegü*, *l. 133*), but since the amount borrowed in grain is aggregated with a similar loan in grain mentioned in IV the exact nature of the transaction cannot be elucidated. The words in *ll. 134-5* seem to indicate that in this case compound, and not simple, interest was charged. It is however clear that the loan was outstanding for a long time. The amount borrowed in IV was only 8 *shih*, in this two separate amounts of 10 *shih* seem to be mentioned. Even taking the higher figure, 28 *shih*, and assuming the interest to be compound interest at the higher of the two rates mentioned in IV, 30 per cent, the total of 100 *shih* implies that the debt had been running for at least 5 years. Taking the price of grain quoted in *l. 72*, 2½ sıtır for a *shih*, the cash value of the debt would have been 5 *yastuk*.

The three persons who died were the son, brother (*kardaş*, a late form of *karındaş*) and a third relative of the writer. The third word, fairly clearly *yengeçim*, presents some difficulty. T. takes it to be a Secondary form of *ekeç*, a Diminutive of *eke*: 'elder sister', listed in *Kaş*., I, 52, but it seems rather to be a Diminutive form, not noted elsewhere, of *yenge*: (*yeŋge*:) 'an elder brother's, or junior uncle's wife' (*Kaş*., III, 380). It is of course quite a different word from *yengeç* 'a crab' (*Kaş*., III, 384), which is a Secondary form of *lengeç*, probably an Indo-European loan word, cf. French *langouste*.

l. 130 The second word seems to be a rather clumsy repetition of the phrase in *l. 127*. It is not clear whether the Toğrıl mentioned here is the same as the one mentioned in *l. 80*. It is possible that he was the brother mentioned in *l. 126*.

l. 131 The second word is hard to read. T. reads *Iŋlamış* and takes it to be the first component in a P.N. This is improbable; there is no known verb *ıŋla*:-; *aŋlamiş* 'understood' makes no sense. I am inclined, very tentatively, to read *ançulamiş* 'presented, gave'. The next word is clearly a P.N.; the first letter looks a little more like *S*- than *K*-.

l. 135 *Kavış*- is an Intransitive verb meaning 'to come together, assemble' (*Kaş*., II, 102); compare *birik*-, same meaning, in *l. 185*.

(*125*) My son, brother and elder brother's wife died on the 11th of the 10th month in the Sheep Year. Financial statement of the funeral (expenses). I borrowed 1 *yastuk* from (PU) Bakınç and used it. I borrowed 10 *shih* of grain for the funeral at interest from (PU) Çinuu. (*130*) Report. Having presented(?) grain for the funeral to Toğrıl, I borrowed 10 *shih* of grain at interest from (PU) Sıla. The aggregate amount of grain borrowed for the funerals of my grandfather(?) Inançu and these three persons together with compound interest (Hendiadys?) came to 100 *shih* of grain.

VI

(PU) *örükke koyn yıl sekizinç ay*
kelin kirdi. iki yastuk béş kırk
sıtır kümüş kabın bérdim. baş
kabından iki sıtırka yürüŋ éşgirti
bir sıtır tartma kümüş üze (PU) *ḏiḏim*
şaş (PU) *aḏnagu kaş étingü kıldı.*
uluğ kiçig (PU) *eŋlikke altı bakır bérdi.*
(PU) *atlığ* (PU) *tişlik üç ületü yürüŋ*
çuğnı altı bakırka aldım. opu kina
üç bakır (PU) *ka kiya tarak kiya* (PU) *şiş alti*
aldim. kalbır (PU) *boğnı béş bakırka aldım.*
(PU) *sürtünç üç bakırka aldım. baş kabın-*
daki koynka bir sıtır bir yarım bakır
bérdim. balık törüsi tép bir sıtır
yarım bakırka koyn aldım. kay kapuda
turğuçıka béş bakır torku alıp bérdim
balık kapuda kapığçıka béş bakır
-ka torku alıp bérdim. Kız kelürgüçi iki
terimke iki yipgin çuğ iki sıtır tört
bakır alıp bérdim. Eşek kelürgüçike
bir sıtır iki bakırka yipgin çuğ alıp
bérdim. alğalı barğuçıka bir koyn
(PU) *tuşğuluk yarım koyn kiçigi bir yarım*
koyn ikinti künki iki koyn béş
koynnuŋ béş sıtır beş bakır aldim.
sokumluğ uḏnuŋ tört sıtır altı
bakırka aldım. (PU) *örükke küḏegü turmış*
takı bir sıtır yéti bakırka kızıl
ésgirti tört sıtır üç bakırka (PU) *çikin-*
(PU)*-lig çuğ aldım. bir sıtır yéti*
bakırka sarığ çuğ (PU) *örmek* (PU) *çoşunluk*
kabın aldım. sekiz bakırka üç ületü
yipgin al aldım (PU) *kerezka kelinke kabın-*

-ı aşı toyı yuŋlağı üç yastuk üç yegirmi sıtır béş bakır boldı. Inançu apamdın tuğmış Sevinç (PU) *kurtğa atlığ kız- -nıŋ* (PU) *Ilik atlığ kıznıŋ bu iki kız- -nıŋ sabı sanka kögürmedin kalmış iki oğulnuŋ üç kıznıŋ bu kızlar- -nı küḏegüke ündürüp oğul kelin alıp korı yuŋlağı ev din yetgürmedin asığka tüşke alıp ağır kala bolup tegürü umadın asığı tüşi üküş bolup yéti yegirmi yastuk yeti yegirmi sıtır tüketi boldi. üç ölüg kötürmisteki yuŋlag ev din yetgür- -medin asığka tüşke alıp bérip umadın asığı tüşi tegmişi tegmeyüki bile birikip yéti yastuk kırk sitir boldi.*

There is a good deal of evidence that this document was copied very carelessly. There are several obvious errors and omissions, some of which can be proved by comparing it with III, which, as already pointed out, it closely resembles. These faults cast some doubt on the quality of the text as a whole. One interesting question is whether the original of III did not serve to some extent as a model for VI. In III the verbs in the main body of the text are all in the 3rd Person, here they are consistently in the 1st Person, except in two sentences (*ll. 141-3*) which are practically identical with *ll. 86-8* except for the sums of money. The following are some of the most obvious errors: *l. 140* the verb (*aldım*) is missing; *l. 145* the amount stated seems insufficient to pay for the goods enumerated; *ll. 146* and *166* the price paid is omitted; *ll. 152*, *156*, *161 bakır* should be *bakırka*; *ll. 161-2 koynnuŋ*, *uḏnuŋ* should be *koynnı*, *uḏnı*; *l. 183 bérip* should be *bérü.*

The heads of expenditure are for the most part identical with those in III but there are interesting details, lacking in III, of gifts to civic authorities and the like. The order of the items is more chaotic; the actual amounts mentioned are fairly small, but it is stated in *ll. 169-71* that the total amount spent was 3 *yastuk*, 13 *sıtır*, 5 *bakır* that is 28 *sıtır*, 5 *bakır* more than the dowry proper.

In the middle of *l. 171* the subject changes to the debts incurred in respect of the weddings of most of Inançu's children. It is not clear whether these are the same weddings as those referred to in I, II and this document. It then turns to the debts incurred in respect of three funerals. It is not clear whether these are the same as those mentioned in V, but the financial details in the two documents are not readily reconcilable.

l. 137 The first word reappears in *l. 163*. Here it might be the name of the bridegroom and would be appropriately in the Dative in association with *kirdi*, but in *l. 163* it should be in the Nominative. This may be another example of careless copying, unless some idiom is involved. It could be read in several ways, but T.'s transcription *örükke* may well be right.

l. 138 In the first word, certainly *kelin* the loop of the *-l-* is missing, another example of carelessness.

ll. 139-140 See the note on *l. 84*.

ll. 141-2 See the note on *l. 87*.

l. 143 See the note on *l. 88*.

l. 144 The first two words are most obscure; *tişlik*, if correctly transcribed, means something to do with teeth, for example a tooth brush; *tizlik* would mean something to do with the knees. *Atlığ* can hardly mean 'famous', so should mean 'belonging to a horse'; the puzzle seems insoluble.

ll. 145-6 *Opu* (?*opo*), probably a Chinese loan word, is 'white cosmetic (*Kaş.*, I, 86); *kına* (?*xına*) is the Arabic word *ḥinnā* 'henna'. The word transcribed *kıya* in both places seems to be the Diminutive suffix; if so *ka* must be a noun, 'vessel, container' (*Kaş.*, III, 211) and *bakır* not a coin but the adjective 'copper'. The penultimate word could be *kaş*, or *şaş* (see *l. 42*), or *şış*, or *kış*; none seems very appropriate; *altı* here is probably 'six' (*sıtırka* or *bakırka* omitted).

l. 147 *Kalbır*, fairly clearly written, seems to be a word, otherwise noted only in some modern languages like Kırgız and Osmanli, meaning 'a sieve'. It is a corruption of the Persian word *girbāl*. *Boğ* means 'a bundle, or bale' (*Kaş.*, III, 127), the meaning here is obscure and the price (5 *bakır*) cannot have paid for anything like 'a parcel of sieves'.

l. 148 T. reads the first word *soğdıç* and connects it with *savdıç* 'a fruit basket' (*Kaş.*, I, 455); to me it looks more like *sürtünç*, a word which is not known to have existed but would have meant 'rubber, polisher'. The meaning of *baş kabındakı* is obscure, perhaps 'forming part of the dowry proper'.

l. 150 *Törü* here seems to mean 'the traditional right, perquisite'; one sheep would not have satisfied the whole population, but perhaps went to a select few.

l. 151 *Kay* is a loan word from Chinese *chieh* 'street' (Giles, *No. 1434*; Middle Chinese *kāi*) fairly common in Uyğur.

ll. 154-8 See the note on *ll. 93-7*.
l. 158 *Alğalı barğuçı* perhaps means '(the man) who went to fetch (the bride)'; he seems to have got one sheep, and another half-sheep on meeting her (?; a possible meaning of (PU) *tuşguluk*), and *kiçigi*, perhaps 'his assistant', 1½ sheep, and the two together got 2 sheep for the next day.
ll. 163-4 See the notes on *ll. 89* and *137*.
l. 167 T. plausibly suggests that (PU) *çoşunluk* is a Concrete Noun in *-luk* from a Chinese phrase *chou shên* (characters not given) and means 'a silk robe', if so *kabın* is here the Accusative with Possessive suffix of *ka:b* 'a container, sack'.
l. 169 The fourth word with a palatal *k-* and a Dative Suffix with a Velar *-k-* is puzzling and perhaps corrupt. It can hardly have anything to do with a loan word *karaza* (with palatal *k-*), meaning 'a monk's robe' noted in F. W. K. Müller, *Uigurica*, III, *A. P. A. W.* (Berlin 1922) 57, *l.* 10 (i).
l. 174 *Sa:b*, which also occurs in *ll. 7* and *12* means 'a turn' (to do something, e.g. to speak; *Kaş.*, III, 145); the phrase *sabı . . . kalmış* seems to mean 'leaving out of account the cases of' (the two daughters). The names of these daughters are uncertain; *kurtğa*: 'old woman' (*Kaş.*, III, 255, 19) seems an odd component in a P. N.
l. 177 *Yetgür-*, a Causative form of *yét-*, 'to overtake', and the like, not noted before the mediaeval period, must here mean 'to make available, provide'.

(*137*) A bride came to (PU) Örük in the 8th month of the Sheep Year. I gave a dowry of 2 *yastuk*, 35 *sıtır* in cash. (*140*) From the dowry proper(?) I bought white embroidered brocade for 2 *sıtır*. With 1 *sıtır* of weighed (or minted?) coin he (*sic*) had a bridal crown, turquoise and various jades made into ornaments(?). He (*sic*) gave 6 *bakır* for a large and small (packet of) red cosmetic(?). I bought . . . . three silk handkerchiefs and a white bag (*145*) for 6 *bakır*. I bought white cosmetic, henna, three small copper vessels and a small comb for 6 ⟨?*sıtır*⟩. I bought a bale (?) for a sieve for 5 *bakır*. I bought a polisher(?) for 3 *bakır*. For the sheep in the dowry proper(?) I gave 1 *sıtır*, 1½ *bakır*. (*150*) I bought a sheep as a perquisite(?) for the town for 1 *sıtır*, ⟨?1⟩ ½ *bakır*. I bought brocade (for) 5 *bakır* and gave it to the man on duty at the street gate. I bought brocade for 5 *bakır* and gave it to the gatekeeper at the town gate. (*155*) I bought two purple bags for 2 *sıtır*, 4 *bakır* and gave them to the two ladies who brought the girl. I bought a purple bag for 1 *sıtır*, 2 *bakır* and gave it to the man who brought the donkey. I bought 5 sheep for 5 *sıtır*, 5 *bakır* (and gave) the man who went to fetch (the bride?) one sheep, for meeting her(?) half a sheep, his assistant(?) one and a half (*160*) sheep and for the next day two sheep. I bought an ox for slaughter for 4 *sıtır*, 6 *bakır*. I bought the bridegroom (PU) Örük's(?) requirements (?) for 1 *sıtır*, 7 *bakır*; red (*165*) embroidered brocade for 4 *sıtır*, 3 *bakır* and a silk bag ⟨for?⟩. For 1 *sıtır*, 7 *bakır* I bought yellow bag fabric(?) and (?) a container for silk robes(?). For 8 *bakır* I bought three silk handkerchiefs purple and scarlet. The expenditure on . . ., the dowry for the bride, (*170*) food and the bridal feast came to 3 *yastuk*, 13 *sıtır*, 5 *bakır*. Of Inançu's children, leaving two daughters, Sevinç (PU) Kurtğa and (PU) Ilik out of account(?), as the cost and expenditure on (*175*) sending the three daughters to bridegrooms, and getting wives for the two sons could not be provided from the family resources, it was borrowed at interest (Hendiadys) and became burdensome. As it could not be paid over, the (accrued) interest (*180*) became large and came to 17 *yastuk*, 17 *sıtır* in all. As the expenditure on the funerals of the three persons could not be provided from the family resources, and as it was borrowed at interest and could not be paid; the interest taking together that already paid (?) and not yet paid (?) has reached the sum of 7 *yastuk*, 40 *sıtır*.

VII

line 187 *atam Basa Toğrıl tiriginde*
bir bakır ma bérim koḏmadın
borluk yér suv ev bark
tükel koḏup Taŋut bardı. ikinti
yılın (PU) *alavéreyin Kuçadın yarım*
yastuk tartma kümüş altmış
san tavar béleg ıḏtı yana
(PU) *babaktakı* (PU) *saman yapığ-* (PU)*-din*
yéti torku béleg ıḏtı. burxan-
-liğ (PU) *sumıtudın bir yastuk*
tartma kümüş béleg ıḏtı . öẕi
oğul kıẕ almadı kıẕ küdegüke
ündürmedi . men (PU) *Taman ağam* (PU) *tavar-*
-ıŋa kıẕ aldım.

This document starts a new line, but may be merely another paragraph of VI, with another change of subject.

Basa Toğrıl, the father of the compiler, and so perhaps the son of Inançu, may be the man of that name mentioned as having made a payment in *USp. 125*; *tiriginde*, 'in his lifetime', implies that he was dead when this document was compiled.

l. 191 T. transcribes the second word *alayitin* and tentatively translates it 'specially', describing it as an Arabic loan word, but without suggesting the Arabic original. To me it looks more like *alavéreyin*, which if this were an Osmanli text could mean 'by buying and selling', but there are obvious objections to assuming an Oğuz *-v-* (for *-b-*) in an Uyğur text, and the problem remains unsolved.

l. 193 *Béleg*, literally 'something wrapped up' is specifically 'a gift sent from abroad, or brought home, by a traveller' (*Kaş.*, I, 385).

l. 194 Is full of difficulties. The first word seems to be a Place Name; the only Turkish noun which looks like it is *borbağ* 'dilatoriness' (*Kaş.*, I, 460), but that makes no sense. The second word seems to have a dot on the last letter, which suggests *saman* 'straw' (*Kaş.*, I, 415) rather than *semiz* 'fat' (I, 365). *Yapığ* has several meanings of which 'covering', and the like is the likeliest here. The last word might be *teg* 'like' or *-tin*/*-din* 'from'. Of the various improbable alternative translations perhaps the least improbable is 'from a straw (i.e. thatched) shelter in (PU) Babak', taking this as one of the places from which he sent presents.

ll. 195-6 The last word of *l. 195* and the first of *l. 196* is clearly a compound Place Name. The obvious reading of the first is *burxanlığ* 'belonging to Buddha'. The *-tu* in the second looks like the Mongolian suffix *-tu* (equivalent to Turkish *-lığ*/*-lig*), and the whole recalls the phrase *burxanu süme* 'a Buddha temple, in *line 7* of the first *Chü-yung-kuan* Inscription (see N. Poppe, *The Mongolian Monuments in ḥP'ags-pa Script* (Wiesbaden 1957) 60). The place might therefore be called 'having a temple to Buddha'; there are the objections that the first letter of the second word looks more like *k-* than *s-* and the second is *-u-* not *-ü-*, but these do not seem insuperable in a text of this kind.

l. 198 The first three words clearly mean 'did not get brides for his sons', but the grammar is rugged, *oğulka* or *oğlıŋa* might have been expected.

l. 199 (PU) *Taman*, cf. *l. 68*, but these seem to be different individuals. *Ağa* (or *aka*), the Mongolian loan word for 'elder brother', which displaced *éçi* after the Mongolian invasion, is further evidence of the lateness of this text; *éçi* still survives in what seem to be the earlier comparable documents in *USp.* but *ağa* appears in the later ones. The last word is probably *tavar* which here must mean 'financial resources' and not, as elsewhere in this document 'horse'. A less probable alternative reading is *tayak* 'support'.

(*187*) My father, Basa Toğrıl, without leaving a single *bakır* of debt (unpaid) left everything, vineyard, landed property, house and household goods, and (*190*) went to Taŋut. The next year, as the result of trading(?) he sent from Kuça half a *yastuk* in weighed (or minted?) coin and sixty head of horses as a gift. Then (*195*) he sent seven pieces of brocade as a gift from a thatched(?) shelter(?) at (PU) Babak. From Burxanlığ (PU) Sumıtu he sent 1 *yastuk* of weighed (or minted?) coin as a gift. He himself never got brides for his sons or gave his daughter(s) to bridegroom(s). I took a bride with (the help of) the financial resources(?) of my elder brother.

C. J. F. DOWSETT

A Twelfth-century Armenian Inscription at Edessa

The city of Edessa, Ruhā in its Arabo-Persian form,[1] has a brief but favourable mention in the *Ḥudūd al-ʿĀlam* translated by Vladimir Minorsky: 'Ruhā, a flourishing town. Most of its inhabitants are Christians. In it stands a church; in the whole world there is none larger, better attended, and more wonderful. To it belongs a flourishing countryside, and in it live numerous monks.'[2] Although the researches of our much regretted friend and colleague were directed more towards the north-eastern fringes of the Armenian area than to those of the south-east, the history of this ancient city involved the destinies of many peoples, Byzantines, Armenians, Syrians, and the finally, as usual, victorious Turks, who claimed his special attention. This commentary on an Armenian inscription on one of the towers of the city, which by reason of its inaccessible position for some years eluded all efforts to secure it on film, is offered as a small tribute to the lasting value of his work for those who, like the present writer, engage in different, though contiguous and parallel, specialities.

The important role played by the Armenians in the eleventh and twelfth centuries in the affairs of Edessa, a city which from the beginning had exerted an influence upon the Christian civilization of Armenia,[3] is well known to every historian of the Crusades.[4] Edessa, or Uřhay as it was known to the Armenians, with its mixed population of Syrians, Armenians and Greeks, passed in the space of seventy years between 1077 and 1146 from the hands of the Byzantines into those of an Armenian veteran of the Manzikert campaign and governor of Marash and Melitene, Philaretos (1077–86), thence into those of the Turks in the persons of the Seljukid Malik-Shah's lieutenant Buzan (1086–94), and the latter's assassin Tutush (1094–5). In 1095 it returned to Armenian rule when one of Philaretos' lieutenants, Thoros son of Hethum, exploiting the dissension of Edessa's Turkish masters, seized the city and governed it alone for three years (1095–8). The Latin state of Edessa was born when Thoros, in 1098, was persuaded to invite the Crusader Baldwin of Boulogne to help him in his struggle against the Turks, obliged to name him as his legitimate successor, and then done to death by the populace. When in 1100 Baldwin became King of Jerusalem, Edessa was ruled by Baldwin of Le Bourg until his own elevation to the throne of Jerusalem in 1118. First entrusting the administration of Edessa to Galeran du Puiset, lord of Biredjik, for a few months, Baldwin II became reconciled with Joscelyn (I) de Courtenay and named him count of Edessa (1119–31). The latter was succeeded by his son Joscelyn II, who was absent from the city when it was attacked by the atabeg Zengi and, in spite of a spirited defence by the Armenians and Syrians, taken by him in 1144. The Armenians tried to assist Joscelyn II to recapture the city in 1146, but the attempt failed; Joscelyn was compelled to flee, and the victorious Turks set about the task of ridding Edessa of its Christian population.

The fall of Edessa in 1144 was understandably felt to be a great tragedy by the Armenians. In the elegy written on this occasion by one of the most celebrated mediaeval poets and churchmen, the Catholicos Nerses IV Shnorhali, the author, who refers to Christ's legendary praise of Edessa as being 'more blessed than any other', holds that there is no other city like it on earth.[5] The city is assured of a permanent place in Armenian literature by producing the historian Matthew of Edessa (Matt'ēos Uṙhayec'i), and an Armenian version, much abbreviated, of the Syriac history of Michael the Syrian. Philaretos and Thoros made Edessa part of Armenian history, and the take-over by their Frankish successors, some of whom, like Baldwin I and Baldwin II, intermarried with Armenian princesses, did nothing to weaken the link. The Armenians' interest in the affairs of Edessa was more vigorously expressed than that of the Syrian inhabitants of the city, who had been to a large extent pushed down and aside by the newcomers. After the fall of Edessa in 1144 the Syrian bishop Basil bar Shumana was willing to collaborate with Zengi, who, it is true, treated the Christians with consideration and showed a great respect, even enthusiasm, for their faith. It was the Armenians, faithful to the De Courtenays, who attempted to bring back Joscelyn II in 1146, a rebellion which brought disastrous consequences to themselves: many of the Armenian inhabitants were banished, to be replaced by three hundred Jewish families who had shown their willingness to collaborate with the Muslims against the Christians.[6] As Grousset says, 'la preuve que les arméniens y trouvèrent leur compte est qu'ils se montrèrent jusqu'au bout les défenseurs fidèles et souvent héroïques du comté d'Edesse'.[7] Given this vital interest, it is not surprising to

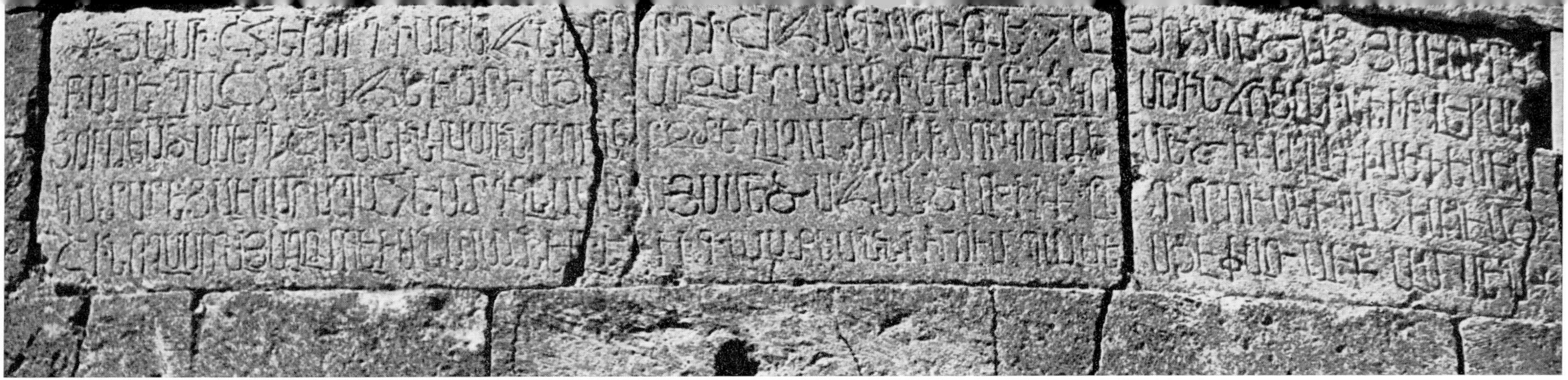

Plate 1. Armenian Inscription on the Bey Kapisi, Urfa. *Photograph by G. Fehérvári.*

Plate 2. Armenian inscription on the Bey Kapisi, Urfa, showing part of the surrounding masonry. *Photograph by G. Fehérvári.*

find evidence that the Armenians were responsible for many of the fortifications of the city. Thoros himself is credited by the author of the *Anonymous Syriac Chronicle* to AD 1234[8] as having built, or rebuilt, 'the lower castle . . . above the East Gate of the city', that which, ironically, became the scene of his own assassination. It is just here that we find further eloquent testimony to the Armenians' role in the defence of the city in the form of a five-line Armenian inscription of AD 1122/3. This is inserted half-way up the outer wall, facing east, of the tower some sixty feet high on the east side of Edessa next to the Bey Kapısı or Bābu'l-'Amīr, the East Gate of the *Anonymous Syriac Chronicle*, also called, by the same source, the Kasas Gate,[9] and, by the much earlier, sixth-century, *Chronicle* of Joshua the Stylite, the 'Great Gate'.[10]

This inscription was mentioned for the first time by E. Sachau in 1882, although, as he explains, he was not able either to read it, or to transcribe it: 'In yet another place I noticed an inscription which I was not able to copy for the same reason [because no ladder was available]. On the east side of Edessa over the so-called *Bek kapusu* rises a rather tall, round, massive tower, in which, a little above half-way up, are set three blocks of stone bearing a well-preserved inscription in Armenian uncials. One can see that they are not in their original setting from the fact that these three stone blocks are in size and shape completely different from the surrounding masonry. The wall now forms the rear of a house belonging to a certain Mahmud oghlu. Should one desire to copy this inscription, one would need a ladder such as is now in use in the fire-brigades of present-day capital cities.'[11] Scholars have visited Edessa since Sachau's day, but, although suitably equipped fire-engines are more common now, they still do not form part of basic field equipment. The inaccessibility of the inscription has until this last summer (1967) thwarted even the modern telescopic lense, for the inscription is awkwardly placed for a photographer. J. B. Segal, who has long been interested in its decipherment in connection with his forthcoming book on the history of the city,[12] and the late D. S. Rice, managed to take useful pictures showing the general position of the inscription in 1959, but it was left to G. Fehérvári to take, in summer 1967, a close-up telescopic photograph of the inscription (Plate 1), and one showing the surrounding masonry referred to by Sachau (Plate 2). It was not possible to take exact measurements at the time. Judging by the available photographs, the three blocks of reddish-brown stone bearing the inscription are of uniform height and vary in length in the ratio of 12.5, 10.1 and 9 from left to right. Judging by the approximate height of the tower, some 60 feet according to J. B. Segal, the blocks are about two feet high and between three and four feet long, with Armenian *erkathagir* ('uncial') capitals *ca.* four inches in height. The inscription reads as follows:

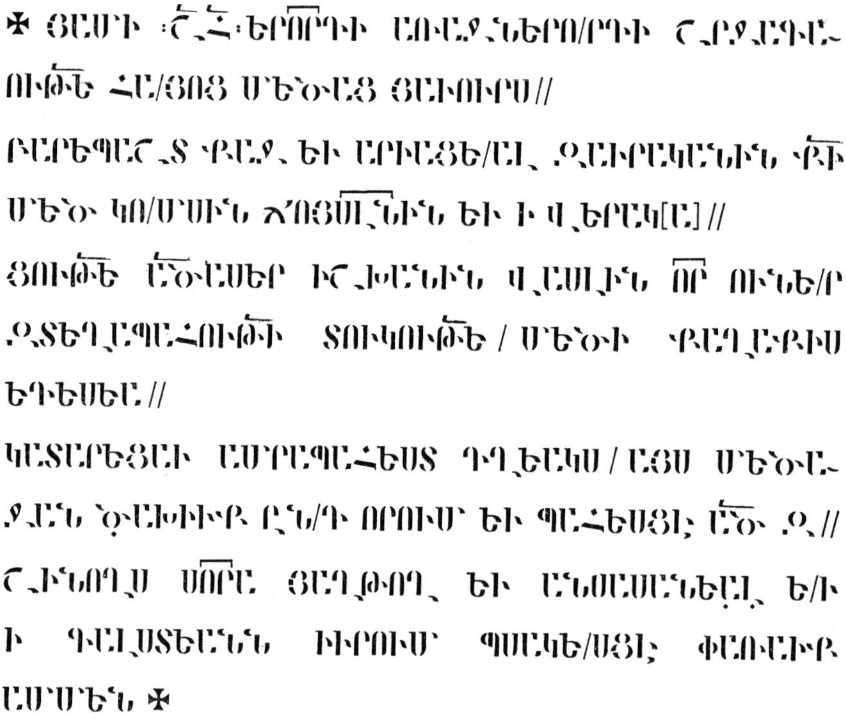

✠ ՅԱՄԻ ՇՀ ԵՐՈՐԴԻ ԱՌԱՋՆԵՐՈ/ՐԴԻ ՇՐՋԱԳԱ-
ՈՒԹԵ ՀԱ/ՅՈՑ ՄԵԾԱՑ ՅԱՄՈՒՐՍ //

ԲԱՐԵՊԱՇՏ ՔԱՋ ԵՒ ԱՐԻԱՑԵ/ԱԼ ԶԱՒՐԱԿԱՆԻՆ ՔՒ
ՄԵԾ ԿՈ/ՄՍԻՆ ՃՈՅՍԼՆԻՆ ԵՒ Ի Վ ԵՐԱԿ[Ա] //

ՅՈՒԹԵ ՑՕՆԱՍԵՐ ԻՇ ԽԱՆԻՆ ՎԱՍԼԻՆ ՕՐ ՈՒՆԵ/Ր
ՕՏԵՂ ԱՊԱՀՈՒԹԻ ՏՈՒԿՈՒԹԵ / ՄԵԾՒ ՔԱՂԱՔԻՍ
ԵԴԵՍԵԱ //

ԿԱՏԱՐԵՑԱՒ ԱՄՐԱՊԱՀԵՍՏ ԴՂԵԱԿՍ / ԱՅՍ ՄԵԾԱ-
ՃԱՆ ՑԱԽԻՒՔ ՕՐ ԱՆ/Դ ՈՐՈՒՄ ԵՒ ՊԱՀԵՍՑԷ ՑՕ Ձ //
ՀԻՆՈՂՍ ՍՈՐԱ ՑԱՂԹՈՂ ԵՒ ԱՆՍԱՍԱՆԵԱԼ Ե/Ի
Ի ԳԱԼՍՏԵԱՆՆ ԻՒՐՈՒՄ ՊԱՐԿԵ/ՍՑԷ ՓԱՌԱՒՔ
ԱՄՄԷՆ ✠

1 ✠ Yami : šh : erordi aṙajnero/rdi šrjaga(y)owtʻe(an) Ha/yocʻ Mecacʻ
   yawowrs //
2 barepašt kʻaj ew ariacʻe/al zawrakanin Kʻ(ristos)i mec ko/msin
   Čoyslnin ew i verak⟨a⟩- //
3 -cʻowtʻe(an) a(stua)caser (*sic: for* -sēr) išxanin vaslin or owne/r (*sic:
   for* ownēr) zteḷapahowtʻi(wn) towkowtʻe(an) / meci kʻaḷakʻis Edesea //
4 katarecʻaw amrapahest dḷeaks / ays mecaǰan caxiwkʻ or ən/d orowm ew
   pahescʻē A(stua)c z- //
5 šinoḷs sora yaḷtʻoḷ ew ansasaneal (*possibly* ansasan ew, *the following* ew
   then being otiose) e/w i galsteann iwrowm psake/ scʻē pʻarawkʻ am[m]en ✠

1 'In the 571st year of the Greater Armenian era (19th February 1122–18th
   February 1123) in the days

2 of the pious, excellent and valorous soldier of Christ, the great Count Joyslin, and in the admini-
3 -stration of the God-loving Prince Vasil who held the locum-tenency of the dukedom of this great city of Edessa
4 this fortified stronghold was completed with great industry and at great expense (*lit.* with greatly industrious expenditure), wherefore may God keep also
5 those who built it victorious and unshaken, and at his (Second) Coming may he crown (them) with glory, Amen.'

Is Sachau justified in considering that the inscription is no longer in its original site? It is a great handicap not to have examined the edifice at first hand, but the question deserves some consideration. It is obvious that the surrounding blocks of stone which might be contemporary are, though often as long, only two-thirds as high as those bearing the inscription (the blocks further to the right are of more recent preparation and differ in colour, as can be seen from Plate 2). The Armenian word employed in the inscription to describe the building thus commemorated, namely *dłeak* 'fortress, dungeon, fort, redoubt' (Bedrossian), translated more neutrally as 'stronghold' above, could well describe the complex comprising the present tower. The statement in the inscription that 'this fortified stronghold was completed (*katarec'aw*)' suggests that the construction was a new one. If so, one may doubt that this refers to the tower, more likely to have been part of Thoros's fortification work round the East Gate; 1122 seems hardly a propitious time for such major work, and there is no mention in the sources of it. If the 'stronghold' was a new one, then one must agree with Sachau that it was in a different site. But it is possible that the phrase in the inscription is to be interpreted to mean that '(reconstruction work on) this fortified stronghold was completed'. No doubt the many encounters in the east of the city, where it was protected by no natural features,[13] had left their mark on the tower, the latest record prior to the date of the inscription of such an assault being in A.D. 1112.[14] It is thus probable that just before 1122, the year in which Joscelyn I was captured, the citizens of Edessa felt that the danger from the Turks was such that the east tower needed urgent repair. It could be this work that the inscription commemorates. That the three blocks did not match the surrounding ones may have offended the canons of good twelfth-century architecture, but the repairers must have been in a hurry; perhaps the inscriptionist chose the blocks, to be worked on the ground, deliberately of extra height to give the inscription added effect, a discernible frame, the fact that, in being placed forty feet above the ground, it would be, as well as undefaceable, illegible from the ground being paralleled by more ancient and celebrated oriental inscriptions. If the inscribed blocks originally formed an integral part of a new section of the twelfth-century fortifications, and were later inserted in the tower, there is no record of any date at which this was done. After the date of the inscription, only twenty-two years remained in which it might be so inserted in the lifetime of the County of Edessa. Thereafter such repair work would have taken place under the Turks, who would be unlikely to specify to the Armenian mason (the fact that the blocks are in their correct order with respect to the text of the inscription presupposes such a man) that an infidel inscription bearing two crosses should stand in such a commanding position, though they may not have managed to prevent it. It seems not impossible that the inscription stands where it was, in 1122/3, intended to stand. The Armenians remained, however, an active element of the population until the present century, and there were no doubt many opportunities, as the city passed from Zengid to Ayyūbid, from Mamlūk to Ottoman, for the blocks to be inserted during repair work on the tower, possibly as a mild nationalistic gesture.[15]

As one could expect, the tower bearing the inscription witnessed a number of momentous events, many of them involving the Armenians. Reference has already been made above (p. 199) to the assassination of Thoros at the lower citadel.[16] The account of the *Anonymous Syriac Chronicle* contains interesting details of this event, deplored by Armenian and Syrian historian alike, not found in the account of Matthew of Edessa: 'Certain lewd townsmen began to provoke strife between the Franks and Theodore till the evil grew and filled their hearts so that they attained the wickedness of plotting to kill their governor and letting the Franks rule over them. They did this not from the love of the Franks but from the bad will of those who disliked Theodore. They raged like wild beasts, excited and influenced one another, gathered in a great crowd, and raised a tumult by the descent from the castle at the head of the spring. When he came to that crowd they rushed at him, and he fled before them to the lower castle which he had built above the east gate of the city. They attacked him, and he asked them to swear that he might depart with his wife and children in poverty. They promised this with an oath, so he opened the gate, but they did not keep their oath and dealt treacherously with him; they went up, beat him, bound him with a rope, and let him down naked, wearing only a loincloth, from a high wall facing the city.'[17]

It was at the East Gate that Edessa was soon after attacked by Kerbogha: 'While the Franks were besieging Antioch, a great chief, Kerbogha (*qr'bg'*) came from the East to Edessa and reached the East Gate'.[18] A more serious attack involving Joscelyn and some twenty Armenian traitors took place in 1112[19] at the same site, which the *Anonymous Syriac Chronicle* justifiably calls 'a corner and open space fit for an adventure'. Mawdūd attacked Edessa during the absence from the city of Joscelyn and 'camped below in the eastern plain round Kasas Castle'. The majority of the inhabitants refused to surrender, but, says the *Anonymous Syriac Chronicle*, 'some twenty Armenians conspired with Mawdūd to betray the city'.[20] Matthew of Edessa refers to the traitors merely as 'certain deceitful men',[21] but the fact that he half excuses them by asserting that 'they were suffering from the severity of the famine, and in their peril did not know what they had done'[22] gives support to the *Syriac Chronicle's* assertion as to their nationality. In accordance with the plan, Mawdūd 'sent some doughty warriors on foot to the place agreed on near the wall on the east of the city inside the lower bridge over the moat over which the water passes. There is a corner and open space fit for an adventure. A great corner tower was there, the guard of it was a well-known citizen named Cyrus. There they met according to agreement; the traitors let down ropes and pulled up strong ladders and tied them to the wall. They began to climb up....'[23] Joscelyn, however, who had been attacking Sarūdj[24] where he killed 150 men during the siege of Edessa, thus causing Mawdūd's temporary withdrawal towards Sarūdj, had returned to Edessa before Mawdūd came back again to be met by the Armenian traitors.[25] 'Joscelyn of Tell Bashīr was in Edessa; he acted like a hero, mounted the wall on that side, and drew near the enemy. When they saw him, they gathered on the big tower, stood on a roof above him, and showered on him arrows and stones. He heartened himself, entered the tower on the roof of which they stood, put his sword through a window made for shooting arrows, and cut down the ladder while many men were on it. . . . Joscelyn mounted on to the roof beside the Turks. Twice they smote him from above with stones and broke his shield. He took a sack full of chaff on which the guards slept, held it over his head, and climbed stoutly among them. They fled. . . . The plot failed, it had hardly begun. Mawdūd went back to his land. The Franks tried the traitors, seized many guilty and innocent, cut off hands and noses; many died, others were executed'.[26]

Joscelyn's bearing at the fight for the east tower in 1112 is a clear demonstration of his meriting the appellation 'excellent and valorous[27] soldier of

Christ' of the inscription. Matthew of Edessa in recounting the event of 1112 uses a nearly identical expression to describe him, viz. 'the victorious soldier of Christ, count J̌oslin' (*yałt'oł zawrakann K'ristosi komsn Čoslin*),[28] speaking also of his 'terrible bravery' (*ahawor k'aǰut'iwn*)[29] displayed at the battle of Beirut in 1111, and elsewhere referring to him as 'a brave man and a powerful warrior' (*ayr k'aǰ ew hzawr paterazmoł*).[30] The *Anonymous Syriac Chronicle*, the author of which often reveals a dislike for the Franks in general, calls him 'a most valiant man' (*gbr' gⁿbr'*).[31] His Muslim opponents concurred, and did not omit to stress another quality, that of resourcefulness, also demonstrated at the fight on the east tower: the *Kāmilu'l-Tawārikh*, while calling him 'one of the demons of the unbelief', refers to his 'bravery and cunning'.[32] Syrians and Armenians alike welcomed him as their leader. The *Anonymous Syriac Chronicle* recounts that when Baldwin I summoned him in 1120 to rule Edessa, it was 'to the delight of the citizens'[33]; had the Syrians not been included, the Syrian chronicler would have said so. The Armenians bore him no ill-will on account of his severity towards those of their race who had sought to betray the city in 1112. On the contrary, he was soon to inspire them to a deed of great valour on his behalf. When, according to the account of the twelfth-century historian William of Tyre, 'certain Armenians of the count's domains', 'fifty of the strongest among them', learned of the capture of Joscelyn and some of his nobles in 1122 by the Turks, 'holding danger as of naught, they launched themselves upon a venture of unheard-of enterprise'.[34] The Old French paraphrase made in the thirteenth century interposes an appreciation of the mood of the Armenians of Edessa which, though without any firm foundation in the text of William's history, may nevertheless be not entirely invalid, as a psychological deduction: 'Il avoit Hermins en la terre Jocelin qui mout l'amoient; grant duel et grant despit en prenoient sur aux de leur seingneur qui einsint estoit priz'.[35] William himself records the view that the Armenian commando may have been inspired partly by the expectation of a large reward.[36] At all events, the capture which was the subject of their action took place on 13 September of the Armenian year 571 in which the inscription was written, i.e. on 13 September 1122, when Joscelyn and Galeran du Puiset were taken prisoner in an encounter with the emir Balaq at the village of Tap't'il in the county of Edessa and taken in chains to Kharberd (Kharput).[37] The Armenian year 571 began on 19 February 1122 and ended with Joscelyn still in captivity. No mention of the captivity is made in the inscription, however. The news of Joscelyn's capture reached Edessa, according to the *Anonymous Syriac Chronicle*, 'on the eve of the Feast of the Cross', i.e. 14 September 1122: 'there was no procession that year, instead all was lamentation'.[38] Vasil's reference to his 'locum-tenency of the dukedom' seems to imply that he, who held the 'office of administrator (*verakac'ut'iwn*)', was acting regent of Edessa. The *Anonymous Syriac Chronicle* reports that 'King Baldwin was in Antioch when he heard this news (of Joscelyn's capture); he at once went to Edessa, stayed there, and put a garrison there under the command of an honoured monk, Godrey Almuin ("le Moine"), until they should know what would happen to Balak's captives'.[39] In fact, he did not go 'at once' to Edessa, the knights of which were 'successfully raiding Moslem territory during the following month'[40]; though ultimately responsible for the government of the county, he did not go there in person until April 1123, after the present inscription had been made, in the following Armenian year in fact; it was then that Geoffrey was given charge of Edessa.[41] Matthew of Edessa does not mention any regency of Edessa on the part of Geoffrey (or on the part of Vasil for that matter), but he knew of him, and speaks of him approvingly.[42] One cannot be sure, of course, that Vasil's 'locum-tenency' (*tełapahu'tiwn*) amounts to a regency,[43] or indeed that Joscelyn was in captivity at the time: as administrator, he may well have been considered 'locum-tenens' whenever Joscelyn was out of the city, doing battle against the Turks, for example. It seems to bear a certain emphasis in the inscription, however, and it appears safe to assume that the inscription was made between Joscelyn's capture and the end of the Armenian year 571, i.e. between 14 September 1122 and 18 February 1123.

The inscription contains a series of titles connected with the administration of Edessa at the beginning of the twelfth century and particularly valuable for being carved on contemporary stone, a more trustworthy witness than ink and paper. The least of these, the Armenian title of *išxan*, 'prince', always somewhat general in import, was borne by a number of persons in Edessa at the same time. Thus, when Thoros, whose position at Edessa will be discussed below, contemplated the assassination of the Turkish nobles Radwan and Aghusiyan, who took refuge in Edessa in 1095, in order to seize the citadel, Matthew of Edessa reports that 'the other princes (*išxank'*) did not consider it opportune'.[44] These 'princes', or the chief among them, could have formed the city or county council of twelve reported by Albert of Aachen as in some way subordinate to the 'duke' Thoros when Baldwin was invited to help Edessa against the Turks in 1098: 'the duke of the city of Rohas, called Edissa, situated in the region of Mesopotamia, sent the bishop of the said city, together with the twelve major prefects of the city by whose counsel every estate of the region was effected, to the same Baldwin'.[45]

The *verakac'ut'iwn* (literally ἐπίσταοις), the office of *verakac'u* (literally ἐπιστάτης) held by the prince Vasil, appears to be the equivalent of Syriac *mĕdabberānūthā*, the office of *mĕdabberānā* 'leader, provost, mayor'.[46] He would seem to be in immediate authority over the city council, if Albert of Aachen is right in discerning one, and the inscription shows that he might on occasions act as the *tełapah* or locum-tenens of the 'duke'. The office could be the equivalent of that of *tesuč'* '(over)seer' and *pahapan* 'protector' the titles given in Matthew of Edessa as those of the general Khaulukh, who was appointed by Malik-Shāh's governor Buzan in 1087–8,[47] though these may merely refer to a temporary military governorship outside the administration of Edessa proper, perhaps merely the command of the citadel. It more probably approximates to the office, admittedly somewhat ambiguous, of *k'ałak'apet* 'city-chief, city-prefect', which was that to which Thoros was appointed by Tutush when Buzan had been assassinated and his head brought to Edessa on a pole in 1094/5: 'and he (Dedush, Tutush) appointed city-chief the prince of the Byzantines (*išxan Hoṙomoc'*) Thoros, whom they call the son of Hethum'.[48] It was while holding this office that Thoros, curopalates, was influenced by the counsel of the *išxank'* in the postponing of his plan to take the citadel referred to above. The office, in regular use during the Byzantine period, is thought by Professor J. B. Segal[49] to go back to the Abgar dynasty; apart from the Vasil in the present inscription, the office is mentioned after the death of Thoros in 1098 only in connexion with one person, namely the Syrian Michael bar Shumana in *c.* 1129. But the rare mention of the office does not necessarily mean that it was not fairly constantly held.

Vasil, then, describes himself as a lord lieutenant of the *tukut'iwn* or 'ducate', dukedom of Edessa, i.e. the office of a Byzantine δούξ or *dux*.[50] When Edessa was captured in 1032 by George Maniaces[51] to form part of the Euphrates Cities theme, to which it thenceforth gave its name, it differed from most other themes (e.g. Antioch) by being administered not by a *duke*, but by a κατεπάνω or catepanus,[52] a subordinate rank. The Armenian authors know this title,[53] and Vardan gives it, correctly, as that of the Byzantine governor appointed for Ani when this city was incorporated into the Empire in 1045,[54] though Matthew of Edessa calls him a *parakoimōmenos* ('Paṙakamanos'),[55] giving the rank of *catepanus* to the contemporary Stephen, general at Ardjīsh.[56] Matthew, however, although clearly familiar with Byzantine titles, even if he does appear to take the rank of *parakoimōmenos* to be a personal name,[57] nowhere refers to his own city as a catepanate, only a ducate. The Bulgarian Basil (*Vasil*), son of Alusianos, he calls 'duke in (*and* of) the city of Uṙhay' in 1069/1070[58]; in 1086/7 when Philaretos's appointed *parakoimōmenos* was assassinated and replaced, according to Matthew by the citizens of Edessa themselves, by Parsama (Barsauma, a Syrian), the historian refers to the office as a *tukut'iwn*,[59] and when Buzan, Malik-Shāh's lieutenant, besieged Edessa, says Matthew, 'the whole city revolted against their duke Parsama', and, having driven him to his death, 'the princes of the citizens [the city council?] went out to Puzan and gave Uṙhay into his hands'.[60] And thereafter Matthew ceases to refer to Edessa as a dukedom. Buzan's representative in the city is called 'prince of the country of Uṙhay',[61] while Buzan himself is called 'the emir' or 'grand emir'.[62] The famous Thoros is nowhere in Armenian sources referred to as *tuk* or 'duke', although this (*dux*) is his usual designation in the medieval Western sources.[63] Fulcher of Chartres, who in 1097, one year before Thoros's death and Baldwin's take-over, had become Baldwin's chaplain and was therefore privier than most to his actions, refers to Thoros as 'dux Edessenus' and 'princeps civitatis Edessae', and represents the group that Albert of Aachen takes to be the city council as Thoros's legation. But he also represents Thoros as having the power to bequeath the city and province as a personal inheritance,[64] which was quite beyond the power of a Byzantine duke,[65] and may explain why the local Armenian sources do not refer to him, or Buzan or Tutush, as *dukes*: they were perhaps more, absolute rulers of Edessa. Matthew of Edessa's reference to Thoros as 'lord of Edessa' (*tēr Uṙhayoy*) suggests as much.[66] Thoros may thus to some extent have followed closely in the footsteps of his former superior Philaretos, who had exploited his Byzantine legitimacy as *curopalates*, perhaps even *sebastos*, the title which had replaced *patrikios* as the honorific of a *dux*,[67] to forge himself a sovereign state from Melitene to Antioch, and including Edessa, which was recognized by the Emperor Nicephorus Botaniates,[68] and subsisted until 1085. Thoros, like Philaretos, held the title of *curopalates*, probably conferred upon him while he was acting as Philaretos's lieutenant at Melitene, at the time of his appointment as *k'ałak'apet* or 'city-chief' by Tutush in 1094/5.[69] After the death of Tutush, he isolates the Turkish garrison (*T'urk' pahapank'*) in the main, 'Maniaces's', citadel (*Manikay klay*), whose general reports to Malik Shāh that Thoros 'has walled up the town from the Sea Gate to (the church of) St Theodore, erecting twenty-five turrets, and has seized the lower citadel, and taken possession of (*tireac'*) the entire city of Edessa'.[70] Victory was not yet sure, however, for it was not before Thoros had, at great personal expense,[71] defended the city against two Turkish emirs including that of Samosata, then against Tutush's son Radwan and the lord of Antioch, then capturing the main citadel with the help of an Armenian defector from the sultan's army, Mekhithar, who held the Byzantine rank of *patrikios*, and finally having the rebellious Alphilak, whom he called in to help him against the sultan, put to death in the hammam, that Thoros became completely master of Edessa: 'and again the curopalates Thoros became lord of Edessa; and the rule (*išxanutʻiwn* 'principate, authority') of Alphilak in Edessa lasted thirty-three days'.[72]

It is difficult to define Thoros's exact status as ruler of Edessa, for it must have varied in the eyes of its several contemporary beholders. Thoros may have looked upon himself as an autocrat after the manner of Philaretos, although the fact that from the beginning to the end of Matthew of Edessa's account he is referred to by his Byzantine rank of curopalates, in addition to such titles as 'prince of the (East) Romans'[73] and 'lord of Edessa',[74] suggests that he considered himself a loyal Byzantine official, though with a now more exalted rank. Alexius I, unlikely to have looked upon him quite as Nicephorus Botaniates had looked upon Philaretos, i.e. as a sovereign vassal, if only because Thoros's domains were much more restricted, would nevertheless probably have confirmed him as *dux* of Edessa, as the Armenian prince Thatul, formerly a Byzantine official, who ruled Marash upon the arrival of the Crusaders in September 1097, was confirmed in his authority.[75] It is difficult to see how the Emperor would have had the opportunity actually to confer the rank upon him officially. As J. Laurent has said, 'Ces titres ne sont que des mots, et nous savons du reste que, de par le monde médieval, il est de nombreux potentats ayant accepté et porté les titres byzantins sans avoir jamais reçu de Constantinople un homme ni un ordre. Or, nous ne connaissons aucun fait nous montrant Thoros subordonné à l'empereur ou recevant de lui un ordre quelconque. De plus, dans la période où Thoros apparaît à Edesse, le gouvernement grec a depuis longemps cessé d'avoir aucune espèce d'autorité en Mesopotamie.[76] The Asian themes had disintegrated,[77] and *duces* in distant parts in these troubled times were best treated with a resigned tolerance, like the rebellious Armenian *dux* of Trapezus and Tebenna in *c.* 1105, Gregorios Taronites (? Grigor Taronacʻi)[78]; the Emperor could do little but be grateful if a self-appointed *dux* considered himself still bound, however tenuously, to Byzantium.[79] Many of the citizens of Edessa themselves, however, a greater reality for Thoros, would regard him as a detestable Byzantine official, and those among them who were Armenian and Syrian Orthodox would reproach him for being, like Philaretos, a member of the Greek Orthodox Church.[80] The arrival of the Franks at Edessa no doubt brought the opposition to Thoros to a head, and whatever Baldwin's own role in his assassination, if any, may have been, they were not slow to profit by it. One notices a tendency in the Western sources to belittle Thoros in order to aggrandize Baldwin, future king of Jerusalem.[81] One passage is particularly interesting in reporting what one might have imagined to be a logical attitude on the part of some of the citizens of Edessa towards the curopalates who was acting like their sovereign. 'The citizens of the city', reads the Old French version of the History of William of Tyre, 'saw that Baldwin was very gracious and wise and doughty and valiant in all things, so that they were much aggrieved that that man who was worth nothing and had done them many wrongs should have risen so far above them and the entire city.'[82] Philaretos, as we know, was himself considered an upstart[83]; why not Thoros? The Old French version, however, was made in the middle of the thirteenth century, a century and a half after the events for details of which William of Tyre himself was dependent on earlier historians. The passage is an example of the way in which the Old French translator, in Runciman's words, 'paraphrased some passages and included comments of doubtful value',[84] for William's Latin original (*c.* 1184) contains no reference to Thoros as *parvenu*, but shows the citizens of Edessa as finding it 'unfitting that one (Baldwin) who was worthy, as the liberator of the city and the securer of peace, to take possession of the whole (city) and judiciously administer all (its affairs), should have a useless man (Thoros) as his equal in the city'.[85] William's complaint, therefore, is that Thoros was inefficient, not an upstart; he elsewhere calls Thoros a 'useless leader' who, unable to deal with the attacks of the Turks, still clung to his 'jurisdiction' over the city even though the citizens urged him to give up the 'administration' of his 'presidency',[86] terms which the Old French paraphraser interestingly, for it is in the vernacular of his time, that no doubt in which William himself thought, renders as *baillie*, roughly 'governorship'.[87] He casts no doubt upon the legitimacy of Thoros as Byzantine governor (*praeses*, O.F. *bailliz*)[88] and duke.[89] On the contrary, William, represents Thoros as a hereditary ruler, for what otherwise would be the significance of the remark that Thoros had no children? A Byzantine dukedom was not, as already remarked, hereditary, any more than a Frankish *baillie* was, and the childless rarely aim at founding a dynasty. An explanation lies in the feudal mentality and political aspirations of the Franks themselves. Baldwin, hungry for land and power, secured, by means of a threat to withdraw his military aid, his adoption as son and heir by the man he observed to wield authority in Edessa. Thoros was probably reluctant to do so. Guibert of Nogent, in his version of the *Gesta Dei per Francos* of *c.* 1109, states that Thoros was ardently desirous of attaching to his cause one of the Frankish nobles, whom he would be willing to adopt, though Guibert makes it clear that he had this information from others.[90] A variant passage in the *Historia Ierusolimitana* by Baudri of Bourgueil, writing between 1108 and 1110 and whose main task was to improve the literary style of the *Gesta*, states that Thoros, being childless, for this reason adopted Baldwin as his son, much impressed by his personality.[91] All the *Gesta Francorum*, first published in 1100 or 1101, says, however, is that Thoros, hearing of Baldwin's steadfastness, sent him a delegation, whereupon 'they became friends, as father and son'.[92] Fulcher of Chartres, who as Baldwin's chaplain would most probably have been present on this occasion in 1098 and who wrote the first instalment of his History in 1101 – and though the most reliable of all was in Cahen's words, 'partial par nécessité', particularly in his account of the affair at Edessa,[93] says roughly the same as the *Gesta*, namely, that Thoros and Baldwin vowed each other lifelong friendship, 'as father and son', but that in the event of Thoros's demise, the city and territory of Edessa would be Baldwin's as a perpetual inheritance.[94] According to Albert of Aachen, Thoros proceeded to the adoption reluctantly, 'willy-nilly', his hand forced by the city council.[95] Albert wrote after 1119, and at second-hand, never having been to the East, but the idea that Thoros was, at least, persuaded into an adoption has a ring of truth. He may not even have grasped, being used to the Byzantine system, the significance of a Frankish move in perfect keeping with the Western feudal system. The adoption ceremony described by three of the above writers seems hardly designed for an adult, being more like a baptism ritual in which Thoros plays the role of godfather; but it also has a certain suggestion of royal investiture which would have appealed to Baldwin.[96] Baldwin, anxious to make himself hereditary and legitimate absolute ruler of the rich city of Edessa, possibly conceived the notion that Thoros himself enjoyed such a status, that a Byzantine dukedom was equivalent to a Frankish dukedom. He might well have been over-concerned with questions of rank and status with which his family was well familiar. His elder brother Godfrey of Bouillon, now, though only as an official, Duke of Lower Lorraine, had seen the duchy, which was a possession of his mother's family, confiscated by the Emperor on her father's death, leaving him with the county of

Antwerp and the lordship of Bouillon. Baldwin's brother Eustace was count of Boulogne, while he himself had been allotted none of the family possessions and had gone for a while into the Church. Guibert, anticipating later events in calling him a count on the occasion of his first meeting with Thoros, divines that the chance of acquiring Thoros's dukedom was a great temptation for the lackland Frank, soul-fellow of the unfortunate Walter Sans-Avoir: 'when he (the soldier contacted by Thoros) inspired him with the hope of acquiring the dukedom, should he permit himself to be adopted by the aforesaid lord, the count believed it, and accompanied by the said soldier, made for Edessa'. When the conspiracy led by Constantine of Gargar, which Guibert, alone, imagines to have been directed against Baldwin also, results in Thoros's death, Baldwin, the historian reports, 'forcefully took possession of the dukedom transferred to him by the adoption'.[97] The take-over is referred to in the baldest of terms by the earliest account of the First Crusade, that of Raymond of Aguilers, composed during the siege of Antioch (1098) and at the end of 1099, therefore within months of the affair at Edessa: 'Baldwin, prior to the capture of Antioch, had marched towards the Euphrates and taken possession of Edessa, a most splendid and famous city'.[98] Perhaps all the truth is there. Raymond's work after all has the advantage of having undergone no subsequent re-editing.[99] But if the adoption story is more than an imaginative frill, the adoption is more likely to have been Baldwin's idea than Thoros's; that the Frank was skilled in all the arts of feudal self-advancement is further demonstrated by his subsequent marriage to the daughter of a wealthy Armenian prince, possibly the brother of Constantine of Gargar.[100]

On Thoros's death, Baldwin, hitherto referred to by Albert of Aachen as a prince,[101] becomes, in the mind of that historian at least, duke and lord (*dux et dominus*) in his place, otherwise duke and prince (*dux ac princeps*), otherwise just duke.[102] Raoul of Caen, who did not arrive in the East before 1108, likewise calls Baldwin duke at Edessa.[103] Fulcher, the closest witness of the affair, says that Baldwin acquired Thoros's principate, nothing more.[104] These are titles, not denoting in themselves any high degree of nobility, well familiar to the inhabitants of Edessa in connexion with the government of their city by the Byzantines. More interesting is the title of *comes* or count which becomes attached to Baldwin, and which he eventually passes on to his cousin Baldwin of Le Bourg when he himself is elevated to the throne of Jerusalem in 1100, and which passes in turn to the Joscelyn of the present inscription, to lapse with his son Joscelyn II in 1146. The occurrence of the title in its Armenian form in the inscription prompts one to wonder how exactly the Byzantine catepanate of Edessa became a Frankish county. The author of a variant passage in the early *Gesta Francorum* calls Baldwin, at the time of his accession to the throne of Jerusalem, *primus consul Edessenus*, which most probably means 'the (chronologically) first count of Edessa'.[105] Ekkehard of Aura, who arrived in Palestine in 1101, calls him 'count in Edessa'.[106]

When did he acquire this title? Sir Steven Runciman writes that, on assuming the government of the city, 'Baldwin took the title of Count of Edessa and made it clear that he intended to rule alone'.[107] But although a man might well declare himself sole ruler of a city, or 'king of the castle', he could hardly arrogate to himself a specific hierarchical and territorial title – for that was what it meant to the Franks, though not to the Byzantines, as will be discussed below – without the approval of his peers. That the question of new titles in Outremer was not considered unimportant by the Franks is shown by the fact that Bohemond and Godfrey assumed respectively no more than the titles of *prince*[108] of Antioch and *advocate* of Jerusalem, strange titles indeed as connected with territorial domains, unlike that of *count*. And whereas Bohemond was already a prince in Italy, Baldwin, a younger son who had been put into the Church when young, had no title at all on his arrival at Edessa. Anna Comnena[109] refers to all the Crusader nobles, including Baldwin, as counts (*comites*) upon their arrival at Constantinople, and Matthew of Edessa calls Baldwin a count (*koms*) before his assumption of power at Edessa (ch. 154), and while he does not specifically give him this title when enumerating the leaders of the Crusaders in 1096, he gives it in anticipation to his successor Joscelyn I (ch. 150); by this title both Anna and Matthew, in accordance with the Byzantine usage, as will be mentioned below, can only have meant *captains* or *military leaders*. This does not mean that the Franks concerned might without further entitlement call themselves counts among their fellows. The problem of Baldwin's acquisition of a *county* has hitherto been somewhat passed over, and although it concerns only one episode in the career of Baldwin between 1098 and 1100, it is not entirely a minor one with respect to the history of the county of Edessa as a whole. H. von Sybel, influenced perhaps by Guibert's anachronism (above, p. 211), is typical in calling Baldwin count (*Graf*) already at the adoption ceremony.[110] Paul Gindler, who devoted a thesis to Baldwin's career as Count of Edessa, follows suit,[111] although he does show some awareness of the hierarchical problem when dealing with the transfer of the county to Baldwin's immediate successor: '[Baldwin presented Edessa to Baldwin of Le Bourg as a fief

(Albert, VII, 31 *in beneficio suscipiens*). Only from this moment on does Edessa enter into a fieffal relationship (*Lehenverband*) with Jerusalem. Hitherto there was never any mention of it]'.[112] *Testimonia ex silentio* being what they are, the fact that there is no mention in the sources of such a relationship does not mean that it, or something like it, did not exist from the beginning. A count was not an independent ruler, and the indications are that Baldwin held this rank with the approval of Godfrey, and after the latter had become virtual king of Jerusalem.

Although he may have considered that Edessa was fully equivalent in status to either of the Frankish counties, Baldwin was never a count as his brothers were counts of Antwerp and Boulogne, that is, within the hierarchy headed by the Emperor Henry IV. His domain lay within that of Outremer and in 1098 the hierarchy of Outremer was in a confused state, if indeed it could be said to exist. It is certainly not clear who was at its head. Raymond of Toulouse's claim to be the secular head, though it had some support among the Crusaders, was not universally recognized, and it was Baldwin's brother Godfrey who in December 1099 was elected to the throne of Jerusalem. The Byzantine Emperor had secured the allegiance of most of the Frankish nobles, including Godfrey and Baldwin, while Raymond de Toulouse, though he had never taken the oath, was his most faithful ally; when Alexius in April 1099 wrote proposing to lead the Crusade to Jerusalem if the army would wait for him until June, there were many ready to recognize in him an indisputable leader of the Crusade.[113] The Pope, who had launched the Crusade, however, had recognized no other leader than himself. Baldwin may have seen a choice of allegiances open to him whereby he might realize his territorial ambitions. A certain caution in his way of proceeding at Edessa indicates that he did not ignore the claims of the Byzantine Emperor upon his loyalty, and he could certainly not ignore those of the Pope and his legate. But it must have been his brother Godfrey who was most influential in securing his recognition, whenever that took place, as Count of Edessa. According to Michael the Syrian, Thoros wrote to Godfrey at Antioch, promising to entrust the city to him, whereupon Godfrey sent Baldwin to take possession of it.[114] Michael's account is unlikely to be exact in so far as direct contact between Thoros and Godfrey is concerned. Nevertheless, there may be some truth in it as far as Godfrey's role is concerned, even if the chronologically separate developments are telescoped and confused. Godfrey would have good reason to look with favour upon the ambitions of his younger brother, especially after Baldwin's consolidation of the new state of Edessa by the capture of Sarūdj almost immediately afterwards. As Gindler says, '[Baldwin was now able to reduce the great deficiencies of the (main) army in front of Antioch. In the course of April 1098 a small detachment led by Gerhard (*privatus et secretarius Balduini*, Albert, IV, 9) left Edessa with money, horses and weapons (Albert, IV, 9). The Armenians from the domains of the count also participated in this aid. So Nicusus sent Godfrey a richly furnished pavillion. A little later Baldwin made over to his brother the revenues of Tell Basher]' (p. 63). The Crusaders had every reason to feel grateful. Furthermore, the dispute that broke out among them over the possession of Antioch,[115] captured on 3 June 1098, less than three months after the beginning of Baldwin's rule at Edessa (10 March), may give some indication of the probable attitude of his fellow nobles (and of the Byzantine Emperor) towards his eventual recognition as Count of Edessa.

Raymond de Toulouse, rightly foreseeing the ill-will that would be caused if they did otherwise, was of the opinion that the city should be restored to the Byzantine Empire; the Pope's legate, Adhemar of Le Puy, in accordance with the Pope's desire to co-operate with Eastern Christendom, agreed with him; it is probable that in any dispute concerning Edessa they would have adopted the same point of view. Bohemond, who like Baldwin had taken the oath to the Emperor, claimed Antioch as his own, and was supported by Baldwin's brother Godfrey, Count Robert of Flanders, and the Genoese; the reasons which probably swayed them to 'interpret' their oath, which Godfrey had taken with the greatest reluctance, would apply equally well to the conditions at Edessa: 'The Emperor was far away. He had not come to their aid. Even his representative had left them [in the case of Thoros, not of his own free will]; and they had taken the city and defeated (the Turk) without his help'.[116] The situation was simplified by the death of Adhemar on 1 April 1098, whereby the Pope, though informed, remained for a long time, until Daimbert's arrival at Antioch in the summer of 1099, without effective representation. Bohemond became independent ruler of Antioch by November 1098, was invested as Prince by the Patriarch Daimbert at the end of 1099, and remained such until finally humbled by Alexius in 1108 and given a Byzantine dukedom. Baldwin would have had supporters other than the nobles mentioned, for he was a potential supplier of lucrative fiefs to the lesser nobles, many of whom had joined him at Edessa while the discussions over the possession of Antioch continued. As far as the Church was concerned, Baldwin would have had no opposition after the death of Adhemar and before the arrival of the next official papal legate, Daimbert, in Jerusalem in December 1099. Arnulf of Rohes, the uncanonical patriarch of Jerusalem elected with the support of Godfrey and Robert of Normandy on 1 August 1099, had no political power. With the arrival of Daimbert in Jerusalem on 21 December, accompanied by Bohemond, and by Baldwin who had joined the pilgrimage at Bulunyas south of Lattakieh, the situation changed. Daimbert was determined to enforce the rights of the Pope. Arnulf was deposed as uncanonically elected, and Daimbert elected Patriarch of Jerusalem in his place. His first act was to appoint Godfrey and Bohemond as rulers of Jerusalem and Antioch respectively on behalf of the Church. There is no record that Baldwin was so appointed to Edessa, before returning thither on 1 January 1100.[117] Anna Comnena says that Godfrey, after having been established as king at Jerusalem, sent Baldwin to Edessa[118]; this might well be interpreted to mean that Godfrey's first official act as acknowledged, indeed consecrated, leader of the Franks of Outremer was to dub his younger brother Count of Edessa within the hierarchy of which he was now the head. This would be the most apt time from which to date Baldwin's title of Count, any references to him as Count of Edessa before the end of 1099, in sources largely written after he had himself become King of Jerusalem, being anticipatory. Daimbert probably had views on Baldwin's suitability, or otherwise, which eventually crystallized into active opposition seven months later when he tried to use Bohemond to prevent him succeeding his brother Godfrey on the throne of Jerusalem. But as long as Baldwin, as Count of Edessa, acknowledged the Advocatus of Jerusalem as his liege lord, and the latter had recognized Daimbert as his spiritual lord, Daimbert had no reason, or perhaps no opportunity, to interfere with Godfrey's appointment.

It is not entirely without significance, even if only for the manner in which Baldwin's rank would be viewed by his new subjects in Edessa, that the title of *count* was well recognized in Byzantine circles, although in the eleventh century it, like that of *duke*, did not mean as much there as among the Franks. The Byzantine rank of *comes rei militaris* was, on its introduction in the fourth century, an elevated one: 'In regard to the titles of *comes* and *dux*, it is to be observed that every *dux* had the rank of *comes*, but usually of the second class. When he was a *comes* of the first class, he was called *comes et dux*, and then simply *comes*.'[119] The governor of the diocese Oriens within the prefecture of the East as organized by Diocletian had the imposing title of *Comes Orientis*, instead of the usual *Vicarius*.[120] In the theme organization of the ninth century, the governor of the Opsikion theme had the title of *Comes*, instead of the usual *Strategus*,[121] but in general the title of *comes* was by then much devalued. In the seventh century *comes* was the title of the military commander of a *banda* or regiment, a colonel, and in the ninth century, according to Ibn Khordādbah at least, that of a company commander[122]; it was the title of the theme quartermaster[123] in the Middle Byzantine period; in the eleventh century it was the title of a ship's captain, the Admiral of the Fleet in 1085 holding the title of *dux*, and a few years later that of *megas dux*.[124] In taking this rank, then, Baldwin would not have appeared to over-reach himself in the eyes of the local inhabitants of Edessa,[125] or, more importantly, of the Emperor. Baldwin was bound to the latter by the oath taken by his brother Godfrey and the lords accompanying him, including himself, almost a year before his assumption of power at Edessa, in April 1097. By this oath the Crusaders undertook to acknowledge the Byzantine Emperor as overlord of any territories they might conquer and to hand over to Byzantine officials any land that had previously belonged to the Empire. Edessa was just such a territory. Alexius seems to have made no plans for the recovery of Edessa, but one might infer from the terms of the Treaty of Devol made between himself and the troublesome Bohemond in 1108 concerning the government of Antioch, wherein the Emperor showed himself prepared to allow frontier districts of the Empire to be ruled by Franks as long as they acted as his vassals, that his attitude towards Edessa was likely to be a similar one. A large measure of Baldwin's success, as one can observe in the manner in which he took over Edessa from the unfortunate Thoros, was due to his skill in the ambiguous art of diplomacy. Having had the Armenian ex-official Bagrat on his staff between Nicaea and Ravendel,[126] he did not lack advice on how to deal with Byzantines. The other Crusaders had shown some respect for their oath: in liberating a number of villages in the neighbourhood of Augustopolis in September 1097, the main army, from which Baldwin had detached himself, handed them over to the Armenian Symeon to rule on behalf of the Emperor; in October 1097 they confirmed the Armenian ex-official Thatul as governor of Marash on behalf of the Emperor. Might not Baldwin, remembering his oath also, perhaps sincerely, perhaps with the view of proceeding cautiously towards ultimate objectives, have decided to adhere to it, and to be, in the first instance at least, the Emperor's man? This would explain the trouble he took to achieve recognition as the heir and successor of the Byzantine official at Edessa, the curopalates Thoros: it was an attempt at self-legitimation. That a Frank might become an agent of the Empire, always possible and implicit in the terms of the oath, had just been specifically demonstrated by the appointment of Peter of Aulps as governor of the liberated Comana, although he himself had already been employed in the imperial service. It is difficult to form a clear picture of Baldwin's character. It is not possible to say that he was insincere; had he been notoriously so, the Crusaders would not have elected him their king at Jerusalem. He may have been more of a realist than anything else, and it is the idealist who is the more single-minded and predictable. Alexius was probably not at all sure what attitude he ought to adopt towards the Frankish noble who had taken the oath of allegiance to himself; had shown, according to his daughter's account,[127] a sensitive concern for the Emperor's dignity in rebuking a fellow Frank for seating himself on the imperial throne; was part of an army which had demonstrated its loyalty to the oath in handing back the captured towns in Cilicia to the Empire; and had now replaced a deceased ex-official of the Empire in Edessa at the request of its citizens. Had Baldwin immediately claimed the rank of *comes* it would not have shocked him, for what more could it have signified to him but 'colonel'? Michael VII had sought to buy Roussel of Bailleul's allegiance in 1073 by means of the superior title of *curopalates* as already mentioned; in 1108 he himself would buy Bohemond's in part by means of the similarly superior title of *dux*.[128] There is no evidence that Baldwin was ever on bad terms with the Byzantine Emperor. In 1102, as King of Jerusalem, he was to write him a courteous letter to beg his support for the Crusades.[129] In 1098 Alexius probably saw no reason to suppose Edessa lost to the Empire.[130] As for the citizens of Edessa, they may well have been unaware of the difference between a Byzantine county and a Frankish county. They soon found out. Armenian estates were given to Franks as personal fiefs, and those who worked them found themselves governed by the stricter feudal system of Europe; only Franks were represented on the county council. By the end of 1098 Baldwin had to put down a plot against his life.[131] But Baldwin was a skilled politician; he did not entirely ignore the feelings and ambitions of his new Oriental subjects; he turned Edessa into a politically and militarily viable unit, the practical success of which formed a solid basis upon which the popularity of the subsequent Count Joscelyn I, to which the present inscription testifies, might rest secure. When on the death of his brother Godfrey Baldwin was crowned King of Jerusalem – the man who had not hesitated to seize a degree of power in Edessa from which his predecessor the curopalates Thoros probably shrank did not hesitate to accept a title his elder brother, the 'Advocatus Sancti Sepulchri', had declined – the new king appointed his cousin Baldwin of Le Bourg count of Edessa; when the latter became in turn king of Jerusalem he appointed Joscelyn I count of Edessa. It seemed that Edessa was in the gift of the king of Jerusalem; when Baldwin II, without male heir, and Joscelyn I died in 1131, there was some doubt whether the latter's son Joscelyn II owed allegiance to the new king of Jerusalem Fulk, Count of Anjou, though the vigorous military action of the latter against Antioch, which was in a similar position, settled the matter in his favour. In 1144 Byzantine and Frankish titles became obsolete in Edessa; the affairs of the city were once again in the hands of a governor, this time a Muslim.

NOTES

1 Cf. Syriac '*Ūrhāy*, Armenian *Uṙhay*. The Old French forms *Rohès*, *Rohas*, etc., reflect the Arabic. In Turkish *Urfa* the aspirate has become a labiodental spirant (cf. English *laugh*, originally pronounced with an ach-laut).

2 P. 141, para. 34, 19.

3 See E. Ter-Minassiantz, *Die armenische Kirche in ihren Beziehungen zu der syrischen Kirche* (Leipzig 1904) pp. 2, 9, 21, etc.

4 For summaries of the Armenian history of Edessa during this period, see Cl. Cahen, *La Syrie du Nord à l'époque des Croisades et la principauté franque d'Antioche* (Paris 1940); R. Grousset, *L'Empire du Levant* (Paris 1949); Sir S. Runciman, *A history of the Crusades* (Cambridge 1951, reprinted Penguin Books, 1965).

5 Ed. E. Dulaurier, *Recueil des historiens des Croisades, Documents arméniens*, t. I, p. 227 lines 37-8, p. 242 lines 484-5.

6 See Runciman, op. cit., 1965, vol. 2, p. 239 and refs.

7 Grousset, op. cit., p. 298.

8 Tr. A. S. Tritton, *JRAS* (1933) pp. 70-1.

9 P. 282.

10 *tarʿā rabbā*, ed. Wright (Cambridge 1882) p. 32 line 1, concerning 'a breach in the wall from the south to the Great Gate' in A.D. 499-500.

11 'Edessenische Inschriften', *ZDMG*, XXXVI, p. 144.

12 *Edessa: the Blessed City* (Oxford 1970); see p. 236 n. 1., and Plate 5b.

13 'From Roman to Seljuk times attacks on Edessa would usually begin in the orchards outside the east walls', J. B. Segal, private communication.

14 See p. 203.

15 There is no mention of any such work in the large book on the Armenian community of Urfa published by a committee of its former Armenian citizens, *Diwcʿaznakan Urfan ew ir Hayordiner* [Heroic Urfa and her Armenian sons], ed. A. Sahakean (Beirut 1955) 1368 + 55 + 77 pp., otherwise useful for certain aspects of Urfa's history.

16 *i nerkʿin klayin veray*, Matthew of Edessa, *History* (ed. Jerusalem 1869) ch. 154, p. 318.

17 Tr. Tritton, pp. 70-1.

18 Ed. Chabot, *CSCO*, xv, p. 58, tr. Tritton, p. 71.

19 Matthew of Edessa, ch. 208, p. 401, dates the event at the beginning of Sahmi, 561 Arm., beginning 23 April A.D. 1112. The *Anon. Syr. Chron.*, the dates of which often require adjustment, has 1417, i.e. A.D. 1110 (p. 82).

20 Tr. Tritton, pp. 84, 82.

21 Ch. 208, p. 401 (*arkʿ omankʿ nengaworkʿ*).

22 Ibid., p. 402.

23 Tr. Tritton, p. 84.

24 The *Anon. Syr. Chron.* (ed. Chabot, pp. 59-60, tr. Tritton, pp. 72-3) has an interesting summary of the local power structure at the end of the eleventh century and the beginning of the twelfth, when Turks held Sarūdj; *R'fn*, tr. Tritton *Rāfin*, is better read as *R'pn*, for *Rōpen*, i.e. Arm. *Ruben* (pron. *Rupen*).

25 Ch. 208, p. 401.

26 Tr. Tritton, p. 84.

27 *ariacʿeal*, lit. 'having acted bravely', implies that his valour had been put to the test, that he was 'well-tried in valour'.

28 Ch. 208, p. 401.

29 Ch. 204, p. 390.

30 Ch. 206, p. 396.

31 Ed. Chabot, p. 70, tr. Tritton, p. 80.

32 *al-shajāʿatu wa'l-makru*, *Recueil des historiens des Croisades*, *Documents orientaux*, t. I, pp. 346, 443.

33 Tr. Tritton, p. 88.

34 *Historia rerum*, XII. 18, *Recueil des historiens des Croisades*, *documents occidentaux* (this collection will be referred to below as *RHC. Occ.*), I, 538.

35 Ibid.

36 quidam tamen asserunt, hos eosdem domini Joscelini diligentia vocatos, et spe remunerationis amplissimae, huic se exposuisse discrimini (ibid.)

37 Matthew of Edessa, ch. 234, pp. 441-2.

38 Tr. Tritton, p. 92.

39 Ibid., p. 91.

40 Runciman, loc. cit., vol. II, p. 161.

41 Ibid., p. 162.

42 'Count Čopʿrē was at that time general of the army of the Franks, a brave and powerful man, a very great believer, and he with great effort and labour kept from the Turks all the provinces of the Franks, Jerusalem, Antioch and Edessa, and comported himself bravely and with great skill', ch. 236, p. 445.

43 The (in Armenian) unequivocal term *payl* (pron. *bayl*) for 'regent' had not yet entered Armenian from Old French *bail*, its earliest attestation being in the Armenian translation of the *Assizes of Antioch* between 1254 and 1265 (see Cahen, *La Syrie du Nord*, p. 29, n. 6). Constantine of Lambron, regent of Armenia 1219–22, is shown as bearing the title in the Chronicle of Hethum of Korikos, 1296: 'In 1220 Philippe roi de France (*ṙē tə Franc'n*) died. . . . Baron Vahram, mareschalc (*marajaxt*) of the Armenians and other princes wished to make Prince (*brinj*, pron. *prints*) Ruben ruler (*baron*) of the Armenians; and Constantine, regent (*payl*) of the Armenians routed them near Sis . . .', *Manr žamanakagrut'iwnner* [Minor chronicles], ed. V.A. Yakobean (Erevan 1951) t. I, p. 79. Another chronicle attributed to the same author calls Balian of Sidon, appointed regent (*bailli*) of Jerusalem by Frederick II in 1229, likewise *payl*, ibid., t. II, p. 67.

44 Ch. 145, p. 300.

45 *RHC. Occ.*, IV, 352.

46 See R. Payne Smith, *Thesaurus Syriacus* (Oxford 1879) vol. 1, col. 817. I owe this identification to Prof. Segal.

47 Ch. 128, p. 282.

48 Ch. 145, p. 300.

49 See *Edessa*, pp. 19, 123, etc.

50 On the use of this Byzantine title in the eleventh century, see E. Stein, 'Untersuchungen zur spätbyzantinischen Verfassungs- und Wirtschaftsgeschichte', *Mitteilungen zur osmanischen Geschichte*, edd. Kraelitz and Wittek, t. II, p. 21: '[Already in the course of the eleventh century the title of *strategus* as that of the governors general of the themes falls gradually into disuse. The last attestation of its use in a specific case is . . . a document . . . of 1079; it is increasingly replaced by the term *dux*, a title borne in the eleventh century and earlier by governors of smaller provinces standing in a position of loose dependence on neighbouring *strategi*]'. The forms *tuk* and *duk* both occur in Medieval Armenian (see Ačaṙean, *Hayerēn Armatakan Baṙaran* [Armenian Etymological Dictionary], vol. VI, pp. 968-9; the first form probably represents a pronunciation *duk*, the final of the strict Cilician transliteration *dug* being unvoiced in Auslaut, though it may possibly represent a Romance form in *-g* (cf. Spanish *dogal*). Grigor Magistros Pahlawuni refers to himself as 'lord (*tēr*) of Mesopotamia, *magistros* of Constantine Monomach, vestiarius (*vēst*), and duke (*tuk*)', the ranks being doubtless arranged in order of their importance at court (*Grigor Magistrosi T'lt'er*, ed. Kostaneanc' (Alexandropol 1910) p. 213). The word always represents a foreign title in Armenian, both Byzantine and Frank; for the latter see, e.g. *Minor chronicles*, t. II, p. 60: '1093: Richard king of England made peace with Saladin . . . and then crossed the sea and was captured by the duke of Austria (*tuk t Awstric'-*)'; the

editor has not recognized Duke Leopold of Austria and has invented a 'tuk Taws tə Ṙičʻ', 'Duke Daws de Rich'.

51 *Cambridge Medieval History*, IV. 1 (1966) p. 196.

52 See G. Ostrogorsky, *Geschichte des Byzantinischen Staates* (1968) p. 261.

53 See Ačaṙean, [Etymological Dictionary], III, 1028-31.

54 *History* (ed. Venice 1862) p. 99.

55 Ch. 66, pp. 112, 114.

56 Ch. 67, p. 116.

57 Again at ch. 128, p. 281.

58 Ch. 101, pp. 234, 235.

59 'and the citizens placed upon the throne of the dukedom (*y-atʻoṙ tukutʻeann*) of Uṙhay his murderer Parsama', ch. 128, p. 282.

60 Ch. 130, p. 285.

61 *išxan ašxarhin Uṙhayoy*, ch. 137, p. 292.

62 *amiray*, ch. 143, p. 297; *mec amiray*, ch. 145, p. 300. 'Grand Emir' was a title used by Tancred after 1101 as regent of Antioch; see Runciman, vol. II, p. 32.

63 dux civitatis Rohas, Albert of Aachen, III.19, *RHC. Occ.*, IV, 352; dux (li dus), William of Tyre, ibid., I, 15. See n. 89.

64 misit ad eum legationem princeps civitatis Edessae . . . si dux ipse Edessenus forte obiret, statim Balduinus, ac si filius esset illius, urbem et terram suam totam in hereditatem perpetuo possideret, ch. XIV, *RHC. Occ.*, III, 337-8.

65 See *Regesten der Kaiserurkunden des Oströmischen Reiches*, ed. F. Dölger, t. I, no. 1012 of A.D. 1078.

66 Ch. 147, p. 305.

67 *Cambridge Medieval History*, IV. 2 (1966) p. 23.

68 See J. Laurent, 'Byzance et Antioche sous le curopalate Philarète', *Revue des Etudes Arméniennes*, t. IX (1929) p. 68.

69 'and he (Tutush) appointed as city-chief the prince of the Byzantines Thoros called son of Hethum' (. . . kʻałakʻapet zišxann Hoṙomocʻ zTʻoros or asēin Hetʻmay ordi), Matt. Ed., ch. 145, p. 300; 'then Thoros the curopalates (*kurapałat*) tried many strategems to become master (*tiranal*) of the city and to save the believers from the infidels', ibid., p. 302; 'Theodorus curopalates son of Hethum' (twdwrws qwrbl't br h'tm), *Anon. Syr. Chron.*, ed. Chabot, p. 54. The once exalted rank of curopalates, held by the presiding princes of Armenia and Iberia in the sixth century (see *Camb. Med. Hist.* [1966] IV.1, p. 603, IV.2, p. 20), used as a tempting bribe to the Armenian Artabazdos (Artawazd), strategus of the Armeniakon theme in the eighth century (see Ostrogorsky, p. 129) had devalued greatly by the time of Alexius I. Nevertheless, the title was offered in 1073 to the Norman rebel Roussel de Bailleul as part of the price of his submission (Dölger, *Regesten*, I, no. 995). The debasement of the titulature went hand in

hand with that of the currency (see Ostrogorsky, pp. 304-5), and it is, *en passant*, interesting to note a tax-collector most probably of Armenian origin, Nicephorus Artabasdos, informing the government in 1106 of varying degrees of confidence in the revalued nomisma (Dölger, *Regesten*, I, no. 1130).

Why, when and in what circumstances Thoros ceased to be administrator of Melitene, now the office of his father-in-law Gabriel, is unknown. It is to Melitene that he wishes to withdraw (ad propria redire, below n. 86) when Baldwin tries to save his life in exchange for abdication, according to William of Tyre.

70 Ch. 145, p. 303.

71 Ch. 146, p. 304.

72 Chs. 146, 147, pp. 303-5. On *Alpʻilak* (ed. Vagharshapat 1898 *Alpʻirak*), see *Belleten*, I (1937) 288 (ref. from M. H. Berbérian).

73 Ch. 145, p. 300: išxann Hoṙomocʻ.

74 Ch. 146, p. 303: tēr Uṙhayoy.

75 Runciman, vol. I, pp. 192, 195.

76 'Des Grecs aux Croisés, Etude sur l'histoire d'Edesse de 1071 à 1098', *Byzantion*, t. I (1924) p. 406.

77 '[Only after the battle of Mantzikert, following which the theme organization in Asia Minor had collapsed together with Byzantine sovereignty, does the process of decay appear to have again intensified]', Stein, loc. cit., p. 19.

78 Dölger, Regesten, I, no. 1221.

79 '[Whoever succeeds in becoming .... *dux* in several of the themes is now tied to the central government only by a loose bond, which easily snaps]', Stein, loc. cit., pp. 22-3.

80 This is the significance of the passages in Western sources which refer to Thoros as a Greek. Fulcher of Chartres knew the difference between the Greeks and Armenians, as his passage on the linguistic heterogeneity of the Crusading army makes clear: Sed quis unquam audivit tot tribus linguae in uno exercitu, quum ibi adessent Franci, Flandri, Galli, Allobroges, Lotharingi, Alemanni, Baioarii, Normanni, Angli, Scothi, Aquitani, Itali, Daci, Apuli, Iberi, Britones, Graeci, Armeni? *RHC. Occ.*, 335-6. In the next chapter (14), he refers to Thoros, whom, as Baldwin's chaplain, he must have seen, as a Greek (ibid., p. 338). Thoros's adopted nationality as a Byzantine official may have given him an aspect quite different from that of his fellow Armenians. Matthew of Edessa reproaches Philaretos for, though 'Armenian by both father and mother', having 'the manners and religion (*varkʻ ew krōnkʻ*) of the Byzantines', ch. 106, pp. 247-8. Thoros, like him a 'prince of the Romans' (n. 73), though Matthew treats him with favour unlike 'that first-born son of Satan, Philaretos', would dress, speak and behave like a Byzantine Greek gentleman, and worship as such. Cf. n. 88 below.

81 The *Anon. Syr. Chronicle*, less concerned, refers to both Thoros and Count Joscelyn I as *princeps* (*'aḥīdā*), ed. Chabot, pp. 54, 70.

82 li citeain de la vile virent que Baudoin estoit mout gracieus et sages et preuz et vaillanz en totes choses; si orent mout grant despit de ce que cil hom qui rien ne valoit et meinz maus leur avoit feiz, estoit venuz si audesus d'els et de toute la vile, IV.2, *RHC. Occ.*, I, 158.

83 See J. Laurent, 'Byzance et Antioche . . .', p. 66; but Matthew does not reproach him for his 'usurpations' (p. 69): Thornik son of Musheł lord of Sasun reproaches him for his 'gross impertinences' (sastik lrbutʿeancʿn iwrocʿ), ch. 106, p. 249.

84 Vol. 2, p. 477.

85 videntes autem cives quod esset dominus Balduinus vir strenuus et in cunctis prospere agens; et indignum reputantes quod qui dignus erat, tanquam liberator urbis et quietis fundator, universa possidere et pro arbitrio cuncta disponere, parem haberet in civitate virum inutilem, *RHC. Occ.*, I, 158.

86 et Turcis supervenientibus antequam praesidatus sui tempus esset evolutum, de necessitate moram facere compulsus, jurisdictionem continuaverat suam, nec ipso ad propria redire volente, nec populo ab administratione eum cedere compellente. Erat tamen praelatus inutilis, a subditis non valens propulsare molestias, aut quietem aliquam procurare, *RHC. Occ.*, I, 155.

87 si estoit remes tosjorz en sa baillie, ibid. On the usage of *payl*, *paylutʿiwn* in Armenian, see above, n. 43.

88 huic autem urbi praeerat quidam natione Graecus, multo confectus senio, utriusque sexus liberis carens, qui, ab eo tempore quo universa provincia Constantinopolitano subjecta erat imperio, missus ad eamdem urbem, praeses fuerat; O.F. en este cite avoit la seignorie uns Grieux qui mout estoit vieux, ne n'avoit fuiz ne fille; il estoit del tens que cele terre fu toute desouz l'empereur de Constantinoble, quar il i fu envoiez pour estre bailliz; *RHC. Occ.*, I, 155.

89 See above, n. 63.

90 apud Edessam, Mesopotamiae urbem, sicut ab his qui ibidem versati sunt accepimus, vir quidam ducatus honore praefuerat, qui Christianam provinciam quam regebat, non tam armis a gentilium incursibus, quam pecuniaria redemptione protexerat. Is senio gravescente jam squalidus, quum esset ei uxor et sine liberis ibentidem anus, dum Francos agnovisset Mesopotamiae contiguos finibus, multo aestu desiderabat quempiam, quem sibi adoptaret, ex Francorum habere nobilibus: qui, quod ipse pretio, hoc ille defensaret armis ac viribus, ch. XIV, *RHC. Occ.*, IV, 165; on this writer, see Cahen, op. cit., p. 9.

91 *RHC. Occ.*, IV, 81 var.

92 *RHC. Occ.*, III, 496-7.

93 Op. cit., p. 10 n. 6.

94 in hereditatem perpetuo possideret, *RHC. Occ.*, III, 338.

95 *RHC. Occ.*, IV, 353.

96 Fulcher, whose silence may be significant, since he was best placed to observe it, mentions no special ceremony, while Matthew speaks only of friendship (like the *Gesta*), gifts, and an alliance (*miabanutʿiwn*), ch. 154, p. 316. Guibert's account is clearly based on hearsay: 'the form of adoption in accordance with the custom of the people is said to have been thus (adoptationis autem talis pro gentis consuetudine dicitur fuisse modus): Introducing him (Baldwin) naked inside his linen undergarment, which we call a shirt, he hugged him to himself (intra lineam interulam, quam nos vocamus camisiam, nudum intrare eum faciens, sibi adstrinxit), and confirmed all these matters with a kiss; the woman afterwards also performed the same ceremony', ch. XIV, *RHC. Occ.*, IV, 165. Baudri of Bourgueil's similar account is also at second hand, Albert of Aachen's at third hand at least (*RHC. Occ.*, IV, 81 var., IV, 353). An Armenian writer has called the reported ceremony 'eigenartig' (peculiar), and appears to prefer to consider it, though the texts do not refer to it as such, as a 'Verbrüderung' (fraternization): Galust Ter-Grigorian Iskenderian, *Die Kreuzfahrer und ihre Beziehungen zu den armenischen Nachbarfürsten bis zum Untergange der Grafschaft Edessa nach armenischen Quellen*, Leipzig Dr.phil. thesis, Weida, 1915, p. 40 n. 128, p. 42. H. von Sybel, *Geschichte des ersten Kreuzzugs*, 2nd ed., Leipzig, 1881, p. 316, looks upon the episode as a legendary glorification of Baldwin. There may be much truth in it, however. What the anonymous eyewitness or eyewitnesses, from whose account those of the historians derive, apparently observed has much in common with the baptism ceremony of the Armenian Church, in which the godfather (*knkʿahayr*), the spiritual adopter of the child, is dressed in the ritual *sapik* or alb (the Franks indeed employed the Late Latin *camisia* to denote the ecclesiastical and the secular garment, shirt, deriving from the Roman tunica; see C. Köhler, *A history of costume*, 1963 reprint, pp. 116, 135, and *NED* under *chemise*). The godfather receives the baptized child on a large cloth (*bṙničʿ*) and holds him to his breast. According to M. Ōrmanean, the *šapik* in former times was open from top to bottom, and was fastened by folding one side over the other at the front; like the alb, it was not the garment next to the skin, but even nowadays the garment has a deep V-line front. Dressed thus, Thoros could well have hugged Baldwin, himself in a relative state of undress though certainly not naked, to his chest, and it is not impossible that their bare skins came into contact. In the Armenian ceremony the baptized child is then passed to the godmother (*knkʿa-mayr*), who dresses it in clothes of her own gift; in Baldwin's case, Thoros's wife may have placed a symbolic vestment upon him, and embraced him; see M. Ōrmanean, *Cisakan baṙaran* (Anthelias 1957), pp. 93, 166 (I owe further details of the Armenian ceremony to my pupil, Father Goriun Kojababian). What the Franks observed, then, was probably a similar religious adoption or baptism ceremony of the

Greek Orthodox Church, of which Thoros was a member, perhaps according to the local Armenian practice (the attempts of the Patriarch Michael Cerularius (1043–59) to standardize usages in the churches of the recently acquired Armenian provinces are unlikely to have had much effect in Edessa). One is led to wonder what might be the ecclesiastical implications of Baldwin's participation in the rites of a church divided in many respects from, if not actually in schism with, his own, although it is true that much of the acrimony had gone out of the controversies by 1095. Baldwin may have thought that 'Edesse vaut bien une messe', while Fulcher, his Latin chaplain, may have considered it prudent to maintain silence on this particular aspect of the adoption. Baldwin was also probably aware that the ceremony had something in common with the investiture ritual at Aachen of his European suzerains, the German emperors, and not only because their coronation robes comprised the alb and other ecclesiastical vestments (see Köhler, pp. 146-8). Viewed against his Flemish background, one could imagine that Baldwin, as an Isengrin, had some degree of contempt for Thoros, a (to him, perhaps) jumped-up Kerel in high office; if he had, he clearly did not allow it to affect his political realism.

97 *RHC. Occ.*, IV, 165.

98 *RHC. Occ.*, III, 267.

99 See Cahen, op. cit., pp. 7-8.

100 See refs. apud Runciman, vol. I, p. 209 n.1.

101 *RHC. Occ.*, IV, 350.

102 Ibid., pp. 354, 355.

103 *RHC. Occ.*, III, 705.

104 Ibid., 338.

105 *RHC. Occ.*, III, 542 var. *Consul* was frequently used by medieval Latin writers as a synonym for *comes*: 'comites, qui etiam possunt dici consules a consulendo', H. de Bracton, *De legibus ... Angliae*, A.D. 1259, cit. *NED*, II, 883c.; cf. M. Bloch, *La société féodale* (Paris 1939), I, p. 126: 'parce que "comte" avait en francais pour cas sujet *cuens*, on le rendait par *consul*'. It is certainly not to be assumed that Baldwin had adopted any such Byzantine title as *hypatos* or *protanthypatos*, though both were still meaningful (see Stein, op. cit., p. 29 n. 3, p. 30 n. 2).

106 That Ekkehard knew little of the events at Edessa is clear from his sanguine account in which Baldwin succeeds 'a most Christian lord deceased at a great age: hoc tempore Baldewinus comes in Rohas ... quae est civitas inclita, immo regio et pars Armeniae, consederat, principatum jam gentis illius consecutus, defuncto scilicet interim grandaevo seniore illo christianissimo, qui naviter gerentem, etiam in filium et haeredem adoptaverat, *RHC. Occ.*, V, 27.

107 Op. cit., vol. I, p. 208. Cf. F. Chalandon, *Histoire de la première croisade* (Paris 1925), p. 176: 'le comte de Flandre [! this was Robert II] entra

en possession d'Edesse'. Gibbon, *Decline*, ch. LVIII (6th ed., London 1921), p. 299, is more cautious: 'Baldwin . . . founded the first principality of the Franks or Latins at Edessa'; cf. also L. Bréhier, *Histoire anonyme* . . . (Paris 1924), p. 5, n. 9: 'Baudouin, plus tard prince d'Edesse et roi de Jérusalem'. Feudal niceties were, or were to be, strictly observed in Outremer: 'la féodalite se présente en Terre Sainte avec une rigueur et une précision que l'Occident na jamais connues' (J. Calmette, *La société féodale* (Paris 1947), p. 210). It is true that Baldwin could have encountered some indulgent attitudes towards feudal sovereignty among his near neighbours at home, the counts of Flanders (cf. J. Flach, 'Le comté de Flandre et ses rapports avec la couronne de France du IXe au XIIe siècle', *Revue Historique*, CXV, 1915), and the German nobles, but Edessa could no more rank as a 'grand fief indépendant', in Luchaire's phrase (cit. ibid., p. 254), than it could an *Allod* or *Sonnenlehen* "fief of the sun" (J. W. Thompson, *Feudal Germany* (Chicago 1928), p. 29).

108 'The title of prince (*princeps*), attached to a territory, was little known in the West, except in southern Italy, where it was used by certain Norman rulers who had taken over Lombard lands and who admitted no lay overlord other than the see of St Peter. It therefore suited Bohemond perfectly' (vol. I, p. 306). It would not have suited Baldwin so well. An Armenian *Genealogy of the Princes of Antioch*, thirteenth century, attributed to Hethum of Korikos, shows an awareness that the title needs explanation: 'and when the city of Antioch was taken and they gave it to Bohemond, because Bohemond himself was Prince of Taranto, he and his successors were called *prince*', [Minor chronicles], t. II, p. 108.

109 *Alexias*, x.x.5, ed. Leib, II, 229.

110 Op. cit., p. 315.

111 *Graf Balduin I von Edessa* (Halle 1901), p. 52.

112 Ibid., p. 38.

113 Runciman, vol. I, p. 272. I follow Runciman's chronology of the First Crusade, based in the main on H. Hagemeyer, *Chronologie de la Première Croisade* (Paris 1902) (see ibid., p. 121 n. 1).

114 XV, vii, tr. Chabot, III, 184, Armenian version (Jerusalem 1871) p. 404.

115 See Runciman, vol. I, p. 249.

116 Ibid.

117 Ibid., p. 293.

118 *Alexias*, XI.vii.3, ed. Leib, III, 33.

119 J. B. Bury, *The Later Roman Empire* (1923), vol. I, p. 36 n. 3.

120 Ibid., p. 27.

121 W. Ensslin, apud *Cambridge Medieval History*, IV. 2, p. 28.

122 Ibid., pp. 37-8.

123 κόμητες τῆς κόρτης 'counts of the Tent', Stein, op. cit., p. 50.

124 Ibid., p. 57.

125 Syr. *kwms* and Arm. *koms* (already fifth century) would reflect Byzantine usage; the Armenian form exactly representing the Frankish rank (e.g. O.F. *cuens*) is *guns* or *gunc'* (pron. *k*-); cf. Ačaṙean, [Arm. Etym. Dict.], II, 322, III, 1311.

126 Bagrat, left as governor at Ravendel, was accused by his fellow Armenian 'Fer', governor at Turbessel, of treachery, and after torture by Baldwin escaped to the territory of his brother Gogh Vasil before Baldwin entered Edessa. Runciman (vol. I, p. 204) suggests that Bagrat's discontent may have been caused by a far-sighted realization that Baldwin's policy would be detrimental to Armenian interests. If so, he would have been considerably more far-sighted than Thoros and the other citizens of Edessa; on the other hand, he knew him better. But the details of Bagrat's act of treachery, if any, are unknown. *Fer* (Albert, *RHC. Occ.*, IV, 351) is not an Armenian form; if really genuine and borne by an Armenian, it could be a Romance version (O.Fr. *fer*) of Arm. *Erkat'* 'Iron' (attested in the fourteenth century, see Ačaṙean, [Dict. of Arm. personal names], II, 143-4, cf. Ašot Erkat', Tigran Erkat'), or a nickname of direct Romance origin (from Lat. *ferus*, cf. O.Prov. *fer* 'wild', O.Fr. *fier?*). (Fulcher and other sources, cit. *RHC. Occ.*, III, 342 n.d., in rendering the name of the captain at Antioch in 1099, given by Arabic sources as *Firūz*, in the forms *Pirrus*, *Pyrus* – which is probably the equivalent of Pers. Arm. *Peroz* – tend to confirm the report that he was an Armenian, a Persian being less likely.)

127 *Alexias*, X.X.5, ed. Leib, II, 229.

128 Dölger, *Regesten*, I, nos. 995, 1243.

129 See Runciman, vol. II, p. 35.

130 Later, when he realized what a Frankish county implied, he may have consoled himself by reflecting on 'the value of the Frankish county there (in Edessa) as an outpost against the Moslem world' (vol. II, p. 16).

131 See Runciman, vol. I, p. 211.

D. M. DUNLOP

The *Mudhākarāt fī ʿIlm an-Nujūm* (Dialogues on Astrology) attributed to Abū Maʿshar al-Balkhī (Albumasar)

Some time ago Dr S. I. Rasool of the Goddard Institute of Space Studies at Columbia University drew my attention to a passage in the *Kosmos* of Alexander von Humboldt where mention was made of a new star seen in Iraq in A.D. 827, or at all events, since the exact year was doubtful, in the first half of the ninth century during the caliphate of al-Ma'mūn (198/813–218/833). Dr Rasool's interest was to find historical evidence regarding the possible temporary appearance of a 'bright new star' in the constellation Scorpio some time in the ninth century. The reason for this interest was the recent observation that the constellation of Scorpio is a source of very strong X-ray emission. One of the explanations of this intense radiation could be that a star located in this region of the sky exploded about 1,000 years ago and it is the small fragment of the centre of the star, though invisible to the eye, that may still be emitting the observed X-rays. Several exploding stars known as novae and supernovae have been observed by the naked eye during the last thousand years, e.g. Tycho Brahe's new star of November 1572, and Dr Rasool's interest was to look for evidence of one such event taking place in the ninth century in that particular region of the sky.

The new star mentioned by Von Humboldt was said to have been observed at 'Babylon', presumably the ruins of the ancient city on the Euphrates, unless Baghdad on the Tigris or simply Iraq in general is meant, by the 'two famous Arabian astronomers Haly and Giafar Ben Mohamed Albumazar'. There was no difficulty about identifying the second of these. Abū Maʿshar Jaʿfar b. Muḥammad al-Balkhī, commonly called Albumasar, spent part of his life in Baghdad and died, over 100 years old, it is said, in 272/886. A well-known astrologer, he may easily have observed at the time and place indicated by Von Humboldt. Haly (ʿAlī) presented more of a problem, since it is at first sight by no means clear which ʿAlī is meant. After a great deal of trouble to Dr Rasool as well as myself, I was able to locate the source of Von Humboldt's statement in the Commentary of Haly (i.e. ʿAlī b. Riḍwān of Cairo who died in 453/1061)[1] on the *Quadripartitum* (*Kitāb al-Arbaʿ*) of Ptolemy, in a passage which implies that ʿAlī b. Riḍwān had as a young man seen such a star,[2] pointing to a date earlier in the eleventh century for the appearance. The matter was subsequently taken up in a paper by Dr Bernard R. Goldstein, in which he determined the date of ʿAlī b. Riḍwān's observation as 30 April 1006.[3]

Abū Maʿshar, on the other hand, had recorded an observation made by him at an unspecified date (I quote the late Professor Lynn Thorndike's translation of the Latin version of Abū Maʿshar's *Kitāb al-Mudhākarāt fī ʿIlm an-Nujūm*): Said Albumasar, 'The philosophers say, and Aristotle himself, that comets are in the sky in the sphere of fire, and that nothing of them is formed in the heavens, and that the heavens undergo no alteration. But they all have erred in this opinion. For I saw with my own eyes a comet beyond Venus. And I knew that the comet was above Venus, because its color was not affected. And many have told me that they have seen a comet beyond Jupiter and sometimes beyond Saturn.'[4]

The net result was that as the basis of Von Humboldt's statement about the new star of A.D. 827 we have notices of two phenomena seen at widely different times and places, one apparently a comet. This is enough to make it certain that the statement, which has frequently been repeated, was ill-founded, and the inquiry, so far as it concerns Arabic literary sources,[5] might appear to be closed. But before leaving the question it seemed desirable to recover if possible Abū Maʿshar's original Arabic. This was the beginning of another inquiry, not connected directly with astronomy, which is the subject of the present paper.

Abū Maʿshar Jaʿfar b. Muḥammad al-Balkhī is a figure of considerable interest about whom not much is known. According to the *Fihrist*, he was originally a traditionist with a house on the west bank in Baghdad near the Khurāsān gate, who had a dislike for al-Kindī because of his philosophical studies and stirred up the common people against him, until at the age of 47, by al-Kindī's contrivance, he began to be interested in the exact sciences and eventually became a famous astrologer.[6] Ibn Khallikān gives his biography, which is, however, largely concerned with reporting an anecdote of the search which he made, from astrological directions, for a man 'upon a mountain of gold in a sea of blood'. It turned out that the wanted man, anticipating that the astrologer would be called in and wishing to baffle him in his search, had taken his seat on a gold mortar placed in a vessel containing blood and remained there for several days (!). Both were afterwards complimented by an unnamed prince for their sagacity.[7] The *Fihrist* gives a long list of Abū Maʿshar's works, of which few have been studied in the original Arabic in modern times. An exception is the *Kitāb al-Ulūf* (Book of the Thousand Year Periods), the existing fragments of which formed the subject of an article by J. Lippert.[8]

Apart from a notice of Steinscheider,[9] the *Kitāb al-Mudhākarāt fi ʿIlm an-Nujūm* (Dialogues on Astrology) was virtually unknown till Professor Thorndike drew attention to it in 1954. It is listed among the works of Abū Maʿshar by Brockelmann,[10] but this is a mistake which has gone uncorrected. In form the work consists, at least for the most part,[11] in conversations on astrology between Abū Maʿshar and one Abū Saʿīd Shādhān b. Baḥr, in which the latter speaking in the first person raises questions, sometimes objections, which are replied to by Abū Maʿshar. That is, the book was compiled by Shādhān b. Baḥr, and it is correctly given as his by al-Qifṭī.[12] Of Shādhān b. Baḥr himself practically nothing is known except what is contained in his book. His own and his father's name (Shādhān, Baḥr) suggest an Iranian origin, and it is consonant with this that he is called in one place al-Kirmānī,[13] i.e. a native of the province of Kirmān, lying immediately east of Fārs (not apparently a native of Kirmān city, which was then called Bardasīr).[14] He may probably have been a pupil of Abū Maʿshar. It is obviously with reference to him that the Latin version of the book studied by Thorndike is called *Albumasar in Sadan* by Peter of Abano.[15] The time and place of the Latin translation and the name of the translator are alike unknown at present. As regards time, the reference in Peter of Abano, which also caught the attention in the Renaissance of the famous scholar Giovanni Pico della Mirandola,[16] is not very important, for at Peter of Abano's date (he was born towards the middle of the thirteenth century) most of the Latin translations from Arabic had already been made, beginning as early as the tenth century.[17]

Several manuscripts of the Latin version were known to Professor Thorndike. The original Arabic, on the other hand, appears to exist in a single Cambridge manuscript.[18] In previous years I had seen and used the manuscript, and had cited from it a curious reference to beetle talismans or scarabs, apparently, as popular in Baghdad in early ʿAbbāsid times.[19] I was again interested in it for the reason mentioned above (p. 230), being unable to recall having seen the Arabic of the passage quoted by Professor Thorndike when the manuscript was previously in my hands. I also wanted to check a statement in the work cited more than once by later authors[20] to the effect that the four most skilful translators in Islam were Ḥunain b.

Isḥāq, Ya'qūb b. Isḥāq al-Kindī, Thābit b. Qurrah al-Ḥarrānī and 'Umar b. Farrūkhān aṭ-Ṭabarī, and in particular to see the context in which the statement was made. (Ḥunain b. Isḥāq and Thābit b. Qurrah many people would be prepared to grant. Ya'qub b. Isḥāq al-Kindī, i.e. the celebrated philosopher, was no translator in the strict sense of the term, though he knew some Greek.[21] 'Umar b. Farrūkhān is very little known.[22]) I accordingly made a request to Cambridge University Library for a microfilm which was soon supplied. This was later printed out at the Goddard Institute of Space Studies, Columbia University, and I got some additional photostats from Cambridge. I should like here to express my thanks to the authorities and experts of both the Library and the Institute.

The manuscript is described by E. G. Browne[23] as containing Abū Ma'shar's *Kitāb al-Mudhākarāt* on folios 1-99. But this is not an exact statement of the contents of these pages, which include several other works not noticed by Professor Browne. On fol. 20a, last line, we have: *tammat hādhihi'l-maqālah bi-ḥamd Allāh wa-'aunihi* (i.e. This treatise is finished with praise to God and his help) and on the next page (fol. 20b) after the *bismillāh* a new work begins: *hādhā ta'līq min auwal kitāb al-Qaiṣarānī* [*sic*] *fi 'ilm al-aḥkām min al-juz' al-auwal*, Annotation from the first Book of al-Qaiṣarānī (read al-Qaṣrānī)[24] on judicial Astrology, part one. Again on fol. 28a after the *bismillāh* we read: *qālā Abū Ṣaqr 'Abd al-'Azīz b. 'Uthmān b. 'Alī al-Qabīṣī al-Mauṣilī*, i.e. the author known to the Latins as Alchabitius,[25] and what follows is his best-known work, the *Madkhal ilā Ṣinā'at Aḥkām an-Nujūm* (Introduction to Judicial Astrology),[26] divided into 5 sections (*fuṣūl*), beginning respectively on fols. 28a, 35b, 41a, 44b and 51a.

This is followed (52b) by a fragment beginning: *mimmā naqala Abī* [*sic*] *'l-Ḥasan b. abī'l-Khaṣīb al-Kūfī fī'l-masā'il 'an ad-dafā'in wa'l-kunūz wa'l-khabāyā wa'l-amwāl*, i.e. Questions on hidden treasures, treasure-trove, buried secrets and wealth, by an author who is apparently the same as the man called elsewhere al-Ḥasan b. al-Khaṣīb.[27] On 53a a new section begins: *i'lam anna burūj as-samā' ithnā 'ashara burjan*, 'Know that the signs of the Zodiac are 12 in number, etc.' Again (58b) we have yet another heading: *Faṣl ibtidā' Nawādir al-Qaḍā' wa-hiya arba'ah wa-'ishrūn bāban*, i.e. Section. Beginning of the Rare Cases in Judicial Astrology, in 24 chapters (*bāb*), but the chapters appear to be considerably more than twenty-four. This is perhaps the same work as the *Nawādir al-Aḥkām wa'l-Masā'il* of Sahl b. Bishr.[28] It appears to extend to fol. 92b, where after the *bismillāh* we find a short catechism on astrology, by way of question and answer.

This extends to fol. 97b, where again after the *bismillāh* we have the *Risālah fi'l-Quṭū'* of Sanad,[29] or Sind, b. 'Alī, to 98b. This appears to be connected with, perhaps a portion of, the *Kitāb al-Qawāṭi'* of Sanad b. 'Alī mentioned by the *Fihrist*.[30]

This part of the manuscript ends (98b): *wa-kāna al-farāgh min naskhihā fī yaum ath-thalāthā' sābi' 'ashrat* [*sic*] *jumād* [*sic*] *al-ākhirah min shuhūr sanah sittīn wa 177 'alā yad al-faqīr ilā raḥmah rabbihi 'Abd ar-Raḥmān b. 'Umar an-nāsikh*, i.e. 'And the completing of the copying of it (sc. the manuscript) was on Tuesday, 17 Jumādā II, of the months of the year 60 and 177, by the hand of him who needs the mercy of his Lord 'Abd ar-Raḥmān b. 'Umar the copyist'. Professor Browne rendered the date 'Tuesday the 7th (or the 17th) of Jumāda II, A.H. 767 (? *sanah sittīn wa 177*)', which remains mysterious. The solution is not plain to me, but two eras, the ordinary Hijrah era, with the hundreds omitted as frequently, and another seem to be involved. I am inclined to think that the year indicated in the second place is (1)177 of the Coptic Era of the Martyrs, which began 29/30 August, 1460,[31] in which case 17 Jumādā II would fall on 31 March, 1461, and would belong to 865 A.H., not 860. We might then suppose that in the text the digit 5 i.e. *khamsah wa-* had fallen out before 60, *sittīn*, or owing to a miscalculation the digit 6, i.e. *sittah wa-*, which would be easier to drop.[32] This dating would at all events be consonant with the further date 927 A.H. corresponding to A.D. 1520–1 given (99b) in a Maghribī hand in a note of ownership, as noted by Browne.

The remainder of the manuscript 'contains astronomical and astrological tables and two brief tracts on eclipses of the sun (fols. 120a-121b) and the motions of the planets (by Abū Isḥāq Ibrāhīm b. Yaḥyā an-Naqqāsh,[33] fols. 140a-145b)'.[34]

From the foregoing paragraphs it is plain that the Cambridge manuscript is not an extensive text of the *Kitāb al-Mudhākarāt* accompanied by tables and two short tractates, as would appear from the *Handlist*, but rather a collection of astrological works of the most varied character, as yet unnoted save for the two mentioned by Professor Browne. The *Kitāb al-Mudhākarāt* itself extends no further than fol. 20a at most, and probably no further than fol. 13a, top, ending: *wa-lā yastaghnī al-Mushtarī 'an Zuḥal wa-lā al-Mirrīkh wa-Allāh a'lam*, since the next portion of the text to fol. 27b is divided into chapters (*bābs*), which are not characteristic of the *Kitāb al-Mudhākarāt*.

If we now compare the Arabic text with the Latin translation as given in Professor Thorndike's article, we find that at least the beginning appears to be the same in both. The opening paragraphs of the Latin, as Professor Thorndike tells us, deal with horoscopes indicative of longevity and the contrary.[35] Quite consonantly, the Arabic begins: 'Stephanus said, The life of all that has breath is according to its line (*khaṭṭihi*) from the sun and the moon', and it goes on to discuss the baneful effects of Mars and Saturn unless joined with a favourable planet (fols. 1b-2a), as given by Thorndike.[36] Curiously enough, the expression in the Latin *almutam* (Arabic *al-mutamm?*)[37] does not occur here in the original.

Next in the Arabic comes a mention of 'mines of iron and high trees like those of 'Ād' (fol. 2a), which according to the Latin translation are signified by Saturn.[38] There comes immediately the following passage:

'Abū Maʿshar said, I once lodged at a *khān* in one of the villages of ar-Raiy with a caravan, and there met a man, a secretary on his way to Iraq. We had previously been friendly, and he had studied astrology. He said to me, "Where will the moon be tomorrow?" I said, "Will you stay tomorrow? The moon is joined with a quartering (*tarbīʿ*) of Mars." "Yes", he replied. "If the muleteers (MS *al-mukārī*, read plural *al-mukārīn*) side with us." We then spoke to them, and they finally agreed, on condition that we provide the fodder. We asked the people of the caravan to wait, but they refused, and began to mock us and deny what we said. So we waited, and they started off. I went up to the roof of the *khān* and took the height of the stars. The ascendant was Mars in Taurus, and the moon was in Leo. I said, "God help them, since they would not agree to wait!" Then I said to the secretary, "These men have destroyed themselves!" We sat down and had our meal, when suddenly a number of the people of the caravan appeared, covered with wounds, having been set upon by robbers two *farsakhs* from the place. Some of them had been killed, and their possessions had been taken from them. When they saw me they took up stones and pebbles, and said, "Infidel! Sorcerer! It is you who have killed our friends and robbed us!", and they began to strike me, till I managed with difficulty to escape from them. I then vowed that I would never again speak to any of the common people and the vulgar herd on matters of astrology. I have kept my oath till now, and I hope that I will continue so till I die.'[39]

This is an authentic picture of an incident in the life of an astrologer in the ninth century A.D., though it is presented almost by accident. What was of importance to Abū Maʿshar and his interlocutor was no doubt the astrological doctrine which the passage contained, and this applies presumably also to the mediaeval Latin translator. We note that the details are clearer in the Arabic. Abū Maʿshar did not go to 'Baldac' (Baghdad) as the translator had it, and the circumstances – very natural in the ʿAbbāsid empire – of a secretary travelling from Raiy to Iraq escape him.

It is in fact characteristic of the Latin version to leave out proper names which the translator did not properly understand or at least had no use for. After a short paragraph in which conjunctions are mentioned, and a question by Shādhān, Can names be derived by means of the ascendant? answered in the affirmative by Abū Maʿshar (both question and answer perhaps omitted in the Latin, or at least not noticed by Thorndike),[40] we have the following:

'Abū Maʿshar said, I was informed by Muḥammad b. Mūsā, the astrologer, al-Jalīs[41] not al-Khwārizmī, that Yaḥyā b. Mūsā an-Nadīm related to us, "I once visited al-Ma'mūn (ʿAbbāsid Caliph as above, reigned A.D. 813–33) when a number of astrologers were with him, also a man who claimed the prophecy, who had already appeared. Unknown to us, qāḍīs and legal experts had been sent for to examine him, but had not yet arrived. Al-Ma'mūn said to me and the astrologers who were present, Go and take an ascendant for a man's claim in a certain matter, and let me know what the angel (*malak*) shows you regarding its (or "his") truth or falsehood. But al-Ma'mūn did not inform us that the man claimed to be a prophet. So we came to a certain castle, and we determined the ascendant and set it formally down. The sun and moon coincided in a single minute and the *pars fortunae* (*sahm as-saʿādah*) and *pars futurorum* (*sahm al-ghaib*) coincided in the same minute as the ascendant, which was Capricorn. Jupiter was in Spica Virginis facing him, with Venus and Mercury facing towards it. All the people who were present asked what the man's claim was, but I kept silent. Al-Ma'mūn said to me, You give your opinion. I said, He is seeking confirmation, and has a proof from Venus and Mercury. But confirmation of what he claims is not complete and not organized. How do you know this? he asked. I said, Because the truth of claims is from Jupiter, and Jupiter is facing him in a favourable manner, only he dislikes this sign and the sign dislikes him. Consequently the verification and confirmation are not complete, and what they say of the proof from Mercury and Venus is merely a kind of adornment and embellishment and imposture which is considered admirable and desirable. He said, Bravo! and went on, Do you people know the man? We said, No. He said, He claims the prophecy. I said, Commander of the Faithful, has he anything to confirm it? So he asked him, and he said, Yes, I have a ring with two bezels. I put it on, and nothing happens. Another puts it on, and begins to laugh and cannot stop laughing till he draws it off. And I have a Syrian (*Shāmī*) pen with which I write. Another takes it, and his fingers do not move. I said, My master, this is Venus and Mercury, they have done their work. So al-Ma'mūn ordered him to do what he claimed. We said, This is a kind of talisman.

"Al-Ma'mūn persisted with him for many days till he confessed and renounced the claim to the prophecy. He described the trick which he had used in regard to the ring and the pen. Al-Ma'mūn gave him 1000 *dīnārs*. I later met him, and he was among the most learned of mankind in knowledge of the stars, and was one of the greatest of the companions of 'Ubaid Allāh b. as-Sarī."[42] Abū Ma'shar said, And it was he who made beetle talismans in many houses of Baghdad.

Abū Ma'shar said, If I had been in these people's place, I should have expressed a different opinion. I should have said, The claim is false, because the sign is reversed. Jupiter is unfavourable, and the moon is on the wane, and the stars are facing the ascendant in a lying sign, the house of oppressors, I mean the several signs of Scorpio.'[43]

This is no doubt more vivid than in the Latin translation.[44] It is not clear whether it is to be connected with accounts given by al-Mas'ūdī of two other, apparently distinct, occasions when al-Ma'mūn had to deal with claimants of the prophecy, each of whom pretended to possess miraculous powers which he was unwilling to demonstrate.[45] Nothing indicates that the account just given is the same as either of the others, but it appears to refer to an actual incident. On the other hand, one would like to have good reason shown, apart from the confusion in religious affairs during al-Ma'mūn's caliphate (of which his adoption of an 'Alid as his heir was symptom as well as cause) for the appearance of claimants of the prophecy at this time.[46]

As already indicated, citations from the *Kitāb al-Mudhākarāt* are to be found in later Arabic books. One of the longest of these is in the *Ta'rikh Sinī Mulūk al-Arḍ wa'l-Anbiyā'* (Chronology of the Kings and Prophets) of Ḥamzah b. al-Ḥasan al-Iṣfahānī, a work completed in Iṣfahān in 350/961.[47] The extract treats of the portents connected with Muḥammad's birth and the duration of Islam and of the Arab empire.[48] It is long enough to permit an estimate of the value of the text of the Cambridge manuscript, and since this portion of the Arabic text is also in the Latin translation,[49] it suggests further remarks on the basis of comparison of the Arabic and the Latin.

There is no doubt that the text in Ḥamzah al-Iṣfahānī is better than that of the manuscript. This can be illustrated in an example or two. In one place Gottwaldt's text of Ḥamzah reads: *falam yajid fī ṭawāliʿihā ṭāliʿan dalla ʿalā an-nubūʾah waʾl-millah waʾd-daulah illā aṭ-ṭāliʿ as-saḥari alladhī fī al-wajh al-auwal min al-mīzān*, i.e. (Muḥammad b. Mūsā al-Khwārizmī) did not find among the ascendants at the date of Muḥammad's birth any which portended the prophecy and the religion (sc. Islam) and the (Arab) empire except the dawn ascendant in the first aspect of Libra.[50] The manuscript in the same place reads: *fa-lam yajid ṭāliʿan fī dhālika ash-shahr yadullu ʿalā an-nubūʾah waʾd-daulah waʾl-millah illā ṭāliʿ al-mīzān wa-dhakara ash-Shajarī* (?) *huwa al-wajh al-auwal min al-mīzān*, i.e. (Muḥammad b. Mūsā al-Khwārizmī) did not find an ascendant in that month which portended the prophecy and the empire and the religion of Islam except the ascendant of Libra. And ash-Shajarī (?) mentioned that it was the first aspect of Libra.'[51] Ash-Shajarī, here taken to be some astrological authority, appears to be pure invention.

Again, we have in Gottwaldt's text: *qāla Abū Maʿshar zaʿama Muḥammad b. ʿAbd Allāh b. Ṭāhir anna fīmā waqaʿa ilaihi min asrār ʿilm an-nujūm anna ʿUṭārida maʿa raʾs aujihi yadullu ʿalā sharf an-nubūʾah*, i.e. 'Abū Maʿshar said, Muḥammad b. ʿAbd Allāh b. Ṭāhir (prominent in politics in the middle of the third/ninth century) asserted that among the secrets of astrology known to him was that Mercury with (or 'in') the head of its apogee portended the glory of the prophecy.[52] In the manuscript on the other hand we find merely: . . . *min asrār ʿilm an-nujūm anna al-kaukab maʿa raʾs aujihi yadullu ʿalā shaiʾ min an-nubūʾah*, i.e. 'the planet (not specified, though here first mentioned) with (in) the head of its apogee portends somewhat of the prophecy',[53] which conveys practically nothing, and is apparently due to careless reading. One may compare the Latin in Thorndike's version. The proper names have disappeared or are garbled. Aposaytes and the 'son of Moses' at the beginning of the passage (not given above) are evidently for Abū Saʿīd, i.e. Shādhān himself, and Muḥammad b. Mūsā, in this case al-Khwārizmī.[54]

Following on this there come in the manuscript the discussion of the probable duration of the Muslim empire and religion (the two are clearly distinguished) with special reference to the astrological views of Māshā'llāh and a longish account of Oriental history before Muḥammad, which cannot be reproduced here (fols. 4a-5b). This is evidently considerably more extensive than the corresponding part of the Latin in Thorndike's translation.[55]

Other matters are then dealt with on fols. 5b-7a, again on a more extensive scale than the Latin,[56] and we next come to a section dealing with the philosopher al-Kindī. His nativity is first given on the authority of Sanad (or Sind) b. ʿAlī. It is in this section that one begins to look for the statement mentioned above about Yaʿqūb b. Isḥāq al-Kindī being one of the four best translators in Islam, but there is no trace of it here or elsewhere in the manuscript. On the other hand, one has the following: *qāla Abū Maʿshar kāna* [sic] *ʿillah Yaʿqūb b. Isḥāq b. Isḥāq at-tarjumān al-Fārisī alladhī kāna yutarjimu kutub al-Yūnān waʾl-Qubṭ annahu kāna fī rukbatihi khāmm wa-kāna yashrabu ash-sharāb al-ʿatīq fa-tāb min ash-sharāb wa-sharaba sharāb al-ʿasal fa-lam tanfatiḥ* (MS *tanqaniḥ*?) *afwāh al-ʿurūq wa-lam yaṣil ilā aʿmāq al-badan wa-asāfilihi shaiʾ min ḥarārah fa-qawiya ʿalaihi al-khāmm... fa-māta ar-rajul*, i.e. 'Abū Maʿshar said, The illness of Yaʿqūb b. Isḥāq the translator, al-Fārisī, who used to translate the books of the Greeks and the Copts was due to an ulcer in his knee. He used to drink old wine, then he stopped for religious reasons and drank a honey drink. But the mouths of the veins were not opened, and no heat reached the internal and lower parts of the body. The ulcer grew worse... and the man died.'[57] While it is of interest to have this account of the last days and death of the philosopher, which are perhaps nowhere else described, what is here said of al-Kindī is little short of astonishing, especially as coming from a contemporary who must have known him well, at least by repute. (I know of no evidence that Abū Maʿshar and al-Kindī ever met. Al-Kindī is said in the *Fihrist* to have induced Abū Maʿshar to turn his attention to science through a third party.)[58] To characterize the philosopher of the Arabs (*failasūf al-ʿArab*) whose descent from the ancient Arabian house of Kindah was well known as 'the Persian translator' is so far off the mark as to lead to the suspicion that someone else altogether is intended. This, however, can scarcely be the case, and we have to allow that the Persian translator who is here said to have translated the books of the Greeks and the Copts is the celebrated al-Kindī, the philosopher. It is plain, even making allowance for some interference with the text,[59] that Abū Maʿshar had no clear idea of what al-Kindī's work consisted in, and if this is so, the loss of the passage where he mentions him with Ḥunain b. Isḥāq and the others is the less to be regretted. Abū Maʿshar appears to have thought of al-Kindī as a translator because he was known to be interested in the non-Arab legacy of the past, and left it at that.

We come now to the passage with which the present inquiry started, concerning the comet which Abū Maʿshar says he saw with his own eyes beyond Venus. This is given by Thorndike, as already mentioned, on his page 29. Now, as it happens, after describing the death of Yaʿqūb b. Isḥāq on fol. 7a, the manuscript continues (fols. 7b-9b) to offer material which can be illustrated from Thorndike's pages 25-27. (This material includes Peter of Abano's passage already referred to about the kings of the Greeks expecting an answer to prayers made at the conjunction of the moon with Jupiter in the head of the Dragon, fol. 8a, but here unfortunately without specific mention of the appropriate constellation, at-Tinnīn = Draco.[60]) Thereafter the next parallel between the Arabic and the Latin does not occur till Thorndike's page 30, i.e. there is nothing in the Arabic for Thorndike's pages 28 and 29, on the latter of which the important passage occurs. That is to say, there is a gap in the Arabic, and it is not possible from this manuscript at least, and at present, as already mentioned, it appears to be the only one in existence, to read Abū Maʿshar's original description of his 'comet'.[61] Thus on the astronomical investigation which has been described at the beginning of the paper the *Kitāb al-Mudhākarāt* throws no additional light, nor can it be said exactly how or at what point the observations of Abū Maʿshar in the ninth and ʿAlī b. Riḍwān in the eleventh century came to be conflated, as was the case for at least several centuries.

Continuing our examination of the text, we read (fol. 10a):

qāla Abū Maʿshar kāna Ḥāmid b. al-ʿAbbās maḥbūsan wa-kānat lahu masʾalah kulliyah ʿajībah ʿamalahā lahu baʿḍ ahl as-Sawād wa-kāna alladhī aujaba ṭūl ḥabsihi bulūgh tasyīr darajat aṭ-ṭāliʿ tilka masʾalah [sic] *ilā muqābalah Zuḥal wa-kāna as-Salmaʿānī* (leg. *ash-Shalmaghānī*) *al-munajjim mulāẓiman lahu fī khidmatihi fa-qāla lahu baʿd ḥabs sanatain au naḥwihā lā arā laka farajan ḥattā tustaufā* (MS *yustaufā*) *arbaʿ sinīn wa-yantaqilu tasyīr hailājika min al-ḥadd alladhī fīhi muqābalah Zuḥal fa-ursila ilā nuskhat al-masʾalah fa-naẓartu etc.*, i.e. 'Abū Maʿshar said, Ḥāmid b. al-ʿAbbās[62] was put in prison, and he had a nice general question (sc. of astrology) which was made for him by one of the people of the Sawād.[63] What necessitated the length of his confinement was the attaining of the direction (*tasyīr*) of the degree of the ascendant (the next two words are out of construction and may be a gloss, "That is the question")[64] to opposition with Saturn. Ash-Shalmaghānī[65] the astrologer was attending him in his service. He said to him after a confinement of two years or thereabouts, I do not see your release till four years are completed and the direction of your *hailāj*[66] moves from the position involving opposition with Saturn. A copy of the question was sent for, and I took the position of the stars, etc.'

This passage is not to be found in Thorndike's version of the Latin, though it may be in the part of the Latin translation which Thorndike omitted.[67] On the other hand the notice of Abū Maʿshar when he and other astrologers were 'with the army of the Cumans', as the version gives it,[68] is not in the Arabic.

The last correspondence of any considerable length involves a passage in the manuscript beginning: *qāla Abū Maʿshar ḥadartu wa-Sulaimah waʾl-Hāshimī wa-kāna az-Ziyādī ustādhan* (MS *ustād*) *fī ʿilm an-nujūm ʿinda al-Muwaffaq wa-aḍmara ḍamīran fa-qāla az-Ziyādī aḍmara al-amīr riyāsatan wa-sulṭānan fa-qāla lahu kadhabta etc.*, i.e. 'Abū Maʿshar said, I was present with Sulaimah and al-Hāshimī, and az-Ziyādī was a master in astrology (sc. and also present), with al-Muwaffaq.[69] He conceived a thought, and az-Ziyādī said, The *amīr* has thought of leadership and power. But he said to him, Wrong!'[70] In the Latin Sulaimah and al-Ḥāshimī appear as Salamas and Thesmies. Az-Ziyādī is Zegedes.[71] (These names in any case are obscure, and only al-Hāshimī perhaps can be identified.[72]) The rest of Thorndike's version of the Latin does not appear to correspond with what we have in the Arabic.[73] There has indeed been some dislocation of the text in one or other, for on fol. 11b we have the remark of Selech (=Abū Saʿīd) that if he had been asked a particular question, he would not have answered it as Abū Maʿshar did, and on fol. 12b the statement of Iṣṭifan (Stephanus) that there is no benevolent star but Jupiter, no malevolent star but Mars.[74] This apparently reverses the order of the Latin, where Iṣṭifan's statement comes before the remark of 'Selech', and of course both in the Latin apparently precede the incident involving Salamas, Zegedes and Thesmies and do not come after it, as in the Arabic text.

The concluding paragraph of the Arabic[75] begins: *qāla Aflīmūn al-mulk* (MS *al-m.lak*) *liʾsh-shams*, 'Polemon said, Sovereignty belongs to the sun' and ends: *wa-lā yastaghnī al-Mushtarī ʿan Zuḥal wa-lā al-Mirrīkh wa-Allāh aʿlam*, 'And Jupiter cannot do without Saturn or Mars, but God knows best'.[76]

What conclusions can we reach from this survey? In the first place the Arabic manuscript is obviously incomplete, since it lacks the passage concerning Abū Maʿshar's observation of 'a comet beyond Venus', also the passage mentioning the four best translators in Islam, which may indeed be wrongly attributed to this particular work, but is of less significance in this connexion since there are plenty of others in Thorndike's version of the Latin which are not in the Arabic, notably an extremely interesting list, but more or less incomprehensible in the Latin, of books on judicial astrology which are said to have been preserved under conditions of secrecy in one of the ʿAbbāsid palaces.[76a] Further, the manuscript is not very correct and is probably late.[77] The Latin translation also, as M. Steinschneider in his time observed,[78] appears to be a shortened or incomplete form of the original, though this is perhaps not so readily demonstrable as in the case of the existing Arabic, because Professor Thorndike signalizes omissions in his version in several places, notably towards the end. A good impression of the original *Kitāb al-Mudhākarāt* can certainly be gained from the Arabic, which as has been shown is not infrequently more precise than the Latin, especially on points of historical or geographical import. The work unquestionably belongs to an early date, and while there is some *a priori* likelihood that it was composed by Shādhān after Abū Maʿshar's death in 272/886 in view of the form in which it is cast, there is no reason to think that it is much later. The authenticity of course goes without saying. At every point where it can be tested it appears genuine. Prose works in Arabic of the third/ninth century, as the *Kitāb al-Mudhākarāt* may be supposed to be, are not very numerous, and such as throw light on ordinary conditions of life are fewer still. It seems to deserve our attention on this account.

But this brings us directly to another consideration. When all has been said about the work in the imperfect state in which it is preserved and about the interest which it possesses even so, there remains the question of its scientific value. Is it a popular or a scientific book? Apart from the baselessness of the main principle of astrology that the stars control events on earth or at least permit the foretelling of future events, which nowadays few would dispute, how far can the accuracy of the observations reported or the correctness of the astrological procedures as such which are here described[79] be relied on? Not very much perhaps, if we are to judge Abū Maʿshar's reliability by what he says about his contemporary al-Kindī. It would appear that he was not always careful in what he said and did not speak always after scrupulous inquiry, or at least that he was badly reported by Shādhān, for we cannot suppose that everything here is due to a faulty manuscript tradition. Should we assume that at least where observation and its reportage are concerned the *Kitāb al-Mudhākarāt* is generally reliable? Perhaps so, for here Abū Maʿshar and following him Shādhān are speaking of his professional work. But what was his profession? The *Fihrist* indicates that he was not a great scientific figure[80] but an astrologer and a very successful one, and a prolific writer on the subject.[81] As such he enjoyed a high reputation during his lifetime and later, especially perhaps, like some other Muslim scholars, in the Latin West.[82] Was he a leading exponent of astronomical theory or a great observer, as some of the astrologers undoubtedly were? There is little to prove this,[83] not certainly his alleged discovery, which was afterwards used to point to the appearance of a new star in the ninth century. On the basis of the present inquiry, which of course has been textual simply, one would be somewhat reluctant to accept a bare statement of the *Kitāb al-Mudhākarāt* on almost any subject without corroboratory evidence. That is to say, it appears as a work of popular astrology, and we should probably regard it in the same way, *mutatis mutandis*, as we should regard a popular book of the present time. There we can always obtain reliable information on what may seem uncertain or defective from some other source. Unfortunately in the case of this ninth-century work such recourse is not available.

It remains to list some proper names in the Latin translation as given by Thorndike, not all of which I have been able to identify (the figures after the names refer to pages in Thorndike's article already repeatedly cited):

Syxyres (23);
John, son of Almusour or Musur (23, 25, 27) = Yaḥyā b. abī Manṣūr (fol. 3b)[84];
Muchinnet, son of Zahac (23, 27), probably Muḥammad b. Isḥāq aṣ-Ṣaimarī[85];
Fizerus (27), perhaps = Phador below, i.e. al-Faḍl b. Sahl[86];
John, son of Talec (23, 29) = Yaḥyā b. Khālid b. Barmak[87];
Phador (29) = Faḍl, i.e. al-Faḍl b. Sahl[88];
Ysaac, son of Salomon (23), possibly Isḥāq b. Sulaimān al-Isrā'īlī[89];
Lenies, king of the Persians (31).

The Arabic also has the following name which I have been unable to identify:

Fahlah al-Hindī (fol. 3b).

NOTES

1 Al-Qifṭī, *Ta'rīkh al-Ḥukamā'*, ed. Lippert, 444, cf. J. Schacht, 'Über den Hellenismus in Baghdad und Cairo', *ZDMG*, XC (1936) 535.

2 *Liber Quadripartiti Ptholemei . . . cum comento Haly Heben Rodan* (Venice 1493), tr. II, ch. ix, 46b-47a. The Arabic original is in Bodleian MS. Marsh 206, fol. 78a, where the phenomenon is spoken of as an *athar*, 'sign, influence' or *naizak*, cf. Dozy, *Supplément aux Dictionnaires Arabes*, s.v. *nzk*, 'Les douze *nayāzik* sont autant de comètes; l'apparition d'une entre elles est le présage d'un événement funeste'.

The passage occurs elsewhere, e.g. in Cardano's Commentary on the *Quadripartitum* (*Cardani Opera*, ed. Spon (Lyons 1663), v, 212, and, in a slightly more complete form, *Hier. Cardani . . . in Cl. Ptolemaei . . . IIII . . . Quadripartitae Constructionis libros commentarii* (Basel 1554) 156), also in an anonymous Latin work of *circa* A.D. 1258 published by Lynn Thorndike (*Latin Treatises on Comets between 1238 and 1368 A.D.* (Chicago 1950) 60), where it is attributed to Haly Abenragel, i.e. ʿAlī b. abī ar-Rijāl, another eleventh-century writer upon astronomical subjects.

3 'Evidence for a Supernova of A.D. 1006', *The Astronomical Journal*, LXX, no. 1 (February 1965) 105-114. Dr Goldstein went into various aspects of the question, and reproduced the Arabic original of ʿAlī b. Riḍwān's description of the phenomenon from Escorial MS 908, fol. 24b, which does not differ materially from the Bodleian MS.

4 Lynn Thorndike, 'Albumasar in Sadan', *Isis*, XLV (1954) 29.

5 Further evidence from another quarter appeared in Bernard R. Goldstein and Ho Peng Yoke, 'The 1006 Supernova in Far Eastern Sources', *The Astronomical Journal*, LXX, no. 9 (November 1965) 748-53.

6 *Fihrist*, ed. Flügel, 277.

7 *Wafayāt al-Aʿyān*, ed. De Slane, 165 = transl. (*Ibn Khallikan's Biographical Dictionary*), I, 325.

8 'Abū Maʿshar's Kitāb al-Ulūf', *WZKM*, IX (1895) 351-8.

9 *Die europäischen Übersetzungen aus d. Arab.* (Graz 1956), II, 37 (§165, i).

10 *Geschichte d. arab. Litteratur, Sup.*, I, 395.

11 For this see below.

12 Ed. Lippert, 242, cf. *Fihrist*, ed. Flügel, II, 111, where correct in n. 2 to p. 245 *wa-dhakara aiḍan Abū Maʿshar fī Kitāb al-Mudhākarāt li-Shādhān b. Baḥrān* (*sic*) *dhā 'r-riyāsatain al-Faḍl b. Sahl etc.* to . . . *li-Shādhān b. Baḥr anna dhā 'r-riyāsatain*, also in the index, p. 230.

13 *Hamzae Ispahanensis Annalium Libri X*, ed. J. M. E. Gottwaldt (Leipzig 1844), 153 (=transl., Leipzig, 1848, 123).

14 G. le Strange, *Lands of the Eastern Caliphate*, 303.

15 Thorndike, op. cit., 22.

16 Cf. *Astrol.* IV, 8, cited in D. M. Dunlop, *Arabic Science in the West*, *Pakistan Historical Society Publication No. 35*, n.d., 83, with Thorndike, op. cit., 25-6.

17 Dunlop, op. cit., 30ff.

18 No. 1028 (Gg.3.19).

19 Dunlop, op. cit., 11. See below, p. 236.

20 Al-Qāḍī Ṣāʿid, *Ṭabaqāt al-Umam*, ed. Cheikho, 37 (=transl. Blachère, 81), and repeated by Ibn abī Uṣaibiʿah, I, 207.

21 See e.g. Matti I. Moosa, 'Al-Kindī's Role in the Transmission of Greek Knowledge to the Arabs', *Journal of the Pakistan Historical Society*, XV (1967) 1-18.

22 Some of his works are in MS in the Escorial, see the Catalogue of H. P. J. Renaud.

23 *A Handlist of the Muhammadan MSS ... in the Library of the University of Cambridge* (Cambridge 1900) 200, no. 1028.

24 Brockelmann, *GAL.*, *Supp.*, I, 392.

25 Ibid., 399.

26 Ibid.

27 Ibid., 394.

28 Ibid., 396.

29 Nallino's vocalization of the name (*Raccolta di Scritti*, V, 295-6), which appears to be right (so also Carra de Vaux, *Le Livre de l'Avertissement et de la Revision*, 70). Most authors have Sind. Both forms are very rare, Sind perhaps unique. For another Sanad, cf. F. Rosenthal, *The Muqaddimah*, III, 18.

30 Ed. Flügel, 275.

31 Mayr and Spuler, *Wüstenfeld-Mahler'sche Vergleichungs-Tabellen* (Wiesbaden 1961) 72.

32 The colophon is evidently carelessly written by the scribe, and such an omission seems possible.

33 I.e. the famous Ibn az-Zarqālah of Cordova, Brockelmann, *GAL*, I, 472.

34 Browne, loc. cit.

35 Ibid., 23.

36 Ibid.

37 Thorndike (loc. cit.) translates 'lord', sc. of the nativity.

38 The Arabic is: *qāla Shādhān qultu li-Abī Maʿshar wa-warada dhikr qaum min ahl hādhihi'-ṣ-ṣināʿah innahu yudallu (yadullu) ʿalā maʿādin al-ḥadīd wa-mithl ash-shajar aṭ-ṭiwāl al-ʿĀdīyāt*, which is defective; mention of Saturn (*Zuḥal*) has dropped out.

39 Fols. 2a-2b = Thorndike, op. cit. 23-4.

40 Op. cit., 24.

41 Al-Jalīs, lit. 'the companion with whom one sits', like an-Nadīm below, 'the companion with whom one drinks', especially with reference to the Caliph. Muḥammad b. Mūsā al-Jalīs, not elsewhere so-called, as far as I have noticed, is apparently Muḥammad b. Mūsā b. Shākir, otherwise simply Muḥammad b. Mūsā the astrologer. See a number of refs. in my article 'Muḥammad b. Mūsā al-Khwārizmī', *JRAS* (Oct. 1943) 248-50 (but the general contention there that Muḥammad b. Mūsā al-Khwārizmī and Muḥammad b. Mūsā b. Shākir are the same person is not right, especially in view of the present passage).

42 Apparently the same as the governor of Egypt ʿUbaid Allāh b. as-Sarī b. al-Ḥakam (from 206/822), expelled in 211/826 (Ṭabarī, III, 1086-93).

43 Fols. 2b-3a.

44 Thorndike, ibid., 24. Again an expression in the Latin, translated by Thorndike 'stichiomatic books' has nothing corresponding in the Arabic text.

45 *Murūj adh-Dhahab*, VII, 36 and 52-53.

46 For an earlier instance see D. M. Dunlop, 'Al-Ḥārith b. Saʿīd al-Kadhdhāb, a Claimant to Prophecy in the Caliphate of ʿAbd al-Malik', *Studies in Islam* (New Delhi) I (1964) 12-18.

47 Brockelmann, *GAL*, *Supp.*, I, 221.

48 Ed. Gottwaldt, 153-54 = transl. 123-24, and fols. 3b, line 13-4a, line 13 of the Cambridge MS.

49 Thorndike, op. cit., 25.

50 Gottwaldt, 153, lines 16-19.

51 Fol. 3b, lines 15-17.

52 Ibid., 154, lines 3-6.

53 Fol. 3b, lines 20-21.

54 Thorndike, op. cit., 25.

55 Ibid.

56 Ibid.

57 Fol. 7a.

58 Cf. at n. 6.

59 E.g. *al-Fārisī* might be an addition of some copyist.

60 The text fol. 8a, line 3, has simply *ar-ra's*, 'the head' for *ra's at-Tinnīn*. For a similar omission cf. above, at n. 53.

61 Thorndike's version of the Latin is given above, p. 230.

62 Evidently the well-known *wazīr* of this name who held power from 306/918 till 311/923 under al-Muqtadir (cf. D. Sourdel, *Le Vizirat ʿabbāside de 749 à 936* (Damascus 1959–60) II, 414ff.). He had a long life, having been born in 223/837 according to Massignon (*Enc. Islam*, new ed., III, 133a), and hence may have been Abū Maʿshar's contemporary for nearly 50 years.

63 The Sawād of ʿIraq, corresponding to ancient Chaldaea, associated with star-gazing from much earlier times.

64 With reference to the 'general question' mentioned above or perhaps with reference to the fact that the ascendent is not named, cf. similar cases above.

65 Apparently the same man as Abū Jaʿfar Muḥammad b. ʿAlī ash-Shalmaghānī, whose later life and death for extreme Shīʿite opinions in 322/934 are given by Ibn Khallikān (De Slane, I, 223ff. = transl. I, 436ff.) from Ibn al-Athīr, *Kāmil*, *s.a.* 322 (Tornberg, VIII, 290ff.).

66 A Persian word, equivalent to Greek *aphetēs*, applied to a planet considered as 'significator' for measurement of time by astrology, cf. *Enc. Islam*, 1st ed., art. *at-Tasyīr*, by O. Schirmer.

67 Op. cit., 29, n. 23.

68 Thorndike, op. cit., 30.

69 Regent for his brother the Caliph al-Muʿtamid till his death in 278/891, and politically important at least since 251/865.

70 Fol. 11a.

71 Thorndike, op. cit., 30.

72 Suter, *Mathematiker u. Astronomen der Araber*, mentions an ʿAlī b. Sulaimān al-Hāshimī (no. 492), who should perhaps be antedated to the ninth century.

73 Op. cit., 31.

74 Thorndike, op. cit., 30.

75 Not in Thorndike, op. cit., 31.

76 Fols. 12b-13a.

76*a* Thorndike, op. cit., 29 n. 25.

77 See the evidence on both these points above.

78 *Die europ. Übers.*, loc. cit.

79 There is in fact little technical detail on how observations were made.

80 *Fihrist*, 277: *wa-dakhala fī dhālika* (*ʿulūm al-ḥisāb waʾl-handasah*, i.e. mathematics) *fa-lam yukmal lahu fa-ʿadala ilā ʿilm aḥkām an-nujūm*, i.e. 'he began the study of the subject, but did not attain mastery of it, so he turned to judicial astrology'.

81 See the list of his works in the *Fihrist*, ibid., also in Brockelmann, *GAL*, Supp. I, 395-96.

82 For the works of Abū Maʿshar (Albumasar, Albumazar) in Latin see Steinschneider, op. cit., 35-39.

83 The tables of Abū Maʿshar are occasionally mentioned, e.g. by J.M. Millás Vallicrosa, *Estudios sobre historia de la ciencia española* (Barcelona 1949) 294, cf. E. Sachau, *Alberuni's India*, I, 304.

84 Brockelmann, *GAL*, Supp., I, 393 (there Yaḥyā b. Manṣūr).

85 Brockelmann, *GAL*, Supp., I, 396.

86 The *wazīr* al-Faḍl b. Sahl was also a noted astrologer (Ibn Khallikān, transl. De Slane, II, 472), which suits the context on p. 27 of Thorndike's article.

87 Cf. Iohannis filii Chaleg, Thorndike, op. cit., 29, n. 25. The identification depends less on this than on the connexion of ʿUmar b. Farrukhān aṭ-Ṭabarī, who is of course the Aomar Tyberiadis or Omar of Thorndike's p. 29, with Yaḥyā b. Khālid b. Barmak mentioned by al-Qifṭī (ed. Lippert, 242), citing the *Kitāb al-Mudhākarāt* (not in the Cambridge MS). See next note.

88 According to al-Qifṭī's citation (see previous note), ʿUmar b. Farrukhān was devoted to Yaḥyā b. Khālid, then to al-Faḍl b. Sahl.

89 Brockelmann, I, 235. According to Ibn Khallikān (transl. De Slane, I, 220), who has a circumstantial account, Isḥāq b. Sulaimān al-Isrāʾīlī was still alive in 341/953, which makes a connexion of his with Abū Maʿshar's circle difficult. Brockelmann, *GAL*, Supp. I, 421, mentions an alternative date, 320/932, for Isḥāq b. Sulaimān al-Isrāʾīlī's death.

L. P. ELWELL-SUTTON

The Influence of Folk-tale and Legend on Modern Persian Literature

Iran, with a history dating back several thousand years, has always been one of the most prolific sources of folk-literature and legend. It is also the home of an ancient and extensive written literature, which at times has drawn heavily on these popular sources, while at others remaining the preserve of an aristocratic and intellectual élite. During the past fifty years Iran has undergone vast and rapid social, economic and political changes. It is therefore a particularly appropriate environment in which to study the interplay of popular and written literature, and the ways in which contemporary writers have reacted to a stiuation of social change.

The use of folk-tales and folk-themes in Persian literature is of course not new. Indeed some of the earliest poetical and prose works of the Islamic 'New Persian' period, dating back to the ninth century A.D., consist of collections of popular tales. Among these are the famous *Kalila va Dimna*, derived originally from the Indian *Panchatantra* and extant in whole or in part in both verse and prose versions. Others of more purely Persian origin are the *Marẕbān-nāma*, the *Sindbād-nāma*, the *Ṭūṭī-nāma*, and the *Bakhtyār-nāma*. Collections such as these were made in the first place for the entertainment and edification of some princely patron, and though they became widely known and read, their appeal was primarily to the limited literate class. This was equally true of more sophisticated adaptations of traditional legends, like the tenth-century *Shāhnāma*, a compendium of the legendary history of Iran, the poetical romances of the twelfth-century poet Nizāmī, *Lailā va Majnūn*, *Khusrau va Shīrīn*, the *Iskandar-nāma*, and so on, and the didactic *Gulistān* of Saʿdī, written in the thirteenth century. Another development was the use of folk-tales to illustrate the mystical ideas of the Ṣūfīs, of which the supreme example is the long mystical *Maṣnavī*, written in the thirteenth century by Jalāl al-Dīn Rūmī.

But by this time both form and content were becoming standardized and stylized, and the art of the writer was directed rather to the elaboration and diversification of established themes. A notable example is the already mentioned *Kalila va Dimna*, which in the fifteenth century reached the apex of ornateness in language in the shape of Ḥusain Vāʿiẓ Kāshifī's *Anvār-i Suhailī*. We cannot therefore speak of popular literature exerting any direct or fresh influence on classical Persian literature after the thirteenth or fourteenth centuries, and we have to come down to modern times before we find the beginnings of a new outlook among the Iranian writers.

The change began with the penetration of European influence into Iran during the nineteenth century, and specifically with the introduction of printing, the spread of education, and the growth of the literate class. The public for a writer's work was no longer limited to the courtier class, and there was an increasing demand for books dealing with the many social and cultural problems created by the impact of new and alien ideas, and still more for a written language that was intelligible to the ordinary man. Early writers of this 'new wave' seem to have had difficulty in finding their feet. The court-poet Qā'ānī (1808–54) wrote the *Kitāb-i Parishān*, a satirical imitation of Saʿdī's *Gulistān*, in which like his predecessor he made use of anecdotes and popular tales, oriented now towards the new age. The reformer Mīrzā Malkum Khān (1833–1908) wrote political pamphlets in a simple straightforward language based on current speech – something not attempted since the earliest prose works of the tenth and eleventh centuries. To him also are attributed several sketches for the stage in the style favoured by travelling bands of players. But for some time the principal influence on new writers came from the translation and imitation of European, mainly French, writers: Molière, Dumas, Jules Verne, Bernardin de St Pierre, Victor Hugo.

By the beginning of the twentieth century writers were starting to look to Iran itself for inspiration. This was the period of the Constitutional Movement, and of growing self-consciousness and interest in political and social problems. One group devoted themselves to the historical novel, with the overt purpose of encouraging national pride and patriotic sentiments. The subjects dealt with ranged from the glories of the Achaemenid Empire in the sixth century B.C. to the exploits of the eighteenth-century Iranian invader of India, Nādir Shāh. Much of the historical content of these works should more correctly be classified as legend, and certainly in the novels of writers like Ṣanʿatīzāda Kirmānī, Muḥammad Bāqir Khusravī and Ḥasan Badīʿ there is no hard and fast line between fact and fiction. Nevertheless, a weakness of all these books was a tendency to draw on the resources of European scholarship rather than on local tradition. In some cases, for instance those by Shaikh Mūsā Naṣrī, the author gives away his sources by using the Franco-Greek forms of his character's names instead of the original Old Persian forms.

Poetry developed rather less notably than prose. There was more interest than formerly in social and political problems, but poems dealing with such themes tended to fall into the dry, didactic mould of the intellectual talking down to the masses. The only poet who seemed to draw his inspiration genuinely from popular folk-songs and poetry was ʿĀrif Qazvīnī, who has been described by one literary historian as the 'Persian Villon'. Strongly nationalist and republican, his songs inspired at least one revolutionary movement. Another poet, ʿIshqī, called on the legendary history of Iran to inspire his fellow-countrymen, notably in the poetic opera *Rastākhīz-i Irān* (The Resurrection of Iran), in which legendary kings and heroes appear and comment vigorously on the present state of their country.

The first prose writer to turn directly to popular speech and story for his material was Muḥammad ʿAlī Jamālzāda, who published his first (and for twenty years his only) volume of short stories in 1921. Significantly, he gave the collection a Persian title, *Yakī būd u yakī nabūd*, exactly equivalent to the English expression 'Once upon a time', the traditional opening to a fairy story. Jamālzāda's method, which he followed also in his later period of literary activity dating from the 'forties onwards, was to make free use of idiomatic and proverbial expressions for the purpose of giving a colloquial colouring to the language of his writings. While the result was undoubtedly an entirely new literary style, and one that had a profound influence on subsequent Persian writing, one also gains the impression that Jamālzāda does not really have an ear for the rhythms and characteristics of colloquial Persian speech; his use of popular phraseology has a slightly artificial air about it, as though he were selecting his material at random from a card-index. It is worth mentioning in this connexion that Jamālzāda has lived abroad for the greater part of his life, so that his knowledge of Persian society is largely second-hand. It is remarkable therefore that his short stories and novels have achieved the high degree of authenticity they have. Some of his plots are based on folk-tale themes; an example is *Dūstī-i Khāla Khirsa* (Auntie Bear's Friendship), in which the traditional cautionary tale of the man who befriended a bear and lost his life in consequence is transmuted into an ironical story of a light-hearted café waiter and a treacherous Russian soldier.

Apart from the linguistic one, there is another marked difference between the school of writing started by Jamālzāda and the historical school. The latter is concerned to build up national consciousness and pride, and while these writers did not always refrain from criticism and condemnation, the general tone is heroic and adulatory. The events and legends they deal with are the great episodes in Iran's history. Jamālzāda's writing however, and even more that of his successors, is primarily satirical. His purpose is not to conceal but to draw attention to the weaknesses and follies of his fellow-countrymen.

The outstanding Persian prose writer of the twentieth century, Ṣādiq Hidāyat, made the big breakthrough on the front already opened up by Jamālzāda. It is interesting that, while Jamālzāda remained silent throughout the twenty years of Rižā Shāh's autocratic domination of Iran, others of this naturalistic school, notably Hidāyat and his friend Buzurg ʿAlavī, first made their name during this period. Hidāyat was even more influenced by folk-literature than his predecessor. Indeed he became immersed in this study even before he started writing fiction, and quite a few of his published works deal with the subject. In particular, he was responsible for the first serious book in Persian on Iranian folklore, *Nairangistān*, published in 1933 at a time when most Iranian intellectuals still looked down on popular literature as beneath the notice of intelligent people. Indeed the book was banned in Iran on its first appearance, and was not reprinted until 1956.

As well as current folklore, Hidāyat also delved into the past. Like some of his predecessors in the historical field, he was obsessed with what he believed to be the baneful influence of the Arab conquest of Iran in the seventh century and the Mongol invasions of the thirteenth. Several of his stories and plays deal with these events, or with the heroic legends surrounding them: *Parvin, Dukhtar-i Sāsān* (Daughter of Sāsān) (1930), *Sāya-i Mughūl* (The Shadow of the Mongol) (1931), *Māzyār* (1933). Later on he learned Pahlavi and translated into Persian a number of books dealing with the legendary history and traditions of the country. All these influences are visible in his creative writing. Like Jamālzāda, he often took his plots from folk-literature. *Murda-khurhā* (The Corpse-Robbers) is an example from his first volume of short stories; a man, buried alive by mistake, escapes from his grave and returns to find his womenfolk squabbling over his property. Here we notice the characteristic blend of the macabre and the satirical that so often marks the folk-tale of Iran.

A little book that Hidāyat wrote in 1933 in conjunction with a friend, Masʿūd Farzād, called *Vaq Vaq Sāhāb* (Mister Bow-wow), shows another aspect of this influence. This is a collection of satirical sketches told in the style of the itinerant storytellers and narrators of popular verse epics, but unlike them dealing with contemporary themes concerned with the arts – the theatre, the cinema, and so on. This deliberate attempt to bring discussion of cultural topics down to the level of the illiterate café audience shocked many educated people of the time.

Hidāyat's most famous novel, *Būf-i Kūr* (The Blind Owl), an extraordinary interior monologue that has not received the attention abroad that it deserves, is a veritable mine of folkloric and mythical motifs. The title itself is a satirical parody of the nightingale of traditional Persian poetry.

After the abdication of Riżā Shāh and the return of democracy and free speech, Hidāyat wrote a pamphlet entitled *Āb-i Zandagī* (The Water of Life). Cast in the form of a fairy tale and based on a traditional legend, it turned in the hands of its author into a biting satire on Iranian society; but in the new political and social atmosphere there was this difference – Hidāyat's normal and characteristic pessimism was displaced for once by an optimistic outcome portraying the triumph of humanity over tyranny and greed.

Hidāyat's ear for the turns of ordinary speech was far superior to Jamālzāda's. Yet even so he wrote for the most part in a simple but strictly literary style, even when reporting dialogue – though occasionally he attempted to reproduce the forms of colloquial speech. It was left to two of his followers in particular to develop this aspect. Ṣādiq Chūbak is entirely a writer of the post-Riżā Shāh period. He published his first book of short stories, *Khaima-i Shab-bāzī* (The Puppet Show), in 1945, but has been most prolific during the past four years, with two novels and two volumes of short stories added to his list. Chubak's characters are drawn mainly from the peasant and worker class, and he is at great pains to reproduce their speech, to a degree of realism that many readers have found offensive. His last work, the novel *Sang-i Ṣabūr* (The Stone of Patience) (the title is that of a well-known Cinderella-type folk-tale, and sufficiently suggests the theme of the book – the sufferings of a young woman who contracts a series of temporary marriages, permitted by Shīʿa law, in order to support her child), is written almost entirely in colloquial language, and is a most unusual blend of low-life realism, folklore motifs, dramatized passages introducing characters from Persian legend and theogony, and even a long quotation from Firdausī's *Shāhnāma*.

Jalāl Āl-i Aḥmad is another writer who has interested himself deeply in folklore and social anthropology, and has published several scholarly studies of rural life in various parts of Iran. Like Chūbak, he makes free use of colloquial dialogue, and he also employs the folk-tale form as a vehicle for his social criticism. Two notable examples are *Nūn va'l Qalam* (the opening words of Sūra LXVIII of the Koran) and *Sarguzasht-i Kindūhā* (The story of the Beehives). The latter, in which the occupants of the beehives act out a satirical commentary on present-day Iranian society, was no doubt suggested by Karel Čapek's *Insect Play*, but is entirely Iranian in style and content, and owes most, apart from the author's own genius, to the inspiration of popular fables.

Before coming to the latest 'wave' of writers, a word must be said about a writer whose fame resides chiefly in his achievements as a collector of folk-tales. Ṣubḥī, after a somewhat stormy life as first of all a Bahai missionary and then a savage opponent of Bahaism, finally settled down as a broadcaster of children's programmes from Tehran Radio, his forte being folk-tales gathered from all over Iran with the help of his young listeners. Ṣubḥī was much criticized by folklorists for recasting these stories in literary form, and it is certainly true that his collections are unsatisfactory from a scientific point of view. However, he did much to bring recognition to the folk-tale as a literary form, though his own attempt at a novel using the folk-tale technique, *Ḥājī Mullā Zulf ʿAlī*, a story of two country youths, is not wholly successful.

These writers came to fruition during the 'democratic' period lasting from the abdication of Riżā Shāh in 1941 to the fall of Dr Muṣaddiq in 1953. Later writers have found themselves inhibited from frank social criticism by a paternalist regime that in general does not encourage too much independence. In consequence the most recent phase in Persian literature has been marked by a change of direction in both poetry and prose. Today's poets, writing in what is known as 'free verse' and is to some extent a departure from the classical forms (though not the rhythms) of Persian poetry, mostly take their lead from the veteran Māzandarānī poet Nīmā Yūshīj (1897–1960). His very nom-de-plume – the first element is the name of an ancient Māzandarānī prince, and the second a dialect form of his place of birth – symbolizes his cult of pre-Islamic Iran and his rejection of the Arabic and Islamic contribution. Starting as a romantic poet, he turned to a stark realism, and wrote much of his own verse in the Māzandarānī dialect; but in his last years he became involved in experiments in 'word-melody' as a substitute for more conventional rhythms that led him deeper into obscurity.

This change of emphasis is also observable in his followers. There is a swing away from the poetry of social criticism or nationalist fervour to something more inward and personal, and if the folklore or legend element enters in, it is rather to symbolize inner feelings and psychological states. Thus Tavallalī gives us a highly subjective impression of the ruins of Shūsh by night; Manūchihr Shaibānī describes with gruesome detail a traditional but long forgotten form of torture; Furūgh Farrokhzād, a young and talented poetess tragically killed in a recent motor accident, uses the legend of a rider by night to illuminate the emotions of a young girl on the verge of life; Suhrāb Sipihrī enters the imaginative world of the child with the image of the Lūlū, the bogeyman used by Persian nurses to frighten children into obedience; and Bāmdād's long poem *Pariyā* (The Fairies) imitates the language and style of a folk-tale. Muḥammad ʿAlī Afrāshta's poems in the Gīlakī dialect deal with the life of the peasants and rice cultivators of the Caspian shores, as do those of Maḥmūd Ṭayyārī, and contain many folkloric references. In all these the primary purpose of the poet is to illustrate psychological ideas – although it is not difficult to read into them implied social criticism.

The new trend in poetry is reflected to some extent in prose. One of the outstanding prose-writers of today is Ghulām Ḥusain Sāʿidī. Significantly, he too has devoted much of his time to the study of dialects, folklore, and village life, and has published several important monographs in this field. His creative writing appears under the pen-name *Gauhar-i Murād* (The Sought-After Pearl), a traditional symbol in Persian poetry, the precious jewel sought vainly in the depths of the sea when all the time it is lying on the shore, symbolizing the truth that the answer to life's problems is to be found within one's self. Sāʿidī has written a number of short stories, and has also had particular success with short plays, mimes and puppet sketches. Most of his scenes are of village life, and there is a marked folkloric element in both language and plot.

Among other writers who are struggling for recognition, the most significant for the theme of this paper are Maḥmūd Kiyānūsh, whose story of his childhood, *Ghuṣṣa-ī va Qiṣṣa-ī* (A Sorrow and a Tale), is full of folkloric allusions that brilliantly illuminate the Iranian scene; and Ṣamad Bihrangī, who has collected a number of the stories, proverbs and riddles of his Turkish-speaking province of Azarbāyjān. His latest work, *Qiṣṣa-i Ūldūz va Kalāgh hā* (Ulduz and the Crows), presented as a story for children, uses mythological and traditional images to express psychological ideas and social criticism. There is the motif, for instance, of the young bird who must fly within a specified time, or it will die (in folk-literature this also appears as the man who must wake by a certain time): here it symbolizes the right of freedom, the need for the child's emotions to be released at the proper time, his right to rebel against his parents and guardians, and by implication the right of a people to escape from paternalism and to work out their own destiny.

(*The above is a paper read at the XXXV International P.E.N. Congress, Abidjan, Ivory Coast, August 1967, under the general theme 'Legends and Mythologies as a source of inspiration in Arts and Literature'.*)

R. N. FRYE

Sasanian Silver and History

As an historian, I have long hoped that an art specialist would turn to questions other than style and composition of subjects, when discussing silver objects. This has not yet happened, so I decided, in honour of our deceased *vozd* in Persian Studies, whom I had known since World War II, to write a survey of the state of our knowledge and certain problems in the investigation of Sasanian silver. I should like to think if Professor Minorsky were alive he would be pleased by the combination of Russian and Near Eastern sources in this brief paper.

In most periods of Iran's history silver has been more prominent than gold, as the precious metal used for decorative objects.[1] The Achaemenid kings had maintained a bimetallic coinage, the gold *daric* and the silver *siglos* or *shekel*, but this was primarily possible because of the great size of the empire, controlling both silver and gold mines. Gold, it would seem, was more closely hoarded than silver, but after the conquests of Alexander gold became more common in the hands of ordinary people. Under the later Hellenistic kings gold again diminishes, to surge up again under the Romans. All of this suggests that gold comes into prominence as the dominant precious metal in times of growing economic prosperity and even political expansion, whereas silver comes to the fore in periods of consolidation, rest or stagnation of a state or empire. Indeed this pattern seems to apply throughout the history of the Near East. The prominence of gold was duplicated again under the Umayyad and ʿAbbasid caliphates, when a great empire united mining and trading centres. Under the Parthians and Sasanians, however, silver was dominant, at least in the production of art objects, not to mention coins. It is not the purpose here to investigate the ebb and flow of the economy of Iran, except to note shortages or influxes of silver and gold which may have influenced the working of silver or gold into plates, jewelry or other objects.

In the Graeco-Roman world, as mentioned above, by the time of

Alexander the Great gold, but especially silver, plate had become common in domestic use. Greek craftsmen exported their products to the northern Black Sea coast, where many have been found, and elsewhere. The Graeco-Roman expansion of production does not seem to have taken place previously in Persia in similar proportions where gold and silver objects were concentrated at the court of the Achaemenid ruler. On the other hand, Persian nobles served in posts all over the empire, and we know that Achaemenid forms influenced Greek artisans, for we have the *rhyton* as an Iranian specialty and the Achaemenid *phiale mesomphalos* as well as the

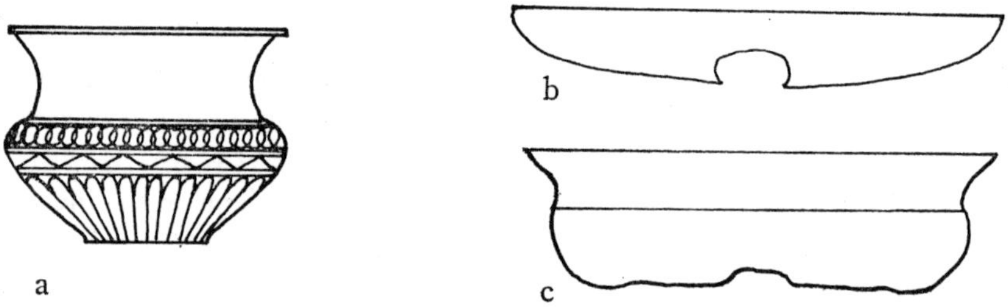

Figure 1. (*a*) Achaemenid deep bowl: (*b*) Greek *phiale mesomphalos*; (*c*) Achaemenid *phiale mesomphalos*.

deep bowl, all of which became very popular in the Greek world even before Alexander[2] (fig. 1). Obviously the king of kings did not hoard all of the gold and silver objects of the empire in his treasury at Persepolis. The use of gold and silver bowls in rituals, such as pouring libations in the temples, should not be underestimated, while gifts of gold and silver objects to shrines or temples are frequently mentioned in Classical sources. Similar conditions, though perhaps not so widespread because of royal demands for the precious metals, seem to have prevailed in the Iranian world. Later, under the Roman Empire vast numbers of silver objects, plates and utensils for the most part, were in private possession. Nothing like this luxury obtained in the Sasanian domains, where there may have been for a time a royal monopoly, or at least regulation of silver objects. Furthermore, both the foreign trade and the desire for articles of luxury in the late Roman Republic and under the Empire far exceeded those of Iran.

There is an interesting parallel between Graeco-Roman silver and Oriental silver in that the largest quantities of both have been found in South Russia and Central Europe. Obviously both Greeks (later also Romans) and Persians traded with the peoples of the north, but the numerous finds of silver in graves in Bulgaria, on the Dnieper and elsewhere in the north

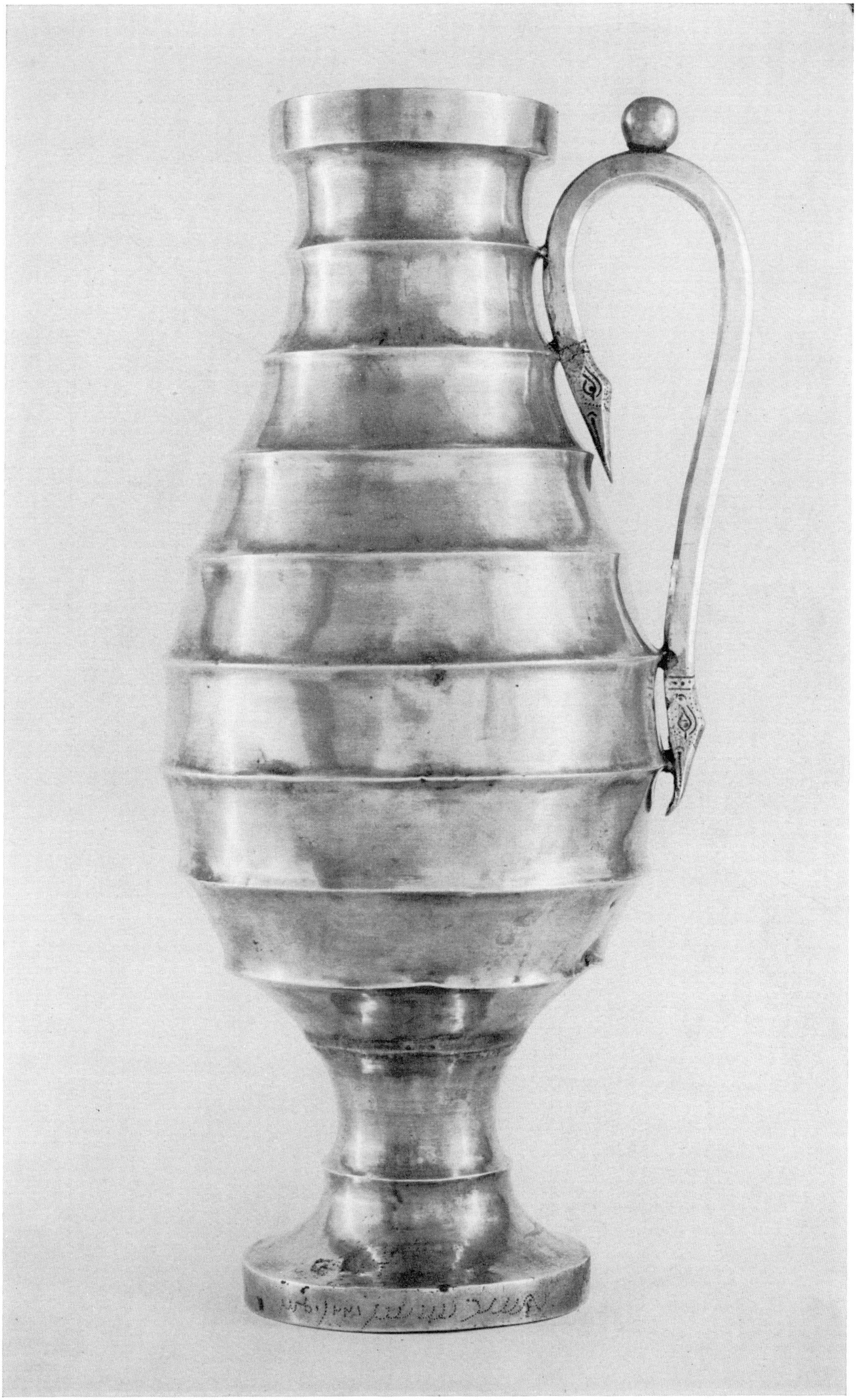

Plate 2. Close up of silver ewer.

Plate 1 (overleaf). Silver ewer (courtesy of the Cleveland Museum of Art).

should have an explanation. One important reason for the abundance of silver and gold objects in those graves was the religious outlook of the peoples of the steppe. Herodotus (IV. 71) described the burial of a Scythian chieftain, and asserted that the Scythians buried gold objects only, excluding silver and other metals. This is not true, however, since silver objects have been found together with the striking gold objects, now the pride of the Hermitage Museum. Perhaps the gold so impressed Herodotus that he overstated its occurrence. In the late Roman Republic and early Empire the demand for gold for the purchase of spices and luxuries from India and farther east, made of Rome a great collecting centre for gold. Silver, on the contrary, was used more for household objects than for trade. One reason for this was the demand by the Indians for gold in exchanges rather than silver, for India always has been a gold-collecting centre. On the other hand, the export of silver to the north by the Romans was noted by Tacitus in his *Germania* 5, where he says the Germans preferred silver over gold since the greater quantity of silver coins served them better for the relative inexpensive wares for which they traded than did the more expensive gold. After all, the ratio between the two was between 13 to 1 and 11 to 1, and silver was thus more available. Taste may have played a role in this preference for silver, which was so widespread among the peoples of northern and eastern Europe extending to China, so much that silver has been characterized as the metal *par excellence* of the steppes. In any case, by Sasanian times there had been a long history of trading of silver by both Romans and Parthians with the northern barbarians. Information on the Parthians, unfortunately, is extremely scant.

We may propose then that silver plates and other objects passed into the northern trade for furs, honey, wax, and the like, because the demand for silver was great there and it was to the advantage of a Persian merchant, for example, to trade silver objects to the north. One may further suppose that the royal practice of giving gifts at a banquet in repayment for services, at the Achaemenid and later at the Sasanid court, put silver objects on the market for such trade.[3] We know from Herodotus IX. 110, the Book of Esther II. 18, in the Bible, and many other sources, that this was a well-known practice at the Achaemenid court. Under the Seleucids and Parthians we hear of silver and gold vessels mentioned in the inventories of Greek and Oriental temples.[4] Obviously silver objects were much used as gifts carried by ambassadors between the Romans and Persians. For example, in the life of Aurelian IV. 2 and V. 5, we find the statement 'When he [Aurelian] had gone as an envoy to the Persians [before becoming emperor in 270] he was presented with a sacrificial bowl on which was engraved the sun god in the same attire in which he was worshipped in the very temple where the mother of Aurelian had been a priestess'.[5] In the same work, Flavius Vopiscus, a contemporary of Diocletian, mentions gifts of silver plates to the Roman court from Iran.[6] From this we may conclude that silver objects were important in trade, in gifts, tribute to Barbarians, in short in the same way as specie.

Relations between the Byzantine and Sasanian Empires, though rarely friendly, were none the less close, and full of respect on both sides. We may see this also in the silver, for the Persians probably borrowed the idea of inscribing silver objects from the Greeks, since the practice of writing names and weights on silver objects is amply attested from the Classical period of Greek history, not to mention Hellenistic and later times. It will be recalled that the first imperial names to appear on Byzantine silver vessels appeared in the reign of Anastasius I (491–518) and this practice continued in force until the reign of Constans II (641–68).[7] It is perhaps coincidental that the reign of Anastasius is parallel in the Sasanian Empire with the reign of Kavad, father of Chosroes Anushirvan, when many reforms and changes in Iran occurred. Among other things an extensive tax and financial reform was started which was carried to completion under Chosroes. During the reign of Justinian (527–65) a new system of control marks for silver was introduced in the Byzantine Empire.[8] If we examine the inscriptions on silver vessels from the Sasanian Empire, we at once see that the overwhelming majority of them date from the late fifth or sixth century, if we judge by the cursive script alone. Stylistic considerations reinforce this view. As a hypothesis it may be proposed that the Sasanians copied the Byzantines in the registration of silver objects for tax or other purposes, and the vast majority of inscriptions on Sasanian silver objects (there are no stamps on Iranian silver vessels) are the result of such a registration. Thus the inscriptions can be used as a *terminus ad quem*, but not as a sure means for dating of the objects, for surely silver antiques were registered as well as contemporary objects at the time of registration.

Byzantine silver has been found in places far from each other. For example, the Byzantine spoon from the Sutton Hoo burial in England has exact parallels in spoons found together with an inscribed Byzantine silver bowl from Amlash, Mazandaran (Caspian Sea Coast) now in the Tehran Museum.[9] Identical spoons are found in the collection of Mohsen Foroughi of Tehran, probably from the same source as the museum objects.[10] All of the Tehran spoons have a monogram on them, in addition to the name

Plate 3. Greek monogram and Pahlavi inscription.

Plate 4. Silver plate. Hermitage, 9-10th centuries. Central Asia.

παυλος.[11] The wide spread of Byzantine objects is thus confirmed by the Sutton Hoo and the Iranian spoons. A fascinating example of the interplay of Byzantine and Iranian interest in the same kind of objects is the silver ewer from the Cleveland Museum of Art (Plates 1, 2). There we find a Greek monogram beside a Pahlavi inscription, both of which probably indicate ownership[12] (Plate 3).

The system of weights used for silver in Sasanian Iran may well have been borrowed from Byzantium if not from Rome. Unfortunately there was no universal system of weights used in the Byzantine Empire, based on the Roman *pondus* and *libra*, and this seems to be reflected in variations of the weight system in the Sasanian Empire. My work on Sasanian silver objects has established the lack of a uniform system which does not help matters in trying to decipher the miserable Pahlavi script of the inscriptions. The *drachme* or *dram* in Iran used for silver varied from 2·5 to 4·0 grams and no pattern of possible geographical or time distribution of objects of varying standards has been as yet established.

What may be of more interest than details of inscriptions and weights of the silver vessels are their historical significance. From the time of Anastasius to Heraclius the Byzantine mints in the eastern part of the empire were not striking regular silver coin. Probably the mint price of silver was lower than the market price, so the mint could not buy silver, which went instead into plates and bowls. This was also the period of great activity on the steppes of South Russia and Central Asia. The Byzantine as well as the Sasanian Empire had to fight, conciliate or bribe the northern barbarians, and with what better means than with silver, which the nomads desired? Baian, the king of the Avars, according to Menander (frags. 27-8) in 567–8 asked for silver objects from the emperor Justin II, and other barbarians were not far behind the Avars.

We know from many Arabic and Persian authors, such as Masʿūdī and Firdōsī, that the Sasanian kings used to hold banquets in which, after having drunk toasts in wine, as their Achaemenid ancestors, in recompense for services rendered to the king, they gave drinking bowls (*phiale*) as presents to their favourites. Surely, as in Byzantium so in Iran, the nomad and barbarian chiefs were similarly honoured. It is difficult to imagine people drinking wine from the flat Sasanian silver bowls, but customs and fads are not always comfortable, witness the slender, high heels of woman in the 1960s. From wall paintings in Panjikant, Tajikistan, and from other indications, it is clear that the flat bowls were used for drinking wine.

The story of silver vessels in Russia is especially fascinating for the large majority of extant bowls has been found in the USSR. In the Russian mediaeval chronicles dealing with the trading city of Novgorod we find confirmation of the supposition that the inhabitants of the upper Volga and Kama Rivers used silver vessels almost like currency. In the year 1194 according to the First Novgorod Chronicle from the fourteenth century, an army of Novgorod attacked the Yugra people in the Perm area. The latter promised to give as tribute to the Novgorodians, among other things, *uzorochiya* or silver vessels with ornamentation.[13] As late as the fourteenth century Sasanian silver plates were known in Novgorod as 'silver from beyond the Kama'. In the Novgorod chronicle for the year 1332 (6840) we find that Ivan Kalita returned from the Golden Horde and turned his anger against that city, demanding from the inhabitants 'silver from beyond the Kama'.[14]

It is fairly easy to establish the reasons for the discovery of so many silver vessels in northern Russia. The local people had furs, honey and wax to trade and in return they wanted that precious metal of civilization which provided both a luxury object and an object which had value anywhere as specie, if not for itself. The Sasanians and Byzantines were happy to obtain expensive furs for their silver. We know that both Byzantines and Persians competed for the lucrative northern trade, for example by objects of both cultures found in the grave of an Avar prince from the Poltava region.[15] It seems that the Sasanians were either more active or their wares were preferred by the northerners, for the vast majority of silver objects found in Russia are Persian rather than Byzantine. We know that the Volga Bulghars later used Caliphal and Samanid coins as currency, and even used their own dies to strike this money. May we not suppose that they also copied Sasanian silver plates? Boris Ilich Marshak has convincingly shown that a famous plate in the Hermitage found in the village of Malo-Amkovkaya in the Perm region in 1909 was probably made in Semirechie in the ninth or tenth centuries[16] (Plate 4). This by itself indicates the continuity of a tradition of making silver vessels long after the fall of the Sasanian dynasty, and in areas far from Iran. More study is needed of the silver manufacture of the upper Volga regions, but there is no reason to doubt the ability of the local inhabitants to copy and manufacture silver vessels of a generally 'Sasanian' type.

Thus we may say that silver objects played an important role in the trade and diplomacy of the Roman (and then Byzantine) and Sasanian Empires with the northern barbarians. Further research is necessary to determine the causes of the decline or rise of silver in history, such as the well-known silver crisis of the eastern Islamic world in the eleventh century A.D. It behooves the historian to devote more time to economic factors in the general picture of the pre-Islamic and early Islamic Near East, for they have been too long neglected. Perhaps then we shall gain a better idea of the international ramifications of trade, surely more developed than hitherto suspected. Although distances and hardships were great, the trade between northern furs and southern spices and luxury objects indicates the willingness of men to endure much for profit from the earliest times.

NOTES

1 By Iran I mean the Iranian cultural area including present Afghanistan, Central Asia and Transcaucasia. 'Persia' is used for the smaller area of western Iran now occupied by the state the capital of which is Tehran.

2 Cf. D.E. Strong, *Greek and Roman Gold and Silver Plate* (London 1966) 75, 100.

3 See E. Benveniste's explanation of the word *τύκτα* in Herodotus as from Iranian **tuxta* meaning 'feast of repayment', in *Bulletin de la société linguistique*, XLVII (1951) 39.

4 Cf. the interesting discussion by M.I. Rostovtzeff in *The Excavations at Dura-Europos*, Fifth Season of Work 1931–2 (New Haven 1934) 307-10.

5 Loc. cit. 308.

6 Mentioned by A. Christensen, *L'Iran sous les sassanides* (Copenhagen 1944) 480.

7 E.C. Dodd, *Byzantine Silver Stamps* (Washington, D.C. 1961) 6.

8 Ibid., 7.

9 On the Sutton Hoo spoons see R.E. Kaske, 'The Silver Spoons of Sutton Hoo,' *Speculum* XLII (1967) 670. The Tehran Museum spoons and plates have not been published.

10 Unpublished, but see a fork found with the spoons; illustration 154 of the catalogue *7000 Years of Iranian Art*, Smithsonian Institution (Washington, D.C. 1964–5) and also G. Belloni, *Iranian Art* (New York 1969) ill. 80.

11 The monogram on the spoons is . On the rim of the bowl in pointillé is the inscription  *ΛΙΘΡΕ*  < *ΧΡΝΓ*. The last two letters may represent the numeral 43, while the *XP* = *χρυσος*? and < = *δραχμη* according to A.D.H. Bivar of London University, whom I wish to thank here. The monogram 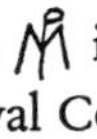 is found elsewhere (e.g. on a silver bowl from the Swedish Royal Collection in Stockholm).

12 The monogram is upside down 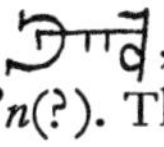, and the Pahlavi inscription, also in pointillé, reads: *nn b'tgw'n*(?). The last word may mean 'wine container'.

13 Cf. Omeljan Pritsak's forthcoming monograph on the Varangians and Rus.

14 *Novgorodskaya Pervaya Letopis* (Moscow 1950) 99 and 344. The word *uzorochiya* means more than just 'decorated [silver]', but in the two contexts here, silver is meant.

15 V. G. Lukonin, *Persia*, II (Cleveland, Ohio 1967) 111.

16 In a lecture before the Institute of Archaeology in Leningrad in the autumn of 1966.

Pseudo-Khaṭā'ī

In Anatolia, in 'Alavī circles whenever a poem bearing the *takhalluṣ* Khaṭā'ī is recited, the women stand up and the men kneel.[1] The poems, which are recited and listened to in such a religious atmosphere, are composed in quantitative or in syllabic metres. These poems, although there has been doubt concerning the authenticity of some of them, have been attributed to Shāh Ismā'īl, the founder of the Ṣafavid dynasty.

The question of the authenticity of these poems obviously could not be examined as long as they were scattered in numerous MSS of various Turkish libraries. In fact, the late Professor Minorsky, who in 1942 contributed a pioneer study on Shāh Ismā'īl's poems,[2] did not touch upon this problem at all. I think in a volume dedicated to Professor Minorsky's memory, it may not be wholly inappropriate to discuss this question on the basis of a collection which has since been made available.

In 1946 S.N. Ergun published a collection of Khaṭā'ī's poems,[3] basing his edition on a MS of Khaṭā'ī's *Dīvān* in the Millet library (Istanbul), and various miscellaneous MSS found in the same and other libraries, both public and private. This collection contains 201 poems, of which 115 are composed in syllabic and 86 in quantitative metres. The *Dīvān* of the Millet library, the only one existing in Turkish libraries, which contains 87 poems in syllabic and quantitative metres, is a recent MS put together from the various miscellanea, and as Ergun himself admits, its text is less reliable than that of some of the other sources used for this edition. This MS of negligible value cannot be considered a *Dīvān* proper.

Ergun mentions two other Turkish poets, besides Shāh Ismā'īl, having the *takhalluṣ* Khaṭā'ī, but he points out that these poets were unknown in their own environments, and hence he has no hesitation in ascribing the authorship of the content of his collection to Shāh Ismā'īl. Ergun concedes that Shāh Ismā'īl was not a Bektashī, nevertheless he finds it natural that Shāh Ismā'īl should take refuge in the spirituality of Ḥājjī Bektash and compose poems in the spirit of Bektashī poetry.

Ergun on the whole is inclined to attribute to Shāh Ismā'īl the poems which have for their subject the *Ithnā-'ashari* creed, and poems which do not contain any notion incongruous with the religious belief propagated by him. Ergun has no doubt about the authenticity of the poems composed in quantitative metre, nevertheless he ascribes those poems of the miscellaneous MSS of the sixteenth to seventeenth centuries, which sometimes bear the *takhalluṣ* of Khaṭā'ī (خطائی) and sometimes Khiṭābī (خطابی) to the latter. However, he has some doubts about the authorship of some poems in syllabic metre, which in various sources are recorded also under the names of Qul Himmet and Pīr Ṣulṭān. He singles them out and gives a list of them; they are very few in number.

This edition of Ergun, though the product of immense labour, does not constitute a solid basis for the study of Shāh Ismā'īl's poetry, for the only MS of the *Dīvān* which he used, was, as we saw, of little value, and the *Dīvāns* of various libraries of Europe were not accessible to him.

The oldest extant MS of Khaṭā'ī's *Dīvān* is Pa (Bibl. Nat. suppl. turc 1307) completed in 948/1541.[4] Pe (Bibl. Nat. suppl. turc 995) completed in the beginning of the seventeenth century[5] and L (British Museum, Or 3380)[6] and Tz (Prof. Minorsky's private library) form a separate group. One hundred and sixty-two poems of it are common to Pa, and fifty-four poems and the *Naṣīḥat-nāma* and the *tuyughs* of it are lacking in Pa. Sixty-six *ghazals* and three *mathnavis* of Pa are not found in this group.

V (Vaticano, Turco 221)[7] maintains an intermediary position between Pa on the one hand and Pe, L and Tz on the other, in that the 103 poems of this MS are common to both Pa and L, Pe, Tz, and twenty-four poems exist only in this MS. Pa contains poems with outspoken utterances such as 'I am the absolute Truth' and 'I am God's eye (or God himself) . . . 'I am the absolute doer' etc.[8] These and technically imperfect poems of this MS are omitted in the later MSS, which have apparently undergone a process of 'expurgation'. The great part of the content of these *Dīvāns* consists of *ghazals*.

Before examining the poems contained in Ergun's collection against the background of the above MSS of the *Dīvān* of Khaṭā'ī, I would like to dwell briefly upon two points: (*a*) three out of eight poems ascribed by Ergun to Khiṭābī exist in Pa and one of them in Pe, L, Tz, and V. There is no doubt that these four poems are by Khaṭā'ī. Ergun's assertion that Khaṭā'ī's poems could not possibly be inserted in the miscellanea of the sixteenth and seventeenth centuries not collected by Bektashīs is untenable. These lyric poems which do not contain Shīʿī propaganda could be, and in fact have been included, in these sources. (*b*) The poem considered by Ergun as composed in syllabic metre,[9] is in fact in quantitative metre.[10] This poem, which is not technically quite perfect, obviously underwent transformation in Bektashī circles so that Ergun was misled about its metre.

Thirty-seven poems out of the seventy-seven poems composed in quantitative metre in Ergun's edition exist in Pa, Pe, L, V, and Tz, and can be regarded as Khaṭā'ī's. The discrepancy between the style and content of the *Naṣiḥat-nāma* which we find also in Pe, L, and Tz, and that of the authentic poems of Khaṭā'ī makes its authenticity very doubtful; it seems to be a later addition. None of the syllabic poems of Ergun's edition exists in the above *Dīvāns*. The argument advanced by Gölpınarlı[11] that these poems, because they were composed in syllabic metre, were not included in the *Dīvān* is not convincing, for Pa in fact contains a poem in this metre.[12]

Shāh Ismāʿīl in general uses the *takhalluṣ* Khatā'ī, but in the syllabic poems besides Khatā'ī, we find also Shāh Kh., Sulṭān Kh., Jān Kh., Darvīsh Kh., Shaykh Kh., Dōst Kh., and even *pīrim* Kh.

In my opinion the syllabic poems contained in Ergun's edition were composed by minor poets of ʿAlavī-Bektashī circles, in which Shāh Ismāʿīl was venerated. The practice of these anonymous poets although unusual, is not unprecedented: Rūmī throughout his poems used the name of Shams, his spiritual *alter ego*.

The problem of the authenticity of Khaṭā'ī's poems will, no doubt, be solved definitively by a systematic examination of the whole material. The above remarks show that the generally accepted opinion that he was 'the most didactic poet of ʿAlavī-Bektashī literature who composed his poems mainly in syllabic metre', must be revised.

NOTES

1 Abdülbâki Gölpınarlı, *Kaygusuz Abdal, Hatayi, Kul Himmet* (Istanbul 1962) 18.

2 V. Minorsky, 'The Poetry of Shāh Ismāʿīl I', *BSOAS*, X (1938–42) 1007a-1053a.

3 Sadeddin Nüzhet Ergun, *Hatayı Divanı, Şah İsmail-i Safevi, Hayatı ve Nefesleri* (Istanbul 1946).

4 E. Blochet, *Catalogue des manuscrits turcs*, II, 229.

5 Ibid., II, 122.
6 Charles Rieu, *Catalogue of the Turkish Manuscripts*, 205.
7 Ettore Rossi, *Elenco dei Mss. turchi della Bibl. Vaticana*, 193.
8 *Il Canzoniere di Šāh Isma'īl Ḫa'ṭā'ī*, ed. T. Gandjeï (Naples 1959) 129 (207).
9 *Hatayı Divanı*, 88 (65).
10 Cf. *Il Canzoniere*, 157 seq. (255).
11 Op. cit., 17.
12 Cf. *Il Canzoniere*, 22 (20).

ILYA GERSHEVITCH

Iranian Words containing *-ăn-*

Two links unite the five words of which a discussion is here presented as a tribute to the memory of Professor Minorsky. The narrower one is no more than a mnemonic device. The general one alone would have sufficed to arouse the interest of the great Orientalist *qui nihil Iranici a se alienum putabat.*

A term for 'kid'

In a wholly delightful article in *MSS*, XXII (1967) 29 sqq., Karl Hoffmann has brought to light three previously unnoticed animal names, and a new form of a fourth, from the Avestan quotation which appears in the Nirangistān and the Dādistān-ī Dēnīk as *yaθa vā azō sčaēniš* (variants *sačainiš sačiniš*) *huš pərəsō.* In *azō* he recognized the Av. equivalent of Ved. *ajá* 'he-goat', in *pərəsō* that of Khot. *pā'sa* 'pig' and Lat. *porcus* 'piglet', the latter being the meaning also of the Avestan word. His conclusion that *huš* must be the nom. sing. of *hū-* 'pig', and *sčaēniš* (or var.) a word for 'kid', is inescapable.

Of the four animal names Hoffmann failed to trace outside Avestan only the one for 'kid', for which he could therefore offer no more than an etymological explanation: assuming that it consisted of *sač-* 'to pass, lapse' and a suffix which in proto-Iranian was either *-ani-* or *-aini-*, he suggested that the original meaning may have been 'ein aus dem laufenden Jahr stammendes (Jungtier)'.

I have long been familiar with the Southern Baškardi word for 'kid', *šen*, whose Bal. cognate is *šinikh*, *šanikh* (Mayer), *šinik* (Grierson). A SBš *e* goes back to OIran. *i* as often as to *a*, but in Bal. it is easier to regard as secondary the first vowel of *šinik(h)* than that of *šanikh*. Accordingly some ten years ago I reconstructed the hypothetical MIran. ancestor of SBš *šen* as **šan*.

Later, V.I. Abayev's suggestion in *AION-L*, II (1962) 37, that Oss.

stæn 'dog' belongs to Wx *skən* (etc.) and Russ. *ščenok* 'puppy', the IE form being **sken*-,[1] induced me to postulate for **šan* an O Iran. form **sčani*-, my reason for preferring an *i*-stem to an *a*-stem being the Bal. suffix -*ik*(*h*). And although I hesitated to follow Abayev to the extent of deriving from **sken*- also Sangl. *štənok* 'kid', seeing that the same language has *ᵊskənok* for 'puppy' and Morgenstierne's etymology of the 'kid' word as from **fštanya*- seemed more than adequate, I did feel tempted to range with Bal. *šanikh*, as Iranian loanwords, Pašai *čhanīk* and Khowar *čhani* 'kid', on the assumption that their initial aspirate might have been due to contamination of the Iranian initial with that of IA *chāga* 'goat', to which Morgenstierne had referred in *IIFL*, III[3], 49 *b*. Similarly Oss. *sænıgk* 'kid' may have *sæ*° instead of **stæ*° by contamination with *sæγ* 'goat', as an alternative to representing an older dialect variant **ša*° < **sča*°, parallel to Bal. *ša*°.

Of Av. *sčaēniš* I never thought in this connexion. But now that Hoffmann has shown its meaning to be 'kid' and its form to have as variants *sačainīš* and *sačiniš*, my secretly reared **sčani*- is ready to join his herd. The three textual variants, together with the form I had reconstructed from living languages, combine to establish two forms as correct Avestan, **sčaini*- and **sčini*-, their coexistence being paralleled by that of *sčandaya*- with *sčindaya*-.

Although Hoffmann did not find a cognate for his *sačaini*-/**sačaēni*- outside Avestan, he did consider (p. 38 n. 15) linking with the Avestan forms a Middle and New Iranian word for 'mountain-goat', viz. MP *p'c(y)n*, NP *pāzan* and (according to Henning, *BSOS*, IX (1937) 86) *pāžan*. If I understand Hoffmann rightly, the link he had in mind was confined to the suffix, his suggestion being that MP -(*y*)*n* corresponds to the -*ani*- of Av. *sač-aini*-.[2] The M Iran. word would then be a derivative of *p'c*- or of an earlier form of it. But since the word means '*mountain*-goat', if one assumes (for etymological proof eludes me) that *pā*- represents a word meaning 'mountain',[3] the second syllable **čin*/*čan* could represent our **sčani*-. It is well known that in Parthian at least, and in postvocalic position, O Iran. *sč* resulted according to dialect in *š* or *č*, see *JRAS* (1954) 125. The *c* of the MP spelling *p'c(y)n* is still heard in Bal. *pāčin* (E Bal. *pāšin*). In intervocalic position the change of *č* to *z* in NP *pāzan* is expected, as would be the change to *ž* in NP *pažan* if the latter was borrowed from Parthian. Forming a compound with an identifiable word for 'mountain' (Pašto *γar*) the same M Iran. **čan* is recognizable before the suffix -*ai* in the Pašto term *γarcanai* given by Morgenstierne s.v. *mountain-goat* in the English-Iranian Index of *IIFL*, II (Orm. *γircanai*, Waz. *γərcanai*, *NTS*, V, 17).

This interpretation implies that the meaning of **sčani-*, or of a descendant of its, had been generalized from 'kid' to 'goat' before the word was joined in a compound with a word for 'mountain', although in certain dialects the original meaning suffered no change. For a parallel one may think of the meaning 'pig' in Romance languages, of the descendants of Lat. *porcus* 'piglet' (cf. Benveniste, *BSL*, XLV (1949) 89), or even more to the point, of Oss. *stæn* which, if Abayev is right, will have developed its sense of matable dog from that of puppy. Underlying our assumption is the view that Russ. *ščenok*, and with it our **sčani-*, belong to Indo-Iran. *kan-* 'young', Gr. *καινός*, and Lat. *recens* (see Max Vasmer, *Russ. etym. Wb.*, III, 448), so that the meaning 'young animal, puppy or kid', and not 'dog/goat', would be the older.

As regards IE **sken-*, the *s*-less forms just quoted, and Welsh *cenaw* 'puppy' and MIrish *cano* 'wolf-cub', show that its *s* was mobile. Would it then be far-fetched to bring in also Lat. *canis*, whose straight derivation from **k̂wen-* is notoriously awkward? If one wished to avoid turning an IE puppy into a Roman dog by spontaneous semantic development, one would not need to go further than to assume that *canis*, although its true ancestor was **k̂wen-*, had the latter's initial *k̂w* replaced with *k* by contamination with the IE word for 'puppy'.

rāna 'belt'

The proof that Sogd. *rāna* (Buddh. *r'n'kh*, Chr. *r'n'*) means 'belt', and not 'jewel', was given in *JRAS* (1946) 180. H. W. Bailey was told of it earlier, and aptly compared Oss. *ron* 'belt' in *TPS* (1945) 23 sq. Later he added Khot. *rrānä* (*AO*, XXX (1966) 33 sq.), which very likely has the same meaning. Etymologically he assumed that the word belongs to Av. *rāna-* 'thigh'.[3a] It has since occurred to me that a semantically more satisfactory derivation would be from OIran. **rāhanā-*, since one could then compare the almost identically formed OInd. noun *rásnā* 'girdle'. The latter has not only the same meaning as Sogd. *rāna*, but also the same gender.

šanman-

In translating in 1959 this Av. noun, attested once only, in the dat.-instr. plur. *šanmaoyō* (*Yt* 10.24), as 'thrust'[4] I was following Henning, who in 1940 had assigned it to the base **šam-* 'to send, throw forward'.[5] However, since 1956 there has been in print an idea of Humbach's,[6] which later, independently occurred also to Henning,[7] that *šanman-* should be equated with the Vedic noun *kṣádman* which in *RV* i 130, 4, denotes an edge-tool usually thought to have been a carving knife (*Vorlegemesser*). This new suggestion was prompted by the Pahl. translation *tēγ* 'sword', originally 'blade (of the sword)', of the Av. entry *šənm* in the Frahang-i Oīm, sect. 302.[8] In the light of it Henning proposed for *šanmaoyō* the translation 'with the edge(s)', this very occurrence of the word in *Yt* 10.24, in a spelling, however, to be reconstructed as **šənmaoyō*, being in his opinion the one which the lexicographer had intended to gloss, although either he, or a later copyist, omitted *-aoyō* as a part of the word irrelevant to semantic identification. To the objection I had raised[9] that, if the Vedic verb *kṣad-*, to which I assumed *kṣadman* belonged, is a cognate of the Ossetic verb *æxsædın* as V. Miller had suggested,[10] one would expect as Av. counterpart of the Vedic noun not *šanman-*, but **xšanman-*, Henning replied (p. 44) that Ved. *kṣad-* means 'to eat or drink, feed' and is therefore remote in meaning from the noun *kṣadman*, while Oss. *æxsædın* means 'to winnow, weed, clean' and is therefore remote from both the verb *kṣad-* and the noun *kṣadman*.

Henning's resolute separation of the edge-tool *kṣadman* from the attested verb *kṣad-*, is an important step forward. It enables us at last to do away with the untidy treatment traditionally accorded to *kṣadman*. Because of the latter's 'sharpness' in *RV* i 130, 4, commentators came to believe that the verb *kṣad-* had somehow derived its eating or feeding connotation from 'carving'.[11] The persistence of this belief, one suspects, owes a good deal to the meaning 'to serve food' of Germ. *vorlegen*, which makes a *Vorlegemesser* appear more relevant to eating or feeding in general, than a *carving knife* would be thought of in English. Now that Henning has stripped the verb of its 'Vorlege'-myth, one wonders why the obvious was not long ago inferred from the compound *svādu-kṣadman*, which occurs as a hapax in *RV* i 31, 15. Its meaning, which undoubtedly is 'Süsses vorlegend' (Grassmann), 'wer süsse Speise vorsetzt' (Geldner), is not even at a superficial consideration accounted for by the supposition that its second component meant 'Vorlegemesser'. By what semantic accident could the essence of a Vorlegemesser, the knife, have disappeared from a compound the meaning of which, to go by the traditional view on *kṣadman*, ought to have been 'whose carving knife is sweet'? But the compound immediately acquires the required meaning if one takes the view that a *-man-* abstract of *kṣad-* 'eat, feed' was almost bound to mean 'food'. The Vedic language therefore had two nouns *kṣadman*, of which the one denoting an edge-tool ought, by the same token as its homonym meaning 'food' belongs to the attested verb *kṣad-* 'eat, feed', to belong to an homonymous unattested verb *kṣad-* that denoted an action performed by means of that tool.[12]

It is here that the Ossetic verb *æxsædın* comes into its own. The meanings 'to winnow, weed, clean' which Henning quoted for it are the ones given in Miller and Freiman's Dictionary. Abayev's entry in his *Osetinsko-russki slovar'* is more detailed: (1) to winnow; (2) to peel, shell, remove husks; (3) to trim, prune, lop (trees); (4) to weed; (5) to clear (Russ. *rasčiščat'*, used for the clearing of undergrowth etc.). Meaning (2) is illustrated in Miller and Freiman's Dictionary by the example *kærdoyı c'ar kærdæi æxsædı* 'he peels the pear with a knife'.

The five meanings have in common the notion of removal, often by means of a tool, of growth obnoxious or inedible. There is no single tool that could be used for all five, but a pruning-knife or bill-hook is required for pruning, and edge-tools are needed to weed, cut through undergrowth, and peel certain fruit. One may guess that 'to winnow', for which activity a quite different tool is required, was the last of the five meanings to develop. If then proto-IA had a verb *kṣad-* that corresponded to Oss. *æxsædın*, its *-man-* noun of instrument could have denoted a pruning-tool. It seems no less legitimate to recognize a bill-hook in Ved. *kṣadman* than a carving knife, and if an Indo-Iranian etymology is desired, a good deal preferable.

To separate the two Vedic bases etymologically, one might think of deriving the one which means 'to eat, feed' from IE **k̑sed-*, so that its Iranian equivalent would be **šad-*. But no such base with the required meaning has so far been recognized in Iranian where, however, Ossetic has a verb *æfsædın* 'to eat one's fill', transitive *æfsadın* 'to feed', past stem *æfsæ/ast-*, whose meaning, and sounds other than *f*, agree with the attested Vedic verb *kṣad-*. Here Bailey, *TPS* (1960) 83 n. 1, proposed to find a base **sat-* or **sad-*. The base **šad-* we are looking for, with the preverb *abi* (or *upa*, cf. below, p. 288 n. 25?), would equally well account for *æfsædın*.[13]

But our main concern is the Iranian cognate of the other base *kṣad-*, the one to which the tool *kṣadman* belongs. If Oss. *æxsæd-* is it, as we may now maintain with better reasons than Miller adduced, then Av. *šanman-* cannot correspond to that tool. In any case, the assumption that the gloss *šənm* = *tēγ* in the Frahang refers to *šanmaoyō* in *Yt* 10.24, encounters two difficulties. The first, a minor one, is that for *šan°* a variant **šən°* would have to be postulated in *Yt* 10.24. The second difficulty is serious. It would be contrary to the usual practice of the Frahang to offer a lemma that consisted of only part of a semantically indivisible word, especially if that part ended in a consonant cluster no Avestan word can ever have had in final position.

The normal noun-entry in the Frahang is equipped with a case-ending, presumably the same as it had in the particular Avestan passage in which the glossator thought that a translation of it would be useful.

šənm does not cease to be an improbable entry in the Frahang through the supposition that it is an incomplete word. To say that Pahl. *tēγ* in the Frahang translates Av. *šanmaoyō* in *Yt* 10.24, amounts to emending *šənm* to *šanmaoyō*, or at least to **šənmaoyō*. But if *šənm* in order to become a probable entry has to be emended, in other words, if it is corrupt, what assurance can there be that the corruption consisted in the omission of the conspicuous ending *-aoyō*, and was not of the type of (*a*) *šustəm* sect. 299, wrong for **xšustəm*, (*b*) *ẓnma* sect. 204, where one expects **ẓnūm*, or (*c*) *pərənm* sect. 457, instead of **pərənəm*? On the strength of (*c*) our lemma might stand for **šənəm*, on the strength of (*a*) + (*c*), for **xšənəm*, either of which would be incompatible with Ved. *kṣadman*, the second also with Av. *šanmaoyō*. It is true that neither emendation would readily account for the Pahl. translation *tēγ*, but there are alternatives that would. On the strength of (*a*), (*b*), and (*c*) one might, for instance, emend *šənm* to **xš*(ə)*nūm*, the acc. of a root-noun belonging to Av. *huxšnuta*- 'well sharpened' (on which see *AHM* 179, 324). And if it is desired to credit the Avestan language with a noun corresponding to Ved. *kṣadman*, why not emend *šənm* to **xšənma*, whose *xš* would agree with both Ved. *kṣ* and the *xs* of Oss. *æxsædın*.

Our conclusion then is, that Bartholomae's translation of *šanmaoyō* as 'with thrusts' is correct, and that the underlying base is either **šam*- 'to send, throw forward', in accordance with Henning's earlier interpretation, or **šan*- with the same meaning, as Bailey has proposed in his recent book *Prolexis to the Book of Zambasta*, 344.

nišān

On the etymology of NP *nišān* 'sign, mark, standard, target', to which in MP and Parth. corresponds *nyš'n*,[14] and which was borrowed by Arm. as *nšan*, by Oss. as *nısan*, the literature is as follows:

(1) Lagarde, *Ges. Abh.* 66, identified Syr. *nyš'* 'sign, standard, target, intention, range of written work (argument, chapter, etc.), metre' with Arm. *niš* 'sign, mark, spot, speckle, point', linking the word, which he considered Iranian, with Arm. *nšan* 'sign, mark, ensign, miracle' and *nšavak* 'target'. All three derived according to him from *šyu*-, *niš* being from **ni-šyu*-.

(2) Hübschmann, *Arm. Gr.* 204-6, while expressing no opinion as to

whether *nšan* belonged to *niš*, kept *nšavak* distinct from both, quoting for it, with due reserve, Lagarde's derivation from *šyu-*.

(3) W. Geiger, *ABAW*, XX (1897) 200, suggested that *nišān* belongs to Bal. *šōn dēagh* 'to show' and to the Pašto verb *ṣ̌ōwul* 'to show'. He referred to neither Arm. *nšavak* nor *niš*.

(4) Bartholomae, *Zum altir. Wb.* 97, took no notice of (3). He approved of Lagarde's connexion of *nšan* with *nšavak*, but not with *niš*, the base of the two former being in his opinion not *šyu-* (*šyav-*) but **šab-*. Thus **nišāvan* < **nišābana-* would be related to Av. *šəmna-*, which he derived from **šabna-*. The meaning of *šəmna-*, which only occurs in the two compounds *ašəmnō.vīd-* and *ašəmnō.jan-* (*Yt* 10.39-40), he had previously, in his *Altiranisches Wörterbuch*, tentatively defined from the context as 'target'. Three different derivatives of a single base, two with *ni* and one without preverb, would thus have existed with the same meaning.

(5) Nyberg, by contrast, accepted from Lagarde only that Arm. *niš* belongs to *nšan*, not also *nšavak* (*Hilfsbuch* II, 147). Arm. *niš*, however, represents in his view not a MIran. **niš*, but **nīš*, a verbal noun belonging to the MP verb *nīš-* 'to see', < **ni-iš-*. The *i* of NP *nišān* would then be the result of a secondary shortening.

(6) Henning, *Mitteliranisch* (1958) 110 n. 3, was concerned only with *nšavak*, whose MIran. source, **nišāwak*, he recognized to be also that of the Khwar. word for 'target', *'š'wk*.[15]

(7) Finally Morgenstierne, in *EVP*, 79, clarified, in respect of (3) above, that Pašto *ṣ̌ōwul* is from *srāvaya-*. Bal. *šōn* reminded him of Orm. *ṣ̌ōm* 'pointing out', which in *IIFL*, I, 409 *a*, he suggested may be connected with Pašto *ṣ̌ōwuna* 'pointing out, showing'. He referred to Geiger's association of NP *nišān* with Bal. *šōn* on both occasions, but did not commit himself to it.

In view of (6) it is safe to rule out that the MIran. ancestor of Arm. *nšavak* belonged either to Bartholomae's **šab-* or to the verb *nīš-* which Nyberg wanted to find in *nšan*. Khwar. *'š'wk* also entitles us to exclude that the OIran. base of **nišāwak* began with *xš*, since this cluster survived unchanged in the Khwar. examples quoted by Henning in *Togan'a Armağan*, 434. What remains uncertain is whether it was to an OIran. base beginning with *h* or with *š* that the preverb *ni* had been prefixed, and whether the *v*/*w* belonged to the base or to the suffix. The last point is relevant to the question whether MIran. **nišāwak* and *nyš'n* are at all related. If for instance the former represented an OIran. word **ni-šā-wa(ka)-* and the latter went back to **nišāna-*, a relationship between the two words would only be plausible if the correct division of the latter were **ni-šā-na-*, and not **ni-šān-a-*. But if it could be shown that *nyš'n* once had a *w* after *ā*, the likelihood of its being a cognate of **nišāwak* would be great.

That *nišān* has lost a *w* would be certain if it could be established that Geiger was right in connecting it with Bal. *šōn*, and that *šōn* is a genuine Bal. word. The latter's *ōn* < **auna* would then stand to the former's *ān* < **āuna*, as MIran. *ōm* (in Arm. *šnom*)[16] < *auma* (in Av. *xšnaoma-*) stands to *ām* (in Sogd. *'xšn'm*) < **āuma* (OIran. **xšnāuma-*).[17]

Of such a loss of *w* after *ā* in either primary or secondary contact with a following consonant, the following examples among others are of interest:

(1) NP *fasān*, *afsāne* 'incantation' < **°sāuna-*, which, as Bailey has recognized,[18] belongs to NP *fusūn*, *afsūn*, MP *'pswn*[19] 'spell' < **°sauna-*. NP *afsāne* is here recalled chiefly in order to stress that it is etymologically unrelated to NP *afsān(e)*, MP *''ps'ng*[20] 'fable' < *OIran. **°sāna-* (to OP *θāti*) or **°sąhana-*.[21]

(2) Sogd. *nm'ny*, Khot. *nimāna-* 'repentance' are shown to be from **ni-māuna-* by Oroš. *nəmāu* 'repentance',[22] Bart., Xuf. *nimaw*, Ruš. *nimōw* (V.S.Sokolova), Šγ *nimů* (Zarubin) 'reproach, scolding, invective'. The verb **ni-maw-* perhaps meant 'to reproach' in the active, 'to repent (reproach oneself)' in the middle. Cf. Parth. *prm'w* 'horror', etc., see Henning apud Ghilain, *Essai*, 82.

(3) MP and Parth. *gr'n* ,Sogd. *γr'n*, etc., 'heavy', is better derived from **grāuna-* (IE **g^{w}r-eH-u-*) than from **grāna-*, since the *u*-extension is the rule with its adjectival cognates; cf. Lat. *gravis*, OInd. *gurú*, and Khot. *ggarkha* < **γaruxa-*[23] < IE **g^{w}r-H-u-* + Iran. suffix *-ka-*.[24]

(4) Oss. *bon* in *mæ bon næu* 'I cannot' etc. (see Abayev, *Ist.-etim. Slov.*, s.v.) is unlikely to have anything to do with *bon* 'day'. Its original meaning may have been 'sufficiency', *bon* being from **bān* < **bāuna-*,[25] to Sogd. *β'w* 'sufficiency' (Henning, *BBB*, 68), Arm. *bavel* 'être en abondance, suffire' (Benveniste, *JRAS* (1933) 32). Thus also the meaning 'rich' of *bondǯın* is accounted for.

(5) Bal. *nawāši* 'to-morrow' is hardly a derivative of Pers. *namāz*, as W. Geiger thought, but goes perhaps back to **nawāušah-* < **nawa-aušah-*. For the use of *nawa-* cf. SBš *náv-insōr* 'next year', *Mélanges Morgenstierne*, 86; on the final Bal. *-ī* see ibid. 84 n. 19.

(6) The MP and NP 2 sg. impt. *bāš* (on which NP *bāšad* was built, v. Henning, *ZII* IX, 239[25-7]) still awaits a satisfactory explanation. I would suggest deriving it from an earlier **bāšd* < OP **bāušdi*, 2 sg. impt. act. of the *s*-aorist of *bū-* (cf. Macdonell, *Vedic Grammar*, paras 520, 526; Renou,

Grammaire de la langue védique, para. 345). As OIr. *ah-* had no injunctive, the prohibitive chosen to match the 2 sg. impt. **ʒdi* 'be' may have been the *s*-aoristal **mā bāuš* 'do not be'[26]; under its influence the *s*-aoristal imperative **bāušdi* may have come, in OP, to replace **ʒdi*.

(7) NP *niʒār*, Arm. *nʒar* 'weak' < **niʒāw(a)ra-* (beside Parth., Sogd. *nyʒ'wr* < **niʒāwara-*), against Bal. *niʒōr* (attested through Brāhūī), MP *n(y)ʒwr* < **niʒaura-*; similarly MP *'bʒ'r* 'strong' < **upa-ʒāw(a)ra-*.[27]

(8) Sogd. *sm''δn* 'perfume' was seen by Bailey, *JRAS* (1958) 105 n. 3 to have *ā* < *āu*, against the *ū/ō* < *au* of Oss. (Ir.) *smudın*, (Dig.) *æsmotun* 'to smell'.[28] Etymologically one may suspect an OIran. **snaud-* (IE **sneud-*, cf. Pokorny, *Idg. Wb.* 768, 972) to have been replaced with **smaud-* by contamination with *baud-*, via, perhaps, a furtively intermediate **sbaud-*.

Although there is thus no difficulty in relating *ān* to *ōn*, Geiger's assumption that Bal. *šōn* belongs to *nišān* is acceptable only if *š* has the same origin in both. If Morgenstierne is right in identifying Bal. *šōn* with Orm. *ṣ̌ōm*, and the latter with Pashto *ṣ̌ōwuna*, then *nišān* can only belong to Bal. *šōn* if its *š* is from *sr*. That this could be the case is shown by NP *ašk* 'tear' and x^{v}*ašū* 'mother-in-law', cf. Horn, *GIP*, 1^2, 88. But *nyš'n* occurs also in Parthian, in which language there seem to be no examples of *š* < *sr*. In Bal., too, there seems to occur no parallel for *š* < *sr*, nor in Orm. for *ṣ̌* < *sr*, so that, in order to connect Bal. *šōn* and Orm. *ṣ̌ōm* with Pashto *ṣ̌owul* it would seem necessary to regard both as loan-words from Pashto.

At all events, if the base of *nišān* were *sru-*, Arm. *niš* and Syr. *nyš'* could no longer be connected with it. For the meaning 'target' of *nišān* would then have to be secondary to that of 'sign'. The meaning 'sign', however, could only be held by causatival forms of *sru-* 'to hear', of whose essential *ā* Arm. *niš* shows no trace. Even **nišāwak* could then only belong to *nišān* if its sole attested meaning 'target' had secondarily developed from 'sign'.

Much therefore depends, if Geiger was at all right in connecting *nišān* with Bal. *šōn*, on whether also Arm. *niš* and Syr. *nyš'* represent cognates of *nišān*. If they do, *šōn* must be separated from Pashto *ṣ̌ōwul* for semantic reasons. If they do not, then the plausibility of Geiger's connexion of Pashto *ṣ̌ōwul* with *nišān* will depend phonetically on whether also Parth. *š* can be from *sr*, and semantically on whether the primary meaning of *nišān* was really 'sign', and not 'target'. There is no way, at present, of answering the first question, but the approach which we are about to attempt, will induce us to hold that the original meaning of *nišān* was 'target'.

The approach consists in taking advantage of a piece of evidence, however slight, which suggests that Bal. *šōn* has a closer link with *nišān* than with Orm. *ṣ̌ōm*. The latter forms the idiom meaning 'to show, point out' with the auxiliary *k*° 'to do, make', the former, which according to information available is not used by itself, with either *dēagh* 'to give'[29] or *dāragh* 'to hold'.[30] The corresponding idiom in Persian is *nišān dādan*; *nišān kardan* would only in exceptional circumstances be translatable by 'to show'.

Taking our cue from here, we shall separate *šōn* from Orm. *ṣ̌ōm* and Pashto *ṣ̌ōwuṭ*, and regard it as a genuine Bal. word related to *nišān*. We shall then not be bound to seek the base *sru-* in *nišān*, and shall have no reason for excluding Arm. *niš* and *nšavak* from relationship with *šōn* and *nišān*. And having already ruled out that **nišāwak*, and therefore, we may now add, also **niš*, *nišān*, and Bal. *šōn*, have *š* < *xš*, we may infer from *šōn* that the base common to all four words began in O Iran. with *š*, and not with *h*. In *šōn*, moreover, the *u* of whose O Iran. ancestor **šauna-* would not have been suffixal, we shall find confirmation that the *w* of **nišāwak* and the lost *w* of *nišān*, belonged to the base, and not to a suffix. If we further take the risk of inferring from the sole meaning 'target' of *nšavak* that this was the original meaning of all four words, the following considerations spring to mind, of which the fifth will provide the solution I would provisionally advocate for this intriguing problem.

(1) The absence of *ni* from Bal. *šōn* need not preclude identity of meaning with *nišān*. For a parallel one may refer to the Iranian words for 'cushion (or sim.)' derived from the base **bṛ̥z-* 'to spread out' (see Benveniste, *Études sur la langue ossète*, 12). On the one hand we have Oss. *nıværzæn* < **ni-b(a)rzana-* (Benveniste, *l.c.*), on the other, without preverb, Yidγa *virzanë* < **bṛ̥zana-ka-* (Morgenstierne, *IIFL*, II, 260), Oss. *baz*, Bal. *barzī*,[31] and NP *bāliš*, < **barziš-*.[32] It has passed unnoticed that NP, too, has a form with *ni*, viz. *nihāl* 'mattress' < OP **ni-barda-* or **ni-bardiš-*, < **ni-barz*°.[33] The meaning 'cushion (or sim.)' being assured for derivatives of both **bṛ̥z-* and **nibṛ̥z-*, it does not seem too far-fetched to suppose that the meaning 'target' could have been shared by derivatives of both **šu-* and **nišu-*, the preverb conveying perhaps in this case the notion of 'into', rather than of 'down' as in **nibṛ̥z-*.

(2) In Bartholomae's view, as we saw (p. 273, sect. 4), also Av. *šəmna-* meant 'target'. The *ašəmnō.vid-* arrows, spears, and sling-stones of *Yt* 10.39 were to him missiles 'which do not find their targets'. To this interpretation I objected in *AHM*, 192, that in fact the targets do seem to have been 'found' by the missiles. But I had overlooked that if one takes °*vid-*, as I

did, in the sense of 'piercing', it becomes unnecessary to conjecture a new meaning for *šəmna-*. The missiles would have been described as *ašəmnō.vīd-* in verse 39, as *ašəmnō.jan-* in verse 40, because although they had been correctly aimed, they had neither 'pierced' nor 'struck' their targets: Miθra had stopped them just short of impact upon the intended victims. In reverting to Bartholomae's interpretation of *šəmna-*, we may give up Darmesteter's notion that the word displays a nasal metathesis (cf. *AHM*, 192). But if the base is simply *šam-*, it cannot be the familiar one for 'to swallow'.[34] Could it then be the only other one known, which we encountered above, p. 269 with n. 5, for 'to send, throw forward, *mittere*'? It seems possible to think of a target or shooting-mark as a notion that could have been expressed by immediate and sole reference to the act of shooting. Just as NP *šikār*, from O Iran. **skāra-*, a verbal noun derived from the base **skar-* 'to hunt',[35] means both 'hunting, hunt' and 'game, prey', the term for the act or skill having been taken to denote also what the act or skill is practised upon, so *šəmna-*, which one expects to have meant 'shooting' or 'shot', may have come to denote also an object upon which shooting is practised.

(3) Southern Baškardi, too, has a word *šōn* which like Bal. *šōn* is only used with an auxiliary. The auxiliary which goes with S Bš *šōn*, however, is not *dah-* 'to give', but *kan-* 'to do', and the meaning of S Bš *šōn kan-* is not 'to show', like that of Orm. *šōm k°*, but 'to send'. The M Iran. antecedent of S Bš *šōn* was more likely **šān* than **šōn*, since on the one hand O Iran. *au* is normally represented in S Bš by *e*, and on the other the closing of *ā* to *ō* is to be expected in S Bš, especially before *n*. Of a M Iran. **šān* several explanations would be possible, including derivation from O Iran. **šāuna-*.

(4) To this **šāuna-* one would have to assign the meaning 'dispatch', or sim., to account for the meaning of S Bš *šōn kan-*. Form and meaning will then immediately call to mind the Parth. verb *frš'w-* / *fršwd-* 'to send', which according to Ghilain, *Essai*, 77, continues the O Iran. causative *frašāvaya-* of *šyu-* 'to go'. This etymology accounts well enough for the form and meaning of *frš'w-*, but the same would be true of an explanation of the Parth. verb as belonging to a base **šu-* which, distinct from *šyu-*, meant 'to send, throw forward, shoot', in one word, '*mittere*'. Such a base, moreover, would be capable of accounting not only for Parth. *frašāw-* and S Bš *šōn kan-*, but also, on the semantic premise suggested under sect. (2) above, for our four words (including, that is, Bal. *šōn*) for 'target'. Equipped with such a base we could feel reasonably safe with Lagarde's explanation of Arm. *niš*, *nšan*, and *nšavak*, the only weakness of which was that the

meaning 'to go', or even 'to stir', of *šyu-*[36] left one at a loss to account for either the meaning 'sign' or 'target'.

(5) A base **šu-* meaning 'mittere' has in fact been recognized in Oss. (Dig.) *ænsonun/ænsudt*, (Iron) *ssonın/ssıd* 'to thrust' and Khot. *ṣun-/ṣva-* (<**šuta-*) 'to throw' by Bailey, *BSOAS*, XXIII (1960) 36 sq. and *Khotanese Texts*, IV, 65, who regards it as cognate with O Slav. *su-* 'to thrust' and Lith. *šáuti* 'he shoots'. It would be natural to derive the Khot. present stem from a regular O Iran. present stem **šun(a)v-* or **šun(ā)-*, but the Oss. pres. stem suggests a different interpretation. Its *o*, since it appears also in Iron, should represent an O Iran. long diphthong *āu* (cf. Oss. *bon* above, p. 274, sect. 4) to which it is hard to believe that the present-formatives *n(a)v* or *n(ā)* would have been added. It seems necessary to assume that proto-Iranian had inherited beside **šu-* a variant **šun-* of the base, with an *n*-determinative lost elsewhere. Its unthematic pres. stem would have had as weak form **šun-*, which would also be a possible antecedent of Khot. *ṣun-*, and as strong form **šāun-* as required by Oss. °*son-*, the relation between the two being as between Ved. *mṛj-* and *mārj-*.

(6) One may then wonder whether **nišāuna-* 'target' and **šāuna-* 'dispatch', the ancestors we have postulated for *nišān* and S Bš *šōn*, instead of containing the nominal suffix *-na-*, should not be regarded as verbal nouns derived, with thematization, from the pres. stem **šāun-* whose existence in **han-šāun-* is virtually guaranteed by Oss. *ænsonun*. Once committed to a variant **šun-* of the base **šu-*, of which a possible thematic pres. stem would have been **šaun-a-*, we may similarly prefer to regard the ancestor **šauna-* of Bal. *šōn* as a verbal noun built on, and identical with, that present stem, rather than as a nominal *-na-* extension of **šau-*. The evidence for the unextended base **šu-* will then be confined (apart from the Oss. and Khot. past stems, and apart possibly from the Av. forms with *-šu-* adduced by Bailey) to the weak unthematic present stem **ni-šu-*, which as a verbal noun became **niš* in M Iran., and to the corresponding strong pres. stem **šāw-*. The latter continued as a verb in Parth. *frašāw-*; it is seen as a noun in M Iran. **nišāwak*, from a thematicized O Iran. **nišāw-a-* derived from the pres. stem **ni-šāw-*, and subsequently extended by the suffix *-ka-*.

The O Iran. ancestors of our words for 'target' from the base **šu-*, which apart from **nišāwa-* came in time to mean also 'sign', would thus all have been verbal nouns directly derived from present stems meaning 'to shoot'. The variety of present stems which these terms for 'target' represent, constarted with the singleness of the procedure adopted for coining the terms, and with the fact that the procedure, if we have at all correctly defined it, is an unusual one, suggests that the terms arose on a common sports-ground frequented by speakers of different dialects. At inter-tribal shooting contests heteroglottic teams would have learned, ultimately perhaps from the original hosts who may have been the same tribe for years, to refer to the target by nouns derived in each dialect from a current present stem of its verb for 'to shoot'.

bāng

To Pers. *bāng* 'voice, call, cry, clamour' belong, as stated already by W. Geiger and P. Horn, Pahl. *wāng*, Arm. *vank*, *vang* 'sound, voice, syllable, tune', Bal. *gwānk* 'voice, sound, echo', and the Bal. verb *gwānǰag* 'to call'. In replacement of the earlier view that its final *g*/*k* was a suffix (cf. Horn, *GIP*, I², 63, Fr. Müller, *WZKM*, VIII (1894) 92), H. W. Bailey proposed in 1937 (*BSOS*, IX, 76 sq.) an analysis of the word as representing the same base **vang-* as he wished to recognize in the Khot. verbs *pyūṃj-* 'to deny, disparage, slander', *byūṃj-* 'to abuse, disparage, slander' (noun *byūṃgga*), and *vaṃj-* 'to dispute'. Recently, in his *Prolexis* (1967) 208 and 262, the same author offered **vank-* as an alternative to **vang-*. R. E. Emmerick, *Saka Grammatical Studies* (1968) 87, gives preference to **vank-*, which he interprets as an *n*-infixed form of the base *vak-* 'to speak'. This is a view which I have held for some time, on grounds which even now it is not superfluous to state. For although the *k* of Arm. *vank* and Bal. *gwānk* supports the connexion with *vak-*, it does not suffice to prove it. And the Khot. verbs, whose *ṃj*, *ṃgg* could be from either *nč*/*k* or *nǰ*/*g*, have meanings which may, but need not have developed from that of 'speaking'.

The proof that the IE base of Lat. *vox* occurs indeed with an *n*-infix in Iranian, is to be found in the Sogd. word for 'voice', Man. *wnxr*, B. *wnyr*, of which a secondary variant without *n*, *wxr*, is found in Chr. and Man. texts. Identity of meaning, and similarity of form, strongly suggest that Sogd. *wanxar* or *wanxr*, and MP *wāng* are related. It would be possible to derive both from a single OIran. neuter stem **wankar-*. MP *wāng* would go back to its nom.-acc. sing., Sogd. *wanx(a)r* to an oblique stem **wanxr-* that would be parallel to Av. *āθr-*. But since the formally almost identical stem **warkar-* 'leaf', whose nom.-acc. sing. survived as *warg* in MP, had **warkar-*, and not **warxr-* as oblique stem surviving in Sogd. *wrkr*,[37] it will be preferable to reconstruct for Sogd. *wanx(a)r* an OIran. vocalic stem **wanxra-* or **wanxri-*. MP *wāng* could then still be from **wankar-*, but a thematic stem **wanka-* would equally well account for it and will be presumed, in what follows, to be its etymon.

The value of Sogd. *wnxr* consists in proving that the *g* of M P *wāng*, and the *k* of Bal. *gwānk*, are not a suffix but belong to the root. This fact, combined with the meaning 'vox' of the three nouns, makes it clear that the root is indeed *vak-* 'to speak', with infixed ***n***. But we still need to explain the long *ā* of M P *wāng*, which, since Bal. *gwānk*, clearly genuine because of its *k*, also has it, must go back to the O Iran. period. Within that period **wānka-* can only have arisen secondarily, from **wanka-*, and the dialect area where it arose, seems to have been a restricted one: it included O P and Old Baluchi, but not, to judge from the later evidence we shall presently discuss, Old Parthian. As far as O P is concerned, seeing that in that language a noun **āwāka-* 'voice' was current, attested through M P *''w'g*,[38] one might think that it was by contamination with it, that the radical *a* of its synonym **wanka-* was lengthened. Since Parth. *''w'c-* 'to shout, proclaim' indirectly points to O Parth., too, having had the noun **āwāka-*, it would not be very daring to attribute it also to O Bal., to which the area of the contamination just mentioned would thus be extended.

What would be a little more daring, but nevertheless deserves preference, is to assume that O P and O Bal. once also had a noun **wāka-* for 'voice', which, contaminated with **wanka-* produced **wānka-*, whereupon both it and **wanka-* fell into disuse. That **wāka-*, with the required meaning, may at an early stage have been current in O P and O Bal., is suggested by Middle Parthian evidence which points to its having existed in Old Parthian. In M Parth., corresponding to the M Parth. verb *pdw'c-* 'to reply' and to the M P verb *nw'c-* 'to sing',[39] the nouns *pdw'g* 'reply' and *nw'g* 'tune' occur. These are on a par with Sogd. *prw'(')k* (see below, p. 284) and Av. *fravāka-* 'pronouncement' and *pāitivāka-* 'reply'[40]: °*w'g*, °*w'k*, °*vāka-* in these compounds, have no semantic status independent of the preverb. But Parthian also has two compounds, *mwrgw'g* 'bird's cry' and *h'mw'g* (< **hāma-wāka-*) 'in unison', whose second part clearly goes back to an O Parth. noun **wāka-* meaning 'voice, call'.

One might hold against our attribution of **wāka-* 'voice' also to O P and O Bal., where we want a contamination of **wanka-* with it to account for **wānka-*, that precisely O Parth., for which **wāka-* is as good as assured, does not seem to have had **wānka-*: the M Parth. word for 'voice' does occur in Manichean texts, but it is *wcn* < **wačana-* (cf. Skt *vacana*), not **w'ng* as in M P. No emergence of **wānka-*, however, would be expected in a language which did not have a noun **wanka-* to contaminate with **wāka-*. And we have no inducement to regard as likely the existence in early O Parth. of a primary noun **wanka-*, unless a reason independent of the M Parth.

evidence, such as the Bal. verb *gwānǰag* may be thought to constitute, should compel us to credit O Parth. with a pres. stem **wānča-*. The possible explanation of the latter as a contamination of a pres. stem **wanča-* with the pres. stem **wāča-* ancestrial to M Parth. *w'c-* 'to speak', would carry with it the further possibility, that beside the primary pres. stem **wanča-* there existed in O Parth. a primary noun **wanka-*.

But if conversely, despite the apparently contrary evidence of M Parth., there did exist in late O Parth. a noun **wānka-* as must have existed in late O P, we would not need to assume that beside the primary noun **wanka-* presupposed by it, O Parth. had a primary pres. stem **wanča-* which in time, through contamination either with the noun **wānka-* ,or, as just mentioned, with the pres. stem **wāča-*, gave rise to a verb **wānča-*. For in late O Parth., as also in late O P, a pres. stem **wānča-* could have been formed directly from the noun **wānka-*, as a denominative.

That this is so, is suggested by the remarkable pres. stems, **pawāča-* in O Parth., **pāwača-* in O P, for 'to purify', attested respectively through M Parth. *pw'c-* (= *pawāž-*) and M P *p'c-* (= *pāz-*).[41] These were evidently denominatives obtained by simply replacing with *ča* the suffix *ka* of the corresponding adjectives for 'pure', O Parth. **pawāka-* (M Parth. *pw'g*), O P **pāwaka-* (M P *p'k*). This clearly secondary, and therefore relatively late, O Iran. treatment of non-radical *ka*, was no doubt modelled on primary, inherited patterns of the type represented by Av. *tača-* 'to run', against *taka-* 'course'. In **wānka-*, it is true, the *ka* would have been etymologically radical. But as the noun, with its long *ā*, could not have been primary, the *ča* of a verb **wānča-* found beside it, would constitute no proof that an *n*-infixed *ča*-verb of the base *wak-* 'to speak', existed before the time when **pawāča-* was coined.

These speculations on the possible origin of an O Parth. verb **wānča-*, which in M Parth. should have become **wānž-* or **wānǰ-*, may seem a digression to no purpose in the absence of **wānž/ǰ-* from the extant Parthian texts. In fact they are a necessary preliminary to a consideration of Bal. *gwānǰag*, in turning to which, however, a further digression will presently become necessary.

It was Geiger who in *GIP*, I², 240, para 12, pointed out that among the Baluchi numerals, *panč* is genuine on account of its *č*. But in *panč* the *č* is final, and might therefore represent a genuine Bal. *ǰ* devoiced. To ascertain whether *panč* really disqualifies the *nǰ* of *gwānǰag* from representing the genuine Bal. outcome of O Iran. *nč*, we need to identify as genuine at least one Bal. word containing in internal position an outcome of *nč*. Such a word has been said to be, and almost certainly is, the Bal. pres. stem *prinč-* 'to press, squeeze' (past stem *pritk-*). But as the etymology proposed for it fails to satisfy on semantic grounds, we shall have to discuss it before we can draw conclusions from *prinč-* in respect of *gwānǰag*.

Geiger, *Lautlehre* 401, divided *prinč-* into *p(a)-rinč-*, assigning it to Av. *raēk-*. Morgenstierne more explicitly printed '*prinč-* < **pati-rinč-*', *TPS* (1948) 77. Hence either the preverb *pati* successively lost its *i* and *t* (like the preposition *pati*, which is represented by *pa* in Bal.),[42] eventually also its *a*, or **patirinč-* became **ptrinč-* in Middle Bal., whereupon in conformity with Henning's Law[43] the initial cluster of three consonants was reduced to two. However, as soon as one contemplates the reconstructed **ptrinč-* and considers its meaning, one is tempted to divide it no longer into **pt-rinč-*, but into **p-trinč-*. For with the latter division the verb, instead of having acquired its meaning indirectly from 'leer machen' as Geiger supposed, would represent a proper base for 'pressing', IE **trenk-* (Pokorny, *Idg. Wb.*, 1093), already known in Iranian from Av. *θraxta-*, Parth. *tryxs-* 'to be oppressed', and Sogd. *βtrync-* (etc.) 'to oppress', cf. *GMS*, p. 22.

We may therefore derive *prinč-* from **upa-tr̥nč-*, provided that there is no evidence that in principle **pati-rinč-* should have become in Bal. **patrinč-*, in which case one would not expect the *t* of **upa-tr̥nč-* to disappear. It may be thought that such evidence is provided by the only word I can find which may be to the point, viz. *patrūšag* 'spark' (Pierce; Mayer *patrushagh*), since on first consideration,[44] without *prinč-* in mind, one would not hesitate to derive it from **pati-ruč-ya-*.[45]

But so long as this etymology would remain the sole obstacle to the proposed etymology of *prinč-*,[46] one may give preference to another possibility, viz. that *patrūš-* derives from M Iran. **paθrūš-*, a metathesis of **parθūš-* as MP *pahrēz* was of **parhēz-*.[47] The base **θu-* is already known to occur with the M Iran. preverb *par* in Sogd. *prδ'w* 'flame' and the past stem *prδwt-* 'to inflame',[47a] see *GMS*, 573. I would think that the same preverb is joined with the base in Khot. *paṭhu-* 'to burn up'.[48] If it is the *s*-extension **θūš(a)-* of **θu-* which survives in Bal. *patrūšag*,[49] one would infer from the meaning 'spark' that in this case the O Iran. preverb was *para* rather than *pari*, a spark being, as it were, an 'off-flame'.[50]

With the Bal. treatment of O Iran. *panča* shown to be genuine by *prinč-*, we may be sure that if Bal. *gwānǰag* at all represents O Iran. **wānča-*, it can only be as a loan-word. The verb would have had to be borrowed before initial *wă* became *gwă* in Bal., from M Parth. (or some other M Iran. dialect behaving like Parthian in respect of O Iran. *č*), where **wānča-* would have become **wānž/ǰ-*. The fact that we know of no **wānž/ǰ-*, or even **wāng*, in M Parth., would constitute no insurmountable obstacle to assuming such a borrowing, as the extant Parthian vocabulary is far from complete. Bal. *gwānǰag* would simply prove, that in the M Iran. language from which it was borrowed there existed a verb **wānž/ǰ-*, and therefore almost certainly also a noun **wāng*. But if that language maintained an inherited **wānǰ-* beside **wāng*, why has Persian no verb **bānz-*, or at least a borrowed **bānǰ-*, beside the noun *bāng*?

The answer can only be that Persian either has lost the missing verb, or never had it. This answer, however, calls for another question: are we really compelled by Bal. *gwānǰag* to attribute a verb **wānž/ǰ-* to Parthian, or to any Iranian language?

In the absence of a verb **bānz-* or **bānǰ-*, Persian uses for 'to call' on the one hand the denominative verb *bāngīdan*, on the other the compound verb *bāng zadan*. Compound verbs with *gwānk* are used also in Bal., and more widely than the pres. stem *gwānǰ-*, which neither Dames in the Vocabulary to his *Textbook*, nor Gilbertson in his *Dictionary*, quote. The Bal. compound verbs are *gwān kanag* and, corresponding to Pers. *bāng zadan*, *gwānk ǰanag* and *gwān ǰanag*. The absence of *k* from the last of these is due to either spontaneous extrusion, or analogy to *gwān kanag*, where the final *k* of the noun was elided before the initial one of the verb.

The past ptc. of *gwān ǰanag* is, as expected, *gwān ǰata*, and in dialects where *t* became *s* (via *θ*), *gwān ǰasa*. To the ear at any rate, the latter does not differ from the past ptc. of *gwānǰag* as known to and given by Geiger, *Etymologie*, 126, *gwānǰasa*. There is no secondary past-stem formation in Bal. consisting in the addition of *-at-* to the pres. stem, but the addition to it of *-it-* for this purpose is common. It is therefore not surprising to find a past ptc. *gwānjitha* quoted by Mayer s.v. 'call'. What is surprising, is that the pres. stem with which Mayer associates *gwānjitha* is not *gwānǰag* (which he does not even mention), but *gwānk janagh*.

It does not take long to see what has happened. The *ǰ* of *gwānǰag* is not an etymological equivalent of the *g* of Pers. *bāngīdan*, as it appears in Geiger's entry, but is the *ǰ* of *ǰanag* 'to strike'. What precedes it is the noun *gwānk* deprived of its *k*. The past ptc. *gwānǰasa* is simply *gwān ǰasa*, heard and written as one word. The pres. stem *gwānǰ-* need be nothing more remarkable than a haplological shortening of **gwānǰan-* = *gwān ǰan-*. But a more elegant explanation is at hand: that palatalized by *ǰ*, the first *a* of the past ptc. *gwānǰata* locally became *i*; and that the resulting *gwānǰita* (Mayer's *gwānjitha*) came to be interpreted as containing the secondary past-stem formative *-it-*. What preceded *-it-* would then have seemed, and came to be used as, a pres. stem alternative to *gwān ǰan-*.

We now turn to the Khot. verbs with the knowledge that their *j* is unrelated to the *ǰ* of Bal. *gwānǰag*, and without being embarrassed by their showing no trace of the latter's long *ā*. Deprived of what was thought to be Western Iranian evidence for a palatal variant of MP *wāng*, do we still wish to connect Khot. *pyūṃj-*, *byūṃj-*, and *vaṃj-* with the MP word? None of the English renderings of the Khot. verbs, 'to deny, disparage, abuse, slander, dispute', is etymologically related to a verb meaning 'to speak'. What is more, O Ind. has both *vañcati* 'goes crookedly' and *vaṅgati* 'limps', respectively from IE **we-n-k-* and **we-n-g-*, two bases whose original meaning is thought to have been 'to bend' (Pokorny, *Idg. Wb.*, 1134, 1148). Would not 'distortion' make as good a semantic etymon of 'slander' as 'speech' (**we-n-kʷ-*)?

The answer is that although this may be so, there is independent evidence that the three Khot. verbs do not by accident look as if they might belong to the base *wak-* 'to speak'. We have seen (p. 280) that Sogd. *wnxr* provides the much-needed assurance that the *k* of Bal. *gwānk* (and of Arm. *vank*) is an unchanged part of the O Iran. root, so that the existence in O Iran. of a variant **wank-* of *wak-* 'to speak' cannot be doubted. We may now add that it is from *wak-* 'to speak' that in Sogdian the noun for 'slander', *prw'(')k*, was derived, as well as the corresponding pres. stem *prw'c-* (to which no past stem is attested). This pres. stem, however, is isolated in Sogdian, where the pres. stem for 'to speak' is *w'β-*, and only the past stem *wyt-*[51] suppletively joined with it, belongs to the base *wak-*.[52]

In Khotanese not even the past stem of any verb for 'to speak' belongs to *wak-*,[53] which base seems to be altogether missing from that language, unless it be present in the three verbs with which we are concerned. These, or at least *pyūṃj-* and *byūṃj-*, have preverbs, going back to O Iran. *pati* and *abi* respectively, which like *pari* can mean 'against'. Sogd. *prw'c-*, from **pari-wāča-*, clearly originally meant 'to speak against'.[54] This fact, and two other facts, viz. that Khot. *-ūṃj-* can phonetically represent **wančaya-*, and that we are entitled to relate this **wančaya-* to *wak-* 'to speak' because the existence of an O Iran. **wanka-* belonging to the same *wak-* is now assured by Bal. *gwānk* and Sogd. *wnxr* jointly, combine to make it virtually certain that also Khot. *pyūṃj-* and *byūṃj-* originally meant 'to speak against'. One would expect the same to be true of *vaṃj-*, which in that case should conceal a preverb. Perhaps *vaṃj-* went back to **awančaya-*, an O Iran. haplological shortening of **awa-wančaya-*, whose meaning would have been close to that of the similarly formed Ved. verb *ava-vad-* 'to speak ill of, *or* against'.

Our case then is, that with the exception of the Sogd. past stem *wyt-*, both Sogdian and Khotanese retained *wak-* 'to speak' as a verb only with preverbs which defined the speaking as hostile, each language having chosen a different pres. stem. Khot. *j* points to an O Iran. pres. stem ending in *-čaya-*, but the noun **abi-wanka-* presupposed by Khot. *byūṃgga*, would have been properly matched only by a pres. stem **abi-wanča-*, of which the stem **abi-wančaya-* required by *byūṃj-* was evidently a mere secondary extension. Between **abi-wanka-* and the original **abi-wanča-* there would have been a relation strictly parallel to the relation between **pari-wāka-* and **pari-wāča-*, the ancestors of Sogd. *prw'(')k* and *prw'c-*. There is likewise strict parallelism between the relation of **abi-wanča-* to **pari-wāča-*, and the relation of **abi-wanka-* to **pari-wāka-*. This relation, manifest in the Eastern Iranian vocabulary, between internal *an* and *ā* forms of *wak/č-* 'to speak', seems to me to put the seal of plausibility on the view expressed above (p. 280), that Western O Iran. **wānka-* presupposes a noun **wanka-* which was contaminated with its internal *ā* variant **wāka-*.

The *n*-infixed forms of *wak-* 'to speak' which we have reconstructed for O Iran., are parallel to the O Ind. ones of *vak-* 'to bend': **wanka-* 'voice' corresponds to *vaṅka* 'river-bed'; **wanxra-* or **wanxri-* 'voice', to *vaṅkri* 'rib'; and *(*pati-*, *abi-*, *awa-*)*wanča*(*ya*)*ti* 'he (gain)says' to *vañcati* 'he goes crookedly'. So long as the *n*-infixation of IE **wekʷ-* remains unattested in other IE languages, one cannot deny that it may have been an Iranian innovation, as may have been the *n*-infixation of IE **merd-* (Av. *mōrənd-*) and **merk-* (Av. *mərənč-*). Yet the suspicion is not easily dismissed, that O Iran. had here preserved a feature of hoary antiquity. As far as Indo-Iranian **wa(n)k/č-* is concerned, the Indo-Aryan elimination of *n*-infixed forms where the meaning was 'to speak', could be explained as due to a striving to avoid homonymity with *vank/c-* 'to bend', while conversely it seems to have been at the expense of *n*-infixation where the meaning was 'to bend',[55] that in Iranian **wank/č-* 'to speak' was retained.

NOTES

1 Morgenstierne, *IIFL*, II, 199, had suggested Asiatic origin.

2 'Der gleiche Ausgang [viz. as in *sačaini-*] könnte auch in *p'cyn* ..., n.p. *pāzan* ... vorliegen.'

3 This meaning was conjectured on the strength of Pašto *γarcanai* (see

presently in text above) by H. W. Bailey in *TPS* (1960) 76, who accordingly suggested that *Pāmir* means 'the hill plateau'.

3a Most recently in *Studia . . . Antonino Pagliaro dicata* (1969), I, 142.

4 *AHM*, 85, 178 sq., 183, 192.

5 *Sogdica* 23 sq.

6 Apud M. Mayrhofer, *A concise etymological Sanskrit Dictionary*, I, 285.

7 *Dr J. M. Unvala Memorial Volume*, 41 sqq.

8 Quoted from Gert Klingenschmitt's new edition, Inaugural-Dissertation (Erlangen-Nürnberg 1968).

9 *BSOAS*, XXVI (1963) 196 *b*. At that time only Humbach was known to hold the view to which I objected.

10 *GIP*, Anhang, 56.

11 Cf. Grassmann's entry s.v. *kṣad*.

12 A third O Ind. base *kṣad-*, corresponding to Khot. *ṣa'-* 'to prepare', <**γẓad-*, has been assumed by H. W. Bailey, see R. E. Emmerick, *Saka Grammatical Studies*, 127.

13 For other explanations of Oss. *æfsædın* see Miller, *GIP*, Anhang, 82, (4) and differently, *IF*, XXI (1907) 325, Morgenstierne, *NTS*, XII (1940) 266, and Abayev, *Ist.-etim. slov.*, I, 480. In favour of Miller's second, and Morgenstierne's, etymology one would now quote Hitt. *išpāy-* 'to eat to satiety', Khot. *spai-/spata-* 'to sate oneself' (see Bailey, *AION-L*, I (1959), 137), but there remains the drawback that the Oss. past stem would then represent an analogical deviation.

14 Translated into Sogdian as *'γšnyrkh*, see Henning, *BBB*, 88. *xšnēr°*< **xšnārya-* 'recognizable', to Lat. *gnārus*.

15 If by 1958 Henning thought that *nišān* belonged to Arm. *nšavak*, he would be bound to have regarded the *y* of M Iran. *nyš'n* as also representing a short *i*, as indeed Arm. *nšan* suggests that it did. Up to 1940 he had followed Nyberg in interpreting the spelling *nyš'n* as standing for *nīšān*, see *Mir. Man.* II, 309 n. 3, *BBB*, 88, *Sogdica* 20.

16 See Bailey, *Prolexis*, 351.

17 Thus on Sogd. *'xšn'm* Henning, *Sogdica*, 33. Later Bailey pointed out (*BSOAS* XII (1948) 327) that the long diphthong of **xšnāuma-* survives, shortened, in Khot. *ṣṣänaumä*.

18 *BSOS*, VII, 284; wrong Junker, *Wissb. Sohn*, 48.

19 Henning, *Sogdica*, 23.

20 Henning, *Sogdica*, 19.

21 Cf., with different preverb, Oss. *æfson* 'cause', *BSOAS* XIV (1952) 484.

22 Lentz, *Pamir-Dialekte*, 77.129, 79.188.

23 With the *u* of **garu-* elided before the suffix, as in Khot. *āska* 'antelope' <**āsuka-*, cf. Bailey, *Prolexis* 21.

24 Bailey, *Prolexis*, 67, compares the suffix of *ggarkha* with the *x* of Sogd. *mẓyx*. But the Sogd. adj. is from **maẓyah-*, a demoted comparative, cf.

AHM 241, bottom, and 330, where add, to the parallel quoted, *MP wtr* (cf. Henning, *BBB*, 116) and the adjectives cited by Wackernagel-Debrunner, *Ai. Gr.* ii 2, 460. It seems possible that the *xa* of Khot. *ggarkha* developed from the suffix *-ka-* of **γaruka-* by assimilation to the initial spirant. Similarly Sogd. *x'x* and Khot. *khāhā* 'source, spring' may reflect a late O Iran. *-kā-* extension of **xā* (from the nom. sg. **xā*^{h}, Av. *xå*), with *k* assimilated to the initial *x*. Cf. already in O Iran. the *x* of O P *amāxam*<**ahmākam*, see Bartholomae, *Ar. Forsch.*, I, 79 n. 1.

Conversely, assimilation to a following spirant may account for initial *x* instead of expected *k* in some of the instances listed by Bailey, *TPS* (1945), 30 (as well as for the *th* of Khot. *thauna* 'cloth'<**tafna-* quoted ibid. 26 sq.): Oss. *xæfs* 'toad, frog' against N P *kašaf*; Oss. *xæf* 'slime', Khot. *khavā* 'foam' against Av. *kafa-*; Oss. *xaun* 'to fall', if from **kaf-*. Add perhaps Pahl. *xaftār* or *haftār* 'hyena', Bal. *haptār*, S Bš *haptōr*, N Bš *hö*^{u}*tar* against N P *kaftār*, N Bš *kaftarg*. As to Oss. *xin* (Dig. *xinæ*) 'trickery, magic', quoted by Bailey, ibid., this is better kept distinct from Av. *kaēnā-* 'vengeance', on semantic grounds, and because it shows *ī* in both Iron and Digoron; Digoron in any case has the expected *kenæ*, beside *kinæ*, for 'vengeance' (see Abayev, *Oset. Yazyk i Fol'klor*, I, 169, 454, and *Ist.-etim. Slov.*, I, 596). Conceivably Oss. *xin* is from **hinya-* (base **hā(y)-*) '(spell-)binding', distinct from Pazand *xīn*, Man. M P *xy(y)n* (*xēn*, see Andreas-Henning, *Mir. Man.*, II, 306, App., n. (2)) 'hatred, malice, enmity', which perhaps represents **ainah-* (Av. *aēnah-*, translated by Pahl. *kēn*), with prothetic *x*?

25 One might even start from O Iran. **bāuθna-* (cf. O Ind. *cyautna*), becoming **bāuna-* in proto-Oss., as there is evidence that O Iran. *θ* was lost before *n* in Ossetic: see *BSOAS* XVII (1955) 481 n. 4 (on *æfsin* 'lady' which I there quoted, Benveniste, *Études sur la langue ossète*, 19, and Abayev, *Ist.-etim. Slov.*, s.v., hold a different opinion, but even they derive *n* in this word from *θn*). Here I must defend my derivation in the same footnote of Oss. *binontæ* 'family, wife' from *hapaθnī-*, to which Abayev, op. cit., s.v., objects that from intervocalic *p* one expects *f*, not *b*. Abayev himself invalidates his objection by accepting Miller's derivation of *bad-* 'to sit' from **upa-had-*, on which I had of course relied, and by insisting, s.v. *bwar*, that '*up* became *b*'. Benveniste, on the other hand, denies (op. cit. 98) that even the preverb *ba-* is connected with *upa*: the preverb 'doit reposer sur une forme ancienne à *b-* initial'. But he neither discloses what that 'forme ancienne' might have been, nor what he thinks of *bad-* 'to sit', while on p. 31 even he derives *bæl* from *upari*. It seems that nobody can manage without occasionally tracing back an Oss. *b* to *p*. To my mind, since as a rule O Iran. intervocalic *p* shares in Ossetic the fate of O Iran. intervocalic *b*, that is, has become *v* (*β*) (with rare exceptions, cf. *BSOAS*, XXIII (1960) 596 *b*), it must in the first place have simply been voiced to *b*. Where such a *b*<*p* is attested in Oss. initial position, the vowel preceding it must have been

lost before intervocalic spirantization began. In the preverb *æv-*, *æf-* < *abi* (sometimes also <*apa*, *upa*?) the loss of the second O Iran. vowel before single consonant other than *h*, caused the initial vowel to remain; subsequent spirantization was due to contact with a consonant.

26 The thematic prohibitive **mā bavah* should have been reserved for 'do not become'.

27 Cf. Bartholomae, *Zum sas. Recht*, v, 52 n. 3. Differently Bailey, *TPS* (1959) 89 n. 5, in whose opinion *nizār* and *aβzār* contain a base *zar-*.

28 For proto-Oss. *θ*<*d* cf. also Oss. *nætīn* 'to groan': Av. *nadant-* (Miller, *IF*, XXI (1907) 329), and Oss. *mætīx* 'locust': Av. *maδaxa-* on which more elsewhere.

29 *šōn dēūn* 'ich will zeigen', W. Geiger, *ZDMG*, XLIII (1889) 581, line 3; *tharā handā šon-deān* 'I will show you the place', *hawān hand šon-dāthaī* 'he showed the place', Dames, *Textbook*, Part I, 15, lines 19, 20; *ānhān . . . nagan šōn dāta* 'they showed (the dog) some bread', Morgenstierne, *AO*, XX (1948) 267; cf. also Dames, op. cit., Vocabulary 67, Gilbertson, *Engl.-Bal. Dict.* s.v. 'show', Mayer s.v. 'point (out)'.

30 Thus according to the three glossaries quoted in the prec. fn. In the Šāh Nāme *nišān dāštan* means 'to be shown, have evidence', not 'to show'. I suspect, therefore, that in Bal. *šōn dāragh* the verb has replaced *dēagh* under the influence of the synonymous idioms *phē(n)-dāragh*, *pezh dārag* (the latter given by Pierce), 'to show, point out'. Note, however, that Yaghnobi has *nišōn dōr-* for 'to show'. [Since this article went into print I received through the kindness of the authors *A Course in Baluchi*, by Muhammad Abd-al-Rahman Barker and Aqil Khan Mengal (Montreal 1969, 2 volumes), based on the Rakhshani dialect of Baluchi. In this dialect *šōn* is used by itself, but only in the meaning 'arrangement, good order', and both *šōn day-* and *šōn kan-* mean 'to arrange', not 'to show' (I, 402 sq.). It is not clear to me whether Rakhshani *šōn* displays a semantic change from 'pointing out' to 'appointing' (as it were), or is a homonym of the word discussed above.]

31 See Morgenstierne, *NTS*, v, 41. The Bal. word means 'saddle-bag'.

32 NP *bāliš*, if it does not continue Pahl. *bālišn*, would have to go back to an OP thematically extended **bardiš-a-*; the same would be true of Pahl. *bālišn* itself, if its *n* is due to wrong analogy and merely inverse spelling as Henning suggested, *TPS* (1944) 117 n. 2. Alternatively one may think of deriving both from an OP stem **bardišana-*, a contamination of **bṛdana-* (cf. Yidγa *virzanë*) and **bardiš(a)-*, whose *-išana-* would have become *-išn* in MP, and further, in NP, *-iš*.

33 *nihāl* seems to be the only Persian word so far identified in which an *h* goes back to O Iran. intervocalic *b*.

34 On which see Bailey, *Rocznik Orientalistyczny* XXI (1957) 61.

35 See *Unvala Memorial Volume*, 91 sq.

36 That the meaning 'to stir' of *šyu-* underlies that of 'action' of Av. *šyaoθna-* was seen by Benveniste, *Donum Nyberg*, 24 sq. It is also discernible in **šyavana-*, the O Iran. form from which according to Henning, *Sogdica*, 23, MP *-šwn* in *'spšwn* derives; the compound can be understood as literally meaning 'horse-stirrer'. Cf. Ved. *cyávana* 'moving' and 'movable', Wackernagel-Debrunner, *Ai. Gr.*, II, 2, 182.

37 See Henning, *Sogdica*, 4.

38 See Henning, *BSOS*, VIII (1936) 584.

39 In Parth. the meaning of *nw'c-* was given as 'to invite' in *Mir. Man.*, III 871.3. But in that passage, and in *M* 4 i v 3 (see Ghilain, *Essai*, 123), the only two quoted, the verb could equally well mean 'to admit, let in'. We would then have also in Parthian, the pres. stem corresponding to Sogd. *w'c-* and Oss. *uadzin* of the base **wak-* 'to let'. The past stem **waxta-* (Sogd. *wyt-*, Oss. *uaxt-*, *uayd-*) had already been recognized in Parth. *'trwḥt* by Henning (*BSOAS*, XII (1948) 605 n. 5), and may be represented by Paz. *vaxt* in *ŠGV*, VI, 3 (cf. Zaehner, *BSOS*, IX, 899 sq., and de Menasce *ad locum*). A trace of **wak-* 'to let' seems to have survived also in Bal., see J. H. Elfenbein, *The Baluchi Language*, 33 n. 20. With Parth. *nw'c* in *Mir. Man.*, III 871.3 one may range the *nw'gyft 'spynj* of the following line, as an 'inn of hospitality'. Cf. NP *nuvāxtan* 'to receive well', and *mihmān-navāz* 'hospitable (*lit.* guest-admitter)'. The preverb is *ni*.

40 Bartholomae regarded also Av. *ažīvāka-* as a compound whose second part was *vāka-*. Its translation as 'snake-bite' by Darmesteter was to him incomprehensible, as it must have been, etymologically, even to its author. Today, however, this rendering is justifiable, as *ažīvāka-* may well be a haplology of **aži-žīvāka-*, with *v*<*b*. Av. **žib-* would neatly correspond to B. Sogd. *zyβ-* (with *z*=*ž*), Man. Sogd. *jβ-*, 'to bite', which verb has a snake as subject in *P* 3, 84 and in Reichelt's *Hdschr. Reste*, I, 58, 16. Acceptance of this etymology would resolve the doubt as to whether the original vowel of the Sogd. verb was *a* or *i* (cf. *GMS*, para. 112), and would lead one to agree more readily with Livshitz that Sogd. *zyβ-* is represented in Yayn. by *živ-* 'to quilt', and not by *žav-* 'to drink, sip' (although the latter, on account of its *v*<*β*, cannot represent O Iran. **žyaw-* as Livshitz wants). [Cf. also B. Sogd. *γr'zβ'k* 'gad-fly' as per *IF*, LXXV (1970) (review of MacKenzie, *SCE*).]

41 See Henning, *BSOS*, IX (1937) 86.

42 Bal. *pa* hardly represents *upa* alone, as Geiger thought, *Etymologie*, 139. But it is possible that in it, as in NP *ba*, O Iran. *upa* and *pati* have coalesced.

43 See Henning, *BSOAS*, XII (1947) 47 with n. 4.

44 By the qualification of a judgement as based 'on first consideration', an author should be entitled to be quoted not for it, or at least not for it alone, but for the judgement he proceeds to deliver on further consideration. On p. 491 of *BSOAS*, XIV (1952) I wrote that 'on first

consideration' at least three different verbs seem to have come to coincide in Oss. *xezun*. On the next two pages I argued at length that in fact only two were involved, one meaning 'to climb, rise across', the other 'to wait, protect, pasture'. Benveniste, *Études sur la langue ossète*, 55 (reprinted from *BSL* (1956)), objects against what he refers to as my threefold distinction that 'on peut s'épargner ces complications', and recommends deriving all the meanings of *xezun* from the single sense of 'to climb'. Abayev, *Voprosy yazykoznaniya*, No. 2 (1959) 148 *b*, rightly rejects Benveniste's over-simplification, but still quotes me as having postulated three homonyms instead of the two he wants. His two, however, are precisely the two for which I had given detailed reasons why they alone should be assumed to have merged in *xezun*.

45 For the use of *pati* with the base *ruk-* cf. Arm. *patroik* 'wick' and Pahl. Ps. *ptlwk* 'splendour', both from **pati-rauka-*. For **ruč-ya-* cf. Bal. *gwaš-* 'to speak' <**wačya-*, Morgenstierne, *NTS*, v, 46. However, the long *ū* of *patrūš-* would remain unexplained.

46 Complications of a different kind arise from two variants of *prinč-* with which Geiger was not acquainted, viz. *prēnč-* in Marw Bal., and the *n*-less pres. stem *prič-* given by Mayer (s.v. 'wring') as *phirrich-*, by Bray (s.v. Brāhūī *princhina*) as *prich-* and (with *ī* by misprint?) *pīrich-*. Both can be explained as secondary if one grants the existence of a further variant, **prinčēn-*, whose causative appearance would merely have emphasized the verb's transitivity, as seems to be the case with Marw Bal. *rēpēn-* 'to deceive' (V. S. Sokolova, *Ocherki po fonetike iranskikh yazykov*, i 65 sq.), against Brāhūī *rēfing*, NP *firēb-*; cf. also Rameški *perüešōn-* 'to sell', against NP *furōš-*. As Bal. *tajēn-* 'to stretch' (against Mīnābi *temzon-*) must be from **tanjēn-* with dissimilatory loss of the first *n*, so from **prinčēn-* there could have arisen **pričēn-*, which in its turn would account for the variant *prič-* of *prinč-*. By analogy to *brēj-* 'to fry', beside *brij-*, there may then have arisen beside *prič-* a form **prēč-*, responsible for the emergence of *prēnč-* beside *prinč-*.

47 See *BSOAS*, XIV (1952) 488.

47a Man. *prδwty* is assigned to the base **du-* by Emmerick, *SGS*, 68. But Chr. *prθwty* (Hansen, *BST*, II, 887.6) confirms that Man. δ here represents theta. To **du-*, by contrast, belongs B.Soghd. *δβ''nh*, *δβ'n* (not δβ'z as in *TSP*, 228), Chr. *db'n* (*BST*, II, 859.27, 860.37.45) 'flame', from **dw-āna-*.

48 Emmerick, op. cit. 66, quotes from Bailey the identification of the base as **θu-*, but offers no explanation of the preverb. To the same base he rightly assigns (p. 43) Khot. *thūs-* 'to kindle'. Add, from Bailey, *haṃthuta* 'burnt up', *E* 21.36 (= *Z* 20.36 in Emmerick's edition, *The Book of Zambasta* (1968) 290). See also Bailey, *Prolexis*, 112, 154.

49 For the long *ū* of Bal. *patrūš-*, unaccountable if from **ručya-*, one would then compare the Vedic *s*-aorist *anūṣ-* of *návate*.

50 On account of the preverb alone, **pati-ručya-* would not make a satisfactory etymology of a word meaning 'spark', cf. above, n. 45.

51 The constant spelling without initial alif suggests that *wyt-* stands for *wayd-*<**waxta-*, and not for *uyd-*<*uxta-*.

52 As part of a compound, however, O Iran. **wāča-* also survived in Sogd. *ẓntw'ch 'mry'* 'singing bird', beside which Sogdian had **ẓandwāβ*, borrowed by Persian. See Henning, *BSOS*, x, 104 sq.

53 Khot. has *hvāñ-* and *pätāy-* for 'to speak', *gvīr-* for 'to talk', *śver-* for 'to tell', see Emmerick, op. cit. s. vv. One wonders if *gvīr-* should not be derived from **vi-b(a)rya-* rather than **vi-varya-*; cf. Sogd. *prβyr-* 'to tell', *prβ'r* 'announcement' (see Henning, *BSOAS*, xi (1943) 68 n. 3), and *wy''βr-* 'to speak, talk' (Henning, *BBB*, 80). To the same base also Khot. *śver-?*

54 I had not realized this in *GMS*, para. 666. Cf. OP *kašči nai adršnauš čišči θastanai pari gaumātam* 'no-one dared say anything *against* Gaumāta' (Bartholomae, Weissbach, Kent: '*about* Gaumāta'), Beh. i 53 sq.

55 Except in the noun Sogd. *yw'nk*, Oss. *iuong* 'joint' as interpreted by Benveniste, *Études sur la langue ossète* 15. Without *n*-infixation, Iranian equivalents of Ved. *vakrá* 'crooked' have been suspected in Pahl. *w'hl* (Zaehner, *BSOS*, ix, 899), Parth. *wxrydg* (Henning, *Mir. Man.*, iii, 908 *b*), and Pers. x^{v}*ahl* [Pahl. Ps. *hwhly*] (Horn, *GIP*, I^{2}, 172 n.). [Six months after the present article was sent to the Editor, *JAOS*, LXXXIX/2 (1969) appeared, where on p. 446 *b* Martin Schwartz assigns Sogd. *wnxr* to the base **vank-* 'to make a sound' assumed by Bailey for NP *bāng*, which he recognizes also outside Iranian, in O Ind. *vaṅkú* 'noisy' and Toch. A *wanke* 'prattle'.]

J. A. HAYWOOD

Urdu Drama
Origins and Early Development

Pakistani and Indian literary critics often exhibit embarrassment in their references to Urdu drama. They sometimes give the impression that they are ashamed of their Marlowes because they were not Shakespeares. Thus, Muhammad Sadiq, in the best guide to Urdu literature yet to appear in a European language,[1] devotes a whole chapter to drama, yet mentions only one dramatist, the pioneer Amānat Lakhnawī.[2] As to the best-known modern dramatist, Āghā Ḥashar Kāshmīrī, he mentions him in a footnote, to illustrate Urdu dramatists' predilection for happy endings, even when adapting Shakespearean tragedy. Mulk Raj Anand, in his *Indian Theatre*, a short monograph for English readers,[3] refers to Āghā Ḥashar[4] as 'a hack... a third-rate poetaster, whose stock-in-trade was blood-and-thunder melodrama, with a dash of morality sufficient to get into the skin of the four-anna audiences and send them home happy, and supposedly uplifted'. Nevertheless, there are some writers in Pakistan who are showing a little more sympathy, and studying Urdu drama with more understanding. Prominent among these are ʿIshrat Raḥmānī[5] and Waqqār ʿAẓīm.[6] A just assessment of Urdu dramatists – especially Āghā Ḥashar – cannot be made by the yardstick of *either*, Classical Sanskrit drama on the one hand, *or* European drama on the other. It must be seen in the context of that popular Indian drama from which it largely sprang. Moreover, other Indian drama of the first half of the nineteenth century – Bengali, Marhaṭṭī, and the like – must come into the picture. The aim of the present article is to draw attention to important factors and land-marks in the history of Urdu drama up to the emergence of Āghā Ḥashar (1879–1935). As the latter's career as a dramatist commenced in 1901, the effective topic of this study is really nineteenth-century Urdu drama.

The *fons et origo* of modern Urdu (and other Indo-Pakistani) drama may be thought to be Classical Sanskrit drama. But the latter was hardly popular, being the 'plaything of princes'.[7] Being devoted to national epic themes, it was largely on too high a plane for the tastes of the masses. The absence of music is cited by Shekhar[8] as one cause for its lack of appeal. Most authorities postulate the existence of some form of popular drama alongside the classical drama. R.A. Jagirdar says[9]: 'Though Sanskrit drama never belonged so much to the common man, we should be wrong in believing that the common man had no dramas of his own.' Monomohan Ghosh[10] in describing an Assamese play of the fifteenth/sixteenth century, Sankaradeva's *Ankīya Nāt*, refers to it as a relic of the old type of drama, the inference being that this 'old type' was the popular drama which existed alongside Classical Sanskrit drama, and that it was not a new form even then. Ghosh reproduces this play (in translation) in full, and it markedly resembles early Urdu drama as exemplified by the *Rahas*[11] and *Indar Sabhā*. Every important speech is followed by a song, and a major role is played by the *Sūtradhāra* (stage-manager, director or chorus – literally *thread-holder*), who gives the stage directions, and explains entrances. He remains on stage throughout, but speaks both Sanskrit and the vernacular for important pronouncements.

An account of Sanskrit drama in decline is beyond the scope of this study. Yet one or two points may be mentioned, because there are examples as late as the seventeenth century. The decline is variously ascribed to dependence on epic themes, lack of music, lack of humour, adherence to the happy ending, a growing preference for dramatic poetry recital rather than drama proper, and the Muslim invasions. All this is speculation. Certainly too much notice need not be taken of the common idea that Islamic prejudice against acting has any great relevance, at least in the Indo-Pak subcontinent. Muslims were prominent in the class of *bhāṇḍ* (strolling player, buffoon), and all the evidence suggests that Muslim audiences were quite content to witness popular drama on Hindu themes. It is probable that the decline of Sanskrit drama was due more than anything else to the growth of the Prākrit vernaculars, which bore a relationship to Sanskrit rather like that of Italian to Latin. The point was reached where Sanskrit drama appealed not to courts, as before, but merely to pedants and scholars. No doubt the stereotyped themes also assisted the decline. But there can be no doubt that drama was performed in the vernaculars, as the Assamese example already quoted shows. One curious bye-product of the decline was the *Bhāna* or monologue as opposed to the *Nātika* or drama-proper. Horace Hayman Wilson[12] describes one such work, Sankara's *Sarada Tilaka*, possibly twelfth-century, in which the sole actor, representing a man of licentious habits, describes his encounters with various people in the streets during a festival. He will ask some imaginary character a question, and then, saying 'What do you say?', repeat the supposed reply. This is the stock-in-trade of the monologue reciter in modern music-hall, and is also exemplified in the type of modern English play which consists merely of one character in a telephone conversation. But for our purpose, its chief importance is that it shows the petrifaction of drama, which finally revived with the Parsi theatrical commercialism which started in Bombay late in the nineteenth century. There melodrama predominated – melodrama inspired largely by English drama, especially Shakespeare. In this liberating process, aimed at drama with real movement and action, Āghā Ḥashar played the major role.

Before dealing with *Indar Sabhā* (1853), by common consent the first Urdu drama worthy of consideration, the forms of popular drama in existence during the first half of the nineteenth century must be mentioned. The performers were itinerant players (*bhānḍ*). These dramas went under a number of names, the differences between which are not always clear. They generally contained singing and dancing, but differed in the amount of acting, and in whether they were unified dramas with a proper plot, or merely varied entertainments resembling Western Music Hall or Variety Shows. Leaving aside the puppet play, we find the *Sawāng*, *Lilā*', *Tamāshā*, *Sangīt*, *Nauṭankī*, and *Rahas* (*Rahs*, *Rās*, *Rāsa*). They were usually performed in the open air, without scenery, and with a minimum of stage 'props'. Anand[13] says: 'In our villages the performance of a play, usually called RAS or NAUTANKI or TAMASHA, though often more vigorous and unpretentious (than in urban theatres), is often a jumble rather like the European revue, consisting of scenes from a religious or a historical play, interspersed with humorous sketches . . . and replete with songs, songs and more songs. The relieving grace is that the . . . players and audience are one . . . often the audience joins in community singing.' In so far as the various forms can be distinguished, the *tamāshā* is the least closely knit. It still exists, and is a variety show, including dancing and singing 'turns', sketches and monologues. In Marhaṭṭī it has been described[14] as 'something like opera, in which, however, obscene and vulgar songs were recited by a boy dressed as a woman. The dances and dialogue were provided as the accompaniment.' The *sawāng* was a pageant, while the *lilā*' was a musical play based on Hindu themes, often concerning Krishna. The latter, with his cowherd-maidens, was a popular figure among Muslim poets – Walī Dakhanī, for example, mentions them in his *Mathnawī* on the city of Surat. The *Sangit* and *Nauṭankī*, were a mixture of song, dance and drama, very popular in Agra and Oudh in the early nineteenth century, the former term being sometimes used especially for the more static performance, while the latter included acting. But it is doubtful whether this distinction was widely recognized. The themes were originally taken from the *Rāmāyan* or *Mahābhārata*. Later, however, other themes were introduced, including Persian and Arab ones, such as *Shīrīn and Farhād* and *Laylā and Majnūn*. The *Rahas* was perhaps the quintessence of all these forms, being poetical drama, usually on Hindu themes, with dancing and singing and making some pretensions to literary merit, especially in Oudh at the time of the Nawab Wājid ʻAlī Shāh in the mid-nineteenth century. He himself is said to have written thirty-six *rahas*.[15] In Bengali, the equivalent of the *rahas* was the *yātrā*, which was often associated with the Krishna theme, but by no means exclusively. Shīva and various other religious and epic themes are encountered.[16] The most famous writer of *yātrās* was Krishna Kamal (1810–88), whose *Svapna Bilās* (Dream Pleasures) of 1835 was so popular that 20,000 copies were sold within a few years.

In view of the importance of Bombay in the history of Urdu drama, it is worth mentioning that probably the earliest popular drama of literary merit in the subcontinent is to be found in Marhaṭṭī. Vishnūpant Bhāve, born in 1818, was the son of an official of the ruler of the state of Sangli. The latter had seen South Indian drama, and suggested that Bhāve write a play. This work, performed in 1841, was called *Sita chooses her husband* (*Sītā svayamvar*). It contained singing and dancing, and was extremely popular over the whole area. By 1880 two genres of Marhaṭṭī drama were recognized, both musical. The *sangīt* was poetical, while the *Nāṭak* had prose dialogue interspersed with songs. Leading examples of both types were performed frequently in Bombay.[17]

But, despite what may be said to the contrary, it is doubtful whether Urdu drama would have made any headway but for the influence of English drama. French influence might also be claimed, were it established that Wājid ʻAlī really did have a French theatrical expert at his court. But Raḥmānī[18] denies this. At any rate, British communities in India in the eighteenth and nineteenth centuries encouraged the performance of English plays, and there is no doubt that these influenced Indians. Macaulay's educational policy, based on the English language (1833/1836), introduced English drama, especially Shakespeare, to an increasing number of Indians. The first English theatre in Calcutta was founded in 1756, and from about 1780 there were frequent performances of Shakespearean, Restoration, and eighteenth-century plays.[19] Garrick is said to have sent out a certain

Massing to take charge of theatrical activities. A Russian adventurer, H. Lebedeff, came to Calcutta, and produced two English plays (*The Disguise* and *Love is the Best Doctor*) in Bengali translation in 1795 and 1796.[20] During the nineteenth century, Shakespeare's best-known plays were translated – or rather, adapted, usually with change of scene and names – into the major Indian languages such as Urdu, Bengali and Marhaṭṭī. Frequently song and dance were added, and tragedies were given happy endings, in accordance with the tradition going back to Classical Sanskrit drama. It is not always realised that when Āghā Ḥashar and his fellow dramatists included these happy endings, they were, in fact, making their adaptations more Indian – surely not automatically a reprehensible practice!

The above will, it is hoped, give some idea of some of the formative influences of Urdu drama. Pakistani writers sometimes also add the epic *mathnawī*, such as the *Mathnawī-yi-Siḥr al-Bayān* of Mīr Ḥasan (1727–86). There is something in this contention, as some *mathnawīs* were very dramatic and contained dialogue of a sort. But one is reminded of those Arab writers who try to see the origins of modern Arabic drama in the *Maqāmāt* of al-Ḥarīrī and Badīʿ al-Zamān al-Hamadhānī.

It is not surprising that Urdu drama in the true sense should have begun in Lucknow, capital of Oudh, at the time of the Nawab Wājid ʿAlī Shāh. As has been shown, this ruler was not merely a patron of drama, but himself wrote a number of *rahas*. Sayyid Āghā Ḥasan Amānat Lakhnawī (1814–58) lost his power of speech owing to paralysis at the age of twenty. After ten years, he recovered, but seldom left his house. It would appear that, though he recovered his speech, he must still have felt selfconscious about it. At any rate, he spent his days alone, and his evenings until midnight with friends and pupils. One of the latter, Ḥājjī Mīrzā ʿĀbid ʿAlī (who used the *takhalluṣ* of ʿIbādat) suggested that he occupy his day-times writing a poem in the form of a *jalsa*. Amānat was dubious about this plan, but set to work in 1851. The more he worked, the more interested he became, and at last, after a year and a half, the play was finished in 1853. This is the story told by Amānat himself in his own *sharḥ*.[21] The first performance was for a certain Shaikh Rajab ʿAlī. The play was published in Lucknow, and soon ran into several editions.

It used to be thought that Amānat was a sort of court poet to Wājid ʿAlī, that *Indar Sabhā* was composed for that ruler, and that the latter actually acted in it at its first performance. But Raḥmānī shows[22] that all this is not true. What seems conclusive is that Amānat makes no mention of it in his *sharḥ*; while Wājid 'Alī in his *tazkira*, while mentioning performances of his own *rahas*'s, does not refer to Amānat or *Indar Sabhā*.

The best accounts of *Indar Sabhā* are that of Waqqār 'Aẓīm[23] and Amānat's own *sharḥ*,[24] which gives a summary with quotations. A study of the play shows clearly that it is a *rahas* – but one written on a high level, in carefully contrived poetry. The singing and dancing are what matter, and are prolonged at the expense of action, which is almost non-existent. In fact the action is mostly described by a *rāwī* – the *sūtradhāra* of Sanskrit drama already mentioned.[25] He announces the entrance of each new character, and remains on stage throughout. Further, before each new character enters, a curtain is lowered, presumably to allow the character to join the scene without actually walking on. Then the curtain is raised again. But even this is not sufficient. The new character begins by announcing who he or she is. One is reminded of the old English morality or miracle play. For example, in the famous *Everyman*, the Prologue warns us that we are to hear God speak:

'For ye shall hear now our Heaven King
Calleth Everyman to a general reckoning.
Give audience and hear what he doth say.'

Death announces himself:

'I am death that no man dreadeth'.

At the opening of *Indar Sabhā*, the Rāwī tells us that we are at Indar's court, and warns us of his approach. Indar (also referred to as the Rajah) is already behind the curtain, which then opens to reveal him in his court. He straight way announces himself, singing:

'*Rājā hūṅ main qaum kā, Indar merā nām,*
Bin pariyon kī dīd ke mujhe nahīṅ ārām.
(I am rajah of the people, Indar is my name,
My sole relaxation is seeing the peris.)'

He calls for his peris, and after the curtain has been closed, the Rāwī announces the coming of the Topaz (*Pukhrāj*) Peri. When the curtain opens again, the Topaz Peri begins singing:

'*Gātī hūṅ maiṅ aur nāch sadā kām hai merā,*
Āfāq meṅ, Pukhrāj Parī nām hai merā.
(I sing, and dancing is my constant task
In Heaven, and Topaz Peri is my name.)'

The Topaz Peri then sings eight songs of varying types: some are termed *ghazal*, while others are named after well-known Hindu song forms or *rāgs*: *basant* (*vasanti*)[26] *chhand*, *ṭhumri*, and *holi*. No plot seems to be emerging, but this is well within *Rahas* tradition. For example, Wājid ʻAlī Shāh's second *rahas*, *Rādhā Kanhaiyā*, composed after *Indar Sabhā*, has as its sole theme the desire of Ṣahrā to see the dance of Rādhā Kanhaiyā once again after an interval of twenty-four years. This wish is gratified, thanks to the intervention of the Saffron Peri and the Red Peri.

Indar rewards the Topaz Peri by seating her at his side.[27] He then calls for the *Nīlam* (Sapphire) Peri. The curtain is closed for the Rāwī to announce her coming, and when it rises again, she introduces herself, and gives a performance similar to that of the Topaz. The Red (*Lāl*) Peri follows, and finally the Green (*Sabz*), who is the heroine of the play. No sooner has she introduced herself, dancing and singing, than she remarks that Indar has fallen asleep[28]:

'*Rājā jī so gāye, diyā na kuchh inʻām,*
Jātī huṅ maiṅ bagh meṅ, yahāṅ merā kiyā kām.
(The Rajah has fallen asleep, without rewarding me.
I am going into the garden, what work have I here?')

She summons the Black Demon, and tells him that she has fallen in love with a mortal, a prince, and asks him to bring him to her. His name is *Gulfām*. The latter is brought, asleep. When he wakes up, after some confusion, he and the Green Peri introduce each other in song-dialogue. All this takes a mere page, as against the previous eighteen pages devoted to the various peris' songs to Indar. This shows how unimportant action really was. Indeed, we are now half-way through the play. Gulfām makes it a condition of his returning of her love that she take him to Indar's court, which is forbidden to mortals. She agrees to this, saying that she will hide him among the trees.[29]

Without more ado, the stage direction informs us that the Green Peri returns to Indar's court, and sings again. The presence of Gulfām is noted by the Red Demon (*Dev*), who has left the court, and gone out into the garden for a walk.[30] Indar is angry, and has Gulfām bound, and expels the Green Peri from his court. The curtain falls,[31] and the Rāwī introduces us to the Green Peri, now wandering on earth disguised as a *Jogan* or female *faqīr*. She sings, and the Black Demon, hearing her, reports to Indar that he is bringing a Jogan with a beautiful voice to sing to him. Indar is enchanted with her singing. Chewing betel, in one of the only three passages of rhymed prose in the play, he reveals the strong effect this strange *faqīr* has had on him.[32] It is significant that Amānat uses rhymed prose (*naṣr-i-muqaffā*) only in this final scene, for dramatic effect. Indar asks the *Jogan* what reward she would like, and she answers: 'My Gulfām'.[33] As might be expected, this wish is granted, and Gulfām is brought in. The lovers are united, and sing a love duet in alternate verses. The curtain descends, and the Rāwī sings a final blessing on the pair.

Muhammad Sadiq's strictures on this play[34] cannot be gainsaid. As he says, the first act is completely static ... the entertainment value lay in the song and dance ... only one Peri, the heroine, is essential to the plot ... the versification is 'unforced but undistinguished'. He is right in maintaining that the whole is frigid save in the final reconciliation scene. Another fault he does not mention is the general naïveté. But Amānat was not a great genius, nor was he in any sense an innovator. He did know, however, that the popular *rahas* could be made into something of literary value: and his final scene, with its rhymed prose, short dialogue verses, and warm feeling, pointed the way to 'live' drama. It is perhaps no accident that Wājid ʿAlī, who had written only one *rahas* before *Indar Sabhā* was produced, wrote a further thirty-five afterwards. And whatever the merits or demerits of the work, its influence was far-reaching. We hear of its being performed in Dacca, then in Bombay, and in other Indian cities. Theatrical companies were formed in a bewildering abundance, especially in Bombay, where by 1861 there were at least nineteen.[35] Frāmjī's Original Theatre Company dates back at least to 1875: it was perhaps the first really famous professional company. It was followed by the Alfred and Victoria Companies. Parsis played a major role in founding and organizing these companies. Mulk Raj Anand speaks scathingly of the 'essentially practical bent of their mind' which 'put commercial success above artistic achievement'. He goes on to say that they 'soon succeeded in vulgarising every theatrical effort'.[36] These Parsis at first concerned themselves with Gujarātī drama: but they soon devoted most of their efforts to Hindustani (Urdu-Hindi) drama. They recruited a number of resident playwrights, often from the United provinces – even from Lucknow itself, Wājid ʿAlī's old capital. Of these Aḥsan Lakhnawī and Betāb Barelwī were the best known.

Plays were based on the *rahas*, Classical Sanskrit drama, and Shakespeare. The latter's plays were seldom literally, or even accurately, translated. Rather were they adapted. The scene and the characters' names were changed to suit Indian audiences. Among Aḥsan Lakhnawī's adaptations were those of *Hamlet*, *Othello* and the *Merchant of Venice*. The tragedies were given happy endings. Betāb Barelwī adapted the *Comedy of Errors*. In technique, dramatists followed first and foremost the *rahas*, such as *Indar Sabhā*. There was much singing and dancing: dialogue tended to be naïve and stilted, and was a mixture of verse and rhymed prose. To the present author, however, it appears that the influence of Shakespeare was decisive. Large numbers of characters, rapid changes of scene, variety evidenced by the intermingling of comedy with tragedy – these were all influenced by Shakespeare, whose plays were studied in Indian schools, as a result of Macaulay's educational policy already mentioned. And even melodrama and bombast which writers like Anand and Sadiq dislike so much can be ascribed to imitation – and Indianization – of Shakespeare. Did not the latter often 'write down to the gallery?' Doubtless, however, it was not merely oriental hyperbole, but also the over-use of poetry, without the saving grace of a verse-form like English blank-verse, which brought out the worst in the playwrights.

This was the theatrical situation in the subcontinent, and more especially in Bombay, when Āghā Ḥashar Kāshmīrī came on the scene. Born in Benares in 1879, the son of a merchant, he soon showed love of both riotous living and the theatre. Seeing the Alfred Theatrical Company perform a play by Aḥsan Lakhnawī in his home town, he voiced his scorn for certain aspects of it in the hearing of members of the company, then sat down and wrote a play himself. He then ran away from home, fearing his father's wrath because of his spendthrift ways, and made for Bombay (1897). In a short time, he became recognized as the leading dramatist, writing over thirty plays, many of which were extremely successful and profitable. His achievement is unparalleled in Urdu drama, whatever his faults.

But Āghā Ḥashar deserves separate treatment. All that need be said in the present study is that, as *Indar Sabhā* was the highest point of the *rahas* and other popular theatre of the first half of the nineteenth century, so Āghā Ḥashar represents the peak of the Urdu professional theatre of the late nineteenth and early twentieth centuries. Taking the composite form of the dancing and singing drama with its roots in the *rahas*, Sanskrit drama and Shakespeare, he developed it to the very limits. It is inconceivable that any further progress should be made along the same lines. But neither can modern drama on purely Western lines take its place. The problem of the modern Urdu dramatist is to find a means of expression which is modern, without entirely abandoning its roots in the past.

NOTES

1 *A History of Urdu Literature* (London 1964).

2 See below.

3 Publ. London. 1953.

4 p. 51.

5 His *Urdū Ḍrāmā – Tārīkh-o-tanqīd* (Karachi 1957) containing substantial extracts from typical dramas, is the best and fullest account so far.

6 This author's *Āghā Ḥashar aur un ke Ḍrāme* (Lahore 1954) though consisting mainly of the text of three plays, contains an important 62-page introduction. Equally important is his edition of Amānat's *Indar Sabhā*, with the dramatist's own commentary, and a 68-page introduction by the editor.

7 I. Shekhar, *Sanskrit Drama, its origin and decline* (Leiden 1961).

8 Op. cit., 139. The author points out that Kalidāsa's *Sakuntalā* only contains one song.

9 *Drama in Sanskrit Literature* (Bombay 1947).

10 *Contributions to the History of Hindu Drama* (Calcutta 1958).

11 See below.

12 H. H. Wilson and others, *The Theatre of the Hindus* (Calcutta 1955). The main part of this book, by Wilson, is, of course, a reprint.

13 Op. cit., 12.

14 Govind Chimnaji Bhate, *History of Modern Marathi Literature, 1800–1938* (Poona 1939) 52.

15 ʿIshrat Raḥmānī, op. cit., 119 ff.

16 P. Guha-Thakurs, *The Bengali Drama* (London 1930) 3ff.

17 Bhate, op. cit., 245ff.

18 Op. cit., 138.

19 Guha-Thakura, op. cit., 40ff.

20 See Herasim Lebedeff, *A Grammar of the Pure and Mixed East Indian Dialects*, ed. Dr Mahadev Prasad Saha (Calcutta 1963) introduction, 13ff.

21 In Waqqār ʿAẕīm's edition, 82.

22 Op. cit., 131ff.

23 *Āghā Ḥashar*, 28ff.

24 In Waqqār ʿAẕīm's ed. of the play 83ff.

25 Amānat does not give him any designation – probably because there was no need: this figure was so familiar in dramatic performances.

26 See A. Daniélou, *Northern Indian Music* (London 1949/54) II, 231ff.

27 Text, 119.

28 Ibid., 131.

29 Ibid., 137.

30 So in Amānat's *Sharḥ*, 94, not in the stage directions.

31 Text, 143.

32 Ibid., 149.

33 Ibid., 151.

34 Op. cit .,394.

35 Raḥmānī, op. cit., 162.

36 Op. cit., 45ff.

WALTHER HINZ

Die spätmittelalterlichen Währungen im Bereich des Persischen Golfes

In meinem Beitrag für die in Teheran erschienene Gedächtnisschrift Vladimir Minorsky habe ich über den Goldwert des Toman im Mittelalter gehandelt. Als Ergänzung hierzu veröffentliche ich hier meine Umrechnung auf Goldbasis der spätmittelalterlichen Währungen im Bereich des Persischen Golfes: in Lār, Hormūz und im muslimischen Indien.

Nur eine Umrechnung orientalischer Währungen auf Goldbasis ermöglicht es dem Historiker, sichere Schlüsse aus den Geldangaben der Quellen zu ziehen. Der islamische Orient hatte im Mittelalter durchgehends eine auf Gold und Silber fußende Doppel- oder Parallelwährung. Allerdings schwankte die Relation zwischen den beiden Edelmetallen häufig. Im 14. Jahrhundert war die Relation Gold zu Silber = 1:12, d.h. ein Gramm Feingold entsprach 12 Gramm Feinsilber. Ungefähr um die Mitte des 16. Jahrhunderts verschob sich diese Relation nach 1:10, d.h. Silber wurde teurer. Etwa um 1622 kehrte die Gold-Silber-Relation zu 1:12 zurück; um 1660 betrug sie 1:13¼, um 1680 sogar 1:15. Diese Schwankungen müssen bei der Errechnung des Silberwertes berücksichtigt werden.

Auszugehen ist in jedem Falle vom Goldwert, da er in seiner Kaufkraft über Jahrtausende hin fast ganz stabil geblieben ist. So kostete beispielsweise zur Zeit des Dareios (522–486 v. Chr.) in der Persis ein Schaf 5.40 Goldmark; rund zwei Jahrtausende später kostete in Anatolien ein Schaf immer noch 5.40 Goldmark. . . .

Bei meinen Berechnungen gehe ich aus von den im ganzen Vorderen Orient gängigen Goldmünzen des mittelalterlichen Italien, also vom *ducato* oder *zecchino* von Venedig und vom *fiorino* von Florenz. Ihr seit 1284 unveränderter Feingehalt (3.559 Gramm 24karätiges Gold) ergibt bei einer Umrechnung in Goldmark ziemlich genau einen Wert von 10.– Goldmark. Dies bewertet das Gramm Feingold mit 2.81 M (M in diesem Aufsatz stets = Goldmark). In der englischen Währung entspricht einer Goldmark ein Gold-*shilling*, in der französischen ist –.81 M = 1 *franc or*.

Lār

Eine der Standardwährungen im Bereich des Persischen Golfes war der *lārī*. Diese anscheinend zu Beginn des 16. Jahrhunderts aufgekommene, eigenartige Münze wurde in Lār, der Hauptstadt des damals noch selbständigen Lārestān (in Südiran) geprägt.[1] Auch für die Maldiven ist diese Prägung (um 1606) bezeugt.[2] Der *lārī* bestand aus einem doppelt gebogenen und beidseitig gestempelten Stück Silberdrahtes von 98 Prozent Feinheit und 5.1 bis 4.8 g Gewicht.[3] Wegen der Reinheit seines Silbers wurde der *lārī* zu einer äußerst beliebten Münze, deren Verbreitung sich von Persien und dem Irak bis an die Westküste Indiens und nach Ceylon erstreckte.[4]

Unser frühester Gewährsmann, der Florentiner Andrea Corsali (um 1517), kennt die Bezeichnung *lārī* noch nicht, sondern nennt diese Münze einfach *tängä*, was auf indischen Einfluß hindeutet; 6 von ihnen gingen zu jener Zeit auf den Dukaten zu 10.– M.[5] Der *lārī* hatte damals somit einen Wert von *1.67 M*.

Im Jahre 1525 gab es bereits *lārī* alter und neuer Prägung: die neuen galten damals 3 *tängä* 10 *dīnār*, die alten 3 *tängä* 9 *dīnār*, wobei 12 *dīnār* in Lār 1 *tängä* ausmachten.[6] Diese kleinen *tängä* dürfen also nicht mit den eigentlichen *lārī-tängä* verwechselt werden. Falls mit den 'alten *lārī*' die von 1517 gemeint sein sollten, die wir mit 1.67 M bewerteten, so wäre 1525 ein 'neuer *lārī*' sogar 1.70 M, ein (kleines) *tängä* 44.4 Goldpfennig (Pfg.) wert gewesen.

Für die Zeit um 1554, für die wir die ausführlichen, unten ausgewerteten Angaben des Antonio Nuñez besitzen, dürfen wir wahrscheinlich *lārī* und indisches *tängä* (d.h. das *tängä* aus dem portugiesischen Herrschaftsbereich Indiens) im Wert gleichsetzen, nämlich zu *1.43 M*.

Hierbei ist folgende Überlegung anzustellen. Zwei portugiesische Quellen, die eine von 1525,[7] die andere von 1554,[8] geben übereinstimmend das Gewicht des *lārī* mit $\frac{1}{45}$ des portugiesischen *marco* (von 229.48 g) an, also mit 5.1 Gramm, und bewerten ihn mit 60 *réis*. Von dem oben ermittelten Wert von 1.67 M für den *lārī* ausgehend, wäre 1 portugiesischer *real* = 2.8 Pfg. gewesen; um 1554 war er aber nur 2.38 Pfg. wert, da damals 420 *réis* auf eine Zechine von 10.– M gingen.[9] Also galt um 1554 der *lārī* nur noch – wie erwähnt – 1.43 M (wie das gleichzeitige *tängä* in Goa oder Diu). Da sich jedoch weder das Gewicht der Münze noch ihr Feingehalt, der Ruhmestitel des *lārī*, geändert hatten, so drängt sich der Schluß auf, daß zwischen 1517 und 1554 eine Verschiebung des Gold-Silber-Wertverhältnisses eingetreten sein muß.

Dieses Verhältnis war um die Mitte des 16. Jahrhunderts sicher 1:10 (wie im Safawidenreich), gemäß folgender Berechnung. Wenn 1 g Feinsilber den zehnten Teil von 1 g Feingold (zum Standardkurs von 2.81 M) wert ist, müssen wir es mit 28.1 Pfg. bewerten; 1 *lārī* von 5.1 Gramm käme danach, wenn er ganz aus Feinsilber bestünde, auf 5.1 × 28.1 Pfg. = auf 1.44 M – in Wirklichkeit aber, da er nur 98 Prozent fein war, auf 1.42 M, also praktisch auf den oben von uns ermittelten Wert. Zwangsläufig ergibt dann ein mit 1.67 M bewerteter *lārī* von 1517 einen Silberpreis von 33.3 Pfg. je Gramm, was eine Gold-Silber-Relation von 1:9¼ voraussetzt.

Dieser Schluß ruht auf der einzigen Angabe des Corsali, und ehe nicht weiterer Beweisstoff beigebracht werden kann, ist die Frage nicht mit Sicherheit zu entscheiden. Möglicherweise stand der *lārī* jener Zeit nicht nur hinsichtlich seiner Benennung als *tängä* unter dem Einfluß des Großmoghul-Reiches, sondern auch hinsichtlich des Gold-Silber-Wertverhältnisses, das zur Zeit Akbars, wie unten zu zeigen sein wird, tatsächlich 1:9¼ betrug.

Völlig sicheren Boden betreten wir ums Jahr 1584. W. Barrett berichtete damals aus Baṣra: 'The duckat of gold is woorth . . . 7 *larines*, and one *danine*'.[10] Aus Gleichungen desselben Gewährsmannes ebenda folgt, daß 1 '*danine*' = 0.3 *lārī* galt, und da eine Zechine = 10.– M ist, so errechnet sich der *lārī* von 1584 auf *1.37 M.*[11]

Der leichte Kursrückgang seit 1554 dürfte mit einer Verringerung des Münzgewichtes um 0.3 g auf 4.8 g zusammenhängen.

Auch im ersten Viertel des 17. Jahrhunderts sank der *lārī* nur langsam ab. Um 1600 gingen 8 *lārī* auf einen 'Xarafy de oro' (*ašrafī*) von 10.– M; der *lārī* galt somit noch *1.25 M.*[12]

Um 1615 bewerteten R. Steele und Th. Barker den Taler (*rial of eight*) mit 5¼ *lārī*.[13] Der Taler galt damals, wie ich anderswo errechnet habe, 6.67 M, der *lārī* somit *1.27 M.* Eine weitere Bestätigung liefert F. Pyrard, der den *lārī* um 1606 mit etwa 8 *sols* bewertet,[14] von denen um 1616 64 auf die Zechine zu 10.– M gingen; 1 *sol* war somit = 15.67 Pfg., der *lārī* also *1.25 M.*[15]

Im Jahre 1627 gibt Sir Th. Herbert[16] dem *lārī* nur einen Wert von 10 d, dem persischen '*abbāsī* einen solchen von 16 d. Da der Toman gegen Ende der Herrschaft des Schah 'Abbās I (1587–1629) – wie ich in meinem Beitrag zur Teheraner Gedächtnisschrift Minorsky gezeigt habe – mit etwa 83.– M zu bewerten ist, der '*abbāsī* also mit 1.67 M, errechnet sich 1 *penny* damals in Iran auf 10.6 Pfg., der *lārī* somit auf *1.05 M.*

Dieser Kurssturz hängt mit einer abermaligen Verschiebung des Gold-Silber-Wertverhältnisses von 10:1 auf 12:1 zusammen, die zwischen 1616 und 1623 erfolgt sein muß. Dadurch büßten alle Silbermünzen ein Sechstel ihres Wertes (gemessen an Gold) ein.

Adam Olearius, der 1637/8 in Persien weilte, gibt zwar keine Bewertung des *lārī*, doch findet sich bei ihm die Notiz, der *lārī* sei die Münze der frühen Safawiden gewesen.[17] Nach dem völligen Aufgehen Lārestāns im Reiche der Safawiden unter den Nachfolgern Schah ʿAbbās' des Großen ging die Prägung der *lārī*-Münzen offensichtlich stark zurück.[18] Die Bewertung folgt seit der Mitte des 17. Jahrhunderts genau der persischen Reichswährung, und zwar galt ein *lārī* soviel wie 125 *dinār* = $1\frac{1}{4}$ *moḥammadī* = $\frac{1}{80}$ Toman.[19] Um 1660 war ein Toman 77.– M wert; somit galt der *lārī* damals –.*96 M*,[20] was (bei 4.4 Gramm Feinsilber) eine Gold-Silber-Relation von 1:$13\frac{1}{4}$ erkennen läßt.

Gegen 1675 galten in Baṣra $5\frac{3}{4}$ *lārī* eine halbe Zechine = 5.– M,[21] der *lārī* wurde also mit –.87 M bewertet. Einen ähnlichen Wert liefert Sparr de Homberg[22] im Jahre 1681, der den *lārī* = $1\frac{1}{4}$ *moḥammadī* und 15 *moḥammadī* = 1 Zechine (10.– M) setzt, was für den *lārī* –.84 M ergibt. Der genaueste Wert dürfte –.*86 M* sein, der sich aus der Angabe J. Fryer's[23] ergibt, wonach eine Zechine = 29 *šāhī* war, also 1 *moḥammadī* = 68.96 Pfg., und somit 1 *lārī* = –.86 M. Dies dürfte einer Gold-Silber-Relation von 1:15 entsprechen.

Die letzte Notierung des *lārī* stammt, soweit ich sehe, vom Jahre 1711. Damals galt 1 *lārī* = 2 *šāhī* 5 *qāz* = $2\frac{1}{2}$ *šāhī*, und auf die Zechine (10.– M) gingen 31 bis 32 *šāhī*.[24] Demnach galt der *šāhī* im Durchschnitt 63.5 Pfg., der *lārī* somit –.*79 M*.

Hormūz

Im Reiche von Hormūz am Persischen Golf bestand im 16. Jahrhundert unter portugiesischer Oberhoheit eine Dinar-Währung, die seit etwa 1550 zur gleichzeitigen safawidischen im Verhältnis 1:4 gestanden zu haben scheint.

Im ersten Viertel des 16. Jahrhunderts liefen an Silbermünzen außer *lārī-tängä* (im Wert von 1.67 M) nur sogenannte *ṣadī* oder 100-Dinar-Stücke um, von denen 20 auf den Dukaten gingen, also jedes –.*50 M* galt. Die sogenannten *hazār* oder 1000-Dinar-Stücke waren damals noch aus Gold und hießen auch halbe *ašrafī*; sie galten einen halben Dukaten oder 5.– M. Die ganzen *ašrafī* waren dem Dukaten gleich, also 10.– M wert; sie hießen auch '*xerafin*'.[25]

Um die Mitte des 16. Jahrhunderts waren die *hazār* oder 1000-Dinar-Stücke zu Silbermünzen geworden. Außer Silber-*ṣadī* liefen noch Kupfermünzen um im Werte von 10 Dinar, *fals* genannt. Zwei *hazār* gingen auf einen Gold-*pardão*, der mit den in Hormūz umlaufenden indischen 5-*tängä*-Silberstücken gleichwertig war.[26] Damals (um 1554) kostete in Hormūz der *meşqāl* feinsten Goldes im Gewicht von 3.825 Gramm[27] 3 *hazār* 2 *ṣadī*[28]; zum Betrag von 2.81 M je Gramm Feingold wäre demnach 1 *meşqāl* = 10.75 M, ein *hazār* = 3.36 M. Somit erhalten wir für die Zeit um 1554:

1 *hazār*	= 3.36 M
1 *ṣadī*	= *0.34 M*
1 *fals* (Kupfer)	= 3.36 Pfg.
1 *tängä* (Silber)	= 1.37 M[29]
1 Gold-*pardão*	= 6.72 M

Hormūz prägte auch weiterhin Gold-*aśrafī* (portugiesisch 'Xerafim', italienisch 'Sarafino'), das Stück mit 300 *réis* bewertet, von denen 420 damals eine Zechine (10.– M) ausmachten, woraus sich der *real* damals auf 2.38 Pfg. errechnet.[30]

Über die zu jener Zeit in Hormūz gültige Gold-Silber-Relation gibt folgende Berechnung Aufschluß. Um das Jahr 1554 bezahlte man für 1 *marco* (= 229.48 g) Silber 9 *pardão* 9 *ṣadī* = 189 *ṣadī*.[31] Setzt man den oben ermittelten Wert von 0.34 M je *ṣadī* ein, so errechnet sich das Gramm Feinsilber auf 28 Pfg. Bezogen auf den Gold-Standardpreis von 2.81 M je Gramm, ergibt dies eine Gold-Silber-Relation von 1:10.

Um 1580 war die Hormūzer Währung genau wie die portugiesische erheblich abgesunken. Der *lārī*, den wir oben mit 1.37 M ermittelten, galt damals 5¼ *ṣadī*,[32] was für einen *ṣadī 26.1 Pfg.*, einen *hazār* 2.61 M und ein *läk* 260.95 M ergibt. Der gleichzeitige Gold-*pardão* errechnet sich aus der Gleichung: 190 *larini* = 38 *pardai* ½ *larino*,[33] nämlich, den *lārī* zu 1.37 M eingesetzt, auf 6.83 M. Der Hormūzer Gold-Xerafim war sogar auf 24 *ṣadī* = 6.26 M abgesunken.[34]

Im Jahre 1618, also kurz vor dem Aufgehen von Hormūz im persischen Safawidenreiche (1622), machten zwar immer noch 5.5 *ṣadī* einen *lārī* aus[35]; aber da damals der *lārī* nur noch 1.25 M galt, so errechnet sich 1 *ṣadī* auf *22.7 Pfg.* Entsprechend galt 1 *hazār* 2.27 M, 1 *läk* 227.– M. Die gleichzeitigen kleinen Kupfermünzen (*folūs*) hatten einen Wert von 0.57 Pfg., da 40 von ihnen auf den *ṣadī* gingen; es waren also nominell 2½-Dinar-Stücke.

Das muslimische Indien

Das Sultanat von Delhi. Die Münzen des Sultanats von Delhi seit der Zeit des Iltutmyš (1211–36) bis zur Thronbesteigung Muḥammad Tuġluqs

(1325) bestanden zur Hauptsache aus *tängä* genannten Gold- und Silberstücken gleichen Gewichtes, und zwar wog ein solches *tängä* 96 *ratī* = 172.8 grains Troy = 11.197 Gramm.[36] Bei einem wahrscheinlichen Feingehalt von etwa 99 Prozent der Goldstücke errechnet sich für das Gold*tängä* ein Wert von 31.44 M. Zum Silber*tängä* siehe sogleich.

Als im Jahre 1325 Muḥammad Tuġluq auf den Thron kam, prägte er Gold-Dinare zu 201.6 grains = 13.06 g, sowie sogenannte *ʿadlī*-Silbermünzen, die aber schon 1328 aus dem Verkehr verschwanden; ein *ʿadlī* wog 80 *ratī* = 144 grains = 9.33 g.[37] Zwölf *ʿadlī* waren, wie es scheint, gleich 10 Silber-*tängä*, was für den *ʿadlī* (gemäß der sogleich anzuführenden Berechnung) einen Wert von etwa 2.60 M ergäbe. Vierzehn *ʿadlī*-Stücke gingen offenbar auf einen der neuen, schweren Gold-Dinare im Werte von 36.40 M, die aber ebenfalls bald aus dem Umlauf herausgezogen wurden, wohl weil sie kein klares Zahlenverhältnis zu den alten Silber-*tängä* aufwiesen.[38]

Nach vorübergehender Münzverschlechterung ergab sich unter Muḥammad Tuġluq für Delhi, Sind und Bengalen um 1335 folgende Währungslage, für die wir die voneinander unabhängigen Zeugnisse des maghrebinischen Reisenden Ibn Baṭṭūṭa und von al-ʿUmarī besitzen.[39]

Die Silber-*tängä* bezeichnet Ibn Baṭṭūṭa durchgehends als 'Dinare'; 10 Silber-*tängä* gingen auf ein Gold-*tängä*. Somit bestand, da beide Münzarten gleich schwer und wohl auch gleich fein waren, im damaligen muslimischen Indien ein Gold-Silber-Wertverhältnis von 1:10.[40] Ein Silber-*tängä* hatte demnach einen Wert von 31.44:10 = *3.14 M.*

Ferner galt – ebenfalls nach Ibn Baṭṭūṭa – ein Gold-*tängä* soviel wie zweieinhalb maghrebinische Gold-Dinare. Diese wogen (seit den Almohaden) 1 *miṯqāl* zu 4.72 g. Ihr Feingehalt dürfte um 94 v.H. gelegen haben, woraus sich für den maghrebinischen Gold-Dinar ein Wert von etwa 12.50 M errechnet. Das Zweieinhalbfache davon kommt unserem oben ermittelten Wert des Gold-*tängä* von 31.44 M recht nahe.

Außerdem liefen kleinere Silbermünzen um, von denen die wichtigste der sogenannte 'Achtfach-Derham' (persisch: *derham-e haštgānī*) war und soviel galt wie ein damaliger ägyptischer oder syrischer *dirham*.[41] Den Wert eines solchen ermitteln wir, da acht *derham-e haštgānī* auf ein Silber-*tängä* von 3.14 M gingen, mit 39.3 Pfg. Die Einheit dazu war der *derham-e yägānī* oder 'Einfach-Derham' = 4.9 Pfg. Dieser wurde auch *ǧītal* genannt und war damals noch eine wirkliche Münze, nicht bloße Rechnungseinheit wie 250 Jahre später unter Akbar. Es gingen also 64 *ǧītal* zu je 4.9 Pfg. auf ein Silber-*tängä* zu 3.14 M.[42]

Der *derham-e dōgānī*, auch *solṭānī* genannt, war dementsprechend = 9.8 Pfg.; der *derham-e šīšgānī* ('Sechsfach-Derham' = 6 *ǧītal*) = 29.4 Pfg.; der *derham-e dawāzdahgānī* ('Zwölffach-Derham' = 12 *ǧītal*) = 58.8 Pfg., und der *derham-e šānzdahgānī* ('Sechzehnfach-Derham' = 16 *gītal*) = 78.6 Pfg. Von den Kupfermünzen gingen 32 auf das Acht-*ǧītal*-Stück (*haštgānī*); ein solcher *fals* galt somit 1.23 Pfg.

Unter Fīrūz Tuġluq (1351–88) trat zu den bestehenden Münzsorten als Neuerung die Präge folgender Silberstücke[43]: *čehel-ō-haštgānī* (Stücke zu 48 *gītal*) = $\frac{3}{4}$ Silber-*tängä* = 2.38 M; *bist-ō-pänǧgānī* (Stücke zu 25 *ǧītal*, leicht legiert) mit $\frac{1}{2}$ 'adlī bewertet, damals = 1.225 M; *bist-ō-čahārgānī* (24er Stücke) = $\frac{3}{8}$ *tängä* = 1.19 M; und *dahgānī* (10er Stücke) = $\frac{1}{5}$ '*adlī* = damals –.49 M. Dazu kamen noch Kupfer-Silber-Münzen für den Kleinsthandel von $\frac{1}{2}$ *ǧītal* = 2.45 Pfg. und $\frac{1}{6}$ *ǧītal* (*mohr-e dāngä ǧītal* genannt) = 0.81 Pfg.

Das Moghul-Reich. Aus dem Silber-*tängä* wurde unter dem Großmoghul Šēr Šāh (1539–45) die Rupie, die unter Akbar (1556–1605) allgemeine Verbreitung gewann und zur Grundlage der indischen Silberwährung wurde.

Ihr Gewicht blieb mit 11.534 Gramm (11$\frac{1}{2}$ *māša* zu je 1.003 g) dasselbe wie beim Silber-*tängä* des 13. Jahrhunderts. Ihr Feingehalt betrug 97 v.H., d.h. die Silber-Rupie enthielt 11.188 g Feinsilber. Ihren Wert in der zweiten Hälfte des 16. Jahrhunderts gewinnen wir aus dem Verhältnis der Rupie zu dem von Akbar um 1562 eingeführten Gold-*mohr* von 11.033 g. Gewicht (= 11 *māša*) und 98 bis 100 v.H. Feingehalt. Auf einen solchen Gold-*mohr* gingen 9 Silber-Rupien.[44] Zum Standardwert von 2.81 M für 1 g Feingold errechnet sich der Akbar'sche Gold-*mohr* im Mittel auf 30.60 M, was für die Silber-Rupie (= $\frac{1}{9}$ *mohr*) einen Wert von *3.40 M* ergibt. Da 9 Rupien 100.692 g Feinsilber enthielten, der gleich-wertige *mohr* aber 10.885 g Feingold, so ergibt sich für die Zeit Akbars eine Gold-Silber-Relation von 1 : 9$\frac{1}{4}$.[45]

Die zur Akbar-Währung gehörige Kupfermünze, *dām* genannt (vor Akbar *paisa* oder *bahlōlī*), galt $\frac{1}{40}$ Rupie, also 8.5 Pfg. Nominell zerfiel ein *dām* in 25 *ǧītal*. Das Gewicht eines Kupfer-*dām* betrug 5 *ṭāṅk* = 20.937 g.[46]

Die genannte Gold-Silber-Relation von 1 : 9$\frac{1}{4}$ scheint sich zumindest bis ins Jahr 1623 gehalten zu haben; denn damals bewertet Pietro della Valle[47] die Rupie noch mit einer drittel Zechine, also mit *3.33 M*.

Die Angleichung an die Verhältnisse in Persien berichtet der deutsche Reisende J.H. von Mandelslo[48] im Jahre 1638: er schreibt, in Persien und Indien gebe man 12 Teile Silber auf einen Teil Gold. Dieser neuen Relation

1:12 entsprechend bewerten wir die Rupie von 1638, deren zwei auf einen Taler (zu 5.50 M) gingen, nur noch mit *2.75 M.*

Im Jahre 1660 setzte J.B. Tavernier[49] den Wert der Rupie mit 1½ *livres* = 30 *sols* an. Da 1 *livre* in Persien damals mit 1.57 M zu bewerten ist, ergäbe sich für die Rupie möglicherweise ein Wert von *2.35 M.* J.B. Thévenot[50] bemerkt allerdings im Jahre 1666, im allgemeinen rechne man zwar die Rupie zu 30 *sols* (= 2.35 M). Alljährlich würden aber neue Rupien geprägt und dabei die des Vorjahres wegen Abnutzung um 1 *paisa* niedriger bewertet. 'Als ich 1666 in Surat ankam, galten die Rupien 33⅓ *pechas* (*paisa*), und als ich abreiste, galten dieselben nur 32½ *pechas.* Es gibt auch halbe und viertel Rupien.' Eine solche Kupfer-*paisa* errechnet sich auf ziemlich genau 7 Pfg.

Auch im Jahre 1681 bestand der Kurs von etwa *2.30 bis 2.25 M* für die Rupie fort. Hier zeigt uns die wichtige Angabe von Sparr de Homberg[51] auch mit Sicherheit die Gold-Silber-Relation im Moghulreich seit etwa 1660. Nach diesem Gewährsmann galt im Jahre 1681 in Surat ein vollwichtiger Dukaten (zu 10.– M) $4\frac{11}{23}$ Rupien. Dies bewertet die Rupie mit *2.23 M*, nämlich gemäß einer Gold-Silber-Relation von 1:13¼. Kupfer-*paisas* gingen durchschnittlich 32 auf die Rupie,[52] also galt 1 *paisā* in Surat 7 Pfg., wie oben erwähnt. In Agra gingen hingegen 56 bis 60 *paisa* auf die Rupie, was für die dortige *paisā* etwa 4 Pfg. ergibt.[53]

Mit aller wünschenswerten Genauigkeit bestätigt ein Bericht von 1695 das Fortbestehen der genannten Wertrelation.[54] Danach galt eine Goldrupie 13¼ Silberrupien oder 6 spanische Taler ('pezze da otto di Spagna'), die damals mit 5.– M zu bewerten sind. Die Rupie hielt also ihren Kurs von *2.23 M.*

Im Jahre 1711 wurde in Surat eine Rupie mit 4 persischen *moḥammadi* von 63.5 Pfg. bewertet,[55] was für die Rupie den vergleichsweise hohen Wert von 2.54 M ergäbe. Trifft dies zu, so wäre damals die Relation zugunsten von Silber wieder auf etwa 1:12½ gestiegen.

Zur Abrundung des oben gezeichneten Bildes der Währungen im Bereich des Persischen Golfes im späten Mittelalter gebe ich anschließend meine Tabelle des *Toman*-Wertes gemäß den Umrechnungen in meinem Beitrag zur Teheraner Gedächtnisschrift für Vladimir Minorsky.

Jahr:	*Wert in Goldmark:*	*Jahr:*	*Wert in Goldmark:*
1300	1 *tomān* = 29 400.–	1593	100.–
1320	24 500.–	1622	83.–
1440	19 500.–	1660	77.–
1452	7 200.–	1680	69.–
1510	270.–	1711	63.50
1522	195.–	1718	66.50
1530	165.–	1800	28.–
1550	133.–	1850	10.–
1577	162.–	1875	8.–
1580	129.–	1907	3.80

NOTES

1 Sir Thomas Herbert, der 1627 in Lār weilte, bemerkt in *Some yeares travels into Africa and Asia the Great* (London 1638) S. 127: 'Neere this Buzzar (Bāzār in Lār) are coyned the *Larrees*, a famous sort of money, shaped like a long Date stone, the Kings name stampt upon pure silver.'

2 F. Pyrard, *Voyage*, in Hakluyt Bd. 76 (London 1887) S. 235.

3 J. Allan, 'The coinage of the Maldive Islands with some notes on the *cowrie* and *larin*', in *Numismatic Chronicle, Fourth Series*, Bd. 12 (London 1912) S. 318-322; zur Feinheit vgl. *Ā'īn-e Akbarī* (*Bibliotheca Indica* N.S. 30 I [Calcutta 1873] S. 38), wonach 1 Rupie 1 *tōla* 2 *sorḫ* reines Silber kaufte oder 1 *tōla* 4 *sorḫ lārī*-Silber, was 2 Prozent Legierung bedeutet.

4 A. Corsali bei G. B. Ramusio, *Navigationi et viaggi* I (Venedig 1563) 188a: 'Hanno anche vna sorte di moneta di tanta finezza, et si buona, che corre per tutte le terre di queste parti, così nella India, et Arabia, come nella Persia. Et parmi che sia poco differente dallo argento di coppella.' W. Barrett (1584) in Hakluyt, *Extra Series* Bd. 6 (Glasgow 1904) S. 12: '... these be the best money in all the Indies'. Pietro della Valle (1622), *Viaggi*, Teil II (Rom 1658) S. 490: '... nè vi è moneta, in somma, in tutti questi parti [in den Reichen der Türken, Perser und des Großmoghuls] che corra più di questa'. J. B. Chardin (um 1670), *Voyages* Bd. 4 (Paris 1811) S. 185/6: 'Il y a une monnoie tout le long du golphe Persique, nommé *larins*, qui est celle dont on s'y sert le plus dans le commerce'.

5 Bei Ramusio, I, 188a.

6 *Lembranças de cousas da India, em 1525* in *JA*, II, xvi (Paris 1920) 206. Bei dem englischen Kaufmann John Newbery findet sich die Angabe, im Jahre 1581 sei in der Stadt Lār 1 'Tanger' = 12 'Pull' gewesen (Purchas, *Extra Series* Bd. 8, S. 460). Nehmen wir für jene

Zeit dasselbe Verhältnis zwischen *lārī*, *tängä* und *dīnār* in Lār an wie 1525, so errechnet sich, da 1 *lārī* um 1580 1.37 M galt, 1 *tängä* ('Tanger' auf –.36 M und 1 *pūl* ('Pull', Kupferstück) auf 3 Pfg.

7 *Lembranças de cousas da India, em 1525*, in *JA*, 11 xvi, 196.

8 A. Nuñez in *JA*, 11 xvi, 90.

9 Ebenda S.75.

10 Hakluyt, *Extra Series* Bd. 6, S. 12.

11 Eine Bestätigung dafür liefert G. Balbi, *Viaggio dell'Indie Orientali* (Venedig 1590) S. 51b, wonach im Jahre 1580 in Hormūz 1 *larino* = *soldi* 26 *piccoli* 8 *venetiani* galt; da 1 *soldo* den 200sten Teil einer Zechine von 10.– M bildete und aus 12 *piccoli* bestand, errechnet sich Balbi's *lārī* auf 1.33 M.

12 *Relaciones de* Pedro Teixeira *d'el origen, descendencia y svccession de los Reyes de Persia, y de Harmuz* (Antwerpen 1610) S. 351. Damals gingen 65 *maravedi* (zu rund 2 Pfg.) auf einen *lārī*: Pedro Teixeira, *Breve Relacion del principio del Reyno Harmuz* (Antwerpen 1610) 77.

13 *Calendar of State Papers, East India Series*, 1513–1616, S. 431; ebenda, 1617–21, S. 155.

14 In: *Works issued by* The Hakluyt Society, Bd. 76 (London 1887) 232.

15 Sieur Bénard, *Le voyage de Hiervsalem* (Paris 1621) 12.

16 *Some yeares travels* (London 1638) 243.

17 *Offt begehrte Beschreibung der Newen Orientalischen Reise* (Schleswig 1647) 425: 'Vor diesem aber haben sie andere Münze, *Lari* genannt, gehabt, war von zusammengebogenem silbern Draht, in der Mitten ein wenig platt geschlagen und darauf geprägt, ... sind etwas schwerer als ein *Chodabende*, soll Schach Ismails I. Münze gewesen sein'. Ein *ḫodābändä* oder *moḥammadī*, von Schah Moḥammad Ḫodābändä 1578 eingeführt, wog 1 *meṣqāl* = 4.63 Gramm.

18 Chardin (*Voyages* Bd. 4 [Paris 1811] 187) behauptet sogar, die Prägung sei ganz eingestellt worden, und man sehe daher kaum noch *lārī*-Stücke kursieren; 'mais on ne laisse pas de compter par cette monnoie en tout ce pays-là, et aux Indes, le long du golphe de Cambaye et dans les pays qui en sont proches'.

19 J. B. Tavernier, *Les six voyages*, Bd. 1 (Paris 1678) 125; Chardin (IV 185): 'Cette monnoie (der *lārī*) est d'argent fin et vaut deux *chayés* (*šāhī*) et demi'.

20 26 *šāhī* zu je 50 *dīnār* galten damals 1 Dukaten = 10.– M, vgl. J. B. Tavernier, *a.a.O.* I 136.

21 John Fryer, *A new account of East-India and Persia* (London 1698) 210. Der gleiche Wert folgt aus Chardin (*Voyages* Bd. 4 [Paris 1811] 185), der den *lārī* mit 11 *sols* 3 *deniers* ansetzt. 1 *sol* galt damals in Persien 7.85 Pfg. (nach Chardin III 219 errechnet, wonach 1 *once* = 30.6 g Feingold mit 56 *francs* zu je 20 *sols* bewertet wurde), 1 *denier* = $\frac{1}{12}$ *sol* = 0.64 Pfg.

22 *JA*, 11 xvi (Paris 1920) S. 112, 113.

23 *A new account of East-India and Persia*, S. 406.

24 Charles Lockyer, *An account of the trade in India* (London 1711) 241.

25 A. Corsale, bei G. B. Ramusio, *Navigationi et viaggi* I (Venedig 1563) 188a: 'Le monete di Ormuz sono *saraffi*, et mezzi *saraffi* d'oro, i quali chiamano *azar*, euui vn'altra qualità di monete d'argento, che loro chiamano *sadi*, de quali vale xx. vno *saraffo*, et x. uno *azar*'. Duarte Barbosa (*Works issued by* The Hakluyt Society, II. Serie, Bd. 44 (London 1918) 99/100) berichtet um 1518, in Hormūz werde Gold und Silber geprägt; 'one coin of very good gold, round like ours, with Moorish letters on both sides, which are called *xerafins*, and are worth 300 *reis*, more or less. The most part of them are coined in halves, each worth 150 *reis*. In silver there is a long coin like a bean, also with Moorish letters on both sides, which is worth 3 *vinteens* (= 60 *reis*), more or less, which they call *tangas*, and this silver is very fine.' Also kennt auch Duarte Barbosa für den damaligen *lārī* nur die Bezeichnung *tängä* (Wert: 1.67 M).

26 *Viaggio dell'Indie Orientali, di* Gasparo Balbi (Venedig 1590) 51b; Antonio Nuñez in *JA*, 11 xvi, 66.

27 Zum Gewicht vgl. meine *Islamische Maße und Gewichte umgerechnet ins metrische System* (Leiden 1955), S. 7.

28 A. Nuñez in *JA*, 11 xvi, 52.

29 Die Bewertung des indischen Silber-*tängä* mit 1.37 M (= dem fünften Teil eines Gold-*pardão* von 6.72 M) wird ungefähr bestätigt durch die Notiz, daß in Goa eine Zechine (10.– M) 6 *tängä* galt, vgl. A. Nuñez in *JA*, 11 xvi, 75.

30 Die Angaben sind entnommen A. Nuñez in *JA*, 11 xvi, 66 und 75.

31 Ebenda S. 52.

32 So übereinstimmend G. Balbi, *a.a.O.* s. 51b, und W. Barrett in Hakluyt, *Extra Series*, Bd. 6, S. 14.

33 G. Balbi, *a.a.O.* S. 51b.

34 W. Barrett, *a.a.O.* VI 14/15: 'There is also stamped in Ormuz a *seraphine* of gold, which is litle and round, and is worth 24 *sadines*, which maketh 30 *medines* of Aleppo'. (30 *mu'ayyadī* waren allerdings 30 x 21.7 Pfg. = 6.51 M, da damals 47 '*medines*' auf einen Dukaten gingen, ebenda S. 10).

35 Th. Barker, Brief vom 2. April 1618, in: *Calendar of State Papers, Colonial Series, East Indies*, 1617–21, S. 155.

36 H. N. Wright und H. R. Nevill in: *Numismatic Supplement* No. 38 (for 1924) des *Journal of the Asiatic Society of Bengal, New Series*, XX (Calcutta 1925) S.37; irrig E. Thomas in: *Athenaeum* vom 3. Febr. 1866 und H. Yule, *Cathay and the way thither*, Bd. I, S. ccxlvii-ccxlviii (Hakluyt Society, *Works* Bd. 36).

37 H. N. Wright und H. R. Nevill, *a.a.O.* S. 35.

38 Ebenda S. 36. Zum Wert des Gold-Dinars vgl. die auffallende Übereinstimmung bei J. A. Bucknill mit Berechnungen der Gold-Rupie aus der Zeit um 1817 (1 Gold-Rupie = 36.36 M).

39 *Voyages d'Ibn Batoutah*, ed. C. Defrémery und B. R. Sanguinetti, Bd. III (Paris 1877) 106/7, 246 und 426 (Delhi); Bd. IV (Paris 1879) 212 (Bengalen). Ferner *Masālik al-Abṣār* von al-ʿUmarī, übernommen von al-Qalqašandī in dessen Werk *Ṣubḥ al-Aʿšā* (Bd. v, S. 84), französisch bei Quatremère, *Notices et Extraits* xiii, 211/2.

40 Auch H. N. Wright und H. R. Nevill geben diese Relation an (*a.a.O.* S. 36); irrig E. Thomas, *Chronicles of the Pathán Kings of Delhi* (London 1871) 231 f.

41 Ibn Baṭṭuṭa IV 210.

42 Die abweichenden Äußerungen von H. N. Wright und H. R. Nevill (*a.a.O.* S. 31) fußen auf dem Mißverständnis einer Stelle bei al-ʿUmarī, wo von der Ilchanwährung die Rede ist ('le *dinar* courant 6 *dirhems*' – gemeint sind aber *dīnār-e rābeḥ*, nicht *rāʾeǧ*, d.h. 'gute Dinare' zu je 6 *derham* der Präge Ghazan Chans von 1300). Die von den genannten Verfassern vorgeschlagene Einsetzung von *šišgānī* für *haštgānī* und – weiter unten – von *tängä* für *sekkä* ist abwegig.

43 Šams-e Serāǧ ʿAfīf, *Taʾrīḫ-e Fīrūzšāh*, im persischen Original angeführt bei E. Thomas, *The Chronicles*, s. 278. Die letzte Münze unserer Aufstellung bezeichnet Thomas irrig als $\frac{1}{4}$ *gītal* statt richtig als $\frac{1}{6}$ *ǧītal*.

44 *Āʾīn-e Akbarī*, *Bibliotheca Indica*, *New Series* Bd. 30, I 28; vgl. auch F. von Schrötter, *Wörterbuch der Münzkunde*, S. 445 und 577.

45 Ähnlich bereits E. Thomas, *The Chronicles*, S. 424, der einen Durchschnittswert von 1:9.4 errechnet hatte.

46 *Āʾīn-e Akbarī*, *a.a.O.* I 31-3, III 125.

47 *Viaggio* III (Rom 1658) 33.

48 *Journal und Observation* (Kopenhagen 1942) 151: 'NS. Sie [die Chinesen] geben noch heuttichen Tages vor 8, aufs högste 9 Silber 1 des besten Goldes. In Persien vnd Indien 12 Silber.' Die Bewertung der Rupie mit einem halben *Rijksdaler* ebenda S. 48 und 152.

49 *Les six voyages...* (Paris 1678) II 392.

50 *Voyages* (Paris 1689) III 54/5.

51 *JA*, II xvi, 105.

52 Ebenda S. 106/7: '1 *ropia*, on peut changer contre 32 *peises*, et quelquefois seulement pour 30, ainsi quelquefois 33 et 34, selon que les vaisseaux ont apporté beaucoup ou peu de cuivre.'

53 Ebenda S. 110.

54 G. F. Gemelli Careri, *Giro del Mondo* (Venedig 1719) III 160.

55 Ch. Lockyer, *An account of the Trade in India* (London 1711) 241.

NIKKI R. KEDDIE

The Assassination of the Amīn as-Sultān (Atābak-i A'zam), 31 August 1907

As is painfully clear to an American in the nineteen-sixties, the question of what forces and persons were responsible for a given political assassination is frequently one that remains cloudy and controversial long after the event. Such controversy has from the beginning surrounded the assassination, during the constitutional revolution, of the powerful prime minister Amīn as-Sultān, also known as the Atābak. Although the young man who is generally believed to have shot the Atābak did so in public and killed himself immediately, leaving a card which identified himself as 'Abbās Āqā, a banker or money changer of Tabriz, 'Fidā'ī no. 41', the question of who inspired the deed has remained controversial. It seemed clear that 'Abbās Āqā was a member of a secret *anjuman* containing other revolutionaries, but already at the time of the shooting there were accusations that the true originators of the assassination were not radical revolutionaries but rather ambitious reactionaries with ties to the court, who were disappointed that the Atābak had not suppressed the national assembly. Such reactionaries hoped to use his assassination as an excuse to put down both the assembly (*majlis*) and the revolutionary clubs, or *anjumans*, which were gaining increasing power all over the country, and especially in the two largest cities, Tehran and Tabriz. Some began to claim that Muhammad 'Alī Shāh was ultimately responsible for the assassination, and also that the Atābak was not as unfriendly to the *majlis* as his enemies had believed, but indeed had aroused the hostility of the Shah by his attempts to adapt himself to the constitutional framework rather than finding an excuse to overthrow the *majlis*, as the Shah wished. Another group rejected this theory, pointing out that those who put it forth were mainly friends of the late Atābak who exaggerated his desire to cooperate with the constitutionalists.[1]

Especially since the actual effect of the assassination was to strengthen the revolutionaries and weaken the reactionaries, progressive Iranians have been loath to believe that an assassination plot originated with Muhammad

ʿAlī Shāh, who they believed to be working hand in glove with the Atābak. Ahmad Kasravī, for example, in his excellent and democratically oriented history of the revolution, says that many silly things have been written about the assassination and sees it as an idea coming wholly from revolutionaries who recognized that the Atābak was trying to kill the constitutional movement.[2]

Mahdī Malikzādeh is one of the few democratically oriented authors who takes a different view. He writes that the Atābak wanted to be a mediator between the Shah and the people in the few months between the time Muhammad ʿAlī Shah recalled the Atābak from abroad and his assassination, but this turned out to be impossible, so that both the Shah and the popular forces became hostile to him. Malikzādeh adds that he has made a long study of the documents and allegations put forth by both sides regarding the assassination, and has concluded that a revolutionary society and the Shah both independently planned to kill the Atābak. Muhammad ʿAlī Shāh delegated three men, who did not include ʿAbbās Āqā, to do the killing, and one of the three recalled the plot in Malikzādeh's presence. Malikzādeh concludes that after ʿAbbās Āqā shot the Atābak one of the men delegated by the Shah claimed the credit in order to get the promised reward, thus giving rise to doubts that ʿAbbās Āqā was the true assassin.[3]

Many other versions of the assassination have also been put forth, and again one familiar with the spate of literature and speculation on recent American assassinations can appreciate the infinite theorizing possible, especially when some of the evidence points to high level or official conspirators. It is the aim of this article to add to the evidence on the case the hitherto unpublished material from the British Public Record Office, which supports the view that the Shah and high-level reactionary courtiers inspired the assassination, but speaks of a single assassination plot rather than the two independent ones adduced by Malikzādeh. Although not utterly conclusive, this newly available documentary evidence supports the probability of high level reactionary involvement. Considering the strong Iranian evidence of an independent revolutionary plot, Malikzādeh's conclusions seem most persuasive.

Before citing this evidence it will be useful to understand the role of the Atābak in Iranian history. The Atābak, who inherited his title Amīn as-Sultān and a court position from his Georgian-born father, was first appointed chief minister by Nāsir ad-Dīn Shāh (1848–96) in 1885 at age 31, and in the first years of his ministry was known as an Anglophil. Devoted primarily to preserving his own power, wealth, and position, which he could do only by meeting the Shah's ever-growing demands for money, the Amīn as-Sultān gained increasing odium among Iranians who objected to his chief means of raising this money – the grant of concessions and loans to foreigners. The Amīn as-Sultān was largely blamed for the concession of a monopoly on Iranian tobacco to a British subject in 1890 which resulted in a successful mass movement that forced the cancellation of the concession early in 1892. Many believed that the Amīn as-Sultān would then be dismissed, but he saved his position largely by giving large bribes and pensions to many of his opponents among the leading '*ulamā*', and by coming to an understanding with the Russians, whose position was strengthened by the successful anti-British tobacco movement. His utility to the crown was demonstrated again in his control of the potentially explosive situation in Tehran after the assassination of Nāsir ad-Dīn Shāh in 1896. The new Shah, Muzaffar ad-Dīn, soon dismissed the Amīn as-Sultān and appointed the reformist Amīn ad-Dauleh chief minister in 1897, but when the latter aroused reactionary opposition and was unable to raise a loan from the British, he was removed and the Amīn as-Sultān recalled. To meet the new Shah's demands for money for foreign trips, the Amīn as-Sultān helped conclude two large loans from the Russian government, in 1900 and 1902, both of which were accompanied by conditions severely limiting Iran's declining sovereignty. The Amīn as-Sultān encountered increasing opposition on both patriotic and religious grounds, for selling Iran to foreign infidels, but the Shah saw him as the only man who could raise the money he wanted and also control the internal situation. In 1902 the Shah conferred on him the higher title of Atābak-i A'zam. When the Atābak was suspected of having one of the Shah's favourites murdered, when he could come up with no more money except by another proposed Russian loan with conditions even he considered too stringent, and when the internal opposition to him increased to the point of including nearly all the leading '*ulamā*' as well as several prominent courtiers, the Shah finally decided to dismiss him in the autumn of 1903. At the time of his dismissal a decree of excommunication signed by the leading Shi'i '*ulamā*', who lived in the shrine cities of Ottoman Iraq, circulated widely in Iran; its authenticity has remained uncertain, but it was generally believed at the time. The Amīn as-Sultān found it prudent to leave Iran and travelled to Japan, the United States, and Europe. During his travels he spoke with several British representatives and Iranians abroad, trying to convince them that he had been a victim of his royal masters, which was partly true, and that his travels had convinced him of the need for reform and Iranian independence of Russia.[4]

Muzaffar ad-Dīn Shāh then turned to a reactionary and anti-foreign relative of his, the 'Ain ad-Dauleh, to be chief minister, and although the opposition was temporarily satisfied by the dismissal of the ex-Atābak, the financial crisis and political chaos continued. The victory of an Asian power, Japan, over Russia, the European power most in control of Iran, followed by the temporary defeat of the Russian government in the Russian Revolution of 1905, gave Iranian nationalists and the small body of constitutionalists new hope that their government might be transformed without the Russian government's being able to intervene. Two massive protest movements in Tehran in December 1905 and in July 1906 resulted in the Shah's acceding to a number of demands by the protesters, the most important of which was the inauguration of a representative and constitutional government. The first *majlis*, or national assembly, was inaugurated in October 1906, as soon as the deputies from Tehran had been elected. Muzaffar ad-Dīn Shāh signed the constitutional law in December 1906, just before his death in January 1907. Crown Prince Muhammad 'Alī Mīrzā had signed the constitution at the same time as his father, but his record as a cruel and despotic governor of Tabriz made many doubt that the new Shah intended to keep his promise not to dissolve the existing parliament for at least two years.

One of Muhammad 'Alī Shāh's first acts was to recall from exile the Amīn as-Sultān to be his prime minister, and there is considerable evidence that the Shah's main motive was a belief that the Amīn as-Sultān would find a way to suppress the *majlis* and the constitution, which is just what many Iranians feared. The Amīn as-Sultān reached the Caspian port city of Anzali (now Pahlavi) by boat from Russia, but there he was stopped from proceeding by the revolutionary local society, or *anjuman*. Telegrams were sent to Sayyid Hasan Taqizādeh and other radical deputies from Tabriz from the *anjumans* of Anzali and nearby Rasht saying that the Amīn as-Sultān was being held up and asking for advice. After heated discussion in the *majlis*, in which the democratic leader Taqīzādeh and a few others stressed their distrust of the Amīn as-Sultān and the dangers of his return, but others saw no way to stop the Shah from choosing his prime minister, the *majlis* voted overwhelmingly that he should be allowed to proceed, and telegrams were sent to Rasht and Anzali to this effect.[5]

Both British and Persian sources indicate that the Atābak had in his years of exile been speaking to sympathetic ears of the need for fundamental reform in Iran, and he now spoke to some of his belief in constitutionalism. Whatever his true feelings, the Atābak had generally acted opportunistically, and his behaviour as prime minister from May through August 1907 can be understood in the same terms. Although the Shah believed that the Atābak would help in the overthrow of the constitution and national assembly, after he arrived he saw that the national assembly had overwhelming support in the country, and set himself to encouraging the conservative party in the *majlis* and mediating between it and the Shah. As an old and trusted friend of Sayyid ʿAbdallāh Bihbihānī, one of the two main ʿ*ulamā*ʾ leaders in the *majlis*, he was soon apprised of the strength of constitutional sentiment even among the religious classes. The Atābak tried to strengthen Bihbihānī and the other more conservative members of the assembly, who were then involved in a struggle with the more secularist party over the terms of the supplementary fundamental law which was to be added to the very brief constitutional law of 1906. The Atābak, however, was still widely considered to be a traitorous tool of the Russians, an idea which was encouraged by his espousal of a new foreign loan as the only way to meet Iran's overwhelming financial problems.

Malikzādeh and other sources show that the Atābak did oppose the Shah on some issues. Specifically, he asked the Shah to dismiss the three most unpopular members of the cabinet, the Farmānfarmā, Kamrān Mīrzā, and the Vazīr-i Humayūn. He also talked the Shah into arresting Rahīm Khān, the tribal leader who with the Shah's connivance had been leading an attack on the revolutionary city of Tabriz and whose acts had caused a concerted public outcry and action.[6] In attempting to steer a compromise path between the Shah and the moderate constitutionalists, however, the Atābak, though temporarily very powerful, managed to arouse bitter opposition on both the radical and the reactionary side.

The story of the radical plot that culminated in the assassination of the Atābak has been told more than once in Persian, including a detailed version that is attributed to an anonymous co-conspirator and accords with what is known from other sources. According to this story, the mastermind of the radical plot was the well-known Caucasian revolutionary who had come to Iran as an engineer before the revolution, Haidar Khān ʿAmū Ughlī. Before discussing Haidar Khān the narrator says that his own *anjuman* had sent him and another member to question the Atābak on his views on the constitution, and to ask him to sign, swearing to his support of the constitution, on the back of a Koran. The Atābak said he supported the constitution but declined to write or sign anything, as he said that he feared they had come on behalf of the Shah. From this they learned that the Atābak feared that the Shah would get evidence of his support for the constitution.

After this the narrator met Haidar Khān and was impressed by his intelligence, bravery, and planning ability. One day Haidar Khān sent him to the Atābak's home, with a petition as a pretext, in order to inspect the area to see its possibilities for an assassination. The narrator concluded that the area was too well guarded for success.

To carry out his planned assassinations Haidar Khān needed brave and experienced men, and finding few in Tehran he turned to Azerbaijan and to Iranians in the Caucasus. He brought some of them to Tehran, but as a precaution did not introduce them to anyone, and dressed them as sayyids or mullas. On 31 August, as the Atābak was coming out of the *majlis* talking to Sayyid ʿAbdallāh Bihbihānī, a shot was fired that killed the Atābak, and at the same time some men threw dust and ashes into the air to make it dark and hard to see. Then came another shot, as the assassin killed himself.

The next day the narrator went to the house of Haidar Khān, but saw it was surrounded by police. Later the author was involved in hiding the assassin's brother, who was the object of a police search. The assassination had affected the brother's brain, and he was constantly pleading to be allowed to kill someone. Haidar Khān tried to spirit him out of the country, but the brother shot himself in Qazvin.

Haidar Khān related to the narrator that a secret circle of the *ijtimāʿiyyūn ʿammiyyūn* (social democrats) of Tehran had taken a vote to kill the Atābak, and had decided to assign ʿAbbās Āqā to the job, with his brother to go along to carry out the task if needed. ʿAbbās Āqā was supposed to escape to the north in the dust and confusion, but he panicked and ran the wrong way, thinking that the fleeing crowd was after him. He then killed himself to keep from being caught. He had also (as the public learned) been given a capsule of strychnine to take in case he were caught. Haidar Khān had secretly been watching the scene, but hurried home immediately afterwards, carefully cleaning the dust and ashes from his shoes so there would be no evidence of where he had been. The police arrested Haidar Khān but could get no evidence against him, and so had to let him go.[7]

A very similar account is recorded as having been dictated by Haidar Khān himself to another revolutionary, Munshīzādeh, who had intended to include it in a book, and whose verbatim handwritten account was passed on to and published by the Iranian scholar ʿAbbās Iqbāl. Haidar Khān recalled that a secret circle of the *ijtimāʿiyyūn ʿammiyyūn* of Tehran, of which the prominent revolutionary orators Malik al-Mutakallimīn (Malikzādeh's father) and Sayyid Jamāl ad-Dīn (Isfahānī) were members, voted to execute the Atābak, giving the job to the 'executive committee' which assigned it to a special terrorist group made up of three groups of four persons each, under Haidar Khān's leadership. The members of this committee drew lots, and ʻAbbās Āqā's name came up. Two other men were deputed to go along with him. The group went several times to the Atābak's summer residence, but were unable to do the job there. One day they heard that the next day the Atābak would go to the *majlis*, and so they went there to do the deed, which Haidar Khān witnessed.

In the same article in which he reprinted this account, ʻAbbās Iqbāl printed a letter from Mukhbir as-Saltaneh Hidāyat, whose brother Sanīʻ ad-Dauleh was president of the *majlis* at the time of the assassination. Both brothers were moderate constitutionalists, friendly to the Atābak after his return, and both claimed to have evidence that the assassination was inspired by the Shah. Mukhbir as-Saltaneh names the three men deputed by the Shah to do the killing (the same three names given later by Malikzādeh), and expresses strong doubt that ʻAbbās Āqā shot the Atābak. In any case, he writes, the Atābak was a martyr for the *majlis*, and the generally accepted opposite version is untrue.

After quoting the above opposite versions of the assassination, and citing some other evidence, ʻAbbās Iqbāl states that there is no doubt that Muhammad ʻAlī Shāh was happy over the assassination and could not hide his joy from those nearest him. Like Malikzādeh, though more tentatively, Iqbāl concludes that both the Shah and the revolutionaries probably had separate agents assigned to do the killing, and that one of the two sides succeeded, but the other agents claimed the credit with their own superiors, thus giving rise to two opposite stories, both with convincing documentation by participants.[8]

The British Public Record Office documents, containing on-the-spot descriptions of events in Tehran, provide some of the most vivid and interesting documentation on the Atābak – material that has not yet been utilized by the Iranians who have written on the subject. After describing the debates in the *majlis* over the fact that ministers were not following its instructions, as the constitutionalists had intended, these documents go on to describe a further *majlis* debate on 6 April 1907, just before the Amīn as-Sultān's return:

> 'Seyed Mohammed [Tabātabā'ī], the Mujtehed, urged the Assembly to insist on the recall of the Ain-ed-Dowleh in order that an inquiry should be held into his administration while Grand Vizier. A Tabreez Deputy (Taki Zade) thereupon made a bold speech, pointing out that if the Assembly had to try all persons who had held Government offices they

would have their hands full, as most of them had betrayed the interests confided to them. He said if one was punished they should all be punished. If Ain-ed-Dowleh was to be put under examination, so should Amin-es-Sultan, who was the greatest traitor of all, and whose proper title was "Khain-es-Sultan" (i.e. the King's traitor), and who nevertheless returning [*sic*] to Persia. A murmur of approval passed round the House as the speaker concluded.'[9]

The British documents also note the attacks on the Amīn as-Sultān by both the press and the secret societies. In mid-May, shortly after his return to the prime ministry, the Atābak told the British he had tried to talk very seriously to the Shah, telling him that:

'there was now a third factor which had to be taken into serious account both by the Government and the Assembly; this third factor was represented by the masses who were rapidly getting out of hand, and to deal with them it was absolutely essential for the Government and the Assembly to cooperate.'[10]

Unable to convince the Shah to cooperate with the predominantly moderate *majlis*, and arousing increasing hostility from the masses because of his advocacy of a new foreign loan, the Atābak in June and July confided to the British his hopelessness concerning finances, his difficulties with both the court and popular parties, and his fears for his own life.

On the day of the assassination, the Atābak and his ministers went to the palace and asked to resign unless the Shah would pledge to cooperate with the government and the *majlis*, which the Shah did in writing. The day before, on 30 August, the Atābak had called on the British Minister, Cecil Spring Rice, and discussed the difficulties likely to arise with the *majlis* over a new foreign loan agreement. He also discussed the policy of the Saʿd ad-Dauleh (who had been a leader of the constitutionalists but was beginning secretly going over to the royalist side). According to the Atābak:

'Saad-ed-Dowleh, whose ambition is to become either Prime Minister or President of the Assembly, is in secret communication with the Shah with the object of upsetting the present Cabinet and forming a new one with himself at the head of it. The object of the Saad-ed-Dowleh, his party, and the Shah, who is very much against the Constitution, is to get the present Assembly dissolved, to bring on a new election, to cause general disorder in the country, and ultimately to get rid of the Assembly, which, on account of the disorder, would be hated by the public in time.'[11]

The Atābak added that a few days before he had wanted to resign, but received letters from secret societies threatening him with death if he did. He said that over two-thirds of the assembly was now with him.[12]

After the 31 August assassination the British representatives at Tehran became convinced that a reactionary court party had instigated it. Some of the bases for this conviction are contained in a memoir by the British Oriental Secretary, George Churchill, who reported in a secret memorandum that Sanī ʿ ad-Dauleh (the moderate president of the assembly and enemy of Sa ʿd ad-Dauleh) had asked to see him. The Sanī ʿ ad-Dauleh's words on this occasion are reported by Churchill as follows:

> 'He said that the murder of the Atabek-i-Azam was proved beyond doubt, by documents he had seen and by the evidence in his possession, to have been the result of the machinations of the reactionary party and, in particular, of his own personal enemy, Saad-ed-Dowleh. One of the accomplices in the murder was a raw youth who was caught soon after the murder with some incriminating papers relating to the Secret Society of which he and the other accomplices were members. His father was chief of the Society and has been arrested. The papers in the father's house showed that Sepahdar, Farman Farma, Ala-ed-Dowleh, Amir Behadur Jang, Naib-es-Sultaneh [reactionary courtiers] and Saad-ed-Dowleh supplied the Society with money and had men in it. The agents of the last named were especially active in the Society and denounced the late Atabek and the President as traitors who had combined to sell the country to the foreigners.... He felt that, as the instigators of the crime were the above-named and were, he felt convinced, backed by the Shah, and as they knew that their complicity would shortly come out through the documents, he had everything to fear, and for this reason he had made up his mind to resign the presidency, which, moreover, he had again been warned to do if he valued his life. He thought that the only thing for him to do was to leave the country, and he wanted to know whether His Majesty's Legation would extend their good offices to him in case of need. He looked upon the situation with pessimism. The enemies of the people in the disguise of democracy and patriotism, and working through agents, had sown the seed of revolution and anarchy in certain Secret Societies. The result had been the wanton murder of a man who was, the ex-President felt convinced, sincerely desirous of working in unison with the assembly for the good of the country.'[13]

Shortly thereafter, Churchill spoke with a foreign officer high in the police department, named Pollacco, who gave an account that confirmed the above story:

> 'He mentioned to me, very confidentially, the names of some of the high officials who are, to his certain knowledge, implicated in the plot. These names included Farman Farma and Saad-ed-Dowleh.'

The Saʿd ad-Dauleh spent the night of the assassination at the home of the Austrian Legation's interpreter, and sent for Pollacco, who had been present when the Atābak died. (The identity of the dead assassin had not yet been established with certainty):

> 'Mr Pollacco told Saad-ed-Dowleh he thought the man was a native of the Caucasus. When Saad-ed-Dowleh heard this his expression seems to have been one of considerable surprise. Mr Pollacco told me that he had called on Saad-ed-Dowleh a few days before the murder, and during the course of conversation on the state of affairs Saad-ed-Dowleh had said that there would soon be a change of Government, and seemed to know of some coming events which would greatly modify the situation.'[14]

With regard to the men who had been arrested and the incriminating documents that had been found, Pollacco confirmed 'that everything is being suppressed and that no serious inquiry will be held'. The men arrested had been released, and the Minister of Justice and the Governor of Tehran evaded all responsibility to pursue the investigation. 'This is attributed to alarm on the part of the authorities lest the names of the high officials involved should get out.'[15]

In addition, already on the day after the assassination Spring Rice reported that the Atābak's family suspected that the deed stemmed from 'certain important persons' rather than the revolutionaries, and the president of the assembly was convinced of the complicity of the Shah himself.[16]

Reporting at length on the situation on 13 September, Spring Rice stated that Churchill and his Russian colleague had seen the Shah the day after the assassination. 'They conveyed the message of condolence, and the Shah replied in a few formal phrases. Neither the Court nor His Majesty seemed to be much perturbed at the sudden death of the Prime Minister.'[17] Spring Rice noted that there were violent feelings against the Atābak on the part of the revolutionaries, who believed him to be in collusion with the Shah to overthrow the assembly and sell the country to Russia. Revolutionary attacks on the Atābak had recently gained in virulence:

> 'The subject was brought up in the House, and a vehement speech denouncing Saad-ed-Dowleh, who was supposed to be the leader of the

movement against the Atabek, was made by the Chief Mujtehed, Seyed Abdullah. The President [Sanī' ad-Dauleh] said that if the Atabek resigned he would resign himself, because the Atabek's resignation would mean the immediate dissolution of the House. The feeling of the majority of the House was in the Atabek's favour, but popular opinion only saw in the support given him by the majority of the Assembly the evidence of a corrupt plot between his Highness and the majority, who were supposed to have been bought, as was certainly the case with Seyed Abdullah. The excitement in the town was intense, and was exploited for their own purposes by the Atabek's personal enemies. These consisted of the coterie of reactionaries who surround the Shah, the principal members of which are the Shepahdar, Minister of Telegraphs, and the Naib-es-Sultaneh, ex-Minister of War, and the Saad-ed-Dowleh, who has no particular political principles, but is revengeful and ambitious.'[18]

Spring Rice reported that the Shah had feared the power of the Atābak and resented his having just forced him to sign a pledge of cooperation with the cabinet and the *majlis*. The Shah, continued Spring Rice:

'according to accounts which have reached me, was in a state bordering on frenzy on the day on which he had been forced to yield by the Atabek and his Ministers. The result of the Atabek's success was to give him control over the Shah and the Assembly, and practically to place the Government of the country under his sole management.

Under these circumstances it was natural that resort should be had to extreme measures. The conspirators appear to have been in communication with one of the Secret Societies which abound in Tehran, and to have secured the admittance of some of their own adherents, who provided money and what appeared to be authentic information from the Court. It was easy to lead the members of the Society to believe that the destruction of the Atabek was the only way to save the country; that he was in corrupt collusion with the Shah and the Russian Legation, and was about to obtain control of the Assembly in order to carry through another Russian loan with the active help of the President. Orders were given to remove him, and the deed was carried out on the very day when, as it appeared, his success was complete.

Popular sentiment approved the murder, and the assassins were regarded as saviours of their country. The streets of Tabreez were illuminated.

. . . the Shah and his party may hope to turn . . . chaos to their advantage. The Assembly have not dared to publish the documentary evidence which is stated to be in their possession, although a fairly plain allusion was made to the intrigues which had caused the Atabek's death in the address delivered to the Shah, . . .'[19]

Although Spring Rice never listed all the sources for his conviction that the Atābak's assassination was plotted by the court, his own close ties with many important Iranians and his judicious analysis of contemporary events in Iran lends credence to his account. Even after it became clear that the revolutionaries were the chief immediate beneficiaries of the assassination, Spring Rice stuck to his account of its planning by the court in his report home on the year's events. He saw the assassination as one of a series of acts undertaken by the Shah in 1907 with the aim of promoting such chaos in Iran that his Russian friends would be forced to intervene and to help him suppress the *majlis*.[20]

Adding slightly to earlier reports on the assassination, Spring Rice reported at the beginning of 1908, 'According to the information which reached me from trustworthy sources I have little doubt that the Shah was privy to the murder, although it was at once hailed as a national victory'. He adds that the Atābak's talk with him on the eve of his death made it plain that the Atābak saw the Shah as the chief cause of the existing internal disorder and the Saʿd ad-Dauleh as the Shah's main instrument. Regarding the Saʿd ad-Dauleh he adds:

'That person, as I ascertained, had been in constant communication with the secret societies, to whom he had conveyed information purporting to prove that the Attabek was in corrupt collusion with the Shah and the reactionaries, for the purpose of overthrowing the Constitution, and that with this object he was obtaining control of the Assembly. The Societies were urged to act at once if they wished to save the country.'[21]

The British Foreign Office documents thus tend to support and carry even further the allegations reported soon after the event by E. G. Browne, who was in close touch with well informed Persian and British sources during the revolution. Browne states:

'The *Amínu's-Sulṭán* had, as we have seen, long been regarded with suspicion by his countrymen as one ready to sell his native land into foreign bondage, but the immediate cause of his death was the discovery by the *anjumans* of certain treasonable documents ostensibly emanating from him, and addressed to the reactionaries in the provinces, inviting them to take action conducive to the overthrow of the Assembly. But it was darkly hinted that the real author of these incriminating documents was, not the *Amínu's-Sulṭán*, but his rival and foe the *Saʿdu 'd-Dawla*, who was playing a double game, and was in close relations with the Court on the one hand, and the *anjumans* on the other. . . .

. . . It was even stated on good authority that Muḥammad ʿAlí Sháh, growing jealous of the *Amínu's-Sulṭán's* growing influence, issued in his name the documents which caused his death, and which were designedly allowed to fall into the hands of the *anjumans*.'[22]

It is true that a major source of information for the British, and possibly also for Browne, was Sanīʿ ad-Dauleh (Hidāyat), a friend of the Atābak and bitter enemy of the implicated Saʿd ad-Dauleh. It is also true that the main proponents of the theory that the assassination was a reactionary, rather than a revolutionary, plot have continued to be friends of the Atābak, especially members of the distinguished Hidāyat family, and that they have yet to provide decisive documentary evidence for their view, despite the Sanīʿ ad-Dauleh's early claim that he had seen the incriminating documents. Nevertheless, it seems quite possible that the incriminating documents were destroyed, and that the story of a reactionary plot, which the British got from Pollacco, the Atābak's family, and possibly other sources as well as the Sanīʿ ad-Dauleh, was a true one. Malikzādeh records the story from a source independent of the Hidāyats – the words of one of the deputed assassins. As the Hidāyats tell the story, however, there was essentially only a reactionary-inspired plot, and the Atābak was a martyr to the constitutionalist cause.[23] This view must be rejected; there were certainly revolutionaries plotting against the Atābak, and it is quite possible, as Malikzādeh concluded after considerable investigation, that there were two independent plots.

The combination of the British Foreign Office documentation with the already known Persian documents and memoirs pointing to collusion in the Atābak's assassination by the Shah and some of his courtiers thus makes such collusion appear very probable. Whether there was a single plot utilizing revolutionaries but hatched primarily by the Saʿd ad-Dauleh, or whether there were two plots, with the purely revolutionary one having prior success, is not entirely clear. The latter alternative fits better with some of the reports that have come down, and could help explain why the revolutionary party on the whole was so sure that only revolutionaries were involved. There is no doubt that the Atābak's whole past history had earned him the profound distrust of the revolutionaries, but there now seems equally little doubt that his typically adaptive posture in relation to a new centre of power in Iran – the moderate constitutionalists – earned him almost equal distrust from the Shah and his courtiers. The policy of retaining his own power by adapting himself to the prevailing forces in Iran had served the Atābak for decades, but it could not cope with the new strength of radical popular forces in polarized opposition to the Shah and his court. In trying to negotiate a conservative but not absolutist compromise between the Shah and the *majlis* leadership against the growing mass demands for a complete break with the imperialist powers and for major democratic political and social changes, the Atābak was understandably perceived as a powerful menace both by the unreconstructed royalists and by the convinced revolutionaries. Even should the future never resolve completely the controversy over his assassination, it seems clear that there were men on both sides who were glad to have it occur.

The research reported in this article was done largely thanks to a John Simon Guggenheim Memorial Fellowship, 1963–4. Thanks are also due to Dr ʿAbd al-Husain Zarrinkūb for criticizing an early draft of the article, and to Ervand Abrahamian and Dunning Wilson for help with references.

NOTES

1 A brief summary of the controversy with references is found at the beginning of ʿAbd al-Husain Navā'ī, 'Az asrār-i qatl-i Atābak pardeh bar mīdārīm', *Ittilāʿāt-i māhāneh*, II, no. 10 (Dey 1328) 23-6, 40-2.

2 Ahmad Kasravī, *Tārīkh-i mashrūteh-yi Īrān*, 3rd ed. (Tehran 1335/1956–7) 447-50. Like many others, Kasravī attributes leadership in the assassination plot to the Caucasian revolutionary, Haidar Khān ʿAmū Ughlī; see below for accounts that claim to describe his plot.

3 Mahdī Malikzādeh, *Tārīkh-i inqilāb-i mashrūtiyyat-i Īrān* (Tehran 1949–53) III, 19-24.

4 See Nikki R. Keddie, *Religion and Rebellion in Iran: The Tobacco Protest of 1891–1892* (London 1966) and 'Iranian Politics 1900-1905: Background to Revolution', *Middle Eastern Studies*, v, 1 (January 1969), 3-31, continued in v, nos. 2 and 3; FO 248/898, Memorandum by G. P. Churchill, enclosed in Spring Rice to Grey, 25 March 1907, No. 58; Mahdī Qulī Hidāyat, Mukhbir as-Saltaneh, *Khātirāt va khatirāt* (Tehran 1329/1950–1), 203, 208.

5 Kasravī, op. cit., 252-8; Malikzādeh, op. cit., III, 9-11; Navā'ī, op. cit., 24-6.

6 Malikzādeh, op. cit., III, 12-13; the British diplomatic dispatches in 1907 give details of the Atābak's clashes with the Shah on such issues.

7 Navā'ī, op. cit., Navā'ī says he is presenting the words of a participant in the plot, who wishes to remain anonymous.

8 'Qātil-i haqīqī-yi Mīrzā 'Alī Asghar Khān Atābak', *Yādgār*, III, 4 (1325/1946–7), 47-51; and 'Haidar Khān 'Amū Ūghlī', *Yādgār*, III, 5 (1325/1946–7), 61-80.

9 FO 371/301, Summary by Churchill, enclosed in Spring Rice to Grey, 26 April 1907, No. 82, Confidential.

10 FO 248/899, Memorandum by Churchill enclosed in Spring Rice to Grey, 21 May 1907, No. 110.

11 FO 371/311, Memorandum by Abbas Kuli inclosure 1 in Spring Rice to Grey, 13 Sept. 1907, No. 200, Secret.

12 Loc. cit.

13 Memorandum by Churchill, inclosure 4, Very Secret, in *ibid.*

14 Loc. cit.

15 Loc. cit.

16 FO 371/311, Spring Rice to Grey, 4 Sept. 1907, Telegram, No. 241, Confidential.

17 FO 371/311, same to same, 13 Sept. 1907, No. 200, Secret.

18 Loc. cit.

19 Loc. cit.

20 FO 371/498, Annual Report, 1907, enclosed in Marling to Grey, 29 January 1908, Confidential.

21 Loc. cit. The British documents disprove the contention of Ibrāhīm Safā'ī, *Rahbarān-i mashrūteh* (Tehran 1344/1965–6), 190 n.1, that only the legation secretary, Churchill, 'twisted the truth' in accusing Sa'd ad-Dauleh, while Spring Rice attributed the assassination to the revolutionary *anjumans*. Safā'ī may have got this impression from published British documents, but it is not supported by reference to the complete unpublished originals.

22 Browne, *Persian Revolution*, 154-5, and 155n.

23 Mahdī Qulī Hidāyat, Mukhbir as-Saltaneh, *Khātirāt va khatirāt*, 203-9; this story implicates the *anjuman-i adamiyyat*, with which the Sa'd ad-Dauleh had been associated, and makes no mention of Haidar Khān and his associates. To take the view that *only* revolutionaries or *only* royalists were behind the Atābak's assassination involves dismissing a mass of evidence coming from witnesses and participants. Some Iranians do this, claiming that this evidence is falsified or fabricated; but to me, as to Malikzādeh and 'Abbās Iqbāl, the evidence for the involvement of both sides seems too strong to be easily rejected.

A. K. S. LAMBTON

The Case of Ḥājjī ʿAbd al-Karīm. A Study on the Role of the Merchant in mid-nineteenth-century Persia [1]

Persian foreign trade in the middle of the nineteenth century, although it was dominated by political considerations arising from Persia's relations with Russia and Great Britain, was not entirely, or even mainly, in the hands of European merchants; and once inside the country merchandise was circulated by Persian, Armenian, and eastern, including Indian, merchants. In Safavid times Multanis had played an important part in the life of the country both as merchants and moneylenders, and had rivalled the Armenians in their wealth. In the disorders after the fall of the Safavids, many of them left the country. By the beginning of the nineteenth century only a few remained in the Gulf ports; somewhat later small numbers were to be found in other parts of southern Persia also. Sir Henry Pottinger recorded in 1810 that there were about forty Hindu merchants from Shikarpur and Sind in Kirmān.[2] In the middle of the century there were some ten Sindi merchants resident in Yazd.[3] On the extension of British conquests in India many of the Indian merchants became entitled to British protection. One such was Ḥājjī Nūr al-Dīn, whose land case with the Persian government, extending over the years 1823–47, I have examined elsewhere.[4] Another was Ḥājjī ʿAbd al-Karīm, whose case is discussed in this article.

Ḥājjī ʿAbd al-Karīm was probably born between the years 1768 and 1777.[5] By 1849 he had been some thirty or forty years in Persia, and therefore presumably came to Persia sometime between 1810 and 1820. In 1849 he was placed under British protection on the grounds that he was a native of Shikarpur.[6] There appears to have been some doubt as to the validity of his claim to British protection. Sir Justin Sheil, who was British minister in Tehran from September 1844 to February 1853, recommended that his claim should not be admitted; his advice was overruled.[7] The Persian government claimed that he was a native of Qandahar, though the circumstances in which they made this claim throw some doubt on its validity. Ḥājjī ʿAbd al-Karīm, himself, finally for reasons of expediency denied, whether truthfully or not, that he was a native of Shikarpur, and acknowledged himself to be a Persian subject. The available evidence shows him to have been a somewhat devious, if not disreputable, character. Mr R. W. Stevens, who was for many years British consul first in Tabrīz and then Tehran, alleged after Ḥājjī ʿAbd al-Karīm's death that he was a notorious rogue[8]; but Stevens, himself, was both credulous and volatile.

During his sojourn in Persia, Ḥājjī ʿAbd al-Karīm amassed great wealth, probably largely by speculating in government bills (*barāt*)[9] and as a moneylender. Part of his wealth was invested in land. He appears to have enjoyed influence and to have had financial transactions with members of the ruling family. One of his wives was a daughter of Fatḥ ʿAlī Shāh, by whom he had two children, who were both minors at the time of his death in 1858. His eldest son, Mīrzā Ghulām Ḥusayn, was nominally in the service of the Persian heir apparent when his father died. Ḥājjī ʿAbd al-Karīm had two daughters, who were in their thirties or forties at the time of their father's death, and another child who was then still a minor. His brother Ḥājjī ʿAbd al-Raḥīm, who also had several children and considerable wealth, was associated with him in his business.

On 1 October 1851 Sheil reported at length to Palmerston on certain money transactions which Ḥājjī ʿAbd al-Karīm had had with Ḥusayn Khān Nāẓim al-Dawleh Muqaddam Marāgheh'ī, the *ājūdānbāshī*, and the difficulties he was experiencing over the collection of his debts.[10] Ḥusayn Khān had been ambassador to England in 1819 and 1839 and subsequently became governor of Yazd.[10a] In 1844 he was appointed governor of Fārs (with the *laqab* of Ṣāḥib Ikhtīār) in succession to Nabī Khān Qazvīnī, who had been appointed in 1843 and under whose governorship there had been numerous disorders, a revival of old feuds and an interruption of the caravan routes.[11] In the spring of 1847 Ḥusayn Khān visited Muḥammad Shāh's court. As was usual on such occasions, he was called upon to make a large payment to the government, whether as a donation to ensure his return to his government, an advance of revenue, or in lieu of arrears of revenue. Colonel Farrant, who became British chargé d'affaires in 1847 reported that Ḥusayn Khān involved himself on this occasion to about £100,000 'to satisfy the rapacity of the Hajee' (i.e. Ḥājjī Mīrzā Āqāsī, Muḥammad Shāh's first minister).[12]

At this time the Persian government was in great straits for money to pay the troops which were to be sent to Khurāsān to put down the rebellion of Jaʿfar Qulī, the chief of Bujnurd, and Sālār al-Dawleh, the son of Āṣaf al-Dawleh, the former governor of Khurāsān, who had been recalled in the spring of 1847. About the beginning of July some troops left Tehran for Khurāsān. Reinforcements amounting apparently to some 5,000 men were to follow, but lack of funds prevented their despatch; they refused to march unless a portion of the arrears due to them was first paid. The sum involved appears to have been small, some 30,000 *tūmāns* (*c.* £15,000), being needed to enable them to set out.[13] Part of the funds borrowed from Ḥājjī ʿAbd al-Karīm by Ḥusayn Khān and paid by him to the government was used to pay the arrears of the troops.[14]

A letter from Ḥājjī Mīrzā Āqāsī to Ḥājjī ʿAbd al-Raḥīm, Ḥājjī ʿAbd al-Karīm's brother, refers to this transaction. It reads,

> 'May God help you my worthy friend, Hajee Abdurreheem. I never was in such distress before. The troops must march, and return before winter. So large a force cannot remain out in the deserts during winter. My income (from his villages) has not reached me. I am in much perplexity, and you have always agreed in a friendly manner to any trouble I have imposed upon you. The governor of Fars Husayn Khan requires money, which is to be given to me. Give him whatever money he wants, with interest (that is, he is to take interest), and I will become a guarantee on the margin of the bond. If pledges are required, I will give you whatever pledges you desire from my own landed property. Assuredly you must get it (the money) by any mode, manner, or means from yourself or from others, and give it. In this manner you must not be guilty of any remissness of any kind, and you will please me very much, very much.'[15]

In addition Ḥājjī ʿAbd al-Karīm had transactions with Ḥusayn Khān over the sale of land and the purchase of government bills. The land transaction amounted to 16,000 *tūmāns* inclusive of one year's interest, which was inserted in the bond.[16] Ḥusayn Khān after his purchase of the land made a gift of it to Ḥājjī Mīrzā Āqāsī, on whose fall after the death of Muḥammad Shāh it was confiscated by the government together with the rest of his property. Ḥusayn Khān admitted that he had entered into an arrangement with Ḥājjī ʿAbd al-Karīm for the purchase of government bills and claimed that this was on a large scale. Ḥājjī ʿAbd al-Karīm on the other hand alleged that the amount involved was small.[17]

A letter from Ḥājjī ʿAbd al-Karīm to Ḥusayn Khān, written apparently after the latter had set out in December 1847 on his return to Fārs from the court, discusses their transactions in *barāts*. It reads,

> '... With regard to the arrangement which you made before leaving that I was to report to you honestly all the Bills (Treasury), which in concert

> with Hajee Boozoorg I might purchase, half of the profit of which was to belong to you and half to me. You have in your last letter told me that the Shah, when you were taking leave, had put you on your oath, and ordered you not to buy bills (*Barat*) as the Moatimed [possibly Manūchihr Khān Muʿtamid al-Dawleh, at one time governor of Iṣfahān] had done because it would be your ruin, I am well pleased that you have changed your mind.... Be assured in all these matters. I will buy with Hajee Boozoorg a number of Bills every year. Bills can do you no harm, because you can pay them from the revenue. I will pass them in the Fars accounts, as you are not here [i.e. in Tehran], when they are wanted that you may not suffer any loss, and I will give the necessary fees to the Moostofees. If your affairs should go wrong, and you are appointed to another office (meaning if you are dismissed from your present post) and my bills should not be paid, I will only regret your misfortune, and will not force money from you....'[18]

A large part of the claims of Ḥājjī ʿAbd al-Karīm on Ḥusayn Khān were guaranteed by Ḥājjī Mīrzā Āqāsī. While this guarantee did not necessarily give the transaction an official character, it suggests that the government, in the person of the first minister, whose functions included the provision of funds for the state to enable it to carry on its operations, had an interest in the conclusion of the transaction between Ḥusayn Khān and Ḥājjī ʿAbd al-Karīm.

In addition to his claims on Ḥusayn Khān, Ḥājjī ʿAbd al-Karīm also appears to have had a claim of 4,000 *tūmāns* on the Persian government for a loan for that amount contracted by Ḥājjī Mīrzā Āqāsī. A bond in the latter's writing existed for this and was not contested.[19]

Ḥājjī ʿAbd al-Karīm held numerous documents supporting his claims. Among these was a promissory note for 61,740 *tūmāns* two *qirāns*, dated 1 Shaʿbān 1263/14 July 1847, payable in eight months. This states that all former accounts had been settled and that Ḥusayn Khān had received the above amount in cash. It also enumerated the various items of property placed in the hands of Ḥājjī ʿAbd al-Karīm, which he was free to sell six months after the eight months had expired. If there was a surplus from the sale, it was to be paid to Ḥusayn Khān; if there was a deficiency, Ḥusayn Khān would continue to be answerable. The property given in pledge consisted of jewels, land, and books, etc., but a large part of the land was in fact never made over. The bond was sealed by Ḥājjī Mīrzā Āqāsī and endorsed in his own hand, as follows: 'What is contained here is true. I make a promise that I will cause the above money to be paid to the above Hajee'.

The bond was further sealed by fifteen of the religious dignitaries of Tehran, who declared that Ḥusayn Khān had acknowledged to them the validity of the bond, and by forty-six other persons of respectability. It was registered in the *dīvān-khāneh* and its authenticity borne witness to by the seals of three of the principal members of the *dīvān-khāneh*, who further declared that Ḥusayn Khān had written a note acknowledging the validity of the bond.[20]

Ḥājjī ʿAbd al-Karīm also had an undated note from Ḥājjī Mīrzā Āqāsī in his own hand, which read,

> 'The light of my eyes, Hajee Abdul Kereem: With regard to the debt which you claim from Hoosseen Khan, the Adjutant-General, Governor of Fars, with the grace of God, and the Prophet, and the Imams, who are our guides, I am in hopes that I shall collect your claim from him and deliver it to you. Your mind may be at rest.'[21]

In addition to these documents, Ḥājjī ʿAbd al-Karīm had in his hands ten *barāts* issued by Ḥusayn Khān as governor of Fārs on the payers of revenue in that province, payable to the agent of Ḥājjī ʿAbd al-Karīm, amounting to 140,500 *tūmāns*, which were collateral proof of Ḥusayn Khān's debt. Ḥājjī ʿAbd al-Karīm also had a promissory note given to his agent by a prominent man in Fārs for 32,500 *tūmāns* as an equivalent for the *barāt* issued on him. In the promissory note it was stated that Ḥusayn Khān had passed the above sum in the accounts of the man concerned. Another document alleged to be in Ḥusayn Khān's handwriting was addressed to one of his secretaries directing him to issue *barāts* to Ḥājjī ʿAbd al-Karīm to the amount of 211,342 *tūmāns*.[22]

After the accession of Nāṣir al-Dīn in 1848 there were renewed outbreaks of disorder in Fārs by the tribes and the townspeople at Shīrāz. The latter issued an ultimatum to Ḥusayn Khān to return to the capital on the grounds that he had been appointed governor by Muḥammad Shāh and therefore no longer had any authority. In 1849 Bahrām Mīrzā was appointed to Fārs to quell the disorders and to succeed Ḥusayn Khān as governor.[23] The latter, who was detained in confinement in Shīrāz for several months after his fall, had therefore little time to reimburse himself for the payments which he had made to the government in Tehran in 1847.

Sheil corresponded with the new prime minister, Mīrzā Taqī Khān Amīr Niẓām, over the case. The latter denied the nationality of Ḥājjī ʿAbd al-Karīm and thereby the right of the British mission to interfere in the recovery of his claims. He contended that Ḥājjī ʿAbd al-Karīm was a native of Qandahar and that he had, during the forty years which he had spent in

Persia, conformed to Persian laws and customs, had bought houses and landed estates, and married a member of the royal family, a daughter of Fatḥ ʿAlī Shāh, and was therefore a Persian subject.[24] The possession of landed property was assumed to prove Persian nationality.[25] It would seem that there was also an attempt to claim by the Persian authorities that anyone marrying a lady belonging to the Qājār royal house automatically placed himself under the jurisdiction of the Shāh. A declaration (*istishhād-nāmeh*) was got up by the Persian government in 1849 alleging that Ḥājjī ʿAbd al-Karīm was a native of Qandahar. The latter prepared a counter document testifying to his British nationality, which was signed by the chief religious dignitaries of Tehran and by natives of Mashhad, Herat, Qandahar, and all the cities in which he had lived. Among the various persons witnessing the document was Ḥusayn Khān, against whom Ḥājjī ʿAbd al-Karīm had large claims and in whose interests it was to refute his British nationality.[26]

When Ḥusayn Khān returned to Tehran about January 1851 Sheil advised him and Ḥājjī ʿAbd al-Karīm to settle their affairs by arbitration and compromise. Several ineffectual attempts were made. By October 1851 only a small portion of the money due from Ḥusayn Khān to Ḥājjī ʿAbd al-Karīm had been repaid. The total amount of his claims by that date, for which he had bonds executed by Ḥusayn Khān, exclusive of interest for the period after which repayment had fallen due, was 135,720 *tūmāns* (some £67,860), of which Ḥājjī Mīrzā Āqāsī had guaranteed 72,540 *tūmāns* (some £36,270). This probably did not wholly represent real debt incurred in return for money or other property, a portion of it being interest calculated in advance and added to the principal.

The other claims of Ḥājjī ʿAbd al-Karīm, not guaranteed by Ḥājjī Mīrzā Āqāsī, for which the Persian government could not be held responsible, amounted to 63,180 *tūmāns* principal, and 114,591 *tūmāns* interest.[27] His total claims, including interest, on Ḥusayn Khān, were by this time over 200,000 *tūmāns* (some £100,000).[28] The total revenue of Fārs in 1849 from taxes on the tribes, land taxes, local taxes and dues, poll-tax on the Jews, the farming of the customs at Shīrāz, and the rent of shops in Shīrāz, after the deduction of certain remissions, amounted in cash and kind to some 336,579 *tūmāns* (nearly £168,290). The total revenue of Persia in the same year was estimated at some 2,775,021 *tūmāns* (nearly £1,388,000) and the expenses of the central government at some 2,267,800 *tūmāns* (nearly £1,133,900).[29]

By 1851 a measure of order had been restored in Fārs and the position was more favourable: the revenue was reckoned at 400,000 *tūmāns* (some

£200,000) of which 50,000 *tūmāns* was expended on troops in the province, 45,000 *tūmāns* on salaries and pensions, 12,000 *tūmāns* on repairs to bridges, buildings, etc., and 60,000 *tūmāns* remitted to the cultivators because of destruction by locusts, leaving a balance of 233,000 *tūmāns* (some £116,500) for remission to the central treasury.[30] Seen in relation to the revenue of the province of Fārs, the sum borrowed by Ḥusayn Khān from Ḥājjī ʿAbd al-Karīm was of considerable magnitude.

Ḥājjī ʿAbd al-Karīm also claimed interest from Ḥusayn Khān on the money which he was owed for the period after the payment of the debt had fallen due. The rate of interest agreed upon by the two parties was 25 per cent per annum. The rate was high but in view of the insecurity of tenure of provincial governors and the fluctuations in provincial revenues, merchants demanded high rates of interest when lending money in this way. Merchants in transactions between themselves usually paid only 12 per cent. In 1844 Muḥammad Shāh had issued a farman prohibiting rates of interest in excess of 12 per cent, but this prohibition was ineffective. It was not even observed by the officials of the state, as shown by some of the bonds guaranteed by Ḥājjī Mīrzā Āqāsī, which specifically mentioned that the rate of interest in the event of a failure to pay by the date stipulated should be at 25 per cent. Most of the bonds were, moreover registered in the *dīvān-khāneh*, which was tantamount to an official recognition of the rate of interest. Jewels to the amount of about 23,000 *tūmāns* were deposited by Ḥusayn Khān with Ḥājjī ʿAbd al-Karīm and were forfeited according to the terms of the bond when Ḥusayn Khān failed to repay the loan.

One of Ḥājjī ʿAbd al-Karīm's difficulties in obtaining repayment was that it was impossible for Ḥusayn Khān to fulfil his engagements from his private funds, since nearly all his property had vanished in bribes, payments and advances on account of the revenue of his governorate to Ḥājjī Mīrzā Āqāsī. He had claims to the amount of 300,000–400,000 *tūmāns* on the Persian government, or on the taxpayers in Fārs, the revenues of the province having been paid by him in advance to the Shah, but these he appears to have been unable to collect.

Ḥājjī ʿAbd al-Karīm finally had recourse to Sheil for official intervention. The latter assumed the guarantee given by Ḥājjī Mīrzā Āqāsī to be official and accordingly demanded payment from the Persian government, since it had confiscated his large private fortune when he had fallen from power on the death of Muḥammad Shāh.

Four months after his return from Shīrāz, Ḥusayn Khān, while admitting the validity of the bonds in the possession of Ḥājjī ʿAbd al-Karīm, attempted to annul their validity by producing two papers in the writing of a clerk of Ḥājjī ʿAbd al-Karīm and allegedly sealed by the latter. One was to the effect that in the event of Ḥusayn Khān's removal from the government of Fārs he would not be responsible for transactions in *barāts* (government bills). Ḥājjī ʿAbd al-Karīm's letter to Ḥusayn Khān quoted above also makes a statement of this kind. The second paper gave a detailed account of the purchase of a large quantity of *barāts*. Ḥājjī ʿAbd al-Karīm denied the authenticity of both documents. Ḥusayn Khān also obtained testimony from a number of witnesses that most of his dealings with Ḥājjī ʿAbd al-Karīm were in *barāts*. The *imām jumʿeh* of Tehran, presumably on the basis of these documents, issued a decree in Ḥusayn Khān's favour, despite the fact that the bonds held by Ḥājjī ʿAbd al-Karīm had been legalized in the presence of the *imām jumʿeh* and by his seal and that he had issued a number of decrees in favour of Ḥājjī ʿAbd al-Karīm's claims.

Sheil questioned the validity of these documents. Pointing out that it was notoriously easy to obtain false evidence, especially in a case in which the government was interested, he expressed the view that Ḥusayn Khān's silence until some four months had passed after his return to Tehran threw some doubt on the validity of the two letters, and added that there was no apparent reason why Ḥājjī ʿAbd al-Karīm should have compromised himself by writing such documents. Further, the clerk who had written the documents had been seduced by Ḥusayn Khān in or about April 1851 from Ḥajjī ʿAbd al-Karīm's service by presents and the promise of larger pay. This same clerk had earlier declared to several persons that he had no recollection of having written a document containing details of the *barāts* purchased, and that such a document, if it existed, must be false.

Ḥusayn Khān, who disputed Ḥājjī ʿAbd al-Karīm's claims in general, also made three specific objections. First he denounced the rate of interest of 25 per cent as being unjust. Sheil when reporting this, pointed out that no one would have lent money to Ḥusayn Khān on lower terms, or indeed on any terms at all. Secondly Ḥusayn Khān alleged that the price of the land sold to him as part of the transaction was exorbitant. Sheil, commenting on this, stated that he believed there was great truth in this assertion, but that Ḥājjī ʿAbd al-Karīm was a trader whose business was gain, and that Ḥusayn Khān had entered into the transaction with his eyes open: Ḥusayn Khān had been reckless and without other resources; and the other had taken the fullest advantage of his extravagance and of the impossibility of his getting money elsewhere or on other terms. Ḥusayn Khān was ready, Sheil reported, to compromise for the land at a just valuation and something more. Thirdly,

Ḥusayn Khān claimed that the transactions in *barāts* were more extensive than Ḥājjī ʿAbd al-Karīm admitted and brought evidence, genuine or not, to prove the purchase of *barāts* and was prepared to bring forward persons from whom the purchases were made. Sheil thought that Ḥājjī ʿAbd al-Karīm's engagement in these speculations had probably been extensive.

When reporting the case to Palmerston in October 1851 Sheil had stated that the first point to be settled was Ḥājjī ʿAbd al-Karīm's nationality. He thought that the Persian government would not recede from its refusal to recognize Ḥājjī ʿAbd al-Karīm's rights as a British subject without a positive and peremptory declaration that the British government would not brook evasion on this point. Unless a member of the mission were to appear at court according to treaty to sustain his rights as a British subject, Sheil thought that he would not enjoy the remotest chance of justice, a view apparently shared by Ḥājjī ʿAbd al-Karīm. The second point to be settled was would the British government consider that the guarantee given by Ḥājjī Mīrzā Āqāsī imposed on the existing government the obligation of discharging responsibilities incurred by him. The property of Ḥājjī Mīrzā Āqāsī (which had been confiscated by the government) was adequate for the liquidation of the claim in his name.

In his report Sheil pointed out that following the practice established by the Russo-Persian commercial agreement concluded under the Treaty of Turkomanchay, the proper course would have been to appeal to the court of justice and the authorities of the religious law and such had been his practice on other occasions of claims between British and Persian subjects. But in this case he was puzzled as to how best to proceed, since he felt it would be a mockery to appeal to the court of justice, since its chief had accompanied Ḥusayn Khān to the house of one of the principal ʿ*ulamā*ʾ and enjoined him to issue judgement against Ḥājjī ʿAbd al-Karīm without hearing the latter's case. In respect of the bonds for which the Persian government was responsible, Sheil recommended that they should be accepted as genuine and their full amount be made claimable, setting against them whatever sums for which Ḥusayn Khān could produce receipts from Ḥājjī ʿAbd al-Karīm or his agents in part payment. With respect to Ḥājjī ʿAbd al-Karīm's other claims, for which the Persian government was not accountable, Sheil saw no alternative but to appeal to the court of justice and the religious law, since this procedure was clearly laid down by treaty. But he thought Ḥājjī ʿAbd al-Karīm ran a great risk of being defeated without any consideration of right.

Sheil also thought that the total amount to be exacted ought to be reconsidered. To offer a compromise would, in his opinion, weaken the case; but to exact the payment of the entire sum would be to support usury and gain acquired by equivocal means. He suggested, therefore, that the entire sum be demanded, but when the matter was on the point of adjustment, that the interest could be reduced to 12 per cent and an allowance be made such as circumstances seemed to justify.[31]

In answer to this despatch Palmerston stated that it was objectionable to encourage British subjects in so corrupt a country as Persia to enter into complicated pecuniary transactions with local people and to expect the British government to step in and help them in their difficulties. Sheil was authorized to give his good offices in bringing about a compromise,[32] but Ḥājjī ʿAbd al-Karīm's claim was not to be supported by the British government since it was contracted before Ḥājjī ʿAbd al-Karīm became a British subject. Sheil, however, did not reveal this decision to the Persian government because he felt it would have deprived Ḥājjī ʿAbd al-Karīm of all chance of compromising with Ḥusayn Khān.[33]

In October 1852 Sheil reported that Ḥājjī ʿAbd al-Karīm had lately engaged in a commercial transaction by which a Persian merchant became his debtor for a small sum. The latter, failing to discharge his obligations, Sheil requested the minister of foreign affairs to send the case before a Persian court of law. His request was refused on the alleged grounds that Ḥājjī ʿAbd al-Karīm was a Persian subject and that Sheil therefore had no right to interfere.[34]

On 28 February 1853 Mīrzā Āqā Khān Nūrī, who had succeeded the Amīr Niẓām as *ṣadr-i aʿẓam* in November 1851, told Sheil that the Persian government could accept Ḥājjī ʿAbd al-Karīm's British nationality provided all previous claims and commercial transactions were to be considered as between Persian subjects and to be adjusted in the religious courts without the intervention of the British mission. Ḥājjī ʿAbd al-Karīm objected on the grounds that this would give him no chance of justice, or of recovery of other large claims on private individuals which he had contracted before the conquest of Sind. Sheil, having requested further instructions, then went home on sick leave after presenting W. Taylour Thomson as chargé d'affaires on 28 February 1853.[35] Thomson was in due course instructed to insist on the nationality of Ḥājjī ʿAbd al-Karīm as a British subject.[36] Later that year, Shafīʿ Khān, the Persian minister in London, made representations to Clarendon (who had become foreign secretary on 21 February 1853) on the subject of Ḥājjī ʿAbd al-Karīm, claiming that he was a Persian subject.[37]

A settlement of Ḥājjī ʿAbd al-Karīm's case was made more difficult by the deterioration, which had by this time taken place in Anglo-Persian relations, mainly over Herat.[38] In the autumn of 1853 further communications took place between Thomson and the Persian government. The latter continued to deny Ḥājjī ʿAbd al-Karīm's British nationality and refused him access to the courts except as a Persian subject. Finally, at Ḥājjī ʿAbd al-Karīm's request, Thomson brought up one of his many claims, that against Fatḥullāh Mīrzā, father of one of the Shah's chief wives.

Ḥājjī ʿAbd al-Karīm had a large house and garden in Tehran. The house was rented and occupied by Fatḥullāh Mīrzā, but the garden was retained and cultivated by Ḥājjī ʿAbd al-Karīm, and the gardener hired and paid by him. Fatḥullāh Mīrzā occasionally received visitors in the garden. The lease for the house had expired in 1851. Ḥājjī ʿAbd al-Karīm had not at first pressed for Fatḥullāh Mīrzā's removal, but eventually he invited him to renew the lease or quit the premises. Fatḥullāh Mīrzā said he would go, but asked for a few days' delay. This was granted. Later he openly announced that he would not pay rent, renew his lease, or quit. Repeated applications by the mission that Ḥājjī ʿAbd al-Karīm's house be restored to him were unavailing. Finally Thomson sent two of his servants in company with one of Hājjī ʿAbd al-Karīm's men with a private note to Fatḥullāh Mīrzā requesting him to cause the house to be evacuated. Thomson's servants had orders to remain in the garden (to which Fatḥullāh Mīrzā had no claim).

Thomson also wrote to Mīrzā Āqā Khān Nūrī, the *ṣadr-i aʿẓam*, telling him what he intended to do. On receiving this note the *ṣadr-i aʿẓam* sent for Mīrzā Ḥusayn Qulī, the Persian secretary to the mission, and in the presence of a number of persons used threatening language. On the following day, 16 October 1853, Thomson's servants and Ḥājjī ʿAbd al-Karīm's man were expelled from the garden by a crowd of women, an event calculated to bring discredit upon the mission. On the previous day the people from the district had repeatedly visited the premises and sought altercation with Thomson's servants. Finally, on the morning of 16 October, 300 women armed with sticks, stones and bricks, accompanied by a man belonging to the *kalāntar* (the headman of the locality), Fatḥullāh Mīrzā's head groom, *mīrẓā*, and one of his eunuchs, rushed into the garden at the instigation of the *kalāntar* and, abetted by some 2,000 persons of the locality, beat the mission servants and turned them out of the garden. Throughout the episode two of the *kalāntar's* men were present, ostensibly as spectators, but they had with them a body of men who, if Thomson's men offered resistance, were to come in under the pretext of protecting the women.

Thomson demanded as reparation that the mission servants should be taken back by the government to the garden from which they had been expelled; that the persons who were the ostensible agents in instigating the women and in assembling them from the various *ḥarams* in the neighbourhood should be punished where the offence had been committed, that the minister for foreign affairs should call on Thomson and apologize on behalf of the government, and that an agreement should be made for the settlement of Ḥājjī ʿAbd al-Karīm's other claims in the courts of law, according to established practice, in the presence of a person deputed from the mission.

The *ṣadr-i aʿẓam* in his reply to this, attempted to introduce the question of ʿAbbās Mīrzā, the Shah's half-brother.[39] Thomson was privately informed that the Shah was inclined to agree to the demands of Ḥājjī ʿAbd al-Karīm if by doing so an arrangement could be made by which he could regain possession of ʿAbbās Mīrzā.

Thomson refused to agree to the introduction of the case of ʿAbbās Mīrzā into the dispute over Ḥājjī ʿAbd al-Karīm. Eventually, having exhausted every argument and been constantly met with evasive replies, Thomson announced that unless satisfaction was accorded in the matter of Ḥājjī ʿAbd al-Karīm, he had no resource but the final one of suspending his diplomatic relations. This produced the desired effect. Farrukh Khān, who later became Persian ambassador to France, and was in 1852 one of the chief men at court and confidential adviser to the *ṣadr-i aʿẓam*, called on Thomson and announced 'officially and in the most formal manner' that Thomson's demand had been acceded to with the exception of the demand for the punishment of Fatḥullāh Mīrzā's servants, and this had been rejected only because Fatḥullāh Mīrzā was a near relative of the Shah. Thomson agreed to this exception. A letter was then sent to Thomson stating that his servants would be allowed to go to the garden for one night, and that the minister for foreign affairs, Mīrzā Saʿīd (who had taken office in February 1852) would call upon him; but only vague references were made to Ḥājjī ʿAbd al-Karīm's claims. Thomson accordingly repeated his former demands and reiterated his intention to suspend diplomatic relations if satisfaction was not given.

Prior to the appearance of Farrukh Khān on the scene, it appeared that the Persian government had obtained its counsels from the Russian mission. Subsequently their communications were carried on ostensibly through the Ottoman ambassador, and with this the determination of the Persian government to resist giving satisfaction seemed to be strengthened. Russo-

Turkish relations were at that time in a critical condition. Russia was pressing Persia to join her against Turkey in the event of hostilities breaking out, and therefore had no interest in encouraging a conflict between Persia and Britain, whereas Turkey may well have taken the view that if Persia was occupied in a dispute with Britain she would be less likely to engage in war against Turkey.

Thomson was unable to obtain satisfaction; on 4 November 1853 he announced that he would suspend diplomatic relations.[40] Sheil in a memorandum on Thomson's dispute with the Persian government, dated 26 December 1853, expressed the view that Thomson had acted with moderation, and that the affront and violence offered had been premeditated and had left no choice to Thomson, but to break off relations. 'It is only by its character and reputation', he wrote, 'that the mission can hold its ground against the *material* preponderance of Russia.' He thought an apology should have been requested from the *ṣadr-i aʿẓam* rather than the minister for foreign affairs and that the *kalāntar* (whose instigation of the tumult recalled the Griboedov affair)[41] should be exiled from Tehran for a period. But he recommended that Thomson should be given some latitude to reduce his demands if he found it would conduce to render Persia less subservient to Russian designs with regard to Turkey.[42]

Thomson's action was approved and Clarendon stated in a despatch dated 17 January 1854 that the British government were prepared to take the strongest measures for obtaining from the Persian government an even greater amount of reparation than demanded by him. Thomson was to make this known to the Persian government in the event of Russian influence again becoming paramount, and 'inducing that government to offer any fresh affront to the British mission'.[43]

Almost immediately after this announcement that he would suspend relations, Thomson received a letter from the *ṣadr-i aʿẓam* and an autograph note from the Shah. The Persian government apparently regretted the course it had adopted but did not admit that the events of which Thomson had complained were established. Mīrzā Saʿīd Khān was to apologize and the *kalāntar* was ordered to be the host of Thomson's servants in the garden for one night. Thomson regarded this as absurd. Meanwhile talk was heard of a proposal that the Shah should send an envoy to settle the case in London.[44]

On 19 November an article was published in the *Tehran Gazette* stating the Persian case with regard to Ḥājjī ʿAbd al-Karīm and regretting Thomson's decision to lower his flag. It stated that Ḥājjī ʿAbd al-Karīm, a native of Qandahar and a well-known merchant in Tehran, had always been considered by the Persian government as a Persian subject. For many years he had been engaged in agricultural pursuits and possessed property, land and houses, etc., which were estimated to be worth 100,000 *tūmāns*. The article alleged that this showed that he was a Persian subject because the right of possessing landed property was denied to foreigners. No question as to his nationality had arisen during the reigns of Fatḥ ʿAlī Shāh and Muḥammad Shāh. During the ministry of Ḥājjī Mīrzā Āqāsī he had been imprisoned and chastised on some account and the British minister had taken no notice and had not raised any question of the right to protect him. Recently the British had claimed that he was a British subject. This the Persian government denied, but Thomson had nevertheless interfered to settle some of his affairs as if he was a British subject.[45]

War had meanwhile broken out between Russia and Turkey. Dolgorouky, the Russian minister, announcing this to the Shah in a private audience said that the Russian emperor would regard the Shah as his enemy if he withheld cooperation and did not make a strong military demonstration against Turkey in Āẕarbāyjān and Kirmānshāh. Orders were given to assemble troops.[46] The Turkish ambassador requested an explanation of this action and when he received an unsatisfactory answer threatened to withdraw.[47] On 20 November Thomson received a private message from the *ṣadr-i aʿẓam* to the effect that the Shah would grant all Thomson's demands with regard to Ḥājjī ʿAbd al-Karīm and that he hoped Thomson would exert all his efforts, to induce the Turkish ambassador not to leave. This Thomson did.[48]

On the following day Thomson reported that Ḥājjī ʿAbd al-Karīm had been invited with some of his relatives to dine with the *imām jumʿeh* of Tehran, who recommended him strongly to renounce his British nationality, assuring him that his pecuniary claims would be settled if he did so. When this had no effect, the *imām* assumed a different tone and talked of the unlimited power of the Shah, alleging that he had been deeply offended and warning Ḥājjī ʿAbd al-Karīm of the risks he ran and that he and all his family might be extirpated. Ḥājjī ʿAbd al-Karīm replied that this made him all the more determined to retain British nationality. The following evening he dined with the deputy-governor of Tehran, the only other guest being to his surprise the *ṣadr-i aʿẓam*. He, too, sought to persuade Ḥājjī ʿAbd al-Karīm with alluring promises to declare himself a Persian subject. Ḥājjī ʿAbd al-Karīm refused.[49]

Three days later on 23 November, the Persian government wrote to

Thomson accepting all his demands with regard to Ḥājjī ʿAbd al-Karīm. This letter stated that from the date of the letter they would recognize Ḥājjī ʿAbd al-Karīm as a dependant of the English government and treat him in the same way as other dependants of the British government were treated. Thomson thereupon resumed diplomatic relations on the assumption that nothing in this would prejudice the distinct acceptance of the demands for reparation.[50] Mīrzā Saʿīd Khān called on Thomson on 26 November and apologized with regard to the affair of Ḥājjī ʿAbd al-Karīm. The persons whose punishment had been claimed for instigating the attack on Thomson's servants were meanwhile sent to the house occupied by Fatḥullāh Mīrzā for Thomson to decide what should be done with them. He did not press for their punishment.[51]

Mr Hector, a British merchant established in Baghdad, commenting on the settlement of the quarrel wrote in a private letter dated December 1853,

> 'The quarrel between Mr Thomson and the Persian government has been arranged by the Persians having agreed to the whole of his demands . . . the cause of England generally has been injured by these discussions, to an extent that it will not be overcome speedily – in fact if England were hated before, she is detested now, as well she may be, considering the conduct of British agents here in the last few years – we owe the arrangement of this quarrel to the skill and ability of the Turkish ambassador – had it not been for him the British Mission would have now been on the way out of Persia.'[52]

Hector, however, was probably not an impartial witness: he had had a bitter quarrel with Thomson because he had been refused use of the mission courier.[53]

The case of Ḥājjī Mīrzā ʿAbd al-Karīm, however, was not yet over. Once more it became caught up in wider political issues. Thomson had been ordered to report at once in the event of the Persian government evincing any disposition to evade giving the reparation demanded in the case of Ḥājjī ʿAbd al-Karīm, or if they persisted in carrying on intrigues in or interfering with the states of Afghanistan, or showed any disposition to side with Russia in the war with Turkey, or to add to the embarrassments of the Porte by menaces on the frontier.[54]

Persia's attitude towards Russia had meanwhile hardened. On 26 January 1854 there was an announcement in the *Tehran Gazette* of Persia's intention to pursue neutrality in the event of war between Britain and Russia. When war broke out the British authorities continued to urge neutrality upon the Persian government. Persian demands made later in the year for an assurance from Britain in the event of a Russian attack met with no definite response except an expression of friendly sentiments, and when the Shah expressed his wish to join the allies against Russia, he was advised to observe complete neutrality. By the autumn, there had been a rapprochement with Russia and a deterioration in Anglo-Russian relations.[55] Quarrels were picked over a number of minor incidents, some of which Thomson considered to be counter blows for the reparation which had been promised in the affair of Ḥājjī ʿAbd al-Karīm.[56]

When Charles Murray, the new minister, arrived in Tehran in April 1855 considerable disappointment and dissatisfaction were shown by Persia that Britain was not prepared to make a clearer and more decisive statement with regard to the future security of Persia.[57] This dissatisfaction was reinforced by the signature of the Treaty of Peshawar with Dost Muḥammad Khān on 30 March 1855. This treaty marked a new phase in British policy for the defence of India and adversely affected Anglo-Persian relations because of its intention to strengthen Afghanistan and the distrust which this policy indicated of Persian good faith.

Meanwhile Ḥājjī ʿAbd al-Karīm's claims remained outstanding. Ḥājjī ʿAbd al-Karīm and Ḥusayn Khān both made frequent representations to Murray and Stevens for a settlement of their claims. While Ḥusayn Khān expressed his readiness to agree to any mode of settlement proposed by Murray, Ḥājjī ʿAbd al-Karīm, according to Murray, 'constantly made every sort of futile objection to my suggestions'. Murray, who had had no experience of Persia, was unwilling to make allowances for differences in custom, and was provoked by Ḥājjī ʿAbd al-Karīm's behaviour. Eventually he decided that the only way of obtaining a just and speedy settlement was to submit the affair to the decision of a British consular court assisted by assessors, three to be selected by each claimant. It was agreed that there should be present at the investigation one attaché of the British mission, one member of the French mission, and one person selected by the Persian government. According to Murray's account Ḥusayn Khān and Ḥājjī ʿAbd al-Karīm both agreed to accept the decision of this mixed court.[58] Sheil, whose views were asked on the case when it came up again in 1857, pointed out that it was an extremely complicated case involving large sums of money, and that it ought not to be left to a consular court from which there was no appeal,[59] but ought to be adjourned until the mission returned to Tehran (it had been withdrawn in December 1855, see below).

Ḥājjī ʿAbd al-Karīm clearly had no confidence in the court.[60] When the time came for it to sit he asked that the case might be deferred, first on the plea of illness, and then owing to the difficulty of selecting assessors in Muḥarram[61]; he then objected to his being confined to the selection of three assessors on the grounds that Ḥusayn Khān might bribe them, and then begged deferment because of an outbreak of cholera. Finally, finding that he could not avoid the meeting, he delivered a paper to the Persian government declaring that he was not a native of Shikarpur and acknowledging himself to be a Persian subject.[62]

Anglo-Persian relations had by this time become strained, and Ḥājjī ʿAbd al-Karīm probably realized that there was a strong likelihood of a rupture taking place. The annoyance of the Persian government against Britain had been mounting for some time. They still hoped to reincorporate Herat into the Persian dominions. The internecine strife prevailing in Afghanistan encouraged them in this design, as also did a belief held by some Persian officials that the population of India would rise against Britain if a Persian army appeared at Jalālābād. In the autumn of 1855 Anglo-Persian relations became critical. The immediate cause was the affair of Hāshim Khān, who had been appointed first secretary to the British mission in Tehran in June 1854. The Persian government had refused to receive him on the pretext that he had not been formally discharged from Persian service. Accordingly another Persian was named in his stead. Later Murray told the Persian government that Hāshim Khān would be sent to Shīrāz as British agent as soon as he had received a formal discharge from the Persian government. On 5 November 1855 Mīrzā Āqā Khān Nūrī informed Murray that the Persian government would seize Hāshim Khān if he set out for Shīrāz, and proceeded to seize his wife, who was a member of the Qājār family. Persian sources meanwhile alleged that Murray had employed Hāshim Khān because he had an intrigue with the latter's wife, and a scurrilous campaign began against him. Murray then threatened to strike his flag if Hāshim Khān's wife was not immediately released. She was not set free and on 5 December 1855 Murray withdrew the mission from Tehran.[63]

A few days before the mission left Tehran Ḥājjī ʿAbd al-Karīm petitioned the Shah to consider him a Persian subject. The Shah agreed and issued orders that Ḥājjī ʿAbd al-Karīm's affairs should in future be entrusted to the management of Niẓām al-Mulk, Mīrzā Āqā Khān Nūrī's son. After the arrangement was made nobody in Tehran, according to Stevens, was 'more lavish in his abuse of the British Government and its agents' than Ḥājjī ʿAbd al-Karīm.[64]

Murray, who was put out by Ḥājjī ʿAbd al-Karīm's action, asked for instructions, and expressed the view that he ought no longer to be given protection. The matter was, however, complicated by the fact that Ḥājjī ʿAbd al-ʿAẓīm, Ḥājjī ʿAbd al-Karīm's brother, and his nephew, who were in Tehran, disclaimed all participation in Ḥājjī ʿAbd al-Karīm's conduct and claimed the continuance of protection. Murray, while not overlooking the possibility that they and Ḥājjī ʿAbd al-Karīm might have come to some secret understanding whereby the latter might make over to his brother and nephew his difficult claims on Persian subjects and in return charge himself with their doubtful claims which the mission could not assist in recovering, considered that they were entitled to protection.[65] Added urgency was given to the case by the fact that Ḥājjī ʿAbd al-Karīm, now in his eighties, was in failing health, and that in the event of his death disputes were likely to arise among his children and the members of his family over the succession to his property.

A Persian expedition had meanwhile proceeded against Herat. Negotiations between the British and Persian authorities proved fruitless, and on 22 September 1856 Clarendon wrote to Stevens instructing the withdrawal of British consuls from Tehran and Tabrīz. On 1 November, Canning, the governor-general of India, declared war on Persia. Ḥājjī ʿAbd al-ʿAẓīm and his son, having refused to give a paper renouncing British protection, were expelled from Persia with other British subjects and went to Baghdad.[66]

Murray, who had also withdrawn to Baghdad, asked for instructions as to whether he was to interfere in the administration of Ḥājjī ʿAbd al-Karīm's estate in the event of his death.[67] The case was duly considered in London by the Foreign Office and the India Board. On 4 March 1857 peace between Britain and Persia was concluded and the mission returned to Tehran on 18 July; Ḥājjī ʿAbd al-ʿAẓīm and his son also returned to Tehran. On 31 October 1857, Clarendon informed Murray that he might extend British protection temporarily to the children and relatives of Ḥājjī ʿAbd al-Karīm.[68]

On 12 April 1858 Ḥājjī ʿAbd al-Karīm died. Correspondence passed between Stevens and the Persian foreign minister regarding his affairs. According to the written testimony of nearly all his relatives, he appointed, immediately before his death, his brother, Ḥājjī ʿAbd al-ʿAẓīm, as administrator of his estate, enjoining him to discharge in the first place all the pecuniary obligations connected with the religious rites observed in the country on death, and willing one-third of the residue of the property to be expended for religious purposes under the supervision of four other persons, one of whom was Ḥājjī Shaykh Murtaẓā (who resided in Najaf).

The remaining two-thirds were to be divided among his heirs according to the provisions of the *sharīʿa*. His estate, consisting of land, jewels, and cash, was estimated by some at a million sterling and by others at a still higher figure.[69] Ḥājjī ʿAbd al-ʿAẓīm was appointed guardian of such of the heirs as might not have attained their majority.[70]

Ḥājjī ʿAbd al-ʿAẓīm and most of the heirs applied to Stevens both before and after Ḥājjī ʿAbd al-Karīm's death, to lend his official assistance, the first to enable him to carry out the provisions of the will, and the latter to secure them from being defrauded of their rights by the arbitrary interference of Mīrzā Āqā Khān Nūrī, the *ṣadr-i aʿẓam*, of whose intentions to get possession of the property they entertained well-founded fears. Mīrzā Ghulām Ḥusayn induced Stevens to invite the cooperation of the Persian authorities and suggested that their joint seals should be placed upon the property until the necessary steps were adopted for its division. The Persian ministers, however, denied Steven's right to interfere.

When the *kalāntar*, Muḥammad Khān, announced the death of Ḥājjī ʿAbd al-Karīm to Mīrzā Āqā Khān Nūrī, the latter ordered him to put a watch on the premises and property; and Nawrūz ʿAlī Khān, a servant of Niẓām al-Mulk, Mīrzā Āqā Khān Nūrī's son, was placed in the house. On the following day Muḥammad Khān and two other men were sent by Mīrzā Āqā Khān Nūrī to Ḥājjī ʿAbd al-Karīm's family with promises of protection, assistance, and favours from the Shah provided they would object to the interference of the English and to the appointment of Ḥājjī ʿAbd al-ʿAẓīm as executor. At the same time a number of servants belonging to Niẓām al-Mulk and the heir apparent and a guard of soldiers were placed on the premises. An offer of Mīrzā Āqā Khān Nūrī to send 500 *tūmāns* for the funeral expenses was refused.

On 14 April, Muḥammad Khān, acting on behalf of the Mīrzā Āqā Khān Nūrī, opposed the application of Mīrzā Āqā Jān, Ḥājjī ʿAbd al-ʿAẓīm's son to the *mujtahid*, Ḥājjī Mīrzā Muḥammad, for a decree declaring the authenticity of the will. When the *mujtahid* offered some objection, Muḥammad Khān hinted at his expulsion from Tehran. The decree was withheld. The *mullā*, Zayn al-ʿĀbidīn, who had drawn up the will and certified its authenticity, was taken by night to the house of Mīrzā Raḥīm, a nephew of Mīrzā Āqā Khān Nūrī, and threatened with violence unless he denied the authenticity of the will. On refusing to do so his turban was removed and put round his neck and, after being nearly strangled, he gave the required denial. In the course of the night a black slave belonging to one of Ḥājjī ʿAbd al-Karīm's sons, who had been left to guard a portion of the premises, was found murdered. Muḥammad Khān ordered his owner to sign a document saying he had died a natural death. He refused, but later a declaration to this effect was given by Mīrzā Ghulām Ḥusayn. Meanwhile an order was issued to the '*ulamā*' not to grant, on pain of punishment, any document to Ḥājjī 'Abd al-'Aẓīm authenticating the will. Niẓām al-Mulk also obtained a document from Ghulām Ḥusayn to the effect that if he were made administrator of the estate he would give a sixth of the property to Mīrzā Āqā Khān Nūrī and 10,000 *tūmāns* to Niẓām al-Mulk.

On 16 April Mīrzā Āqā Khān Nūrī ordered the *mujtahid*, Shaykh 'Abd al-Raḥīm, to issue a *fatwā* annulling the appointment of Ḥājjī 'Abd al-'Aẓīm as executor of the will on the grounds of his being under British protection and therefore an infidel incapacitated from administering the state of a Muslim. The *fatwā* was promised but not given. Two days later, a *ghulām* and a *farrāsh* from the British mission were placed on the premises at the request of the executor and the heirs. Ghulām Ḥusayn gave notice of this to Mīrzā Āqā Khān Nūrī, who had them ejected. On the following day Shaykh 'Abd al-Raḥīm was taken before Mīrzā Āqā Khān and again ordered to issue a decree. He temporized. On 24 April Mīrzā Āqā Khān Nūrī drew up a document, to be signed by the '*ulamā*', annulling the appointment of Ḥājjī 'Abd al-'Aẓīm on the grounds of his connection with the English and declaring that since Ghulām Ḥusayn was unfit to act as administrator of the estate, the '*ulamā*' had delegated the office to Mīrzā Āqā Khān Nūrī, his two sons, Niẓām al-Mulk and Mīrzā Dā'ūd Khān, and his scribe, Mīrzā Zamān. The Shah meanwhile sent a message to the '*ulamā*' warning them not to act contrary to the wishes of Mīrzā Āqā Khān Nūrī. The '*ulamā*' thereupon held a meeting and decided not to sign such a document unless under positive compulsion. Mīrzā Āqā Khān Nūrī meanwhile issued orders to the inhabitants of the late Ḥājjī 'Abd al-Kārīm's villages, forbidding them to pay the revenues to Ḥājjī 'Abd al-'Aẓīm. On the 25 April he caused Ḥājjī 'Abd al-'Aẓīm to be informed that the Persian government would withdraw all opposition in the matter, provided he signed a paper disclaiming for himself and all his relatives all future connection with the British government.[71]

Further correspondence on the case of Ḥājjī 'Abd al-Karīm and his heirs of a somewhat testy nature ensued between Murray and Mīrzā Āqā Khān Nūrī.[72] Meanwhile the opinion of H.M. Advocate Attorney and Solicitors General was taken and as a result Murray was instructed to desist from contending that Ḥājjī 'Abd al-Karīm was entitled on his death to British protection or that his succession was to be considered a British succession.

So far as Ḥājjī ʿAbd al-Karīm's children and other family were concerned, each case for British protection was to be decided on its merits.[73]

On 30 August 1858, Mīrzā Āqā Khān Nūrī fell from office and Murray, while he avoided in accordance with his instructions all official discussion with the Persian government on the case of Ḥājjī ʿAbd al-Karīm, had hopes that an arrangement might be reached between the administrator of his estate and the Persian government, who, he thought, would probably be satisfied with a douceur less heavy than that which the former *ṣadr-i aʿẓam* would have insisted upon.[74] Murray now urged the view that the British government was bound to protect the right of the heirs of Ḥājjī ʿAbd al-Karīm against the exploitation meditated by the Persian government, and asked for the case to be reconsidered.

In October 1858 Murray left Tehran. Doria, who became chargé d'affaires, reported on 31 December that no settlement had been reached and asked for instructions.[75] Stevens, who had been instructed by Murray to grant protection to those members of Ḥājjī ʿAbd al-Karīm's family who had previously enjoyed it and to avoid discussion with the Persian government, also reported on the same date that his efforts to effect an amicable settlement had been fruitless and that the affair had led to repeated squabbles with the Persian authorities, who contended that they had the right to act without reference to the British consulate. Stevens also reported that some of Ḥājjī ʿAbd al-Karīm's heirs had signed documents declaring themselves Persian subjects, while others had not renounced British protection.[76]

The affair now became still more complicated by the proceedings of the interested parties. Ghulām Ḥusayn withdrew his contestation of Ḥājjī ʿAbd al-ʿAẓīm's claim to be the executor of the will in exchange for a document by which Ḥājjī ʿAbd al-ʿAẓīm engaged not to sue Ghulām Ḥusayn for the large amount of money and valuables which he was alleged to have stolen to the detriment of his brothers and sisters. The latter petitioned the Shah against this transaction and as a precautionary measure the Shah ordered seals to be placed on the property and premises concerned.

Stevens meanwhile agreed to a proposal made through the minister for foreign affairs that since all parties to the disputed succession were Muslims the case should be referred to the religious courts without the interference of the consulate. He also withdrew protection from Ḥājjī ʿAbd al-ʿAẓīm on the grounds that he could not be protected in the dispute without interference in the succession of Ḥājjī ʿAbd al-Karīm, which had been distinctly forbidden by the Foreign Office. Ḥājjī ʿAbd al-ʿAẓīm appealed against this decision to Doria, while Ghulām Ḥusayn took refuge in the shrine at Shāh ʿAbd al-ʿAẓīm.[77]

Reporting the proposal from the ministry for foreign affairs on 15 January 1859, Stevens recalled the views expressed earlier by Murray, Clarendon and others that interference was undesirable, and alleged that Ḥājjī ʿAbd al-Karīm was a notorious rogue, who had amassed his wealth by dishonest means. He declared that an examination of his books would show that many of the claims he preferred against Persian subjects, 'nearly all of whom were members of the royal family', were unjust or fictitious. As for Ḥājjī ʿAbd al-ʿAẓīm, Stevens asserted that he was less disreputable than his brother and that he had refused to forgo British protection to which the family had been admitted in 1849. When he and his son had been expelled from Persia on the outbreak of the Anglo-Persian war, their commercial affairs had been interrupted, and their house in Tehran plundered; people owing them money had been ordered by Mīrzā Āqā Khān Nūrī not to pay, and the lands belonging to them seized and not returned. Stevens hoped that instructions would be issued to the commissioners to be appointed for the settlement of the pecuniary claims of British subjects on the Persian government, under Article 11 of the treaty concluded after the Anglo-Persian war, stating that they should insist on their claims being settled,[78] apart from those arising out of Ḥājjī ʿAbd al-ʿAẓīm's connection with his late brother's will.

Doria, who had been unaware of Steven's intention to withdraw protection, disapproved of his action. He expressed the view that if the decision to deprive Hājjī ʿAbd al-Karīm's family of British protection was to be carried out it should have been done with reference to the decision of the crown lawyers. This would have avoided the reports current in the capital that were calculated to lower the British name and influence for having withdrawn at the last minute 'without any ostensible reason, at least made known to the public, our protection from persons in whose cause the British flag had been once hauled down to obtain redress for them from the Persian government'.[79]

Stevens finally reported on 19 January 1859 that since he had withdrawn his interference the heirs of Ḥājjī ʿAbd al-Karīm were gradually settling their disputes, and the question which existed between some of them and the Shah, who was to receive a certain sum of money, was also being settled. The bulk of the property was to be divided between the heirs in conformity with Muslim law under the supervision of an employee of the Persian ministry for foreign affairs and the religious authorities in Tehran.[80]

Thus ended a long and complicated case. It had led to much acrimonious discussion between the Persian and British governments and at one point caused the British minister to haul down his flag. The case, when it was fought, turned out to be weak, and the transactions of those for whom the right of British protection was claimed, although sanctioned by the participation of the highest in the land, were somewhat shady. But it was not upon the nature of these actions that the case turned, but upon the right of the British mission to protect merchants who claimed British nationality. Its main interest lies in the information which it gives concerning contemporary methods of financing the state and the difficulties faced by the merchant in the conduct of his business. In the nineteenth century the activities of the state and its institutions were gradually extending into new fields, but new methods of financing the state had not yet been devised. Its operations were still largely financed indirectly; and the state depended to a large extent upon the merchant for the provision of funds. The profits made by the merchants, in which the authorities of the state shared, were high; so also were the risks they ran. The transactions in which they engaged, with the connivance of the authorities of the state, were often of a somewhat curious, if not dubious, nature.

The case also illustrates how the position of the merchant was affected by Persia's foreign relations. The question of the nationality of merchants was not of vital importance in the mediaeval Persian state. Privileges were granted from time to time to foreign merchants, but their sovereign governments had no permanent diplomatic missions in the country and could not therefore afford them effective or constant protection. The position of foreign merchants was, therefore, not very different from that of Persian merchants. In the nineteenth century the position began to change. European nations established permanent missions in Persia and extra-territorial rights were granted by treaty. Protection arising from the new concept of nationality was thus added to the existing concept of protection, which had arisen from the custom of sanctuary. Such protection, gave the merchant a privileged position. This, coupled with the more favourable conditions for trade accorded to foreign merchants by treaty, contributed to, if it did not cause, some of the changes in the pattern of trade which began to take place in the nineteenth century.

NOTES

1 Transcripts of Crown-Copyright records in the Public Record Office in this article appear by permission of the Controller of H.M. Stationery Office.

2 Curzon, *Persia and the Persian Question* (London 1892) II, 244.

3 See FO 60:165. Notes on the Trade, Manufacture, and Productions of Persia, visited by Mr Consul Abbott in 1849–50. Cf. also Pelly, who states that the Indian traders in southern Persia were mainly from Multan and on the Herat and Bukhara line principally from Shikarpur (*Report on the Tribes, etc., around the Shores of the Persian Gulf* (Calcutta 1874) 22n).

4 See 'The case of Ḥājjī Nūr al-Dīn, 1823–47: a study in land tenure', *BSOAS*, XXX, pt. 1 (1967) 54-72.

5 Cf. FO 60:216. Murray to Clarendon, No. 16, Baghdad, 2 April 1857, in which it is stated that Ḥājjī ʿAbd al-Karīm was over eighty.

6 FO 60:143. Palmerston to Farrant, No. 20, Foreign Office, 13 June 1849.

7 See FO 60:225. Sheil to Hammond, London, 2 Chester Square, 19 January 1857.

8 FO 60:241. Stevens to Stanley, No. 1, 15 January 1859.

9 It was customary for the central government to send a budget at the beginning of the year to the provincial governor. If there was a surplus of receipts this was at the disposal of the central government; if there was a deficit the central government had to remit this to the provincial governor. At the end of the year the governor submitted his accounts, which were then examined by a special official, whose duty it was to exact the payment of any sums held to be due from the provincial governor. The salaries of government servants and other government expenses were largely paid by drafts (*barāts*) on the revenue. Thus, someone having a claim on the government would be given a draft, or payment order, on the governor of a province, and this would be noted in the central government register against the revenue due from the province. The issue of *barāts* under Muḥammad Shāh far exceeded the total revenues of the kingdom. Their value was therefore nominal and the holders, unless they were persons of influence and able to insist on the payment of their claims before those of other persons, were glad to sell them at a discount of 70 or 80 per cent. The principal governors had their agents in Tehran to purchase the *barāts* drawn on their provinces. The full amount of them was afterwards charged in their accounts with the government, although only a small part of them may in reality have been paid (cf. FO 60:125. Sheil to Palmerston No. 117, Tehran, 20 November 1846). Georgian merchants were also involved in transactions over government bills. For example, when Nabī Khān was appointed governor of Iṣfahān in 1847 he took upon himself the payment of government bills due by Muḥammad Shāh and Ḥājjī Mīrzā Āqāsī to Georgian merchants to the amount of 40,000 *tūmāns* (FO 60:132. Farrant to Palmerston, No. 8, Tehran, 12 November 1847).

10 FO 60:163. Sheil to Palmerston, No. 175, Camp near Tehran, 1 October 1851. He was sent by Muḥammad Shāh as his personal envoy

to the courts of Austria, France and England in 1837 to complain of the conduct of the English envoy, John McNeill, and to demand his recall. The government in London, however, refused to receive him officially.

10*a* See ʿAbd al-Ghafūr Ṭāhirī, ʿTazkireh-i Jalālī' (ed. Iraj Afshār) in *Farhang-i Īrānzamīn*, XIII, fascs. 1-4 (1966), 152, who states that he was governor of Yazd from 1258/1842–3 to 1262/1846. If these dates are correct, he presumably continued to hold the governorship of Yazd for a period after his appointment to Fārs.

11 Cf. FO 60:104. Sheil to Aberdeen, No. 66, Tehran, 12 June 1844. See also Fasā'ī, *Fārs-nāmeh-i Nāṣirī*, I, 298ff.

12 FO 60:136. Farrant to Palmerston, No. 29, Tehran, 27 March 1848.

13 FO 60:131. Sheil to Palmerston, No. 74, Camp near Tehran, 30 July 1847, and FO 60:132. Farrant to Palmerston, No. 21, Tehran, 24 December 1847.

14 FO 60:163. Sheil to Palmerston, No. 175, Camp near Tehran, 1 October 1851.

15 Ibid. Incl. No. 22 in Sheil to Palmerston, No. 175 of 1 October 1851.

16 It was a common practice to include in the bond interest as well as the principal. Thus, if a man borrowed 1,000 *tūmāns* at 10 per cent to be repaid in one year, the bond would be made out for 1,100 *tūmāns*.

17 FO 60:163. Sheil to Palmerston, No. 175, Camp near Tehran, 1 October 1851.

18 Ibid. Translation of a letter from Hajee Abdul Kereem to Hoossein Khan (translated by Ronald F. Thomson), incl. No. 33 in Sheil to Palmerston, No. 175, Camp near Tehran, 1 October 1851.

19 Ibid. Sheil to Palmerston, No. 226, Tehran, 17 December 1851.

20 Ibid. Incl. 1 in Sheil to Palmerston, No. 175, Camp near Tehran, 1 October 1851.

21 Ibid. Incl. No. 22 in Sheil to Palmerston, No. 175, 1 October 1851.

22 Ibid. Incl. No. 29 in Sheil to Palmerston, No. 175, Camp near Tehran, 1 October 1851.

23 *Fārs-nāmeh-i Nāṣirī*, i, 301ff.

24 FO 60:163. Sheil to Palmerston, No. 175, Camp near Tehran, 1 October 1851 and enclosures.

25 See my article '*The case of Ḥājjī Nūr al-Dīn, 1823–47*: a study in land tenure', op. cit.

26 FO 60:178. Sheil to Russell (signed by Thomson in the absence of Sheil), No. 42, Tehran, 28 February 1853; and see FO 60:164. Sheil to Palmerston, No. 201 of 14 November 1851, and FO 60:225. Sheil to Hammond, London, 2 Chester Square, 19 January 1857.

27 FO 60:163. Sheil to Palmerston, No. 175, Camp near Tehran, 1 October 1851.

28 See FO 60:180. Memorandum by Sheil, London, 25 July 1853, Relative to Hajee Abdul Kareem.

29 See FO 60:144. Sheil to Palmerston, London, 29 January 1849. The governor of Fārs farmed the revenue of the province, a portion of which he levied in grain, but the payment made by him to the central government was in money. The *tūmān* was worth about ten shillings at this time.

30 FO 60:158. Sheil to Palmerston, No. 22, Tehran, 12 February 1851.

31 FO 60:163. Sheil to Palmerston, No. 175, Camp near Tehran, 1 October 1851.

32 FO 60:157. Palmerston to Sheil, No. 130, FO, 18 December 1851.

33 FO 60:180. Memo by Sheil, London, 25 July 1853. Relative to Hajee Abdul Kareem.

34 FO 60:172. Sheil to Malmesbury, No. 142, Tehran, 2 October 1852.

35 FO 60:178. Sheil to Russell (signed by Thomson in the absence of Sheil), No. 42, Tehran, 28 February 1853, and FO 60:180. Memo by Sheil, London, 25 July 1853. Relative to Hajee Abdul Kareem.

36 FO 60:177. Clarendon to Thomson, No. 2, Dft., FO, 4 May 1853.

37 FO 60:177. Clarendon to Thomson. No. 25, Dft., FO, 6 August 1853.

38 Anglo-Persian relations worsened after the accession of Nāṣir al-Dīn for a variety of reasons. Britain's interest in maintaining the independence of Persia was reiterated by Palmerston in a despatch to Sheil dated 24 June 1851 in which he stated, 'it is the policy of the British government to maintain the Persian monarchy in its separate existence and to render it as independent as possible of its powerful northern neighbours . . .' (FO 60:157. Palmerston to Sheil, No. 73, FO, 24 June 1851). Russian encroachments on northern Persia were, however, increasing, and the fact that the indemnity imposed by Russia on Persia by the Treaty of Turkomanchay had not yet been paid off, provided Russia with a ready means of putting pressure on Persia, if she proved intransigent to Russian demands. Tentative approaches to Britain by Persia for a defensive alliance against possible encroachments by Russia were made in the summer of 1852 and rejected (FO 60:168. Malmesbury to Sheil, No. 18, FO, 28 June 1852). The question of Herat meanwhile continued to be a source of annoyance and dispute between the two governments, and when in the early summer of 1852 Persian troops advanced on Herat and assumed possession of the city, intercourse was broken off with the Shafīʿ Khān, the Persian envoy in London, until Persian troops evacuated the city. On 25 January 1853 the Persian government signed an agreement in which they engaged to abstain from all interference in the internal affairs of Herat and to relinquish all claims to the coinage and the *khuṭbeh* in Herat, but relations were not finally renewed until 7 May 1853 (FO 60:176. Malmesbury to Sheffee Khan, Dft. FO, 27 October 1852, and same to same FO, 3 November 1852, and FO 60:177. Clarendon to Thomson, No. 8,

Dft., FO, 7 May 1853). Various incidents, including disputes over the question of protection, occurred in 1853, and further disturbed Anglo-Persian relations. Mīrzā Āqā Khān Nūrī, the *ṣadr-i aʿẓam*, and the Shāh both evinced considerable irritation at British interference. Perso-Turkish relations in 1851 were also not good and the fact that both Russia and Britain used their influence to persuade the Shāh not to attack Turkey, had caused added irritation.

39 On the death of Muḥammad Shāh, Khadījeh Khānum, his favourite wife and mother of his second son, ʿAbbās Mīrzā, had asked for asylum on behalf of herself and her son in the British mission. ʿAbbās Mīrzā, who was then some twelve years of age, was later banished to Qumm. In the late summer of 1852 it was believed that his life was in danger so he was sent with a British passport to Baghdad, the Shah agreeing to his departure on condition that Sheil would engage that the British consul-general in Baghdad would forbid or impede ʿAbbās Mīrzā's return to Persia without the Shah's consent (FO 60:172. Sheil to Malmesbury, No. 116, Camp near Tehran, 5 September 1852).

40 FO 60:182. Thomson to Clarendon, No. 129, Camp near Tehran, 5 November 1853 and inclosures. A pencil note to Thomson's despatch reads: 'Did not the Turk seek to bedevil matters between the parties, in order that Persia having a quarrel with England on her hands might be less disposed to trouble Turkey?' In this despatch Thomson suggested that if the mission were to be withdrawn, England should protect her commercial interests by the presence of a small body of troops on the Island of Karrak (Kharg). Sheil thought this proposal 'highly judicious' not only because it would hasten the settlement of the present dispute but also with reference to Afghanistan. He further suggested that Kharg should not be evacuated without an express arrangement with the Persian government that it would cease from all interference with Herat. Such action would also, he thought, be a useful intimation to the Shah that Great Britain would not allow him to join Russia with impunity against Turkey (FO 60:183, Memo by Sheil on Thomson's dispute with the Persian government, Paris, 26 December 1853).

41 See D.P. Costello, 'The Murder of Griboedov', in *Oxford Slavonic Papers*, VIII, 1958.

42 FO 60:183. Memo. by Sheil on Thomson's dispute with the Persian government, Paris, 26 December 1853. See also FO 60:184. Correspondence between the *ṣadr-i aʿẓam* and Clarendon, in which the former complained of Thomson's actions.

43 FO 60:188. Clarendon to Thomson, No. 2, Dft., FO, 17 January 1854.

44 FO 60:182. Thomson to Clarendon, No. 130, camp near Tehran, 8 November 1853.

45 *Tehran Gazette*, 17 Ṣafar 1270/19 November 1853.

46 FO 60:182. Thomson to Clarendon, No. 132, Camp near Tehran, 11 November 1853.

47 FO 60:182. Thomson to Clarendon, No. 133, Camp near Tehran, 12 November 1853.

48 FO 60:182. No. 144, Tehran, 20 November 1853, and same to same, No. 145, Tehran, 20 November 1853.

49 FO 60:182. Thomson to Clarendon, No. 147, Tehran, 21 November 1853.

50 FO 60:182. Thomson to Clarendon, No. 150, Tehran, 26 November 1853 Inclosures.

51 FO 60:182. Thomson to Clarendon, No. 158, Tehran, 11 December 1853. Clarendon approved this decision (see FO 60:188. Clarendon to Thomson, No. 13, Dft., FO, 17 February 1854).

52 FO 60:199. Extract from letter from Hector to Stirling, December 1853. Incl. Memo of Thomas Stirling Esquire, Merchant, Sheffield.

53 Messrs Hector and Company had also come into conflict with Sheil in 1847. Muḥammad ʿAlī Mīrzā when governor of Kirmānshāh had contracted a debt of *c.* 10,000 *tūmāns* to a Turkish subject, Gaspar Khān. Muḥammad ʿAlī Mīrzā was succeeded on his death by his son, Muḥammad Ḥusayn Mīrzā, who gave bills on the revenue payable by the tribes of Luristān in payment of his father's debt. Muḥammad Ḥusayn Mīrzā and Gaspar Khān both died without the debt being discharged. The heirs of Gaspar Khān then apparently transferred their claims to Messrs Hector and Company, who had recourse to Abbott, the British consul in Tehran for assistance in the recovery of the claim. Sheil, unwilling to sanction speculations of this nature or to lend official support to an attempt to extort payment in favour of British subjects of revenue bills which could be purchased for a trifling sum from their holders (to whom they were worthless), instructed Abbott to withhold his assistance (FO 60:131, Sheil to Palmerston, No. 72, Camp near Tehran, 22 July 1847). In 1847 Hector had concluded a deal with Ḥājjī Mīrzā Āqāsī for the supply of 200,000 muskets (FO 60:130. Sheil to Palmerston, No. 62, Camp near Tehran, 18 June 1847). When Ḥājjī Mīrzā Āqāsī was dismissed and his property confiscated, Mīrzā Taqī Khān Amīr Niẓām, his successor, persuaded Hector to annul the contract and make a new one with the Persian government for the supply of 20,000 muskets, which he did subject to payment being made for the 5,000 already imported (FO 60:145. Farrant to Palmerston, No. 40, Qulhak, 25 May 1849).

54 FO 60:188. Clarendon to Thomson, No. 6, Dft., FO, 17 January 1854, marked secret and confidential.

55 FO 60:195. Thomson to Clarendon, No. 195, Tehran, 3 November 1854, and same to same, No. 203, Tehran, 28 November 1854.

56 FO 60:201. Thomson to Clarendon, No. 7, Tehran, 20 January 1855.

57 FO 60:202. Murray to Clarendon, No. 9, Tehran, 23 April 1855.

58 FO 60:208. Murray to Clarendon, No. 16, Tabrīz, 25 January 1856.

59 FO 60:225. Memo by Sheil, London, 16 March 1857.

60 Cf. FO 60:210. Note by Sheil on Murray to Clarendon, No. 105, Baghdad, 18 November 1856, and FO 60:213. Sheil to Hammond, Boulogne, 18 Grande Rue, 29 September 1856, and FO 60:227. Memo by Sheil sent to Hammond, 19 September 1857, Kingston, in reply to Hammond's note of 18 September 1857, ref. Murray's No. 62 of 21 July 1857.

61 Muḥarram 1272 fell in September-October 1855.

62 FO 60:208. Murray to Clarendon, No. 16, Tabrīz, 25 January 1856.

63 See G. H. Hunt, *Outram and Havelock's Persian Campaign* (London 1858), for a more detailed account.

64 FO 60:212. Stevens to Murray, No. 8, Tehran, 19 January 1856, incl. in Stevens to Clarendon, No. 4, Tehran, 20 January 1856.

65 FO 60:208. Murray to Clarendon, No. 16, Tabrīz, 25 January 1856.

66 FO 60:216. Murray to Clarendon, No. 16, Baghdad, 2 April 1857; and FO 60:218, same to same, No. 62, Camp near Tehran, 21 July 1857.

67 FO 60:209. Murray to Clarendon, No. 61, Baghdad, 27 June 1856.

68 FO 60:216. Clarendon to Murray, No. 148, Dft., FO, 31 October 1857.

69 FO 60:231. Murray to Malmesbury, No. 68, Tehran, 30 April 1858.

70 FO 60:234. Stevens to Malmesbury, No. 4, Tehran, 25 April 1858.

71 FO 60:234. Stevens to Malmesbury, No. 4, Tehran, 25 April 1858 and Inclosures.

72 FO 60:231. Murray to Malmesbury, No. 76, Tehran, 15 May 1858 and inclosures.

73 FO 60:228. Malmesbury to Murray, No. 55, Dft., FO, 21 July 1858.

74 FO 60:232. Murray to Malmesbury, No. 120, Camp near Tehran, 14 September 1858.

75 FO 60:233. Doria to Stanley, No. 6, Tehran, 31 December 1858.

76 FO 60:234. Stevens to Stanley, No. 4, Tehran, 31 December 1858.

77 FO 60:238. Stevens to Doria, Tehran, 26 January 1859, incl. in Doria to Stanley, No. 10, Tehran, 1 February 1859.

78 FO 60:241. Stevens to Stanley, No. 1, Tehran, 15 January 1859. Some days later Stevens disclosed in another despatch that some months previously, when with Murray's sanction he was unofficially endeavouring to bring about a settlement between the Persian government and the heirs of Ḥājjī ʿAbd al-Karīm, the Persian government had promised him that if he succeeded justice would be done to his brother, George Stevens, who was established as a merchant in Tabrīz and had a number of pecuniary claims on the Persian government. When Stevens told the minister for foreign affairs that he would agree to the case of the heirs of Ḥājjī ʿAbd al-Karīm being referred to the religious courts, the minister for foreign affairs said that the termination of this dispute, which had been a source of great irritation to the Shah, would afford

such satisfaction that he would grant Stevens any favour he would ask. Stevens in reply said that he wanted none but the fulfilment of the promise given regarding his brother's claim (FO 60:241. Stevens to Stanley, No. 2, Tehran, 16 January 1859). Stevens was reprimanded for his action in mixing public and private interests in thus taking advantage of the anxiety of the Persian government to be relieved of the interference of the British government in the case of Ḥājjī ʿAbd al-Karīm to suggest to the minister for foreign affairs a settlement of the claims of his brother upon the Persian government (FO 60:237. Stanley to Doria, No. 19/79, India Office, 7 April 1859).

79 FO 60:238. Doria to Stanley, No. 10, Tehran, 1 February 1859. It is not without interest that when strenuous efforts were made by Nāṣir al-Dīn to induce Sayf al-Dawleh Mīrzā and Mīr ʿAlī Naqī Khān to renounce British protection in 1859 they were told to take warning from the example of the case of the heirs of Ḥājjī ʿAbd al-Karīm 'who had been abandoned by the English government' (FO 60:238. Doria to Stanley, No. 3, Tehran, 27 January 1859).

80 FO 60:241. Stevens to Stanley, No. 3, Tehran, 19 January 1859.

Pahlavi, Pârsi, Dari
Les Langues de l'Iran d'Après Ibn al-Muqaffaʿ

I

Le plus ancien témoignage d'époque islamique sur la situation linguistique de l'Iran est celui d'Ibn al-Muqaffaʿ (mort en 139 hég./757 ap. J.-C.), qui nous est transmis par le *Fihrist* d'Ibn al-Nadīm (vers 377/987)[1]:
wa-qāla Ibn al-Muqaffaʿ luġat al-fārisiyya al-fahlawiyya wa-l-dariyya wa-l-fārisiyya wa-l-xūẓiyya wa-l-suryāniyya fa-ammā al-fahlawiyya fa-mansūb ilà Fahlah ism yaqaʿu ʿalà xamsat buldān wa-hiya Iṣfahān wa-l-Rayy wa-Hamaḏān wa-Māh Nihāwand wa-Āḏarbāyǰan wa-ammā al-dariyya fa-luġat mudun al-Madāʾin wa-bihā kāna yatakallamu man bi-bāb al-malik wa-hiya mansūba ilà ḥāḍirat al-bāb wa-l-ġālib ʿalayhā min luġat ahl Xurāsān wa-l-mašriq luġat ahl Balx wa-ammā al-fārisiyya fa-yatakallamu bihā al-mawābiḏa wa-l-ʿulamāʾ wa-ašbahuhum wa-hiya luġat ahl Fāris wa-ammā al-xūẓiyya fa-bihā kāna yatakallamu al-mulūk wa-l-ašraf fī-l-xalwa wa-mawāḍiʿ al-laʿb wa-l-laḏḏa wa-maʿa al-ḥāšiyya wa-ammā al-suryāniyya fa-kāna yatakallamu bihā ahl al-Sawād wa-l-mukātaba fī nawʿ min al-luġa bi-l-suryānī fārisī.
Ce qui se traduit littéralement, en donnant aux noms de langue leur forme persane[2]:
Ibn al-Muqaffaʿ dit: La langue pârsi [*comprend*] *le* pahlavi, *le* dari, *le* pârsi, *le* xuzi *et le* soryâni. *Le* pahlavi *se rapporte au Fahlah, nom qui s'applique à cinq régions, à savoir Ispahan, Rey, Hamadan, Māh Nihāvand et Aẓerbaïdjan. Le* dari *est la langue des villes de Madāʾin; il était parlé par ceux qui étaient à la cour du roi;* [*son nom*] *se rapporte à la présence à la cour; parmi les langues des gens du Khorassan et de l'Orient c'est celle des gens de Balkh qui y domine. Le* pârsi *est la langue que parlaient les* mowbad, *les savants et leurs semblables; c'est la langue des gens du Fars. Le* xuzi *est la langue que parlaient les rois et les nobles dans le privé et dans les moments de jeu et de plaisir, et avec leur entourage. Le* soryâni *est la langue parlée par les gens du Sawād; la correspon-aance se faisait dans une sorte de langue en* soryâni [*appelée?*] pârsi.

On lit dans le *Mafātiḥ al-ʿulūm* de Xwārizmī (mort en 375/985) une notice presque identique[3]:

wa-min luġat al-furs al-fahlawiyya wa-bihā kāna yaǰrī kalām al-mulūk fī maǰlisihim wa-hiya luġa mansūba ilà Bahlah wa-Bahlah ism yaqaʿu ʿalà xamsat buldān Iṣfahān wa-l-Rayy wa-Hamaḏān wa-Māh Nihāwand wa-Aḏarbāyǰān wa-min luġatihim al-fārisiyya wa-kāna yaǰrī bihā kalām al-mawābiḏa wa-man kāna munāsiban lahum wa-hiya luġat kuwar Fāris wa-l-dariyya luġat ahl mudun al-Madāʾin wa-bihā kāna yatakallamu man bi-bāb al-malik fa-hiya mansūba ilà ḥāḏirat al-bāb wa-l-ġālib ʿalayhā min bayna luġāt ahl al-mašriq luġat ahl Balx wa-l-xūziyya luġa mansūba ilà kuwar Xūzistān wa-bihā kāna yatakallamu al-mulūk wa-l-ašrāf fī-l-xalāʾ wa-mawḍiʿ al-istifrāġ wa-ʿinda al-taʿarrī fī-l-ḥammām wa-fī-l-abzan wa-l-muġtasal wa-l-suryānī luġa mansūba ilà kuwar Sūristān wa-hiya sawād al-ʿIrāq wa-l-suryāniyyūn hum allaḏīna yuqālu lahum al-nabaṭ wa-bihā kāna yaǰrī kalām ḥāšiyyat al-mulūk iḏā iltamasū al-ḥawāʾiǰ wa-šakaw al-ẓulāmāt li-annahā amlaq al-alsina.

Parmi les langues des Persans il y a le pahlavi; *c'est en cette langue que s'exprimaient les rois dans leurs séances; elle se rapporte au Bahlah; Bahlah est un nom qui s'applique à cinq régions, Ispahan, Rey, Hamadan, Māh Nihāvand et Azerbaïdjan. Il y a aussi le* pârsi, *langue dans laquelle s'exprimaient les* mowbad *et gens de même sorte; c'est la langue des districts du Fars. Le* dari *est la langue des villes de Madāʾin; c'est dans cette langue que s'exprimaient ceux qui étaient à la cour du roi;* [*son nom*]*se rapporte à la présence à la cour; parmi les langues des gens de l'Orient c'est celle des gens de Balkh qui y domine. Le* xuzi *se rapporte aux districts du Khouzistan; c'est dans cette langue que s'exprimaient les rois et les nobles en privé, dans les moments de détente, et lorsqu'ils se déshabillaient au bain ou lors de l'usage de l'aiguière et de la baignoire. Le* soryâni *se rapporte aux districts du Sūristān, c'est-à-dire du* sawād *irakien; les* soryâni *sont ceux qu'on appellent* [*aussi*] *Nabatéens; c'est dans cette langue que s'exprimaient les courtisans du roi quand ils présentaient une supplique ou se plaignaient d'une offense, car c'est la plus caressante des langues.*

Comme on voit cette notice coïncide très largement celle du *Fihrist*. Les seules différences notables concernent l'usage du *soryâni*, sur lequel le *Fihrist* est moins clair, mais sans doute plus sérieux, et le *pahlavi*, à propos duquel Xwārizmī donne une précision supplémentaire: il était employé dans les 'séances' des rois.

Enfin Yāqūt (mort en 626/1229), dans le *Muʿǰam al-buldān*,[4] citant Hamza Iṣfahāni (mort en 360/970), donne presque textuellement les mêmes renseignements que le *Mafātiḥ al-ʿulūm*.

Il est évident que ces trois notices remontent à une même source, qui doit être Ibn al-Muqaffaʿ. La mention des 'villes de Madā'in' et de la cour du roi indique qu'elles réfèrent aux temps préislamiques: la situation décrite est sans doute celle de la fin de l'époque sassanide.

Ibn al-Muqaffaʿ, Iranien originaire du Fars, traducteur de nombreux ouvrages pehlevis en arabe, devait savoir de quoi il parlait. Et pourtant cette notice, bien connue et souvent citée, a embarrassé les commentateurs et donné lieu à des interprétations discutables. C'est qu'elle est loin d'être claire à première vue. Les cinq langues sont énumérées avec une belle symétrie, qui suggère qu'elles se partagent harmonieusement à la fois le territoire de l'Iran et les fonctions dans la société: le *pahlavi* est langue du Fahla et des 'séances' royales, le *pârsi* celle du Fars et des prêtres, le *dari* celle de la capitale et du Khorassan et celle des courtisans, le *xuzi* celle du Khouzistan et des usages familiers, le *soryâni* celle de la Mésopotamie et de la correspondance. Une telle image est certainement fausse. Elle manifeste trop bien pour n'être pas suspecte le goût du système bien connu dans la tradition iranienne. En outre la répartition géographique du *dari* est bizarre: qu'est-ce que cette langue dont le domaine comprend à la fois la ville de Madā'in et le Khorassan, qui sont séparés par les vastes zones occupées par le *pahlavi* et le *pârsi*? On ne peut se représenter l'Iran sassanide comme une sorte de Suisse, dont le territoire aurait été réparti entre plusieurs langues d'importance comparable et de droits égaux.

Mais la difficulté principale réside dans l'interprétation des noms de ces langues. Deux d'entre eux n'appellent guère de discussion, l'un, *soryâni*, parce qu'il est clair, l'autre, *xuzi*, parce qu'on n'en peut dire grand chose. Le *soryâni* est évidemment l'araméen. Quant au *xuzi*, on a pu supposer sans absurdité qu'il s'agit d'un vestige de l'élamite.[5] Mais les noms de *pahlavi*, *pârsi*, *dari* sont autrement litigieux. Rien n'est plus équivoque que les dénominations de *pahlavi* et de *pârsi*. La notice du *Fihrist* elle-même en fournit une illustration: lorsque l'auteur dit que la langue *pârsi* comprend plusieurs idiomes, dont justement le *pârsi*, le même mot est nécessairement pris dans deux sens différents. Dans les textes arabes et persans les termes de *pahlavi* et de *pârsi*, employés comme noms de langue, réfèrent, selon les époques et les auteurs, à des réalités diverses. Pour clarifier les données il importe de cerner aussi étroitement que possible les différents emplois de ces noms. On essaiera dans ce qui se suit de préciser, à l'aide des attestations les plus claires, quelles réalités ont pu recouvrir les mots *pahlavi*, *pârsi* et *dari*, puis on tentera, en étudiant comment ils sont associés ou opposés, de définir les significations et d'apercevoir les infléchissements ou les bouleversements qu'elles ont subis au cours du temps. On sera alors en mesure de proposer une interprétation de la notice d'Ibn al-Muqaffaʿ.

V. Minorsky s'est toujours intéressé aux langues et dialectes de l'Iran. En 1962 encore il publiait, dans un appendice à sa fameuse étude sur *Vis-o Râmin*, quelques pages intitulées 'Pahlavi and the language of Fahla'.[6] Il écrivait: 'The problem of the history of the term *Pahlavi* was considered by Professor Ohlshausen in "Parthava and Pahlav", in *Monatsberichte der Preuss. Akad.*, 1877, 727-83, but since then a mass of new material has awaited a new examination. The classification of languages by I. Muqaffaʿ still remains obscure.'[7] Puisse le présent article répondre à son vœu!

II

Le nom de *pahlavi* et sa variante *pahlavâni*, qui a le même sens,[8] ont été employés pour désigner quatre réalités différentes.

(1) Etymologiquement et anciennement *pahlav(ân)i* désigne la langue parthe. Le mot est par chance attesté dans un texte manichéen en moyen perse qui fait le récit d'une mission d'évangélisation au Khorassan[9]:

k' prystgrwšn 'ndr hlwn šhryst'n bwd xwnd 'w mry 'mw hmwc'g ky phlw'[ny]g dbyryy ['w]d 'ẓw['n d'n]yst hm m[...]ynyn ''šn'g 'w 'bršhr pryst'd 'b'g 'rdβ'n wyspwhr 'wd br'dr'n dbyr'[n] nbyg'n ng'r'b'g

Quand le Messager de Lumière (Mani) se trouvait dans le chef-lieu de Holvān, il appela Mar Ammō le Maître, qui savait l'écriture et la langue pahlavâni *et était familier aussi avec.... Il l'envoya à Abaršahr avec le prince Ardaβān et des frères-scribes, ainsi qu'un peintre de livres.*

Ce texte bien connu, dont il existe aussi une version sogdienne mentionnant également la langue *pahlavâni* (en sogdien *pyl'w'n'k*),[10] est un témoignage précieux sur la situation linguistique de l'Iran au IIIe siècle ap. J.-C. Mani, en Mésopotamie, prêchait en moyen-perse et en araméen; c'est dans ces deux langues qu'il rédigea ses livres. Mais pour porter, oralement et par écrit, la bonne parole au Khorassan (Abaršahr est l'ancien nom de la région de Nichapour), il fallait un apôtre qui sût la langue du pays, le *pahlavâni*, c'est-à-dire le parthe. Mani prend soin d'ailleurs d'adjoindre à la mission un prince de la dynastie arsacide. La version sogdienne raconte ensuite comment Mar Ammō, à Abaršahr et à Marv, convertit beaucoup de princes, princesses et seigneurs divers. Et l'on sait quel développement a pris par la suite la littérature manichéenne en parthe.

(2) A l'époque islamique le mot *pahlavi* est employé le plus souvent pour désigner le moyen-perse littéraire, c'est-à-dire la langue que l'on appelle encore couramment le 'pehlevi'.[11] Les attestations sont nom-

breuses: on se bornera ici à citer quelques passages dont le sens n'est pas douteux.

Le géographe Iṣṭaxrī (vers 330/951), décrivant le Fars, indique que trois langues y sont en usage[12]:

wa-lahum ṯalāṯat alsina al-fārisiyya allatī yatakallamūna bihā wa-ǰamiʿ ahl Fāris yatakallamūna bi-luġa wāḥida . . . wa-lisānuhum allaḏī bihi kutub al-ʿaǰam wa-ayyāmuhum wa-mukātabāt al-maǰūs fi-mā baynahum huwa al-fahlawiyya allatī taḥtāǰu ilà tafsir ḥattà yaʿrifahā al-furs wa-lisān al-ʿarabiyya allatī bihā mukātabāt al-sulṭān wa-l-dawāwīn waʿ-āmmat al-nās.

Ils ont trois langues: le pârsi *qu'ils parlent – tous les habitants du Fars parlent la même langue . . . –; la langue dans laquelle [sont rédigés] les livres des Persans, leurs histoires et la correspondance des mages entre eux, à savoir le* pahlavi, *langue qui nécessite une explication pour que les Persans la comprennent; la langue arabe, dans laquelle est rédigée la correspondance de l'administration, des bureaux et de la masse de la population.*

pârsi désigne ici clairement le persan parlé et *pahlavi* le moyen-perse littéraire, qui déjà, comme on voit, passait pour fort difficile à lire.

La préface du *Livre des Rois* en prose persane d'Abu Mansur (346/957 –8), évoquant le précédent du livre de Kalila et Dimna, rapporte comment le calife Ma'mun s'en fit raconter l'histoire par Ibn al-Muqaffaʿ, son secrétaire (*dabir*)[13]:

goft nâmei az Hendustân biâvard ângah Borzuye-ye tabib az hendovi be pahlavi gardânide bud tâ nâm-e u zende šod miân-e jahânián. . . . Ma'mun ân nâme bexâst va ân nâme bedid farmud dabir-e xiš-râ tâ az zabân-e pahlavi be zabân-e tâzi gardânid

[Ibn al-Muqaffaʿ] dit: Il (Anuširavân) fit venir ce livre de l'Inde; Borzuye le médecin l'avait ensuite traduit de l'indien en pahlavi, *de sorte que sa renommée (celle du roi) survécut parmi les humains. . . . Ma'mun demanda ce livre. Il le vit et ordonna à son secrétaire de le traduire du* pahlavi *en arabe.*

L'histoire du livre de Kalila et Dimna est racontée également dans le *Šâhnâme* de Ferdowsi (achevé vers 400/1009–10[14]), qui appelle aussi *pahlavi* ou *pahlavâni* la version rédigée sous le Sassanide Xosrow Ier Anuširavân.[15] Il s'agit évidemment du moyen-perse littéraire ou pehlevi.

Cette langue est également appelée *pahlavi* dans le plus ancien texte zoroastrien en persan, le *Zarâtoštnâme*, dont C. Rempis a montré qu'il avait été composé à Rey un peu avant 978 de notre ère.[16] Dans l'introduction l'auteur parle de sa source pehlevie (dist. 14)[17]:

yeki daftari didam az xosrovi

be xatti ke xâni varâ pahlavi
J'ai vu un livre du temps de l'Empire
Dans l'écriture qu'on appelle pahlavi.

Un peu plus bas un *mowbad* l'exhorte à mettre ce livre en persan (dist. 23 et suivants):

hami bini in qessehâ -ye kohon
k-az u yâd n-ârad kasi asl-o bon
nadârad bedin xat kasi dastgâh
betarsam ke gardad be yek rah tabâh
hamân beh ke in-râ be nazm âvari
be pâkize goftâr-o xatt-e dari
Tu vois ces récits anciens
Dont personne ne rappelle le début et la fin.
Personne ne connaît cette écriture:
Je crains que [cette histoire] ne disparaisse tout entière.
Il vaut mieux que tu la mettes en vers,
En belle langue et en écriture dari.

On voit que dès la deuxième moitié du xe siècle de notre ère la connaissance de l'écriture pehlevie et par conséquent de la langue pehlevie était peu répandue même parmi les Zoroastriens. Trois quarts de siècle plus tard Gorgâni, dans son *Vis-o Râmin*, composé en 446/1054 à Ispahan, décrit le *pahlavi*, c'est-à-dire bien sûr le pehlevi, comme un véritable casse-tête[18]: l'histoire de Vis et de Râmin, dit-il, rédigée par six savants, est fort intéressante,

valikan pahlavi bâšad zabân-aš
nadânad har ke bar xânad bayân-aš
na har kas ân zabân niku bexânad
v-agar xânad hami ma'ni bedânad
farâvân vasf-e har cizi šomârad
co bar xâni basi ma'ni nadârad
Mais sa langue est le pahlavi:
Quiconque la lit n'en saisit pas la signification.
Tout le monde ne sait pas bien cette langue,
Et [même] si on la lit, on ne voit pas le sens.
[L'auteur] accumule beaucoup de descriptions de toute chose,
Mais quand on lit, cela n'a guère de sens.

Toutefois, ajoute Gorgâni (dist. 39-40), 'dans ce pays' (donc à Ispahan) on est amateur de pehlevi[19] et l'on s'y exerce dans ce livre:

dar in eqlim ân daftar bexânand

bedân tâ pahlavi az vey bedânand
kojâ mardom dar in eqlim hamvâr
bovand ân lafz-e širin-râ xaridâr
Dans ce pays on lit ce livre
Pour y apprendre le pahlavi,
Car les gens de ce pays toujours
Sont amateurs de cette douce langue.

(3) Le mot *pahlavi* ou, plus souvent, la forme arabisée *fahlavi* (pluriel *fahlaviyyât*) est appliqué à la poésie dialectale. Le témoignage le plus circonstancié est ici celui de Šams-e Qeys, auteur d'un traité de versification en persan (VIIe/XIIIe siècle),[20] qui mentionne le *fahlavi* à plusieurs reprises et lui consacre même des discussions assez détaillées. Les *fahlaviyyât* dont parle cet auteur sont des vers qui présentent deux traits caractéristiques:
(*a*) ils sont composés non en persan littéraire, mais en dialecte, comme le montrent bien les exemples qu'il en cite;
(*b*) ils ont une forme métrique particulière, proche du hazaj, mais admettant certaines variations sans exemple ailleurs en persan comme en arabe (⏓ — — — ⏑ — — — ⏑ — — — / — ⏑ — —; Šams-e Qeys critique d'ailleurs vigoureusement ces libertés, irrégulières au regard de la métrique arabe et persane); en outre ils sont généralement groupés en quatrains.

Fahlaviyyât semble donc être un terme technique désignant les vers qui répondent à cette définition. En fait il signifie 'compositions en *fahlavi* (*pahlavi*)', comme *fārsiyyat* chez les auteurs arabes désigne des 'compositions en persan'. *fahlavi* (*pahlavi*) est un nom de langue. On le voit bien lorsque Šams-e Qeys, parlant du mètre dit *mošâkel*, écrit (p. 128): *aš'âr-e fahlavi dar in bahr biš az aš'âr-e pârsi ast* 'ce mètre est plus fréquent dans les vers *fahlavi* que dans les vers *pârsi*', ou lorsqu'il dit, à propos du poète Bondâr-e Râzi (p. 131): *zabân-e u be loqat-e dari nazdiktar az fahlavi ast* 'sa langue est plus proche du *dari* que du *fahlavi*'. Par *pârsi* et *dari* l'auteur entend sans aucun doute le persan littéraire. Le mot *fahlavi* désigne par opposition au persan, langue commune, le dialecte, non pas, sans doute un dialecte strictement défini, mais toute forme dialectale employée en poésie. De fait les exemples cités portent certains traits des dialectes du nord-ouest de l'Iran.[21] Et lorsque Šams-e Qeys parle des auteurs ou des amateurs de *fahlaviyyât*, il mentionne *ahl-e Hamadân va Zengân* 'les gens de Hamadan et de Zendjan' (p. 131), ou encore *ahl-e Arâq* 'les gens de l'Irak (persan)' (p. 129), qui tous, dit-il, vibrent beaucoup plus à l'audition de vers *fahlavi* qu'aux meilleurs poèmes en arabe (*arabi*) ou en persan (*dari*). Il est clair que pour lui le nom de *fahlavi* réfère aux formes littéraires des dialectes de l'Irak persan ou Jabâl, c'est-à-dire de l'ancienne Médie.

Le même sens apparaît, par exemple, plus anciennement chez le poète Bondâr de Rey (mort en 401/1010):

lahn-e urâman-o beyt-e pahlavi
zaxme-ye rud-o samâ'-e xosrovi.
La mélodie urâman *et les vers* pahlavi
Le son du luth et la musique xosrovi,[22]

et, plus tard, dans la biographie du šeyx Safiyyoddin Ardebili, ancêtre des Safavides (650–735/1252–1334), par Ebn-e Bazzâz (759/1358), qui raconte qu'une femme disciple du šeyx, saisie d'un élan d'amour pour celui-ci, *zabân begošâd va in pahlavi enšâd kard* 'ouvrit la bouche et récita ces vers *pahlavi*': suit un quatrain dialectal.[23]

Le mot est resté en usage pour désigner la poésie dialectale par opposition à la poésie en persan, par exemple au Guilan.[24] Il s'est trouvé parfois appliqué à d'autres dialectes que ceux du nord-ouest: c'est ainsi que des vers de Boshâq-e At'eme, poète du IXe/XVe siècle, en dialecte de Chiraz, sont appelés *fahlaviyyât* dans l'édition du divan de ce poète par Mirzâ Habib Esfahâni (1303/1885).[25]

Sans référence à la poésie, le mot *pahlavi* est clairement employé comme nom de dialecte par Hamdollâh Mostowfi (VIIIe/XIVe siècle), qui dit que le langage des habitants de Zendjan est du 'pur *pahlavi*' *zabânešân pahlavi-e râst ast*, celui de Maragha du '*pahlavi* mêlé d'arabe' *zabânešân pahlavi-e moarrab ast*, et celui du Goštâsfi (région située sur la côte caspienne au nord de l'Araxe et qui faisait partie du Chirvan) un '*pahlavi* proche du parler du Guilan' *zabânešân pahlavi-e be jilâni bâz baste ast.*[26] Il s'agit, comme on voit, de dialectes de l'Azerbaïdjan.

(4) En poésie persane le mot *pahlavi* désigne parfois tout simplement le persan, ainsi presque certainement chez Adib-e Sâber (mort vers 540/1145)[27]:

gar soxan-râ qeymat az ma'ni padid âyad hami
ma'navi bâyad soxan ce tâzi-o ce pahlavi.
Si c'est le sens qui fait le prix de la parole,
Il la faut pleine de sens, qu'elle soit arabe ou pahlavi,

et à coup sûr chez Jâmi (817–98/1414–92), lorsqu'il définit ainsi le célèbre Masnavi (persan) de Jalâleddin Balxi dit Rumi[28]:

masnavi-e ma'navi-e Mowlavi
hast Qor'ân dar zabân-e pahlavi.

Le Masnavi spirituel de Mowlavi,
C'est le Coran en langue pahlavi.

III

Moins protéiforme que le nom de *pahlavi*, celui de *pârsi* n'en est pas moins susceptible de désigner plusieurs langues différentes.[29]

(1) Dans la rivayat pehlevie d'Ēmēd ī Ašavahištan (vers 900 ap. J.-C.),[30] on lit cette explication du mot avestique *hāθra-*, qui est le nom d'une mesure de longueur: *hāθra vāz-ē i avastāyig, pad ēvāz i pārsig frasang xvānand* '*hāθra* est un mot avestique, en langue *pārsig* on appelle [cela] *frasang*'. *frasang* est le mot moyen-perse. *pārsig* (= pn. *pârsi*) est donc en moyen-perse même (pehlevi) le nom de cette langue.

C'est le nom que lui donne en arabe Ibn al-Muqaffa', traducteur de nombreux ouvrages pehlevis. On lit à la fin de la préface de sa traduction du livre de Kalila et Dimna[31]: *wa-innā lammā ra'aynā ahl Fāris qad fassarū hāḏā al-kitāb wa-axrajū min al-hindiyya ilà al-fārisiyya alḥaqnā bāban bi-l-'arabiyya* 'pour nous, quand nous avons vu que les Persans avaient interprété ce livre et l'avaient fait passer de l'indien en *pârsi*, nous y avons adjoint un chapitre en arabe'.

Le même emploi est abondamment attesté chez les auteurs arabes. On sait par exemple que, après la conquête de l'Iran par les Arabes, l'administration financière est restée longtemps aux mains de secrétaires iraniens et que l'arabe n'est devenue la seule langue administrative qu'en 78/697–8 (ou 82/701–2) dans l'ouest et en 124/741–2 au Khorassan. Auparavant, dit Balāḏurī (mort en 279/892),[32] *lam yazal dīwān xarāj al-Sawād wa-sā'ir al-'Irāq bi-l-fārisiyya* 'les registres du tribut du Sawād et du reste de l'Irak était toujours en *pârsi*'. Jahšiyārī (mort en 331/942) écrit de même[33]: *wa-lam yazal bi-l-Kūfa wa-l-Baṣra dīwānāni aḥaduhumā bi-l-'arabiyya ... wa-l-āxar li-wujūh al-amwāl bi-l-fārisiyya* 'il y avait toujours à Kufa et à Basra deux divans, l'un ... en arabe, l'autre pour les questions financières en *pârsi*'. Et plus loin[34]: *wa-kāna awwal man naqala al-kitāba min al-fārisiyya ilà al-'arabiyya bi-Xurāsān Isḥāq ibn Ṭulaiq al-kātib* 'le premier qui dans les écritures substitua l'arabe au *pârsi* fut Isḥāq ibn Ṭulaiq'. Le *pârsi* en question ne peut être que le moyen-perse littéraire (pehlevi).

Il en va de même chez tous les auteurs qui parlent des ouvrages traduits, avant le ɪvᴇ/xᴇ siècle, du *pârsi* en arabe. Par exemple, Mas'ūdī (mort en 345/956) mentionne dans les *Murūj al-ḏahab*[35] *al-kutub al-manqūla ilaynā wa-l-mutarjama lanā min al-fārisiyya wa-l-hindiyya wa-l-rūmiyya* 'les livres qui nous ont été transmis et qui ont été traduits pour nous du *pârsi*, de l'indien, du *rumi*'. Plus précisément il dit dans le *Tanbih*[36] avoir vu au Fārs un livre contenant l'histoire et les portraits des rois sassanides: *wa-kāna ta'rix hāḏā al-kitāb annahu kutiba mimmā wujida fi xazā'in mulūk Fāris li-l-niṣf min Jumadà al-āxara sanat 113 wa-nuqila li-Hišām ibn 'Abd al-Malik ibn Marwān min al-fārisiyya ilà al-'arabiyya* 'Le livre que j'ai vu avait été rédigé d'après les documents trouvés dans le trésor des rois de Perse et achevé au milieu du second Djoumada de l'an 113. Il fut traduit pour Hicham fils d'Abd-el-Malik fils de Merwân du persan en arabe' (traduction Carra de Vaux; 'persan' traduit mécaniquement *al-fārisi* sans prétendre l'interpréter). Ibn al-Nadīm consacre un chapitre de son *Fihrist* à l'énumération des traducteurs du *pârsi* en arabe, chapitre intitulé *asmā' al-naqala min al-fārisī ilà al-'arabī* 'noms des traducteurs de *pârsi* en arabe'.[37] Ailleurs il dit que 'Mani est l'auteur de sept livres, dont un est en *pârsi* et six en *suri* (araméen)' *li-Mānī sab' at kutub aḥaduhā fārisi wa-sitta sūrī.*[38] Nous savons que le livre de Mani en *pârsi* est le *Šābuhragān*, qui était en moyen-perse (mais en écriture manichéenne, non en écriture pehlevie).

Cet emploi se trouve encore chez Ferdowsi. Sous le règne de Hormozd, fils de Xosrow Anuširavân, un conseiller révèle au roi l'existence d'un écrit de son père[39]:

conin dâd pâsox ke dar ganj-e šâh
yeki sâde sanduq didam siâh
nehâde be sanduq dar hoqqei
be hoqqe darun pârsi roq'ei
nebešta-st bar parniân-e sepid
bedân bâšad Irâniân-râ omid
be xatt-e pedar-t ân jahândâr šâh
to-râ andar ân kard bâyad negâh.
Il répondit: dans le trésor royal
J'ai vu un coffre simple de couleur noire.
Dans le coffre est placée une boîte,
Dans la boîte un écrit pârsi
Tracé sur de la soie blanche.
Il porte l'espoir des Iraniens.
[*Il est*] *de la main de ton père, ce roi maître du monde.*
Tu dois le regarder.

Ferdowsi savait parfaitement que l'écriture persane (arabe) n'était pas en usage en Iran au temps des Sassanides[40]: cet écrit *pârsi* ne peut être pour lui qu'un écrit en moyen-perse (pehlevi).

(2) *pârsi* désigne le persan, c'est-à-dire la langue commune et littéraire

de l'Iran islamique. C'est ordinairement le cas en persan même, mais souvent aussi en arabe.

Abū Ḥātim de Rey (mort en 322/934), dans une page savoureuse de son *Kitāb al-zīna*[41] déclare que nul peuple ne possède une poésie comme l'arabe; les chants (*aġānī*) des Iraniens sont intermédiaires entre la prose et la poésie (c'est-à-dire qu'ils ignorent la prosodie et la métrique quantitative); les Iraniens ne savent pas ce qu'est la poésie, *wa-dalīl ʿalà anna al-šiʿr lam yakun fī-l-ʿaǧam anna al-šāʿir lā yūǧadu lahu ism fī-l-fārisiyya* 'la preuve qu'il n'y a point de poésie en Iran, c'est qu'on ne trouve pas de mot en *pârsi* signifiant *poète*'. Jusqu'ici le nom de *pârsi* reste ambigu, mais l'auteur ajoute quelques lignes plus bas: *wa-ammā allaḏi aḥdaṯūhu al-ān min al-šiʿr bi-l-fārisiyya fa-huwa kalām lā maʿnà lahu wa-lā ḥuǧǧa fīhi wa-lā nafʿ bihi wa-lā dīwān lahu ʿinda al-ʿaǧam* 'la poésie qu'on a récemment inaugurée en *pârsi* n'est qu'un discours sans signification, sans titres et sans utilité, et il n'en existe pas de divan chez les Persans'. Cette fois Abu Ḥātim fait clairement allusion aux débuts de la poésie persane classique, dont il ne prévoyait pas le brillant avenir. Dans un autre passage[42] il reproche au *pârsi* de manquer de mots pour beaucoup de notions, si bien qu'on doit recourir aux mots arabes: ici encore c'est le persan qui est visé.

Muṭahhar Maqdisī (mort en 355/966) cite deux fois des vers persans de Mas'udi Marvazi[43] en les annonçant par ces mots *fī qaṣīdatihi bi-l-fārisiyya* 'dans son poème en *pârsi*'.[44]

Cet emploi de *pârsi* apparaît en persan dès les débuts de la littérature. Bal'ami, dans son adaptation des Annales de Ṭabarī (352/963–4), s'apprêtant à citer des lettres échangées par le calife Mansur et un vassal révolté, déclare[45]: *agar be tâzi va be pârsi har do nebešti derâz šodi va pârsixân-râ del tang šodi* 'il serait trop long de les citer à la fois en arabe et en *pârsi* et le lecteur de *pârsi* s'ennuierait'. Meysari, auteur d'un poème médical intitulé *Dânešnâme* et composé en 367–70/978–81, dit dans l'introduction qu'il s'est demandé en quelle langue écrire son ouvrage[46]:

ke cun guyam-š man tâ dir mânad
vo har kas dâneš-e u-râ bedânad
beguyam tâzi ar na pârsi naqz
ze har dar man beguyam mâye-o maqz.
Comment le rédigerais-je afin qu'il vive longtemps
Et que chacun ait accès au savoir qu'il contient?
L'écrirais-je en arabe ou en pârsi *élégant*
Pour donner de chaque sujet la substance et la moëlle?

Puis il s'est dit que, vivant en Iran, où la plupart des habitants sont *pârsidân*, l'arabe ne serait pas compris de tous : l'ouvrage est donc en persan. Ferdowsi se glorifiant de son œuvre, remarque[47] :

nabinad kasi nâme-ye pârsi
nevešte be abyât sad bâr si.
On ne voit pas de livre persan
Qui compte trois mille distiques.

La mention de 'distiques' (*abyât*) assure qu'il s'agit ici du persan.

Dans tous ces textes *pârsi* désigne le persan écrit, littéraire. Mais le mot était également appliqué au persan parlé, dès avant la naissance de la littérature. Ṭabarī (mort en 310/923),[48] rapportant un événement de l'année 67/686–7, cite une phrase persane : *qālū bi-l-fārisiyya 'in bâr doruq gofť' yaqūlūna hāḏihi al-marra kaḏaba* 'ils dirent en pârsi : *in bâr doruq goft*, c'est-à-dire : cette fois il a menti'. Cette phrase, qui appartient à la langue parlée du Ier/VIIe siècle est d'ailleurs identique à du persan classique et même à du persan moderne. Ibn al-Muʿtazz (mort en 296/908) cite de même un mot persan de langue parlée[49] : *qāla lahum bi-l-fārisiyya 'dehid' yaʿnī iḍribū* 'il leur dit *dehid*, c'est-à-dire : frappez'. Le géographe Maqdisī (vers 375/985) commence en ces termes une description du langage des habitants du Khouzistan[50] : *wa-laysa fī aqālīm al-aʿājim afṣaḥ min lisānihim wa-kaṯiran mā yamzuǰūna fārisiyyatahum bi-l-ʿarabiyya* 'Il n'y a pas dans les pays iraniens de langue plus élégante que la leur ; souvent ils mêlent leur *pârsi* d'arabe'. Les citations qui suivent montrent que le *pârsi* en question est bien le persan. On a cité plus haut (p. 365) un passage d'Iṣṭaxrī où *pârsi* est employé dans le même sens.

(3) Dans le *Târix-e Boxârâ*, ouvrage composé en arabe en 332/943–4, mais qui n'est conservé que par une traduction persane de 522/1128–9,[51] on lit ceci :

mardomân-e Boxârâ be avval-e eslâm dar namâz Qor'ân be pârsi xândandi va arabi natavânestandi âmuxtan va cun vaqt-e roku' šodi mardi budi ke dar pas-e išân bâng [*kardi*] bknyt' nkynt *va cun sajde xâstandi* [*kardan*] *bâng kardi* nkwny' nkwny.

Au débuts des temps islamiques, les gens de Bokhara pendant la prière lisaient le Coran en pârsi, *car ils ne pouvaient comprendre l'arabe. Quand venait le moment de s'incliner, un homme derrière eux criait* bknyt' nkynt, *et quand ils devaient se prosterner, il criait* nkwny' nkwny.

Les deux expressions citées, dans la mesure où elles se laissent interpréter, sont en sogdien.[52] On en conclut que *pârsi* désigne ici le sogdien. Il n'est pas impossible cependant que ce mot réfère au persan, qui avait sans doute déjà pénétré à Bokhara : on devra alors admettre que le Coran était lu en persan et les commendements donnés en sogdien. Mais cette hypothèse n'est pas suggérée par le passage, car on attendrait dans ce cas devant les citations sogdiennes une expression telle que 'dans leur dialecte, dans le parler du pays'.

IV

A la différence de *pahlavi* et de *pârsi*, le mot *dari* n'est pas ambigu : il désigne toujours le persan.

Muṭahhar Maqdisī, déjà cité, dans un passage traitant des noms de Dieu dans différentes langues,[53] écrit : *qawl al-aʿājim bi-lisān al-dariyya 'xodây' wa-'xodâvand' wa-'xodâygan'* 'les Persans disent en langue *dari xodây, xodâvand, xodâygân*'. Ce sont les mots persans. Meysari, auteur du *Dânešnâme*, dans le passage mentionné plus haut (p. 371), déclare dans les termes suivants qu'il a décidé de composer son poème en persan :

dari guyam-š tâ har kas bedânad
vo har kas bar zabân-aš bar berânad.
Je l'écrirai en dari, *afin que chacun le connaisse*
Et que chacun le récite.

L'auteur du *Zarâtoštnâme*, dans les vers cités ci-dessus (pp. 365-6), use de même du mot *dari* pour dire que son poème est en persan ; un peu plus bas (dist. 40) il met dans la bouche de l'envoyé céleste Soruš cette exhortation :

yeki tâze kon qesse Zartošt-râ
be lafz-e dari-o be nazm-aš farâ.
Rajeunis l'histoire de Zartošt
En langue dari et en vers.

Ferdowsi, présentant Zahhâk, écrit[54] :

hamân Bivarasb-aš hami xânedand
conin nâm bar pahlavi rânedand
kojâ bivar az pahlavâni šomâr
bovad dar zabân-e dari dah hezâr.
On l'appelait aussi Bivarasb ;
Tel est le nom qu'on lui donnait en pahlavi,
Car bivar *dans la manière de compter* pahlavâni
Signifie en langue dari *dix mille.*

dah hazâr est l'expression normale en persan, par opposition à *bivar*, présenté comme *pahlav(ân)i* (quelle que soit la valeur que l'on donne ici à cette dénomination : nous y reviendrons).

Dans ces quelques passages le mot *dari* est employé seul. Mais le plus souvent il est associé à *pârsi*, dans l'expression *pârsi-e dari* ou quelquefois *pârsi-o dari*, qui désigne toujours également le persan. La traduction persane du tafsir de Ṭabarī, élaborée entre 350/961–2 et 365/975–6, commence ainsi[55]: *va in ketâb tafsir-e bozorg-ast az revâyat-e Mohammad ebn-e Jarir at-Tabari . . . tarjoma karde be zabân-e pârsi-o dari râh-e râst* 'Ce livre est le grand Commentaire selon Mohammad b.Jarir Tabari, traduit correctement en langue *pârsi* et *dari*'. De même Bal'ami, au début de son adaptation des Annales de Tabari (352/963–4), dit dans son introduction en arabe[56]: *fa-qad tarjamtuhu biluġat al-fārisiyya al-dariyya* 'j'ai traduit ce livre en *pârsi dari*'. Ferdowsi, dans le passage déjà rappelé sur le livre de Kalila, écrit[57]:

be tâzi hami bud tâ gâh-e Nasr
bedân gah ke šod bar jahân šâh-e asr
gerânmâye Bolfazl dastur-e u
ke andar soxan bud ganjur-e u
befarmud tâ fârsi-o dari
be goftand-o kutâh šod dâvari
[*Ce livre*] *resta en arabe jusqu'au temps de Nasr,*
Jusqu'à ce qu'il devînt le grand roi de son temps.
Son ministre le noble Bolfazl,
Qui en belles-lettres était son trésorier,
Le fit réciter en pârsi *et* dari
Et la question fut réglée.

Le roi Nasr est le Samanide Nasr b. Ahmad (301–30/901–42) et la traduction en question celle que mit en vers le poète persan Rudaki.[58]

V

Les attestations des mots *pahlavi*, *pârsi*, *dari*, qu'on vient de passer en revue ont été choisie entre bien d'autres parce qu'elles se laissent interpréter clairement. On voit que *pahlavi* peut désigner: (*a*) le parthe, (*b*) le moyen-perse, (*c*) le persan, (*d*) des dialectes; *pârsi* de son côté peut référer: (*a*) au moyen-perse, (*b*) au persan, (*c*) à une autre langue (sogdien). *dari* désigne le persan. On résume les données considérées dans le tableau suivant.

	pahlavi	*pârsi*	*dari*
parthe	texte manichéen (IIIe s.)		
moyen-perse		rivayat pehlevie (v. 900)	

	pahlavi	*pârsi*	*dari*
		Ibn al-Muqaffaʿ (av. 757)	
		Balāḏurī (av. 892)	
		J̌ahšiyārī (av. 942)	
	Iṣṭaxrī (v. 951)	Masʿūdī (av. 956)	
	Šâhnâme d'Abu Mansur (957–8)		
	Zarâtoštnâme (av. 978)	Fihrist (v. 987)	
	Ferdowsi (av. 1010)	Ferdowsi (av. 1010)	
	Vis-o Râmin (1054)		
persan		Ibn al-Muʿtazz (av. 908)	
		Ṭabarī (av. 923; événement de de 686–7)	
		Abu Ḥātim (av. 934)	
		Muṭahhar Maqdisī (av. 966)	Muṭahhar Madqisī (av. 966)
		Bal'ami (963–4)	Bal'ami (963–4)
			Tafsir-e Tabari (961–76)
			Zarâtoštnâme (av. 978)
		Meysari (978–81)	Meysari (978–81)
		Muḥ. Maqdisī (v. 985)	
		Ferdowsi (av. 1010)	Ferdowsi (av. 1010)
	Adib-e Sâber (av. 1145)		
	Jâmi (xve s.)		
autre dialecte iranien	[dialectes du N.-O.]	[sogdien]	
	Bondâr (av. 1010)	Târix-e Boxârâ (953–4, trad. 1128–9)	

pahlavi	*pârsi*	*dari*
Šams-e Qeys (XIIIe s.)		
Ebn-e Bazzâz (1358)		
Mostowfi (XIVe s.)		

Ainsi, *pahlavi* et *pârsi* peuvent tous deux référer au moyen-perse, et tous deux au persan, qui peut aussi être désigné par le nom de *dari*. L'ambiguïté semble à son comble au Xe siècle, puisqu'on trouve à cette époque *pahlavi* et *pârsi* pour le moyen-perse, *pârsi* et *dari* pour le persan; ces quatre emplois sont attestés à la fois chez Ferdowsi.

Pour sortir de la confusion il faut partir du principe que, malgré les apparences, ces noms ne sont pas synonymes; s'ils réfèrent aux mêmes réalités, ils ne s'équivalent pas. 'Paris' et 'la capitale de la France' désignent bien la même ville, mais les deux expressions n'ont pas la même valeur. Nous avons vu quelles langues désignent les mots en question dans différents emplois; nous devons maintenant tenter d'apercevoir quelle valeur ils avaient pour ceux qui les employaient. Autrement dit, pour user du langage des sémanticiens, nous avons, pour chacun des emplois, précisé le 'référent'; il reste à définir la 'signification'. Celle-ci ne peut être établie que par des oppositions. Il faut donc chercher dans quelles oppositions entrent les termes considérés, comment, à diverses époques, ils s'opposent entre eux ou à d'autres noms de langue.

VI

Au IIIe siècle ap. J.-C., au moment ou l'empire sassanide remplaçait l'empire parthe, l'opposition majeure était certainement, pour les langues comme pour les peuples, entre parthe et perse, entre *pahlav(ān)ig* et, très vraisemblablement, *pārsig*. Parthe et perse (moyen-perse) étaient les langues impériales, l'une l'ancienne, l'autre la nouvelle. Elles avaient toutes deux leur tradition et leur écriture, dérivée de l'araméen selon des voies différentes, mais parallèles; elles étaient égales en dignité. Cette relation bipolaire est illustrée de manière éclatante par les inscriptions des premiers rois sassanides, où deux versions, parthe et perse, se répondent symétriquement. De ce temps, et même des siècles antérieurs, date l'opposition *pahlavi-pârsi* qui a persisté pendant des siècles dans la conscience iranienne, survivant même au changement des conditions sociales et politiques qui l'avaient fait naître.

Celles-ci en effet n'ont pas tardé à se modifier dès l'époque sassanide. Le parthe, déchu de son rang de langue impériale, entraîné dans la disgrâce systématique qui a atteint tous les souvenirs des temps arsacides, a tôt sans doute perdu de son prestige. Après Narseh (293–302) les inscriptions royales sont uniquement en perse. Cette langue devient la seule langue officielle. C'est aussi la langue religieuse et celle de la littérature écrite.

Sur le terrain, le perse parlé, dont l'aire originelle était le sud-ouest, s'est peu à peu répandu dans l'ensemble de l'Iran. Ce mouvement, continué à l'époque islamique, a gagné jusqu'à la Transoxiane, où il a presque complètement éliminé le sogdien. On sait que le parthe a disparu sans laisser de trace: aucun dialecte moderne n'en est le vestige. Au Khorassan, qui, comme on a vu, était au IIIe siècle le domaine propre du parthe, on ne parle aujourd'hui que le persan, continuation du moyen perse. L'élimination du parthe dans cette région a dû s'opérer, au moins en partie, dès l'époque sassanide: on l'a attribuée à l'installation, par les rois sassanides, de colonies militaires aux marches orientales.[59]

Cependant le parthe ne s'est peut-être pas éteint si tôt. Le domaine administré directement par les souverains arsacides comprenait aussi la Médie; vers la fin de leur empire le nom de Parthie (*Pahla*(*w*), forme arabisée *Fahlah* ou *Bahlah*) s'est trouvé étendu à cette région.[60] Chez les écrivains des premiers siècles islamiques il ne désigne plus que le nord-ouest de l'Iran,[61] où subsistent d'ailleurs aujourd'hui de nombreux dialectes historiquement plus proches du parthe que du perse. Il est possible qu'une forme plus ou moins pure de la langue parthe y ait survécu longtemps.[62] On sait d'autre part que le parthe fut l'organe d'une riche poésie orale: les ménestrels ou poètes-musiciens parthes (*gōsān*) furent renommés.[63] Il est douteux qu'une telle tradition ait disparu rapidement. Divers indices suggèrent 'that the *gōsān* played a considerable part in the life of the Parthians and their neighbours, down to late in the Sasanian epoch'.[64] Vraisemblablement cette poésie est restée cultivée, sinon au Khorassan, du moins en Médie, soit dans un parthe évolué, soit dans quelque forme de langue intermédiaire entre le parthe et les dialectes locaux. Si les œuvres, orales, ont disparu, cette activité dut être fort vivace, car elle n'a pas été interrompue par la conquête arabe et l'islamisation du pays et elle s'est continuée dans la littérature des *fahlaviyyât*. L'attachement, noté par Šams-e Qeys, des 'gens d'Irak' à leur poésie dialectale doit être un héritage direct de leurs ancêtres des temps préislamiques et le dernier avatar de la glorieuse poésie parthe.

Tout ceci permet d'entrevoir la signification qu'avait pu prendre à la fin de l'époque sassanide le couple traditionnel *pahlavi-pârsi*: il opposait le perse, langue commune et langue écrite, à la langue ou aux dialectes parlés dans le nord-ouest de l'Iran et dont l'usage littéraire (oral) préservait et affirmait l'individualité face à l'idiome officiel. C'est probablement en ce sens qu'il faut interpréter le seul passage du *Šâhnâme* où *pârsi* et *pahlavi* sont mis en parallèle. Il se place dans l'histoire du règne de Širuye; Xosrow Parviz détrôné est prisonnier et le roi son fils donne des instructions à son geôlier[65]:

ke hamdâstâni makon ruz-o šab
ke dar piš-e Xosrow gošâyand lab
magar ânke goftâr-e u bešnavi
agar pârsi guyad ar pahlavi.
N'accepte pas, de jour comme de nuit,
Que l'on parle à Xosrow
Sans que tu entendes la conversation,
Qu'elle se tienne en pârsi *ou en* pahlavi.

VII

Après la conquête arabe les perspectives changent complètement. L'opposition principale n'est plus entre Parthes et Perses et leurs langues, mais entre Arabes (*al-ʿarab*) et Iraniens (*al-ʿajam, al-furs*). Elle se manifeste avec éclat dans la querelle de la *šuʿūbiyya*. En Mésopotamie et en Iran les deux pôles des relations linguistiques sont désormais la langue des Arabes (*al-ʿarabiyya*) et celle des Iraniens (*al-fārisiyya*). Car telle est maintenant la valeur du mot *pârsi*: par opposition à l'arabe, *al-fārisiyya* est proprement la 'langue des Iraniens' (*al-furs*), en général et quelle qu'elle soit.

En fait on savait bien, naturellement, que ce 'langage des Iraniens' comportait plusieurs variétés. En cas de nécessité on pouvait les spécifier par un qualificatif. Masʿūdī distingue le *pârsi* ancien et le *pârsi* moderne[66]: '*derafš*' *bi-l-fārisiyya al-ūlà al-rāya wa-bi-hāḏihi al-fārisiyya išfà al-xarz* '*derafš* en *pârsi* ancien signifie étendard et en *pârsi* moderne il signifie l'alène du savetier'. Et à propos de Zoroastre[67]: *wa-kataba fī iṯnay ʿašara jild ṯawr bi-quḍbān al-ḏahab ḥafran bi-l-luġa al-fārisiyya al-ūlà wa-lā yuʿlamu aḥad al-yawm yaʿrifu maʿnà tilka al-luġa wa-innamā nuqila lahum ilà hāḏihi al-fārisiyya šay' min al-suwar* 'il écrivit son livre en creux avec des verges d'or sur douze mille peaux de bœufs, et dans l'ancienne langue *pârsi* dont personne aujourd'hui n'a plus l'intelligence; on a traduit en *pârsi* moderne seulement quelques parties des chapitres'. L'expression *al-fārisiyya al-ulà* désigne ici l'avestique; mais le sens est simplement 'la langue ancienne des Persans'.

Le plus souvent on ne se donnait pas la peine de préciser. Lorsque Abū Ḥātim de Rey, comparant les mérites des langues arabe, hébraïque, araméenne (*suryāniyya*) et *pârsi*,[68] porte au crédit de cette dernière le fait que les Mages ont un prophète avec un livre, *wa-inna kitābahu kāna bi-l-fārisiyya* 'et son livre est en *pârsi*', il dit simplement qu'il existe une Ecriture en 'langage iranien' tout comme il y en a en hébreu et en arabe. Il en va de même dans les gloses: quand un auteur dit que tel mot est *pârsi*, il serait vain de se demander à quelle langue iranienne il le rapporte; il veut dire seulement que ce mot est d'origine iranienne ou employé par les Iraniens. Au demeurant les diverses langues iraniennes ne sont aux yeux des auteurs arabes que des variétés d'un même langage, des nuances sur un fond commun. Masʿūdī dit bien, parlant de l'Iran:

> 'Tous ces pays constituaient un seul royaume régi par un seul roi, ils parlaient la même langue, sauf de légères différences que présentaient leurs idiomes; en effet des idiomes sont une même langue, lorsque les lettres que l'on écrit y sont les mêmes et qu'elles y sont composées de la même façon, bien que toutes les autres particularités ne s'accordent pas, comme on le voit dans le Pehlevi, le Déri, l'Adéri et les autres idiomes perses.'[69]

Pârsi signifie donc 'le langage des Iraniens'. Cependant ce sens général est susceptible de se particulariser selon les contextes; de là vient pour le lecteur moderne l'ambiguïté du terme, ambiguïté qui ne met pas en cause sa signification propre. Quand, avant le xe siècle, il est question de littérature et de livres, par exemple des ouvrages traduits en arabe ou des documents de la science et de la morale iraniennes, *pârsi* désigne la seule langue littéraire écrite de ce temps, le moyen-perse ou pehlevi: cet emploi rejoint le sens originel du mot. Quand il s'agit de la langue parlée dans telle province, il peut désigner un dialecte; nous avons vu l'exemple du *Târix-e Boxârâ*, où *pârsi* semble référer au sogdien. De même, lorsque Iṣṭaxrī écrit[70]: *wa-lisān Āḏarbayǰān wa-Armaniyya wa-l-Rān al-fārisiyya wa-l-ʿarabiyya ġayra anna ahl Dabīl wa-ḥawālīhā yatakallamūna bi-l-armaniyya wa-nawāḥī Bardaʿa lisānuhum al-rāniyya* 'les langues de l'Azerbaïdjan, de l'Arménie et de l'Arrān, sont le *pârsi* et l'arabe, si ce n'est que la population de Dabil et des environs parle arménien et que la langue de la région de Bardaʿa est l'arrāni', il a peut-être en vue, en parlant de *pârsi*, le dialecte iranien de la région, c'est-à-dire l'âzari; nous avons vu que Masʿūdī mentionne ce dialecte parmi les langues iraniennes aux côtés du *pahlavi* et du *dari*, et lui reconnait ainsi une certaine importance. Au ve/xie siècle, Nâser-e Xosrow, dans son *Safar-nâme*,[70a] décrit ainsi un maître qu'il a vu enseigner à Semnan: *mardi javân bud soxan be zabân-e fârsi hamigoft be zabân-e ahl-e Deylam* 'c'etait un homme jeune qui parlait *pârsi* dans la langue des Deïlamites'. Il faut entendre: il enseignait non pas en arabe, mais en langage iranien, dans le dialecte deïlamite (c'est-*à*-dire, probablement, celui de Semnân, dialecte septentrional, considéré comme une variété du deïlamite).

Cependant, dans la plupart des cas où le mot *pârsi* est employé pour désigner une langue parlée, il réfère naturellement à la langue de communication de l'ensemble des pays iraniens, celle qui était sentie comme la langue parlée des Iraniens par excellence, le persan. Après la naissance de la littérature, il désigne aussi bien sûr le persan écrit. Cet emploi deviendra de plus en plus fréquent et finira par éliminer les autres. *pârsi* (*fârsi*) deviendra le nom propre du persan: le mot aura alors changé de signification.

VIII

Le mot *pahlavi* à l'époque islamique a subi une évolution singulière et divergente. D'une part il est resté la désignation des dialectes de l'ancienne Médie, dont les formes littéraires étaient utilisées dans les *fahlaviyyât*. C'est probablement ce sens qu'il faut lui reconnaître dans le passage, cité ci-dessus (p. 379), où Mas'ūdī le mentionne sur le même plan que le *dari* et l'*âzari*, tous deux dialectes vivants. Dans le cadre des langues parlées de l'Iran et hors de toute référence à l'arabe, l'opposition entre *pahlavi* et *pârsi*, entre dialectes du nord-ouest et persan gardait assez fidèlement sa signification ancienne. Plus tard le nom géographique de Pahla (Fahlah) étant tombé en désuétude et le sens propre de *pahlavi* oublié, ce mot pourra s'appliquer à d'autres dialectes: le couple *pahlavi-pârsi* opposera dialecte et langue commune.

D'autre part les emplois du mot *pahlavi* dépassaient largement son utilisation comme nom de langue. C'était un qualificatif que l'on trouve chez Ferdowsi appliqué à des héros, à leur corps ou à leur équipement, à leurs festins, à la religion antique.[71] Il évoque la prestance des guerriers, la magnificence de leurs vêtements et de leur table, le caractère vénérable de la religion des ancêtres. Le trait commun de ces diverses acceptions est une référence à l'antiquité iranienne, au temps prestigieux des *pahlavân*. Les idées de souche iranienne, d'antiquité et de noblesse sont étroitement associés dans la signification du mot. On aperçoit comment celui-ci a pu en venir à désigner la langue des livres anciens, de ceux qui contenaient la sagesse des aïeux, le moyen-perse littéraire ou pehlevi. C'était la langue des temps anciens,[72] de l'époque glorieuse de l'empire iranien, dont le souvenir brillait d'un si vif éclat sous les Abbassides. Lorsque Ferdowsi parle de messages royaux ou de documents antiques, il ne manque guère de préciser qu'ils étaient rédigés en *pahlavi*, dans la langue noble des temps héroïques; et quand il fait parler ses héros, ceux-ci s'expriment en *pahlavi* c'est-à-dire en 'iranien ancien'.

A quelle époque ce nouveau sens s'est-il instauré? Nous l'avons trouvé bien établi au milieu du xe siècle, chez Iṣṭaxrī. Il faut probablement le reconnaître aussi chez Mas'ūdī (mort en 345/956) lorsqu'il parle des anciens livres étrangers traduits en arabe, tel Kalila, *wa-sā'ir al-kutub al-qadīma min al-yūnāniyya wa-l-rūmiyya wa-l-fahlawiyya wa-l-fārisiyya wa-l-suryāniyya* 'et autres ouvrages anciens, grecs, rumi, pahlavi, pârsi et syriaques'[73]; *pahlavi* et *pârsi* sont employés pléonastiquement, comme *yūnānī* et *rūmī*, et désignent tous deux le pehlevi. Il en va de même lorsque, quelques pages plus loin,[74] il mentionne les ouvrages de Mani, Bardésane et Marcion, *mimmā naqalahu 'Abd Allah ibn al-Muqaffa' wa-ġairuhu wa-turjimat min al-fārisiyya wa-l-fahlawiyya ilà al-'arabiyya* 'qui furent traduits par 'Abd Allah ibn al-Muqaffa' et d'autres du *pârsi* et du *pahlavi* en arabe'.

Il semble bien que le mot *pahlavi* soit déjà employé pour désigner le moyen-perse dans un passage, souvent cité, où Ǧāḥiẓ (mort en 255/868) expose, sans les prendre à son compte, les arguments par lesquels les *šu'ūbiyya* voulaient prouver la supériorité des Persans[75]:

wa-qad 'alimnā anna axṭab al-nās al-furs wa-axṭab al-furs ahl Fāris wa-a'ḏabahum kalāman wa-ashalahum maxrajan wa-aḥsanahum dallan wa-ašaddahum fihi taḥakkuman ahl Marw wa-afṣaḥahum bi-l-fārisiyya al-dariyya wa-bi-l-luġa al-fahlawiyya ahl qaṣabat al-Ahwāz.

Nous savons bien que les hommes les plus éloquents sont les Persans et que parmi eux les plus éloquents sont les gens du Fars, que ceux qui ont le langage le plus doux, l'élocution la plus aisée, les plus habiles a s'exprimer, les plus incisifs dans l'argumentation sont les gens de Marv, et que ceux qui pratiquent le plu élégamment le parsi dari *et le* pahlavi *sont les gens de la ville d'Ahvaz.*[76]

Comme on n'imagine pas que les habitants d'Ahvâz aient manié les dialectes médiques, il faudrait admettre que Ǧāḥiẓ a ici en vue le pehlevi. Cependant, comme il semble s'agir seulement de langue parlée, il n'est pas impossible qu'il reproduise quelque 'dit' traditionnel d'époque sassanide remontant au temps où l'opposition *pahlavi-pârsi*, celle des deux langues nobles, était bien vivante, et exprimant à l'aide d'une expression toute faite, l'habileté des gens d'Ahvâz en toute langue et en tout style.

Comment faut-il comprendre le mot *pahlavi* dans les passages où un auteur, glosant un mot, le donne pour *pahlavi* ? par exemple dans les vers, cités plus haut (p. 373), où Ferdowsi explique le mot *bivar*?[77] Faut-il entendre que le mot en question est dialectal ou qu'il appartient à la langue ancienne?[78] Il est de fait que certains de ces mots sont dialectaux, voire authentiquement parthes: c'est le cas de *gusân* cité par le *Mojmalottavârix* (520/1126) 'ménestrel'.[79] Le linguiste moderne le sait: les glossateurs anciens le savaient-ils? Ce n'est pas sûr. Le certain, c'est que pour eux les mots en question n'appartenaient pas à la langue commune, normale. C'est peut-être tout ce que pour eux signifiait le mot *pahlavi*, associant, dans une représentation assez vague, par opposition à la langue courante (*pârsi-e dari*), les formes de langue anciennes et dialectales. Une telle association n'est pas étrange: la conscience populaire rattache volontiers le dialectal à l'antique; tous les dialectologues de l'Iran sans doute se sont une fois ou l'autre entendu dire que dans tel ou tel canton on parle 'l'ancienne langue'.[80] Il est fort possible que dans le passé aussi le sentiment linguistique ait uni les deux sens du mot *pahlavi*, 'antique, archaïque' et 'dialectal', en une seule signification, qui serait: 'iranien non persan, hors de la norme'.

Reste à expliquer l'emploi de *pahlavi* pour désigner au contraire le persan. Il appartient à un autre registre. Nous avons vu que ce mot, employé comme qualificatif, unit les idées d' 'iranien' et d' 'antique'. La deuxième idée a donné naissance à l'emploi de *pahlavi* pour 'pehlevi, moyen-perse'. Mais la première pouvait aussi se trouver au premier plan, lorsque *pahlavi* s'opposait à d'autres noms ethniques, ainsi chez Ferdowsi décrivant le champ de bataille couvert de morts de toutes races[81]:

ze Cini-o Šogni-o az Hendovi
ze Saqlâb-o Harri-o az Pahlavi,
Chinois, gens du Shughnan, Indiens,
Slaves, gens de Hérat et Pahlavis,

ou des tissus précieux[82]: *ze rumi-o cini-o az pahlavi* '*rumi*, chinois et *pahlavi*'. C'est de la même façon que, par opposition à *arabi* ou *tâzi* 'arabe', *pahlavi* a pris le sens de 'langue des Iraniens'; après l'essor de la littérature, cette langue ne pouvait être que le persan. *pahlavi* est opposé explicitement à *tâzi* 'arabe' chez Adib-e Sâber, et implicitement chez Jâmi, qui met en parallèle le Masnavi et le Coran. *pahlavi* n'est pourtant pas strictement synonyme de *pârsi*. C'est un mot noble appartenant à la langue poétique. Il évoque encore en quelque mesure le peuple des *pahlavân*, et l'on force à peine le sens du distique de Jâmi en le traduisant: 'le Masnavi, c'est le Coran dans la langue des *pahlavân*'.

IX

Le *dari* est le persan, non seulement le persan écrit, mais aussi, bien avant la naissance de la littérature, le persan parlé dans toute l'étendue des pays iraniens. Cette langue était la continuation du perse parlé qui à l'époque sassanide s'était répandu en Iran vers le nord et vers l'est. Le mouvement avait continué de plus belle dans les premiers siècles islamiques, à la faveur de la conquête musulmane On sait quelle fortune cette langue d'origine occidentale a connue dans l'est: elle y a supplanté presque tous les dialectes locaux alors qu'ils subsistent nombreux dans l'ouest; et c'est dans l'est, au Sistan, au Khorassan et en Transoxiane, qu'elle a été élevée au rang de langue littéraire.

Lorsque se constitua le moyen-perse écrit, il devait être à peu près identique à la langue parlée. Mais cette dernière évoluait tandis que la langue écrite restait fixée. Vers la fin de l'époque sassanide l'écart devait être déjà assez grand entre la langue écrite et la langue parlée commune. On appela celle-ci 'langue de la Cour' (*dar* 'la Porte').[83] Le *dari* (mp. **darīg*), langue quotidienne de la cour royale et de la capitale, ainsi que d'une bonne partie de la population de l'empire, était ainsi opposée d'une part au *pârsi* (*pârsig*), langue des documents et des livres, des prêtres et des savants, et d'autre part au *pahlavi* (*pahlav*(*ān*)*īg*), le principal dialecte.

On trouve encore un reflet de cette opposition du *pârsi* au *dari*, c'est-à-dire du pehlevi à la langue parlée commune, chez Muṭahhar Maqdisī.[84] Après avoir mentionné les noms de Dieu chez les mazdéens (*hurmuẓ*, *īẓad*, *yaẓdān*), il dit avoir vu au Khouzistan un fragment de l'Avesta: *fa-qara'ū 'alayya bi-lisānihim wa-fassarū 'alayya bi-mafhūmihim al-fārisiyya* '[les prêtres] me le lurent dans leur langue et me l'expliquèrent avec ce qu'ils comprenaient de *pârsi*'; suit une citation indéniablement en pehlevi. Puis quelques lignes plus bas, vient le passage que nous avons cité ci-dessus (p. 373) et contenant la mention du *dari*: *wa-qawl al-a'ājim bi-lisān al-dariyya xoḏây wa-xoḏâvand wa-xoḏâygân* 'les Persans disent en langue *dari xodây*, *xodâv and*, *xodâygân*'. L'auteur distingue clairement *pârsi*, c'est-à-dire le pehlevi, et *dari*, c'est-à-dire le persan.

Mais à l'époque islamique les relations entre *pârsi* et *dari* sont en général tout autres. Les deux mots ne sont pas opposés, mais souvent associés, comme on a vu, dans l'expression *pârsi-e dari* (*pârsi-o dari*). *pârsi* signifiant 'le langage des Iraniens' en général, le mot *dari*, plus précis, vient le spécifier.

Le *dari* est une variété de *pârsi*; *pârsi-e dari* est 'la forme *dari* du *pârsi*'. Cette relation d'inclusion est énoncée explicitement chez le géographe Maqdisī[85]: *wa-kalām ahl hāḏihi al-aqālim al-ṯamāniya bi-l-ʿaǧamiyya illā anna minhā dariyya wa-minhā munġaliqa wa-jamīʿuha tusammà al-fārisiyya* 'la population de ces huit climats parle *ʿaǧamī* (non arabe, iranien), partie en *dari* et partie en des dialectes obscurs; l'ensemble s'appelle *pârsi*'. On ne saurait être plus clair.

Le Qâbusnâme (475/1082–3) distingue encore de la même manière *pârsi* et *dari*. Dans un chapitre sur le style épistolaire,[86] on lit la recommandation suivante: *agar nâme-ye pârsi bovad pârsi-e motlaq manevis ke nâxoš bovad xâsse pârsi-e dari ke ma'ruf nabovad ân xod nabâyad nevešt* 'si la lettre est en *pârsi*, n'écris pas en *pârsi* pur, car ce style est déplaisant, surtout s'il s'agit de *pârsi dari*, où cette manière n'est pas estimée; il faut absolument s'en abstenir'. L'auteur veut dire qu'il ne faut pas se limiter au vocabulaire iranien et éviter systématiquement les mots arabes. Si l'on se rappelle que c'était un homme du Tabaristan, région dont le dialecte avait connu un certain développement littéraire, on comprend qu'il songe à d'autres langues iraniennes que le persan; pour lui, par opposition à l'arabe (mentionné d'ailleurs un peu plus bas: *nâme-ye tâzi*), *pârsi* s'applique à l'ensemble de ces langues; le *dari*, la plus prestigieuse, n'est cependant que l'une d'entre elles.

Mais bientôt les relations vont encore changer. L'usage littéraire des dialectes sera abandonné, excepté dans le folklore; les livres pehlevis seront oubliés et la littérature persane vivra sur ses propres traditions. Le nom de *pârsi* étant dès lors réservé au persan, celui de *dari* deviendra inutile. Il ne survivra que comme un synonyme littéraire de *pârsi*. C'est ainsi qu'au XIIIe siècle en use Šams-e Qeys, lorsque, selon le style désormais à la mode, ils emploie l'un et l'autre mot dans des expressions symétriques et équivalentes, par exemple: *tabaqe-ye zorafâ va halqe-ye šoarâ ke dar e'jâz-e nazm-e pârsi dam-e isavi zanand va dar ebrâz-e âyât-e maâni-e dari yad-e musavi nemâyand* 'le groupe des beaux esprits et le cercle des poètes qui font des miracles dignes de Jésus dans la poésie *pârsi* et des prodiges dignes de Moïse dans la rhétorique *dari*'.[87]

X

Revenons à la notice d'Ibn al-Muqaffaʿ. Nous voyons maintenant qu'elle représente bien la situation à la fin de l'époque sassanide.

Le nom de *pârsi* tout au début est employé dans le sens général qu'il avait sous la plume des musulmans des premiers siècles, et même dans un sens plus large encore, puisqu'il embrasse non seulement les langues iraniennes, au sens moderne du terme, mais diverses langues usitées sur le territoire de l'empire d'Iran, y compris l'araméen et le *xuzi*. On traduira: 'Les langues de l'Iran sont . . .'.

Dans la suite, *pârsi*, langue 'des *mowbad*, des savants et de leurs semblables' est évidemment le moyen-perse littéraire ou pehlevi. Le mot est pris dans le sens qu'il avait à l'époque sassanide.

Le pays de Pahla, défini comme la région comprenant Ispahan, Rey, Hamadan, Māh Nihāvand et l'Azerbaïdjan, est l'ancienne Médie. Le *pahlavi*, langue du Pahla, est le parthe, s'il y vivait encore comme langue de littérature orale, ou les dialectes locaux, ses proches parents. Xwārizmī et Yāqūt ajoutent que ce *pahlavi* était employé dans les 'séances' royales. On peut penser qu'il s'agit de séances de divertissement, comme on en a tenu en Iran de tout temps, c'est-à-dire de 'banquets' où l'on buvait du vin en écoutant des vers et de la musique. Dans de telles 'séances', les célèbres ménestrels parthes ou leurs successeurs, qui chantaient en parthe ou dans les dialectes qui le continuaient, avaient leur place tout indiquée.

Le *dari*, langage de la capitale et de la cour royale, est la langue parlée commune, qui se distinguait dialectalement du *pahlavi* et plutôt stylistiquement du *pârsi*.

Restent deux indications à élucider, celle qui donne le *pârsi* comme langue du Fars, et celle qui concerne les relations du *dari* avec le Khorassan.

Comment le *pârsi* était-il la langue du Fars? Il est exclu que le pehlevi, langue des écrits, ait été le langage parlé ordinaire de cette province. Pas plus qu'ailleurs on n'y parlait comme les livres. Dans l'usage quotidien on s'exprimait soit comme ailleurs dans la langue commune, le *dari*, soit dans les dialectes locaux, historiquement proches du moyen-perse et du persan, mais aujourd'hui de structure assez différente du persan. Plusieurs explications, qui ne s'excluent pas, sont possibles:

(*a*) Ibn al-Muqaffaʿ ou l'auteur qu'il suit fait un rapprochement étymologique;

(*b*) il gardait le souvenir de l'origine du moyen-perse littéraire, constitué bien des siècles plus tôt en pays perse;

(*c*) le Fars était un important centre religieux et le pehlevi y était cultivé de manière particulièrement active (ceci est assuré en tout cas pour les premiers siècles islamiques);

(*d*) peut-être les dialectes du Fars étaient-ils vers les VIIe-VIIIe siècles sentis comme spécialement proches du moyen-perse littéraire par leur vocabulaire et leur structure grammaticale plus archaïque que celle du *dari*.

La mention de Balkh et du Khorassan à propos du *dari* n'est pas incompréhensible, puisque le *dari* non seulement s'est répandu dans l'est, mais est devenu la langue unique dans la plus grande partie du pays. Elle détonne cependant dans cette notice, dont l'horizon est par ailleurs borné à l'Iran occidental. En outre la formule n'est pas claire et paraît bien particulière: on attendrait plutôt un renseignement plus général, par exemple que le *dari* est aussi la langue du Khorassan et des pays de l'est. Au lieu de cela Ibn al-Muqaffaʿ dit seulement de manière allusive et obscure que parmi les parlers de l'Orient c'est celui de Balkh qui domine dans le *dari*. Comment interpréter cette indication? Le géographe Maqdisī dans l'intéressant aperçu qu'il donne des parlers de l'Iran oriental, dit que celui de Balkh est le meilleur et qu'il convient au style épistolaire.[88] Il s'agit certainement du persan local, non de l'ancien dialecte bactrien. Ce parler était donc considéré, au xe siècle, comme le plus élégant de la région. Peut-être avait-il cette réputation depuis longtemps et Ibn al-Muqaffaʿ ne veut-il pas dire autre chose. Il faudrait alors entendre: de tous les parlers *dari* usités au Khorassan c'est celui de Balkh qui a la primauté. Il n'en reste pas moins que cette note cadre mal avec le reste du texte. On a le sentiment qu'elle n'est qu'une remarque incidente, puisée à une autre source et ajoutée à un tableau plus ancien.

NOTES

1 Ed. Flügel (Leipzig 1871–2), 13.

2 Je transcris les mots et les noms persans selon la prononciation moderne d'Iran et conformément au système simplifié proposé par le 'Premier congrès international d'études iraniennes' (Téhéran 1966).

3 Ed. van Vloten (Leyde 1895) 116-17.

4 Ed. de Beyrouth (1957), IV, 281, s.v. *fahlaw*.

5 Spuler, *Iran in früh-islamischer Zeit* (Wiesbaden 1952) 243.

6 *BSOAS*, XXV (1962) 278-82.

7 Ibid., 278 n.3, où sont rappelées aussi les remarques de Nöldeke, 'Pehlevi' dans *Aufsätze zur persischen Geschichte* (1887).

8 On le voit bien chez Ferdowsi, qui emploie indifféremment les deux formes, par exemple à la fin de l'histoire du livre de Kalila et Dimna (*Šâhnâme*, éd. de Téhéran, Beroukhim, 1934–5, p. 2506, dist. 3492 et suiv.):

neveštand bar nâme-ye xosrovi
nabod ân zamân xat bejoz pahlavi
hami bud bâ arj dar ganj-e šâh
bedu nâsezâ kas nakardi negâh

conin tâ be tâzi soxan rânedand
az ân pahlavâni hami xânedand.
On le copia sur un livre royal:
Il n'y avait alors d'écriture que pahlavi.
Il resta précieusement dans le trésor du roi:
Les gens indignes ne pouvaient le regarder.
Jusqu'au temps où l'arabe se répandit
On le lut ainsi dans ce texte pahlavâni.

Et, trois distiques plus bas:

Kalile be tâzi šod az pahlavi
bar ân sân ke aknun hami bešnavi
Kalila fut traduit du pahlavi *en arabe*
Comme tu l'entends raconter aujourd'hui.

Cf. aussi 1283.22 (ci-dessous n. 78), et 28.95-96 cités plus bas.

9 Andreas-Henning, 'Mitteliranische Manichaica, II', *Sitzungsberichte der preuss. Akad. der Wissenschaften, phil.-hist. Klasse* (1933) 302-3.

10 V. Henning, 'Mitteliranisch' (dans Spuler, *Handbuch der Orientalistik. Erste Abt.*, *Vierter Band*, *Iranistik*, *Erster Abschnitt*, *Linguistik*, Leyde-Cologne 1958) 94.

11 C'est dans ce sens traditionnel qu'on emploiera ici la forme française *pehlevi*; la forme *pahlavi* sera réservée à la transcription du mot persan sans préjuger de son sens.

12 *Masālik al-mamālik*, éd. de Goeje, *Bibliotheca geographorum arabicorum* (*BGA*) I (Leyde 1870), 137.

13 M. Qazvini, *Bist maqale*, II (Téhéran 1313/1934) 22. Le nom d'Ibn al-Muqaffaʿ est ici un anachronisme.

14 Rypka, *History of Iranian Literature* (Dordrecht 1968), 156 et n.74.

15 V. ci-dessus n.8.

16 *Mélanges Massé* (Téhéran 1963) 337-42.

17 Ed. Dabirsiâqi (Téhéran 1338/1959) 2.

18 Ed. Minovi (Téhéran 1314/1935) 26, dist. 33 et suiv.

19 Ce témoignage est en quelque mesure corroboré par Šahmardân b. Abelxeyr, qui, dans son *Nozhatnâme*, ouvrage composé au début du VIe/XIIe siècle, dit avoir vu à Ispahan des textes étendus sur la légende de Rostam traduits du pehlevi en persan par un certain Piruzân sur l'ordre du kakouyide Farâmarz b. Alâoddowle (v. Lazard, dans *Mélanges Massé*, 227).

20 *Almo'jam*, éd. Qazvini et Modarres Razavi (Téhéran 1935) 22, 77-80, 128-32.

21 Etudiés par Adib-e Tusi, *Rev. de la Fac. des Lettres de Tabriz*, VI (1333) 471-8.

22 *Farhang-e Jahângiri*, s.v. *urâman*; *Majma'olfors* s.v. (éd. Dabirsiâqi, t. I, Téhéran 1338/1959, 76). Šams-e Qeys, op. cit., 132, associe les mots *urâman* et *fahlavi* dans une anecdote où des *fahlaviyyât* sont chantés au rythme du tambourin.

23 *Safvatossafâ*, cité par Adib-e Tusi, *Rev. Fac. Lettres Tabriz*, VII (1334) 468.

24 Chodzko, *Specimens of the popular poetry of Persia* (Londres 1842), 454, 474 n.2, 478 n.1.

25 V. Browne, *JRAS* (1895) 787.

26 *Nozhatolqolub*, éd. Le Strange (Londres-Leyde 1915, *Gibb Mem. Ser.* 23), 62, 87, 93 (trad. 67, 88, 94).

27 Dehxodâ, *Loqatnâme*, s.v. *pahlavi*.

28 Ibid.

29 Q. Sadiqi, *Rev. Fac. Lettres Téhéran*, XIII/4 (1345), 65 n.2, donne une une liste de références pour l'emploi du mot *pârsi* chez les auteurs arabes des premiers siècles de l'islam en distinguant les sens suivants: iranien, pehlevi, persan, langue du Fars. Pour ce dernier sens, les seules références sont la notice du *Fihrist* et celle de Yāqūt citées plus haut au début de cet article: je ne crois pas, comme on verra, que ce sens doive être retenu. – On laisse de côté dans ce qui suit l'emploi du mot *pârsi* pour désigner la transcription du pehlevi en écriture persane.

30 Ed. Anklesaria (Bombay 1962) 46. Je dois cette référence à l'amabilité de M. J.-P. de Menasce.

31 Ed. ʿAzzām (Le Caire 1941) 12.

32 *Kitāb futūḥ al-buldān*, éd. de Goeje (Leyde 1866) 300.

33 *Kitāb al-wuzarā' wa-l-kuttāb*, éd. Ibyārī et Šilbī (Le Caire 1357/1937) 38.

34 Ibid., 67.

35 Ed. trad. Barbier de Meynard (Paris 1865) IV, 89.

36 Ed. de Goeje (Leyde 1894, *BGA*, VIII) 106, trad. Carra de Vaux (Paris 1896) 151.

37 Op. cit., 244.

38 Ibid., 336.

39 Op. cit., 2577. 201-40.

40 *nabod ân zamân xat bejoz pahlavi*, v. ci-dessus n. 8.

41 Ed. Ḥamdānī (Le Caire 1957) I, 122-3.

42 Ibid., 71.

43 Sur cet auteur, v. Lazard, *Les premiers poètes persans* (Téhéran-Paris 1964) I, 22.

44 *Le livre de la création et de l'histoire*, éd. trad. Huart (Paris 1899–1919) III, 138 et 173.

45 MS Bibliothèque Nationale Persan 63 p. 612.

46 Lazard, *Premiers poètes persans*, I, 167, II, 182.

47 Op. cit., 2868.3420.

48 *Annales*, éd. de Goeje (Leyde 1879–1901), secunda series, 724.

49 *Ṭabaqāt al-šuʿarā'*, éd. Eghbal (Londres 1939, *Gibb Mem. Ser.* N.S.13) 10.

50 *Aḥsan al-taqāsīm*, éd. de Goeje (Leyde 1906, *BGA* III), 418.

51 Ed. Schefer (Paris 1892) 47.
52 Frye, *The History of Bukhara* (Cambridge, Mass., 1954) 48 et n.184.
53 Op. cit., 63.
54 Op. cit., 28.95-96.
55 *Tarjome-ye tafsir-e Tabari*, éd. Yaqmâi, I (Téhéran 1339/1960) 5.
56 Celle de la version la plus ancienne; citée par Grjaznevič et Boldyrev, *Sovetskoe vostokovedenie* (1957) fasc. 3, 53.
57 Op. cit., 2506.3498-500.
58 On trouvera une série d'autres citations attestant l'emploi du mot *dari* chez Boldyrev, 'Iz istorii razvitija persidskogo literaturnogo jazyka', *Voprosy jazykoznanija* (1955), fasc. 5, 78-92.
59 Christensen, *Contributions à la dialectologie iranienne* I (Copenhague 1930) 4-5. L'usage littéraire du parthe comme une langue vivante par les manichéens semble avoir cessé vers 400 ap. J.-C.: le dernier texte daté est de 386; dans les textes manichéens plus tardifs, issus de Transoxiane, le parthe est une langue morte, v. Ghilain, *Essai sur la langue parthe* (Louvain 1939) 24-30.
60 Henning, 'Mitteliranisch', 95.
61 V. les notices d'Ibn al-Muqaffaʿ (dans le *Fihrist*), de Xwārizmī et de Yāqūt citées ci-dessus. De même Ibn Xurdāḏbih, *Kitāb al-masālik wa-l-mamālik*, éd. trad. de Goeje (Leyde 1889, *BGA*, VI), 57 (trad. 38) définit ainsi le pays des Pahlavis (*bilād al-bahlawiyyīn*): 'Ray, Ispahân, Hamadhân, le Dynawar, Nèhâwand, Mihridjânkadhak, Mâsabadhân, Kazwyn . . . Puis Zandjân . . . Enfin le Babr, le Tailasân et le Dailam' (trad. de Goeje). Autres références et discussion chez Olshausen, *Monatsber. d. kgl. pr. Akad. zu Berlin*, 1876 [1877] 741 et suiv.
62 On peut objecter que Mani ne recourt au parthe que pour une mission au Khorassan, plus à l'est. Mais nous n'avons pas de renseignements sur l'évangélisation de la Médie. En outre il se peut que dès le IIIe siècle ap. J.-C., à la différence du Khorassan, le moyen-perse y ait été déjà plus ou moins répandu et suffisamment compris, ce qui n'exclut pas la persistance de dialectes septentrionaux.
63 V. Boyce, 'The Parthian *gōsān* and Iranian minstrel tradition', *JRAS* (1957) 10-45.
64 Ibid., 16.
65 Op. cit., 2913.74-5.
66 *Tanbih*, éd. de Goeje 86, trad. Carra de Vaux, 124.
67 Ibid., 91, trad. Carra de Vaux, 132.
68 Op. cit., I, 61.
69 *Tanbih*, trad. Carra de Vaux, 112-13. Texte: éd. de Goeje, 78.
70 Op. cit., 191-2.
70*a* Ed. de Berlin (1923) 5.
71 Je compte revenir ailleurs sur les emplois du mot *pahlavi* dans le *Šâhnâme*.

72 Explication déjà indiquée par Tavadia, *Die mittelpersische Sprache und Literatur der Zarathustrier* (Leipzig 1956) 13-14.

73 *Murūj*, VIII, 291.

74 Ibid., 293.

75 *Kitāb al-bayān wa-l-tabyīn*, éd. Muḥammad Hārūn (Le Caire 1368/1949) III, 13.

76 C'est ainsi que comprend Rescher, *Excerpta . . . aus den Schriften . . . Ğāḥiẓ* (Stuttgart 1931), 32; de même Pellat, *Cahiers algériens de littérature comparée*, I (1966) fasc. 1, 99. Goldziher, *Muhammedanische Studien* (Halle 1888–90) I, 170, traduit librement 'das eleganteste Persisch ist der Derīdialekt, das beste Pahlawī sprechen die Bewohner des Kreises von Ahwāz', ce qui est une interprétation arbitraire. Bahâr, *Sabkšenâsi* (Téhéran 1947) I, 150, rattache *wa-afṣaḥahum bi-l-fārisiyya al-dariyya* au membre de phrase précédent et entend: 'les gens de Marv sont aussi les plus élégants en *pârsi dari*, et en *pahlavi* ce sont les habitants d'Ahvâz'. Bahâr croyait que le *dari* était propre à l'est iranien et ne pouvait être usité à Ahvâz: c'est ce qui l'amène à traduire ainsi. L'interprétation que nous adoptons est la plus naturelle et la plus conforme au mouvement du texte.

77 Autres gloses analogues chez Ferdowsi, op. cit. 51.325 (*Arvand*, nom du Tigre), 52.342 (*Gang-e Doẓhuxt*, nom de Jérusalem), 1283.220 (*Kondoẓ*, nom de ville), 2205.1606 (*peydâvasi*), et ʿAbdulqâdiri Bagdâdensis *Lexicon Šahnâmianum* (éd. Saleman, St Pétersbourg 1895) n°2644 (*Varaẓrud*, nom de la Transoxiane); dans le *Târix-e Tabari* de Bal'ami, éd. Bahâr (Téhéran 1341/1962), 152 et 180 (t'rx, nom *pahlavi* du père du prophète Abraham!), et MS Bibl. Nat. Persan 63 p. 474 (*âẓar* 'feu', à propos de l'étymologie du nom de l'Azerbaïdjan); dans le *Tafsir-e Tabari*, éd. Yaqmâi V (Téhéran 1342/1963), 1155 (*derafš*); chez Bīrūnī, *Chronologie*, éd. Sachau (Leipzig 1878), 99 ligne 22 (*gar* 'montagne'); dans le *Mojmalottavârix*, éd. Bahâr (Téhéran 1318/1939), 69 (*gusân*).

78 Pour Ferdowsi, c'est plutôt la langue ancienne, comme on voit en 1283.222-23:

varâ nâm Kondoẓ bodi pahlavi
agar pahlavâni soxan bešnavi
konun nâm-e Kondoẓ be Peykand gašt.
[*Cette ville*] *portait le nom* pahlavi *de Kondoẓ,*
Si tu entends la langue pahlavâni.
Aujourd'hui *le nom de Kondoẓ a été changé en Peykand.*

79 V. Boyce, op. cit., 11.

80 Déjà Browne, *A literary history of Persia*, I (réimpr. Cambridge 1929) 80.

81 Op. cit., 994.580.

82 Ibid., 976.970.

83 C'est l'étymologie donnée par Ibn al-Muqaffaʿ lui-même, ainsi que par

le géographe Maqdisī, op. cit., 335. Sur les monnaies et dans les inscriptions pehlevies, *dar* désigne Ctésiphon, la capitale, v. Herzfeld, *Paikuli* (Berlin 1924) 151.

84 Op. cit., 62-3.

85 Op. cit., 259.

86 Ed. Levy (Londres 1951, *Gibb Mem. Ser.* N.S.18) 119.

87 Op. cit., 18.

88 Op. cit. 334-5.

KENNETH A. LUTHER

Rāvandī's Report on the Administrative Changes of Muḥammad Jahān Pahlavān

The reign of the last Seljuq Sultan of Iraq, Ṭughril (571/1176–590/1194), during the period when he was under the control of the Great Atabeg, Muḥammad Jahān Pahlavān (571/1176–582/1187), is troublesome for the historian. There is very little recorded for the period of Pahlavān, even in the summary fashion of the reporters of the time, such as Muḥammad Rāvandī, the unknown author of the *Akhbār al-Dawlat al-Saljūqīyah*, and the universal historian Ibn al-Athīr. Most of what occurred is lost to us forever, and this circumstance makes it necessary for us to subject the material we have to as thorough a scrutiny as possible. The chief purpose of this article is to examine some of the material in Rāvandī's *Rāḥat al-Ṣudūr*, verify it, and make an attempt to assess its significance in the light of the other relevant evidence. Before proceeding to this, however, I should like to take a few lines to throw Rāvandī's report into relief by noting the substance of the other contemporary and near-contemporary reports on Western Iran (ʿIrāq ʿAjamī) during the period of Pahlavān.

The *Saljūqnāmah* of Nīshāpūrī terminates essentially with the accession of Ṭughril. The only important bits of information on this period are that the amirs of the various regions of the Iraq Sultanate (which, it must be understood, no longer included Arab Iraq), held aloof from Pahlavān while he faced threats from two *maliks*, the Seljuq Muḥammad ibn Ṭughril and, presumably, the King of Georgia. Pahlavān was able to defeat these two with his own personal following, it seems, and this put him in a position of power which the amirs of the Sultanate were forced to recognize. They found themselves too weak to oppose him, and, according to the formula, '. . . put their feet firmly on the path of sincere friendship and affection'.[1] Pahlavān, for his part, according to this source, treated them kindly and increased their livings and *iqṭāʿs*. The end of this source is the same in all versions, concluding by wishing Ṭughril a long reign and noting that the amirs are his partisans.[2] Rāvandī follows the *Saljūqnāmah* tradition to the end also but adds to its statements so as to give the impression that Pahlavān treated the *raʿiyat* and the *dihqāns* well, not the amirs.[3]

Except for Ibn Isfandiyār, whom I shall save for the main part of my discussion, none of the other contemporary sources in Persian has very much more to give us. The *Ẓayl* of the *Saljūqnāmah* by Muḥammad ibn Ibrāhīm begins with the death of Pahlavān. From the section, 'Ḥavādis̱-i Ayyām' in *Tarjamah-'i Tārīkh-i Yamīnī* one learns only that order in the Iraq Sultanate ended with the death of Pahlavān.[4] The *Tārīkh al-Vuzarā'*, which was written shortly before the end of the Iraq Sultanate, again has very little of a specific nature on Pahlavān's period of rule and only says the usual, that the troubles began with his death.[5]

Of the sources in Arabic, one might expect *Akhbār al-Dawlat al-Saljūqīyah* to have the most material on Pahlavān's rule but, again, there is very little. We are told that Pahlavān was in control while Ṭughril was a child, that he moved against the Georgians, that he made his brother Qizil Arslān ʿUthmān his deputy in Āzarbāyjān, that the *khuṭbah* was given in Ṭughril's name in a great many places, and that he was continually sending messages of submission and presents to the caliph until his death.[6] Nothing of real importance is to be found in the summary treatment in *Zubdat al-Nuṣrah* or in the scattered notices of Ibn al-Athīr, Ibn al-Jawzi, or Sibṭ ibn al-Jawzi.

Rāvandī, after he ceases to copy the *Saljūqnāmah*, is the one who gives us the most information on the internal condition of the Iraq Sultanate during the period of Pahlavān. He couples his report with observations which represent a kind of casual explanation for the chaos which overtook Western Iran after the death of the Atabeg. I shall devote the remainder of this discussion to an attempt to evaluate and interpret what he says about the period.[7]

In his remarks about the period of Ṭughril under Pahlavān, Rāvandī first tells us that Sultan Ṭughril had security and the trouble-free enjoyment of his realm for a period of ten years, provided by the Atabeg who exerted himself in procuring for this Sultan that which even Malikshāh and Sanjar did not have. Pahlavān secured the *khuṭbah* and *sikkah* for Ṭughril in 'the lands', and he was able to keep the caliph from meddling in the internal affairs of Iraq, as afterwards happened. Then Rāvandī continues,

> 'And by means of the glory (*farr*) and good fortune of such an Atabeg, the Sultan became the envy of the people of the world, he in banquet and merry-making and the Atabeg in battle and toil. And when, at the beginning of his world-conquering, the Atabeg made two attacks, one

in the direction of Āzarbāyjān and the other toward Iṣfahān, and had caused two *maliks* to reach the abode of ruin on account of their coveting the realm, by means of conciliating (*istimālat*) he seized (*ba-dast āvard*) the amirs who were in rebellion (*dar darj-i sar-kashī*) and removed [them] according to his rightly guided opinion and placed his slaves in their places. He raised up sixty or seventy chiefs (*ʿalam*) from his slaves in the kingdom and appointed each one to a city and a region (*nihāyat*) in the hope that "since they are slaves they may keep my children safe from enemies". The obstinacy[8] of the offspring entered their heads and those same slaves made the kingdom miserable for his sons and the Sultan, and they cut off their rule from the *vilāyat* and the cities by reason of their [the slaves] holding *iqṭāʿs*, and each slave became the ruler in a region, and the glance of strangers fell on the kingdom from [different] sides, and the results of that became apparent after the death of the Atabeg. And the Atabeg made these slaves established and powerful (possessed of followings) and honoured from the plunder of Pārs and the riches of those regions ... and that was an inauspicious move which was the uprooting of the muslims of those regions, and it turned back with reverse motion on ʿIrāq (? *va ba-tarājuʿ bā-ʿirāq gardīd*). And these same slaves did the same to Iraq with the pretext of the Khvārazmīs. And they gave their heads and households to the winds with their own hands.'

Rāvandī mentions how they plundered *waqfs* and *madrasahs* and libraries, then had their own names put in books which they gave to one another as presents. He continues,

'... the open corruption in Iraq came from the fact that among the Turks each slave who seized a *vilāyah* did not know a law (*qānūn*) from the lives of his ancestors in regard to kingship, according to which he might proceed. Whatever he wanted and was possible he did until affairs came to that. And that fortunate Atabeg used to look upon a prospering realm far from trouble, and he did not imagine it would come to this. He sought the peace of the kingdom in the present and he used to say, "in the end let it remain this way".'

Our author goes on to tell how Pahlavān was very fond of his wife and children, wanted to make each one of them powerful and a ruler and was under the influence of his wife, Inānj Khātūn, who wanted her own sons (Inānj Maḥmūd and Amīr Amīrān ʿUmar) to rule. After telling how Pahlavān prepared to meet the threat of Ṣalāḥ al-Dīn, Rāvandī reports that the Atabeg fell ill on his return from the confrontation with the Ayyūbid and died at Rayy.[9] With this he ends his report of Jahān Pahlavān whom all contemporaries seem to feel was a great keeper of the peace, but to whom little space is devoted in their works.

Part of what Rāvandī refers to in the passage happened after the death of the Atabeg. It is difficult to tell whether or not Pahlavān gave his sons some sort of control over specific regions before his death. If he did so, the *mamlūks* may have begun to take control into their own hands before he actually died.[10] In any case, it is clear that Rāvandī sees Pahlavān's handling of his slaves, his appointing them to high administrative posts, as the root cause of the troubles which afflicted Western Iran during the last years of the Iraq Sultanate and on down to the time in which he himself was writing (*c.* 601/1204–5). Moreover, this action on the part of Pahlavān represents a sudden, far-reaching administrative change capable of leading to permanent changes in the political and social order. We may never be able to learn much about the details of Pahlavān's dispensation, for the sources we have now are far too thin to even suggest them. But some things can be said from what we do have.

We do have other evidence, some of it direct, most of it indirect and circumstantial, which converges in support of Rāvandī's description of what happened. The first bit is right to the point and is in itself a kind of interpretive statement which parallels that of Rāvandī. In his *Tārīkh-i Ṭabaristān*, Ibn Isfandiyār has a report from Pahlavān's last visit to Rayy, a city frequently mentioned in his work. Pahlavān was seated with the son of ʿAlī Vār. They heard the cry of *chāvūshes*, and Pahlavān, on asking who is coming, is informed that it is his slave Qāymāz. Ibn Isfandiyār then has Pahlavān say, 'Qāymāz has also reached a station in life where he has *chāvūshes*, but what do you say in regard to my slaves and the positions which I have given them?' The report continues with the reply, ' "May the life of the Great Atabeg be eternal. You have caused the slaves to reach such a position that after you they will obey no son of yours, and one will not greet another. And as long as one of these slaves shall live, Iraq shall have no peace." Tears came into the Atabeg's eyes, and he said, "You are right. Now what is to be done?" He said, "For this time is necessary in order to see what the command of God, whose glory is exhalted, may be." ' Shortly after this Pahlavān sickened and died, according to the report.[11]

It seems clear that Ibn Isfandiyār's view of the way in which Pahlavān had raised his slaves to positions of power and influence was essentially the same as Rāvandī's. Moreover, by means of the prophecy in the mouth of ʿAlī Vār, he took the same view of the consequences. There is more to be said about the correctness of their assessment of these consequences, but I shall defer that until I have dealt with the other evidence which supports Rāvandī's description of the change which Pahlavān carried out.

First of all, it can be argued that Pahlavān had every reason for making a large-scale administrative change of this nature, that is, for dislodging the older amirs of Western Iran and replacing them with his own slaves. Ever since his father, Shams al-Dīn Eldigüz[12] had become the power in the Iraq Sultanate in 555/1160 and had instituted a kind of dyarchy, in which the Sultan indispensably reigned while the Atabeg ruled, there had been opposition to the Atabeg from the amirs of Persian Iraq who owed their positions not to him but to the situation which had prevailed prior to his taking power. Right after he had placed his charge, the Seljuq Arslānshāh, on the throne, he had to face serious opposition from the Iraqi Amirs in 555–6/1160–1,[13] and one of the leaders of this revolt, Inānj, rebelled again during the years 561–4/1165–9.[14] Again, immediately after the death of Eldigüz in 571/1175, the amirs of Iraq are reported to have started Arslānshāh on an attempt to invade Āzarbāyjān and overthrow Pahlavān.[15] The Sultan is supposed to have been poisoned on account of this,[16] but, again, some of the amirs of Iraq were willing to support the Seljuq pretender Muḥammad ibn Ṭughril in a second attempt to seize the throne from Pahlavān's choice, Ṭughril ibn Arslānshāh. Pahlavān was forced to defeat this pretender with his own personal troops, apparently, while the amirs of Iraq either held back, waiting to see who would win.[17] This, according to Rāvandī, was the occasion which actually prompted Pahlavān to make the change in administration of the districts of the Iraq Sultanate. Thus we can count at least four certain occasions on which Eldiguz and his son were given good cause for wishing to have other servants in their army and administration.

Turning to the slaves themselves, one can gather a respectable contingent of prominent *mamlūks* whom the sources indicate as being members of Pahlavān's group. Their names come from reports of the period after the death of Pahlavān, down to the final Khvārazmian conquest of Western Iran in 614/1217–18. The relatively large number of individuals who can be identified as Pahlavān's *mamlūks* and the prominent role which they played in this '*mamlūk* period' in Iran's history are the strongest kind of evidence for Pahlavān's having done as Rāvandī says. We cannot come near the figure of sixty or seventy which he mentions, but, given the abridged nature of sources and their general lack of detail, we can come up with enough individuals to admit the existence of a slave corps of sizeable proportions, a group which could easily have had sixty or seventy men of enough rank and stature to be in charge of districts. In drawing up the list, the only criteria which the sources allow us are that the men mentioned be connected with Pahlavān with reasonable certainty and that there be some evidence for calling them slaves. One must say 'some evidence', since the sources do not make clear distinctions between free men, freedmen and slaves. The persons mentioned are often called only amirs. In naming the known members of Pahlavān's corps of *mamlūks*, I shall try to group them in the way in which they appear in the sources. They are mentioned in the sources for their role in events after the death of Pahlavān, of course. Except for Ibn Isfandiyār's account of Qāymāz, none of them appears by name in the very short accounts of Pahlavān's decade as Great Atabeg.

Two parties emerge within Pahlavān's following right after his death when Sultan Ṭughril is bidding for power against Qizil Arslān ʿUthmān, the brother and would-be successor of Pahlavān as Great Atabeg. Three important men in this group opposed an attempt on the part of Ṭughril, supported by Inānj Khātūn for her own reasons, to assume power. They were the Amīr Bār,[18] Nūr al-Dīn Qarā,[19] ruler of Qazvīn, and Nūr al-Dīn Qur'ān-Khvān who is associated with the region of Naṭanz.[20] Others also supported Ṭughril, Inānj Khātūn, and her son Qutlugh Inānj. They were Jamāl al-Dīn Āy Abah Chāshnī-gīr, *mamlūk* and high-ranking military commander,[21] Sayf al-Dīn Rūs, the same,[22] and Jamāl al-Dīn Az Abah, again the same.[23] Ibn Isfandiyār adds four others to this pro-Ṭughril group: ʿIzz al-Dīn Miyāq and Qarāgūz, both of whom are called *atābakīs*, plus Bashīr and Savinj Abah.[24] Two other great amirs who are known to be *mamlūks* and heads of districts are Sarrāj al-Dīn Qāymāz, Pahlavān's governor of Rayy until shortly before the latter's death,[25] and Jamāl al-Dīn Ulugh Bārbak Āy Ābah Farrazīnī, ruler of Karaj-i Abū Dulaf and holder of the great castle of Farrazīn, as well as *Malik al-Umarā* for the Atabeg.[26] Other *mamlūks* of Pahlavān who appear in the sources after the death of Ṭughril and the end of the Seljuq dynasty, are Nūr al-Dīn Kūkjah and Āytughmish, both identified by Ibn al-Athīr as *mamlūks* of the *Bahlawāniyah*.[27] Others identified as *atābakīs* are Qayāpah and Shūmlah-kash.[28] Badr al-Dīn Dizmārī, who was probably governor of the castle of Kuhrān, may well have been a *mamlūk*.[29] There are other individuals who, although not directly slaves of Pahlavān, belong in the following of his slaves: Jamāl al-Dīn ʿAlī, nephew of the Amīr Bār,[30] the son of Nūr al-Dīn Qarā,[31] at least two sons of Nūr al-Dīn Qur'ān Khvān,[32] a slave of Qarāqūz, Fakhr al-Dīn Qutlugh,[33] and a slave (*ghulām*) of Jamāl al-Dīn Āy Ābah Farrazīnī, Sayf al-Dīn Tukuz.[34] Thus we have as many as twenty-four individuals who can be associated with Pahlavān's corps of *mamlūks*.

As I have said before, considering the abbreviated nature of our sources, this is a profusion of names. Some of them are mentioned but once. There is enough material on others to allow one to devote small individual notices to them. Here it is impossible to do more than state below some of the more general characteristics of the group.[35] In any case, considering that there are approximately twenty-nine other amirs or military types mentioned in the sources, of which four belonged to Pahlavān's sons Abū Bakr and Uzbak, some thirteen seem to have been in Sultan Ṭughril's service, and some twelve others are difficult to assign to a specific group, this profusion alone indicates that Pahlavān did indeed have a large corps of 'politically prominent' *mamlūks*.

As noted above, they did not all hang together in the troubled years following the death of Pahlavān. They could be found on different sides and in different factions between their master's death and the final conquest of the Khvārazmshāh. In the statements of Rāvandī and Ibn Isfandiyār, it is clear that they were noted for their divisiveness as well as for disobedience and, in the case of Rāvandī's report, their rapacity. Even so, enough of them cooperated in their *mamlūk* fashion for Ibn al-Athīr to single them out as *al-Bahlawānīyah*, the *mamlūks* of Pahlavān.[36] It is clear in his reports that his sources caused him to see them as one very important group out of several groups which strongly affected the course of Western Iranian history throughout this period. This, of course, is additional support for Rāvandī's statement.

There is perhaps some measure of confirmation in Qazvīnī's *Nuzhat al-Qulūb* for Rāvandī's statement that the number of cities and districts involved in Pahlavān's change was sixty or seventy. If we assume that Rāvandī was referring to the two principal regions under Pahlavān's direct control, al-Jibāl and Āzarbāyjān, using Qazvīnī's figures of forty cities for (Persian) Iraq,[37] i.e. Jibāl, and twenty-seven for Āzarbāyjān,[38] we come up with the number of sixty-seven. This assumes, of course, that Mongol administrative divisions were similar to those of the late Seljuqs, something which demands proof in itself. It is also admitting a bit of circularity to say that Rāvandī's figures support this idea of continuity in the administrative divisions, but the figures in the two sources do seem to suggest this.

Taking all points together, that is, Ibn Isfandiyār's relation, the obvious necessity for dealing with the recalcitrant Iraq amirs, the large number of *mamlūks* prominently mentioned in the sources, Ibn al-Athīr's mention of *al-Bahlawāniyah*, and the way in which Rāvandī's figure compares with those of Qazvīnī, it seems that we can rely on Rāvandī's description of what took place. Pahlavān did indeed use his slaves to set up a system of *mamlūk* governorships in Western Iran, and in doing this he brought into being a specific élite group which was to play a dominant role in the area for some thirty years after his death. I hope to deal with their history in detail elsewhere. Here I shall confine myself to what we can say of Rāvandī's assessment of their role in history and to what we can say about this situation during the period of Pahlavān himself.

There are many instances in the *Rāḥat al-Ṣudūr* where Rāvandī laments the political confusion in Persian Iraq after the death of Pahlavān, and the plundering of the region by the *mamlūks*, by the army of the Khvārazmians, and also by the troops in the Caliph's army, especially when it was under the control of the *vazīr*, Mu'ayyad al-Dīn, whom Rāvandī found especially obnoxious.[39] In the course of the report of Rāvandī under discussion here, as quoted above,[40] he makes it clear what he feels the effects of Pahlavān's slave system were. In general, the drift of his statement is that Pahlavān sought to make the kingdom secure for his children but that the result was just the opposite. Their power was too great, their positions were too high, and they were ignorant of any principles of rulership, so did as they pleased, and the results were disastrous. There was 'open corruption', and the glance of strangers fell on the land.

It is quite clear from the history of the succeeding period that Rāvandī's assessment of the results of Pahlavān's efforts is a reasonable one. In the struggle between Sultan Ṭughril and the Great Atabeg Qizil Arslān, 583/1187–587/1191, there were great *mamlūks* on both sides, although, in the end Ṭughril had alienated and killed so many on his side that most of them ended up with the Atabeg, and this made it possible for him to seize and imprison the Sultan. In the final phase of Sultan Ṭughril's career (587/1191–590/1194) when Qutlugh Ināṇj, son of Pahlavān and Inānj Khātūn, fought the Sultan, the slaves appeared on all sides of the question but principally with Qutlugh Inānj, many of them following his lead and resorting to the Khvārazmshāh, one of the 'strangers whose eye had fallen on Iraq', who came and administered the *coup de grâce* to the moribund Seljuq Sultanate.[41]

In the following eighteen years the results of Pahlavān's elevation of his slave corps become even more evident.[42] To summarize, from 591/1194–5 to 595/1198–9 the *mamlūks*, under the ostensible control of the Atabeg of Āzarbāyjān, Abū Bakr, and his brother Uzbak who was supposed to be '*malik*' of Persian Iraq, contested Miyājiq, the deputy of Takash Khvārazmshāh, for control of the province. One of the more important *mamlūks* of Pahlavān, Jamāl al-Dīn Ulugh Bār-bak Āy Abah, was *Malik al-Umarā* for Uzbak during these years. He exerted considerable influence on affairs in Hamadān. Presumably, he was supposed to be the commander-in-chief of all the amirs, but only a few were usually cooperative with Jamāl al-Dīn at one time. Later, another Pahlavānī *mamlūk* who was powerful from the start, Nūr al-Dīn Kūkjah, became ruler of Persian Iraq after Khvārazmī influence was eliminated in 595/1198–9. For all practical purposes he was independent ruler of Persian Iraq until 600/1203–4 when a dispute among the *mamlūks* resulted in his deposition and murder. Another Pahlavānī *mamlūk*, Āytughmish, who had been Kūkjah's right-hand man, became 'Khāqān'[43] of Iraq until 608/1211–12 when the *mamlūks* went over to Mingli, who, though a *mamlūk* of Uzbak and not of Pahlavān, belonged to the same system by this time and had actually been raised to a position of prominence by Kūkjah, who is said to have regarded Āytughmish as a brother and Mingli as a son.[44] There is some indication here that the generations were changing. By 608/1211–12 the *mamlūks* of Pahlavān themselves were some twenty-six years from the death of their master, and they were beginning to give way to the *mamlūks* of his sons Abū Bakr and Uzbak. It is certainly the same group of military élite, however, consisting of the *mamlūks* of Pahlavān, Abū Bakr and Uzbak as well as others, perhaps some of the aging *ghulāms* of Sultan Ṭughril. Mingli incurred the wrath of the Caliph al-Nāṣir who organized a grand coalition against him, and when he was done away with, the last *mamlūk* of this series, Ighalmish, slave of Abū Bakr, had control of ʿIrāq ʿAjamī as Uzbeg's *Malik al-Umarā* in the years 608/1211–12 to 611/1214 or 612/1215–16.[45]

Most of what we know about these slaves and their behaviour is from this *mamlūk* period after the death of Pahlavān. However, certain things can be learned about their situation in the Pahlavān period. That the sources really mean 'slave' when they say *bandah* is generally clear, and, in one case at least, people are quoted as saying that Pahlavān bought Jamāl al-Dīn Āy Abah Ulugh Bār-bak for two or three hundred *dīnārs*.[46] We can also be certain that some were governors of cities and districts. There is the case of Sarrāj al-Dīn Qāymāz who was Pahlavān's governor of Rayy. He held this post until a short time before his master's death when his suggestion that Pahlavān should intervene directly in the affairs of the Shah of Māzandarān caused the Atabeg to remove him and substitute one Savinj Abah.[47] Qāymāz must have been able to use his post to amass great wealth, since, according to Rāvandī, Qutlugh Inānj was able to obtain 160,000 *dīnārs* from his effects.[48] It is difficult to associate many of these *mamlūks* with specific regions, but, again, it is possible to do so in some cases. Nūr al-Dīn Qur'ān-Khvān chose as his base the castle at Naṭanz after the death of Pahlavān, and it is likely that he was associated with this region previously.[49] I have already remarked about Jamāl al-Dīn Ay Abah Ulugh Bar-bak and Farrazīn, and in his case it seems that he held it at least as early as the last years of Ṭughril. The general difficulty remains, however, there is a lack of precise terminology even when we have some indication, as in yet another case, that of Nūr al-Din Qarā who is called only the '*ṣāḥib*' of Qazvīn.[50] In going along with Rāvandī one tends to conclude that these associations of particular *mamlūks* with particular areas is a result of administrative positions assigned to them by Pahlavān, although the implication in what Jurfādaqānī says is that these *mamlūks* sought the castles and gained control of them *after* the death of Pahlavān.[51] The trouble with Jurfādaqānī's report is that, in his attempt to discuss the causes and moral lessons of twenty years of strife, he is not much interested in matters of chronology, and one cannot make such an inference without other, chronologically reliable statements.

These men were usually called amirs. The greatest of them seem to have commanded contingents of a thousand, as in the case of Jamāl al-Dīn Āy Abah Chāshnī-Gīr, Sayf al-Dīn Rūs and Jamāl al-Dīn Āy Abah.[52] They must have been given *iqṭā' s* by means of *manshūrs* issued to them, for there is reference to this in the period after Pahlavān's death.[53] Some of them had *sarāys* in Hamadān, such as the *sarāy* of the Bār-bak, or *amīr-i bār*.[54] One can infer from one passage in Rāvandī that the most important ones may have had retinues which actually formed quarters in Hamadān, since he reports that a quarter of Hamadān was plundered in connection with Ṭughril's seizure of Sayf al-Dīn Rūs.[55] They are generally characterized as rapacious, of course, but some of them, notably Jamāl al-Dīn Āy Abah Ulugh Bār-bak were of good repute and even pious. This Jamāl al-Dīn built a *madrasah* in Hamadān which he used to visit whenever he came to the city.[56] Some of the members of this class apparently had at least the elements of a literary education, but, again, there is too little to allow one to generalize. One can only say that they had the opportunities for education which money, power, and high position allowed.

In sum, the Great Atabeg Shams al-Dīn Muḥammad Jahān Pahlavān made a change in the administration and control of the Seljuq Sultanate of Iraq which was to have far-reaching effects. The military slave system was much older than this, of course, but Pahlavān did make a clean sweep, and he thus rid himself of liabilities resulting from uncertain and conflicting loyalties of the older amirs of diverse origin. He used his power and position to set a new group of *mamlūks* in motion, and these were to affect the history of Western Iran for a generation.

Slaves and freedmen had dominated the history of Western Iran during the whole of the twelfth century and had made it ever more difficult for the Seljuqs to assert the claims of their dynasty, their sultanate. The Sultans relied upon a trio of concepts which in theory brought them loyalty from Muslims of varying classes and backgrounds. The concept of the Sultan, deputy of the Caliph wielding power in his name; the idea of the Persian king, the good *kadkhudā*; and the image of the Turkish Khān. But by the end of the century all of these were giving way to a slave system in which the only really enduring institutional tie was that between slave and master. It was on this that Pahlavān consciously based his government. He maintained the Sultan and used whatever loyalty the Seljuqs still inspired, but he relied on his slaves. In doing so he laid the basis for a 'Mamlūk Period' in the history of Western Iran.

NOTES

1 Ẓahīr al-Dīn Nīshābūrī, *Saljūqnāmah* (Tehran 1332 Sh.) 83. A useful control for this poor edition is Ahmed Ateş's edition of Rashīd al-Dīn Faẕl Allāh, *Jāmi' al-Tavārīkh*, Jild 2, Juz' 5, *Ẕikr-i Tārīkh-i Āl-i Salchūq*, Türk Tarih Kurumu Yayınlarından, III. Seri, No. 6 (Ankara 1960) here p. 177. Compare also Muḥammad al-Rāvandī, *The Rāḥat-uṣ-Ṣudūr wa Āyat-us-Surūr: Being a History of the Saljūqs*, ed. M. Iqbāl, *GMS*, N.S. II (Leyden 1921) 332 and note.

2 *SN* (*Saljūqnāmah*), 84.

3 *RS* (*Rāḥat-uṣ-Ṣudūr*), 332.

4 Abū al-Sharaf Nāṣiḥ ibn Ẓafar Jurfādaqānī, *Tarjamah-'i Tārīkh-i Yamīnī*, ed. Ja'far Shi'ār (Tehran 1345 Sh.) 422, also 4.

5 *Tārīkh al-Vuẕurā'*, Dār al-Kutub, 7 Ta'rīkh Fārsī Ṭal'at, f. 219b. Short notice in *Fihris al-Makhṭūṭāt al-Fārisīyah*, 'Al-Qism al-Awwal (Alif-Shīn)' (Cairo 1966) 52-3. Also my article, 'A new Source for the History of the Iraq Seljuqs: The Tārīkh al-Vuzarā'', in *Der Islam*, XLV (1969), 117-28.

6 Ṣadr'uddīn Abū'l Ḥasan Alī ibn Nāṣir ibn Alī, *Akhbār 'ud-Dawlat 'is-Saljūqiyya*, ed. M. Iqbāl (Lahore 1933) 171-2.

7 *RS*, 334-6.

8 Reading *khvudsarī* for *khvudsar-hā-yi* in the text, 335.

9 *RS*, 337.

10 In *ADS* (*Akhbār 'ud-Dawlat 'is-Saljūqiyya*), 173, one gets the impression that Pahlavān made a plan for dividing the sultanate among his sons earlier, but did not have it carried out until his death.

11 Bahā' al-Dīn Muḥammad ibn Ḥasan ibn Isfandiyār, *Tārīkh-i Ṭabaristān*, ed. ʿAbbās Iqbāl (Tehran 1320) (second sequence of page numbers) 151-2.

12 On the reading of this name, see V. Minorsky, *Studies in Caucasian History* (London 1953) 92n.2.

13 *RS*, 286. Al-Bundārī, *Zubdat al-Nuṣrah wa Nukhbat al-ʿUsrah*, vol. II of *Recueil de textes relatifs à l'histoire des Seldjoucides*, ed. M. T. Houtsma (Leyden 1889) 297-8. Ibn al-Athīr, *al-Kāmil fī al-Ta'rīkh*, IX (Cairo, printing of Maktabat al-Tijārīyah al-Kubra, n.d.), 73-4.

14 *RS*, 292-3. *ADS*, 147-8. Regarding corrections in the chronology of the *ADS* account, see Kenneth A. Luther, *The Political Transformation of the Seljuq Sultanate of Iraq and Western Iran: 1152–1187* (unpubl. dissertation, Princeton University 1964) 173 n.59.

15 *ADS*, 168-9.

16 *RS*, 348-52.

17 *RS*, 332, 335.

18 *RS*, 338. *ADS*, 179. The references for these individuals in this note and the following ones are not inclusive but are those which bear directly on the present discussion.

19 *RS*, 338 and n.2. *ADS*, 179.

20 *RS*, 338. Jurfādaqānī, *Tarjamah*, 428, regarding Naṭanz.

21 Muḥammad ibn Ibrāhīm, *Ẕayl-i Saljūqnāmah*, publ. at the end of *SN*, 85-92 and as part of Rashīd al-Dīn Faẕl Allāh's *Jāmiʿ al-Tavārīkh*, II, pt. 5, *Ẕikr-i Tārīkh-i Āl-i Salchūq*, ed. Ahmed Ateş, cited above, p. 403, n.1, 181-194; using the latter edition, 182. Jurfādaqānī, *Tarjamah*, 427. The *Ẕayl* has the title *chāshnī-gīr*. The name 'Y 'BH is written and rendered various ways. See J. A. Boyle's translation, *The History of the World Conqueror* of ʿAla-ad-Din ʿAta-Malik Juvaini, I (Cambridge, Mass. 1958) 148n.26. Also Muḥammad Qazvīnī in his edition of *Ta'rīkh-i-Jahān-Gushā* of Juwaynī, Part II, *GMS*, XVI, 2 (London 1916) 15n.9. In general I have simply transliterated one version of each of these Turkish names without attempting to involve myself in the problems of reconstruction. I have included some of the reconstructions in parentheses to aid in identification.

22 *Ẕayl*, 182. *Tarjamah*, 427.

23 *Ẕayl*, 182. *Tarjamah*, 427. *Ẕayl* has Uzapah, *Tarjamah*, Az Abah.

24 *TT2* (*Tārīkh-i Ṭabaristān*, second page sequence), 152. Qarāgūz is called *atābakī* by *RS*, 375. Savinj Abah is my reading of SWNJBH.

25 *TT2*, 146-52. *ADS*, 179.

26 *RS*, 379. *Tarjamah*, 431.

27 Ibn al-Athīr, *al-Kāmil*, IX, 232, 265. Kūkjah: Minorsky has Kökčä in 'Uzbek', *EI*, IV, 1063-4. Āytughmish: Minorsky, 'Uzbek', has Aytoghmish. Shiʿār, ed. of *Tarjamah*, has Āytughmish (p. 5). See also Mojtabā Minovi in his edition of Shihāb al-Dīn Muḥammad Khurandizi *Sīrat Jalāl al-Dīn Mīnkubirnī* (Tehran 1344 Sh.) 397, for Āydughmish and related names.

28 *Ẓayl*, 190. Ateş, the editor, has vowelled QY'PH as Qayāpah. The second name reads ŠMLH KŠ in the text.

29 *RS*, 364. *Ẓayl*, 189. *ADS*, 182. He and Maḥmūd-i Anāsūghlī ('N' SWĠLY) freed the Iraq Sultan Ṭughril from his captivity after the death of Pahlavān's brother and successor, Qizil Arslān. One has the impression that they were both in the service of the atabegs. According to *ADS* Maḥmūd was a Turkoman and (presumably?) not a slave. In the *Ẓayl* Dizmārī is other than the governor of the castle. The accounts do not agree, and it is difficult to be certain what positions they had.

30 *RS*, 384.

31 *RS*, 389.

32 *RS*, 389.

33 *RS*, 362, 365.

34 *RS*, 379.

35 Below, pp. 401-2.

36 Ibn al-Athīr, *al-Kāmil*, IX, 234, 305.

37 Ḥamd Allāh ibn Abī Bakr ibn Muḥammad ibn Naṣr Mustawfī Qazvīnī, *Bakhsh-i Nakhust az Maqālah-i Sivvum-i Nuzhat al-Qulūb*, ed. Muḥammad Dabīr-Siyāqī (Tehran 1336 Sh.) 51.

38 Mustawfī, *Nuzhat*, 85.

39 *RS*, 381-82.

40 Above, pp. 394-5. One other writer sees Persian Iraq's troubles as the result of the actions of Pahlavān's *mamlūks*, although he does not discuss the way in which the Atabeg had raised them up in his own time. This is Jurfādaqānī who, in the introduction to the *Tarjamah*, 4-5, says, 'Nearly a hundred of . . . his important *mamlūks*, each one of which was an *ʿifrīt* from the *ʿifrīts* of mankind (*ʿafārīt-i ins*), . . . stepped off the path of rectitude, and all of them made greed strong in the realm of Irāq, and conquered a castle in a region and opened the door for the people of destruction and corruption . . . and for nearly twenty years the space of this strife and the substance of this calamity increased . . .'.

41 *ADS*, 171-96. *RS*, 337-71. *Ẓayl*, 181-94.

42 The first part of this period is the subject of *RS*, 375-403. There is information in the 'Khātimah', or 'Ḥavādiṣ-i ayyām', of the *Tarjamah*, 420-42, but it is not clearly separated from the last years of Ṭughril. Jurfādaqānī was attempting to explain the whole period of chaos from the death of Pahlavān to his own time. A chronology for the rest of the period can be gained from Ibn al-Athīr, *al-Kāmil*, under the years 599–612.

43 *Tarjamah*, 5.

44 *TT* 2, 169.

45 One of the first to point out the '*mamlūk*' character of the régime in Iran after the death of the last Seljuq Ṭughril was Muḥammad Qazvīnī on pp. 407-11 of his edition of the *Ta'rīkh-i-Jahān-Gushā* (Part III). His list of the *Mamlūks* of Western Iran consists of Kūkjah, Miyājiq (Khvārazmī commander in Iraq), Āytughmish, Mingli, and Ighalmish (p. 411). I hope to do more work on this question, but at present it seems that Jamāl al-Dīn Ay Abah of Farrazīn should also be included in the list, since he was dominant at least at one point after the death of Ṭughril (*RS*, 388-9). Regarding the position of Ay Abah, see also V. Minorsky, 'Uzbek', *EI*, IV, 1063.

46 *Tarjamah*, 431.

47 *TT* 2, 151.

48 *RS*, 380.

49 *Tarjamah*, 428.

50 *Ẓayl*, 189. *RS*, 338n.2.

51 *Tarjamah*, 4.

52 *Tarjamah*, 427.

53 *RS*, 363.

54 *RS*, 350, where the author speaks of 'sarāy-i har mihtari', and 365, the *sarāy* of the Amīr Bār.

55 *RS*, 344.

56 *RS*, 379.

D. N. MACKENZIE

The Vocabulary of the Lahore *Tafsīr*

After the appearance of G. Lazard's comprehensive work on the earliest New Persian prose[1] – one of the many fields in which our deeply regretted friend V. M. contributed so much – it is practically superfluous to describe the language of a further text of the period. This text, a seemingly unique fragment of 46 folios of a *Tafsīr* of the Qur'ān, bequeathed by the late Mahmud Sherani[2] to the University of Lahore, has now been published in facsimile,[3] with an introduction by M. Minovi. It is thus possible to turn directly and conveniently to the vocabulary, which contains some very interesting words.

The portion of the manuscript which has survived contains a translation, with a long commentary, of the verses 65-151 (Flügel, 61-146) and 233 of the second surah, *al-Baqarah*. Thus forty or so folios are lost from the beginning, and an unknown number from the end, and with them all indication of the original title, the author, or the source of the work. Minovi justly estimates, on the evidence of the writing, spelling, and style, that the work was composed about 450 A.H., say A.D. 1050, possibly earlier, somewhere between Khorasan and Ghazni. It does not seem to have any of the dialectal characteristics that Lazard connects with Herat.[4] It does, however, have much in common with the Cambridge *Tafsīr*, described in detail by E. G. Browne,[5] including some of the Mazdean vocabulary noticed by Lazard.[6] Since, as will be seen, the vocabulary also includes elements of distinctly eastern Parthian, and even Soghdian, origin it is likely that its provenance is to be sought in the region of the Oxus.

I

Many of the peculiarities of the text are simple variants, either archaic spellings[7] or dialect forms, of well-known words, such as *'βgndn* 'throw' 3.24, 80.12 (Lazard § 2), *'βz'y-* 'increase' 5.18, *frstydn* 'send' 20.10, 41.11 (L. § 333), *fryšth* 'angel' *passim* (L. § 130).

There are many words which, though found in the dictionaries, occur but rarely in texts, while others are employed in unusual senses. There are also some previously unknown words. If the following list, though shorter than Sherani's (loc. cit. 41-78), should still err on the side of fullness, this may be forgiven in view of the continuing backward state of early Persian lexicography. Etymologies are suggested, where possible, to supplement those quoted in M. Moʿin's edition of the *Borhān-e Qāteʿ*, or Lazard, op. cit.

''hnǰ- 'extract', 76.17 *yā rabb, tō-ē ʿaziz, ay ki kīna āhanǰē az ān kas ki nagirawaδ* 'O Lord, thou art mighty; that is, thou takest vengeance on that person who does not believe' (L. § 140).

''wnd 'vessel', *v.* 88 *qālū qulūbunā γulfun* = 23.26 *ǰahūδān guftand ki dilhā-yi mā čūn āwandhā-st mar gūna gūna ʿilmhā rā wa γilāfhā-yi ʿilm ast* 'the Jews said, Our hearts are like vessels for various kinds of knowledge and they are cases for knowledge'.

''z'dy nmwdn 'give thanks', 69.5 *az xuδāy ... bisyār āzāδi wa šukr namūδ* 'she gave many thanks to God' (Browne, 440).

'fsws, fsws 'mockery', *v.* 67 *qālū 'a-tattaxiδunā huzū'an* = 3.9 *guftand, yā mūsā, bar mā fusōs mē kunē* 'they said, O Moses, dost thou mock at us?' (cf. Ṭabari,[8] *mē girē mā rā ba fusōs*); 4.21 ... *ki bar mu'minān afsōs kunam, ki harki bar mu'minān afsōs kunaδ ō az ǰumla-yi ǰāhilān bāšaδ* '(God forbid) that I should mock at the believers, for whoever mocks at the believers is of the ignorant' (*'fsws*, Br. 443).

'lfydn, 'lfnǰ- 'gain, amass', *v.* 81 *man kasaba sayyi'atan* = 15.81 *harki baδi alfanǰaδ, ay ki pa xuδāy ... širk āraδ* 'whoever gains evil; that is, brings partners to God'; *v.* 95 *bi-mā qaddamat aydīhim* = 29.25 *paδān sabab ki dānand ki ēšān či alfayda-and mar xwēštan rā* 'because they know what they have gained for themselves'; 78.26 *alfaydand ... alfanǰēδ* (Br. 443; L. § 331; Henning, *BSOS*, 10, 105).

'ngštyrh 'ring', e.g. 34.2 *har bārē ki sulaimān pa āb-xāna andar šuδē az ḥurmat mar ān angustīra rā bā xwaδ nadāštē* 'every time Solomon entered the privy, out of respect he would not have that ring with him'.

'skrd, v. 11 *infra*.

'st'xy 'impudence', 38.2 *pēš az ān hēč dēwē rā zahra nabūδē ki pa nazd-i sulaimān āmaδē yā bā way ustāxī kardē* 'before that no demon had the gall to approach Solomon or to make free with him' (L. § 55).

'w = NP *āyā*, 23.18 *guft, yā ǰahūδān, u har bārē ki pa sōy-i šumā az man rasūlē firistīδa āyaδ ... ēšān rā kuštan girēδ* 'He said, O Jews, whenever

a prophet is sent to you from me . . . do you take to killing them?' (L. § 733-4).

b'yst w n' b'yst, v. *š'yst w n' š'yst*.

b'z zd krdn 'prohibit, abrogate', *v.* 85 *wa huwa muḥarramun 'alaykum 'ixrājuhum* = 19.6 *ān bērūn kardan-i šumā mar-ēšān az xānahā-šān ḥarām būδ bar šumā, ya'nī bāz-zaδ karda būδ šumā rā* 'your expelling them from their homes was forbidden to you, that is it was prohibited for you'; 49.16 *ammā nāsix ān ast ki pēš az ān āyatē āmaδa bāšaδ wa paδān kār farmūδa pas-i ān āyatē digar āyaδ wa kārē digar farmāyaδ wa-z ān kār-i pēšīn bāz-zaδ kunaδ* 'now (the meaning of) abrogating is that formerly a verse has been revealed and in it actions commanded, then another verse comes and commands another action, and abrogates that former action'; 51.20 *ānči xwāhaδ farmāyaδ wa-z-ānči xwāhaδ bāz-zaδ kunaδ* 'He commands what He wills and prohibits what He wills'.

bnj 'base', 72.11 *wa firēšta az binj-i kōh sang āwurd* 'and the angel(s) brought stone(s) from the base of the mountain(s)'.

brdgy 'captivity', e.g. 33.22 *duxtarē az ān-i malik-i kāfirān pa bardagī girift wa pas ō-rā āzāδ kard* 'he took a daughter of the king of the infidels captive and then set her free' (*brdh*, Br. 447; *varda*, L. § 8).

brxš-, v. II *infra*.

**bydh*, v. II *infra*.

b^{a}yd^{u}xt 'Venus', 43.8 *nām-i īn zan pa tāzī zuhara būδ wa pa pārsī baiδuxt wa pa zabān-i 'ibrī anāhīδ* 'the name of this woman [who later became the planet Venus] was Zuhara in Arabic, Baidukht in Persian, and Anahid in Hebrew [!]'.

byhdh 'vain', 13.11 *ān bēhuδahā-yi tarfandhā* 'those vain, idle things' (L. § 127). No MP **abē-hōdag* is known, but cf. Pāzand *aβēhangī* (*ŠGV* iv, 81) for Pahl. *'*pyhwdyh* = *abēhōyih* 'futility' and **hwdk* 'cause, reason' in *GB* 100.12 *az ān *hōyag (ī) margīh pad tan ī gayōmart andar šud harwisp dāmān ō frašegird margīh abar mad* 'for that reason, that death entered the body of Gayomart, death came upon all creatures until the Restoration'; also Central Kurd. *hō* 'cause, means'. Perhaps a specialization of Av. *aoδa-* 'source (of water)' > 'cause', and 'without cause' > 'futile', in which case the NP form would be from a Parth. **abē-hōδag*.

by-stwn, v. *xstwn*.

bzh mndy 'sinfulness', *v.* 85 *bi-l-'iθmi wa-l-'udwāni* = 18.8 *pa bazamandī wa sitamgārī* 'with sin and oppression' (cf. Ṭabarī, *ba baza wa sitam*); *v.* 233 *fa-lā junāḥa 'alayhimā* = 40.26 *bar-īn māδar wa piδar či tangī nēst wa bazamandī nēst* 'on this mother and father there is no constraint and no sin' (Br. 447).

β'm 'debt', 17.13 *wājib šuδan-i zakāt rā haft šarṭ ast . . . čahārum bēβāmī* 'there are seven conditions for the (giving of the statutory) alms to be obligatory . . . the fourth is not being in debt' (L. § 14).

d'nšwmnd 'learned', 11.20 *gurōhē az dānišōmandān gufta-and ki ān suxun ham az xuδāwand-i taʿālā šunīδand* 'some learned men say that [Moses and his companions] heard those words directly from God'; also 12.12 ff.

dšxw'r 'difficult', 5.3 *wa l(ē)kin bar xwaδ dušxwār giriftand* 'but they made things difficult for themselves'; *v.* 143 *wa 'in kānat la-kabīratan* = 86.16 *īn rōy gardānīδan-i tō az qibla-yi baitu-l-muqaddas pa sōy-i baitu-l-ḥarām saxt dušxwār āmaδ bar dil-i gurōhē az jahūδān* 'this thy turning of the face from the *qiblah* of Jerusalem to the direction of Mecca was very hard on the hearts of some of the Jews' (Br. 461).

dwk'n, in its original sense of 'platform of flattened earth', Ar. *dakka* 'crush, flatten', 72.10 ff. *ādam ānjā dukkānē binā kard . . . ēzaδ-i taʿālā xāna-yi zarrīn az zēr-i ʿarš pa sōy-i ādam firistāδ bā haftāδ hazār firēšta tā ān xāna rā bar miyān-i dukkānē binihāδand* 'Adam there built a platform . . . God sent a golden house from beneath (His) throne towards Adam, with seventy thousand angels, so that they set that house down on the middle of a platform' (L. § 133).

dwžx, e.g. 14.26 *ātaš-i dōžax* 'the fire of hell' (L. § 42).

dyw'l, e.g. 1.24 *dēwālē bar kašīδand* 'they raised a wall'; cf. Taj., Afghan Pers., Pashto *dēwâl* (Br. 463; L. § 63).

frywl, *frwyš*, v. II *infra*.

frym'n- 'deceive', 37.20 *xwāst ki mar-ō-rā bifirēmānaδ* 'he wanted to deceive her': 37.17 *mar-ō-rā mē firēft* 'he used to (try to) seduce her'; cf. Br. 478 *firēwān-* (L. § 5).

grdn bᵘrd 'disobedient', *v.* 114 *wa man 'azlamu* = 58.12 *kēst az mardumān bar xwēštan bēdāδgartar wa-z xuδāwand-i taʿālā gardan-burdtar wa bar xuδāwand-i xwaδ dilērtar* 'who of men is more unjust to himself and more disobedient to the Lord and more insolent to his own Lord?'; similarly 83.7 = *v.* 140 *ditto*.

gw' 'witness', *gw'yy* 'testimony', e.g. 85.24 *tā rasūl mar šumā rā guwā bāšaδ* 'so that the apostle may be a witness for you'; 85.15 *nūḥ īn ummat rā pa guwāyī xwānaδ tā az bahr-i ōy guwāyī dihand* 'Noah calls this people to witness so that they may give testimony on his behalf' (L. § 95).

gw'žh, v. II *infra*.

hw'zy, *v.* 145 *'innaka 'iδan la-mina-z-zālimīna* = 89.19 *tu hawāzī āngah az jumla-yi bēdāδgarān bāšē bar xwēštan* 'thou wilt then surely be among those unjust to themselves'. The dictionary definition of *hawāzī*, 'suddenly', does not seem to be well established; in all traceable occurrences the meanings 'then, thus' would pass muster, so perhaps < Av. *awaθā* + *zī*, cf. Cent. Kurd. *wahā* 'thus' (Br. 493).

j'dw 'sorcerer', *j'dwy* 'sorcery', *v.* 102 *wa mā kafara sulaymānu* = 41.14 *ay mā saḥara sulaymānu, guft, sulaimān kāfir nabūδ wa jāδū nabūδ az-ē-rā-ki harki jāδūī iʿtiqād kard murtadd wa kāfir gardaδ* 'and Solomon did not disbelieve – that is, S. did not use sorcery; he said, S. was not an infidel and not a sorcerer, for whoever believed in sorcery becomes an apostate and an infidel'.

k'rbnd 'attentive', *v.* 121 *yatlūnahu ḥaqqa tilāwatihi* = 65.12 *mē xwānand taurāt wa injīl rā wa kārband mē bāšand čunānki sazā-yi ān-ast wa dar xwur-i ān-ast* 'they recite the Torah and the Evangel and apply themselves to it as is fitting and appropriate'.

k'sky, 2.12, 64.7 *kāskē* [sic] *bidānamē* 'would that I knew' (L. *kāški*, § 47). Pahl. *kāč (ka)* < OP **kac(č)i* = Skt *kaccid* 'I hope that' < **kad-čid*. NP *kāš-*, *kās-* should be northern and southern dialect forms resp., cf. Parth. *čiš* : Pers. *tis* < OP *čišči* < **čid-čid*; *kās-* therefore seems out of place in this text.

kdyjk, v. 11 *infra*.

kšn, v. 11 *infra*.

kpy 'ape', e.g. 1.25 *ēzaδ-i taʿālā ān qaum rā ki māhī girifta būδand kapiān gardānīδ* 'God turned that people who had caught fish into apes' (Br. 480).

m'yg'n 'month', e.g. 50.9, 84.5 *hafdah māyagān* 'seventeen months' (L. *māhagān*, § 150; but see my note, *JRAS*, 1966, 69 n.3).

n'xw'h'ny 'indifference', *v.* 130 *wa man yarγabu ʿan millati 'ibrahīma* = 76.21 *kēst ki nāxwāhānī kunaδ mar dīn-i ibrāhīm* 'who is there that turns away from the faith of Abraham?'.

nš'xtn 'seat, set', 46.11 *šab andar āmaδ, du sag yā du gurba biyāwurd ... yakē xwaδ bar nišast wa yakē ma-rā nišāxt, raftēm* 'night came, she brought two dogs, or two cats, sat on one herself and set me on one, and we went ...'.

nwsb'sy [!] 'ingratitude', *v.* 90 *'an yakfurū bi-mā 'anzala-llāhu* = 25.19 *nuspāsī kardand niʿmatē rā ki xuδāwand-i taʿālā mar-ēšān rā dāδa-ast* 'they were ungrateful for the bounty that God has given them' (Br. 490).

nyrng 'magic', 33.18 *ān nibištahā rā ki dēwān nibišta būδand az jāδūīhā wa nēranghā andar waqt-i mulk-i sulaimān ... pēš giriftand* 'they followed those writings which the demons had written about sorcery and magic during the reign of Solomon'.

nznd 'humbled', 80.24 *saranjām xuδāwand-i ta'ālā īn γam wa šuγl-i jahūδān az pēš-i dil-i tu bar girδa wa ēšān-rā nizand wa zalīl-i šumā gardānaδ* 'in the end God will remove this sorrow and concern with the Jews from thy heart and make them humbled and contemptible before you' (Br. 490). A Parth. form; v. Benveniste, *TPS*, 1945, 73 (s.v. Arm. *hnazand*), and Henning, *BSOS*, 11, 722 (s.v. Sogd. *nyz'nt*).

p'šn' 'heel', e.g. 86.10 *pa jāyē mē rawaδ pas az ānjā bar pāšnā bāz gardaδ* 'goes to a place, then turns back on his heels from there'.

p'yw'h, v. 11 *infra.*

prdh, v. 11 *infra.*

prgst, *v.* 67 *qāla 'a'ūδu bi-llāhi* = 4.20 *mūsā guft ... pargast bāδā wa ān rōz mabāδā* 'Moses said, God forbid and may that day never come!'; = Pahl., < **para-gasta-* 'extra loathsome', cf. OP *gasta-*, Parth. *gst* <√*gand* 'smell'.

ps'y- 'touch', *v.* 80 *wa qālū lan tamassanā-n-nāru 'illā 'ayyāman ma'dūdatan* = 14.26 *guftand jahūδān ki napasāyaδ mā rā ātaš-i dōzax juz ki rōzē čand-i šumurda* 'the Jews said, The fire of hell will not touch us except for a few, numbered days' (cf. Ṭabarī, var. *nh bs'wd*, and Br. 448, s.v. *bswδn*). *ps'y-* : Sogd. *ps'w-* 'touch', as NP *sāy-* 'rub' : Parth. *s'w-* 'crush', < **sāwaya-*.

pst 'low', 66.7 *az-ān yakē nāxun past kardan* 'one of them (is) to trim the nails'.

pštg'n 'supporter', 65.6 *āngah mar tu-rā juz az xuδāy 'azza wa jalla ki bāšaδ dastgīrē ... wa yā puštagānē ki mar tu-rā yārī dihaδ* 'who then except God will be a helper for thee, or a supporter who will give thee help?'.

pšt w'rh 'load', 7.24 *čūn rōz šuδē puštwāra-ē hēzum āwurdē wa ān rā bifurōxtē* 'when day broke he would bring a load of firewood and sell it'; also 38.14.

py'ft'dn 'understand', 48.5 *aknūn pa āškārā dušnām mē dihēm-u mē gōyēm rā'inā, ō xwaδ pay nayuftaδ. sa'd ... luγat-i jahūδān pay uftāδē* ' "Now we shall abuse him openly and say *rā'inā*; he will not understand". Sa'd understood the language of the Jews' (Br. 442, s.v. *'ft'dn*, with *by*).

pyywlh 'corner', 69.24 *wa īn sang dar paiyōla-yi masjid būδ pa rōzgār* 'and this stone was in the corner of the mosque for ages'; < **pati-gaušaka-*, cf. NP *gōša*, *-š-* > *-l-* as in *frywl*, q.v.

r'st' in *pr'st'y* 'with regard to', 16.14 *farmūδēm tā pa-rāstā-yi xwēš wa paiwandān nēkōyihā kunand* 'We commanded that they should act kindly with regard to relatives'; 92.20 *tā nēkōyihā-yi xwēš pa-rāstā-yi šumā tamām gardānam* 'that I may complete my bounties towards you' (Br. 447; L. § 711).

r'st xyz 'Resurrection', e.g. 10.17 *hamčunīn zinda gardānāδ mar murdagān rā pa rōz-i rāst-xēz* 'so will He bring the dead to life on the Day of Resurrection'.

r'š 'cubit', e.g. 71.20 *bālā-yi xāna nuh riš kard wa pahnā-yi ān si riš* 'he made the height of the house 9 cubits and the width of it 30 cubits' (Br. 463); = Pahl. *'ršn* 'cubit', MP *''ryšnwg* 'elbow', < OP *ărašni-*.

Ar. *skynh*, 73.2 *ēzaδ-i ta' ālā firēšta-ē rā bā way firistāδ wa sakīna rā bā way rawān kard wa muryē andar miyān-i sakīna tā injā rasīδ ki jāy-i xāna ast, sakīna gird-i ān bar tanīδ cunānki' ankabūt tanaδ wa mury az miyān-i ān āwāz dāδ, yā ibrāhīm . . . dar barābar-i man xāna binā kun* 'God sent an angel with him, and the *sakīna* with a bird within it, until he reached this place where the Kaaba is; the *sakina* spun (a web) round it, as a spider spins, and the bird cried from within it, O Abraham, build a house before me'; the concept defies translation.

sry', v. II *infra*.

swn, v. II *infra*

sxwn 'speech', e.g. 2.6 *pa zabān saxun natawānistandē guft* 'they could not speak' (Br. 469; L. § 61).

š'rst'n 'city', 1.6 *ān čunān ki qaumē būδand andar šāristān-i ailah andar ayyām-i dāūd* 'it was so, that there was a people in the city of Elath in the days of David' (Br. 472).

š'w'n-, v. II *infra*.

š'yst w n'š'yst 'right and wrong', 32.14 *āyathā-yi qur' ān padīd karda-and rōy-i bāyist wa nā-bāyist wa šāyist wa nā-šāyist* 'the verses of the Koran have made manifest (the truth) concerning what it is necessary and proper to do and what it is not' (Br. 473).

škrwf, v. II *infra*.

škyb- 'be patient', 21.7 *in 'iyāl-i man būδa-ast wa dil-i man dar way basta-ast wa bē way namē šikēbam* 'this was my wife and my heart is bound to her and without her I cannot bear (life)'[9]; = Parth. *'škyb-*, cf. Pahl. *škyp'kyh* 'patience'.

šngl, v. II *infra*.

t'rh 'dark', 60.6 *yārān-i paiyāmbar . . . waqtē dar biābānē bimāndand, tāra mēyē bar āmaδ, āsmān bipōšiδ* 'once the companions of the prophet stopped in a desert; a dark cloud came up and covered the sky'; cf. Sogd. *t'ry*, Yaghn. *tóra* < **tāθraka-*.

t^{u}n^{u}k 'tender', 20.21 *ahl-i ō tunuk-dilī-yi bisyār mē kardand. dil-i ʿisā tunuk šuδ, bar sar-i gōr-i ō āmaδ wa duʿā kard* 'the people (of Lazarus) were sorely grieved. Jesus' heart softened and he went to his tomb and prayed.'

trfnd 'vain, idle', v. s.v. *byhdh*; also 55.25, 70.11.

xstwn 'confessing', *n'xstwn*, *by xstwn*, and *by stwn* 'disbelieving', e.g. *v.* 84 *θumma 'aqrartum* = 17.26 *šumā xustūn šuδēδ ki bar šumā ʿahd ham bar-ān gūna būδa-ast ki yāδ kardēm* 'you confessed that the covenant had applied to you also, as we mentioned'; *v.* 90 *wa li-l-kāfirīna ʿaδābun muhīnun* = 26.17 *mar in bē-xustūnān rā pāywahē buwaδ andar dōẓax xwār kunanda* 'for these infidels there is a humiliating punishment in hell'; *v.* 85 *wa takfurūna bi-baʿḍin* = 19.9 *wa pa baʿẓē bē-stūn wa nā-xustūn šawēδ* 'and in a part you disbelieve' (Br. 458). Cf. JP *xwstw*, etc., *BSOAS*, 31, 253.

yk'nh, v. II *infra*.

ywb-, *ywbh*, v. II *infra*.

ẓ^{a}hy 'breeding, brood-', 17.15 *haftum agar čahārpāy buwaδ čunān bāyaδ ki ẓahī bāšaδ yā aẓ bahr-i tijārat* 'the seventh (condition for the giving of the statutory alms), if cattle are concerned, they must either be for breeding or for trading'.

II

The following words are of special interest, either for their uniqueness or for their parallels in other Iranian languages.

'^{a}sk^{a}rd 'obligatory', *v.* 83 *wa 'aqīmu-ṣ-ṣalāta wa 'ātu-ẓ-ẓakāta* = 17.6 *bar pāy dārēδ, ay ki tamām guẓārēδ namāẓhāyē rā ki bar šumā askard karda-and, ay ki wājib karda-and . . . wa bidihēδ ẓakāt, ay ki dihišē ki bar xwāstahā-yi šumā askard karda-and* 'establish, that is carry out fully, the prayers which have been made obligatory for you . . . and give the alms, that is the donations which have been made obligatory upon your wealth'. Possibly related is Sogd. *'sk'rt-* 'rent' (Mugh, B-4, 10; v. Gershevitch, *CAJ*, VII, 2, 84), if 'forced (payment)' < **uẓ-kṛta-*; alternatively cf. Sogd. *skrtyy* 'victorious, overpowering' (v. Henning, *Sogdica*, 37), if 'imperious' > 'imperative'. The word reappears in Taj. colloquial as *iskard*,[10] with the further development of meaning

'without exception' > 'invariably', e.g. *vay iskard hamin gapro taqror mekunad* 'he always repeats these words'.

$b^{u}r^{u}$*xš-* 'shine', 8.5 *gāwē saxt zard čunānki gōyē az rang-i mōy-i way āftāb mē buruxšaδē* 'a cow so yellow that you would say the sun was shining from the colour of its hair'; NP *ruxš-*, *raxš-*, with *mē* + *bi-* (L. § 357), or < *wiruxš-* = Chr. Sogd. *wyrw*[*x*]*š-*?

**bydh*: unless a haplography for **tā* ⟨*pā*⟩*yinda* or the like be assumed, this seems the only possible reading in the following passage, *v.* 150 *wa li-'utimma niʿmati ʿalaykum* = 92.19 *tā bēδa gardānam nēkōyihā-yi xwēš bar šumā, in-jahāni wa ān-jahāni* 'so that I may complete my bounties upon you, of this world and of that' (v. further s.v. *r'st'* above). This actually corresponds to an Arabic gloss *li-'ukammila*...; thus *bēδa* seems to be a survival of MP **abēdag* < **upa-ita-ka-* in its original sense of 'arrived' > 'perfected', cf. NP *rasida*. In the more common sense of *upa*√*i*, 'to be necessary', only Parth. *'byd* 'in need' and Pahl. *'pyt'n* 'necessary' are attested.[11]

f^{u}*rywl* 'negligence', and

frwyš 'forgetfulness'. *v.* 74 *wa mā-llāhu bi-yāfilin ʿammā taʿmalūna* = 11.12 *nēst xuδāwand-i taʿ ālā az kardahā-yi šumā bē xabar, wa guft ki xuδāwand-i taʿ ālā az kardahā-yi šumā furyōl-kār nēst, guft ay ki farwiš-kār nēst* 'the Lord is not unaware of your actions; and he said, God is not neglectful of your actions; he said, that is, He is not forgetful'; *v.* 85 *ditto* = 19.21 *xuδāy ʿazza wa jalla az pāywah-i ēšān farwiš-kār nēst* 'God is not forgetful of their punishment'. On *furyōl*, v. Henning, 'Sogdian loan-words in New Persian', *BSOS*, 10, 100, n.1. The *-l-* < *-š-* suggests a more eastern form than Parth. *frgwš-*. *farwiš* recalls Sogd. *frāwə*(*š*)*či* 'forgetfulness' < **frāmušti-*, but *-m-* > *-w-* only occurs (sporadically, cf. Yaghn. *firōmič*/*š*) after *-ā-* in Parth. and Sogd., so Pers. *farwiš* is not entirely explicable.

gw'zh 'greed', g^{u}*w'zgn* 'greedy', *v.* 96 *wa la-tajidannahum 'aḥraṣa-n-nāsi ʿalā ḥayātin* = 30.4 *ēšān rā har-āyina az mardumān-i digar bar zindagāni hariṣtar yābē, ay ki guwāzgintar yābē. pārsi-yi ḥirṣ guwāza kardan bāšaδ wa maʿni-yi ḥirṣ sēr našuδani bāšaδ az yāftan-i čizē agar bisyār yābaδ* 'you will find them in all ways greedier of life than other men, that is you will find (them) more covetous. The Persian for 'coveting' is *guwāza kardan* and its meaning is not being satisfied with obtaining something, (even) although one obtains much (of it)'. This must be a different word from *guvāza* 'rebuke' < **wi-wāčaka-*[12]; perhaps <√**gū* 'want', v. Benveniste, *BSOS*, 9, 514.

kdyǰk 'hut', 73.23 *hāǰar aȥ xāšāk-i kōh wa-ȥ xārbunān-i wādī xwēštan rā kaδičakē sāxt* 'Hagar made herself a hut from the straw of the mountain and the thorn bushes of the river bed'. This word, a diminutive of MP *kadag* 'house', has been confused in the *Borhān-e Qāṭeʿ* (followed by Br. 481) with *gurič(a)* 'pit', Parth. *gryhcg* (v. Henning, 'List', *BSOS*, 9, 83).

k^{i}*š*^{i}*n*, 74.18 *bandagān-i xuδāwand-i taʿālā aȥ aṭrāf-i ȥamīn īnǰā āyand, labbaik gōyand, sarhā kišin šuδa wa gard-ālūδ gašta wa gird-i ān xāna ṭawāf kunand* 'the servants of the Lord will come here from all parts of the earth, they will say, "I am here", their heads *shaven and dust-stained, and they will circumambulate that house'. An unknown word, < **kṛšna-* < **kṛθ-na-* <√*kart* 'cut'?

p'yw(')h 'punishment', e.g. *v*. 85 *fa-mā ǰaȥā'u man yafʿalu δālika minkum* = 19.13 *či bāšaδ saȥā-yi ān-kas ki īn čunīn kunand ǰuȥ pāywah wa ruswāyi andar īn ǰahān* 'what is the due of persons who act so, except punishment and disgrace in this world?'; *v*. 114 *wa lahum fi-l-'āxirati ʿaδābun ʿaȥīmun* = 59.18 *wa mar-ēšān rā xwāhaδ būδ pa rōȥ-i pasīn, ay ki paδān ǰahān, pāywāhhā-yi buȥurg* 'and for them there will be on the Last Day, that is in the other world, great punishments'. Despite the obvious similarity to MP *pādifrāh* (NP *bāδafrāh*) < **pati-frāθa-*, it would be necessary to assume an unparalleled contraction of *-fr-* to connect the two words. A possible alternative etymon is Av. *paitī.wyādā-*, lit. 'recompense', though it is only attested in a beneficial sense.

p^{u}*rdh* 'accused', v. 76 *li-yuḥāǰǰūkum bihi ʿinda rabbikum* = 12.22 *tā ēšān paδīn bar šumā pa qiyāmat pa xuδāy-i taʿālā bahāna gīrand wa mar šumā rā paδīn purda* [here *brdh*] *gardānand* 'so that they may thereby find a pretext against you and accuse you thereby before God at the Resurrection'; 13.1 *ēšān rā ḥuǰǰat wa bahāna bāšaδ wa šumā andar īn purda šawēδ* 'it will be an argument and a pretext for them and you will be in the wrong thereby'; 92.3 *pārsī-yi ḥuǰǰat bahāna-ē buwaδ ki xaṣm rā purda gardānaδ* 'the Persian for *ḥuǰǰat* is "a pretext which puts the antagonist in the wrong" '. Steingass has *purda* 'enigma', source unknown: probably from a misunderstanding of a similar context, say **purda kardan* taken as 'to confuse, baffle'. The word continues either MP *'pwrdg* 'guilty' < **apa-pṛtaka-* or the simple participle of √*par* 'condemn', without a preverb, cf. Sogd. *'prtk* (pronounced *əpte*).

s^{a}*ry'g'n* 'cantors', 13.11 *taurāt-i xwaδ nadānand ǰuȥ ān bēhuδahā-yi tarfandhā ki aȥ saryāgān-i xwēš wa dānišmandān-i xwēš mē šinawand* 'they do not know their own Torah, except for the vain, idle things they hear from their cantors and wise men'. *saryāgān* < **srāyăgān*, cf. Parth. *sr'wg* 'singer' < *sr'w-* : MP *sr'y-*, NP *sarūdan*.

swn alternates with *swy* 'side, direction' (once 12.3 *b-šwy* in error), e.g. 35.4 *bar yak sūn-i anguštīra nibišta būδ* 'on one side of the ring was written . . .'; 84.7 *wa čūn pa madīna āmaδ ham bar-ān sūn namāz̨ mē kard* 'and when he came to Medina he still prayed in that direction'. Also *brswn* 'upwards', *v.* 144 *qad narā taqalluba wajhika fi-s-samā'i* = 88.1 *dīδēm wa mē bīnēm ān rōy gardānīδan-i tu pa sōy-i āsmān wa barsūn nigarīstan-i tu andar namāz̨* 'We saw and see thy turning the face towards heaven and thy looking upwards during prayer' (Br. 447 *brsw*). Perhaps contamination of *sōy* < MP *sōg* and MP *rōn* < **(h)rawan-*, or a by-form of the latter. The connexion between the two words, if any, remains unclear. ['*sūn* 'côté' se trouve dans At, QN, Garšasbnâme (éd. Yaqmâi 488), et en tadjik dialectal (Rastorgueva, *Očerki*, fasc. 5).' Note from G. Lazard of 12/67; v. L. § 699.]

š'w'n-, *v.* 126 *θumma 'aḍṭarruhu 'ilaʿ aδābi-n-nāri* = 71.14 *wa l(ē)kin kāfir rā wā bišāwānum andar-ān jahān pa pāywāhē dardnāk* 'but the infidel I shall drive into a painful punishment in that world'. A NP causative in *-ān-* from the caus. stem Av. *šāwaya-*, cf. Parth. *frš'w-* 'send', corresponding to the intransitive MP, NP *šaw-* 'go'.

š^u^krwf 'loser, in trouble', *v.* 121 *wa man yakfur bihi fa-'ūlā'ika humu-l-xāsirūna* = 65.20 *ān-kashā ki pa hūasti-yi xuδāwand-i taʿālā bē-stūn gaštand . . . ēšān-and z̨iyān-z̨adagān-i šukrūfān* 'those who have become disbelievers in the existence of the Lord . . . they are sufferers, losers'. The word, ultimately from √**skar-f*, cf. Parth. *ʿskrfyšn* 'stumbling', MP *ʿškrw-*, NP *šikarf-* 'stumble', reproduces very closely the Sogd. form *'škrwβ*, whose pronunciation it clarifies. This occurs once in *SCE* 21, *'XRZY 'sty ZKZY Z Kw šyr wnty rty 'škrwβ šwt rtyms 'sty γwnγ 'kyZ Y Z Kw γnt'k wnty rty wr'kh βyrt*, where *'škrwβ šwt* corresponds to Chin. 致過 'results in transgression', so 'then there is the one who does good and gets into trouble, and there is the one who does evil and achieves success'.

š^u^ng^u^l 'hoof', *v.* 69 *'innahā baqaratun ṣafrā'u fāqiʿun lawnuhā* = 5.10 *ān gāwē-st ki hama pōst-i ō z̨ard ast, z̨ard-i z̨ard tā šungulhā wa surūn-iš* [!] *nēz̨ z̨ard ast* 'that is a cow the whole of whose skin is yellow, as yellow as can be, and even its hooves and horns are yellow'. Cf. Pashto *ṣ̌ōngáray* 'cloven hoof' (Morgenstierne, *EVP* 78), or Yidgha *čogulo* 'hoof' (*IIFL*, ii, 201 a)?

yk'nh, *yg'nh* 'submissive', *v.* 128 *rabbanā wa-jʿalnā muslimayni laka* = 75.5

yā rabb, mā har du rā yakāna-yi xwaδ gardān 'O Lord, make us both submissive to thee'; *v.* 131 *qāla 'aslamtu li-rabbi-l-'ālamīna* = 77.11 *guft ibrāhīm . . . xāliṣ gardānīδam dil-i xwēš rā wa yagāna gaštam az bahr-i xuδāwand-i xwēš rā* 'Abraham said, I have made my heart pure and become submissive for my Lord'. The meaning corresponds exactly to Pahl. *'ywk'nk'* = *ēkānag* (distinct from Man. MP *'ywg'ng* = *ēw(a)gānag* 'sole, unique'), e.g. *M X* ii, 6 *andar xwadāyān ēkānag ud framān-burdār ud rāst-gōwišn bāš* 'be submissive and obedient and veracious towards lords'.

ywb- 'long for', *ywbh* 'longing, desire', *v.* 125 *wa 'iδ ja'alna-l-bayta maθābatan li-n-nāsi* = 67.13 . . . *mahwan li-qulūbi-l-mu'minīna . . . čūn mā mar xāna-yi ka'ba rā maṣāba gardānīδēm wa yōba-gāh-i dilhā-yi mu'minān gardānīδēm, ay ki dilhā-yi mu'minān sōy-i ān yōbān gardānīδēm, či agar kasē bisyār dīδa bāšaδ ham yōbān-i ān bāšaδ wa agarči rafta bāšaδ bāz digar bāra ārzō baraδ* 'when We made the Kaaba a place of resort and made it the place of desire of the hearts of the believers, that is We made the hearts of the believers yearning towards it, so that if anyone should have seen it much he would still yearn for it, and although he should have gone (there) he would desire (to go) again another time'. The passage not only confirms the word *yōba*, against doubts that it was a misreading of *bōya*,[13] but introduces the verbal stem *yōb-*, here in a present participle. This parallels exactly the Parth. verb *ywb-*, thus to be translated 'yearn for, mourn', verbal noun *ywbšn* 'yearning, mourning' (*Mir. Man.*, III).[14]

zlyfn 'threat', *v.* 119 *bašīran wa naδīran* = 63.26 *muždakān dihanda firistīδēm tu-rā mar girawīδagān rā pa bihišt wa pa zalīfan kardan firistīδēm mar tu-rā mar nāgirawīδagān rā pa dōzax* 'We sent thee as a giver of good tidings to the believers about heaven and We sent thee to threaten the infidels with hell' (Br. 465). Henning ('Mitteliranisch', 112 n.5), discussing Khwarezmian *'zwyz(y)-* 'threaten', Chr. Sogd. *zwydm'* 'threat', has recognized the Pers. word as a loan from an E. Ir. language, presumably with metathesis from **zfyln* < **zβyδn* < **uzwaidana-*, cf. Av. *uzwaēδaya-* 'threaten'.

NOTES

1 *La langue des plus anciens monuments de la prose persane* (Paris 1963).

2 Who contributed a full description, in Urdu, to the *Oriental College Magazine*, VIII, 3 (Lahore 1932), 1-96, with many quotations. [See

now also, Dr ʿAbbās Zaryāb Xui, ʿTafsīr-e Qor'ān-e pāk', *Yaymā*, no. 214 (xix, 2 of 1345), 57-63.]

3 *Tafsir-e Qor'ān-e pāk*, published by the Bonyād-e Farhang-e Irān (Iranian Culture Foundation) (Tehran, XII/1344=III/1966), and graciously presented to participants in the International Congress of Iranologists, IX/1966. Citations are by page and line.

4 Op. cit., 93 n.8.

5 'Description of an old Persian Commentary on the Ḳur'án', *JRAS* (1894), 417-524; quoted hereafter Br[owne], with page.

6 Op. cit., 58.

7 Note that *majhul ē* is very commonly marked with a superscribed *alef*, that *b*/*p* and *k*/*g* are almost always distinguished, and *β* is written with a triple-dotted *f*; δ, however, is only rarely distinguished from *d*. The transcriptions here are, therefore, to some extent normalized.

8 Quoted from *Tarǰoma-ye tafsir-e Ṭabari*, ed. Ḥabib Yaɣmā'i, I (Tehran 1339=1960); see Lazard, 41-5.

9 From the story of the young man for whose sake Jesus raised his wife from the grave, whereupon she deserted him for another man. Morgenstierne records several versions from the east of Iran; see *Acta Or.*, XX (1948) 269 ff., 272 n.1.

10 Rahimi and Uspenskaja, *Tadžiksko-Russkij slovar'* (Moscow 1954) 166.

11 A similar word, the Parth. *hapax leg.* (*Mir. Man.* III, m 28) *'pydg*, may be a borrowing from the Mazdean technical vocabulary, Pahl. *'pytk*. This may be read *apēdag* 'lost, strayed (of animals)', cf. Parth. *'pyd* 'disappeared', < **apa-ita-*, and Av. +*ap(a)ita*, which it glosses, *Nir.* 54, = *kē-š bahr andar nē būd ēstēd* 'which does not belong to him'. The treatment of such animals, by the *apēdagdār*, was ordained in the *Apēdagānestān*, a lost portion of the Avesta summarized in *Dēnkard*, VIII (*DkM* 762-6); v. also *DkM* 709.6, 658.6.

12 Or **wat-wāčak?*, recognized by Henning in Pahl. *(w)tw'ck* (*Kārnāmag*, Antia, 27): *pad absōs, riyahrīh ud ēwēnag wadwāzag ud brahnag abāz ō pēš Ardašīr frēstīd* 'he was sent back to A. with shame, mockery and various kinds of abuse, and naked'.

13 Which comes into doubt instead. No MP **bōyag* is attested, only *bōy*, 1 'smell' < Av. *baoδi-*, 2 'sense, insight' < Av. *baoδah-*, both < √*baud* 'perceive'. There is no proof of Ghilain's derivation (*Essai*, 80) of Parth. *pdbws-*, MP *pyws-*, NP *payōs-* 'hope, long for' from an inchoative **pati-baud-sa-*, which might otherwise support a NP **bōya* 'desire'.

14 Parth. *ywbhr* 'sickness' (v. Benveniste, *JA*, CCXXVIII (1936) 201; Boyce, *Hymn-cycles*), however, probably represents another root; Skt √*yup* 'efface' does not help.

V. L. MÉNAGE

Three Ottoman Treatises on Europe

1. Kātib Čelebi's *Irshād al-ḥayārā*

A formerly unknown work of Kātib Čelebi, *Irshād al-ḥayārā ilā ta'rīkh al-Yūnān wa 'l-Rūm wa 'l-Naṣārā*, 'Guide of the perplexed towards the history of the Greeks, the Byzantines and the Christians', was briefly described in 1957 by O. Ş. Gökyay, following Mesut Koman's description of a manuscript in Konya.[1] A second manuscript, formerly owned by Professor Süssheim and now in the Staatsbibliothek, Marburg, has recently been described by Dr Barbara Flemming.[2] A third is preserved in the library of the Türk Tarih Kurumu at Ankara (no. 15).[3] This last consists of 32 fols. with 21 lines to the page, written in a small *neskh*, and is undated. In spite of inevitable corruptions, nearly all the numerous Latin names and terms which the author has transcribed are identifiable; and in what follows I tacitly restore the Latin spellings.

In a preface, Kātib Čelebi explains his reason for writing the work: although the Christians of Europe are numerous and powerful, the Muslim histories recount of them only lies and fables; therefore in order to rouse his fellow-Muslims from their 'sleep of negligence' he has compiled it 'from the *Atlas Minor* which I have translated and from other works', beginning it on 14 January 1654 (i.e. 24 January 1655, N.S.) in his 'residence (*menzil*) and library' between the mosques of Sultan Meḥemmed and Sultan Selīm.[4]

The first quarter of the work consists of an introduction in two sections (*ḳism*). The first, dealing with the Christian religion, describes the four Gospels and the five bases (*ḳawā'id*) of the faith – baptism, the doctrines of the Trinity and the Incarnation, the Eucharist, and Confession. The passage on the Trinity mentions three main sects (*medhheb*), Jacobites, Melkites and Nestorians, and quotes in Arabic the Nicene Creed (without the *filioque* clause). Two sources are mentioned in this frankly polemic section, both Arabic works by converts from Christianity: *Tuḥfat al-arīb fī 'l-radd 'alā ahl al-ṣalīb* (composed in Tunis in 823/1420 by 'Abd Allāh b.

ʿAbd Allāh al-Mayorḳī, a former Franciscan)[5] and *al-Naṣiḥa al-īmāniyya fī faḍīḥat al-milla al-Naṣrāniyya* (by Naṣr b. Yaḥyā, of whom it is known only that he was a physician).[6]

The second section summarizes the system of government in Europe in the form of a series of definitions – of the terms *monarchia*, *aristocratia*, and *democratia*; of secular ranks from *imperator* to *comes*; and of ecclesiastical titles from *papa* and *patriarcha* to *papas*. One point of interest here is that the author seems to regard monarchy, aristocracy and democracy as 'political' *medhhebs*, connected (*mensūb*) with Plato, Aristotle and Democritus(!) respectively (for him Venice is an aristocracy, while democracy is represented by England and Holland). Some of his renderings of Latin terms may also be of significance for the history of political ideas in Turkey: he distinguishes *status politicus* (*siyāset-i medeniyye*) and *status ecclesiasticus* (*siyāset-i dīniyye*), which refer to the *laicus* (*ʿawāmm*) and the *clericus* (*khawāṣṣ*) respectively. The introduction concludes with short sections on the episcopal courts and the languages of Europe.

The inspiration for this section presumably came from a passage in the *Atlas Minor*[7] where Hondius speaks of the 'gradus Imperatorius aut regius, quem ordine subsequuntur Dux, Comes . . .', and later of 'Monarchia, Aristocratia, Democratia'; but the details – the explanations of the Latin terms[8] and of ecclesiastical affairs – were no doubt supplied to Kātib Čelebi by his French-born amanuensis Sheykh Meḥemmed Ikhlāṣī, for there are a few pointers in the text to show that his informant was a Frenchman[9] (and, incidentally, a former Roman Catholic[10]).

The body of the work consists of nine *faṣl*, of greatly varying length, on the Papacy, the Empire, France, Spain, Denmark, Transylvania, Hungary, Venice and Moldavia. Only the Venetian system of government is described in any detail.[11]

The chapter on the Papacy (fols. 9v-15r) consists of little more than a numbered list of the Popes, with the years (A.D.) of their election and the lengths of their pontificates, from (*1*) *Petrus* to (*232*) *Paulus III*; of the last it is said only that he became Pope in 1535, an indication that Kātib Čelebi's source for the list had appeared before this Pope's death in 1549. A similar list of Emperors (fols. 15r-18v) begins with the seven Kings of Rome, from (*1*) *Romulus* to (*7*) *Tarquinius Superbus*, again with their dates (B.C.) of accession and the lengths of their reigns, and proceeds immediately with a list of 117 names from (*1*) *Gaius Julius Caesar*. This list changes its character after (*112*) *Maximilianus* 'who succeeded in 1473 and ruled for 33 years' [sic][12]: the length of the reign of (*113*) *Carolus V* 'who succeeded in 1519' is not stated, but a brief description of his appearance is given. For Charles's successors no dates at all are given, but only a similar 'description'; the last name is (*117*) *Ferdinandus III* 'who is now Emperor and whose heir died in 1655' (in fact his eldest son Ferdinand, elected King of the Romans in 1653, died in 1654). Again there is the implication that a source of the mid-sixteenth century had been used, but this time extended (perhaps, as Dr Flemming suggests, from a book with portraits). The same significant break is found in the list of Doges (fols. 27v-30r): it extends to (*82*) *Franciscus Donatus*, Doge 'from 1545' (he died in 1553), after whom comes only the unnumbered *Franciscus Contarin*, Doge 'from 1623' (he died in 1625).

The main source for these lists must have been the 'Catalogus Regum, Caesarum, Pontificum ...' which was first appended to Johann Carion's 'Chronicle' in the Paris edition of 1548 – the edition which Kātib Čelebi and his amanuensis translated from Latin, in these same months, as *Ta'rikh-i Firengi*.[13]

Two lists (fols. 18v-24v), following different traditions, are given for France. The first, in five dynasties (*ṭabaḳa*) to *Henricus* (scil. Henri II, 1547–59), is said to reproduce the account of *Hunibaldus*, *Tritemius*, *Paulus Aelius Aemilius* and (?)*Freigius*. The second, following *Gaguinus*,[14] becomes more and more detailed – in some sort an outline history of France – until *Ludovicus XI* (1461–83); to this paragraph is appended merely the names of the kings from *Carolus VIII* to *Ludovicus XIV*.

Of the remaining chapters, only that on Spain (fols. 24v-26v), mostly based on the description in the *Atlas Minor* (pp. 154 ff.), is of any length. The others are a hotch-potch of fragments of information, some, as occasional Hijra dates indicate, taken from Ottoman sources.

Kātib Čelebi may have intended this work to supplement his *Dustūr al-'amal*, written two years earlier to expose the causes of the internal weaknesses of the Empire, by a warning of the growing power of its external enemies; in fact, however, it is no more than a slight and rather naïve parergon – perhaps never completed[15] – to his translation of the *Atlas Minor*. It is of some interest as an indication of the European works available, directly or at second-hand, to Kātib Čelebi – and perhaps also, by its very triviality, as an index of the ignorance of Europe which prevailed in his day among Ottoman men of learning.

2. *Ijmāl-i aḥvāl-i Avrūpā*

An anonymous short treatise with this title, 'Summary account of European affairs', is preserved in Turkey in at least four manuscripts: Esad Ef.

2062/1,[16] Atif Ef. 1885, Revan 1648[17] and Kayseri, Raşid Ef. 1220/5.[18] The Esad Ef. MS (whose text I follow here) consists of 30 fols., written in an elegant and clear *nesta'lik* hand, with the numerous foreign names carefully vocalized. The *wakf*-seal of Maḥmūd I (1730–54) on fol. 1r suggests that this is a 'royal copy'. The date of composition, stated on fol. 4r, is 1138 (beg. 9.ix.1725). The text begins: *Erbāb-i joghrāfiyā memālik-i dünyāyi kısmet-i ūlāda dört iklīme kısmet edüb* . . . and ends: . . . *bu jümleyi tafṣīl u īżāḥ bir 'uluvv-i himmetüŋ himmet-i bi-hemtāsına menūṭdur*. This dedicatee is presumably the Grand Vizier Dāmād Ibrāhīm Pasha (1718–30).

Like Kātib Čelebi's *Irshād al-ḥayārā*, this work begins with a series of definitions of ranks, both ecclesiastical (*fīmā beynehüm 'ulemā'*) and secular (*'avāmm*). The ecclesiastical ranks (2r-3r) are six: *papa*, *cardinal*, *archiepiscopus*, *episcopus*, *abbatia*, and the heads of monastic orders (*medhāhib u āyinlerinde vāki' firak-i kethīrenüŋ ser-ṭariklarɪ*); the secular ranks (3r-4r) are eight: *imperator* (the rank of the Austrian Emperor and, outside Christendom, of the Ottoman Sultan), *čāsār* (the title also of the Austrian Emperor, and of the Czar of Russia), *kırāl* (the rulers of France, Spain, Sweden, etc.), *principe*, *duca*, *marchio*, *comes*, and *baron*.

The body of the work consists of a statistical digest of the states of Europe. It begins with a long, detailed, and (necessarily) complicated exposition of the territories subject to the Emperor (4r-10r); starting with Upper and Lower Austria and ending with Cleves, it is rounded off by the statement that the Emperor rules a total of 82 provinces (*eyālet*), containing 610 cities. Now follow the territories of what the author calls the Emperor's 'seven dukes' (*yedi hersekleri*), i.e. the Electors (10v-13r): Bavaria, Saxony, Hanover, Brandenburg, Mainz, Trier, Cologne and the Palatinate.[19] Finally come the princes belonging to the Empire 'who hold their lands in perpetuity and are independent but who must on succeeding obtain a *berāt* from the Emperor'; these are the Dukes of Holstein, Bremen, Mecklenburg, etc.

The author then turns to the states outside the Empire. Beginning with the independent states of Italy (Venice, Genoa, Lucca, etc.), he passes via Switzerland to France, Spain, Portugal, and Malta, and so to *Memālik-i Ingiliz* (23v-24v). So far the names have nearly all been carefully transliterated, from their Latin or German forms, so that they are easily identifiable; but the author is completely at sea when he deals with the British Isles: the king is named as William II (whereas William III had died in 1702), and the place-names are much distorted.[20] He is more at home on returning to the mainland, with Holland, Denmark, Sweden, Poland, and

European and Asiatic Russia. He concludes his account by enumerating (29v) those territories of the Ottoman Empire which count as part of Europe, and sums up with a series of grand totals: Christian Europe contains 15 *ḳrallık* (or *regnum*), 122 *eyālet* (or *principatus*), 656 *livā* (or *provincia*) and 3,865 *shehir* (or *civitas*); and the holders of rank (*rütbe erbābı*) are 1 pope, 87 archbishops, 314 bishops, 10 abbots, 1 emperor, 1 *čāsār*, 10 *ḳıral*, 57 princes, 87 dukes, 16 margraves, 114 counts, 5 barons and 29 *titulus* (which he explains as *zuʿamā*).

It cannot be denied that in general the work is extremely dull. Of some interest is the author's definition of *jumhūr* (with reference to *Jumhūr-i Venedik*, 14v), apparently meaning 'democracy': 'in such a state there is no single ruler, but all affairs are dealt with by the agreement of its leading men; and these leading men are elected by the choice of the populace'.[21] Switzerland (19r) is defined as *jemāhīr-i müttefiḳa*, each canton being a *jumhūr*. Poland (26v) is both a kingdom and a *jumhūr*, as its kings are neither independent nor hereditary. Holland (*Felemenk*, 24v) is governed as a 'stadt' – 'this is like a *jumhūr*; indeed the country is also known as the *jemāhīr-i müttefiḳa*; but whereas in a *jumhūr* executive power lies with several men, in a *stadt* a single man is entrusted with carrying out the decisions of the leading men'. It is perhaps also noteworthy that he uses the term '*bash-vekīl*' – of Prince Eugène of Savoy (3v).[22]

The author is well-informed: he knows, for example, that the Archbishop of Cologne is the son of the Duke of Bavaria (12v); that Mecklenburg had 'recently' been occupied by the Russians (14r) – as it was in 1716; that the 'dead Czar' (Peter the Great, d. 1725) had taken most of Livonia and Ingria from Sweden (i.e. by the Treaty of Nystad, 1721); and that Prussia had taken part of Pomerania (i.e. by the Treaty of Stockholm, 1720) (26r). His identification may best be considered after another similar, and apparently related, treatise has been described.

3. *Ijmāl al-safā'in fi biḥār al-ʿālam*

At least three manuscripts of this work, 'Summary account of the navies in the seas of the world', exist in Istanbul: Esad Ef. 2062/2, Esad Ef. 2035, and Arkeoloji Müzesi 537. Esad Ef. 2062/2, in 22 fols. (32v–53r), is written in the same hand and with the same arrangement as the first work in the MS, the *Ijmāl-i aḥvāl-i Avrūpā*, but it was, before re-binding, a separate booklet, having on fol. 32r the seals of Maḥmūd I and Selīm III. In all three MSS, on a blank recto before the text begins, is a note which reads, in its fullest form: 'A learned monk recently came from Toulouse in France and embraced

Islam in the presence of the Grand Vizier. Since he had made numerous voyages and was fully acquainted with world affairs, this treatise has been drawn up from his deposition.'[23] The work is mentioned by Bursalı Meḥmed Ṭāhir[24] and has been briefly discussed by Meḥmed ʿĀrif[25] and Adnan Adıvar.[26]

The text begins: *Umūr-i ʿāleme ve aḥvāl-i benī Ādama ān^an fa-ān^an iṭṭilāʿ dan ḳalb-i ḥaḳiḳat-shināṣ* . . . and ends: . . . *taʿdād u taḥrīre jūrʾ et olunub ʿafv-i taḳṣīrāt aṣḥāb-i keremüŋʿ uluvv-i shānına ḥavāle olundı*. The 'deponent' begins by saying that information on the rulers who hold the coasts and ports of the world and possess fleets, on their warships, merchantmen and arsenals, and on the numbers of their garrison-troops, their peacetime standing armies and their total forces in wartime is recorded in their (?) newspapers,[27] and that many of these matters have been personally witnessed by him in the course of long travels; he has therefore drawn up this summary report and transmitted it to the Grand Vizier; he has omitted the Ottoman Empire, since as yet he has little knowledge of it.

He deals principally with the powers of Europe, in the order: Austrian Empire, Venice, Savoy, Genoa, the Papal States, Florence, France, Spain, Malta, Portugal, Holland, England, Hamburg, Denmark, Sweden and Russia; but he ends the work with short sections on European settlements and naval strength in Africa (48v-50r) and Asia (50r-52v) (the various American settlements having been mentioned in connexion with the appropriate European powers).

The author shows no special acquaintance with naval affairs and uses few technical terms; but his little work is remarkably full of contemporary detail. For example: 'Ostend is a large port which can take 50 ships. There are 25 ships there which belong not to the Emperor but to various evildoers who have fled to his protection . . . they trade to the East and the West Indies, and pay customs to the Emperor in return for protection. . . . The tides there are strong, and a sandbar has blocked the harbour-mouth, but they are building quays and barriers (*ḳapular*) at the entrance. . . . In twenty or thirty years it will be (?)dredged (*takhliye*) and extended to become an excellent harbour' (33v); 'At Trieste the Emperor has begun to construct an arsenal and to build ships, laying down two warships at his own expense for the state (*mīrī*), and at Fiume nearby one warship has been laid down; they have not yet been launched. The Emperor wants to develop these ports to promote commerce in the Mediterranean, and has constructed a great highroad to them from Vienna. Trieste could indeed become a great port, but it is full of worms which will destroy the wood of ships unless they can find a way of destroying them or sheathe their ships with metal as some English do' (34r); 'At the present time, England is the strongest maritime power. She has two flourishing ports and arsenals, Gravesend and Bristol, where there are 500 warships, each carrying 50 to 120 guns. These ships are built with wooden pegs, not with iron nails.... They have also 24 warships at Gibraltar and at Porto Mahon in Minorca, and three in the New World at Barbados, near Brazil, for protection against pirates...' (46v); 'The Emperor of India has 14 great warships at Aḥmad-ābād and Ṣūrat in Gujarat, which he has bought from the English, and 60 ships called "proa(?)", which are like frigates' (51r).

A first approximation for the date of the work can be reached from the facts that the war of the Spanish Succession (mentioned, 40r-41v, in connexion with the siege of Toulon [1707]) is over and past; Philip v (1700–46) is described as King of Spain; and Eugène of Savoy (d. 1736) is called – as in the other treatise – 'now' *bash-vekīl*. A closer indication is given by a passage (35r) discussed by Adnan Adıvar[28]: 'Last year (*gečen senede*) the Spanish fleet was defeated by the English fleet, and two of the warships taken by the English were bought by the Emperor and stationed at Naples; they remain anchored just as they are and no start has been made on repairing them'. This sentence can only refer to the battle of Cape Passaro, in August 1718, when the Spanish fleet was destroyed by Byng; yet in spite of the *gečen senede* (? to be understood 'in a recent year'), the work must have been composed a few years later still, for the passage on Ostend summarized above evidently relates to the activities of the short-lived Ostend Company, which received its charter in 1722 but had it suspended in 1727; similarly too the passage on Trieste and Fiume must refer to their development as free ports (from 1719 and 1723 respectively). This treatise is therefore nearly contemporary with the other, which has the precise date 1138/1725–6.

Indeed, apart from the fact that the two sections of MS Esad Ef. 2062 were written by the same copyist, the two treatises have much in common, both in style and content. The proper names and titles in each are usually given after their Latin forms, but with *-s-* regularly transliterated by *-sh-*: *Evgeniyūsh* for Eugenius, *ḳomesh* for *comes*, *Lūdōviḳūsh* for Ludovicus, etc.; and some identical fragments of information are given in each: that Eugène is 'now' *bash-vekīl*; that Switzerland consists of 13 *jumhūr-i müttefiḳa*; that Paris is 120 hours' journey from the Mediterranean, etc. The two are in effect complementary, the first setting out the political and territorial extent of the states of Europe, and the second their naval, commercial and (to some degree) military strength. There can be little doubt that the compiler of the first is identical with the redactor who drew up the second from the information of the French renegade.[29]

The transliteration of the proper names suggests that the deposition had been made in Latin, and the reproduction of *-s-* as *-sh-* suggests a native speaker of Hungarian. When we look for a Hungarian-born Muslim with a knowledge of Latin, who was active in the 1720s, we come immediately to Ibrāhīm Müteferriḳa as the compiler of both treatises: born in 1674 and taken prisoner by the Turks in 1692, he first appears on a diplomatic mission – to Prince Eugène – in 1715; the first books which he printed were issued in 1729; he died in 1158/1745–6. This identification is supported by an aside, in the *Ijmāl-i aḥvāl-i Avrūpā*, that printing and the science of geography – Ibrāhīm's principal interests – arose in Mainz.[30]

There is a further, and at first sight perhaps tenuous bibliographical link between one of these treatises and Ibrāhīm Müteferriḳa, in that one copy of the *Ijmāl-i aḥvāl-i Avrūpā* survives in the Raşid Efendi library at Kayseri. This library was founded in 1792 by Meḥmed Rāshid Ef. (b. 1162 or 1167/1749 or 1754, d. 1212/1798), who was the son of a certain Ja'fer Fevzī of Kayseri and who, although he made his career in government service in Istanbul, left his library to his native town. He rose to be Re'īs ül-Küttāb for three short periods.[31] In about 1782 he and Wāṣif Ef. (later the official historiographer) bought the equipment of the Müteferriḳa Press, which had been lying idle for 25 years; printing was re-commenced, and the years 1783–94 saw the appearance of six books.[32] This manuscript 1220 – one of the 'foundation' MSS of the library – might therefore well be part of the stock of the press which the partners had bought.

This possibility draws our attention to the four other works in the MS. They are listed by Z. V. Togan[33] as (1) a treatise on the pantometer; (2) a treatise on the art of war; (3) an abridged translation of the book of Montecucculi; and (4) a treatise on fortification, being a partial translation of a book of mathematics in 28 sections written by a monk named 'Gişbar Işkut'. The source for the last is clearly the *Cursus mathematicus . . . in libros XXVIII. digesta* (first ed. Würzburg 1661) by the Jesuit Gaspar Schott (1608–66), whose *Pantometrum Kircherianum . . .* (Würzburg 1660) probably lies behind the first. The content and nature of these other works makes it fairly safe to ascribe all the contents of the MS to Ibrāhīm Müteferriḳa.

The third and fourth of these treatises lead us to consider two Paris manuscripts. Supp. turc 226 is a translation of the Vienna 1718 edition of Montecucculi's *Commentarii bellici*; and Supp. turc 227 is a treatise on the art of war, dedicated to Maḥmūd I (1730–54), among the sources of which are Montecucculi's *Commentarii* and, once again, Schott's *Cursus mathematicus*.[34] Blochet believed, from the style of the two works, that the compiler of the second was also the translator of the first, and suggested that this author was Ibrāhīm Müteferriḳa. Both works are indeed characterized by the 'Hungarian' *-sh-* in their transliterations; and the new link of common sources (Montecucculi and Schott) connecting them with the Raşid Ef. MS and hence with Ibrāhīm's continuator at the press gives very strong support to Blochet's suggestion.[35] These would seem to be two further works to be added to the list of translations made by Ibrāhīm.

There is perhaps a tendency to allow Ibrāhīm's pioneering activity at the press to overshadow the many other contributions which this enthusiastic, industrious and well-read convert offered to his adopted country. Dry as they are, the two short works described here have at least the merit that they presented to the Ottoman authorities, perhaps for the first time, really up-to-date and factual information on the contemporary Christian world, collected by one who – unlike Kātib Čelebi – was conversant at first hand with the languages and the thought of Europe. In the slow history of Turkey's modernization these treatises may take their minor place with the similar reports made in the following years – and perhaps with as little immediate effect – by Ibrāhīm's fellow-convert Bonneval.[36]

NOTES

1 *Kâtip Çelebi: hayatı ve eserleri hakkında incelemeler* (TTK, VII. seri, no. 33) (Ankara 1957) 57, referring to an article by M. Koman in *Konya Halkevi aylık kültür dergisi*, no. 79 (May 1945), 20 ff.

2 *Türkische Handschriften der Staatsbibliothek*, in *Orientalische Handschriften: Forschungsberichte 10* (Wiesbaden 1966) 5; and now in *Türkische Handschriften: Teil 1* (*Verzeichnis d. Orientalischen Handschriften in Deutschland*, XIII/1) (Wiesbaden 1968) No. 117.

3 On a visit there in 1959 I took notes of its contents and, by the kindness of the librarian and the authorities of the Millî Kütüphane, obtained a microfilm.

4 K. Č. was at this date still working on his translation of the *Atlas Minor*, the *Lawāmiʿ al-nūr*, for he says in its *Khātime* (MS Nuruosmaniye 2998 [the autograph], f. 423v) that the marginal explanations

(*ṣaḥīfaların sharḥı*) were finished on Friday 25 Ramaḍān 1065 'which is the Christian date 20 Temmūz 1655' (30.VII.1655, N.S.) and that he will now begin inserting the legends in the maps (many of which are in fact left uncompleted in the MS) and writing further comments.

5 *Kashf al-ẓunūn*, ed. Flügel, no. 2541; Brockelmann, *GAL*, G II² 322-3, S II 352.

6 *Kashf al-ẓunūn*, no. 13830; *GAL*, S II 145. The absence of the *filioque* clause in the Nicene Creed indicates that Naṣr was a convert from the Eastern Church.

7 *Atlas Minor, Gerardi Mercatoris à I. Hondio . . . auctus atque illustratus* (Amsterdam 1610) 190 ff. (section headed 'Studioso et benevolo lectori', introducing 'De politico statu regni Galliae'). The edition which K. Č. used, Arnheim 1620 (cf. MS Nuruosmaniye 2998, f. 423v), is not available to me.

8. E.g. (f. 6r): '*imperator* is a Latin word meaning *emr ediji*; the *maṣdar imperare* means *emr eylemek*'; '*seẓār* [Caesar] is from the Latin word *sed.re* [*caedere*] which means "to cut" '.

9 Thus K. Č. mentions that in French *episcopus* is '*evek*'; the passage on languages approaches precision only in reference to France, where are spoken 'on the Mediterranean coasts Gascon and Provençal, on the coasts of the [Atlantic] ocean . . . (?) and Breton, and in the centre French'; and the passage on the episcopal courts mentions the dress worn 'in France' by the *praeses*, *stator*, etc.

10 The tacit assumption – certainly not derived from the Dutch *Atlas Minor* – is that all Christendom is comprehended by the Church of Rome: the Orthodox Patriarchs, of Constantinople, Antioch, Alexandria and Jerusalem, are defined as *Papa ḳā'immaḳāmları*, 'deputies of the Pope', in Muslim lands, and there is only one oblique reference to Protestantism, in the note that the English, the Danes and the Swedes do not acknowledge the authority of the Pope.

11 K. Č. speaks of the 'Great Dīvān' (i.e. Maggior Consiglio) 'with 2,000 members over 24 years old, who vote with buttons called *ballotta*', the Council of Ten, etc.

12 Maximilian was in fact Emperor for 26 years, 1493–1519.

13 The only copy known, in Bay İzzet Koyunoğlu's library at Konya, is described by O.Ş. Gökyay (op. cit. in n.1), 54-6. Its introduction contains K. Č.'s statement (which I copied in 1959, when İzzet Bey kindly showed me the MS) that Carion 'completed the work in 1531 and had it printed (*basdırmıshdır*) in 1548'. This edition of 1548 (the only Latin edition of that year was printed in Paris) is not available to me; but although the lists (not identical) in the Paris editions of 1550 and 1551 have no Doges and neither tallies exactly with K. Č.'s names and figures for the Popes and the Emperors, yet K. Č.'s list of the kings of Rome shares with them a significant inconsistency, for which the 1548 edition must be the common source: K. Č. states that (*1*) *Romulus*

became king in 571 B.C. [sic] and ruled 37 years, to be succeeded by (2) *Numa Pompilius* in 714 B.C.; and the slip '571' (for '751') is found also in the 1550 and 1551 Paris editions of Carion, where the lists begin 'Reges incipiunt ante Christum ann. 571'.

14 Four are chroniclers of French history, named in the British Museum catalogue as Hunibaldus, Johann Tritheim, Paulus Aemilius (Veronensis) and Robert Gaguin, while Joannes Freigius is the author of a short *Historiae synopsis* (Basle 1580).

15 The text ends abruptly, with the appointment (in 1620) of the Moldavian voyvoda Alexander.

16 This MS, described in *Istanbul Kütüpaneleri tarih-coğrafya yazmaları katalogları*, I/3 (Istanbul 1945) 327, no. 210, contains three further short works: (2) (fols. 31-53) *Ijmāl al-safā'in fī biḥār al-ʿālam* (see below); (3) (fols. 55-74) *Ta'rīkh safar al-Baṣra ...*; (4) (fols. 76-91) *Ijmāl safar Nahr Dhiyāb.* (3) and (4), written in the same hand, describe the campaign in ʿIrāḳ of 1701 (Hammer, *GOR*, VII, 31-4).

17 See F.E. Karatay, *Topkapı Sarayı ... türkçe yazmalar kataloğu*, I (Istanbul 1961) no. 1395.

18 See Z.V. Togan, in *TD*, I/I (1949) 68-9. These four MSS certainly present the same text. Cevdet Türkay (*Istanbul kütübhanelerinde ... coğrafya eserleri bibliyografyası* (Istanbul 1958) 37) lists as having the same title MS Bağdadlı Vehbi 1030, but he gives no indication whether this is the treatise considered here or a later work (*c.* 1800) with the same title which is preserved in MS Esad Ef. 2063 (*sic*, not 2603 as in *Ist. küt ... katalogları*, I/3, no. 211).

19 He thus in fact names eight (whereas they were nine): to the original seven Bavaria had been added in 1623 and Hanover in 1708; the author omits Bohemia at this point, but includes it (7v) among the 'subject territories'.

20 'Ingiltere' consists of three kingdoms: '*Biritāniyā-i kebīr*' (as distinct from '*Küčük Britānyā*' (20r) = Brittany), Scotia and Hibernia. The first consists of six *eyālet* or *büyük principatus*, each divided into several *livā* or *provincia*: Middlesex has 9 *livā* and 40 cities, its capital [*ḳāʿide*] is London; Wessex has 11 *livā* and 43 cities, and its capital is Southampton; Wales has 12 *livā* and 40 cities and its capital is (?) Flint; etc.

21 *jumhūr dedikleri devlet oldur ki ol devletde müstaḳill ḥākim olmayub her umūr u khuṣūṣ rijālinüŋ ittifāḳiyle ve re'y ü tedbīrleriyle görilür, ve ol rijāl tenfīẕ-i aḥkām içün ʿāmmenüŋ re'y ü ittifāḳiyle intikhāb olunub naṣb u taʿyīn olunur.*

22 The term had been used as early as 1683 in an Ottoman document, referring to the Margrave of Baden (see F. Babinger, in *Archiv Orientální*, IV (1932) 27 and 30 ('Ministro Primario') = *Aufsätze*, II, 21 and 23); and a document of 1804 (*Belleten*, XIII/51 (1949) 641) uses it of Lord Hawkesbury (who was in fact Foreign Minister). For the history of the term from 1838 onwards, see *EI*², s.v. *başvekil* (by B. Lewis).

23 *Frānča diyārında vāḳiʿ Tūlūzha nām shehirden gečen günlerde bir rāhib-i pür-maʿārif gelüb ḥuzūr-i Āṣafīde sherefiyet-i Islām ile sheref-yāb olub* [+ (MS Ark. Müz. only) *merḳūmuŋ seyāḥat-i keṣīresi ve tamāmen aḥvāl-i ʿāleme vuḳūf-i tāmmı olmaghla*] *ishbu risāle anuŋ taḳrīrinden tesvīd olunmushdur.*

24 ʿ*OM*, III, 316.

25 *TOEM*, part 20, p. 1283.

26 *Osmanlı Türklerinde ilim* (Istanbul 1943) 122 n.2 (expanded version of *La science chez les Turcs ottomans* (Paris 1939), where this note does not appear).

27 *jerīdelerinde*. If the author really does mean 'newspapers', this is a very early attestation (cf. *EI*², art. *djarīda*).

28 Loc. cit. in n. 26. Adıvar, thinking the informant might be Kātib Čelebi's French-born amanuensis Meḥmed Ikhlāṣī (which is impossible), suggested that the passage refers to Blake's activities in the Mediterranean in the 1650s.

29 Meḥmed ʿĀrif suggested (loc. cit. in n. 25) that the informant was Aḥmed Pasha Bonneval. Adıvar rightly rejected this, as Bonneval had never been in ecclesiastical orders. Furthermore, Bonneval did not enter Ottoman service until 1729 (*GOR*, VII, 367); Meḥmed ʿĀrif, it is true, dates the work to about 1746, on the ground that it refers to battles fought in the last years of the reign of Philip V of Spain (1700–1746), but I cannot find any such passage: Philip V is mentioned only once (41r), in connexion with the War of the Spanish Succession.

30 *Kütüb basması ve funūn-i joghrāfiyā Moghunčiya* (= Moguntia) *shehrinde peydā olmushdur* (12v).

31 For his biography, see Jevdet, *Taʾrīkh*², VI, 269-70.

32 Nos. 19-24 in Hammer's list (*GOR*, VII, 586); cf. S.N. Gerçek, *Türk matbaacılığı*, I (1939) 94-8.

33 Loc. cit., in n. 18.

34 Blochet, i, 271-2; Adnan Adıvar, *İlim*, 162 = *Science*, 144. I am unable to identify the 'Alain Manson' whose three-volume work in French is also mentioned as a source.

35 Adnan Adıvar (*İlim*, 162-3 = *Science*, 144, n.1) objected that the language of supp. t. 226 was too modern for Ibrāhīm to be the translator; but since another MS of the Montecucculi translation, Nuruosmaniye 3237, though undated and unfinished, bears the *waḳf*-seal of ʿOṣmān III (1745–7) and so belongs to the original 'foundation' collection, the translation could well have been made during the lifetime of Ibrāhīm (d. 1158/1745–6).

36 The translation of a report by Bonneval, dated 1146/1733–4, on the recent history of the Empire, Hungary, Spain and France, is preserved in MS Ali Emiri 70 (see *Ist. küt. . . . kataloglari*, 1/3, no. 209); Meḥmed ʿĀrif (loc. cit.) describes a similar, rather later report (MS Esad Ef. 3889), and quotes (pp. 1283–6) two short reports of 1159/1746. For

Ottoman interest in Europe in the eighteenth century in general, see B. Lewis, in B. Lewis and P. M. Holt (edd.), *Historians of the Middle East* (London 1962), 188 ff. (Incidentally, the 'Kosmo Komidas' mentioned there must be Cosimo Comidas da Carbognano, dragoman of the Spanish embassy in Istanbul, who translated the catalogue of the Ahmed III library for Toderini (*Letteratura Turchesca* (Venice 1787) II, 52) and is the author of *Descrizione topografica ... di Constantinopoli* (Bassano 1794) and *Primi principi della grammatica turca ...* (Rome 1794).)

G. M. MEREDITH-OWENS

An Early Persian Miscellany

The *Mu'nisnāmeh*, a collection of Traditions, maxims, tales and anecdotes of an ethical character, is a work which has hitherto escaped notice. It is preserved in an apparently unique manuscript in the British Museum copied probably not later than the sixteenth century.[1] In the preface the author, Abū Bakr ibn Khusrau al-Ustād, about whom nothing is known, begins with a eulogy of the reigning sovereign, Nuṣrat al-Dīn Abū Bakr ibn Muḥammad ibn Īldigiz[2] (Atabeg of Azerbaijan, 591/1194–5–607/1210–11), and states that he is well aware of the superiority of verse to prose as a literary medium. He quotes Rashīd-i Vaṭvāṭ, Sanā'ī and some verses from his own composition, the *Nuzhat al-majālis*, in support of this view. In the case of the present work, the *Mu'nisnāmeh*, however, he prefers to write in prose so that it can be more readily understood, combining pleasure with instruction. On fol. 2b he mentions six earlier works of his but refrains from giving any details except in one case.[3] All of them are associated with the Eldigüzid line:

1. *Kitāb-i Ṣanam u 'Ajam* in verse, dedicated to Qizil Arslan (581/1185–6–587/1191–2).
2. *Naqīḍeh-i Kitāb-i Alfīyeh va Shalfīyeh*, dedicated to the same, which must have been a counterblast to the erotic work of that title by Azraqī.
3. *Mihr u Mushtarī*, unfinished at the time of writing. This was probably a romance in verse and a forerunner of the well-known mas̱navī on this theme by 'Aṣṣār of Tabriz.
4. *Rāḥat al-rūḥ*, in verse, dedicated to Nuṣrat al-Dīn Abū Bakr ibn Muḥammad.
5. *Nuzhat al-majālis* 'the disputation between the youth and the maiden', in prose, dedicated to the same. From this he quotes a few verses earlier in the preface as mentioned.
6. *Dāstān-i Manṣūr u Marjān*, dedicated to the late Atabeg Muḥammad (570/1174–5 – 581/1185–6).

Having listed all his previous works, the author goes on to say that he wishes to leave the *Mu'nisnāmeh* as an abiding memorial (*yādgār*), dedicated to Atabeg Abū Bakr, containing attractive stories (*ḥikāyāt-i marghūb*). It is divided, according to the table of contents, into the following *bāb*:

1. Traditions and sayings of ʿAlī (5a), each of which is provided with a Persian translation, sometimes in verse such as:

   من سلّ سیف البغی قُتل به و من حفر بئرًا لاخیه وقع فیه

   of which he gives quite a pleasing rendering:

   هرکه تیغ ستم کشید برون   فلکش هم بدان بریزد خون
   وآنکه بهر برادران در راه   چاه سازد خود اوفتد در چاه

2. Injunctions of ʿAlī to Ḥusain (6a).
3. Names of Shaikhs and holy men (9b).
4. Short biographies of the same (10b).
5. The *Risālat al-ṭair* of al-Ghazālī (31a).
6. Anecdotes concerning justice and equity (34b).
7. On generosity, particularly that of the Barmecides (35b).
8. On the wise counsels of the sages of Rūm (41b).
9. The admonitions of King Hūshang to his son with the aphorisms of Hippocrates and others (42b). These and the succeeding sections are derived for the most part from the *Jāvīdān-i khirad* which is quoted several times as an authority.
10. The sayings of Anūshīrvān the Just, his minister Buzurgmihr and the wise men of India (44b).
11. The wisdom of the Persian sages, including the advice of Jamshīd to his governors all over the world (49a).
12. Words of wisdom from various sources and the counsels of Balīnās (Apollonius of Tyana) (50a).
13. More of the wisdom of Balīnās (52b).
14. The wisdom of Aesop (یوسباس) (52b).
15. Counsels for those who serve kings (55b).
16. On Aflāṭūn and his counsels together with the sayings of Rābiʿah al-ʿAdawīyah, Fuḍail ibn ʿIyāḍ, and others (56a).
17. On the sayings of great men and stories which contain a moral truth (61a-365a).

Nothing further need be said about any of these sections apart from Nos. 4, 5, and 17, which are clearly the most interesting parts of the book. Most of the biographical notices in *Bāb* 4 are extremely short, especially towards the end where they consist merely of a few sayings of the saint mentioned. A few on the other hand contain several fairly long anecdotes which are derived from such works as the *Risālah* of al-Qushairī and the *Lawāqiḥ al-anwār* of al-Sha'rānī as they do not appear in the *Kashf al-maḥjūb* of Hujvīrī and the *Ṭabaqāt* of Anṣārī. Eighty-nine notices appear in this section. Two of those which are found in the table of contents (Abū 'Umar al-Dimashqī and Abū Ḥamzah al-Khurāsānī) are not represented by biographies, owing to carelessness on the part of the copyist.

The attribution of the *Risālat al-ṭair* to Aḥmad al-Ghazālī (d. 520/1126) found in *Bāb* 5 of this manuscript and elsewhere is probably correct. It seems likely that the Arabic recension of this tract is an abridged version of a Persian original, as Professor Ritter suggests.[4] Whether written by Aḥmad al-Ghazālī or not, this short allegorical tract is of considerable interest and a further investigation made in the light of this manuscript would be desirable.[5]

The last *bāb* opens with some sayings of 'Alī and a few lines of verse by way of introduction. The stories amount to thirty-one:

1. The adventures of Faḍlullāh of Mosul (62b).
2. The story of the builder of Bam, his wife and the minister of the King of Kavāshīr (77a).
3. Abū'l-Qāsim, the generous man of Basrah, the Amīr of Basrah and his vizier (93b).
4. The Vizier and the daughter of the King of Daryābār (103a).
5. Naṣr-i 'ayyār of Baghdad and the Prince of Khurāsān (110b).
6. Prince Zain al-Aṣnām and the King of the Jinn (115b).
7. The sons of the King of Ḥarrān and the brothers of Khudādād (128a).
8. The three youths, the old man and the daughter of the King of Kavāshīr (134a).
9. The King in search of a man without sorrow (140b).
10. The goldsmith's wife, the *Faqīh*, the *Muḥtasib*, the *Shiḥneh*, the *Vāli* and the *Qāḍi* (150a).
11. The story of the carpenter and the weaver (158b).
12. Isḥāq-i Mauṣilī, the Caliph of Baghdad and the kiosk (167a).
13. Balqīs, the King's daughter and the Peri (172a).
14. The story of Manṣūr ibn 'Abd al-'Azīz, the jeweller of Baghdad (176a).
15. Ṭāhir of Basrah and the witch Shamseh (missing in the text).
16. The daughter of the King of Kashmir and the merchant of Khurāsān (missing).

17. The *Qāḍi* of Baghdad and Hārūn al-Rashīd (missing).
18. Shāpūr the brickmaker and Muẓaffar the merchant (190a).
19. The three princes who buried their father's money, the Turkoman and the *Qāḍi* (201a).
20. The King who cast a minister to the man-eating dogs every year (204a).
21. Levvāḥeh of Nīshāpūr and Bishr the money-changer (206a).
22. The miser, the caravan and the tomb of Ḥātim Ṭā'ī (209a).
23. Various tales about Sulṭān Maḥmūd (210a).
24. Prince Khalaf and the daughter of the Faghfūr of China (missing).
25. The garden of Iram, Saif al-Mulūk and Badī' al-Jamāl (missing).
26. The Seven Sleepers of Ephesus (214a).
27. The dispute of Sulaimān and the Sīmurgh on fate and predestination (243b).
28. The story of Khālid the jeweller and his boon companions and the advice which they gave him (266a).
29. The story of Abū'l-'Alā Kirmānī and his son and their expedition to Nakhchuvān (309a).
30. Arvīyeh, the devout woman, her brother-in-law, the black slave, the honest youth and the merchant (320b).
31. Balūqiyā and 'Affān's quest for the ring of Sulaimān (349a).

Between Stories 28 and 29, another story, that of Manṣūr and Yūsuf the phlebotomist, has been added – presumably by the copyist as it does not appear in the table of contents and the author states that there are thirty-one tales.

With one exception, all the tales belong to the anonymous cycle of forty-two generally called *al-Faraj ba'd al-shiddah*, not to be confused with the work of the same title by al-Tanūkhī. These tales are best known in their Turkish recension of which copies are quite numerous.[6] Manuscripts of the Persian original are much less common.[7]

Story No. 29 has apparently been included because of its local interest. Its presence among the tales is possibly a compliment to the ruling Eldigüzid house owing to their championship of Islam against the Christian kings of Georgia. The story may have been re-edited from various themes in folklore (cf. the legend of Becket's father and his romance with the Saracen's daughter). In view of this a summary might not be out of place in this article.

A certain ruler of Kirmān named Abū'l-'Alā had a son named Mukhtār who was handsome and accomplished. One day in the middle of a festive gathering, Mukhtār reproached his father for wine-drinking. Abū'l-ʿAlā was filled with repentance and vowed to go on a pilgrimage to Mecca, giving up wine from henceforth. His son suggested that it would be better to make a foray into Infidel territory beyond Nakhchuvān. The King accepted this advice and they set off. Mukhtār, leaving his father in occupation of Nakhchuvān, pressed on against the capital of the Infidel King, ʿAbd al-ʿUzzā, which was called Kharshana (Charsianon) at that time but the narrator adds that it is the modern Tiflīs.[8] At first he was successful and reduced the fortress of Sharzāb (?) but later he fell into an ambush and was taken prisoner by ʿAbd al-ʿUzzā. On hearing this, Abū'l-ʿAlā was filled with grief and thought that he would never see his son again. The unfortunate youth was loaded with fetters and confined in a dungeon for a year. One day the Infidel King's daughter heard the lamentations and prayers of the prisoner from her room in the palace which was near the prison. She looked down through an opening in the prison wall and fell in love with him at first sight. She could understand Persian, like her nurse who was her confidante. The nurse was very resourceful and soon devised a pretext to find out the identity of the prisoner. She kept him supplied with food and clothing without saying a word to ʿAbd al-ʿUzzā. By means of a cord and basket she let down the princess from the palace roof so that she could visit Mukhtār by night. After some time the princess bore a son whom she called Vafā. The faithful nurse looked after the child in secret for two years. Then one day the princess, her son and the nurse were captured by a raiding party of Abū'l-ʿAlā's men while she was on her way from the bath. They took them back to Nakhchuvān in triumph where the princess fell to the share of Abū'l-Alā as a prize of war. She asked the King if she could be reunited with her son and the nurse and he consented. ʿAbd al-ʿUzzā was enraged and came in pursuit to rescue his daughter, but without success. In the meantime Mukhtār remained in prison completely unaware of what had taken place. When he heard the ill tidings he fell down insensible. Abū'l-ʿAlā made advances to the beautiful captive but she repulsed him, saying that her love was only for another. At last, in sheer desperation she told the King about Mukhtār and they at once began to discuss ways and means of saving him from the Infidels. It was decided that the princess dressed as a man should go with ten cavaliers to Kharshana. When they arrived there, ʿAbd al-ʿUzzā rejoiced to see his daughter safe and sound. She told him that she had escaped from captivity after overpowering her guards. Her first task was to visit Mukhtār and to bring about his release. He made his way out of prison disguised with a veil and reached his father at Nakhchuvān. ʿAbd al-ʿUzzā once more led his men on a punitive expedition against the Muslims but Mukhtār slew him in single combat and put his army to flight. After ten days of feasting Mukhtār married the Infidel princess and the Muslims then returned in triumph to Kirmān. The story-teller remarks that only a hundred Muslims fell in the battle with the Infidels and they were buried at the gate of Nakhchuvān. Those who make a pilgrimage to their tomb which is called Kūhleh (?)[9] have their dearest wishes fulfilled. The moral of the story is that he who worships God will not lack help in the hour of his need and he who is patient will achieve his desire.

The early date of this collection makes it extremely important for the study of this cycle of tales in their Persian recension. As the stories are too long to be quoted in full, it is more convenient to give in conclusion an anecdote from one of the biographical notices as an example of the style. In this case there is no attempt at literary artifice although the stories are written in the *sabk-i razmī* which reflects the popular taste of the period. This anecdote concerns Abū Turāb Nakhshabī and is told by ʿAṭṭār[10]:

حکایت آورده اند که یکبار در سفری بود آرزو کرد که دو سه تخم مرغ با نان گرم بخورد بهوس این آرزو از راه بگردید و بدیعی تا مگر در آن دیه این آرزو یابد قضارا جماعتی دزدان برآن دیه دست یافته بودند و بسیار متاع برده ومردم دیه بچپ و راست طلب دزدان میکردند چون ابو ترابرا دیدند بگرفتند و گفتند تو دزدی یاران خودرا بنمای او جواب داد که من مردی راه گذری ام از دزدان خبر ندارم اورا هشتاد چوب بزدند مردی اورا بشناخت بانگ بر آورد و گفت شیخ ابو تراب نخشبی است مردم گرد آمدند و اورا از زخم چوب خلاص کردند وعذر خواستند آن مرد که اورا شناخته بود اورا بخانهٔ خود برد چندانکه در خانه طعامی طلب کرد که پیش وی برد غیر نان و تخم مرغ چیزی نیافت بر گرفت و پیش او نهاد ابو تراب اورا گفت تا هشتاد چوب معتبر نخوردم بیك آرزوی نفس نرسیدم

NOTES

1 Or. 9317, consisting of 365 fols. in a fair *Nastaʿlīq* hand. It is undated and lacks the first folio. There are lacunae after fols. 183b and 213b. Unfortunately the manuscript has suffered much from rough usage and many of the section headings have been obliterated. It was purchased in 1920 from Mr Ter Avetissian and bears a few notes in Russian, one of which reads 'The Thousand and One Days'.

2 More correctly Eldigüz.

3 All these appear to be unrecorded.

4 *Das Meer der Seele* (Leiden 1955) 8. The Arabic version is published in *Majmūʿat al-rasāʾil* (Cairo 1328) 537, and may have been written by Muḥammad al-Ghazālī or Aḥmad's pupil ʿAin al-quḍāt al-Hamadānī.

5 Copies are scarce. In the absence of a published text, Professor Ritter consulted for his analysis of the work a manuscript belonging to the Royal Asiatic Society of Bengal (No. 875/10).

6 See Rossi, *Elenco dei manoscritti turchi*, 120-2 where a list is given of the manuscripts recorded. To this should be added a further copy in the Library of New College, Edinburgh (No. 8) described by J.R. Walsh in *Oriens*, XII/1-2 (1959).

7 One containing a collection by Ḥubbī of uncertain date is in the British Museum (Rieu, II, 760).

8 Written Tiblīs here.

9 کوهله.

10 *Tazkirat al-auliyā* ed. Nicholson, 295-6. In the *Mu'nisnāmeh* (20b) it has been inserted by the copyist in the notice of Abū'l-Qāsim Junaid.

GEORGE C. MILES

The Coinage of the Bāwandids of Ṭabaristān

The Bāwandid princes of the Caspian region of Ṭabaristān, also known as Māzandarān after the eleventh century, ruled for nearly 700 years from early in the first century of the Hijrah until 750 H/AD 1349, when control of the area was taken over by another local family, that of the Afrāsiābs. There were three lines of Bāwandids: the Kā'ūsiyyah who ruled from 45/665 until 397/1007 when the region was temporarily occupied by the Ziyārid Qābūs b. Washmgīr (or Vushmagīr); the Ispahbadiyyah, who annexed Gīlān to the east of Ṭabaristān, and whose rule lasted from 466/1074 until 606/1210 when the famous Khwārizmshāh Muḥammad overran the land; and the Kīnkhwāriyyah, vassals of the Mongols, ruling from 635/1238 until 750/1349. To our knowledge coins were issued by members of only two of these dynasties, the first and the second. In 1914 E. von Zambaur summarized, but did not describe in detail, the then existing numismatic evidence.[1] Since that date the only additional contribution to our knowledge of the coinage is contained in an article by Paul Casanova entitled 'Les Ispehbeds de Firîm'. R. Vasmer mentioned the Bāwandid coinage in an addendum to the article on Māzandarān in the first edition of the *Encyclopaedia of Islam* but added nothing new. V. Minorsky's interest in and profound knowledge of the history and geography of Māzandarān and of neighbouring lands are well known[2] and it occurred to me that a corpus of Bāwandid coins, with a brief commentary, might make a suitable contribution to a volume devoted to the memory of a great gentleman and scholar and a personal friend.

My own interest in the series was aroused by the acquisition in 1954, 1964 and 1965 by the American Numismatic Society of a few specimens of the coinage of Rustam b. Sharwīn, and then, quite by accident, two groups of gold coins of Shahriyār b. Qārin and 'Alī b. Shahriyār turned up in the trade in New York in 1967 just at the time when I was about to compile the corpus. Coins of these rulers were hitherto unknown and their discovery offered another inducement to undertaking the project.

All the coins in the corpus, with the exception of the dinars of Shahriyār b. Qārin and ʿAlī b. Shahriyār, are silver dirhems.

A. Rustam b. Sharwīn
c. 353–69 H/*c.* AD 964–80

The approximate dates of Rustam's rule are arrived at solely on the basis of the numismatic evidence. Lane-Poole in *The Mohammadan Dynasties* (London 1894) omitted the Bāwandid dynasty entirely. Zambaur in his *Contributions III* made no attempt to assign dates to this Rustam and pointed out that he was evidently not considered one of the regular line of the house of Bāw. In his *Manuel* he gives him approximate dates of 335 to 370 H. The initial date must have been based on a supposed coin of the year 335,[3] but I do not believe this coin exists. Casanova (in 'Les Ispehbeds', 121-4), sorting out the conflicting names and ambiguities in the chronicles, gave two dates for Rustam (355 and 367) on the basis of the coins, demonstrating that on this evidence we know at least that Rustam was ruling in these years. M. Rabino (in *JA* (1936) 418-19) gave no dates, nor does C. E. Bosworth in *The Islamic Dynasties*.

As Zambaur observes (*Contributions III*, 138), the fact that Rustam does not place his name in the field of the coin, the customary location of a ruler's or a vassal's name, but hides it in a very unusual position within the mint-date formula (see below) tends to corroborate the conclusion that he was not in the regular line of succession.

Firīm (sometimes spelled Firrīm), the mint name which appears on the following coins, was a stronghold in the mountains known as Jibāl-i Qārin on the northern slopes of Demavend, south of Āmul. It was the residence and treasury of the Bāwandid princes.[4] Its exact location is unknown. Paul Casanova[5] suggested that it might be identified with Fīrūzkūh on the road between Tehran and Sāri. He argues the case with erudition and in considerable detail; archaeological evidence might clinch the argument.[6] Minorsky (*Ḥudūd*, p. 387) thought that Firīm (Pirrīm in the text) was situated on the western branch of the Tijīn River.

The earlier preserved issues of Rustam have never been described in full, but it is evident that they all carry the Shīʿite formula *ʿAlī walī allāh*, as do all the other coins of his that have been described in detail or that I have actually seen. Earlier commentators (Fraehn, Dorn, Casanova) have of course remarked on the fact. The Bāwandids were ʿAlid sympathizers, but so also were the Būyids whom the Bāwandids recognized as their overlords but who out of deference to the ʿAbbāsid caliph never announced their unorthodox leanings on the coinage. Although the Bāwandids too paid lip service to the caliph in Baghdād, they evidently felt secure enough in their mountain fortress to broadcast their Shīʿite convictions.

1. Firīm. 353 H/AD 964. Names of Caliph al-Muṭīʿ, Rukn al-Dawlah and Rustam b. Sharwīn.

(*a*) Markov, *Inventory*, p. 977, no. 1. No description: 'Rustem'.

(*b*) Gozdowski *et al.*, p. 56, no. 86, a fragment with mint effaced. The authors compare it to one published by R. Vasmer in *I. Imp. Arch. Kom.*, 51, pp. 62-64, with marginal legend: بامر رستم بن شروين سنة . . .

(*c*) A specimen in the Cabinet des Médailles, Paris, communicated to me by M. Raoul Curiel. Æ 31 mm. Pl. I, 1

Obverse	*Reverse*
لا اله الا الله	لله
المطيع لله	محمد
ركن الدولة	رسول الله
	على ولى الله

Inner margin: بسم الله ضرب هذا الدرهم بفريم بامر رستم بن شروين سنة ثلث و خمسين وثلث . . .

Margin: Qur'ān IX, 33

Outer margin: Qur'ān XXX, 3-4

2. Firīm. 355 H/AD 965–6. Names of Caliph al-Muṭīʿ, Rukn al-Dawlah and Rustam b. Sharwīn.

(*a*) Fraehn, *Recensio*, p. 600, a (digit خمسة questioned, شروين transcribed شرويه) = Lindberg, *Essai*, 233, no. 51 (cf. Defrémery in *RN* (1847) 167, and Casanova, 'Les Ispehbeds', 125).

(*b*) Dorn, *Collections Scientifiques*, IV, 152, no. 13. Zambaur, *Contributions III*, 137, says 'la même pièce' as (*a*), but does he mean the same specimen?

(*c*) Markov, *Inventory*, 977, no. 1a (no description). This could be the same specimen as (*a*).

(*d*) A specimen in the Cabinet des Médailles, Paris, communicated to me by M. Raoul Curiel. Æ 31 mm. Pl. I, 2.

Obverse	*Reverse*
Area and outer margin similar to no. 1.	لله
Inner margin: بسم الله ضرب	محمد
هذا الدرهم بفريم سنة خمس	رسول الله
و خمسين وثلثة مائة	على ولى الله
	رستم بن شروين
	Margin: Qur'ān IX, 33

3. Firīm. 356 H/AD 966–7.
(*a*) Markov, *Inventory*, 852, no. 0. No description.
(*b*) Ibid., 977, no. 1^{c}. No description except mint effaced and 'variant' of the 355 issue.

4. Firīm. 35X H [356 or 358]/AD [966–7 or 968–9]. Names of Caliph al-Muṭī', Nāṣir al-Dawlah [sic, doubtless Rukn al-Dawlah misread] and Rustam b. Sharwīn.
(*a*) Lane-Poole, *NC* (1892) 170 (Avent Collection). Mint-date formula: بفريم امر [sic] رستم بن شروين سنة . . . وخمسين وثلثمائة

5. Firīm. 360 H/AD 970–1. Names of Caliph al-Muṭī', Rukn al-Dawlah and Rustam b. Sharwīn. Reading of mint-date formula varies (see below).
(*a*) Zambaur, *Contributions III*, no. 472. Mint-date formula transcribed: بفريم رستم شروين سنة ستين وثلثمئة Zambaur proposed to read 'bi Firîm-i-Rostem-i-Scherwīn, avec l'Isâfet persan'.
(*b*) Markov, *Inventory*, 310, no. 1. No description.
(*c*) Ibid., 977, no. 1^{e}. No description except 'variant' of the 355 issue.
(*d*) Covernton, *NC* (1909) 233, no. 2. Covernton transcribed the mint-date formula: بفريم (?) ملم . . . (?) سنة ثلث وستين وثلث مائة (?) and remarked, 'The mint-name in part resembles that on the previous coin [one of "335", but probably 365, see below], but it evidently consists of more words, and the latter part is indistinct. The date is also obscure'. This coin has now been acquired by the Ashmolean Museum, and Miss Helen Mitchell writes me: 'بامر is very clear, but رستم is more doubtful. The space available is right, but I cannot really see the initial ر (unless it is very close to the ر of بامر). I think Zambaur's amended reading [*Contributions III*, 138] بفريم ملك رستم شروين is not possible.' Miss Mitchell reads the date سنة ستين وبلم.

6. Firīm. 361 H/AD 971–2. Names of Caliph al-Muṭī', Rukn al-Dawlah and Rustam b. Sharwīn.

(*a*) Erdmann, *Numi Asiatici*, 233, mint and date not read, attributed to the Ḥamdānids; corrected by Fraehn 'in second volume of his manuscripts' (according to Tiesenhausen) to read بفريم بامر رستم followed by the date 361 (see Casanova, 'Les Ispehbeds', 125).

(*b*) ANS 54.122. Æ 30 mm., 6·62 gr.↗ . Pl. 1, 3.

Obverse	*Reverse*
*	لله
لا اله الا الله	محمد
المطيع لله	رسول الله
ركن الدولة	على ولى الله
Inner margin:	Margin: Qur'ān IX, 33

بسم الله ضرب هذا الدرهم بفريم بامر رستم
سنة احدى ستين ثلثمائة

Outer margin: Qur'ān XXX, 3-4

(*c*) ANS 65.243. Æ 30 mm., 4·14 gr.↗ (pierced). Same dies as (*a*).

7. Firīm. 36(3?) H/AD 973–4? Names of Caliph al-Muṭīʿ, Rukn al-Dawlah and Rustam b. Sharwīn (?).

(*a*) ANS 65.243. Æ 30 mm., 3.47 gr. ↖. Pl. 1, 4.

Obverse	*Reverse*
ب	Same die as nos. 6 (*b*) and (*c*).
لا اله الا الله	
المطيع لله	
ركن الدولة	

Inner margin:

بسم الله ضرب هذا الدرهم بفريم بامر رستم (؟)
سنة ثلث (؟) وستين ثلثمائة

Outer margin: Qur'ān XXX, 3-4.

The obverse is badly struck and the reading of the digit of the date must be considered doubtful, though probably correct.

8. Firīm. 365 H/AD 975–6. Names of Caliph al-Muṭīʿ, Rukn al-Dawlah and Rustam b. Sharwīn.

(*a*) Covernton, *NC* (1909) 232, no. 1. Æ 27 mm., 2.65 gr.

Obverse	*Reverse*
بامر رستم (miniscule)	الله (?) (interlaced *lām*'s?)
لا اله الا الله	محمد
المطيع لله	رسول الله
ركن الدولة	على ولى الله
	ح

Inner margin: Margin: Qur'ān IX, 33

بسم الله ضرب هذا الدرهم بفريم سنة خمس وستين وثلثمائة

Outer margin: Qur'ān XXX, 3-4.

The legends are transcribed in full above as there are a number of errors in Covernton's description. He read the miniscule legend in the observe area as شا هان شاه and the date as 335, although he observed that the decade looked more like sixty than thirty. He was tempted to read thirty because, as he remarked, al-Muṭīʿ died in 363 H. The floral scroll Covernton mentions on the reverse is a flourish on the د of محمد. The coin is now in the Ashmolean Museum and I have had the benefit of Miss Helen Mitchell's first-hand reading.

(*b*) Lane-Poole, 'Fasti Arabici', *NC* (1892) 165 (J.M.C.Johnston Coll.) = Sotheby auction catalogue July 16-18, 1906, 27, no. 311 (not described but from the Johnston collection). Lane-Poole's abbreviated description follows:

Obverse	*Reverse*
لا اله الا	لله
الله	محمد
المطيع لله	رسول الله
ركن الدولة	على ولى الله
	رستم

Margin: بفريم سنة الخ Outside: و / ع / ل / حـ

Outside: ه / ۰ / ه / ک

(*c*), (*d*), (*e*) Markov, *Inventory*, 310, no. 2, 977, nos. 2^a and 2^b, no descriptions, the last a 'variant'.

9. Firīm. 366 H/AD. 976–7.
(*a*) Markov, *Inventory*, 310, no. 3. No description.
(*b*) Ibid., 310, no. 4. No description other than:

ضرب هذا الدرهم بفريم بيد رستم الخ

10. Firīm. 367 H/AD 977–8. Names of Caliph al-Ṭā'i', 'Aḍud al-Dawlah, Mu'ayyid al-Dawlah and Rustam b. Sharwīn.
(*a*), (*b*) Lane-Poole, 'Fasti Arabici', *NC* (1892) 171. Two specimens (J. Avent Collection).

Obverse	*Reverse*
لا اله الا الله	الطائع لله
محمد رسول	عضد الدولة
الله على ولى الله	ابو شجاع مو
رستم بن	يد الدولة
شروين	ابو منصور
Margin: Qur'ān IX, 33	Inner margin: 'date and mint normal' Outer margin: Qur'ān XXX, 3-4

(*c*) Cabinet des Médailles, Paris. Æ 29 mm., 3.75 gr. ↗. Mentioned but not described by Casanova, 'Les Ispehbeds', 117, 125. Pl. 1, 5.
Similar to (*a*) and (*b*). Mint-date formula: سنة سبع وستين وثلث مائة يسم الله ضرب هذا الدرهم بفريم Outside the border enclosing the obverse marginal legend three isolated letters are preserved: و at 12 o'clock, حـ at 3 o'clock, د at 6 o'clock. Outside the border on the reverse, preserved: ح at 12 o'clock, . at 9 o'clock.
(*d*) ANS 64.12. Æ 29 mm., 3.20 gr. ↘. Pl. 1, 6.
(*e*) ANS 65.243. Æ 30 mm., 4.01 gr. ↘.
Similar to (*a*) and (*b*), the reverse inner marginal legend reading:

بسم الله ضرب هذا الدرهم بفريم سنة سبع وستين وثلث مائة

The above two specimens are from the same dies. There appears to be an oranment or letter above the obverse area. Outside the border enclosing the obverse marginal legend, four isolated letters, reading clockwise from the top: و حـ د ء. On the reverse: ابو منصور is written cursively; outside the marginal legends, clockwise: ح. ک. .
ANS 64.12 was illustrated and briefly described in the *Annual Report of the American Numismatic Society* for 1964, pl. IV, 4 and p. 9.
(*f*) Markov, *Inventory*, 310, no. 5. No description.

11. Firīm. 368 H/AD 978–9.
(*a*), (*b*) Markov, *Inventory*, 977, nos. 5[a] and 5[b], the latter a 'variant'. No description.

12. Firīm. 369 H/AD 979–80. Names of Caliph al-Ṭā'i', 'Aḍud al-Dawlah, Mu'ayyid al-Dawlah and Rustam b. Sharwīn.
(*a*) ANS 65.243. Æ 29 mm., 4.42 gr. ↘. Pl. 2, 1.

Obverse (partly double-struck)	*Reverse*
∴	حر
لا اله الا الله	الطائع لله
محمد	عضد الدو
رسول الله	لة وتاج الملة
على ولى الله	ابو شجاع مو
	يد الدولة
Margin: Qur'ān IX, 33 There are traces of letters or symbols in the four quarters outside the margin as on 10 (*d*) and (*e*).	Margin: بسم الله ضرب هذا الدرهم بفريم رستم بن شروين سنة تسع وستين وثلث . . . Outside the margin traces of letters or symbols at 7, 9 and 11 o'clock, the last probably an ع.

(*b*), (*c*) Markov, *Inventory*, 977, nos. 5[c] and 5[d]. No description.

13. Mint effaced. 36X H/AD 971–80. Names of Caliph al-Ṭā'i', Rukn al-Dawlah and Rustam.
(*a*) In a hoard of Sāmānid and Būyid dirhems unearthed at Ra's al-Khaimah in the Trucial Oman. N. M. Lowick and J. D. F. Nisbet in *NC* (1968) 240, no. 42. Æ 30 mm., 3·48 gr.

Obverse	*Reverse*
بامر رستم (miniscule)	K لله K
لا اله الا الله	محمد
الطائع لله	الرسول له
ركن الدولة	على ولى الله
Inner margin: بسم الله ضرب . . . ستين وثلثمائة Outer margin: Qur'ān XXX, 3-4	Margin: Qur'ān IX, 33

B. Shahriyār III b. Dārā
c. 358–396 H/*c.* AD 969–1006

Zambaur in his *Contributions III* and in the *Manuel* gives 358–396 H for Shahriyār b. Dārā, and these dates are accepted by Bosworth. Casanova, however, in 'Les Ispehbeds' (p. 124) assigns him the dates 382–397, but these dates, he admits (p. 125) are not certain and are based on an attempt to accommodate the chronology to genealogical lists which give no precise dates but only the length of each ruler's reign. Rabino (op. cit., p. 418) cites Zambaur's dates but otherwise states only that Shahriyār b. Dārā ruled 35 years, according to Ẓāhir al-Dīn al-Marʿashi, was defeated by Rustam b. Marzbān and died in prison in 397.

14. Firīm. 376 H/AD 986–7. Names of Caliph al-Ṭā'iʿ, Fakhr al-Dawlah and Shahriyār b. Darā.

(*a*) Ashmolean Museum. Æ 24 mm., 4·62 gr.

This unique coin has recently been described in full by Miss Helen Mitchell in *NC* (1965) 220. It was found in a hoard reportedly from Ardekan.

The area legends read:

Obverse	*Reverse*
لا اله الا الله	محمد رسول الله
وحده لاشريك	على ولى الله
له الطائع لله	الامير السيد
شهريار بن درا[ى]	فخر الدولة
	وفلك الامة

An individual by the name of Sharwīn b. Muḥammad, presumed to be a Bāwandid, should be deleted from the list of princes of the dynasty. Markov (*Inventory*, 310, nos. 6-7) attributed to the Bāwandids a dirham of 401 H, mint effaced, and another with date effaced but the mint name read as Shamhār (a town, exact location disputed, in the Jibāl-i Qārin), both bearing the names of Sharwīn b. Muḥammad and of Bahā' al-Dawlah. A similar dirhem, mint and date effaced, is listed in Casanova, *Princesse Ismail*, no. 1123; and an unpublished specimen, dated 401, mint effaced, is in the Cabinet des Médailles in Paris. On the basis of these attributions Zambaur (*Contributions III*, 137, and *Manuel*, 187 and 189) included Sharwīn in his dynastic tables. The issue is complicated by Markov's attribution of a similar dirhem of 401 to Parwīz b. Muḥammad (cf. Zambaur, *Manuel*, 136) under the Marwānids. It is now believed that all these coins are to be assigned not to the Bāwandids but to a certain Sharwīn b. Muḥammad at Mayyāfarīqīn. I am indebted to M. Raoul Curiel for photographs of the Paris specimen and to Dr Alexander Bykov not only for casts and photographs of the Hermitage specimens but also for a literary reference to the individual in question. An article might well be devoted to a detailed study of these rare issues.

C. Shahriyār b. Qārin
c. 466–504 H/AD 1073–1111

Zambaur (*Contributions III* and *Manuel*), Rabino (p. 422) and Bosworth all give Shahriyār's dates as 466–503 H. These dates are based on Ẓāhir al-Dīn's statement that Qārin died in 466 and was succeeded by Shahriyār in that year,[7] and that Shahriyār ruled for 37 years. We are told that in 500 H as a result of his refusal to cooperate in exterminating the Assassins, the Seljūq overlord Muḥammad b. Malikshāh sent the amīr Sunqur of Bukhārā against him but the latter failed to subdue him and subsequently Sultan Muḥammad persuaded him to send one of his sons to his court in Iṣfahān where he would be treated with honour. This son was ʿAlā al-Dawlah ʿAlī (see below, pp. 456-7).[8]

No coins of Shahriyār b. Qārin were known to exist until a hoard came to my attention in June 1967. Most of the specimens hereunder described were acquired by the American Numismatic Society. Photographs of three specimens (nos. 16 (*b*), 17 (*a*) and 18 (*a*)) were kindly communicated to me in 1967 by Mr Cheragh Ali Azami of Teheran. No. 21 enables us to extend the period of Shahriyār's rule by one year to 504 H. The contents of the entire hoard, at least so far as it was intact when it was shown to me, is summarized below, p. 456.

It will be noted that on all the issues Shahriyār recognizes the Seljūqs Barkiyāruq and Muḥammad as overlord. The ʿAlid formula *ʿAlī walī allāh* no longer appears on the coins; we do not know when he or his predecessors dropped the sentence from the coinage. On one of the issues (no. 16) Shahriyār appears to take the title *malik ʿādil*.

No. 21, the issue of 504 H, is of particular interest, not only because of the date which informs us that Shahriyār was still ruling a year later than heretofore accepted, but also because at the sides of the obverse area there appears the name of Jalāl al-Dīn Aḥmad. There can be little doubt but that this is a son of Sultan Muḥammad's known as Malik Aḥmad. According to

Ibn Isfandiyār, Muḥammad sent Aḥmad, under the care of an amir named Sunqur-i Kūchak, to Rayy, making him governor of Rayy itself and of the towns of Āwah, Sāwah, Arrān, Khwār, Samnān, Ruyān and Lārījān, as well as of Ṭabaristān and Gurgān. Evidently Aḥmad and his tutor had difficulty in persuading Shahriyār's son, Najm al-Dawlah Qārin, in Āmul, to accept Aḥmad's authority and eventually Qārin's brother ʿAlā al-Dawlah ʿAlī (see below) was named governor of Ṭabaristān providing he would recognize Aḥmad.[9] No date is given by Ibn Isfandiyār for these events, but at least the coin informs us that in 504 Shahriyār was recognizing Aḥmad. This is the first recognition of the young prince's name on a coin, and we also learn that he called himself Jalāl al-Dīn.

The mint name Sāriyah is clear. Sāriyah (today Sārī) was an important town and alternated with Āmul as the capital of Ṭabaristān.[10] Coins of other dynasties struck at Sāriyah (or Sārī) are known: Būyid, Ziyārid, Ilkhānid, Sarbadar, Tīmūrid, Ṣafavid, Afshār and autonomous bronze city issues under the Qājārs.

15. Sāriyah. 499 H/AD 1105–6. Names of Caliph al-Mustaẓhir, the Seljūq Muḥammad, and Shahriyār.

(*a*) ANS 67.261. AV 18 mm., 0·94 gr. ↘. Pl. 2, 2.

Obverse	*Reverse*	
عدل	لله	
لا اله الا	المستظهر بالله	Sword or
الله محمد	السلطان المعظم	dagger
رسول الله	غياث الدين	at right
شهريار	•6 محمد 9•	
Margin: ... ضرب هذا الدينار بسارية سنة تسع وتسعين واربع ما ...	Margin: Qur'ān IX, 33 (partially preserved)	
4 pellets on double linear border between area and margin.	4 annulets on double linear border between area and margin.	

16. Sāriyah. 499 H/AD 1105–6. Names of Caliph al-Mustaẓhir, the Seljuq Muḥammad, and Shahriyār.

(*a*) ANS 67·261. AV 21 mm., 2·05 gr. ↖. Pl. 2, 3.

Obverse	*Reverse*
عدل	لله
لا اله الا	المستظهر بالله
عادل الله محمد	السلطان المعظم Scroll
رسول الله	غياث الدين
شهريار	* محمد *

Inner margin: بسم الله ضرب هذا الدينار ية (sic) سنة تسع وتسعين و . . . مئة	Margin: Qur'ān IX, 33

Outer margin: Qur'ān XXX, 3-4 (partially preserved)

The word at the left of the obverse area is in all probability *ʻādil*. The cursive *dāl* is to be compared with the *dāls* in the reverse marginal legend. The mint name is almost certainly Sāriyah. It would appear that the die-engraver forgot the letters سا, having just engraved the word الدينار, the end of which looks like سار.

(*b*) Collection of Mr Cheragh Ali Azami, Teheran. AV 25 mm. Pl. 2, 4. Similar to (*a*) but بسارية, in full; probably same reverse die as (*a*).

17. Sāriyah. 499? H/AD 1105–6? Names of Caliph al-Mustaẓhir, the Seljūq Muḥammad, and Shahriyār.

(*a*) Collection of Mr Cheragh Ali Azami, Teheran. W 24 mm. Pl. 2, 5.

Obverse	*Reverse*
عدل	لله
لا اله الا	المستظهر بالله
الله محمد	غياث الدين
رسول الله	محـ[ـمد]
شهريار	

Margin: . . . ضرب هذا الدينار بسارية سنة تسع (؟) و	Margin: Qur'ān IX, 33 (mostly preserved)

18. Sā(riyah). Date effaced. Between 487 and 498 H/AD 1094–1105. names of Caliph al-Mustaẓhir, the Seljūq Barkiyāruq, and Shahriyār.

(*a*) Collection of Mr Cheragh Ali Azami, Teheran. AV 26 mm. Pl. 2, 6.

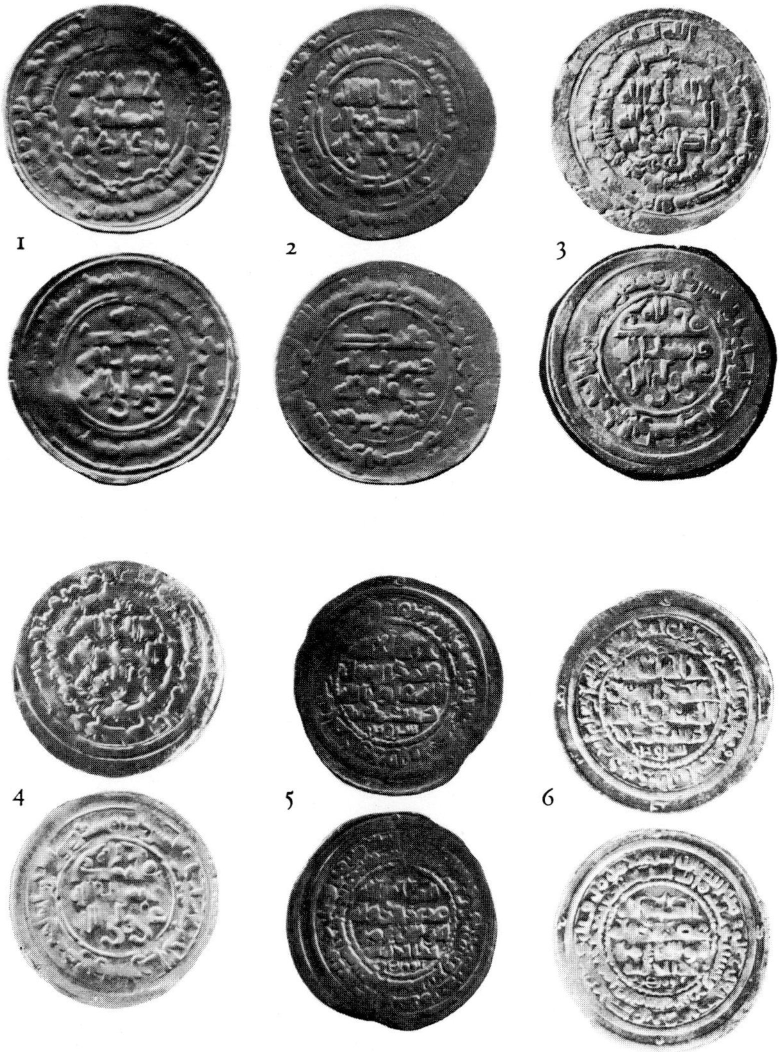

Plate 1. Bāwandid coins. Rustam b. Sharwīn.

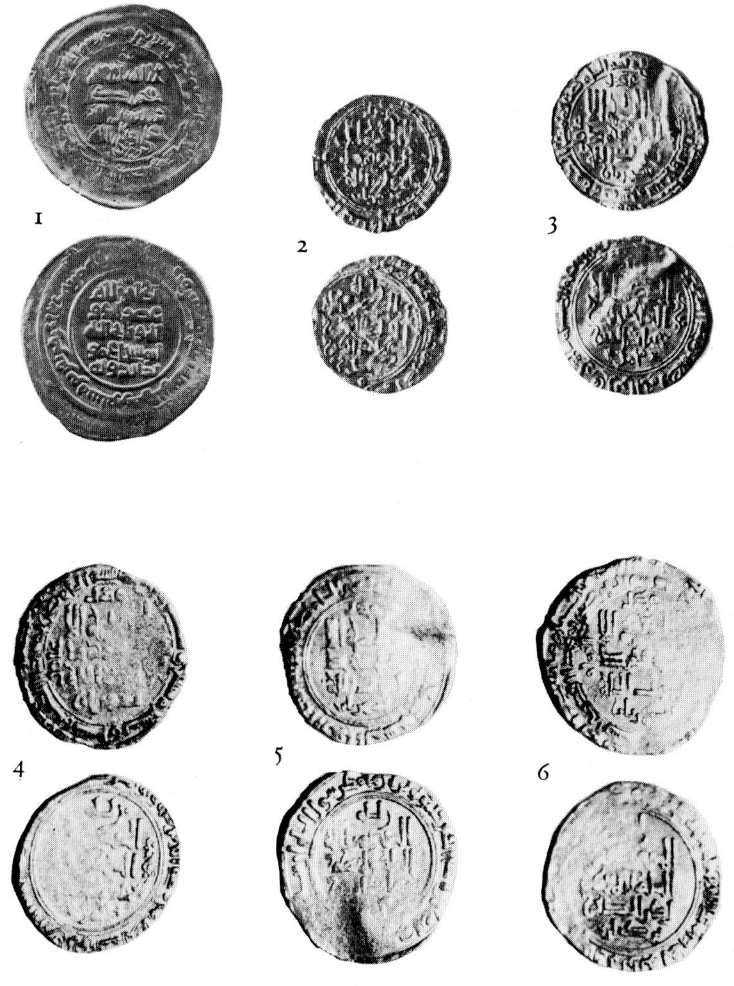

Plate 2. Bāwandid coins. 1, Rustam b. Sharwīn; 2-6 Shahriyār b. Qārin.

Obverse	*Reverse*
عدل	لله
لا اله الا	المستظ[ـهر بالله]
الله محمد	السلطان المعظم
رسول الله	ركن الدين
شهريار	بركيارق

(Left margin of obverse: الدولة; dotted border)

Inner margin:

ضرب هذا الدينار بسا . . . . . .

Margin: Qur'ān IX, 33

Outer margin: Qur'ān XXX, 3-4

The inclusive dates given above are those of the Seljūq Sultan Barkiyāruq.

19. Sāriyah. 500 H/AD 1106–7. Names of Caliph al-Mustaẓhir, the Seljūq Muḥammad, and Shahriyār.

(*a*) ANS 67.261. AV 22 mm., 2·64 gr. ↙. Pl. 3, 1.

Obverse	*Reverse*
Area similar to no. 17. Partly double-struck.	Area similar to nos. 17 and 18, but no ornaments.
Margin: بسم الله ضرب هذا الدينار بسارية سنة خمس مائة	Margin: Qur'ān IX, 33 (mostly preserved as far as كره.

20. Sāriyah. 501 H/AD 1107–8. Names of Caliph al-Mustaẓhir, the Seljūq Muḥammad, and Shahriyār.

(*a*) ANS 67.261. AV 21 mm., 2·70 gr. ↘. Pl. 3, 2.

Obverse	*Reverse*
Area similar to no. 17.	Area similar to nos. 17 and 18, but
Inner margin:	only ornament a scroll at right.

بسم الله ضرن هذا الدينار

بسارية سنة احدى وخس (sic) مائة

Outer margin: Qur'ān XXX, 3-4 (mostly preserved).	Margin: Qur'ān IX, 33 (preserved as far as يظهره).

21. Sāriyah. 504 H/AD 1110–11. Names of Caliph al-Mustaẓhir, the Seljūq Muḥammad, Shahriyār and Jalāl al-Dīn Aḥmad.

(*a*) ANS 67.261. AV 20 mm., 0·92 gr. ←. Pl. 3, 3.

Obverse	*Reverse*
عدل	لله
لا اله الا	المستظهر بالله
الله محمد	السلطان المعظم ٥
رسول الله	غياث الدين
شهريار	* محمد *
(right field, vertical: احمد ٥; left field, vertical: جلال الد . . .)	

Inner margin: اربع وخمس مائة
بسم الله . . . . . سارية سنة

Margin: Qur'ān IX, 33 (partially preserved).

Outer margin: Qur'ān XXX, 3-4 (partially preserved).

The composition of the hoard of Shahriyār's dinars referred to on p. 452, above, is as follows:

Sāriyah, 499 H: 5 specimens, including the two acquired by the ANS. Weights: 2·16, 2·15, 2·05, 1·99, 0·94 grams.

[Sāriyah], 499 H: 7 specimens. Weights: 2·55, 2·27, 1·78, 1·61, 1·57, 1·50, 1·29 grams.

Sāriyah, 4XX H: 1 specimen. Weight: 2·60 grams.

Sāriyah, 500 H: 1 specimen, acquired by the ANS. Weight: 2·64 grams.

Sāriyah, 501 H: 14 specimens, including the one acquired by the ANS. Weights: 2·70, 2·67, 2·59, 2·32, 2·18, 2·12, 1·94, 1·85, 1·80, 1·80, 1·75, 1·62 1·12, 1·11 grams.

[Sāriyah], XXX H: 1 specimen. Weight: 1·54 gram.

Sāriyah, 504 H: 1 specimen, acquired by the ANS. Weight: 0·92 gram.

[Sāriyah], 504 H: 2 specimens. Weights: 1·68, 1·31 grams.

[Sāriyah], 50X H: 2 specimens. Weights: 1·66, 1·65 grams.

Sāriyah, XXX H: 3 specimens. Weights: 2·51, 1·40, 1·27 grams.

[Sāriyah], XXX H: 5 specimens. Weights: 2·23, 1·79, 1·71, 1·58, 1·34 grams.

Where the name of Sāriyah is enclosed in square brackets, the mint is effaced, but the similarity in style and fabric is identical with those where the name is preserved and there can be no doubt that they are from the same mint.

D. ʿAlī b. Shahriyār
c. 511–34 H/*c.* AD 1117–40

The dates are those given by Zambaur in his *Contributions III* and in his *Manuel*, repeated by Rabino[11] and Bosworth. According to Ibn Isfandiyār and Ẓāhir al-Dīn, ʿAlā al-Dawlah ʿAlī b. Shahriyār reigned 21 years. A few fixed dates are known: on the death of his brother Qārin he received permission from his Seljūq overlord Muḥammad to proclaim himself sovereign in Ṭabaristān. After some dispute he returned to Ṭabaristān in 512. In 521 he defeated Sultan Sanjar's nephew Masʿūd. At the age of 75 he was forced by his son Shāh Ghāzī Rustam to abdicate in his favour, and three years later he died. During his reign a number of Ghaznavid, Seljūq, Khwārizmshāhī and other princes sought refuge at ʿAlī's court.

Coins of this ruler were unknown until June 1967 when a lot of eight dinars came to my attention. They may perhaps have formed a part of the hoard of dinars of Shahriyār b. Qārin (see p. 452, above); in any case they came from the same source. All eight specimens are exceptionally thin (note the weights), crudely designed and badly struck, and the legends are almost barbarous. The name Shahriyār on the first two specimens is almost illegible and on the other dies the final letters are crowded or actually omitted, so that the name appears to be spelled شهرر or شهرير. The د of الدولة is only faintly visible on the first two specimens, but the word is clear on the others.

I have no idea how the mint name is to be read. The letters seem not to suit any of the known mint names of Ṭabaristān. Note the strange rendition of the caliph's name, al-Mustarshid on the reverses. The *thā* of al-Ḥārith has three dots over it and ends in a flourish similar to the last letter on the two preceding lines.

22. Mint? 519? H/AD 1125? Names of Caliph al-Mustarshid, the Seljūq Sanjar, and ʿAlī b. Shahriyār.

(*a*) ANS 67.261. AV 23 mm., 1·36 gr. ↗. Pl. 3, 4.

	Obverse	*Reverse*	
[الد]ولة (vertical, at left)	عدل	لله	
	لا اله الا	المسارشد (sic) بالله	
	الله محمد	السلطان الاعظم	Sword or dagger at right
	رسول الله	شاهانشاه	
	على بن شهريار	ابو الحرث	
		سنجر	

Inner margin:
بسم الللہ (sic) ضـ . . . . بسعحم (بالسلحم or) سنة تسع عشـ و

Margin: traces of Qur'ān IX, 33?

Outer margin: Part of Qur'ān XXX, 3-4 (?) preserved.

(*b*) ANS 67.261. AV 24 mm., 1·34 gr. ↑. Pl. 3, 5.

Apparently from the same dies as (*a*) but double-struck, the second (?) striking of the obverse about 150 degrees at variance with the other, and the reverse showing nearly 180 degrees of variance. The mint name is not preserved but the date appears to be as on (*a*).

23. Mint? Date? Names as on no. 22.

(*a*)-(*d*). ANS 67.261. AV 24 mm., 1·77 gr. ↑; 26 mm., 1·10 gr. ↑; 24 mm., 1·01 gr. ↓; 25 mm., 0·99 gr. →.

Four specimens apparently from the same pair of dies.

Obverse

Similar to no. 22. الدولة is mostly clear. I can make nothing of the mint and date, even on those specimens on which a number of the letters are preserved.

Reverse

Similar to no. 22, but * at right of area in place of sword. There are no dots over the *thā* of al-Ḥārith.

24. Mint? Date? Names as no. 22.

(*a*), (*b*) ANS 67.261. AV 24 mm., 1·55 gr. ↖; AV 24 mm., 1·49 gr. ↖. Pl. 3, 6.

Two specimens from the same pair of dies. Obverse and reverse similar to no. 23. The mint سمنه is quite clear, but on neither specimen is the date preserved.

E. Shāh Ghāzī Rustam b.ʿAlī
c. 534–560 H/*c.* AD 1139–1165

The dates are those given by Zambaur in his *Manuel*. In his *Contributions III* he gives 534–558. Rabino (op. cit., 427-8) has 558 or 560 as the terminal date, and Bosworth adopts 558, the date given by Ẓāhir al-Dīn who says that Shāh Ghāzī ruled 24 years. Ibn Isfandiyār wrote that he was the greatest and richest of the Bāwandid rulers. Among his possessions was the great city of Rayy, where he is said to have spent more than 120,000 dinars on buildings in the Zādmihrān quarter.[12]

Zambaur, *Manuel*, 187, indicates that a dinar of Rustam's is known, dated 551 or 552 H, and Rabino (op. cit., 427), doubtless relying on Zambaur, writes 'nous avons un *dīnār* de Rustam b.ʿAlī.' Unfortunately Zambaur does not give the location of the coin and I have not been able to trace it.

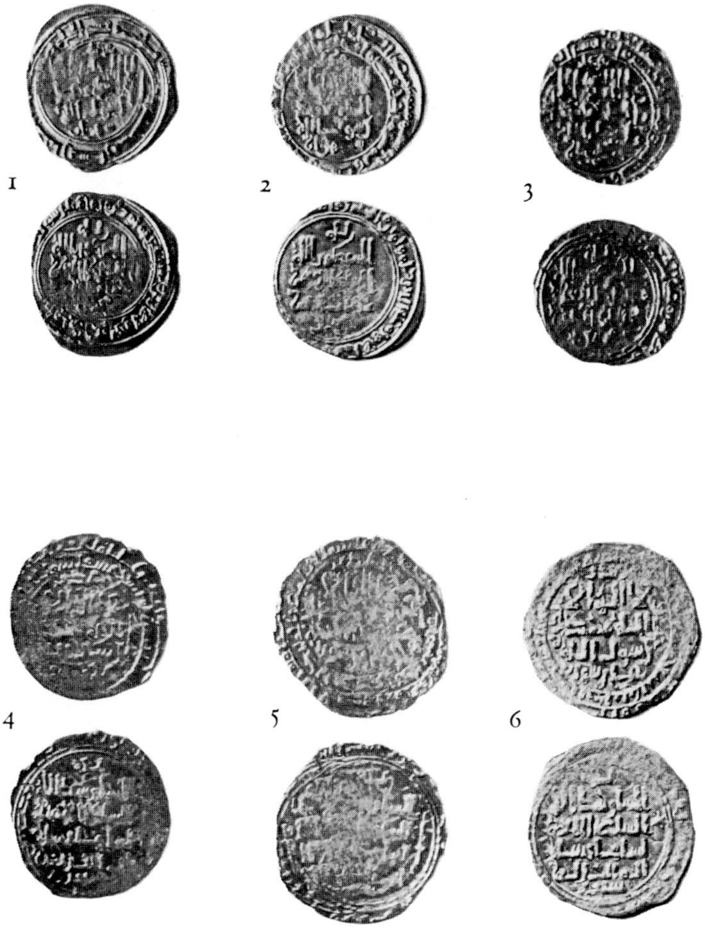

Plate 3. Bāwandid coins. 1-3, Shahriyār b. Qārin; 4-6 ʿAlī b. Shahriyār.

NOTES

1 'Nouvelles Contributions à la Numismatique orientale', *NZ* 1914, pp. 136-40. The following abbreviations are used in the body of the present article: ANS = American Numismatic Society; Bosworth = C.E. Bosworth, *The Islamic Dynasties* (Edinburgh 1967); Casanova, 'Les Ispehbeds' = Paul Casanova, 'Les Ispehbeds de Firîm', in T.W. Arnold and Reynold A. Nicholson, *A Volume of Oriental Studies presented to Edward G. Browne* (Cambridge 1922) 117-26; Casanova, *Princesse Ismaīl* = P. Casanova, *Inventaire sommaire de la collection des monnaies musulmanes de S.A. la Princesse Ismaīl* (Paris 1896); Dorn, *Collections Scientifiques* = L'Académicien Dorn, *Collections Scientifiques de l'Institut des Langues Orientales du Ministère des Affaires Etrangères* (St. Petersburg 1881); *EI* = *Encyclopaedia of Islam*; Erdmann, *Numi Asiatici* = F. Erdmann, *Numi Asiatici Musei Universitatis Caesareae Literarum Casanensis* (Kazan 1834); Fraehn, *Recensio* = C.M. Fraehn, *Recensio Numorum Muhammedanorum* (St Petersburg 1826); Gozdowski *et al.* = Marian Gozdowski, A. Kmietowicz, W. Kubiak, T. Lewicki, *Wczesnośredniowieczny skarb srebrny z Maurzyc pod Łowiczem* (Wrocław 1959); Ibn Isfandiyār = E. G. Browne, *An abridged translation of the History of Tabaristán... by Muḥammad b. al-Ḥasan b. Isfandiyár* (Leyden & London 1905); Le Strange, *Lands* = G. Le Strange, *The Lands of the Eastern Caliphate* (Cambridge 1930); Lindberg, *Essai* = J. C. Lindberg, 'Essai sur les monnaies coufiques frappées par les émirs de la famille des Bouides et les princes de leur dépendance', in *Mém. de la Soc. Royale des Antiquaires du Nord* (1844) 193-271; Markov, *Inventory* = A. Markov, *Inventarniy katalog musulmanskikh monet* (St Petersburg 1896–1904); Minorsky, *Ḥudūd* = V. Minorsky, *Ḥudūd al-ʿĀlam* (London 1937); *NC* = *The Numismatic Chronicle*; *RN* = *Revue Numismatique*; Rabino, *JA* (1936) = M. Rabino, 'Les Dynasties du Māzandarān', in *Journal Asiatique* (1936) 397-474; Zambaur, *Contributions III* = E. von Zambaur, 'Nouvelles contributions à la numismatique orientale', in *Numismatische Zeitschrift* (1914) 115-90; Zambaur, *Manuel* = E. de Zambaur, *Manuel de Généalogie et de Chronologie pour l'Histoire de l'Islam* (Hanover 1927).

2 See for example his many articles in the first and second editions of the *Encyclopaedia of Islam*, including Māzandarān (in the first edition), 'La domination des Dailamites' (*Conference faite à la Société des Etudes Iraniennes, Paris, le 28 mai, 1931*), printed in *Iranica* (Publications of the University of Tehran, vol. 775, 1964).

3 Zambaur, *Contributions III*, 137, referring apparently to Fraehn, *Recensio*, p. 600a, but this coin is dated 35(5?). See below.

4 Iṣṭakhrī, 205; Yāqūt III, 890; Le Strange, *Lands*, 372-3; Zambaur, *Contributions III*, 138, 140.

5 'Les Ispehbeds', 117-21.

6 R.N. Frye, s.v. Fīrūzkūh in *EI*², writes that Mirza Muḥammad Qazwīni in his edition of Juwayni, refutes Casanova's identification.
7 Cf. Rabino, *JA* (1936) 421.
8 Ibn Isfandiyār, 241-2; cf. Rabino, op. cit., 422.
9 Ibn Isfandiyār, pp. 244-5; cf. Rabino, op. cit., 423.
10 Le Strange, *Lands*, 370.
11 *JA* (1936) 425; Rabino also cites Sachau, who gives 512-33 H.
12 Rabino, *JA* (1936) 428.

R. M. SAVORY

A Curious Episode of Ṣafavid History

Introduction

On 27 Jumādā I 984/22 August 1576 Shāh Ismā'īl II was enthroned at Qazvīn with the support of the united *qizilbāsh* tribes. The *qizilbāsh* had only belatedly come to realize that their dominant position in the Ṣafavid state was threatened, not only by their old rivals the Tājīks, but also by the new Circassian and Georgian elements. Between 947/1540–1 and 961/1553–4 Shāh Ṭahmāsp sent four expeditions to Georgia, and from the last of these alone, 30,000 prisoners were brought back to Persia. In the main, these prisoners consisted either of boys, who were trained for service in the Ṣafavid administration and were known as *ghulāms* ('slaves of the shāh'), or of women, who were taken in marriage by the *qizilbāsh* and whose offspring were trained in a similar way. Some of the women were admitted to the royal *ḥaram*, where their intrigues to secure the advancement of their respective sons meant the introduction of a type of dynastic dispute previously unknown in the Ṣafavid state, and also led to the *ḥaram*'s obtaining an increasing degree of political influence, and interfering to a growing extent in the affairs of state. In addition, members of the Georgian nobility, either voluntarily or perforce, entered Ṣafavid service, and rapidly rose to positions of importance in the state.

In 982/1574, when Shāh Ṭahmāsp fell ill, rival factions took advantage of the situation to press the claim of their particular candidate to the succession. In 982/1574, and 983/1575, the *qizilbāsh* tribes had not necessarily supported a '*qizilbāsh*' candidate, that is, one born of a Turcoman mother. For instance, Sulaymān Mīrzā, whose mother was a Circassian, and Ḥaydar Mīrzā, whose mother was a Georgian slave, each had their supporters among the *qizilbāsh*, and this situation continued during the dynastic struggles which followed the death of Shāh Ṭahmāsp on 15 Ṣafar 984/14 May 1576. Only at the last moment, as stated above, did the *qizilbāsh* perceive that the position was no longer that which obtained in 1524 and the subsequent years. Then, the question had been, which *qizilbāsh* tribe would succeed in dominating the ruling institution? In 1576 the question was, would the *qizilbāsh* succeed in maintaining their dominant position in the state, or would the new Georgian and Circassian elements usurp it? In an effort to maintain it, the *qizilbāsh* placed Ismāʿīl II on the throne.

Only two choices had been available to the *qizilbāsh*, once they decided to support a '*qizilbāsh*' candidate, for only two of the nine sons of Shāh Ṭahmāsp had been born of a Turcoman mother. Neither of the alternatives, however, was satisfactory as the ruler of the Ṣafavid empire. Muḥammad Khudābanda, Ṭahmāsp's eldest son, had weak eyesight and was consequently initially passed over as a possible shāh. Ismāʿīl Mīrzā, on the other hand, had been incarcerated in the fortress of Qahqaha in Qarābāgh for twenty years, and it was suspected that his mind had been affected by his long imprisonment. Once on the throne, Shāh Ismāʿīl II speedily provided the evidence to substantiate these suspicions. In his brief reign of fifteen months, Ismāʿīl II put to death some nine Ṣafavid princes. The only members of the Ṣafavid royal house to escape were his elder brother Muḥammad Khudābanda and his three sons, and they escaped only because of an historical accident; Ismāʿīl II died before his orders for their execution had been carried out.

Even worse, from the *qizilbāsh* point of view, was Ismāʿīl's policy of ordering wholesale executions of their own number. Not only did Ismāʿīl II vent his rage on the Ustājlū tribe, which had supported Ḥaydar Mīrzā in the succession struggles of 1575, but he also put to death many *qizilbāsh* officers who were guilty only of holding office under his father, Shāh Ṭahmāsp. In the past, when the privileged position of the *qizilbāsh* in the Ṣafavid state had been threatened by a Tājīk official, the *qizilbāsh* had frequently resorted to assassination as a means of removing the threat. The fact that in this instance they were prepared to assassinate the Shāh himself is an indication of the extent to which they felt the Shāh was undermining their position. The Shāh's pro-Sunnī tendencies provided the *qizilbāsh* with a more respectable motive for assassinating him, and his addiction to narcotics suggested a method which would enable them, with reasonable plausibility, to attribute his death to natural causes. The Shāh, in the company of a few boon-companions, was in the habit of consuming a mixture of the expressed juice of the opium poppy and Indian hemp. On the eve of 13 Ramaḍān 985/24 November 1577, poison was inserted in this mixture, and in the morning the Shāh was found dead.

The *qizilbāsh* then placed on the throne the only other available '*qizilbāsh*' candidate, namely, Ismā'īl's elder brother Muḥammad Khudābanda, originally passed over because of his defective eyesight. Proclaimed shāh at Qazvīn on 5 Dhu'l-Ḥijja 985/13 February 1578, Sulṭān Muḥammad Shāh, as he was entitled, reigned until 10 Dhu'l-Qa'da 996/1 October 1588, but his rule was weak and ineffective. For the first eighteen months, he was dominated by his ambitious wife, Mahd-i 'Ulyā, and her pro-Tājīk party. On 1 Jumādā I, 987/26 July 1579, the *qizilbāsh* murdered Mahd-i 'Ulyā and assumed control of the state for the remainder of Sulṭān Muḥammad Shāh's reign.

The four pseudo-Ismā'īls

In 988/1580–1, three years after the murder of Shāh Isma'īl II, the first of four pseudo-Ismā'īls made his appearance. His name was Qalandar Muzavvar,[1] and his centre of activity was Kūh Gilūya. The *Tārīkh-i 'Ālam-ārā-yi 'Abbāsī* gives the following account of 'this strange incident':

A qalandar, *who resembled Ismā'īl Mīrzā*[2] *in every particular, and who, like Ismā'īl, had only two teeth (or, in order to avert suspicion, had himself pulled out (the others) – God alone knows! –) went among the Lurs of Kūh Gilūya and opened the doors of deception and deceit. He declared: 'I am Ismā'īl Mīrzā, whom a group of ingrates conspired together to kill. On grounds of expediency, I had no course left open to me except to flee and conceal myself.'*

'On a certain night in Ramaḍān, when I was sleeping in the house of Ḥalvājī-oghlu,[3] *I noticed that a group of people, who had enmity for me in their hearts, had surrounded my bedroom and intended to break in. I broke the window-shutters of that house, and hurled myself outside. Divested of the garb of sovereignty and kingship, I clothed myself in the costume of dervishes and* qalandars, *and concealed myself in a (remote) corner. That group (i.e., the conspirators) produced (the body of) a strangled* ghulām *who looked like me, and announced and proclaimed that Shāh Ismā'īl* (II) *was dead.'*

'For about two years I was absent from Iran, dressed as a qalandar. *I travelled around a lot, particularly in Asia Minor. I observed with close attention the good and bad points of that (i.e., the Ottoman) Empire. Until this moment I have not revealed to anyone the secret which I have carried in my head. I have waited patiently, with the result that most of my enemies have, one by one, paid the penalty for their crime.'*

'When the time came for me to manifest myself, and my mind was completely set at rest regarding the machinations of my enemies and the guile of my foes, I revealed myself. If God wills, I will take revenge on the rest of my enemies.

Then, with my true supporters and like-minded friends who exist on the periphery of Asia Minor, I shall set out to conquer the Ottoman empire, and I shall do this and that.'

During his youth, (*Qalandar Muzavvar*) *had used Indian hemp* (Cannabis indica), *of the type used by foreign beatniks* (bang-i lūthā-yi bīgāna), *and had allowed corrupt thoughts to enter the mansion of his brain. He used to utter foolish boasts, and make fine promises to all and sundry. Each man was nominated to a post in the government or financial administration of one of the provinces of Iran, Tūrān or Rūm. Those ignorant rustics were deceived by the absurd utterances of that fool who had turned aside from the path of reason.*

When the incident of the death of Ismā'īl Mīrzā occurred without any doubt, people remote (*from the scene*), *who were not fully informed of all the details of the affair, thought that those delirious ravings and lack-lustre, lying stories were probable, and gradually his* (*i.e., Qalandar Muzavvar's*) *fame spread among the Lur tribes. From concealment, he came out into the open. People flocked in from all sides, bringing offerings and presents. The above-mentioned Qalandar, seeing a favourable opportunity for* (*the furtherance of*) *his plans among that unintelligent group of people, laid the foundations of kingship and spread out the carpet of royalty. Everyone who visited him to pay his respects was expected to prostrate himself and kiss his foot in the traditional manner. People in every tribe brought their beautiful daughters as an offering to him, so that they might have the honour of sharing his bed.*

In short, that madman, who had the appearance of sanity, adorned the shop of sovereignty and kingship with deception, and decked it out with folly. He appointed to high office the leading men (khavāṣṣ) *of each class* (ṭabaqa),[4] *and gave orders for the mobilization of the army.*

When the size of his army, which was composed of the Jākī, Javānakī, Bandānī[5] *and other Lur clans and tribes, reached 20,000, he marched with this large force, which he had ready for action, to Dihdasht,*[6] *which is the seat of the Governor of Kūh Gilūya. The Afshār tribes informed Khalīl Khān,*[7] *the governor of that province, who was in the royal camp* (urdū), *of the fact of Qalandar's revolt.*

To resist Qalandar, the sons of Khalīl Khān, the leader of whom was Rustam Beg, assembled, and major battles were repeatedly fought by the two sides. Qalandar's men were sometimes victorious, sometimes defeated. A large number of Afshārs and Lurs were killed in these battles. By divine decree, Rustam Beg, the son of Khalīl Khān, was killed. His death resulted in the triumph and ascendancy of Qalandar, and the Afshār tribe was no longer able to resist him. Many of them had been killed in this campaign. Qalandar's men took prisoner many Afshār women and youths. (The Qalandar) sent orders (aḥkām) *and letters-patent* (manāshīr) *to all parts of Fārs and Khūzistān, and summoned his partisans. Since the royal retinue was far off, engaged in important operations on the Ādharbāyjān frontier, Qalandar's writ ran everywhere. The people of most of the neighbouring districts, seeing no course open to them but submission, bowed to the expediency of the moment, and sent gifts. Since Qalandar was an unintelligent fool, as indicated by the hemistich: 'the lamp of falsehood gives no light', the falsity of his words gradually became apparent as the days went by, and the wiser men among that tribe (the Lurs) began to have doubts in their minds regarding him. Also, the approach of Khalīl Khān (himself) was reported. Qalandar, becoming suspicious and mistrustful of some of the Lurs, abandoned (the idea of) fighting, and went to Ḥavīza and Dizfūl, to seek help from Sayyid Shujāʿ al-Dīn, as the Mushaʿshaʿi* shaykhs *were at that time governors of Ḥavīza and its dependencies in the province of ʿArabistān.*[8] *Dismissing the Lurs to their homes, (Qalandar) ordered them to be ready when he summoned them.*

When Khalīl Khān, who was at Court, heard the news of Qalandar's revolt, he obtained permission to proceed in that direction. When he reached those parts, he was intercepted by a group of ill-starred Samāyandānī[8a] *Lurs, partisans of Qalandar. They ambushed Khalīl Khān in a mountain valley which had only one road through it and, as he was passing through the valley, they hurled large rocks down from the top of the hills, and fired arrows and muskets. By divine decree, an arrow struck and killed Khalīl Khān. At his death, the Afshār* ghāzīs *were thrown into confusion, and the Lurs turned to killing and plundering. This event increased the rebelliousness and audacity of the Lurs.*

When the news of the death of Khalīl Khān reached Qalandar, he returned from Dizfūl to Kūh Gilūya. Once again, a great multitude rallied round him at Dihdasht. He wished, during the short space of time available to him before the news of his action was reported (to the Shāh),[9] *to take his fill of carnal pleasures and to live on borrowed time* (giravī az rūzgār gīrad). *When the news of the death of Khalīl Khān, and the destruction of the victorious Afshār* dūdmān *(family), was spread far and near, and reached the ears of the Shāh, the Shāh appointed Khalīl Khān's nephew, Iskandar Khān, Governor of Kūh Gilūya, and despatched him to those parts. He further ordered Ummat Khān,*[10] beglerbeg *of Fārs, and the Dhu'l-Qadar* amīrs *who were (subordinate) governors in Fārs, to suppress Qalandar and to aid Iskandar Khān.*

The following year (989/1581–2), *when the royal standards went to Khurāsān, Ummat Khān sent a detachment of the Fārs army, under the command of Dawrāq Khalīfa, to Kūh Gilūya. Iskandar Khān and the Afshār tribe joined them, and they marched together on Dihdasht. The large crowd and throng which had initially gathered round Qalandar dispersed and scattered. When the Fārs army moved rapidly to repulse him, since his design was by that time completely revealed, and the faith of the Lur chiefs in him had been severely shaken, no one came to his support. Qalandar was forced to shut himself up behind the walls of that fortress, and for a few days (he and) the small group of men who were with him waited like animals for the slaughter. The Dhu'l-Qadar* ghāzīs *made an assault and penetrated the fortifications, and slew a number who opposed them. Qalandar was seized in his house and dragged outside. The Dhu'l Qadar tribe wished to send him alive to the Court, but the Afshār* ghāzīs *fell on him and slew him against the will of the Dhu'l-Qadars, and sent his head to Court. It was delivered to the Shāh (Sulṭān Muḥammad Shāh) while he was encamped at Turbat-i Ḥaydariyya in Khurāsān, engaged in laying siege to the fortress of Turbat.*[11] *Thus the fires of the sedition of that hemp-addict were extinguished in Kūh Gilūya.*

In a word, after the episode of the above-mentioned qalandar, *other hemp-addicted* qalandars *took it into their heads to pretend to be Ismāʿil Mirzā. Tumult and disturbance occurred in several places. Every few days an 'Ismāʿil Mirzā' would appear in some province or other, and people would rally round him and then disperse again. (The second pseudo-Ismāʿil) made his appearance in Luristān and Chamchāl. The ill-starred Kurds and Lurs of the Hamadān district rallied round him, and his army soon numbered 10,000 men. He appointed* amīrs *and officers* (arbāb-i manāṣib), *and began to cause trouble on those confines. He sent a messenger to Sūlāgh Ḥusayn Takkulū*[12] *directing him to obey and submit, and sent an order (appointing) him to the* vikālat, *so that he might be* vakīl *and* rukn al-salṭana *in place of Chūha Sulṭān Takkalū.*[13]

Sūlāgh Ḥusayn, as intelligence dictated, considered it better and more advisable to deal with him by first of all (pretending to) obey him and submit to him. He accepted his terms, and verified his claim to be Ismāʿil Mirzā. He declared his sincere devotion to and complete support of him, and sent him a supply-train (bārkhāna), *and begged him to visit him. He (further) sent him tents and equipment fit for a king, and went in person to meet the* qalandar. *The wretched* qalandar *believed him, and set off for Chamchāl with the greatest pomp and circumstance.*

Sūlāgh Ḥusayn and the Takkalū nobles entered his presence, and went through the ceremony of prostration and foot-kissing. By using their intelligence and sagacity, they dispersed the (qalandar's) *followers and, when they saw their chance, they seized him and imprisoned him. When the Shāh, on his return from Khurasan, encamped at Qazvin, Sūlāgh Ḥusayn sent the* qalandar *to*

Court. Ḥamza Mirzā, in the Khiyābān-i Maydān-i Asp, put a 'gunpowder shirt' on him and detonated it. Despite that (cruel) method of punishment, the qalandars *were not completely finished, and another (the third)* (qalandar) *had similar ambitions in Ṭavālish. A group of ignorant people with no future gathered round him and went to Ardabil, where they incurred the penalty for their actions.*

Another (the fourth pseudo-Ismā'il) appeared in Ghūr and on the borders of Farāh in the province of Khurāsān. A large number of people of that region who were bankrupt of intelligence and were mischief-makers, rallied round him and started causing trouble. Ḥusayn Sulṭān Afshār, the Governor of Farāh, moved to suppress this revolt, and an engagement was fought between the two sides. The Ghūris won, and Ḥusayn Khān was killed in the battle. The Afshārs fled in confusion back to Farāh. When the news was received at Court, Husayn's brother, 'Ali Khān Sulṭān, who at Court was a yūzbāshī *of a group of Afshār qūrchīs, was appointed to his brother's post, and went to Farāh. To avenge his brother's death he went after the* qalandar *to Ghūr. The* qalandar's *followers prepared to fight, and after several struggles 'Ali Khān Sulṭān too was killed, and once again the Afshār tribe had failed to achieve anything.*

Yakān Sulṭān[14] *of their tribe (the Afshārs) became governor of Farāh. After his arrival there, he was still pondering how to deal with (the* qalandar) *when the spuriousness of the latter became manifest to his followers, and in the end they themselves killed him.*

In short, for the first four or five years of the reign of Muḥammad Khudābanda, whispers and rumours concerning Ismā'il Mirzā were on the tongues of men.[15]

Commentary

The persistent appearance of these pseudo-Ismā'īls – no less than four during the first four or five years of the reign of Sulṭān Muḥammad Shāh, that is, between 1578 and 1582–3 – raises many puzzling questions. In the first place, the occurrence of these revolts may postulate dissatisfaction with the rule of Sulṭān Muḥammad Shāh, or it may merely be indicative of his weakness. A weak ruling institution always affords opportunity for revolt, but why did these particular revolts assume this form? Challenges to the authority of the reigning shāh usually took the form of a revolt by one of the Shāh's sons or brothers, or by a group of powerful *amīrs* attempting to put on the throne a prince of the royal blood who was still a minor. The revolt of the Ustājlū-Shāmlū coalition on behalf of 'Abbās Mīrzā in 989/1581, and that of the Turkmān-Takkalū coalition in 993/1585 in favour of Ṭahmāsp Mīrzā, were of the latter type. Apart from serious challenges of this nature to the ruling institution, any extensive breakdown of the authority of the central government might, of course, be accompanied by less serious local revolts of tribal chieftains and others who wished to increase their own power in a particular area but had no real thought of overthrowing the ruling institution (though local revolts, if unchecked and allowed to proliferate, might result in its collapse).

The revolts of the pseudo-Ismāʿīls do not fall obviously into either category. Revolt I rapidly developed into something far more than a local rebellion. The Afshār *qizilbāsh* troops in the area were unable to deal with the situation, and Khalīl Khān Afshār, the powerful leader of the Afshār tribe, when he arrived from the royal camp to take charge of the operations, fared no better. Dhu'l-Qadar *qizilbāsh* troops had to be brought in from Fārs, but the revolt continued to spread, and pseudo-Ismāʿīl I soon had adherents, not only in Luristan, but also in Fārs and Khūzistān. In revolt IV, which occurred in Ghūr, the rebels were also too much for the *qizilbāsh* forces in the area.

Two features in particular of these revolts are curious and, as far as I know, without parallel in the Ṣafavid period. The first feature is the impersonation of a former shāh, namely, Shāh Ismāʿīl II. Pseudo-Ismāʿīl I went to great lengths to improve on what was apparently already a good likeness; he may even have pulled out all his own teeth except two, so that the resemblance might be more perfect. The circumstances attending the death of Shāh Ismāʿīl II had been obscure – the *qizilbāsh* had wished them to be so, in order to divert suspicion from themselves – and this lent an air of credibility to the claims of the various pretenders. The desire to impersonate a man thought to be dead, however, has a strangely messianic quality more proper to extremist Shīʿite and other heterodox beliefs than to the prosaic question of the succession to the Ṣafavid throne. This brings us to the second feature which is peculiar to this series of episodes. All these pseudo-Ismāʿīls are described by the *Tārīkh-i ʿĀlam-ārā-yi ʿAbbāsī* as *qalandars*. *Qalandars* were wandering dervishes, not attached to any *silsila* or Ṣūfī Order, not acknowledging the authority of any *shaykh*, and not considering themselves bound by any conventional patterns of behaviour.

One thing is very clear: the pseudo-Ismāʿīls had no backing from the *qizilbāsh*. Considering that it was the *qizilbāsh* who had murdered Shāh Ismāʿīl II, this at least is logical. The common denominator in all the revolts seems to have been support of the pseudo-Ismāʿīls by Tājīk elements. The power of pseudo-Ismāʿīl I was based on Luristān, where he was supported by the Jākī, Javānakī, Bandānī and Samāyandānī Lurs, but he also had (unspecified) support in Fārs and Khūzistān. Pseudo-Ismā'īl II was supported by the Kurds and Lurs of Hamadān and other districts. Support for pseudo-Ismā'īl III was centred on the district of Ṭavālish in Gīlān, and pseudo-Ismā'īl IV drew his followers from the mountainous district of Ghūr on the borders of Khurāsān. All the tribes and clans mentioned are Tājīk, non-Turcoman, tribes. Clearly, therefore, this is not a case of support for one '*qizilbāsh* candidate' against another '*qizilbāsh* candidate' – in fact, these tribes obviously are not supporting the pseudo-Ismā'īls because they are '*qizilbāsh* candidates' at all. Their motive for supporting them must be quite other than this. In other words, the tribesmen can only indirectly have been supporting the pseudo-Isma'īls as potential *pādishāh*; they must have been supporting him as actual *murshid-i kāmil*. If Shāh Ismā'īl II were still alive, he must necessarily still be the *murshid-i kāmil*, and Sulṭān Muḥammad Shāh must be a usurper. In 998/1589–90 the conspiracy of the Ṣūfīs against Shāh 'Abbās I turned on a very similar point. The view of the Ṣūfīs was that, since Sulṭān Muḥammad Shāh was still alive, he was still officially their *pīr* and *murshid-i kāmil*; 'Abbās had usurped this position and (consequently though indirectly) that of *pādishāh* also. Shāh 'Abbās had no answer to this argument except that of force.[16]

Ṣūfīs had no particular reason to love Shāh Ismā'īl II. In a head-on confrontation with an ambitious *khalīfat al-khulafā* in 984/1576, Shāh Ismā'īl II had put to death 1,200 Ṣūfīs who were followers of this *khulafā*. Nevertheless, I suggest that the fact that each of the four revolts involving a pseudo-Ismā'īl was led by a *qalandar* is the key to understanding the motive underlying the revolts. I suggest that, like the Ṣūfī conspiracy against Shāh 'Abbās I referred to above, they represent attempts to reassert the principle that the *murshid-i kāmil* was at least as important as, if not more important than, the *pādishāh*. It was the fanatical belief of the supporters of the Ṣafaviyya in the infallibility and invincibility of their *murshid-i kāmil* which had provided the impetus which had swept the Ṣafavids to power, and which had formed the basis of the 'dynamic ideology' of the theocratic government of the early Ṣafavid period. Although this 'dynamic ideology' had largely spent itself by the end of the reign of Shāh Ismā'īl I, there persisted in certain quarters an atavistic desire to return to the early theocratic form of government and to restore the position of the Ṣūfī organization of the Ṣafavid revolutionary period. I regard it as highly significant that it was the ambition of pseudo-Ismā īl I to mobilize supporters in Asia Minor and to attack the Ottoman Empire. Such aspirations, again, hark back to the theocratic period of Ṣafavid government, when the network of Ṣafavid *murids* in Ottoman territory in eastern Anatolia represented a genuine threat to the Ottoman Empire, and recall the Ṣafavid campaigns of 917–18/1511–12 in that area.[17] The desire to reinstate the *murshid-i kāmil* existed mainly among the politically less sophisticated elements of society, and it was precisely among such elements, among the Lurs and the Kurds, and in the mountains of Ghūr, that the claims of the *soi-disant murshids* found ready acceptance. Fortunately for the Ṣafavid state, none of the pseudo-Ismāʿīls was of sufficient calibre to constitute a serious threat to its existence. The pretenders, having acquired local power, soon demonstrated that this represented the limit of their ambitions. The realization of this fact eventually disillusioned their supporters, as did the grossness of their behaviour as they enjoyed the fruits of their success.

A further argument in support of the view that the basis of the pseudo-Ismāʿīl revolts was religious rather than political, lies in the method employed to execute the second pseudo-Ismāʿīl, the only one of the four to be sent to the capital, Qazvīn, for formal execution. Pseudo-Ismāʿīl I was killed by the Afshārs against the wishes of the Dhu'l-Qadars, obviously in revenge for the losses inflicted on the Afshārs by the pretender. We are not told how Pseudo-Ismāʿīl II met his end, but he was probably killed when his revolt was crushed at Ardabīl. Again, the choice of Ardabīl as his objective surely had religious and emotional overtones within the context of the early history of the Ṣafavid Order. It may be significant, too, that the native, non-Turcoman tribes of Ṭālish had been supporters of the Ṣafavids from the time of Shaykh Ṣafī al-Dīn himself.[18] Pseudo-Ismāʿīl IV was put to death by his own followers when his pretensions were revealed to be a sham. Pseudo-Ismāʿīl II, however, was taken alive and publicly executed at Qazvīn. Two aspects of this execution are significant: first, the method, designed to ensure the destruction of the body; second, the cruelty of the method used. Throughout history, the most cruel penalties have generally been reserved for religious, rather than political, offenders. The Ṣafavid period was no exception. I have suggested elsewhere that the ferocity with which Ismāʿīl I dealt with the rebellion of Amīr Ḥusayn Kiyā Chulāvī in 909/1504 was due to the fact that Ismāʿīl viewed this particular rebel as a potential rival on the religious plane.[19] Religious pretenders must not only be thought to be dead; they must be seen to be dead by as many people as possible. It was, after all, the obscurity surrounding the circumstances of the death of Shāh Ismāʿīl II which had led to the emergence of the pseudo-Ismāʿīls. To sum up, therefore, I consider this curious episode of Ṣafavid history must be viewed as a series of attempts, however crude and ineffectual, on the part of certain non-Turcoman elements in the state, to return to the theocratic government of the early Ṣafavid period.

NOTES

1 W. Hinz, *Schah Esmaʿil II*, in *Mitteilungen des Seminars für orientalische Sprachen*, XXXVI (1933) 97.

2 I.e. Shāh Ismāʿīl II; possibly because his reign was so short (fifteen months), some Ṣafavid chroniclers never made the change from Ismāʿīl Mīrzā.

3 Ḥasan Beg Halvājī-oghlu, one of Ismāʿīl II's boon-companions (*Tārīkh-i ʿĀlam-ārā-yi ʿAbbāsī*, Tehran 1334 s./1955, I, 218). See the unflattering description of him in the *Rawḍat al-Ṣafā*, VIII, 170.

4 Hinz, op. cit. 97 says that a certain Dīv Sulṭān was appointed *vazīr* ('Reichshofkanzler').

5 The following four Lur tribes and clans are mentioned by the *Tārīkh-i ʿĀlam-ārā-yi ʿAbbāsī* in the course of its account of the pseudo-Ismāʿīls: Jākī, Javānakī, Bandānī, Samāyandānī. I have been able to identify only one of these: the Jākī tribe is one of three large tribes forming the Kūhgīlū'ī division of the Lurs (the other divisions being the Mamāsanī or Mamasanī; the Bakhtīārīs; and the Lurs proper, i.e. those living in modern Luristan). The Jākī, Javānakī, and Bandānī are mentioned in two other places in the *Tārīkh-i ʿĀlam-ārā-yi ʿAbbāsī*: I, 503 lists them together with other Lur and Bakhtīārī tribes, and I, 525 (the Khānkī of the text is almost certainly a mistake for Jākī) refers to the 'Jākī, Javānakī, Bandānī and other Lurs who were always causing trouble in that province' (i.e. Kūhgīlūya). The *Sharafnāma* of Amīr Sharaf Khān Bidlīsī (ed. Muḥammad ʿAbbāsī), 47, lists the Javānakī among the tribes of Luristān. Twenty-eight tribes are mentioned in this passage, and after twenty-seven of these the editor has placed a number apparently intended to refer to a regrettably non-existent footnote. Mr C. J. Edmonds, the greatest living authority on Luristān, informed me in a personal communication that he had been unable to find in his diaries and travel notes any trace of the four tribes mentioned in connexion with the pseudo-Ismāʿīls (Jākī, Javānakī, Bandānī, Samāyandānī).

6 Dihdasht is situated eight *farsangs* (approximately 30 miles) N.-E. of Bihbihān. See Baron Clement August de Bode, *Extracts from a Journal kept while travelling, in January 1841, through the country of the Mamásení and Khógilú (Bakhtiyárí), situated between Kázerún and Behbehán*, in *Journal of the Royal Geographical Society*, XIII (1843) 87.

7 Khalīl Khān Afshār, described by the *Tārīkh-i ʿĀlam-ārā-yi ʿAbbāsī* (i, 219) as 'a benevolent greybeard, blessed by fortune', is listed by the

same source (I, 140) among the most powerful Afshār *amīrs*. Khalīl Khān was governor of Kūh Gīlūya, and chief of 10,000 Afshār families. His nephew, Iskandar Khān, who succeeded him as governor of Kūh Gīlūya, is also mentioned as a prominent Afshār *amīr* (see also *Tārīkh-i Qizilbāshiyya*, fol. 74b).

8 According to V. Minorsky, article *Musha'sha'* in *Encyclopaedia of Islam*, 1st edition, *Supplement*, the Musha'sha'ī governor of Ḥavīza in 988/1580–1 was Sajjād b. Badrān. He had been appointed governor by Shāh Ṭahmāsp in 948/1541, and apparently continued in office until his death in 992/1584. I have translated the *pidarān-i musha'sha'ī* of the text as 'Musha'sha'ī *shaykhs*', as the sense seemed to require something like this.

8*a* See above, n.5.

9 Lit., 'before the veil was removed from his actions'.

10 Mentioned by the *Tārīkh-i Qizilbāshiyya*, fol. 65a; according to this source, Ummat Beg (Khān) Dhu'l-Qadar, after the defeat of the Turkmān-Takkalū coalition (in 993/1585 by Ḥamza Mīrzā), fled to Yazd, where he was executed by Maqṣūd Beg, the *vazīr* of the *qūrchī-bāshī* Qulī Khān Afshār. Ummat Beg was appointed governor of Fārs in 990/1582 (*Tārīkh-i 'Ālam-ārā-yi 'Abbāsī*, I, 279).

11 This dates this event precisely to the winter of 990–1/1582–3. Turbat-i Ḥaydariyya was held by the powerful *qizilbāsh amīr* Murshid Qulī Khān Shamlū who, together with 'Alī Qulī Khān Shāmlū, the governor of Harāt, had raised the standard of revolt on behalf of 'Abbās Mīrzā.

12 Sūlāgh Ḥusayn Takkalū had been appointed governor of Kurdistān by Shāh Ismā'īl II in 985/1577 (*Aḥsan al-Tavārīkh*, ed. Seddon (Baroda 1931) 492).

13 On the face of it, pseudo-Ismā'īl II's information was a little out of date, since Chūha Sulṭān Takkalū had been killed in 937/1530–1, over fifty years previously. I assume the meaning is that Sūlāgh Ḥusayn Takkalū was invited to aspire to a position as important as that held by Chūha Sulṭān, who was *vakīl* and *amīr al-umarā* and for more than three years was the virtual ruler of the state (see R. M. Savory, *The Principal Offices of the Ṣafawid State during the reign of Ṭahmāsp I* (930–84/1524–76), in *Bulletin of the School of Oriental and African Studies*, XXIV, part I (1961) 68-9, 77-8).

14 Yakān Sulṭān is listed by the *Tārīkh-i 'Ālam-ārā-yi 'Abbāsī*, I, 140, as one of the leading Afshār *amīrs*, and is described as the governor of Farāh and Isfizār.

15 *Tārīkh-i 'Ālam-ārā-yi 'Abbāsī*, I, 272-5. The episode of the pseudo-Ismā'īls is mentioned, extremely briefly, by Aḥmad Kasravī, *Tārīkh-i pānṣad-sāla-yi Khūzistān*, 3rd ed. (Tehran 1330 s./1951) 60-4.

16 See R. M. Savory, *The Office of khalīfat al-khulafā under the Ṣafavids*, in *Journal of the American Oriental Society*, LXXXV, no. 4 (Oct.-Dec. 1965) 501.

17 See R. M. Savory, *The Consolidation of Ṣafawid Power in Persia*, in *Der Islam*, XLI (October 1965) 82 ff.

18 See *Tadhkirat al-Mulūk*, translated and explained by V. Minorsky. (London 1943) 189.

19 R. M. Savory, *The Consolidation of Ṣafawid Power in Persia*, in *Der Islam*, XLI (October 1965) 74.

J. SCHACHT

On the Title of the *Fatāwā al-ʿĀlamgīriyya*

I knew the late Professor Minorsky for more than thirty years and have always admired his scholarly work, but our fields of research have hardly ever coincided. So in order not to remain quite outside the scope of this commemorative volume, I venture to offer the following slight remarks on a subject which has at least some Indian and Iranian connotations.

The *Fatāwā al-ʿĀlamgīriyya*, compiled by order of the Mogul emperor Awrangzīb ʿĀlamgīr (1067/1658–1118/1707) during the years 1075/1664–1083/1672, is not a collection of *fatwā*s but of authoritative passages and accepted decisions from the recognized works of the Ḥanafī school. It is in this sense, which corresponds to the expression *ʿalayhi l-fatwā*, that the terms *aftā* and *fatwā* are used in the preface twice: *an yuʾallifū kitāban ḥāmishan li-ẓāhir al-riwāyāt allati ttafaqa ʿalayhā wa-afyā bihā l-fuḥūl*, and *mawsūm bi-ʿalāmat al-fatwā wa-simat al-rujḥān.* No one who has opened the work, can be in doubt about its character.[1] I should not insist on this were it not that the erroneous view that it is a collection of *fatwā*s is still being given currency in certain writings. Al-Murādī, too, although he uses the term *fatwā* somewhat loosely, is really unequivocal (*Silk al-durar*, IV, 114):

> 'He commanded the Ḥanafī scholars of his country to collect under his name *fatwā*s which should comprise the totality of the doctrine of their school concerning the rules of the sacred law of which people were in need; they were collected in a number of volumes, and he called them *al-Fatāwā al-ʿĀlamgīriyya*; the work became famous in Hijaz, Egypt, Syria and Rūm, it was widely used, and became a work of reference for muftis.'[2]

The *Fatāwā al-ʿĀlamgīriyya* thus presents two extraordinary features: that a prince should appear officially as the sponsor of a work of Islamic law in its title, and that, being in reality a collection of extracts from authoritative works, it should be called *Fatāwā*.

A precedent in both respects appears to be at first sight the *Fatāwā al-Tātārkhāniyya*, compiled by order of Tātārkhān (d. soon after 752/1351), a nobleman at the court of sultan Muḥammad II Ṭughlāq (726/1324–752/1351).[3] Whereas the compilation of the *Fatāwā al-ʿĀlamgīriyya* was carried out by a group of scholars under the direction of a certain Shaykh Niẓām (d. 1090/1679), the *Fatāwā al-Tātārkhāniyya* is the work of a certain ʿĀlim b. ʿAlāʾ (al-Dīn) al-Ḥanafī who is otherwise unknown. I recently had occasion to consult some copies of this work in the libraries of Istanbul (Ragıp Paşa 610-13, of 987; Aya Sofya 1551–3, of 1017; Muratmolla 1110–11; all very large volumes).[4] The author does not mention himself at the beginning but he starts at once by referring to Tātārkhān, who had commissioned the work, in the most extravagant terms: *ammā baʿd fa-qad ashāra ilayya man ishāratuh ḥukm wa-iṭāʿatuh ghunm wa-amruh yutalaqqā wa-khiṭābuh yutaṣaddā wa-kalāmuh masmūʿ wa-khilāfuh marfūʿ wajaba lahu l-idhʿān ʿalā kulli qāṣin wa-dān fa-aṣbaḥa man aṣbaḥa muqallida amrih wa-amsā man amsā muqayyada ḥukmih fal-falāḥ kull al-falāḥ li-man inqādahū wa-wālāh wal-wayl kull al-wayl li-man ʿāṣāhu wa-ʿādāh a-lā wa-huwa l-majlis al-ʿālī al-mutadarriʿ bi-durūʿ al-majd wal-maʿālī al-mutaṣarrif fī maṣārif al-ayyām wal-layālī al-ghālib ʿalal-aʿdāʾ bil-qawāḍib wal-ʿawālī ẓāʾir al-ḥaramayn al-ʿayn lil-insān wal-insān lil-ʿayn al-Khān al-aʿẓam wal-Qahramān al-muʿaẓẓam TĀTĀRKHĀN alladhī alqā ilayhi l-dahr qiyādah fa-qāma bi-amr al-mulki wa-mā ādah*, and he goes on to describe the character of his commission: *an attasima bi-jamʿ kitāb jāmiʿ lil-fatāwā wal-wāqiʿāt ḥāwi l-aḥkām wal-riwāyāt mughni l-nās ʿan al-rujūʿ ilal-muṭawwalāt wal-mukhtaṣarāt li-mā bih min al-shafaqa wal-ḥadab ʿalā arbāb al-arab fa-rubba dhī irba lā yuḥaṣṣil gharaḍah fil-fiqh min kitāb wa-kitābayn wa-lā yajid maṭlūbah fī aṣl wa-aṣlayn fa-lā jaram yatʿab fī jamʿ al-kutub wa-yaghtamm bi-hādha l-hamm.* The emphasis is thus laid on collecting decisions on cases which might arise in practice, in a book which would obviate difficult research in a number of works. The author then mentions his sources, an account of which can be found in the Catalogue of the Bankipore Library; he says that he has arranged his subject-matter according to the arrangement of the *Hidāya* (*wa-rattabt abwābah ʿalā tartīb abwāb al-Hidāya*), just as we read in the preface to the *Fatāwā al-ʿĀlamgīriyya* that its compilers have chosen to follow the arrangement of that work (*wa-khtārū fī tartīb kutubihā tartīb al-Hidāya*); and finally he states explicitly that he has called his work *al-Fatāwā al-Tātārkhāniyya*. This disposes of the two suppositions, mentioned by Ḥājjī Khalīfa, that ʿĀlim al-Ḥanafī should have omitted to give a title to his book, so that it came to be called *al-Fatāwā al-Tātārkhāniyya* by default, or that its real title, given to it by the author, was *Zād al-musāfir*. The practice of naming a work of religious law after a prince therefore goes back in India to the first half of the eighth century of the hijra.

The *Fatāwā al-Tātārkhāniyya* is similar to the *Fatāwā al-ʿĀlamgīriyya* in being essentially a collection of quotations from authoritative works of the Ḥanafī school, but it differs from it in containing also considerable doctrinal developments by the author himself. From the enumeration of the sources of the *Fatāwā al-Tātārkhāniyya* it appears that systematic works on Islamic law, if they concentrated on questions arising in practice, even if not technically collections of *fatwā*s, were apt to be called *fatāwā*, particularly in the Central Asian and Indian regions.

The literary form of presenting systematic statements of Islamic law in the semblance of *fatwā*s, however, can be traced in a much more explicit manner to the *Fiqh-i Fīrōz-Shāhi*, a work published at the command of sultan Fīrōz Shāh (752/1351–790/1388), the successor of Muḥammad II Ṭughlāq. I had occasion to consult this work in the seemingly unique manuscript 2987 (Persian) of the Library of the former India Office.[5] The manuscript bears the date 1061, *fī sulṭān al-barr wal-baḥr Awrangzīb ʿĀlamgīr pādishāh ghāzi* [sic], but this applies only to the first and the last leaf by which the manuscript was completed; its main part is itself a composite of two manuscripts. According to the introduction, the author, Mawlānā imām-i humām Ṣadr al-milla wal-dīn Yaʿqūb Muẓaffar Kirāmī, had only made a draft (*sawād*) when he died; this remained for a long time neglected in the hands of his heirs until, by order of sultan Fīrōz Shāh, the manuscript was revised, enlarged and published in its present form. The editor does not mention his name.

The work presents itself as a collection of *fatwā*s, but this is merely a literary form. The author declares in the preface that he has collected his material from fashionable works (*az naw-dahisht kutub*), taking care to give only the soundest opinions and omitting everything doubtful, a consideration which recurs with force in the introduction of the *Fatāwā al-ʿĀlamgīriyya*. The problems are formulated in Persian, introduced by *istiftāʾ* or by *mā qawluhum*; this is followed, in the best style of *fatwā*s, by a short decision, *bāshad* or *kunad* or *shawad* or *tuwānad*, or their negatives, always with *wallahū aʿlam*, and then by quotations from one or several of the authoritative works. I have been unable to find the name of the author or the title of the work or a reference to sultan Fīrōz Shāh having sponsored it, in any of the obvious sources or works of reference.

A different but closely related version of this last work is called *Fatāwā-i*

Qarākhānī and attributed to a certain Qabūl Qarākhān in a manuscript of the Asiatic Society of Bengal,[6] and a copy of the same work, incomplete at the beginning and identified only by the mention *Fatāwā-i Qarākhānī* in the colophon, exists in the Library of the former India Office.[7] The author, who calls himself Qabūl Qarākhān, relates in the introduction that the original version of the work was produced by Ṣadr al-dīn Ya'qūb Muẓaffar Kirāmī, that this last suddenly died, leaving the work unfinished and unarranged, and that he, Qarākhān, undertook to give it its present form.[8] The lists of the chapters of the *Fiqh-i Firōẓ-Shāhī* and of the *Fatāwā-i Qarākhānī* are rather different although they have a certain family likeness, and there can be no doubt about the close connection of both these works, although their beginnings are quite different. Either Qarākhān committed flagrant plagiarism, or we are in the presence of a most remarkable coincidence. I have been unable to find any reference to Qarākhān either, or come across other manuscripts of his work, and it is not clear to me why Ivanow should have called it 'the well known treatise on the system of *fiqh*'.

So this line of research runs out somewhat inconclusively, but I hope to have shown that there are precedents in the Indian region for the two extraordinary features of the title of the *Fatāwā al-'Ālamgīriyya*.

NOTES

1 Cf. A. S. Bazmee Ansari, art. 'al-Fatāwā al-'Ālamgīriyya', in *EI*².

2 In another passage of 'Ālamgīr's biography (ibid., 113) al-Murādī calls him 'the sultan of India in our time, the Commander of the Faithful (*amīr al-mu'minīn*) and the *imām* of the believers'; although al-Murādī died in 1206/1791, he may well have spoken of 'Ālamgīr as the great sultan of India in his time; the caliph's titles which he attributes to him are obviously meant to be of local application only.

3 *Catalogue, Cairo*¹, III, 87 f.; *Catalogue, Bankipore*, XIX/2, No. 1715; Ḥājjī Khalīfa, II, No. 2039; *GAL*, S, II, 643.

4 I should like to thank the curators of these collections, and indeed of all the libraries in Istanbul, Üsküdar and Ankara which I had the privilege to use, for their unfailing helpfulness and courtesy.

5 Cf. H. Ethé, *Catalogue of Persian Manuscripts in the Library of the India Office*, I, No. 2564.

6 W. Ivanow, *Concise Descriptive Catalogue of the Persian Manuscripts in the Collection of the Asiatic Society of Bengal*, No. 1034.

7 MS 3069 (Persian); Ethé, No. 2971. This copy is dated 1099, again in the reign of 'Ālamgīr, and that of the Asiatic Society of Bengal is of 1150.

8 I take this information from Ivanow's *Catalogue*.

Khurāsān at the Time of the Arab Conquest

Students of Islamic History are greatly indebted to Professor Minorsky's valuable studies on the geography of the Islamic Empire. Eastern Iran seems particularly to have interested him, the more so because he realized, perhaps more than other scholars, the extremely important role that this part had played in the early history of the Islamic Empire. It is with such a problem that I shall concern myself here.

As 'Khurāsān' means literally the land of the east, it was meant sometimes to cover all the lands of eastern Iran almost to the borders of China; at others it covered only parts of Khurāsān as we know it now. Yāqūt observed that the Arab geographers were misleading in their definition of Khurāsān, because they included under this name all the lands which used to be under the Arab governors of Khurāsān. Nevertheless the Arabs themselves must have realized this discrepancy and for this reason introduced such terms as 'Khurāsān wa mā warā' an-Nahr', 'Khurāsān wa' l-Mashriq', or simply 'al-Mashriq'.[1] The confusion was not so critical then, since these lands were parts of one political domain, though sometimes under separate governors. The problem arises when one tries to follow the Arab conquests in the east. Then it is essential to establish the political geography of the area with all its differences in political institutions, sovereigns and populations with various interests. All these are certainly important factors in understanding the problems which faced the Arabs in their conquest and colonization of these parts and the subsequent historical developments.

It has been established that, at the time of the Arab conquest, the Murghāb river formed the eastern boundary of the Sāsānian Empire.[2] In other words, Khurāsān of the Sāsānians was then only the districts of Nīsābūr, amongst which the districts of Qūhistān were included, and the two towns of Marw and Marw-ar-Rūd with their immediate vicinities west of the Murghāb; indeed the last two towns were the outer posts of the eastern borders.[3] It is not without significance that though we have a very detailed account of the conquest of the district of Nīsābūr, in the Arabic sources, yet when the same sources speak about the conquest of Marw and Marw-ar-Rūd, there is only the mention of one *Rustāq*, at most, along with each of these cities.[4] In the narratives concerning the Arab conquest of Khurāsān we do not find any trace of a Sāsānian governor general there, although a *Pādhūsbān* is mentioned by Ibn Khurdādhbeh as the *Iṣbahbadh* of all of Khurāsān.[5] We only find *Marzbāns* alongside with the *Kanārang*, which was the title of the hereditary governor of all the region of Nīsābūr, and who may have been descended from a pre-Sāsānian dynasty.[6] It is possible, if we accept Christensen's suggestion that this title carries with it the connotation of a 'governor of a province', that the *Kanārang* was not only the governor of Nīsābūr but the governor of the whole province of Khurāsān.[7] As we find *Marzbāns* in Sarakhs and Abīward, we also find *Marzbāns* in Marw and Marw-ar-Rūd. These *Marzbāns*, who were chosen from the local nobility, were charged with the administration of their districts; and because Marw and Marw-ar-Rūd were frontier outposts, their *Marzbāns* had also the military obligation of defending these borders. The *Kanārang* also had the military duty of defending the countryside which was always exposed to the raids of the Ephthalites from Bādghīs, and for this reason he made his residence in Ṭūs which occupied a central position, a fact which caused the Arab narrators to identify him with this later city.[8] With the collapse of the central government of the Sāsānians, each *Marzbān* became independent and had to act on his own, as a representative of his district, in regard to the new invaders. Most of them offered no resistance to the Arabs, and were only glad to conclude peace treaties with them, assuring the continuation of their authority under the new régime. In Khurāsān of the Sāsānians, as in the rest of the Empire, the *Dihqāns* who formed the local nobility held the upper hand, and their principal function was the allocation and collection of taxes. According to the Sāsānian system, they, as well as the warriors, the priests, and the civil servants, were exempted from the poll tax. The burden of the taxes fell heavily on the shoulders of the peasantry, who had also to serve in the infantry in the army. In the cities, the bourgeoisie was in a better situation; they paid the poll tax but they did not have to serve in the army.[9]

It is important to keep in mind always the fact that the Murghāb was the easternmost border of the Sāsānian Empire when trying to follow the Arab conquest of Khurāsān, because the Arabs must have realized that once they conquered the 'small' Khurāsān of the Sāsānians and advanced east of the Murghāb they were coming in conflict with completely different sovereigns, if not peoples. Although these latter peoples were also of Iranian origin, yet, owing to separate historical development, they had different social, political and cultural, backgrounds. The Arabs must then have realized that they were opening new fronts against enemies who proved by their resistance to the conquerors that they had better-organized armies than the remnant forces of the Sāsānian Empire. The choice of Marw as the base for the Arab armies, and later the capital of the Arab governors, is the best indication of the Arab recognition of this fact. In the beginning, their intention, as heirs of the Sāsānian Empire, was probably to maintain the Murghāb as their eastern border, while raiding the areas to the east in order to keep their armies busy in the field. As it later turned out, and following the same pattern of the previous conquerors from the west, they were compelled to advance not only to the Oxus but even further, to the Jaxartes, bringing under Arab dominion the lands in which had flourished previously the Greco-Bactrian, the Kūshān and the Ephthalite Empires. In contrast to the previous conquerors, the Arabs were able to integrate these areas into their empire, and in due course of time they became great centres of Islamic civilization.

Although the Chinese sources throw some light on the history of these regions, yet, in spite of the many researches done in this field, the history of the area and its peoples is still to some extent a matter of speculation on the part of the historians.[10] From the earliest times, there had been successive waves of emigration of nomadic tribes of Iranian origin from central Asia westwards to settle down in the area, rightly called 'Outer Iran'.[11] These nomads were soon assimilated to sedentary life, though some of them were not fully assimilated and led a kind of semi-nomadic life. We are concerned here with the last wave of these nomads, mainly the Ephthalites.

I must acknowledge my debt to the very well-documented study of R. Ghirshman, *Les Chionites-Hephtalites*. It is due to his painstaking work that we are now able to form some opinions about these little known people. They probably appear for the first time among the armies of the later Kūshāns, helping them against the Sāsānians. It is now generally accepted that they were of Indo-European origin, and they took their name from the name of their eponymous ancestor, or perhaps the founder of their empire.[12] One factor distinguishes the Ephthalite empire from the empire of Bactria and the Kūshāns, and had a great influence on the history and development of this area; in contrast to the two previous empires, which in the course of their expansion southwards had to stop for some time to the north of the Hindū-Kūsh, the Ephthalites occupied both areas, the north and the south of these mountains, at much the same time. It seems that the Ephthalite tribes were divided in two major divisions – the northern tribes, who kept the name Ephthalites, and the southern tribes, whose tribal name was the 'Zābulites' from whom the area of Zābulistān took its name.[13] These southern Ephthalites, the 'Zābulites', expanded successfully south-eastwards in India, and the northern tribes, the Ephthalites, had to go westwards for their expansion and they clashed with the Sāsānians. After a period of half a century of fighting against the latter, the final victory rested with the Ephthalites, and they became virtually the masters of Persia, from which for half a century they exacted a heavy annual tribute in cash. The Ephthalite empire in the first half of the sixth century A.D. extended over Soghdiana, the Oxus basin and the lands to the north and south of the Hindū-Kūsh. There is ample evidence that the trade which flourished under the Kūshāns continued under the Ephthalites and became one of the major sources of income to their Empire; and the Soghdians also continued to play a major role in this trade.[14] Though the Sāsānian influence on the life and culture of the Ephthalites cannot be denied, Buddhism was still the predominant religion of the whole Empire. However, due to the religious tolerance of these people, other religions were found among them, like Zoroastrianism, Manichaeism and even Christianity, and at the time of Yuan Chwang, the Chinese pilgrim, Buddhism was very strong south of the Iron Gate, though north of it among the Soghdians, Zoroastrianism was gradually taking its place.[15]

Finally, the Sāsānians had to seek the alliance of the rising new power beyond the Jaxartes, namely the Western Turks, to rid themselves of the Ephthalites' domination. The two allies were able to defeat the Ephthalites (A.D. 563–8), and the result was the partition of their empire between the two victors and for a brief moment the Oxus became the boundary between the Iranians and the Turks. The Sāsānians were not able to hold their newly acquired lands for very long, and owing to their gradual weakening and the rising power of the Turks, the latter were able to extend their suzerainty southwards to include the Ephthalite lands north of the Hindū-Kūsh. Apparently, the Ephthalites of the south were able to escape the fate of their brethren in the north, only to meet their final destruction later at the hands of the Arabs, but not until after a stubborn resistance which lasted well over two hundred years.[16]

The defeat of the Ephthalites in the north of the Hindū-Kūsh did not mean their disappearance from the scene. They continued to live side by side with, and probably more assimilated into, the previously settled population. In some places where they were not fully assimilated and the semi-nomadic element was more dominant, they were able to form their own principalities, probably encouraged by the Turks, and they continued to give the Sāsānians much trouble on their north-eastern frontiers.[17] In fact, as we are told by Yuan Chwang, he found on his way to India in A.D. 630 that all the Ephthalite territories south of the Iron Gate, which came under Turkish suzerainty, were divided up in twenty-seven principalities with separate chiefs,[18] but, owing to the lack of a strong centralized government and the frequent internal conflicts among the Turks, these principalities were left with almost a semi-independent status.[19] The oldest son of the *Jabghū* of the Western Turks was appointed as a general in command, with the title of *Shād*, and had his residence near Warwālīz possibly with the principality of Huo (Qunduz) and the city of Balkh under his governorship. From A.D. 630, when the Chinese government started its intrigues against the Western Turks until the latter's final destruction at the hands of the former in A.D. 658, there was a period of near-anarchy in this region. A son of the former *Shād* founded the dynasty of the *Jabghūs* of Ṭukhāristān which ruled over the district we know as Ṭukhāristān proper. The other chiefs in the rest of the principalities, and probably others who seized the opportunity to form new principalities, recognized the new *Jabghū* as their suzerain, though his authority could hardly have been anything but nominal.[20] The Chinese sources inform us that in A.D. 661 the government of China, after formally annexing the territories between Khotan and Persia, tried to re-organize them in sixteen governments under Chinese suzerainty. But the Chinese attempt failed because of Tibet's advances in Central Asia, and China had to devote all its energy to check the new danger.[21] If Turkish interference in the administration of the subject territories was limited to the appointment of military governors and the collection of tribute, Chinese interference was practically nothing more than diplomatic manœuvres, and thereafter these principalities enjoyed an even greater measure of independence and were only linked together by accepting the nominal suzerainty of the *Jabghū* of Ṭukhāristān.[22]

Among these principalities, the principality of Ṭukhāristān occupied a dominant position, yet it seems rather difficult to define what Ṭukhāristān was. Professor Gibb draws our attention to the fact that the name Ṭukhāristān is used very loosely in the Arabic records with misleading effects. Barthold suggests that it was used in two different senses: the first and narrower sense is to define the area east of Balkh and west of Badakhshān south of the Oxus; the second and larger sense is to define the area east of Balkh on both sides of the Oxus.[23] The Chinese sources give a larger definition than that of Barthold, even in his larger sense. Yuan Chwang, speaking about the land of the Tu-hou-lo (Ṭukhārā), defined it as reaching on the east to the Tsung-ling, on the west to Persia, on the south to the great mountains (the Hindū-Kūsh), and on the north to the Iron Gate; the river Oxus flowed through the middle of it from east to west.[24] We find that al-Balādhurī used the word Ṭukhāristān in a similar sense, indicating that the lands immediately to the east of the Murghāb were considered at the time of the Arab invasion as part of Ṭukhāristān.[25] In spite of the numerous researches done on Ṭukhāristān and the Ṭukhārā people, no satisfactory conclusion has been reached.[26] It is beyond the scope of this article to decide the origin of the Ṭukhārā people, but it seems that they were part of the Iranian peoples who emigrated to this region in earlier times. At the time of the Arab invasion they formed a part of the settled population and, as observed by Professor Gibb, they were 'noted in the Chinese annals for their commercial enterprise.'[27] Here reference will be made to Ṭukhāristān as the principality known under this name, i.e. the district which lies east of Balkh and west of Badakhshān to the south of the Oxus, in contrast to the principalities of Ṭukhāristān as meaning the principalities under the suzerainty of the *Jabghū* of Ṭukhāristān at the time of the Arab invasion.

Among the principalities of Ṭukhāristān, the various Ephthalite principalities seem to have had a rather important place, but the problem arises when we try to define their location or number. It is certain, from the evidence of the later activities of Nēzak, that Bādghīs was an Ephthalite principality or at least part of one. The name Bādghīs seems to be associated with Harāt and Būshanj, which makes it a principality of considerable size. From the fact that when Nēzak made peace with Qutaybah ibn Muslim he made stipulations in regard to Bādghīs alone,[28] it is tempting to conclude that there was more than one principality in this district of Harāt, Būshanj and Bādghīs. It could be argued that this peace was made long after the Ephthalites were reduced to the sole principality of Bādghīs, but it is more probable that there were numerous principalities in this region which were subjected to the Arabs at different stages. From the list of the titles of the kings of Khurāsān and the East provided by Ibn Khurdādhbeh,[29] we gather that the prince of Nasā (Yahūdiyyah of Jūzjān[30]) used to have the title of *Abrāz*, the prince of Gharshistān had the title of *Barāz-Bandeh* and the prince of Harāt, Būshanj and Bādghīs was called *Barāzān.*[31] On certain coins which were identified as Ephthalite coins belonging to the second half of the seventh century A.D., the word *BRZ* was found on the obverse.[32] It is possible to conclude that *Barāz* or *Abrāz* was the title of the princes of the Ephthalite principalities, *Barāz-Bandeh* was the title of the lesser princes subject to *Barāz*, and *Barāzān* simply meant the plural of *Barāz*. The principality of Nasā (Yahūdiyyah) was probably one of many principalities formed around the different towns in the district of Jūzjān, in which the Jūzjān-Khān,[33] the most powerful prince, held the supreme authority. In the area of Harāt, Būshanj and Bādghīs there could have been many principalities with separate princes each of whom was a *Barāz*, and of whom Nēzak Ṭarkhān later distinguished himself as the leading Ephthalite prince against Arab domination. Gharshistān was a lesser principality under a weaker prince subject to the more powerful *Barāz*, probably from the district of Jūzjān. Thus, in the area west of Balkh extending southwest to include all of Jūzjān, the upper course of the Murghāb south of Marw-ar-Rūd to Gharshistān, and then extending west to reach the middle course of the Harāt River, there were a number of Ephthalite principalities, which were ruled by their own princes, but subject to the nominal suzerainty of the *Jabghū* of Ṭukhāristān.

From the information that has come down to us, particularly in the Chinese annals, but sometimes supplemented by the Arabic sources, most of the rest of the principalities can be identified as follows:

1. Shūmān, which also includes Akhrūn. Its prince was said to be of Turkish origin in the Chinese sources.[34]
2. al-Qūmid (Karategīn) in the Surkhān valley to the north-east of Ṭukhāristān. Its prince was also a Turk.[35]
3. al-Khuttal. Its prince was called as-Sabal according to Arabic sources.[36]
4. Ṭukhāristān, which included the towns of Baghlān, Khulm, Siminjān and its capital Warwālīz.
5. Badakhshān.
6. Kuwādhiyān.
7. Wakhān.
8. Ṭālqān.
9. Chaghāniān.

All these last five principalities, though they were under separate princes, seem to have had a close relationship with Ṭūkhāristān.[37] Yuan Chwang on his way back from India in 644 spoke about the king of [illegible]uh, who was a Turk and ruled over the small states south of the Iron Gate moving about from one to another.[38] It is possible that the princes of these principalities had formed some sort of a defensive military alliance with the *Jabghū* of

Ṭukhāristān, a fact which is also indicated by the preservation of the office of *Shād* as late as A.D. 710[39]; this *Shād* was identified by Professor Gibb as the king of Chaghāniān (Chaghān-Khudā) and not as the *Jabghū* himself.[40]

10. Shughnān to the north of Wakhān. It was divided into five autonomous valleys, but all under one prince. The people there were nomads who used to raid the merchants on the road to Tibet via Wakhān.[41]
11. Tirmidh. Under the rule of the Tirmidh-Shāh.[42]
12. Āmul. To the west of the Oxus.[43]
    These two principalities were mainly cities with strong fortresses to control the main trade routes at the crossings of the Oxus.
13. Bāmyān, north of the Hindū-Kūsh. Its prince was called Shīr-ī-Bāmyān.[44] This principality was at the southern end of the lands which were under the suzerainty of the *Jabghū* of Ṭukhāristān.

The kingdom of Zābulistān (ar-Rukhkhaj) with its capital Ghaznah,[45] where the king, Zunbīl[46] or Rutbīl[47] resided, is mentioned in the Chinese sources as under the suzerainty of the *Jabghū*,[48] but this could only be taken as an exaggeration often found in these sources, particularly when we notice that this is mentioned in the events of the year A.D. 718, when it was impossible to have been the case. This kingdom had always defended its independence with great zeal and proved that it could still do so, even when the Arabs penetrated Western Sijistān and concentrated their attacks against it.

In addition to the already mentioned principalities of Ṭukhāristān, there may have been other principalities which cannot be identified under the names given by the Chinese sources,[49] but were most probably minor principalities or possibly parts of the bigger principalities.

It must be mentioned that the city of Balkh did not seem to hold the pre-eminence it had in earlier times or the importance it was given later by the Arab historians and geographers.[50] According to Yuan Chwang, at the time when he was going to India in A.D. 630 it was thinly populated and it was part of the governorship of Qunduz.[51] Warwālīz seems to have taken its place as the seat of government and the only explanation is that this city was, from a military point of view, easier to defend than Balkh.

The mass of the population in the principalities of Ṭukhāristān were people of Iranian origin who had previously emigrated into this area in successive waves of nomadic tribes. When they settled down in the seat of the old Bactrian Hellenistic civilisation, they were gradually assimilated and became known to us under different names – Ṭukhārā, Kūshāns or Ephthalites. Under the Kūshān Empire, Buddhism became the predominant religion and it continued thus until it was replaced by Islam. Because the Ephthalites were the last to come to this region, assimilation had not taken its full course among them, particularly among those who had settled in the rich pasture lands of Jūzjān and around Harāt and Bādghīs, and who posed the greatest problem to the Arabs at the time of the invasion.[52] It is to be expected that in all these petty principalities the political institutions were certainly different to those in the Sāsānian domain. These small princes were probably nothing more than military lords who imposed their authority over the local population by virtue of their arms. Certainly the expenditure involved in maintaining separate courts and armies would have created a heavy burden on their people, and these people would only be happy to see a chance for a change in their desperate conditions. Such conditions added to the political disunity of the area and were naturally in favour of the Arab invasion.

Moving northwards through the Iron Gate, the regions open into the rich cultivated lands of the Zarafshān river. In spite of the great differences in almost every respect between the Oxus and the Zarafshān valleys, we find in Soghdiana a political disunity not dissimilar to that south of the Iron Gate. The country was divided in a number of small independent principalities, but though each had its own prince, all the princes belonged to what is known in Chinese sources as the Shao-wu clan. They formed together what was best described as 'a loose confederacy in a manner strikingly reminiscent of the Hellenic city-states'.[53] Between A.D. 605 and 611 the king of the chief city of Soghdiana, Samarqand, who was the head of the Shao-wu clan, married a princess from the Turkish royal family.[54] Whether this was out of policy or ambition, he ended up by being a vassal of the Western Turks. It is uncertain what the origin of the Shao-wu clan was, but it is clear that during their long rule, about six or seven hundred years, all these princes had fully identified themselves with their Iranian subjects. Moreover, in contrast to the princes of the principalities of Ṭukhāristān, their authority was much limited by the great power of the *dihqāns* and the rich merchants, and as suggested by Professor Gibb, 'the "kingship" was not a real monarchy but rather the primacy in an oligarchical system'.[55] The Soghdians were famous for their commercial enterprise, and they were highly interested in the Chinese silk trade, the centres of which were at Samarqand, Paykand, and Kish, and they worked as intermediaries between East and West. Sūq aṣ-Ṣughd (the market of the Soghdians) was one of the most ancient quarters of the city of Marw.[56] The population of the cities as well as that in the countryside, was of Iranian elements reinforced by emigrants from the Sāsānian dominions. Professor Gibb singles out the merchant families of Paykand as probably being Kūshāns.[57] In Samarqand, probably not all the people were Zoroastrians, but they were evidently not Buddhists at the time of Yuan Chwang's visit.[58] However, among the Soghdians, Christianity and Manichaeism lived side by side with Zoroastrianism.

It was against these people of Iranian origin that the Arabs had to fight for almost a century, in order to conquer and establish their rule in the lands to the east of the Sāsānian Empire. In the Arabic sources they were wrongly referred to as Turks. In fact, the Turks did not come to their help against the Arabs until the rise of the Türgesh power in A.D. 716,[59] and even then their resistance to the Arab armies did not last more than twenty years, at the end of which they were finally dispersed in 119 A.H./A.D. 737.[60]

NOTES

1 Yāqūt, *Mu'jam al-Buldān*, ed. F. Wüstenfeld (Leipzig 1924), II, 409-10; Ibn Khurdādhbeh, *Al-Masālik wa'l-Mamālik*, ed. M. J. De Goeje (Leiden 1889) 18.

2 J. Marquart, *Ērānšahr*, in *Abhandlungen der Königlichen Gesellschaft der Wissenschaft zu Göttingen*, III (1901) 74-5; H. A. R. Gibb, *The Arab conquests in Central Asia* (London 1923) I.

3 Ya'qūbī, *Al-Buldān*, ed. M. J. De Goeje (Leiden 1892) 278; Balādhurī, *Futūḥ al-Buldān*, ed. De Goeje (Leiden 1866) 403-5; Ibn Sa'd, *Aṭ-Ṭabaqāt al-Kabīr* (Leiden 1905–21) V, 33; Ibn Ḥawqal, *Ṣūrat al-Arḍ*, ed. J. H. Kramers (Leiden 1938–9) II, 434; E. Chavannes, *Documents sur les Tou-kiue (Turcs) occidentaux* (St Petersbourg 1903) 251.

4 Balādhurī, *Futūḥ*, 406.

5 Ibn Khurdādhbeh, *Masālik*, 18.

6 Marquart, *Ērānšahr*, 74-5; A. Christensen, *L'Empire des Sassanides*, in *Mémoires de l'Academie des Sciences et des Lettres de Danemark*, 7th ser., I (1907) I, 27; Minorsky, *Encyclopaedia of Islam*, Article 'Ṭūs'.

7 Christensen, *L'Iran sous les Sassanides* (Copenhagen 1936) 102n.3.

8 Marquart, *Ērānšahr*, 74-6; Balādhurī, *Futūh*, 334; Ya'qūbī, *Tārīkh*, ed. M. T. Houtsma (Leiden, 1883) II, 129.

9 Christensen, *L'Iran sous les Sassanides*, 107, 315, 316.

10 W. M. McGovern, *The Early Empires of Central Asia* (Chapel Hill 1939) supplementary notes, 471-83.

11 R. Grousset, *The civilization of the East* (New York 1931–35).

12 R. Ghirshman, *Les Chionites-Hephtalites* (Cairo 1948) 74, 115 ff.

13 Ibid., 128.

14 Ibid., 129-30.
15 Ibid., 67, 129-30; T. Watters, *On Yuan Chwang's travels in India*, (London 1904–5) I, 95.
16 Balādhurī, *Futūḥ*, 402; Ghirshman, op. cit., 133.
17 Gibb, *The Arab conquests in Central Asia*, 3; Ghirshman, *Les Chionites-Hephtalites*, 96.
18 Watters, *Yuan Chwang*, I, 102.
19 Chavannes, *Documents*, 263-4, 299.
20 Watters, *Yuan Chwang*, I, 75-6, 106-9; Gibb, *Arab Conquests*, 8.
21 Chavannes, *Documents*, 274, 287.
22 Ibid., 263, 264, 287, 299.
23 Gibb, *Arab Conquests*, 8; Barthold, *Encyclopaedia of Islam*, Article 'Ṭukhāristān'.
24 Watters, *Yuan Chwang*, I, 102.
25 Balādhurī, *Futūḥ*, 406.
26 See the excellent note by W. M. McGovern in his *Early Empires of Central Asia* on Dahia and Tachari, 479-83.
27 Gibb, *Arab Conquests*, 2.
28 Ṭabarī, II, 1184-5.
29 Ibn Khurdādhbeh, *Masālik*, 39.
30 Marquart, *Ērānšahr*, 67.
31 Ibn Khurdādhbeh *Masālik*, 40.
32 Ghirshman, *Les Chionites-Hephtalites*, 23.
33 Ibn Khurdādhbeh, *Masālik*, 39.
34 Chavannes, *Documents*, 275.
35 Ibid., 278.
36 Ibn Khurdādhbeh, *Masālik*, 39; Ṭabarī, II, 1224.
37 Watters, *Yuan Chwang*, II, 270-7.
38 Ibid., 270-1.
39 Ṭabarī, II, 1224.
40 Gibb, *Arab conquests*, 9.
41 Chavannes, *Documents*, 163.
42 Ṭabarī, II, 1147.
43 Marquart, *Ērānšahr*, 310-11.
44 Ibn Khurdādhbeh, *Masālik*, 39.
45 Marquart, *Ērānšahr*, 250, 287-9.
46 M. Bahār, *Tārīkh-i-Sīstān* (Teherān 1314 A.H.), 92n.2.
47 Ibn Khurdādhbeh, *Masālik*, 39. He calls him Rutbīl, the king of Sijistān, ar-Rukhkhaj and Bilād ad-Dāwar.
48 Chavannes, *Documents*, 291.
49 Watters, *Yuan Chwang*, II, 267-74.
50 Ya'qūbī, *Buldān*, 287.

51 Watters, *Yuan Chwang*, I, 108-9.

52 Gibb, *Arab Conquests*, 14n.6.

53 Ibid., 5.

54 Chavannes, *Documents*, 135.

55 Gibb, *Arab Conquests*, 6.

56 Ibn Khurdādhbeh, *Masālik*, 178; Ibn al-Athīr, *al-Lubāb* (Cairo 1357), I, 37.

57 Gibb, *Arab Conquests*, 5.

58 Watters, *Yuan Chwang*, I, 95.

59 Chavannes, *Documents*, 284-5.

60 The topics discussed in this article are further elaborated in the book of M. A. Shaban, *The ʿAbbāsid revolution* (Cambridge 1970).

S. A. SKILLITER

The Hispano-Ottoman Armistice of 1581

In 1578, less than seven years after the celebrated Christian victory at Lepanto, Philip II, Most Catholic king of Spain and champion of the Inquisition, succeeded, after a long secret negotiation, in reaching an agreement not to engage that year in armed combat by land or sea with the Ottoman Sultan Murād III, Caliph and leader of the Muslim Jihād. Such an agreement would appear to be an astonishing and significant denial by both parties of the faiths upon which their empires had been founded. Be that as it may, no less astonishing, diplomatically, is the form of the armistice document itself, to be studied here on the basis of its second renewal, of 4 February 1581. The work of the Imperial dragoman Khurrem Beg, it is an undertaking between the deputy of the Grand Vizier and the Spanish ambassador on behalf of their royal masters and is valid in two languages, Ottoman and Italian.

The present writer wishes to record, with affection, her gratitude for the friendship and inspiration accorded her for so many years by Professor Vladimir Minorsky and humbly offers these unworthy pages to his dear memory.

The documents which will concern us comprise folios 123-4 (the armistice) and folios 121-2 (the list of the Spanish allies) of British Museum, Additional MS 28,415.[1] The armistice, in Ottoman and Italian with between and below the certification of the authenticity of both the texts by their author Khurrem Beg, is written on one side of a piece of Oriental paper, without a watermark, 37 cm wide and 57 cm long. It has been guarded into the volume in its full length and numbered 123 (top half) and 124 (lower half) – although it is only one folio – and has then been folded up and across to fit the volume (26 cm × 36½ cm). It had been folded originally in the Oriental manner, over and over from the base, and its eleven foldings of 5 cm increasing to 5½ cm at the top can still be seen. At some time the paper must have been subjected to damp and as a result part of the Ottoman text has offset on to the certificate. On the back (f. 124v) is the following endorsement, in the hand of the Spanish clerk at Venice:

+

> Copia de la capitulacio*n* en turquesco y Italiano de la suspensio*n* de armas concluyda a 4 de hebrero 1581 entre In°. de Marglia*n* en no*m*bre de su mag*esta*d y el chause Pascia Vesire en no*m*bre del gran turco por tres años q*ue* se acabara*n* en fin del año de 83.

The Hispano-Ottoman armistice renewed on 29 Dhū'l-Ḥijja 988/4 February 1581, at Constantinople.
British Museum, Add. MS 28,415, ff. 123-4, see plate 1.[2]

1. Ottoman text (f. 123r).

(1) هو

(2) دولتلو وزير سياوش پاشا فاتّوليقه مايستانك ايلچيسي اولان قدوة اعيان الملّة
المسيحية نامدار جوان مارليانله مباشرت اولنان ويره خصوصنده بعضى مشكلّلر واقع
اولوب اول مشكللرى مزبور قاتّوليقه مايستايه دانشماق لازم كلوب (3) و وقت طار
اولماغن بونك كبى خيرلو مصلحت بوزولممق ايچون مشار اليه دولتلو وزير سياوش
پاشا مزبور ايلچى اولان نامدار جوان مآرليانله قولّلشديلر كه افنديلرينك اجازتلريله
اوّلا مزبور ايلچى ذكر اولان مشكلّلرى واروب قاتوليقه مايستا ايله (4) مشورت
ايليه ايكنجى كلاجك اوچ ييله دكين كه ١٥٨٣ ييلنده دچمبريز آينك آخرنده كه
اهل اسلام تاريخي اوزره سنه ٩٩١ ذى الحجه سنك آخرنده تمام اولور ايكى
پادشاهلرك[3] دريادن دونمه‌لرى وقره‌دن عسكرلرى (5) بربرلرينك و ولايتلرينك وبو
ايكى پادشاهلره مخصوص اولان مملكتلرك وايكى جانبندن بو ويره‌ده معا داخل
اولاجقلرك قصد مضرّتلرينه چقمايه و طرفيندن بو ويره‌ده معا داخل اولاجقلرك اسملرى
باشقه باشقه تمسّكلر اولنوب (6) و بو تمسّكلرى دولتلو وزير سياوش پاشا ومزبور ايلچى
جوآن مارليان كندولرينك امضالرى ومهرلرى ايله امضاليوب ومهرليوب بربرلرينه
تسليم ايدرلر فامّا بو ايكى پادشاهلرك دريادن دونمه‌لرى وقره‌دن عسكرلرى
كندولرينك (7) ساير مصالحلرينه چيقالر ومشار اليه دولتلو وزير سياوش پاشا ومزبور
نامدآر ايلچى بربرينه شويله متعهّد اولمشلردر كه افنديلرينك جوانبندن اقرارلرينه
طوروب وجه مشروحه مغاير ايش اولنميه بونك صحّتينه توركجه اوچ تمسّك يازيلوب

Plate 1. The Hispano-Ottoman Armistice of 1581. BM Add. MS 28,415, ff. 123-4.

دولتلو وزیر سیاوش پاشا قاتولیقه مایستانک ایلچیسی اولان [illegible]

[illegible]

[illegible] ۱۵۸۳ [illegible] سنه ۹۹۱ [illegible]

[illegible]

Io Aurrem dragomanno dico [illegible] sopra iscritto scrittura e la copia a fronte della iscrittura turchesca che a data il S.re Sianuse pascia vesire al S.re giovanni Margliani imbasciatore di sua Mtà C.ca e medemamente dico che la sotto iscrittura turchescha e la copia a fronte della iscrittura Italiana che a' data il ditto S.re giovanni Margliani inbasciatore al sopradetto S.re Sianuse pascia vesire fermate e sillate delli sigilli [illegible] in esse si contiene e di piu dico l'una essere tradutione dell'altra Tradutte da me [illegible] sopra scritto

Essendo nato qualche difficultà sopra il negotio della tregua il quale si tratta fra il Ill.mo Sianuse pascia vesire e l'Ill.mo e honorato fra le generationi credente al Messia giovanni Margliani imbasciatore della Mtà C.ca le quali era necessario consultare con detta Mtà per che per mancamento di tempo no si perda uno si santo negotio il Ill.mo Sianuse pascia vesire e l'Ill.mo giovanni Margliani imbasciatore sono convenuti con licentia delli suoi principi — primo che detto imbasciatore vada a consultare con S. Mtà dette difficultà — Secondo che per 3 anni a venire li quali finiranno alla fine del mese di dicembre del 1583 che secondo il conto delli musulmani sara l'anno 991 a l'ultimo della luna di Zilhigge no uscisca armata per mare ne essercito per terra dell'una e l'altra Mtà per andare a li danni l'uno de l'altro ne delli Regni e stati a dette Mtà pertinenti ne di quelli che anno da essere compresi in detta tregua da' ambi le parte li nomi delli quali si scriveranno in iscritture separate le quali il Ill.mo Sianuse pascia vesire e giovanni Margliani imbasciatore daranno l'uno a l'altro fermate e siggillate del loro segno, ma per altri loro affari le due Mtà possino cavare armate per mare e esserciti per terra e cosi li sopradetti il Ill.mo vesire Sianuse pascia e l'Ill.mo imbasciatore giovanni Margliani hanno promesso l'uno a l'altro che li loro principi non contravenirano e manteneranno quanto di sopra si e detto, e per fede si sono fatte tre iscritture in turchesco fermate e siggillate dal detto Ill.mo Sianuse pascia vesire, e tre in italiano fermate e siggillate dal detto imbasciatore le italiane resteranno in mano del Ill.mo Sianuse pascia vesire e le turchesche in mano di detto Ill.mo giovanni Margliani imbasciatore

Fatta in Costantinopoli a di 4 febraro 1581

Io Aurrem sopra iscritto afermo quanto di sopra

(8) دولتلو وزیر سیاوش پاشانک مهری و امضاسیله امضالیوب ومهرلنمشدر و اوچ
تمسّک داخی ایتالیانجه یازیلوب مزبور ایلچینک مهر و امضاسیله امضالنوب مهرلنمشدر
و ایتالیانجه یازیلانلر دولتلو وزیر سیاوش پاشانک اُلّلرنده قالا (9) وترکجه اولانلری
مزبور نامدآر ایلچی اولان جوان مارلیانک النه تسلیم اولنه تحریرا فی الیوم التاسع
و العشرین شهر ذی الحجة سنه ثمان وثمانین وتسعمائه

بمدینه
قسطنطنیه
المحروسه

2. Certificate of authenticity by the translator

(10) Io Hurrem draghomanno dico che la sop*ra* iscritta iscrittura è la copia à punto della iscrittura turche (11) scha che à data il S*igno*re Siauuse Pascia Vesire al s*igno*re giouanni Marglani Imbasciatore di sua (12) M*aest*a C*attolic*a et medemame*n*te dico che la sotto iscritta iscrittura e la copia à punto della iscrittura (13) Italiana che à data il ditto s*igno*re giouan*n*i Margliani in basciatore al sop*ra* detto s*igno*re siauuse (14) Pascia Vesire fermate et bollate dalli sop*ra* ditti si come in esse si contiene et di piu dico l'una (15) essere tradutione del'altra Tradutte da me Hurrem sop*ra* scritto

3. Italian text (f. 124r)

(16) Essendo nata qualche di ficultà sop*ra* il neghotio della tregua il quale si tratta fra il Ric*chissi*mo siauuse (17) Pascia Vesire et l'Ill*ustrissi*mo et honorato fra le generationi credente al Messia giouanni Margliani in (18) basciatore della M*aest*a C*attolic*a lequali era necessario consultare con detta M*aest*a P*er*che p*er* mancame*n*to (19) di tempo no*n* si p*er*da uno si santo neghotio il Ric*chissi*mo Siauuse Pascia Vesire et l'Ill*ustrissi*mo giouanni (20) Margliani in basciatore sono conuenuti con licentia delli suoi p*r*incipi – Primo che detto in (21) basciatore vada à consultare con s*ua* M*aest*a dette di ficulta – Seghondo che p*er* 3 anni à uenire (22) li quali finiranno alla fine del mese di dicenb*re* del ·1583· che seghondo il conto delli musulmani (23) sara lanno ·991· à lultimo della luna di Zilhiggè no*n* uscisca Armata p*er* mare ne esercito p*er* terra (24) del'una et l'altra M*aest*a p*er* andare à li danni l'uno de l'altro ne delli Regni et stati à dette M*aest*a p*er*tine*n*ti (25) ne di quelli che anno da essere comp*re*si in ella tregua dà anbi le parte li nomi delli quali si iscriue (26) vanno in iscritture separate le quali il Ric*chissi*mo Siauuse Pascia Vesire et giouanni Marigliani in (27) basciatore daranno l'uno à l'altro fermate et siggillate del'loro segno, mà p*er* altri loro affari le

(28) due M*aesta* possino cauare Armatà p*er* mare et eserciti p*er* terra et cosi li sop*ra* detti il Ric*chissi*mo Vesire (29) Siauuse Pascia et l'Ill*ustrissi*mo in basciatore giouanni Margliani hanno promesso l'uno al'altro che li loro (30) p*r*incipi non contraueniranno et manteneranno quanto di sop*ra* si è detto, et p*er* fede si sono fatte (31) tre iscritture in turchesco fermate et siggillate dal detto Ric*chissi*mo Siauuse Pascia Vesire, et tre (32) in italiano fermate et siggillate dal detto in basciatore le italiane Resterara*nn*o in mano del Ric*chissi*mo (33) Siauuse Pascia Vesire et le turchesche in mano di detto Ill*ustrissi*mo giouan*n*i Margliani in basciatore (34) Fatta in Costantinopoli à di 4 feb*r*aro i58i

(35) Io Hurrem sop*ra* iscritto affermo qua*n*to di sop*ra*

English rendering of no. 1, the Ottoman text

line 1 HE (is God)

lines 2-3 Certain problems having arisen in the matter of the truce which is being negotiated by the fortunate Vizier Siyāwush Pasha[4] and the ambassador of the Catholic Majesty (Qāttūlīqa Māyestā),[5] the model of the notables of the Messiah's religion, the celebrated Juwān Mārliyān,[6] it was necessary to confer about those problems with the aforesaid Catholic Majesty. However, since time was pressing, in order that such an excellent agreement as this should not be cancelled, the above-mentioned fortunate Vizier Siyāwush Pasha and the aforesaid ambassador, the celebrated Juwān Mārliyān, agreed together, with the permission of their masters:

lines 3-4 1. That the aforesaid ambassador should go and consult with the Catholic Majesty about the above-mentioned problems.

lines 4-6 2. That for the next three years, expiring at the end of December (Dechembrīz) 1583 which will be, according to the Muslim reckoning, at the end of Dhū'l-Ḥijja 991, the navies of the two Padishahs by sea and their armies by land shall not go forth with the intention of harming one another, or their countries, or the provinces which are in a special relationship with these two Padishahs, or with those who from the two sides shall be included together in this truce. When the names of those who from both sides are to be included together in this truce have been inscribed in separate documents and when the fortunate Vizier Siyāwush Pasha and the aforesaid ambassador Juwān Mārliyān have signed and sealed these documents with their own signatures and seals, they shall hand them over, one to another.

lines 6-7 Nevertheless, the navies of these two Padishahs by sea and their armies by land may go forth upon other enterprises of their own. Moreover, the above-mentioned fortunate Vizier Siyāwush Pasha and the aforesaid celebrated ambassador have thus engaged together that, acting on behalf of their masters, their decision shall be maintained and no act shall be performed contrary to the aforesaid.

lines 7-9 In confirmation whereof three receipts have been written in Turkish and have been signed and sealed with the signature and seal of the fortunate Vizier Siyāwush Pasha, and three more receipts have been written in Italian and have been signed and sealed with the seal and signature of the aforesaid ambassador. The receipts in Italian shall remain in the keeping of the fortunate Vizier Siyāwush Pasha, and the receipts in Turkish shall be handed over to the aforesaid celebrated ambassador Juwān Mārliyān.

line 9 Written on the twenty-ninth day of the month of Dhū'l-Ḥijja of the year nine hundred and eighty-eight (i.e. 4 February 1581).

In the city
of Constantinople
the (divinely) protected.

Margliani's list of those who are to be included with Spain in the truce.[7]
British Museum, Add. MS 28,415, ff. 121-2.

The document, written in Italian, consists of two sheets of watermarked, European paper, 22 cm wide and 32 cm long. The list and its certificate of authenticity by Khurrem Beg are on f. 121r, ff. 121v and 122r are blank, and the endorsement is on f. 122v.

(f. 121r) (1) Li nominati dal Ill*ustrissi*mo Amb*asciato*re di Sua M*aes*ta Catt*oli*ca Giouanni Margliani, li quali hanno da essere compresi (2) nella tregua, et sono compresi in q*ue*sta Capitulacione, sono li sequenti,

(3) Il Papa,
L'Imperatore,
(5) Li Arciduchi ferdinando et Carlo,
L'İmperio,
Il Re di francia,
La Republica di Venecia, tutte le sue cose, li suoi statti, et vasalli,
Malta et Religione di S*an*to Giouanni,
(10) La Republica di Genoua,
La Republica di lucha,
İl Duca di Sauoia,
İl Duca di fiorenza,
İl Duca di ferrara,
(15) İl Duca di Mantua,
İl Duca de parma,

İl Duca de Urbino,
İl S*igno*r de piombino,
Tutti li pensionarij di Sua M*ae*sta et feudatarij dell' İmperio in Italia
(20) fatta in Const*antinopo*li Alli 4 di febraro 158İ.

Certificate of authenticity by Khurrem Beg, in his hand

(21) Io Hurrem draghomanno dico che la sopra iscritta iscrittura
(22) è la copia a punto della iscrittura che il S*igno*re giouan*n*i Marglia*n*i
(23) hà data al s*igno*re Siauuse Pascia Vesire.

Endorsement, in the hand of the Spanish clerk at Venice

(f. 122v)

+

Copia de los q*ue* han de ser comprehendidos en la tregua, y lo son en esta capitulacion dada por In° Marlian a 4 de hebrero 1581.

Historical Commentary

The events leading up to the cessation of the state of war between Spain and the Ottoman Empire from 1577 to 1584 have been studied on the basis of published and unpublished documents by F. Braudel in *La Méditerranée et le monde méditerranéen à l'époque de Philippe II.*[8] Our object is to summarize the events prior to the issue of the 1581 truce, referring the interested reader to Braudel's work for greater detail but taking the opportunity to complement or clarify his account whenever possible. This object has been facilitated by the discovery of Giovanni Margliani's report to Philip II on his forty-month long embassy in Constantinople,[9] the text of which follows as an appendix to this article.

A truce between the Christian and Muslim powers in the Mediterranean seems to have been a cherished although necessarily secret Spanish ambition long before its realization in 1578. Braudel cites several unsuccessful tentatives by Philip II from 1558,[10] and the much-vaunted victory at Lepanto in 1571 appears to have in no way diminished his desire to negotiate with the Turk. The first Spanish agent to achieve any success, however, was a certain Don Martín de Acuña,[11] who returned to Spain from Constantinople in June 1577 with a document dated 18 March,[12] enumerating the Turkish terms for peace, and a letter to Philip II from the Grand Vizier Ṣoqollu Meḥemmed Pasha,[13] promising that the Turkish fleet would not go out against Spain that year. This promise, gained exceptionally quickly and probably at the expense of a similar promise made on behalf of

Spain, at least assures Don Martín's name a place in the negotiation. But the document was certainly not a truce, and the presence of a Spanish ambassador in Constantinople must have been stipulated before a truce could be concluded.

In November a Spanish agent, Fabio Romanus, left Constantinople with two letters, written by the dragoman Khurrem Beg, from the Grand Vizier to Don Martín, requesting a reply to the first letter and again urging an embassy.[14] It would seem that Don Martín, returned to Spain, had claimed a greater success for his agency than the facts warranted and so, when the long-awaited envoy, Giovanni Margliani, arrived in December 1577, Khurrem Beg met him with these indignant words: 'Si j'étais Chrétien, je ferais le signe de la croix devant ces menteries qu'a imaginées Don Martín. Le pacha attend un ambassadeur: c'est ce qu'on a écrit à S. M., c'est ce qu'a promis Don Martín ici même, c'est ce que Don Martín a fait enfin annoncer par un homme venu jusqu'ici. Le pacha ressentira grandement qu'on ait ainsi changé d'avis.'[15]

Before vouchsafing the truce, which Spain obviously desired so eagerly, the Turks expected to be wooed by a splendid embassy. Margliani, unassuming in person and secretive in his mission, was an immediate disappointment.[16] The Imperial ambassador, David Ungnad, vividly describes the situation, as follows: 'Die Spanier wolten gern das *pacem* nur in der Sacristeyküsse/aber Sultan Murat als hoher Priester beruffte sie vor den hohen Altar/daß sie auch mit andern Leuten zum Opffer gehen sollen. Sie müssen auch opffern/sonsten gebe man ihnen das *pacem* nit zu küssen.'[17]

Giovanni Margliani, the despised Spanish envoy, was a native of Milan.[18] He had fought, under his cousin Gabrio Serbelloni, at the siege of La Goulette, and had lost an eye. When the fort surrendered to the Turks on 13 September 1574, he, Serbelloni and Don Martín were taken prisoner,[19] and he was not redeemed until 1576. The Turkish officials were astounded at the Spanish choice of such a man, one-eyed and so recently their prisoner, to negotiate the truce in Constantinople, and he was frequently the target of abuse.[20] The French ambassador in Constantinople, de Germigny, in a memorial to be presented to the Sultan, attacks him with the following bitter words: 'Questo Giov. di Mariliani, huomo da nulla, schiavo ultimamente riscattato in questa città di Constantinopoli, et tale che ogiuno lo cognosce a tal, che si vede un grandissimo dispreggio che fà il re d'Ispagna di sua altezza di mandar a un potentissimo imperadore, per cosa così importante come è questa pace, un huomo da niente a trattar con esso'.[21] However, the French ambassador in Rome, de Foix, has a clearer judgement of

Margliani when he says of him: 'Il est estimé homme d'entendement & fort habile négociateur',[22] for, in spite of all the unfavourable circumstances, he was successful in negotiating the first Hispano-Ottoman armistice, concluded on 7 February 1578, only a few weeks after his arrival in Turkey. To achieve this Margliani had been fortunate in winning the powerful and able assistance of Khurrem Beg,[23] the chief dragoman of the Porte.[24] Although these two men, the leading characters in this strange drama, represented nations as geographically and culturally diverse as Spain and Turkey, they were in fact fellow-Italians, almost neighbours, Margliani being a native of Milan and Khurrem Beg a native of Lucca.[25] Under the title 'Gottlose Rede eines Welschen (i.e. an Italian) Mamelucken' Gerlach gives the following brief but illuminating glimpse of the renegade, enjoying hospitality in the Imperial embassy: 'Huram Beg/Dolmetscher/sonsten ein Welscher/den mein Gnädiger Herr zu Gast hatte/sagte ob der Mahlzeit ganz Epicurisch: Er wolle hier thun/was dieser Welt-Brieff außweise/fressen/sauffen/huren; wann er in jene Welt komme/woll er auch sehen/was sie dorten für eine Weise halte/da woll er sich auch einschicken'.[26] And so the two Italians, one serious and retiring, the other a worldly cynic, schemed together and achieved Philip II's object.

A copy of the 1578 armistice is preserved in Simancas, as Braudel indicates.[27] Its contents we know from Ungnad's detailed report[28] and from the remarks of the French ambassador l'abbé de Lisle.[29] The Venetian Bailo Nicolò Barbarigo also discusses the armistice, and under the title 'Copia del concordato dato al Marigliano' he gives the text which will be quoted here in a slightly abbreviated form. The document, addressing Margliani, is listed under five headings, as follows:[30] (f. 456r) 'In conclusione fatta col signor Bassà[31] è

1. Che l'Illustrissimo signor Bassà scriva, et prometta à Sua Maestà,[32] che per quest'anno 1578 non uscirà armata soltante per guarda dell'Isole, et à servitio delli loro Regni, si come vostra Signoria[33] hà preghato, et similmente vostra Signoria hà promesso da parte di Sua Maestà, che non cavera armata per quest'anno à danni del Serenissimo gran Signor,[34] et per questo lei resterà qui per sicurezza.
2. Che tutti quelli, che vostra Signoria hà nominati, che siano inclusi in la tregua, facendola, piacendo al Signor Dio, da parte di Sua Maestà, l'Illmo signor Bassà si contenta in questo modo, che l'Imperator, et la Signoria di Vinetia siano nominati ancora, et inclusi da parte del S^mo^. gran Signor, si come hanno la pace con esso lui, et tutti gli altri si contenta, quali sarano nominati qui sotto, fuor del Rè di Portogallo resta indeterminato, se ben

l'Illmo. signor Bassà dice, et promette, che l'armata del S^{mo}. gran Signor non anderà à dani del sopradetto fin che durerà la tregua con Sua Maestà per il Stretto di Gibilterra, et (f. 456v) chi sà quello, col farà per il mar rosso per molte cause et ragioni dette, come vostra Signoria hà inteso dell'Illmo. signor Bassà. (Here follows the list of the Spanish allies, i.e. the Pope, Malta, the Order of St John, the Republics of Genoa and Lucca, the Dukes of Savoy, Florence, Ferrara, Mantua and Urbino, the Lord of Piombino, and all the Spanish possessions in Italy.)

3. (The allies nominated by the Grand Vizier, on behalf of the Sultan, as follows: the Emperor, Venice, the Kings of France and Poland, the Prince of Fez – se bene non fà bisogno, portando lui la bandiera del S^{mo}. gran Signor, et li renda obedientia.)
4. Tutto questo conciede, et promette l'Illmo. signor Bassà, con che habbia à venir uno honorato, et degno Ambasciator mandato da Sua Maestà à questa Eccelsa Porta, per far la capitulatione. Ancora promette l'Illmo. signor Bassà, et il S^{mo}. gran Signor mandar un'Ambasciator à Sua Maestà con la capitulatione, si come è il costume di questa Eccelsa Porta.
5. L'Illmo. signor Bassà si contenta, che se Sua Maestà non vuole il commercio, sia come li piace.

Fatta in Constantinopoli à 7 di Febbraio 1578'.

From this we see that the document is an agreement on peace by sea during 1578 between the Grand Vizier and Margliani, on behalf of their royal masters and their nominated allies. It is probable that the 1577 document sent to Spain was in the same form, but without reference to the originals nothing more can be said on these extraordinary documents. Certainly a Spanish ambassador is still demanded by the Turks before the 'capitulatione' can be concluded, and then a Turkish ambassador will also be sent to Spain. Ungnad notes that, although the Grand Vizier has not mentioned a present, the matter must have been arranged verbally.[35] Spain is not to be forced into a trade-agreement, and Margliani is to remain in Constantinople as hostage.

That Margliani himself regarded the privilege he had obtained as sufficient is evident from his report.[36] He calls the 1578 agreement 'una suspensione', which he was able to keep valid for 1579 without further agreement. On 21 March 1580 a new armistice was issued, also termed 'una suspensione' by Margliani. However, this time there was a Spanish ambassador in Constantinople – Margliani – who, owing to the non-arrival of the appointed ambassador Don Juan de Rocafull,[37] had been sent the ambassadorial licence and the gifts to be presented to the Sultan.

It may be presumed that the form of the 1580 truce is identical with ours of 1581, although no text of it is available.[38] De Germigny describes its contents, and adds: 'Ledit Mariglian allant à l'audience du bassa, print pour seureté dudit accord de la main dudit bassa l'arz en turquesque qu'il avoit présenté au seig^r^, signé par icelluy bassa, et en bailla réciproquement un au bassa en italien signé de sa main'.[39] Similarly the Venetian secretary Gabriel Cavazza only reports on the armistice, but gives the following description of its form: 'Di questo ne sono state fatte due scritture simili: l'una in Turco, et l'altra in Italiano segnate delli sigilli del magnifico Bassà et del detto signor Marigliani: il qual anco si è sotto scritto et appresso di lui è rimasta quella in Turco: et quella in Italiano appresso il magnifico Bassà: Nel principio di detta scrittura vien detto, che vertendo certe difficultà nel negotio delle tregue, che si tratta fra queste due Maestà accioche il signor Ambasciator Cattolico possi haver tempo di avisarne il Serenissimo suo Rè, et di riceverne sopra esse l'ordinamente di Sua Maestà'.[40]

After yet another year spent in fear of his life, Margliani was successful, in collaboration with Siyāwush Pasha,[41] the Second Vizier who was acting as deputy to the Grand Vizier Sinān Pasha during his absence on campaign, in concluding a three-year armistice, on 4 February 1581.

The 1581 Hispano-Ottoman armistice

Braudel lucidly summarizes the circumstances of the issue of the 1581 agreement,[42] allowing us to confine ourselves here to a discussion of the document. It is not an Imperial or official Ottoman document; it is not a treaty, nor a capitulation, nor even, as de Germigny suggested in 1580, an *'arẓ-u ḥāl*, although it may well be based on a petition from the Vizier to the Sultan. It is a simple receipt – *temessük*[43] – confirming, in Ottoman and Italian, the agreement reached between Siyāwush Pasha and Giovanni Margliani, on behalf of their masters, for peace to be maintained by land and sea between Turkey and Spain for three years. The document under consideration here must be the master-copy, since it contains both texts and the certificate of their authenticity by their compiler Khurrem Beg. As we are told, three copies of only the Italian receipt, signed by Margliani, were to be kept by the Vizier, and three copies of the Turkish receipt, signed by Siyāwush Pasha, were to be kept by Margliani. It is probable that the master-copy was also in Margliani's possession, since it was later kept in the papers of the Spanish ambassador in Venice. Braudel, however, gives no indication of any text preserved in the archives of Simancas. Yet the Bailo Paolo Contarini devoted his despatch of 4 February 1581 to a study of the armistice and enclosed a copy of the Italian text, which is identical with ours except that it has the following date: 'Data in Constantinopoli a primo gennaio 1580 (*more veneto*: = 1 January 1581) che vien ad esser secondo il conto de Mussulmani all'ultimo della luna di Silcadel l'anno 988'.[44] From this we may suppose that the separate receipts made from the master-copy were back-dated to when the armistice had theoretically begun.

In short, the document is so uniquely strange, having no parallel except, presumably, the other renewals in the same series, that we are led to the conclusion that it is the invention of Khurrem Beg, to meet the exceptional circumstances. The future possibility of a proper truce, said to be still under negotiation, is kept in sight; until then, this concocted document will have to serve. By this furtive agreement the pressing need of both sides can be judged – that Spain could ask, that Turkey could give so easily. Margliani even boasts that he had avoided the audience with the Sultan.[45] It is all most clearly the Spanish 'Sacristeyküsse' which David Ungnad so wittily prophesied![46]

There can be no doubt that the Italian text and the certificate are in Khurrem Beg's hand; he has signed them. Equally we may suppose that he wrote the Ottoman text, in a very clear and developed calligraphy which gives no hint of a European scribe. Indications of a non-Ottoman composer can be found in the text, however: for example, Philip II is called 'Qāttūlīqa Māyestā', a straight transliteration of the Italian, instead of the expected 'Ispānya qırālı' (king of Spain); the Sultan is given no honorific titles and he and Philip II are referred to, equally, as 'Padishah'; the Christian date of expiry is given first and the Muslim date is related to it; the name of the month is again a transliteration, from the Latin 'decembris'. Particularly remarkable, in a sixteenth-century composition, is the use of 'Türkce' to indicate the Ottoman language and 'Ītāliyānca' to indicate the Italian language. Above all, the exchange of receipts bilingually valid, the Ottoman as much a translation of the Italian as the Italian of the Ottoman, is probably unique in Ottoman diplomatics.

Contarini's copy of the armistice, referred to above, consists of three documents: the receipt in Italian, the list of the Ottoman allies nominated by Siyāwush Pasha and, thirdly, the list of the Spanish allies nominated by Margliani. We know from the receipt that an integral part of the agreement was the exchange of copies of these two lists, signed and sealed, between the Vizier and the Spanish ambassador. Only Margliani's list, which is identical with Contarini's copy, is included in the British Museum manuscript;[47]

therefore, to complete the armistice we must quote Siyāwush Pasha's list here:[48]

(f. 410v) 'Seconda scrittura, li nominati dal ricchissimo Sciaus bassà Visir, li quali hanno da esser compresi nelle Tregue, et son compresi in questa capitulacione, sono li seguenti,

Il Re di Fessa

l'Imperator

li Arciduchi Ferdinando, & Carlo,

Il Re Christianissimo

Il Re di Polonia

li Signori Venetiani con Tutte le loro cose, Stati, Regni, et Vassalli.'

Contarini's report also enables us to solve the enigmatic 'Essendo nata qualche difficultà' with which the Italian receipt opens. The difficulty was the eternal problem of rank and precedence, as the Bailo explains: 'Nel particolar di Vostra Serenita fusse stata fatta distinta mentione, come havea prommesso l'Ambasciator et essendo poi nata difficoltà sopra la dinominatione de principi, et delli titoli, volendo l'Ambasciator che il Re di Spagna fosse il primo, fu accordato di far due scritture separate, et che ogni uno sopra la sua nominasse senza titoli chi le piace le quali essendo state mandate dentro al Signor, et essendosi Sua Maestà contentata di esse, hoggi si sono sotto scritte'.[49]

With the difficulties resolved and thanks to the clause stressing the necessity of his consultation with the king, Margliani prepared for departure which, he says, 'desidero più di quello chi si può credere'.[50] Philip II had already indicated that he did not wish to maintain a resident ambassador in Constantinople.[51] By early June 1581 Margliani had arrived in Rome.[52] He did not return to Turkey, and died at the beginning of 1588.[53]

That the armistice was effective can be proved by reports sent to the Spanish Viceroy of Naples in 1581.[54] Peace in the Mediterranean had by now become essential for Spain and Turkey. The two powers, as the representatives of Christianity and Islam, after the climax of Lepanto, had abandoned their traditional struggle in the Mediterranean and had both turned away and engaged themselves in attempts to suppress enemies within their own faiths. Thus Turkey was engrossed from 1578 until 1588 in the crippling war with Persia, her attention turned towards the Caspian and the suppression of the Shiite heretics. On the other hand, after the annexation of Portugal in 1580, for which, Margliani claims, the 1580 armistice with Turkey was an important factor,[55] Philip II's interest turned towards the Atlantic, the Netherlands and the expedition against England.

The English agent William Harborne,[56] during his first visit to Turkey from 1578 to 1581, observed the Spanish intrigues, as he later reported: 'The Spanyarde, att that time the highest capitall enemie to her Mag^{tie}, whoe being by themperor his Ambassador certified my first couert coming thether (as he and the rest of the Christian Ambassadors falslie imagined, to be for procuring the turke by sea to have inuaded the Spanishe dominions, to divert him from the conquest of Portugall), sent thether the Earle Gio Marillano to craue A truce for five years, wthin thend of two years, corrupting the Bassaes, and not gainesaide of me then in private estate, or of anie other (then the ffrenshe nott prevayling) he obtayned'.[57] In spite of this denial, however, the French ambassador de Germigny in his despatch of March 1580 gives this hint of Harborne's anti-Spanish activity: 'J'eus advis que cest Anglois avoit remonstré au bassa l'importance de l'agrandissement du roy d'Espaigne, mesmes où il s'impatroniroit de Portugal et des terres despandantes dudit royaume voisines à ce seig^{r} au Levant, comme du royaume d'Ormus et autres païs'.[58]

Harborne left Turkey in July 1581 and did not return until April 1583, this time as the first English ambassador to Turkey. On 27 January 1584 he reported the renewal of the 'league with Spain' for one year,[59] adding the following information in his despatch of 15 February: 'Giovane Stephano [Ferrari], sometime comptroller of Gio. de Marilano's house, is sent away with prolongation for one year of the late truce, otherwise expiring this next month, which is obtained with great charge in nine months time that he stayed only about the same granted of the Grand Signor to the end he may the more conveniently pursue the ancient enemy the Persian with greater security and advantage, for that of Christian princes he fears none other'.[60] In spite of the newly made truce, however, it seems that Harborne was successful in winning a solemn promise from the Sultan's councillors that if England should go to war with Spain the Sultan would likewise declare war.[61] In the spring of 1585 he received instructions from Walsingham to incite Turkey to war with Spain, and from that time he worked energetically to prevent the renewal of the truce – thus obliging Spain to keep forces in the Mediterranean – and to persuade the Sultan to provide a fleet to attack Spain or the Spanish dominions of Apulia, Calabria and Catalonia simultaneously with an attack by England from the Atlantic. To make this possible Walsingham advised Harborne to urge the termination of the war with Persia, which had drained the Turkish resources.[62] In this he was strongly assisted by Saʿdu'd-Dīn, the historian and the Sultan's tutor,[63] himself a Persian and keen to divert the Sultan from the Persian war to an attack against Spain.[64]

Yet Harborne never succeeded in securing Turkish naval intervention; in fact, he confessed afterwards that it would have been unjustifiable so to set the Infidels against the Christians of Spain.[65] Nevertheless, after he and Saʿdu'd-Dīn had petitioned the Sultan, he was instrumental in having Ferrari, the Spanish agent who had returned to Constantinople to renew the truce of 1584, sent away empty-handed in April 1587. That Khurrem Beg was still active we know from the following remark of the Venetian ambassador Lorenzo Bernardo: 'After the departure of the Spanish Agents I have had occasion to learn from Orembey, the dragoman, all the particulars about the truce, which was first concluded and then broken off'.[66]

In September 1587 Margliani submitted a report to Philip II, by request, giving his opinion on the necessity of the renewal of the Hispano-Ottoman truce before the sailing of the Armada. He emphasized the importance of the truce to secure Spain's flank, adding 'If the truce is concluded the Turks will not send their fleet to invade Naples and Sicily while the King is engaged on his enterprise, as the Queen of England is doing her best to secure'.[67] Good advice, but Harborne sat scheming in Constantinople, and so when the Armada had to set sail in May 1588 there was still no truce and no absolute security for Spain in the Mediterranean.

Dates of issue of the truces

1. 7 February 1578.	For one year, but kept valid for 1579.
2. 21 March 1580.	For one year.
3. 4 February 1581.	For three years.
4. January 1584.	For one year.

APPENDIX

Giovanni Margliani's report to Philip II of Spain on his services rendered in negociating the Hispano-Ottoman armistice for six years, petitioning for adequate remuneration. Undated, probably 1583.
Holograph original (?) in British Museum, Add. MS 28,415, ff. 1-4.

The document, written in Italian, consists of four sheets of European paper, without watermark, $21\frac{1}{2}$ cm wide and $30\frac{1}{2}$ cm long. The report occupies ff. 1r-3v, f. 4r is blank and f. 4v has the following address and signature, in the same hand as the report, probably Margliani's:

S.C.R.M.
Giouanni de Margliano

Beside it is the endorsement, in the hand of the Spanish clerk at Venice:

✝
Venecia A Su Mag*estad*
Juan Margliano

Summary. Margliani's report to Philip II on his Constantinople mission is divided into three parts:

1. (ff. 1r-2r) Complaint about the insults offered him.

He was referred to the Viceroy of Naples, the Marquis of Mondéjar, with orders not to confer with him, which he obeyed, thinking that the Viceroy would be informed by the King, or Aurelio di Santa Croce, or Bartolomeo Brutti. The Viceroy resented this secrecy and plotted against Margliani, who left Naples and reached Constantinople (December 1577), where he presented the letters and gifts, received through Aurelio di Santa Croce, to the Grand Vizier, Ṣoqollu Meḥemmed, and Khurrem Beg. By inscriptions on the covers his mission was at once revealed, endangering it and his very life. He obtained the originals and had them sent with a despatch to the King, by Giovanni Stefano Ferrari; he was taken by Fabricio de Sangre at Barletta and the despatch was removed and sent to Naples. Margliani continued to advise the King through Ferrari sending, as ordered, copies of the letters to the Viceroy, who never replied until he was ordered to do so by the King, and then insultingly, giving Margliani the same title as Ferrari, his servant. The King then decided to appoint Don Juan de Rocafull as Ambassador, disappointing Margliani and dishonouring him before the Turks; even so he promised to help and serve Rocafull. The King changed his mind, detained Rocafull, sent the present via Ragusa, and the letters and patents made in Rocafull's name were sent to Margliani – an unheard of thing, and very dangerous for him. Thus he had to resort to bribery and friends to achieve his end. But the whole success of his mission is owing to the prudent direction of Mondéjar's successor Zúñiga, the Commander of Castille (appointed to Naples 1579). Margliani came to Naples (*c.* June 1581) with hopes of recognition inspired in him by Don Juan de Idiáquez, but he waited there twenty months, during which time one of his brothers-in-law was unjustly displaced from his office of senator. Finally (1583), he was referred to Nuestra Señora de Guadalupe, then to Madrid, where he was unfairly treated by the Cardinal de Granvelle.

2. (f. 2r) Statement of the dangers he endured.
He was close to drowning for a day and a night crossing the Gulf (of Venice). Fearing the treachery of Santa Croce and Brutti he lived fifteen months in Constantinople confined to two rooms, his only pastime being to look out of the window. He was doing this when news came of the King of Portugal's crossing over to Africa (1578), and his house was stoned. Every time the King raised a fleet the French ambassador suggested that it was for the conquest of Algiers, and Margliani's life was in danger. He arranged with the Grand Vizier Aḥmed Pasha that, as he was sending the present to the King of Spain in his own name and not the Sultan's, then Margliani would give the present to the Sultan in his own name, not the King's (1580). However, the High Admiral, Ūlūj ʿAlī, wanted to give the present himself and Margliani had to oppose him. He spent forty months in Constantinople, always in great danger, up to the moment of departure.

3. (ff. 2v-3r) The services he has rendered.
He describes the reaction of the Grand Vizier, on his arrival in Constantinople, to Don Martín de Acuña's claim to have negotiated a secret armistice. Margliani won his confidence so that he granted an armistice for 1578, which was maintained for 1579. When Ṣoqollu Meḥemmed died Margliani gained the goodwill of his successor Aḥmed Pasha and they made the armistice for 1580, an important factor in the King's annexation of Portugal. He made the latest armistice with Siyāwush Pasha for three years, thus saving the King great expense over six years and instituting a proceeding which will probably be beneficial for years to come. As it was to Spain's advantage that no Italian state should have diplomatic relations with the Porte he had obstructed the negotiations of the Duke of Tuscany. He had made the Viziers think that all the Italian states were in allegiance to the King. He had put the Republic of Venice under obligation to him. He had found a way to poison Ūlūj ʿAlī and had a suitable compound been sent he would have put it into the Admiral's goblet which he had in his house. He brought in the present. He had never conceded a point to the French ambassador. He refused to have audience with the Sultan, risking his life for the King's honour, because he knew that he would have to buy cloth and other gifts and everybody would understand that they were presented by the King. He had left excellent relations in Constantinople, such as the Emperor Charles v had spent huge sums to establish. He had been able to convert to his own use the 12,000 escudos which he had been keeping to give to Ṣoqollu Meḥemmed, who had died before taking them up. In spite of the necessity of pleasing the Pope, Margliani had conducted Brother Christo-

pher Pérez of Seville to Rome, although there was a brief out for his death. Above all he has accomplished the Constantinople mission by skill, without even a letter of credit from the King, only spending 12,000 escudos in the forty months, going, staying and returning. He ends (f. 3r-v) by petitioning the King to fulfil his hopes of an adequate reward; although he has been granted the four vallies and feudal domain of Intelvi, its income of 400 escudos is not sufficient. He had to disburse his own money in Constantinople and, with his business interests neglected, he has lost 8,000 escudos since he departed from Milan, and is ruined. The Marquis of los Vélez and Antonio Pérez gave him higher expectations, assuring him that the King would have ransomed him from danger or rewarded his children to the extent of the value of his domain had he died in service. He implores the King to use his services in the future and to deliver him from the difficulties accruing from his services in the past.

(f. 1r) S*acra* C*attolica* R*eal* M*aestà*

Non ho mai pensato di douere hauere à dire à V*ostra* M*aes*ta li disgusti riceuuti, et, i, periculi passati, doppo che mi commando andasse in Constan*tinopo*li, ne che mi douesse essere neces*sari*o narar, i, mei seruigi minutam*en*te alla M*aes*ta V*os*tra, si perche ho sempre tenuto per fermo, che mi douesse far tal mercede, che se desinganeria il mondo, come perche ho creduto, che non conuenesse à bon creato, et uasallo, farsi scudo al suo principe, con li seruigi fatti; Il modo, con che sono statto tratato, mi obliga à fare l'uno et l'altro officio con V*ostra* M*aes*ta.

Fui rimesso al Marchese de Mondejar Vicere di Napoli,[68] con ordine di non hauere à comunicar seco alcuna cosa, obedi, come conueneua, ò, ch'egli hauesse noticia del nego*zi*o, per uia delli despachi de V*ostra* M*aes*ta, ch'egli mi prese, ò, di Aur*eli*o santa croce,[69] et Bartolameo Brutti,[70] et sdegno, di che andasse riseruato, mi fece infiniti tiri, è causo molti periculi; Parti finalm*en*te et gionto in Constan*tinopo*li, et dato le letere, et robe, che portaua dil detto Aur*eli*o, per il Basa,[71] et Hurrembei,[72] fra poco scopersi, che haueua portato con me la morte, perche le coperte delle robe erano scritte, dando auuiso di tutto il mio disegno, et animando, et machinando contra la persona mia, et al Real seruigio della M*aes*ta V*ostra* hebbi modo di hauere li stessi originali, et li mandai à V*ostra* M*aes*ta. Mi conuenne mandar Gio*vanni* stef*ano* de Ferrari[73] con un despacho, inarriuando in Barleta, fu preso da Fabricio de Sangre, le fu leuato il Despacho, et mandato sotto custodia in Napoli; Inuiato det*to* Gio*vanni* stef*ano*, andai auuisando à V*ostra* M*aes*ta le cose che succedeuano, scriuendo d*al* (f. 1v) orden*amento* à detto Marchese, et mandandoli copia, per maggior osseruanza, delle l*ett*ere, che scriueua à V*ostra* M*aes*ta mai si degno di respondere à una l*ett*era mia, et quando hebbe ordine da V*ostra* M*aes*ta di farlo, mi scrisse, tratandomi differentem*en*te di quello conueneua, et per smacarmi, daua nell'istesso tempo il medemo titulo à Gio*vanni* stef*ano* mio creato; Piacque à V*ostra* M*aes*ta di far elle*tio*ne di Amb*asciato*re, et nomino Don Gio*vanni* De Rocaful,[74] col*l*a qual nomina uenne io à essere ten*u*to in poco concetto, perche si uenne à confermare il mondo nella oppenione presa, che fusse stato mandato come huomo che si hauesse in poca consideracione, con tutto cio, anteponendo il serui*zi*o di V*ostra* M*aes*ta alla reputacion mia, scrissi à V*ostra* M*aes*ta, che assisterei, accompagnerei, et seruirei, à detto Don Gio*vanni* in tutte le occasioni; Si muto pensiere, et si tratenne Don Gio*vanni* mandando il p*res*ente in Ragusa, et à me, le patenti, et l*ett*ere, ch'erano fatte in credenza di detto Don Gio*vanni*, perche con esse tratasse nego*zi*o di simile qualita, cosa mai piu sentita, che poteua distrugere il tutto, et farmi capitar male, presi altro espediente, quale fu di satisfat*io*ne, poi che quei ministri mostrarono fede in me; Di q*ue*sta manera si procedete meco sin alla uenuta dil Com*mendat*or maggiore,[75] quale in auanti tenne tal stile, che debbo dire, se si è fatto cosa di bene, che si ha da reconosere, dalla prudencia, et discrecione di quel sig*no*re; Venni à Napoli, diedi conto à detto Com*mendat*or maggiore di quello haueua passato, q*u*ale mi fece instan*z*a, che uenesse da V*ostra* M*aes*ta; Sono statto tratenuto uinti mesi, con le speranze, che Don Gio*vanni* Idiaquez[76] mi ha dato, con la sua solita modestia, et bonta, nel qual tempo fu nominato un cugnato mio per senatore, quale era statto nominato delle altre uolti, et haueua seruito in tutti li offici biennali di q*ue*llo stato, come conuie (f. 2r) ne, honoratissimam*en*te, fu posposto à chi non haueua per eta, per ualore à fare con lui; Fui alla fine rimesso à N*ostra* S*ignora* di Guadaluppe, poi à Madrid, doue il Card*ina*le di granuela,[77] in luogo di hauer compas*sio*ne à mei stenti, trauaglij, et spese, ha proceduto meco in tutto differentem*en*te; Ho detto li disgusti, diro li periculi;

Pasando il Golfo, stette tutta una notte et un giorno in punto per annegarmi; Hauendo scoperto quanto ho riferto di Aur*eli*o santa croce, e Bartolomeo Brutti, per desinganar q*ue*lle genti, stetti circa xv me*si* in due camere, ne hauendo altro transtullo, che uenire à una fin*estra* quando il Re di portugalle passo in Africa,[78] essendo comparso *à* q*ue*lla finestra, mi fu lapidata la casa, dicendo parole ingiuriose, et facendo segno di assaltarla; Tutte le uolti che V*ostra* M*aes*ta ha fatto armata, mi sono trouato in periculo, perche l'Amb*asciato*re di Franc*ia*[79] persuadeua che si pensaua all'Inpresa de

Algeri; Dissi in facia à Acmat Bassa,[80] tratando egli, di che darebbe il presente in suo nome, et non del gran Turco, che la persona mia ualeua in quel caso, tanto come la sua, perche se lui rapresentaua la persona del Imp*erato*re de Musulmani, io q*ue*lla del maggior Re de Christiani, et che uolendo egli dare p*rese*nte in suo nome, io lo daria nel mio; Quando Alluchali[81] penso di mettermi paura, perche dasse detto p*rese*nte, et si leuo in piede contra di me, non li cedete punto, se bene con molto mio periculo; In fatti sono statto quaranta mesi in Constan*tinopo*li, sempre con periculo manifesto, et il proprio giorno che parti, mi uidi in termine de perdermi; Ho detto li periculi, diro adesso li seruigi;

(f. 2v) La p*rim*a risposta che mi fu data, quando arriuai in Constan*tinopo*li, dal Basa,[82] furono le formate parole; Se fusse Christiano mi farei il segno della croce, facendosi le marauiglie, che Don Mar*tin*o de Acuña[83] hauesse riferto à V*ostra* M*aes*ta Che il Turco faria una suspensione secreta, con destrezza andai desinganando il Basa, et guadagnando la uolunta, à tal che feci una suspens*io*ne per q*ue*llo anno, che fu l'anno del, $\overline{78}$, quale mantenni l'anno del $\overline{79}$ ancora, con la paciencia, et ressolut*io*ne mia; Mori Mehemet Basa, al quale successe Acmat, la cui uolunta guadagnai ancora in processo di poco tempo, di modo che feci una suspen*sio*ne per l'anno del $\overline{80}$, che fu di tanta Importan*z*a à V*ostra* M*aes*ta como si sa, essendo occupata nell'acquisto del Regno di Portugalle; Feci l'ultima Intel*ligen*z*a per tre anni con Schiaus Basa,[84] di manera, che con la persona mia, et con la reputacione mia, ho liberato V*ostra* M*aes*ta da una spesa eccessiua de sei anni, et incaminato una pratica, che potra V*ostra* M*aes*ta per mio giudicio, ualersi di detta Intel*ligen*z*a per maggior tempo; Hauendo consideracione, che non conuenesse, che alcun potentato de Italia hauesse Intel*ligen*z*a con q*ue*lla porta, andai mettendo difficulta nella pratica, che procuraua il Gran Duca di Toscana,[85] et potero tanto le mie diligencie, che non hebbe effetto; Ho lassato quei ministri in oppenione, che V*ostra* M*aes*ta commandi à tutti li sig*no*ri de Italia liberam*e*nte; Ho datto tanta satisfat*io*ne alla Rep*ubli*ca di Ven*ez*i*a, che si chiamano obligatis*si*mi; Ho raccordato, procurato, et trouato forma, che si auenenasse Alluchali, et se me fusse stato mandato composito à proposito, si sarebbe essequito, per che hebbi commodita di hauere in casa il uaso, in che beueua, per uedere la quantita che teneua, per poterla auuisare, come feci; Ho rapportato il p*rese*nte; Non ho (f. 3r) ceduto in un minimo punto all'Amb*asciato*re di Franc*i*a; Non ho uoluto uedere il gran Turco, anteponendo la reputac*io*ne di V*ostra* M*aes*ta alla uita, perche preuiddi, che il giorno che andaua à fare q*ue*sto compimento, uoleuano far comparere una quantita de drappi, et altre cose, et publicare, ch'erano cose che V*ostra*

M*aesta* haueua mandate di p*resen*te; Ho lassato una bona corrispondencia in Constan*tinopo*li, che l'Imp*erato*re Carlo quinto Inuittis*si*mo di fe*lice* Me*moria*[86] spese gran quantita de danari, per hauere una Intel*ligenz*a di gente sicura, et fidele; Ho putoto conuertire in mio uso li xij mille scuti, che mi furono datti, per donare à Mehemet Basa, quali egli mi lasso in custodia, et morendo senza pigliarli, nc ho dat*o* conto; Conosendo, che conueniua molto dar sodisfat*io*ne à S*ua* S*ant*ita,[87] presi la ressolut*io*ne, che V*ostra* M*ae*sta si deue raccordare, con Frate Christoforo perez di Siuiglia conducendolo in Roma, con molto mio periculo, se bene haueua hauuto breue per farlo morire; È quello V*ostra* M*ae*sta ha di tenere in molto, è l'hauere redotto à segno una tanta negociacione, solo con il modo di trattare è senza che sia restato in Constan*tinopo*li, pure una l*ette*ra della M*ae*sta V*ostra* di credenza, ne altra scrittura; Et alla fine, non ho speso piu de xij mille scuti, nell'andare, stare, et ritornare, ne ui arriuano in quaranta mesi;

Questi sono et molti altri li seruigi, con che ho procurato seruire à V*ostra* M*ae*sta, et se sono ueri, mi debbo pur promettere dalla benignita di V*ostra* M*ae*sta, che non debbano restare inremunerati, ne che habbia à parere ad alcuno, che la Mercede che V*ostra* M*ae*sta mi fece delle quatro ualli, et contado de Intelue,[88] che uano allargando per deshonorarmi, sia troppo, ne à bastanza, non eccedendo, 400, scuti de intrata, promettendomi dalla sua Real mano molto piu, poi che, se bene q*ue*sto satisfa à un certo modo all'honore, trouandomi consumato, per hauere fatte molte spese del mio in Constan*tinopo*li, et per essere state mal gouernate le mie faculta, con l'hauere speso da scuti otto mile doppo partij di Mil*ano*, resto distrutto; Et (f. 3v) le speranze che mi furono datte dal Marchese de los Velez,[89] et da Ant*oni*o perez,[90] erano di maggior qualita, et mi assicurauano, che V*ostra* M*ae*sta non hauerebbe quardato à spesa per leuarmi di periculo, et che se Iddio hauesse disposto di me, hauerebbe V*ostra* M*ae*sta fatto mercede à mei figl*io*li; la quale non si poteua sperar meno dil ualore delli Feudi sopradetti;

Prego et humilm*ente* sup*pli*co V*ostra* M*ae*sta habbia consideracione al tutto, et che non sono inhabile per seruire à V*ostra* M*ae*sta in qual si uoglia occas*io*ne, che me inpiegara, è che per cio resti seruita farmi despachare, come meglio à S*ua* M*ae*sta parera, è N*ostro* Sig*no*re la Cat*toli*ca Real persona di V*ostra* M*ae*sta conserui è guardi;

NOTES

1 This is one of the 170 volumes of state-papers from the archives of the Altamira family acquired by the BM in 1870. Its contents are described

in the *Catalogue of Additions to the manuscripts in the British Museum in the years MDCCCLIV–MDCCCLXXV*, II (London 1877), 480, as: 'Letters, despatches, *etc.*, originals and copies, from Don Christoval de Salazar, Ambassador at Venice, chiefly to Philip II, on affairs of Venice and of the Turks; 1579–1595, with a few of later dates. Paper. Folio.'. Ours is the only Ottoman document in the volume. The volume is catalogued, from the endorsements of the documents, in P. de Gayangos, *Catalogue of the manuscripts in the Spanish Language in the British Museum*, III (London 1881) 598-602.

2 The author wishes to make grateful acknowledgement to the Trustees of the British Museum for permission to publish the following material from their collection.

3 MS پاشا هلرك

4 The Second Vizier, acting as deputy to the Grand Vizier who was absent on campaign; see below, n. 41.

5 Philip II of Spain.

6 Giovanni Margliani: on him, see below, p. 497.

7 For Siyāwush Pasha's list of the Ottoman allies see Commentary, below, p. 499.

8 2nd ed., 2 vols. (Paris 1966): cited hereafter as 'Braudel'. The relevant chapter is in Vol. II, 431-68.

9 BM, Add. MS 28, 415, ff. 1-4.

10 Braudel, II, 348-9, 431-7.

11 On him and his agency see ibid., 437-9.

12 Braudel, ibid., 438, says that the document, which is preserved in Simancas, must be a translation, but he does not indicate a Turkish original.

13 On him see EI^1 *s. v.* Ṣoḳolli, Muḥammad Pasha (art. by J.H.Kramers).

14 The letters are described and discussed in Gerlach, *Tagebuch* (Franckfurth a.M. 1674), 404-5. For Gerlach's coverage of the Don Martín agency, see ibid., 319-20, 322-3, 325, 363-4.

15 Quoted in Braudel, II, 440, from Margliani's report of February 1578; cf. also his report, below, p. 509, where, writing years later, he puts a similar exclamation into the mouth of the Grand Vizier.

16 See Gerlach's comments, *Tagebuch*, 460-1.

17 Reported by Gerlach on 22 February 1578: ibid., 461.

18 On him and his embassy see Braudel, II, 439-50. The French secretary, Juyé, speaks of the revenues granted him by Philip II 'à Milan, d'où il est natif': Charrière, *Négociations de la France dans le Levant*, III (Paris 1853) 769n.

19 Gerlach, *Tagebuch*, 460.

20 See de Germigny's report, of 12 February 1580, of the violent scene when the Grand Vizier threatened to throw Margliani into irons (Charrière, *Négociations*, III, 870-2nn.) and, of the same month, when

the High Admiral expressed the wish to remove his other eye (ibid., 876n.).

21 Undated memorial, perhaps of 1580, in Charrière, *Négociations*, III, 919n. For Margliani's modest and secretive mode of life see ibid., 760, 769n.

22 Paul de Foix, *Lettres* (Paris 1628) 36-7.

23 The 'Hurrem' of our document; variously known in contemporary reports as Oram-Bey, Orembey, Orimbei, Horembey, Huram Beg, Orunbey, etc.

24 De Germigny writes of him, on 30 March 1580, as 'Oram-Bey, premier truchement de ce Seig[r].': Charrière, *Négociations*, III, 891n.

25 See the anonymous Venetian Relation of 1582, in Albèri, *Relazioni*, Ser. 3, Vol. II (Florence 1844) 224-5, '. . . era in compagnia nostra il dragomanno del Gran Signore, chiamato Orimbei, lucchese rinnegato, e ex-dragomanno della signoria.' Note the inclusion of the Republic of Lucca in the list of Spanish allies; see below, p. 495.

26 *Tagebuch*, 461.

27 Vol. II, 441.

28 To the Emperor, 2 March 1578, in Gerlach, *Tagebuch*, 539-41.

29 In his reports to Henri III of 22 January and 12 February 1578; Charrière, *Négociations*, III, 708-14.

30 In Venice, Archivio di Stato, *Senato*, *Secreta*, Despatches from Constantinople, *filza* II, ff. 456-7, enclosed in Barbarigo's despatch of 10 February 1578, ibid., ff. 458-61.

31 The Grand Vizier Ṣoqollu Meḥemmed Pasha.

32 Philip II of Spain.

33 Giovanni Margliani.

34 The Sultan Murād III; on him see *EI*[1] *s.v.* Murād III (article by J.H. Kramers).

35 In Gerlach, *Tagebuch*, 540.

36 See below, p. 509.

37 On him see Braudel, II, 443-4.

38 The text in Simancas E° 490, which Braudel (441n.2) suggests is a copy made in 1579 of the 1578 agreement, is more likely a copy of the 1580 armistice. The terms of the treaty seem to have been discussed in the Sultan's letter of August 1580; the Chancery copy, in the Istanbul State Archives, MD 43, p. 177, no. 322, is noted in Hess, 'The Moriscos: an Ottoman fifth column in sixteenth-century Spain', *American Historical Review*, LXXIV/i (1968), 22.

39 In his report to Henri III of March 1580; Charriére, *Négociations*, III, 888.

40 In his despatch of 24 March 1580, in Venice, A. di S., *Senato*, *Secreta*, Despatches from Constantinople, *filza* 14, f. 34.

41 A native Hungarian or Croat, he was deputy from 7 August 1580 to

22 July 1581. On him see Ṣureyyā, *Sijill-i ʿOṣmānī*, III (Constantinople, A.H. 1311), 116. An excellent description of him in the Anonymous Relation of 1582, Albèri, *Relazioni*, Ser. 3, vol. II, 242-3.

42 Vol. II, 447-50.

43 Thus the document terms itself: see lines 7 and 8 of the Ottoman text. For 'temessük' see Meninski, *Lexicon* (Vienna 1680) col. 1392 *s.v.*: Handschrifft / Obligation / Schuldschein / Schein / Quittung.

44 Despatch in Venice, A. di S., *Senato, Secreta*, Des. Con., *filza* 14, f. 409. Copy of the agreement, ibid., f. 410. Contarini promised, f. 409v, ll. 1-3, to obtain an Ottoman text of the treaty from Margliani, but the present writer could not find any Ottoman texts of the armistices in Venice. To be noted, also in *filza* 14, f. 363, is the copy of the letter from the Viceroy of Naples, Don Juan de Zúñiga, to Siyāwush Pasha, of 19 November 1580, confirming the armistice.

45 See his report, below, p. 509.

46 Quoted above, p. 497.

47 Given in full above, pp. 495-6.

48 In *Senato, Secreta*, Des. Con., *filza* 14, f. 410.

49 Contarini's despatch of 4 February 1581; ibid., f. 409r. See also Margliani's despatch of 4 February in *Cartas y avisos dirigidos á Don Juan de Zúñiga Virey de Nápoles en 1581* (Madrid 1887) 55.

50 His despatch, ibid., 56.

51 Ibid., 55.

52 The French ambassador, de Foix, in his report of 12 June 1581 says that Margliani had arrived there a few days before; *Lettres*, 36.

53 His death is reported in *Cal. S. P. Ven., 1581–91*, p. 339: no. 627; despatch of Hieronimo Lippomano, Venetian ambassador in Spain, of 13 February 1588.

54 See *Cartas y avisos*, 133 (Report from Caller, 22 May 1581), 250 (From Constantinople, 20 August), 262-8 (From Tabarca, 14 August), 296-7 (From Algiers, 22 September).

55 See his report, below, p. 509.

56 For Harborne see the rewritten *D.N.B.* article by E. S. de Beer in *Bull. Inst. Hist. Res.*, XIX, 160-2.

57 In *William Harborn his seruice to her Magestie and Commons*, published in Rawlinson, 'The embassy of William Harborne', *Trans. R. Hist. Soc.*, Ser. 4, vol. V, p. 22.

58 In Charrière, *Négociations*, III, 885n.

59 Despatch to Walsingham in *Cal. S.P. For., 1583–4*, 329.

60 Despatch to Walsingham, ibid., 355.

61 In his petition of 9 November 1587 Harborne reminds the Sultan of this promise, made four years previously; English version of the Latin petition, calendared under its date of receipt, 9 February 1588, in *Cal. S.P. For., 1586–8*, 508-9.

62 Walsingham to Harborne, 8/18 October 1585, in Read, *Mr Secretary Walsingham*, III (Oxford 1925) 226-8.

63 On him see *EI*[1] *s. v.* Khodja Efendi (article by F. Babinger).

64 On his part in the negotiation see Kurat, 'Hoca Sâdeddin Efendinin Türk-İngiliz münasebetlerinin tesisi ve gelişmesindeki rolü' in *Fuad Köprülü Armağanı* (Istanbul 1953) 305-15.

65 In *William Harborn his seruice*, Rawlinson, op. cit., 24.

66 Despatch to the Doge and Senate of 16 April 1587, in *Cal. S.P. Ven., 1581–91*, 267: no. 502. For the part played by Harborne see Bernardo's despatch of 4 April 1587, ibid., 263: no. 496, and Harborne's account in Rawlinson, op. cit., 23.

67 Margliani's report is enclosed in the despatch of Hieronimo Lippomano, Venetian ambassador in Spain, of 4 September 1587, *Cal. S.P. Ven., 1581–91*, 310: no. 576 (despatch), 577 (report).

68 Don Iñigo Lopez Hurtado de Mendoza, Marquis of Mondéjar; Viceroy of Naples, 1575–9.

69 Agent for Spain, and a merchant; also known as Aurelio de Santa Cruz, but probably an Italian.

70 An Italianized Albanian, seen here working for Spain but at the same time in the pay of Venice and the Imperialists and, later, of the English. He became the principal official of the Moldavian prince, Peter the Lame.

71 I.e. Ṣoqollu Meḥemmed Pasha, Grand Vizier from 1565 until his assassination on 12 October 1579.

72 Khurrem Beg, the chief Interpreter at the Porte; on him see Commentary above.

73 A member of a famous Milanese family, Ferrari was a devoted servant and collaborator; after Margliani's death in 1588 he took over responsibility for the Spanish negotiations in Constantinople.

74 On him see Braudel, II, 443. He was apparently a native of Valencia, and at one time a commander in the Neapolitan fleet.

75 I.e. Don Juan de Zúñiga y Requesens; Commander of Castille, 1578–1586, and Viceroy of Naples, in succession to Mondéjar, 1579–81.

76 Don Juan de Idiáquez (d. 1614), minister and secretary of Philip II and Philip III.

77 Antoine Perrenot de Granvelle (1517–86), Franc-Comtois cardinal, a high-ranking member of the Spanish administration under Philip II.

78 Margliani refers to the arrival of Sebastian of Portugal in Morocco before the Battle of the Three Kings at al-Qaṣr al-Kabīr on 4 August 1578.

79 Jacques de Germigny, baron de Germoles, French ambassador at the Porte, 1579–84.

80 Semiz Aḥmed Pasha, Grand Vizier from 13 October 1579 until his death on 28 April 1580.

81 Ūlūj ʿAlī, born in Calabria about 1500, died in 1587. He was appointed Qapudān Pasha and named Kılıç ʿAlī in recognition of his salvation of the Ottoman fleet after its defeat at Lepanto.

82 Cf. note 71.

83 On him see Braudel, II, 437-9.

84 Siyāwush Pasha, Second Vizier, was acting as Qāyimmaqām during the absence on campaign of the Grand Vizier Sinān Pasha from August 1580 to July 1581.

85 Francesco de'Medici, Grand Duke of Tuscany, 1574–87.

86 Charles V (1500–58), Holy Roman Emperor, 1519–56.

87 Gregory XIII, Pope from 1572 to 1585.

88 Intelvi is a valley region with a village between Lakes Como and Lugano.

89 Luis Fajardo de la Cueva, marqués de los Vélez.

90 Antonio Pérez (1540–1611), secretary of Philip II from 1568 to 1579.

BRIAN SPOONER

Notes on the Toponymy of the Persian Makran

In an article published in 1957 Professor Minorsky made it his 'direct purpose . . . to stimulate a more systematic approach to the toponymy of the old land of Iran'. He maintained that 'as a subsidiary instrument of work for historians, toponymy should occupy its due place, by the side of numismatics and epigraphy'.[1] This paper is written not by an historian (nor for that matter by a philologist) and cannot press too hard the claim to be systematic. It does, however, owe much to the constant encouragement of Professor Minorsky[2] and it may claim to present new material from a particularly little known area. My main purpose is to publish a representative selection of toponyms – names of settlements, areas and natural features – from that part of the Makran which lies within the present borders of Persia. I have, therefore, little if anything to offer the historian who seeks modern identifications of ancient place names (the more important ones have anyway all been identified), and the philologist will no doubt spot many points in the names I list which I fail to note in my comments on them. Probably none of the points I make myself are entirely new, but they have not before been noticed for the area here discussed, and certain historical processes may be more clearly visible from this material than elsewhere. The point of such an approach is to make the first step in a direction which may lead us to an understanding of how a particular environment has been classified by its inhabitants. An important point of interest here is that it is obvious from the beginning that different ethnic elements – if not successive populations – have each contributed to the present situation. The final picture to be gained is not of any *system* of analysis or classification of the environment but of a number of processes existing side by side, some still active, many fossilized into archaisms. At the same time the list should provide useful data not previously available to Iranian philologists.

The factual basis of what follows derives from field work in the area between 1962–7. As a social anthropologist I have of course a particular interest in the material and should like to regard the article as an introductory case study in the sociology of toponymy.

I

Throughout historical times a certain aura of mystery seems always to have surrounded the Makran whatever its administrative status. Compare:

> 'Thou showest me the road to Makran, but what a difference there is between an order and its execution: I will never enter this country, as its name alone terrifies me' –

the lament of Sinān ibn Selāma, the second Arab governor of the Makran, and:

> 'The Ichthyophagi, as their name implies, live on fish. They inhabit deserts where not a tree grows, and where there are not even wild fruits. They construct their dwellings with the backbones of fish. They have shaggy hair all over their bodies, and go practically naked.'

from Arrian's Periplus (both taken from Sykes, *Ten thousand miles in Iran*, 98, 109), with:

> 'RASK, the chief place of the district of Jurūj [on the lower part of the Sarbāz river before it becomes the Mazan Kaur; the spelling of the name of the district is disputed]. It is prosperous and very populous, and is a place possessing many merchants'

from the *Ḥudūd al-ʿĀlam*, and Muqaddasī's account of the Port of Tīs as having many palm-groves, large crowded inns, and a beautiful mosque.

A first-hand acquaintance with the area today leads one to suppose that each of these accounts must be, at best, misleading exaggerations, for despite the fact that they spread over some thirteen centuries it is extremely unlikely that the natural environment could have supported such wide variations. The discrepancy between these reports illustrates a general problem in the assessment of literary evidence for the reconstruction of Persian historical geography: the judgements passed tend to be in vague subjective terms, to which no absolute value can be attached without a knowledge of the writer's criteria – which we seldom have, and which is difficult to determine generally from the context. This situation throws into particular relief the value of the study of toponymy for reconstructing the historical geography and the history of the Makran perhaps even more than the Iranian plateau in general and other regions. For it shows not only which places were agricultural rather than nomadic, but which were more significant agricultural areas, and what differences there may have been other than occupational between the inhabitants of different villages and areas. If we may briefly, at this stage, dispose of the quotations:

(1) It seems natural that the name of the Makran was terrifying to people coming from the cities because it was separated from the provinces to the west and north of it by long stretches of desert, which where we have historical evidence have always been roamed by pastoral, nomadic, more or less outlaw groups.[3] Within the Makran itself the climate is difficult and settlement is *possible* only in certain definite places. These are defined by natural conditions – in particular the availability and coincidence of water and soil, and are often widely separated.

(2) The majority of the population on the coast itself – though all are now called Baluch – is ethnically distinct, retains a distinct (supra-) tribal name (Mēd), which is attested on the coast and in the Indus valley as far back as the early Islamic geographers. They are now the only part of the population which look toward the sea rather than inland, and are mainly fishermen. Throughout the coastal plain fresh water is generally obtainable only by catching rain water, and rainfall is very irregular, though the general humidity supports a certain amount of tree life. The ubiquity of fish (which is mostly dried in the sun in and around Mēd settlements before further use) and its attendant effluvia might account for the remainder of this report.

(3) Rāsk is at the end of a natural corridor through the Makran range, which must have been the main artery for both east-west and north-south traffic west of Kēch (now in West Pakistan). The corridor carries a river, which though not perhaps strictly perennial is never completely dry, and which is bordered for much of its course by long ribbons of rice fields and palm groves. Rāsk is thus ensured a certain degree of prosperity except in the case of prolonged drought, but this is nevertheless only relative and there are no signs that there has ever been any very large settlement in the vicinity.

(4) Tīs is historically the most important port on the Makran coast. The Portuguese built a fort there, but no trace (that I noticed) remains of the inns or the mosque. We may therefore surmise that its prosperity was one of quantity rather than quality, and it may have looked bigger but otherwise little different from its condition a decade ago.

I believe the same is true for the other Makran 'towns' for which we have any historical detail. And these 'towns' are the main sites of agricultural settlement and exploitation now (at least until the introduction of the motor pump) as previously, and their names have remained unchanged (except for a few artificial changes made in the 1930's) despite obvious (though perhaps only partial) changes in the ethnic composition and general structure of the population.

The name Makran no longer has any formal meaning or official usage in Persia, and among the Baluch themselves it is generally used to denote the south-western province (bordering Persia) of the former State of Kalāt (now West Pakistan) because of administrative usage. The modern province which covers most of the extent of the Makran within the modern borders of Persia is called *Baluchistān and Sīstān* (hereafter referred to as 'the Province') since it stretches north to include the distinct oecological region of the Helmand delta. The name Baluchistan derives from the fact that the vast majority of the population call themselves Baluch. Practically nothing is known of the area of any sociological or ethnographic import before Safavid times at the earliest, and I have not found the name used before that. This I feel to be simply one of a number of factors which throw doubt on the generally held view (based mainly on philological reasoning about the history of the Baluchi language and scattered historical references to people called Baluch up to the eleventh century A.D.) that the Baluch were driven into the Makran from the north-west by the Seljuqs. I hope to treat the historical process, and, more particularly, what can be known of the history of the Baluch within Persia, in a future publication. The present article will merely touch on certain geographical aspects of this process which arise from the toponymy. The literature on the mediaeval geography of such a relatively unimportant and isolated area is of course not vast, but is nevertheless too much to be even summarized here. Details of the more significant studies are given in the course of the article, and I am obliged to assume some degree of familiarity with them as I write, though I only comment on or cite them when their content seems pertinent to the point I wish to make.

'The earliest mention of the Makran, called Maka, is in the old Persian cuneiform inscription of Darius at Behistun and Persepolis'.[4] It is sometimes mentioned as part of India, but was generally claimed as part of the Persian Empire at least until Nāṣiru'd-Dīn Shāh accepted the border agreement with India and the Khān of Kalāt in 1871. The border has been redefined twice since, but with only minor alterations, and it is interesting that its rationale is one of basically internal tribal politics: it has little or nothing to do with any of the non-human aspects of geography. To mediaeval geographers the Makran was one definite administrative region, though of varying status, indefinite borders, and very little known. Accord-

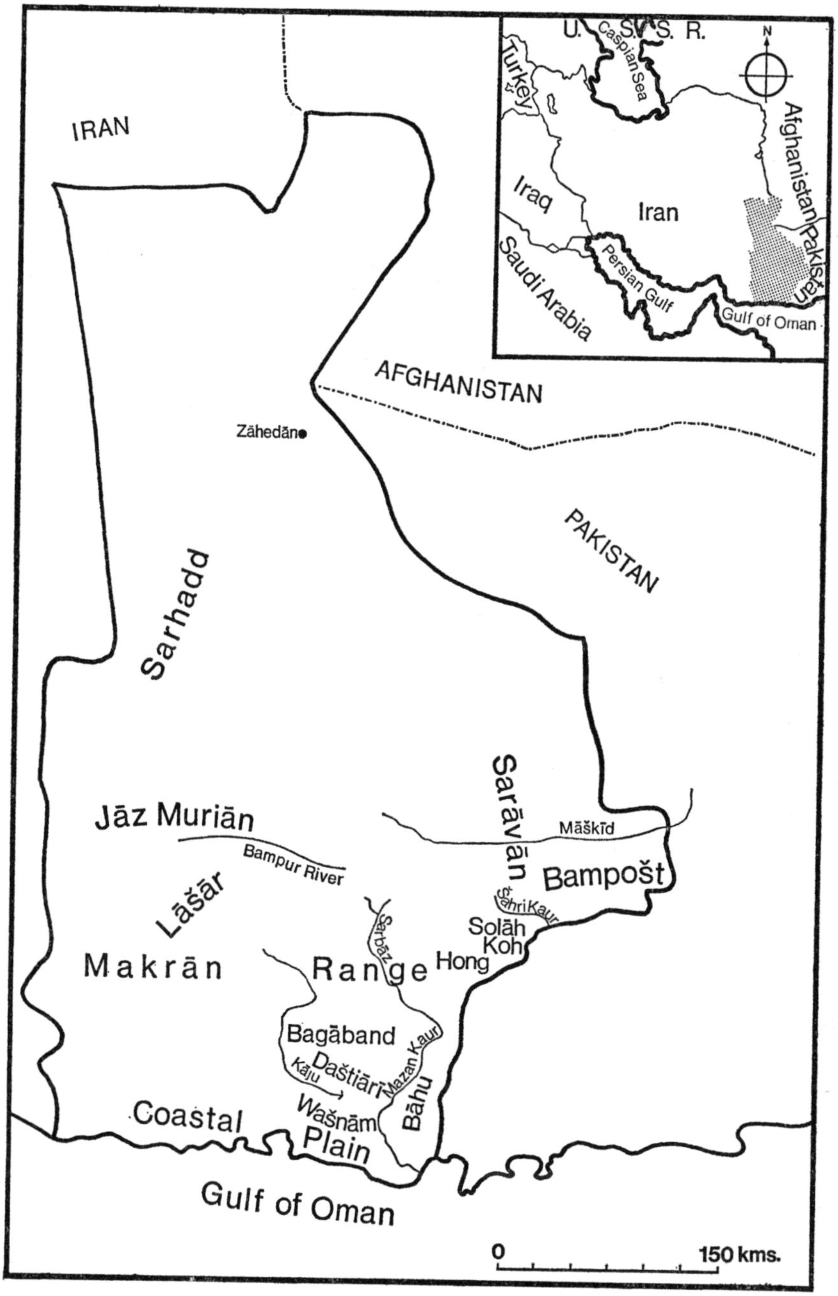

Map showing area described as Persian Makran.

ing to Ibn Khordādbih, Ardashīr (in the first half of the third century A.D.) set up a *Makrān Shāh*, who must presumably have put the province on an equal footing with its neighbour Kermān, ruled by a Kermān Shāh. Later it was always – at least in theory – dependent on Kermān. Within Persia it appears always to have included the coastal plain and the 'Makran range' of mountains behind it at least as far west as Bashkard, and north-west it shaded into Kermān and to the north into Sīstān. North of the Makran range there appears to have been a flourishing agricultural population at the eastern end of the Jāz Muriān depression around Bampūr, probably coinciding with the Harappan period.[5] Around Bampūr cultivation has always been possible because of the river but elsewhere in the depression *qanāts* are required; yet *qanāts* do not appear to have been introduced until the last century at the earliest.[6]

With the possible exception of Sarāvān (which also needs *qanāts* but may have acquired them a little sooner, cf. my forthcoming history of the Baluch in Persia) all the country north of the Makran range must have been very sparsely populated, and what population there was must have been almost exclusively pastoral and therefore nomadic. Since there are no natural boundaries in this country it is therefore natural that the borders between the Makran and Kermān and Sīstān should fluctuate according to the relative political and military strength of each. The no man's land between these three traditional territorial divisions contains very few traditional settlements. All of these except one are situated very close to the semi-active volcano (Kūh-i Taftān 13,000 ft). The three most significant ones were definitely known by the same names in the early centuries of Islam as they bear still. They are Damandān (or Tamindān), Khwāš (Baluchi: Wāš(t)), and Sipi. Damandān is mentioned as belonging to Kermān in Ibn Faqīh, but to Makran by Muqaddasī, while in the *Ḥudūd*, Khwāš – some 20 miles to the south-west of Damandān – is linked with Rīqān (now Rīgān, an outpost of Narmāšīr, south-east of Bam and north of the Jāz Muriān, and generally considered to belong to Kermān) and the two together are called 'two little towns in the desert'. Sipi is now called Noṣratābād and lies on the motor road from Bam to Zāhidān. It is mentioned in several pre-Mongol sources under forms varying from Sanīj to SBH[7] but the name Sipi was until recently still used by the Baluch of the area.[8] It is generally mentioned as a town in the desert, sometimes as dependent on Kermān. Damandān and Khwāš probably owe their antiquity to their proximity to the mines of the Kūh-i Taftān complex previously known as Damāvand (cf. e.g. Ibn Faqīh), and Sipi must have been an important stage on the route from Kermān to Sīstān, and perhaps also a turning-off point on that route for the mines of this southern Damāvand. The names of the remaining traditional settlements in this area (cf. Lādez, Junābād) are almost certainly equally old but have not been found in any pre-Mongol texts. The region between and around these settlements is oecologically distinct and has for long been differentiated in the local toponymy by the name Sarḥadd – literally 'the border country' (cf. e.g. *Iḥyā' ul-Mulūk*,[8a] *passim*), and in recent Baluch times at least it has developed rather differently from the Makran to the south. Nevertheless, so far as can be ascertained it has always been much more closely linked with the Makran than either Kermān or Sīstān, perhaps because routes south do not have to cross desert.

Makran is a place name of unknown (but suspected Dravidian) etymology that lives on today after at least two and a half millennia of continuous usage with its meaning apparently unchanged. This stability in the toponymy is not unusual in the Iranian area and is not unknown, but no one has so far to my knowledge followed up its implications. The archaeological sites found by Stein[9] and others that have come to my notice, increase this impression of continuity. Similarly, the reed dwellings which abound in the Makran today are attested at least as far back as the early centuries of Islam.[10]

However, the toponymy also reflects the vast and complicated demographic changes, which are suggested by, but not yet fully explored in, the literature. I have already drawn attention[11] to the fact that place-names in the Makran may be seen to fall easily into three categories. To characterize them briefly these are:

(i) Names of Baluchi origin – or at least fully Baluchized. These are almost exclusively names of natural features, e.g. rivers, streams, rocks, mountains (but not the two highest peaks in the Province – Damāvand *alias* Kūh-i Taftān *alias* Kūh-i Ceheltan and Kūh-i Zenda *alias* Kūh-i Bazmān – which must have provided unforgettable landmarks and perhaps watering places, from very early times on important arterial routes passing north and perhaps also south of them), and small areas. These can be seen to suggest the toponymy of a pastoral, nomadic people.

(ii) New Persian formations, e.g. ending in the suffix *-ābād*. These belong almost entirely to small, new agricultural settlements started since the renewed Persian (i.e. non-Baluch) interest in the Province in the middle of the last century.

(iii) Names which do not fit into either of these categories. This last category, which I have defined so negatively, consists exclusively of names of agricultural settlements, and many of them were in use in pre-Mongol times and therefore almost certainly in pre-Islamic times also. Simply by virtue of the fact that these names are neither Baluchi nor of any obvious alien origin, we can assume that they are pre-Baluch, i.e. that they were there before the Baluchi language began to dominate the area (which may or may not have been the same as the time when the name Baluch was imported, for not only do we not know the origin of the word Baluch or the Baluchi language or the people who brought the language into what is now Baluchistan, we also do not know when or how the name came to be applied to either the people or the language). It is therefore very likely that at least a number of the names in this last category are pre-Iranian. And anyway who knows how late the Iranians effectively colonized the Makran? Since the names in this category do not appear to be philologically homogeneous either, it is surely reasonable to speculate that some of them may be of even greater antiquity, and it is possible even that some may derive from one of the pre-Iranian strata of population which having once benefited from commercial relations with the Harappans, perhaps their cousins, and produced the Bampūr wares,[12] are now disguised as Baluch peasants.

II

In making the selection which forms the following lists, and in the transliteration, I have followed the same principles as in my article on the vocabulary,[13] of which this article is in a sense a continuation. I have thought it sufficient simply to indicate very generally the area to which each toponym relates, and only areas and important rivers are written in on the map. Each name relates to a settlement except where otherwise indicated. *q* indicates that the settlement contains a fort of some historical significance, and * that the name is known from a pre-Mongol text. For convenience I have used the name Jāz Muriān (said to derive from the names of particular shrubs) to cover the whole of the central depression, although it properly denotes only a small part at the western end of the central sump.

A. Alphabetical list of constituent toponymical elements and geographical terms.

1. *-ābād* settlement; see below, III, 3, d.
2. *āp* water
3. *-ān* plural, but cf. W. Eilers, *Archiv. Orientální*, XXIV (1956) 183
4. *baluc* shepherd

5. *band* small dam of earth or stones to catch rain or river water and silt
6. *bāzār* group of huts in agricultural area (no commercial connotation)
7. *cēr* below
8. *cīl* natural drainage line in plain
9. *cok* baby
10. *ḍakk* pass
11. *ḍann* plain
12. *dap* entrance (lit. mouth)
13. *dar* exit
14. *dēm* face
15. *gwalm* pool left in river bed
16. *halk* group of tents (Arabic: *khalq*)
17. *jahl* low
18. *kahn* qanāt
19. *kalāt* fort
20. *kaur* river
21. *koh* mountain
22. *lāp* middle (lit. stomach)
23. *mētag* group of nomad (occasionally peasant) dwellings
24. *mac* date palm
25. *pošt* behind (lit. back)
26. *sar* above (lit. head)
27. *šēp* small *kaur* (in mountains)
28. *šahr* cultivated land or date palm grove
29. *šur* friable, crumbling rock
30. *tāb*/*tāp* (P. *āftāb*) sunlight
31. *talār* firm solid rock
32. *tomp* mound (archaeological)
33. -*zai* denotes tribal name. In Daštiārī and Bāhu some villages are known by the name of the tribe or lineage which founded and peoples them

B. Alphabetical list of selected toponyms. I have felt it desirable here to indicate (by means of Roman numerals) to which of my three categories I think each name may belong. However, I have done this with some trepidation, and many of the allocations are tentative in the extreme. I realize also that in some cases I may have allowed my theories to influence my allocation in lieu of any other evidence. I have decided nevertheless that the risk was worth taking, since this article will achieve nothing if it does not indicate patterns. No names are included from category II, since they are all imported ready-made from a known alien (linguistic) origin, and their enumeration will not therefore add anything. All names are of settlements unless otherwise indicated. As a general rule the settlements with names from category I are smaller than those with names from category III. (I have included a few popular etymologies.)

1. *Ābander* Sarbāz, ?I
2. *Afšān* Sarāvān, III
3. *Anzā* Sarbāz, ?III
4. *Apter* Jāz Muriān, *q*, III
5. *Ārāmkān* Sarbāz, I
6. *Āšār* Sarāvān, *q*, III
7. *Āspīc* Sarāvān, ?III
8. *Bādk* Sarbāz, I
9. *Bahtāk* Sarbāz, *kaur*, I
10. *Bāhu* area of plain shown on map, ?III
11. *Bāhu Kalāt* Bāhu, *q*, ?III
12. *Bampur* Jāz Muriān, *q*. *, III

13. *Bampošt* mountain range, cf. map, III
14. *Bapātān* Sarbāz, I
15. *Baškard* western end of Makran range, ? I (cf. Eilers 1956: 187)
16. *Bazmān* Sarḥadd (cf. Eilers 1956: 183), III
17. *Benkal* Hong, I
18. *Bent* Makran range, *q.* *, III
19. *Berēs/an* Berēs is a port; Berēsan is a *kaur* in Salah Koh, I
20. *Bozdrangī* Salāh Koh, šep, I
21. *Bog/ān* Makran range (several occurrences), ?III
22. *Cahbār* port (Persian: Cāh Bahār), III
23. *Cāmp* Lāšār, III
24. *Daj* Daštiārī, I
25. *Dalgān* Jāz Muriān and Daštiārī, I
26. *Damāvand* (*Dunbāvand*) former name of Kūh-i Taftān in Sarḥadd (cf. Eilers, *AO* [1954] 269), III
27. *Dapkod* Šahri Kaur, I
28. *Daštiārī* area of plain, cf. map, III
29. *Daurak* Sarbāz, ?I
30. *Dāzandar* Šahri Kaur, I
31. *Delīg Kaur* Bagāband, I
32. *Dermān* Daštiārī, ?I
33. *Dezak* Sarāvān, *q*, III
34. *Dogdānok* Salāh Koh, *šēp*, I
35. *Drugī* Salāh Koh, *šēp*, I
36. *Ērafšān* Šahri Kaur, *q.* (16 miles from Afšān; Bal. *er* down), *q*, I/III
37. *Eškastagān* Sarāvān, I
38. *Espaka* Lāsār, *q*, *, III
39. *Espakānī* Salāh Koh, *šēp*, I
40. *Espētk* Salah Koh, *šēp*, I
41. *Ezbandak* Sarbāz, I
42. *Fannuc* (pronounced by Baluch: Pahnuc) Makran range, *q*, III
43. *Fīrūzabād* Sarbāz, *q*, III
44. *Gazab* ruined fort in Bāhu, I
45. *Gazaoz* Šahri Kaur, I
46. *Gazbastān* Salāh Koh, *kaur*, I
47. *Geh* (now renamed Nīkšahr) Makran range (P. Beh), *q*, *, III
48. *Gētān* Salāh Koh, *šēp*, I
49. *Gošt* Sarāvān, *q*, III
50. *Gunekān* Sarbāz, I
51. *Gureng* Sarbāz, I
52. *Gweimark* Sarbāz, I
53. *Gwāmīcdām* Salāh Koh, *šēp*, I
54. *Gwangī* Salāh Koh, *šēp*, I
55. *Gwartāb* Salāh Koh, *kaur*, I
56. *Gwasurkān* Sarbāz, I
57. *Gwātr* Bāhu, port, ?III
58. *Hamant* Makran range, *koh*, ?I
59. *Hansān* Salāh Koh, *šēp*, I
60. *Hēduc* Sarāvān, III
61. *Hīt* Sarbāz and Kāju, both with forts, ?III
62. *Hīcān* Makran range, I
63. *Homeiri* Kāju, I
64. *Hong* cf. map, I
65. *Hunak* Sarbāz, I
66. *Hušak* Sarāvān, *q*, ? III
67. *Īdk* Sarbāz, I
68. *Jaganī* Salāh Koh, *kaur*, I
69. *Jālq* Sarāvān, *q*, *, III
70. *Jamīdar* Sarbāz, I
71. *Jammīz* Salāh Koh, 2 rivers flowing N and S from one watershed (*jan* = woman, and *mīzag* = urinate)
72. *Jaurak* Sarāvān, *šēp*, I
73. *Jauren* Salāh Koh, *šēp*, I
74. *Jāz Muriān* cf. map, I
75. *Jazān* Sarbāz, *kaur*, I
76. *Junābād* Sarḥadd, III
77. *Kahīr* coastal plain (= name of tree), I
78. *Kajdar* Sarbāz, I

79. *Kāju kaur* cf. map, ? I
80. *Kallagān* Sarāvān, *q*, III
81. *Kallēnk* Jāz Muriān, I
82. *Kalpurkān* Sarāvān, ? III
83. *Kān* Sarbāz, I
84. *Kandez* Sarbāz, ? I
85. *Kant* Sarāvān, *q*, III
86. *Karagīn* Sarbāz, I
87. *Kāšok* Salāh Koh, *šahr* (= P. *qāšoq*), I
88. *Kātār* Sarbāz, I
89. *Kaurān* Sarāvān, I
90. *Kekkī* Sarāvān, I
91. *Kīškaur* Sarbāz, river and its basin, I
92. *Koh Birg* Sarāvān, *koh*, ? I
93. *Konārak* port (= diminutive of name of tree), I
94. *Kopk* Sarbāz, I
95. *Kozur* mountain range adjoining Salāh Koh, I
96. *Krucī* Salāh Koh, *kaur* (kruc = non-pedigree date palm), I
97. *Kuca* Daštiārī, small area (obl. Kucé-ā), ? I
98. *Kupag* Sarāvān, I
99. *Lādez* Sarḥadd, *q*. (cf. Eilers 1954:351), III
100. *Lāšār* cf. map, ? I
101. *Magas* Sarāvān, *q*, III
102. *Mamjor* Salāh Koh, I
103. *Margān* Salāh Koh, *šēp*, I
104. *Margu* Sarāvān, *šahr*, I
105. *Māškīd kaur* cf. map, ? III
106. *Maškotān* Sarāvān, ? III
107. *Maskotān* Makran range, ? III
108. *Mazakān* Sarbāz, I
109. *Mīnān* Sarbāz, I
110. *Mirjāwa* Sarḥadd, ? III
111. *Mog* Sarbāz, I
112. *Mordān* Salāh Koh, *šēp*, I
113. *Muredān* Salāh Koh, *kaur*, I
114. *Murtan/Multān* Sarāvān and W of Hong, I
115. *Nāgpahn* small nomadic area in Sarāvān (*nāg* = name of shrub), I
116. *Nāhuk* Sarāvān, *q*. (said to derive from *nāg*. cf. 115), ? I
117. *Nalēṭ* Daštiārī, *kaur*, I
118. *Naṛgwaḍ* Daštiārī, I
119. *Naskant* Sarbāz, III
120. *Nigwar* Daštiārī, I
121. *Nud* Sarbāz, I
122. *Nukdar* Šahri Kaur, I
123. *Ošnā* Salāh Koh, *šēp*, I
124. *Pahra* (P. Fahraj, now renamed Īrānšahr) Jāz Muriān, *q*, *, III
125. *Panān* Sarbāz, I
126. *Parkān* Sarbāz, I
127. *Pārud* Sarbāz, ? II
128. *Pāsele* Bagāband, I
129. *Paskoh* village in Sarāvān, *q*, III
130. *Patkān* Sarāvān, I
131. *Pendak* Sarbāz, I
132. *Pēšāmak* Sarbāz, I
133. *Pīp* Lāšār, I
134. *Pīrdān* Sarbāz, I
135. *Pīrsīr* Sarāvān, I
136. *Pīšīn* Sarbāz, III
137. *Pollān* Daštiārī, I
138. *Porrakant* Sarāvān, III
139. *Potān* Sarbāz, I
140. *Pozm* port, ? III
141. *Pukī* Salāh Koh (*puk* = crazy), I
142. *Qaṣr-i Qand* Kāju, *q*, *, III
143. *Rāsk* Sarbāz, *, III
144. *Rek* Bagāband, *kaur*, I
145. *Rīmdān* Bāhu, I
146. *Rudānī* Salāh Koh, *šēp*, I
147. *Salāh Koh* cf. map, I
148. *Salāt* Salāh Koh, *šēp*, I
149. *Salug* Salāh Koh, name of highest peak, I
150. *Sāmorān* Salāh Koh, *kaur*, I

151. *Samsur* Sarḥadd, plain, I
152. *Sand* Daštiārī and Bāhu, I
153. *Sānīc* Sarbāz, I
154. *Sarāvān* cf. map, I
155. *Sarbāz kaur* (cf. map) and basin, III
156. *Seb* (Persian: Sīb) Sarāvān, *q*, III
157. *Seken* Salāh Koh, I
158. *Sīnukān* Sarāvān, I
159. *Sulān* Sarbāz, I
160. *Suldān* Bāhu, I
161. *Surān* Sarāvān, I
162. *Sirjā* Bāhu, I
163. *Sirkup* Daštiārī, I
164. *Sīsād* Bāhu, I
165. *Šastun* Sarāvān, *q*, (P. Šahestān >Šahrestān), III
166. *Šurenkān* Sarāvān, I
167. *Šurgwaz* Bāhu, I
168. *Šušgel* Salāh Koh, *šahr*, I
169. *Talāng* Daštiārī, ? I
170. *Tamindān* Sarḥadd (= Damandān) * cf. Eilers 1954:284-5 and 334, III
171. *Tāp* mountainous area adjoining Salāh Koh to the south, I
172. *Tāpdēm*-Sarāvān, nomadic area, I
173. *Tīs* port, III
174. *Tongī* Salāh Koh, *koh*, I
175. *Tudak* Sarḥadd, I
176. *Urāmān* Sarbāz, I
177. *Warrāmdar* Salāh Koh, *kaur*, I
178. *Wāš*(*t*) Sarḥadd (P. Khẉāš, now written Khāš), *q*, *, III
179. *Wašnām* coastal plain, small area, I
180. *Weiag* Salāh Koh, *kaur*, I
181. *Zāmorān* extension of Salāh Koh eastwards over Šahri Kaur, I

III

I conclude this article with an enumeration of points of apparent sociological import – whether modern or historical – which have occurred to me at some stage of my work. Each begs one or more philological questions which I am not qualified to answer. My justification is that there is always a sociological reason for begging the philological question, and begging may not be an altogether unsuitable, even though abject, means of gaining an eventual answer.

(1) The first point is suitably introductory, and tentative. Beside some names in the list I have indicated the existence of a fort or at least the ruins of one. Since forts were not always built according to the same design, some were more conspicuous than others, some have been allowed to fall into more complete ruin than others, and during my work in the area I was not looking for forts, there are no doubt several others in places which I have not marked. Those I have so marked have two points in common: they are all among the more important centres of agriculture in the Province (in itself not so surprising since agriculture would obviously have been the most important thing to defend and the most difficult); and they all have names which would fall in the last of the three categories defined above. Names which occur in extant early Islamic texts are marked with an asterisk.

In most cases these coincide: a name with an asterisk also has a *q*. (One exception – Rāsk – may in fact be only apparent, since Rāsk was the main town of the (pre-Mongol) district known as Khoruj, the boundaries of which cannot be known for certain. Sarbāz is the name of the river that flows through Rāsk, and is applied as a regional name to include all the settlements which are watered by the river or its tributaries, from its sources down to where it changes names just below Rāsk. What is now known as 'the fort of Sarbāz' (in Persian simply Sarbāz) is a settlement (which includes the remains of an old fort) at a strategic confluence of the river with one of its main tributaries some way above Rāsk.) No category I names have forts, but the traditional Baluch political system was centred on the forts. It is tempting therefore to formulate the hypothesis that the Baluch political structure has assimilated itself to the structure which existed before the Baluch came, even though their ethos (of pastoral nomadism) is probably diametrically opposed to that of the original population which first built the forts in agricultural centres.

(2) In the Sarāvān region there is a much larger proportion of names which fall into the third category than elsewhere, yet none of them, save one – Jālq, in fact occur in the early texts. This might be taken to show that the region was one of the latest to be Baluchized, and also that it was more closely joined to the rest of Persia than the remainder of the Province. The topography tends to support this view, since it is the Makran range which constitutes the great barrier to communications. It is interesting also that the dominant family in the region during much of the last century (the Bārakzai) is of Afghan origin. We have already noticed that there are very few traditional settlements in the Sarḥadd. Most of these, similarly, are not to be found in the early texts. There is no obvious topographical border between the Sarḥadd and Sarāvān, and it is interesting that we should notice this similarity in the toponymy for if we turn to the *Iḥyā' ul-Mulūk* we see that they are both together treated as an appendage of Sīstān, and there are very few references to Baluch anywhere. But in this book most of the village names in Sarāvān are already mentioned. It is interesting also that apart from the eastern end of the Jāz Muriān depression Sarāvān is the only part of the Province which contains important clusters of villages depending entirely on *qanāts* for irrigation.

Similar factors are evident at the eastern end of the Jāz Muriān depression. Here there are large clusters of villages with a quite heterogeneous selection of names, but the three main centres – each with one of the only three forts – are Bampūr, Fahraj (Bal.: Pahra), and Apter, of which the first two are asterisked in the list, and all are category III. Once again, they are north of the Makran range and stand at the main entrance to the Province from the north and west.[14] The fort at Bampūr is the oldest and is situated by the stretch of the river which is perennial.

(3) The following names are duplicated outside the Province: (*a*) The case of Damāvand is perhaps the most obvious, though it is no longer used in the Province, (*b*) A less well known case is Multān which occurs twice in the Province, and again as the name of a famous city on one of the tributaries of the Indus (I have marked it category I in the list, because both Multāns within the Province appear to be Baluch foundations). (*c*) Hīt is another. Again it occurs twice in the Province, and once outside as the name of an historically famous city in Mesopotamia. (*d*) Another example is Junābād, which must surely be the same word as Gonābād. Gonābād is in Khorāsān north of the Qā'ināt and traditionally includes all the villages on a stretch of fertile plain sandwiched between salt desert and a range of mountains. In the mediaeval geographers (e.g. Yāqūt) it is Junābidh. It is perhaps relevant that Fīrūzābād is the only other toponym ending in -ābād in the Province, which is of any antiquity. (*e*) Eilers suggests[15] that the Halīlrud which flows into the Jāz Muriān depression from the north-west is a corruption of the name born by the Harē-rud and Harāt in Afghanistan. The place-name Harāt also occurs in Fārs. (*f*) Another case which might be included here is the question of the relationship between Gwātr and Gwādar, the former Muscadine port which lies just across the border in West Pakistan. (*g*) The Sipi already mentioned at Noṣratābād in the Sarḥadd recalls the Sibi and Siwi in Pakistani Makran, Sīb (Bal.: Seb) in the region of Sarāvān, and the adjective 'white' (P. sipīd – Bal. commonly drops final *d*; Bal. spēt). (*h*) Another example is Fahraj, of which there are several occurrences in Iran. Three are relatively well known: one near Yazd; one in the district of Narmāšīr, south-east of Bam; and the one listed here some fifteen miles east of Bampur in the Makran, which is in Bal. Pahra (though now officially renamed Īrānšahr). The name originally (in Middle Persian) meant 'watch', 'guard(-post)'. The last of these three occurrences is often mentioned in the geographers as Fahlfahra – though the first vowel is not certain. Bampur is sometimes written Banfohl. The *-pur* of Bampur means bridge, or perhaps ford. We could therefore read Fohlfahra and understand 'the watch on the ford'. It is surprising that a river as important as the Bampur river should not have a name of its own, but it is not surprising that a natural feature of such agricultural importance should carry a pre-Baluchi name. It appears to be related to two other names: Bam, and Bampošt. It seems possible

that Bampur and Fahraj were originally one settlement, or at least in one place and not fifteen miles apart, since the fort at Bampur was obviously (from its ruins and mound) a far older and more important construction than that at Fahraj, and Bampur was the more important settlement until some 75 years ago when it finally lost to Fahraj its function as military headquarters – because of the insalubriousness of its water supply, which came straight from the river. Fahraj lies above that part of the river which has perennial flow, and relies on *qanāts*. This is, in fact, another indication in the same direction, for Fahraj could not have been an important settlement before the arrival in the area of the skill of *qanāt* digging. It is possible, therefore, that at one time Bampur was the main settlement at the eastern end of the depression and situated at the site of the bridge over the river, and Fahraj was the appellation of a military post, and gradually became a proper name as a settlement grew up around it. It is, however, difficult to understand why there should ever have been a bridge or even a ford anywhere near Bampur, since the river is now only perennial for a very short stretch. The remainder of its course is subject to occasional torrential floods but these soon dry out, and there is no evidence for such climatic factors having been any different in the past. The only simple solution would be if *-pur* could indicate a dam, for the existence of at least some form of rudimentary dam is essential to any measure of agricultural use of the water and is thought to have existed for a very long time. (*i*) There are two areas called Sarāvān: one is the area within Persia drained by the Māškīd river and its tributaries; the other is a more important mountainous area in Pakistani Baluchistan. The Baluch say that in Pakistan the name denotes upland country as distinct from the neighbouring lowlands, but this does not seem to fit the Sarāvān in Persia. (*j*) There are at least two places called Dalgān; one in Daštiārī, and one at the north-east corner of the seasonal swamp in the Jāz Muriān depression. Both settlements rely on extremely rich alluvial soil as a major factor in their (agricultural) economy.

Professor Minorsky accounted for the existence of a second Damāvand in Baluchistan 'by the southward migration of the Baluch who seem to have left traces of their language in the oases of the Central Iranian Desert'.[16] This explanation, though attractive, seems to beg some historical questions, and would mean that the Baluch had 'Baluchized' names on their migration route and then planted an Iranian name (Damāvand) in the area where they finally came to rest. Besides, this mountain is called Damāvand before the Baluch are *supposed* to have arrived.

(4) The toponymical suffix *-kanθ*, of Sogdian origin, has been discussed by Minorsky.[17] Morgenstierne has related it to Kant and there exist also Naskant, Porrakant, and Qaṣr-i Qand (Bal.: Kasər Kand) in the Persian Makran.[18] If the derivation stands it could be a sign of Turkish influence. There are also Turkish elements in the vocabulary, though their acquisition is not easily explained. However, other forms of the root occur in other Iranian languages.

(5) Daurak also occurs in the Bakhtiārī mountains.[19]

(6) Finally, it should be noted that a few names have survived in pre-Mongol texts which are no longer identifiable.

Despite the inconclusive nature of the arguments presented in this article it will nevertheless be more than justified if it helps to re-open the question of the historical movements of 'the Baluch people' and the Baluchization of what is now called Baluchistan, and to strengthen existing impressions of the great historical and sociological complexities of the area.

NOTES

1 'Mongol place-names in Mukrī Kurdistan (Mongolica IV)', *BSOAS*, XIX (1957) 81.

2 Dr I. Gershevitch and Dr D. N. MacKenzie, have also very kindly advised me on some etymologies and have brought some references to my notice. I take this opportunity to express my gratitude for their help. They are not, of course, responsible for anything I have written.

3 This is discussed at greater length in Spooner, 'Politics, kinship and ecology in Southeast Persia', *Ethnology*, VIII/2 (1969) 139-52.

4 R. N. Frye, *Encyclopaedia of Islam*², art. 'Balūčistān'.

5 Cf. Sir Aurel Stein, *Archaeological reconnaissances in N.W. India and S.E. Iran* (London 1937).

6 Cf. Spooner, op. cit.

7 The variety of forms is discussed by P. Schwarz, *Iran im Mittelalter*, III, 250 ff.

8 Cf. also I. Afshār, in *Rāhnamā-i kitāb*, X/I (1967).

8*a* Ed. Manūchihr Sotūdeh (Tehran 1966).

9 See Stein op. cit.

10 Cf. the references gathered in Sa'īd Nafīsī, ed., *Tārīkh-i Baihaqī*, 1074.

11 In my 'Notes on the Baluchī spoken in Persian Baluchistan', *Iran* V (1967) 53.

12 Cf. Stein, op. cit., and B. de Cardi, 'Excavations at Bampur, S.E. Iran', *Iran*, VI (1968).

13 Spooner, 'Notes on the Baluchi spoken in Persian Baluchistan'.
14 See the discussion in Spooner, 'Politics, kinship and ecology in South-east Persia'.
15 'Der Name Damawend', *Archiv Orientální*, XXII (1954) 330.
16 'Mongol place names in Mukrī Kurdistan', 60.
17 Ibid., 78.
18 'Baluchi miscellanea', *Acta Orientalia*, XX (1948) 289.
19 Personal communication from Mr David Brooks.

S. M. STERN

Ya'qūb the Coppersmith and Persian National Sentiment

I. The Persian Nation in Islam

The part played by the Persians in Islamic civilization is one of the great themes of its history, and the forms in which Persian national sentiment accommodated itself to Islam are an important aspect of this theme. I shall deal here with one episode of this development of Persian national sentiment under Islam, but it will be useful for the appreciation of the episode to give an overall sketch of the development, at least so far as the early centuries of Islam are concerned.[1]

The great conquests of the seventh century (and to a large degree also their extensions in the eighth) were Islamic and Arab at the same time; in the first generation the terms Muslim and Arab were synonymous. The territories conquered by the Arab tribesmen under the Meccan-Medinan leadership were exploited in favour of the conquerors. From the very first moment some of the conquered accepted Islam, but significantly enough this could only be done by affiliation to one of the Arab tribes; the converts became 'clients' (*mawālī*), or second-class Arabs. Thus 'to become Muslim' could then on occasion be described by the phrase 'to become Arab'. Social and economic inducements had a great share in the conversion of the subject peoples, but one should not underestimate the religious element, especially since the different motives cannot be kept apart easily: the very success of the Muslim Arabs in imposing their domination could be taken, and was presumably often taken, as a proof of the truth of Islam. Moreover, whatever were the prevailing motives of the converts themselves, the next generations could not but be sincere and often fervent Muslims, and many of the great religious figures of early Islam were descendants of non-Arab converts. In view of the gradual levelling of conquerors and conquered, and their amalgamation into a common Islamic society, it was inevitable that the distinction between pure Arab and client should disappear. In the Umayyad period the clients strove against discrimination on the one hand by political action, on the other – in the field of ideas – by insisting on the common brotherhood of all Muslims. In the ʿAbbāsid period actual discrimination had more or less disappeared; instead of the 'Arab Empire' of the early caliphs and the Umayyads, we have an Islamic Empire. The Arab feeling of superiority lingered on but was of little practical importance.[2]

The gradual abolition of the barrier between Arab and client meant in some parts of the Islamic world the disappearance of national feeling among the clients; they were Muslims, and their national past meant little or nothing to them. This is all the more understandable, because it so happened that the national coherence of some of the peoples conquered by the Arabs was based on religion. The natives of Egypt showed their resistance to the Byzantine ruling class by adopting and clinging to a particular form of Christianity, Monophysitism, as opposed by the Orthodox Church of Byzantium. There was no secular Egyptian culture, and so when a Christian Egyptian was converted to Islam, he had no, or hardly any, 'national' traditions to preserve. The case of the Berbers is rather different; in contrast to the converted population of Egypt – and those of Syria, Mesopotamia and ʿIrāq, whose story was similar – they preserved their language and much of their social organization, so that they appear throughout Islamic history with a highly distinct character of their own. But since the Berbers also had no historical traditions of a national kind, this attachment to native institutions never took the form of an articulated national sentiment.

Of all the peoples incorporated into the Islamic empire the Persians possessed the strongest national identity. They could look back to a millennium of national history and their national sentiment was reinforced by their religion. Zoroastrianism was the state religion of the Sāsānian empire, and though orthodox Zoroastrianism was opposed by various heresies, they themselves showed a definitely Iranian character. It is not surprising that while many Persians joined the Arab ruling class and were integrated into Muslim society, others, remaining faithful to their ancestral religion, and full of nostalgia for the times when that religion had been dominant, would revolt against Islam and attempt the restoration of a Zoroastrian state. We are reminded of the rebellions of the Christians of Egypt in the middle of the eighth century and those of the superficially Islamicized ex-Christians of Spain (who made common cause with the Christians) as late as the turn of the ninth-tenth centuries. (In Spain the social discrimination against the *muwalladūn* – the new converts to Islam, corresponding to the *mawālī* of the East – continued much longer than elsewhere; this explains their making common cause with the Christians, a case to which there is no parallel in the East.) The last Persian revolts conducted in the name of the old national religion were put down by the end of the third decade of the third century A.H. (ninth century A.D.), and while a small minority of Persians continued to hold fast to Zoroastrianism, the majority came finally to terms with Islam.

Yet this did not mean that the Persians were giving up their national identity. They differed from all the other peoples which joined Islam by having a secular and not merely religious tradition of national life, strong enough to survive the change of religion. If a Copt, whose sense of identity was based on his belonging to a particular Christian Church, turned Muslim, he merged with the rest of the Muslims, and retained little of his former traditions. It was another matter with the Persians. Though in the first centuries of Islam the language of administration and culture – indeed the only language in which a Muslim could write anything – was Arabic, Persian remained the vernacular of Iran. But that was not all. The Berber language retained the same position in North Africa, but yet there was no 'Berber revival', comparable with the Persian revival. The Persians had something more, though I am not sure whether I can give a full account of this. They had historical traditions such as the national heroic epos, which kept alive the sentiment of a national past of Iran, from the mythical times till the times of the Sāsānid dynasty, and certainly this played a great part in not letting the Persians forget their identity however perfectly Islamicized they were. It seems that the descendants of the old Persian nobility were among those who preserved these heroic stories. Thus the Persian nation, though submerged in the common civilization of Islam, continued to exist.

Persians who occupied prominent positions as members of the bureaucracy in the Islamic empire and as men of letters, that is of Arabic letters, introduced Persian traditions into Arabic literature, so that many Persian elements became an integral part of the Arabic literature which formed the basis of Islamic education.[3] Some of these people went further and pointed with pride to the magnificence of Iran at the time when the Arabs were no better than savages. These protagonists of the Shuʿūbiyya lived at the time when the *de facto* emancipation of the Persian 'clients' had been accomplished and men of Persian ancestry occupied the highest positions in the Islamic empire. In so far as the Shuʿūbite movement had a concrete social purpose beyond being the literary expression of a romantic glorification of the Persian past, this can be found in the opposition to the still lingering idea of social superiority of men of pure Arab descent. A high-ranking official in government service might have to face a taunt by a pure Arab about his Persian origin; it was satisfactory to be able to retort that after all the Persians were better people than the Arabs.

The Shuʿūbiyya was a literary movement; the developments which led to profounder results occurred in other spheres, though they were made possible by the same motive which gave rise to it, that is the permeating presence of Persian national feeling. One of the important developments was the breaking up of the ʿAbbāsid caliphate and the rise of local dominions through governors who made themselves independent. This is a tendency which can be observed in all the provinces of the ʿAbbāsid Empire in the third/ninth century, from North Africa to Transoxiana, and is not an intrinsically Iranian development; owing, however, to the permanence of Iranian national traditions in their dominions, the local dynasties of Iran were led to foster them, thus assuming a part for which there is no parallel in the other lands of Islam. The poem to be discussed by us provides an instructive example of how an Iranian adventurer made use of Shuʿūbite notions in order to provide an ideology for his rule; its importance lies in the establishment of a link between the Shuʿūbiyya and the rise of the independent dynasties in Iran.

The most prominent symptom of the tendency of these local rulers to foster Persian culture, was their share in the revival of Persian literature. The earliest Persian poets appeared at the courts of the Ṭāhirids, Ṣaffārids, Sāmānids and Buwayhids. Since the analysis of the poem to which this article is chiefly devoted sheds new light on the attitude of the founder of the Ṣaffārid dynasty to Persian national sentiment, it is appropriate to examine also the evidence about his role in the rise of panegyrical poetry in Persian (below, section III). In the fourth/tenth century, when Persian poetry steadily gained ground, there arose also a prose literature in Persian, and by the eleventh century Persian literature, both in poetry and prose, reached full maturity.

In the fourth/tenth century successful dynasties of Persian origin – especially those from Gīlān and Daylam, lands recently converted to Islam and where Persian traditions were particularly alive – harked back to features of Persian antiquity. Thus, to mention two examples, Mardāwīj, descendant of the royal clan of Gīlān, is said to have adopted Sāsānid symbols of royalty, such as a crown of Sāsānid pattern, and to have aimed at the restoration of the Persian realm,[4] and the Daylamite Buwayhids introduced the old Persian title of *shāhānshāh*.[5] This revival of Persian traditions (however external) is a significant characteristic of the century which has been described with some justification as the 'Persian intermezzo' of Islamic history.[6] This development was, however, checked by the final emergence in the eleventh century of the Turkish military ruling class which henceforth dominated Islam. By that time, however, the Persian cultural revival had reached such an advanced stage that the Turkish rulers themselves fell under its spell and acted as its promoters. Largely through their action the eleventh century also saw a considerable territorial expansion, and it was of far-reaching consequence that the new provinces gained for Islam – such as India and Anatolia – though governed by Turkish military rulers (and in the case of Anatolia populated by Turks), became 'colonial territories' of Persian culture. Thus the Persian renaissance initiated in the third/ninth century and brought to maturity in the course of the next century, proved successful not only in Iran, but beyond it. This development proved of crucial importance for the whole later history of Islamic civilization. During its first centuries, Islamic civilization was unitarian, based on the Arabic language which was the medium of religious instruction as well as of secular literature. (This secular literature did incorporate, as we have seen, elements of Persian tradition, but in Arabic garb.) On the level of everyday life there were large differences between the various provinces of the Islamic world, but on top of this diversity at the lower level lay the single higher civilization. This unity was now breached, because the Persian literary creations remained unknown in those parts of the Islamic world which kept to Arabic as the only vehicle of literature.[7] The disruption of the unity was of course only relative, since, for one thing, Arabic and Arabic literature continued to play some role (even though diminishing) in the Persian and Turkish parts of the Islamic world, and provided a kind of binding factor between the different cultural provinces. Nevertheless, this breaking-up of the unitarian Islamic civilization into distinct cultural provinces – together with the final emergence of the Turks as the military masters of the greater part of the Islamic world, and the territorial extension of Islam beyond the limits it reached during the first great conquests – give the later centuries of Islam beyond the watershed of the eleventh century an aspect different from the first centuries.

II. Ibrāhīm b. Mamshādh's poem for Yaʿqūb the Coppersmith

For the convenience of the reader, I begin by recapitulating the main facts about Yaʿqūb, son of Layth, surnamed al-Ṣaffār, the Coppersmith.[8] Arriving at Zaranj, capital of Sijistān, from the countryside, he began as a coppersmith, joined the *ʿayyārūn* (gangs of young men), and gradually assumed a leading position in that milieu, until he was proclaimed in 247/861 amīr of the province and was recognized as such by the Ṭāhirid government of Khurāsān and by the caliph. In 250/864 he defeated the Zunbīl, the native ruler of al-Rukhkhaj (ancient Arachosia), the eastern neighbour of Sijistān, and in 251/865 the Khārijite leader ʿAmmār. In 255/869 he invaded the province of Fārs, but was persuaded by the caliph to evacuate it and to turn instead to the eastern marches of Khurāsān: he was appointed governor of Ṭukhāristān and Sind in addition to Sijistān. When, however, Yaʿqūb turned against the Ṭāhirid ruler of Khurāsān, Muḥammad b. Ṭāhir, captured his residence at Nīshāpūr, and took him prisoner (259/873), relations deteriorated between Yaʿqūb and the caliph, who objected to his high-handed usurpation of the governorship of Khurāsān. Yaʿqūb occupied Fārs and marched through Khūzistān to ʿIrāq, aiming at Baghdad itself. The regent al-Muwaffaq, brother of the caliph al-Muʿtamid, defeated him, however, near Dayr al-ʿĀqūl, on 2 Rajab 262/1 April 876. Yaʿqūb was wounded and retreated to Jundīshāpūr in Khūzistān. He succeeded in reoccupying Fārs, but died in Jundīshāpūr on 9 Shawwāl 265/4 June 879.

The poem discussed in the present article is by Abū Isḥāq Ibrāhīm b. Mamshādh,[9] a native of Isfahan. As such he figured in the famous *History of Isfahan* by Ḥamza al-Iṣfahānī, an author of the fourth/tenth century; his book is lost, but it was used copiously by Yāqūt in his *Dictionary of Learned Men*. The article on Ibrāhīm b. Mamshādh in Yāqūt's *Dictionary* is also taken from Ḥamza's work. Ḥamza states that Ibrāhīm was a secretary, and later a boon-companion of the caliph al-Mutawakkil (232–47/847–61), and gives two different accounts of the way in which he left the court of Baghdad to join Yaʿqūb the Coppersmith. According to one story he disliked the unsettled conditions after the murder of al-Mutawakkil and decided to seek his fortune in Sijistān, whereas according to another account he was sent with an embassy to Yaʿqūb by the caliph al-Muʿtamid (258–79/870–92) and the regent al-Muwaffaq (261–78/875–91), and was persuaded by Yaʿqūb to remain. Yāqūt decides in favour of the second alternative, because he thinks it is borne out by the poem with which we are concerned. The poem was written by Ibrāhim on behalf of Yaʿqūb who was supposed to pronounce it. The violent attack on the ʿAbbāsid caliph suggests that the poem was written after Yaʿqūb's final break with the caliph, probably in the course of the invasion of ʿIrāq (Jumādā II 262/March 876); it is not likely that it belongs to the period after Yaʿqūb's defeat: the enmity to the caliph would be understandable, but the confident tone less so. To tell the truth I cannot quite see how the poem can help to decide whether Ibrāhim went to Yaʿqūb's court after al-Mutawakkil's death, i.e. at an early date of Yaʿqūb's career, or just before the invasion of ʿIrāq; but at any rate this point is of little importance. Be that as it may, if we believe the end of the story as told by Ḥamza, the high favour which Ibrāhīm found with Yaʿqūb proved fatal to him, since his envious rivals accused him of treacherous intelligence with the caliph's government, and the poet was killed.

Here is the poem, first in the original,[10] then in an English translation.

انا ابن الأكارم من نسل جم   وحائز إرث ملوك العجم
ومحيى الذى باد من عزّهم   وعفّى عليه طوال القدم
وطالب أوتارهم جهرةً   فمن نام عن حقّهم لم أنم
يهمّ الأنام بلذّاتهم   ونفسى تهمّ بسَوْق الهمم
الى كل أمر رفيع العماد   طويل النجاد منيف العلم
وانى لآمل من ذى العلا   بلوغ مرادى بخير النسم
معى عَلَم الكابيان الذى   به أرتجى ان أسود الأمم
فقُلْ لبنى هاشم أجمعين   هلمّوا الى الخلع قبل الندم
ملكناكم عنوة بالرما   ح طعنا وضربا بسيف حذم
وأولاكم الملك آباؤنا   فما إن وفيتم بشكر النعم
فعودوا الى أرضكم بالحجاز   لأكل الضباب ورعى الغنم
فانى سأعلو سرير الملوك   بحدّ الحسام وحرف القلم

I am the son of the noble descendants of Jam, and the inheritance of the kings of Persia has fallen to my lot.

I am reviving their glory which has been lost and effaced by the length of time.

Before the eyes of the world, I am seeking revenge for them – though men have closed their eyes and neglected the rights of those kings, yet I do not do so.

Men are thinking about their pleasures, but I am busy with directing my aspirations

To matters of high import, of far-reaching consequence, of lofty nature.

I hope that the Highest will grant that I may reach my goal through the best of men.[11]

With me is the banner of Kābī, through which I hope to rule the nations.

Say then to all sons of Hāshim: 'Abdicate quickly, before you will have reason to be sorry:

We have conquered you by force, by the thrusts of our spears and the blows of our sharp swords.

Our fathers gave you your kingdom, but you showed no gratitude for our benefactions.

Return to your country in the Ḥijāz, to eat lizards and to graze your sheep;

For I shall mount on the throne of the kings, by the help of the edge of my sword and the point of my pen!'

This precious document, hidden in Yāqūt's great biographical dictionary, has been hitherto neglected by historians, although it is true that a few lines, known from other authors before the publication of Yāqūt's text, did not pass unnoticed. Lines 1, 7-8 and 11-2 are quoted in Rāghib al-Iṣfahāni's anthology *Muḥāḍarāt al-Udabā'* (Cairo 1287/1870) I, 219-20. A portion of this anthology was published and translated much earlier by G. Flügel; misled, however, by the Vienna MS which served as the basis for his edition, the text was published by him as a work by al-Thaʿālibī and under the fictitious title of *Vertraute Geselle des Einsamen* (Vienna 1827). The lines from our poem are found on p. 272, but proved too much for the youthful editor, whose translation is rather faulty. The verses quoted by Rāghib (or as they thought, by al-Thaʿālibī) were used by two eminent scholars of the nineteenth century. F. Rückert translated the lines in an appendix of his famous German translation of the *Ḥamāsa*, published in 1846 (II, 245), and I. Goldziher availed himself of them in his classical study on the Shuʿūbiyya (*Muhammedanische Studien*, I, 164).[12] But the quotation in the anthology did not allow a true appreciation of the poem, not so much because only a few lines are reproduced, but chiefly because the circumstances of its composition are obliterated. Rāghib says that these lines, as well as a verse from another poem, are by 'al-Mūbad'. Flügel writes 'al-Mowebbed', Rückert 'Elmu'ebbed (Elmobed)', Goldziher 'Mu'bad', taking this as the name of the poet. This is obviously not what the anthologist meant; he nonchalantly attributed the verses, which exalt the glory of Persia, to 'the *mūbad*', the Zoroastrian priest. (Indeed, he quotes yet another verse by 'the *mūbad*', which in reality is a famous verse by Bashshār

b. Burd, who boasts in it of his noble Persian ancestry, but also of his status as a client of the Arab tribe of the Banū ʿĀmir b. Ṣaʿṣaʿa: 'My branches belong to those noble men the Banū ʿĀmir, while my root is among the Quraysh of Persia'. The verse is often quoted in the name of Bashshār, e.g. in the *Aghānī*, III, 21.) Rückert fancifully assigned our poem to the period of the Arab conquests under Abū Bakr and ʿUmar. Goldziher did not follow him in this error, but, without having the information about its background, naturally enough saw in it a conventional expression of Shuʿūbite ideas. He shed light on its literary antecedents by putting it against the background of the Shuʿūbite movement, from whose literature various features of the poem – the pride in noble Persian descent, the exaltation of the Persian nation, and the mocking of the Arabs with their Bedouin ancestry – are derived. Now that we have the full text (or let us say a fuller text, since we cannot be absolutely sure that Ḥamza or Yāqūt have not omitted some verses) and know the true background of the poem – that it comes from the entourage of Yaʿqūb the Coppersmith and is meant to express his own aspirations – we can appreciate its full meaning and its great importance.

The poet puts his verses into the mouth of Yaʿqūb the Coppersmith himself, and this fiction raises the question how far the ideas expressed in the poem are really those of the ruler and how far those of the poet. Put, however, in this form the question rather misses the point. We have here a piece of political propaganda, and as in all cases of propaganda it is more important to ask what effect it was meant and expected to achieve among the public than to try to assess how seriously it was taken by the ruler whose interests it promoted or by the poet who actually wrote it.

The Coppersmith is represented as the descendant of the ancient kings of Iran. Jam, better known under the fuller form of Jamshīd, was the mythical ancestor of all the Iranian kings. Thanks to the *History of Sīstān* we know in detail the noble lineage claimed for Yaʿqūb: Yaʿqūb, son of Layth, son of al-Muʿaddal, son of Ḥātim, son of Māhān, son of Kay Khusraw, son of [the Sāsānid king] Ardashīr, son of Qubād [better known as Shīrūya], son of Khusraw (II) Aparwīz, the famous Sāsānid king, whose genealogy is of course derived, through a long chain, from Jamshīd.[13] Similar tributes to the strength of the Iranian national traditions were paid also by other local dynasties before and after the Ṣaffārids. The Ṭāhirids claimed descent from the great hero Rustam, the Sāmānids from Bahrām Chūbīn. Later, the Ziyārids – who came from the 'royal' clan of Gīlān – claimed descent from the Sāsānid king, while the Daylamite Buwayhids –

mere upstarts, even in comparison with the Ziyārids – had a genealogical tree fabricated which traced them back to the Sāsānid king Bahrām Gūr.[14]

The line 'With me is the banner of Kābī, through which I hope to rule the nations' alludes to an even more concrete symbol of the old Iranian glory. I must, however, insert here a textual parenthesis. In the edition of Yāqūt's book (based on a unique and late MS) the first words read *'indī 'alamu' l-kā'ināti* 'With me is the banner of the things that are', which does not make much sense.[15] On reading Yāqūt's text, I have emended the words and read *'alamu'l-kābiyāni*, 'the banner of Kābī' – Kābī being the archaic form of the name Kāwī. I am perhaps permitted the slight vanity of mentioning this, though I soon found out that the emendation had been made before me. Flügel printed the words in question in his *Vertraute Geselle*, discussed above, as *'alima' l-kābyānu*, which makes no sense at all, but gives the clue; and the correct form and the true meaning were recognized by Rückert, who made a note in his translation (also referred to above): 'Read *'alam ulkabiyani*'. The archaic form *kābiyān* for *kāwiyān* is often found in Arabic writers.

The 'Banner of Kāwī', *drafsh-i kāwiyān* in Persian, was the imperial banner of the Sāsānids.[16] It was captured by the Arabs in the battle of Qādisiyya in the year 636 or 637; an account of its capture and destruction is to be found in historians such as al-Ṭabarī and al-Mas'ūdi,[17] who also give some details about its appearance (it was made of panther skin and was twelve cubits long and eight broad). According to Christensen's plausible hypothesis the name *drafsh-i kāwiyān* originally meant 'imperial banner' (derived from *kāwī*, later *kay* = 'king'). When the true etymology was forgotten, the word gave rise to legends about the smith Kāwa in the distant past who gave the sign of revolt against the monster Dahāk by hoisting his leather apron as a banner; the expression *drafsh-i kāwiyān* was taken to mean 'the banner of Kāwī'.

It is not quite clear what exactly the poet means by saying that Ya'qūb had with him the banner of Kāwī. Did Ya'qūb really have a banner made in imitation of the old imperial banner, or have we to reject such a literal explanation and assume that the phrase wished to say no more than that Ya'qūb was renewing the glory of Iran? I do not dare to commit myself to either of the alternatives.

Thus the former coppersmith, who by the time Ibrāhīm b. Mamshādh's poetry was composed had become a great lord indeed, ruler of many of the Iranian provinces of the caliphate, claims to be a descendant of the Sāsānid kings and boasts of raising again their banner which had been torn by the victorious Arabs in the battle which put an end to the glory of Iran. He is the legitimate heir of the ancient kings and strives to take revenge for their lost inheritance. It is idle to speculate how far the claim to be a descendant of the Sāsānids was taken seriously by Yaʿqūb himself, the poet, or even the public. It is a different matter when Yaʿqūb claims to act as a restorer of ancient Persian glory. Obviously the main spring of his activity was to acquire power; but it is not impossible, it is even probable, that he aimed at being more than a successful adventurer and delighted in seeing himself as the heir of the Persian monarchs of old. To be sure, most likely such ideas would not come to him on his own, but would be suggested to him by his entourage – by Shuʿūbite men of letters coming to his court (such as our poet) and local supporters among whom Persian traditions had remained alive. Indeed, the three interested parties – the ruler (subject of the propaganda), the poet (who gives expression to it), and the public (at whom it is aimed) are inextricably involved in the spreading of such ideas.

It is essential to keep in mind that the poem is not merely a general piece of propaganda aiming to boost Yaʿqūb's prestige, but a political manifesto with a quite particular objective. It is impossible to say at which stage of his career from the leadership of a small gang to the rule over vast tracts of land, had Yaʿqūb adopted the ideology of Persian national restoration. This poem at any rate was written at a late stage in his life when he was engaged in hostilities against the caliph, and its edge is turned against the ʿAbbāsid dynasty. The contrast between the old civilization of Iran and the barbaric state of the Arab Bedouins is a commonplace of Shuʿūbite literature, in which the Arabs are railed at for their diet of snakes, mice and lizards.[18] Here this old chestnut of the Shuʿūbiyya is used with deadly effect against the ʿAbbāsids who are admonished to relinquish their throne to Yaʿqūb, leader of the victorious Persian armies. There is an additional feature, of great interest. The ʿAbbāsids are accused of ungratefulness, since it was 'our fathers' who had put the rule into their hands. The reference is to the Khurāsānian armies which had defeated the Umayyads; these consisted, as is well known, only partly of elements of Persian origin, so that the argument is not quite correct. But propaganda need not be based on accurate facts in order to be effective.

III. The revival of Persian poetry under the Ṣaffārids

Ibrāhīm b. Mamshādh's poem, preserved by luck in Yāqūt's compilation, informs us of the strength of Persian national sentiment under Yaʿqūb and how he made use of it for political purposes. The eleventh-century *History of Sistān*, which is in general an important source for the history of the Ṣaffārids (we have already quoted it in connection with Yaʿqūb's genealogical claims), contains invaluable information about the part taken by Yaʿqūb and other members of the Ṣaffārid dynasty in the rise of classical Persian poetry. There existed a rich Persian literature in the pre-Islamic period, but the conversion of the Persians to Islam cut them off from both religious and secular books written in what we call 'Middle Persian', which remained comprehensible only to those who kept to Zoroastrianism. The vernacular spoken in Iran remained Persian – but the only literary language employed by Muslims was Arabic. Naturally enough, Arabic books – in addition to the copious loan-words borrowed by Arabic from Persian – frequently quote Persian phrases used by Persians, and they have also preserved some verses in Persian spoken on different occasions. These short pieces are not, however, evidence for a Persian poetical literature. If someone or other composes a ditty in the vernacular, we may appreciate the linguistic interest of these documents, we may even ask how far there are traces in them of the ancient Iranian versification – but we cannot consider them as signs of a conscious will to create again a literature in the Persian language in the full sense of the word.[19] It is only about the middle of the third/ninth century[20] that we find professional men-of-letters who begin to compose poetry in Persian, and since they were brought up on Arabic poetry and wrote it themselves, the Persian poetry written by them follows Arabic prosody and is also in its contents deeply influenced by Arabic poetry.

The author of the *History of Sistān* claims to know the first poem composed in Persian and attributes it to an Arabic poet who lived at the court of Yaʿqūb the Coppersmith. His story is (pp. 209 ff.) that after the conquest of Herat by Yaʿqūb and the execution of ʿAmmār the Khārijite in 253/867, an Arabic poem was composed in honour of the victorious amīr:

> God has honoured the inhabitants of the city and the province through the rule of Yaʿqūb, a man full of bounty and strength.
>
> His valour gives security to the population and his glorious appearance is a protection sent by God to the cities and the province.[21]

Since Yaʿqūb had no education, he was unable to understand the poem when it was recited in his presence, and he exclaimed: 'What is the use of saying to me things which I cannot understand'. The narrator tells:

> At that time no literature (*nāma*) existed in Persian. . . . Muḥammad b. Waṣīf began to compose poetry in Persian. He was the first to do so,

and no one had done so before him; because as long as they were Zoroastrians (*Pārsiyān*), there were recited for them compositions to the accompaniment of music, in the *khusrawānī* mode[22]; when the Persian rule was destroyed and the Arabs arrived, poetry was written amongst them [the Persians] in Arabic, and everybody possessed the knowledge of Arabic poetry. No great man worthy of having poems composed in his honour arose among the Persians before Yaʿqūb, excepting Ḥamza b. ʿAbd Allāh the Khārijite, who was a scholar and knew Arabic, so that his poets composed their verses in Arabic; moreover, most of his army were Arabs and Arabic-speaking (*Tāziyān*).[23]

When Yaʿqūb killed Zunbīl[24] and ʿAmmār the Khārijite,[25] took Herat, and was granted Sīstān, Kirmān and Fārs,[26] Muḥammad b. Waṣīf composed the following poem[27]:

O amīr, to whom the amīrs of the world, noblemen and commoners, are but slaves, servants, clients, dog-keepers and valets!

There is an inscription on the Tablet from all eternity: 'Give the kingdom to Abū Yūsuf Yaʿqūb b. Layth, the mighty hero'.

Zunbīl came with . . . and a thump like a panther[28]; the army of Zunbīl was broken and his den turned into dust.

You recited, O amīr: 'To whom belongs the kingdom', in confident faith; with 'a small party' . . . your desire of that army.[29]

ʿAmmār's life desired you, and denounced its allegiance to him; your sword was an arbiter between the mild animals and the beasts of prey.

His lifetime came to you, so that you may live as long as Noah. His body is on the Ākar Gate, his head on the Ṭaʿām Gate.[30]

The rest of the poem is not reproduced by the author of the *History of Sīstān*. On the other hand he quotes another panegyric on Yaʿqūb by a certain Bassām Kūrd composed under the inspiration of Muḥammad b. Waṣīf's poem (pp. 211-12), and yet a third poem on the same events by Muḥammad b. Mukhallad (p. 212), as well as further poems by Muḥammad b. Waṣīf from later years, alluding to an event in the career of Yaʿqūb's brother and successor, ʿAmr b. al-Layth (pp. 253, 260), as well as to the captivity of ʿAmr's two grandsons, Ṭāhir and Yaʿqūb (296/908–9); this poem (pp. 286-7) is the latest one preserved by Muḥammad b. Waṣīf, and written almost half a century after his first known poem, must belong to his old age. There is no need to quote these poems (some of which are difficult to interpret) since our aim is not a philological or literary exegesis of the early poetry. The question which is relevant for us is whether the account of the *History of Sīstān* about the rise of Persian poetry is likely to be true. I think the story bears all signs of verisimilitude – one feels that something like this must have happened. We have an uneducated ruler, who can make no head or tail of the Arabic panegyrics composed in his honour, and a secretary trained in Arabic eloquence and poetry who conceives the idea of composing a panegyric in Persian, imitating Arabic prosody and poetical style. Since we have seen that the entourage of Yaʿqūb showed pride in their being Persians, we may well suspect (although the *History of Sīstān* says nothing of the sort) that poetry in Persian was favoured also because of a sentimental attachment to the national language.

Two other questions which occur are whether Muḥammad b. Wāṣīf's poem of 253/867 is indeed the first poem in Persian (in the sense explained above: a poem in 'classical' Neo-Persian composed according to Arabic prosody) and if so whether other attempts at writing Persian poetry were due to his inspiration. I do not think we can give definitive answers to these questions. The poet Ḥanẓala of Bādghīs is said to have been in the service of the Ṭāhirids, and thus to have belonged to an older generation than Muḥammad b. Waṣīf. A verse by him is said to have incited the adventurer Aḥmad al-Khujistānī to engage in the profession of arms; if this indication were reliable, the verse could be dated before the middle of the century. The authenticity of the verse is doubtful, but there is no reason to deny that the attribution of the poet to a period before Muḥammad b. Waṣīf could be correct. The fragments ascribed to him are lyrical verses, so that it would be possible to conclude that lyrical poetry in Persian was written before the panegyrics.[31] Is there a connection running through the rise of the various genres, in other words, was the first poet to write verses of a certain genre – for example the first writer of panegyrics, Muḥammad b. Waṣīf, if he was the first – inspired by the existence of earlier Persian poetry even if belonging to another genre (say lyrical poetry)? Also, within the same genre, were poets belonging to a subsequent generation necessarily acquainted with the work of their predecessors and have we to assume the existence of one originator who was followed by later poets? Or ought we to envisage, instead of a single common source, the possible existence of several independent sources? We have far too few texts from the earliest period to be able to decide such delicate problems. The author of the *History of Sīstān* is positive about Muḥammad b. Waṣīf being the first poet in Persian – or at least the first poet of panegyrics. But he obviously has his own province in mind; when he says that there was no great man before Yaʿqūb the Coppersmith excepting Ḥamza the Khārijite, we have to supply 'in Sīstān', rather than 'in Iran'. Thus if there existed panegyrics in Persian in other provinces, they might have been beyond his ken.

I should like to draw attention to a text dealing with the beginnings of Persian poetry which, though it does not give the answer to the questions posed by us, is of some interest.

The passage is found in the introduction of the theologico-philological glossary by the famous Ismāʿīlī leader Abū Ḥātim al-Rāzī, the *Kitāb al-Zīna*, which contains a section where the author – though he says that Persian was his native tongue – wishes to establish the superiority of Arabic language above other languages, and more especially Persian.[32]

> 'We find that no other nation has metrical and regular poetry like the Arabs. The texts used by the Persians for their songs are something between poetry and prose, not having the metre and the regularity of Arabic poetry. These texts are composed as rhymed prose and adapted to melodies; when they produce them they enjoy themselves and lengthen their voices in singing them. The texts do not follow the metre and rhyme of poetry, but are merely aimed at causing enjoyment and raising desires in the soul. They contain no panegyric, satire or boasting; they do not describe wars and battles, do not fix genealogies, are not concerned with glorifying noble deeds and memorable actions, enumerating titles for glory or shame, describing horses, camels, wild animals, deserts, wind, rain, wanderings to find pasture, and other subjects of poetry which would take too long to enumerate in detail.
>
> That the Persians had no poetry can be proved by the fact that the Persian language has no word for "poet" (*shāʿir*); similarly, only Arabic has a word for "poetry" (*shiʿr*). When al-Aʿshā paid a visit to the king of Persia and the king asked who he was, they told him *surūd-gū ba-tāzī*, i.e. "a singer in Arabic".'

Abū Ḥātim tells the story about the king's comment on al-Aʿshā's famous verse 'I am sleepless – whence comes this sleeplessness which keeps me awake, though I am not ill and not in love?' (*Dīwān*, xxxiii, 1): 'He must then be a brigand'. Abū Ḥātim is indignant about the ignorance of 'that barbarian', who, though being a king whose office must have caused many worries, did not know that someone who is neither ill, in love, or a brigand, can still suffer from sleeplessness.

> 'Al-Aʿshā was described to him as *surūd-gū ba-tāzī*, because they had no name for "poet", and neither knew poetry nor had they collections of

poetry. That poetry in Persian which they have now invented is meaningless speech which cannot serve as proof, is useless and is not collected among the Persians as poetry is collected among the Arabs, whose poetry has manifest usefulness and evident excellence. It [modern Persian poetry] is a new-fangled, not an old, thing: when they heard poetry in Arabic they pretended to imitate it in this fashion. I have heard from various knowledgeable people that the first man to compose poetry in Persian was a certain person from Nīshāpūr, not a very long time ago. In contrast, the old songs in Persian had no metres and followed no rhymes, as we have said above. They said to the king of Persia *surūd-gū ba-tāzī*, which means "a singer in Arabic": "singing" is not the same as poetry but a separate word. Only that part of poetry is called "singing" which is about soft subjects, love-poetry addressed to women, concerned with such matter alone. In poetry too we find something like this, e.g. the verse by Jarīr: "Those eyes with their white and black colour strongly delineated have killed us, nor did they revive those dead among us". Poetry, however, has many other branches in addition to singing, such as those subjects which, as we have said, the Arabs have cultivated: panegyric, satire, etc., or incitement to strive after the other world and encouragement to do good and show kindness to people and to avoid sins and such actions which would be shameful if known to others – such as is the verse by Labīd: "Every man will one day know what he has striven for, when the actions will be laid bare in the presence of God". This is something quite different from singing which encourages sins and makes one reckless in doing forbidden and shameful actions and incites one to indulge in them, as the poet [al-Aḥwaṣ] says: "If you do not enjoy yourself and do not take part in dissipation, be a dry, hard piece of stone!" This kind of verse may be called "song", but the other kinds are not songs and cannot be called by that name. Many kings, as well as other eminent and pious men have composed and recited poems, and it is permissible for them to know poetry, the knowledge of which is in fact part of their education and adds to their excellence; if they compose or recite poetry, we are not allowed to say: So-and-so is a singer, or so-and-so sings, but this would be injurious and humiliating for them. Thus it is clear how different poetry is from singing. One who composes poetry or recites it is by no means to be described as a singer, and stands high above the lowly state of singers and the low repute which they are given by learned and intelligent people.'

This account of ancient Persian poetry (which is not considered as true poetry at all) has some points of contact with the account in the *History of Sīstān*. The author of that *History* says that in the Sāsānid period the Persians had poems set to music; but he implies that such compositions are not poems in the proper sense of the word. This is the main idea of Abū Ḥātim, who explains in detail that the songs of the Persians cannot be considered as poetry. The argument is of course based on a *petitio principii*, since it is implied that by definition 'poetry' is that which conforms to the characteristics of Arabic poetry: is based on quantitative metre and shows the conventional contents of Arabic poetry. Thus, naturally 'we find that no other nation has metrical and regular poetry like the Arabs'. This generalization also shows whence Abū Ḥātim and the *History of Sīstān* derive their thesis about the absence of 'Poetry' among the ancient Persians. It was the protagonists of the supremacy of the Arabic language against the Shuʿūbiyya who insisted that only the Arabs did possess poetry. The conclusion was reached on *a priori* arguments rather than on empirical knowledge of other literature; it is typical that one of the defenders of the thesis pretends to have examined Greek poetry and found that it had no prosody :[33] Thus we need not assume by any means that those who laid down the law about the ancient Persians having had no poetry based their judgement on an actual knowledge of poetical texts from the Sāsānian period (although it is correct that ancient Persian verse was not quantitative but was based on counting of the syllables).[34] It was enough that they knew about the existence of music in that period and concluded that its poetry was merely meant as text for it and was unworthy to be called real poetry.[35]

Abū Ḥātim quotes in support of this theory an anecdote also known from an earlier writer, Ibn Qutayba,[36] according to which the famous Arab poet al-Aʿshā was described to the Sāsānid king as 'one who recites songs in Arabic'. (Incidentally, Abū Ḥātim's text allows us to restitute the corrupted Persian phrase in Ibn Qutayba's text: we have to read *asrūdh-gū badh tāẓī*. The Middle Persian form of the preposition 'in' was *pat*, and *badh* may be the Arabic spelling for *padh*, a later form of *pat* – Abū Ḥātim gives for the older *padh tāẓī* ['in Arabic'] the modern form *ba-tāẓī*.)[37] The argument is of course rather weak and suggests that the speculations of these authors were not really based on a knowledge of actual poetical texts from the Sāsānian period.

On the other hand, Abū Ḥātim and the author of the *History of Sīstān* are perfectly right in saying that Persian poetry in Arabic style began sometime in the middle of the third/ninth century. The historian of Sīstān asserts that it was born in his country; Abū Ḥātim quotes a story according to which the first Persian poet in the new style was a man from Nīshāpūr. Unfortunately he is so vague that we cannot do much with this piece of information. Does the story refer to Ḥanẓala of Bādghīs? Or some other poet of Nīshāpūr of the Ṭāhirid or Ṣaffārid period? It is idle to speculate.

We have seen two sides of Yaʿqūb's role as a promoter of Persian revival. He posed as a restorer of the ancient Persian kingdom; in this role he found some successors, but on the whole such aspirations led to no significant results. On the other hand through the impetus which he gave to the development of neo-Persian poetry he counts among the initiators of a historical process of the first importance.

NOTES

1 The various processes summarized here are on the whole well known, but I may perhaps claim to have arranged them in a better logical order than is usually done and to have put in a clearer light one or two features. References to the sources and modern literature can be found in various chapters of B. Spuler's *Iran in früh-islamischer Zeit* (Wiesbaden 1952). ('The progress of the Islamisation of Persia', 133ff.; 'National sentiment', 225ff.; 'Linguistic conditions', 237ff.). The details are not always accurate.

2 On the Arab feeling of superiority and the contrasting ideology of equality in Islam, I. Goldziher has assembled a documentation of marvellous richness in his essay ''Arab and 'Ajam', *Muhammedanische Studien*, I, 101ff. (English translation–with annotation brought up to date–edited by S. M. Stern (London 1968) 98ff.)

3 For this and the conflict between the promoters of Persian and Arabic literary traditions, respectively, cf. H. A. R. Gibb, 'The Social Significance of the Shuʿūbiyya', *Studia Orientalia Ioanni Pedersen ... Dicata* (Copenhagen 1953) 105-14 (= *Studies on the Civilization of Islam*, 62-73). The classical study on the Shuʿūbiyya is Goldziher's essay in the *Muhammedanische Studien*, I, 147ff. (English translation, I, 137ff.)

4 Al-Masʿūdī, IX, 27-8; Miskawayh, I, 316.

5 See M. Kabir, 'The Assumption of the Title of Shahanshah by the Buwayhid Rulers', *Journal of the Asiatic Society of Pakistan.* (1959) 41-8; S. M. Stern, 'The Coins of Āmul', *Numismatic Chronicle* (1967) 264.

6 This was a favourite idea of Minorsky and was expressed by him in *La Domination des Dailamites* (Paris 1932) 21, and elsewhere.

7 Gibb closes his article on the Shuʿūbiyya with the following passage: 'The Persian materials admitted [into Arabic literature] by Ibn Qutaiba closed the canon, as it were. All later Arabic works relating to government and courtly life draw on him, directly or indirectly. Of the later

Persian works, such as the *Shāhnāma* of Firdawsī or the *Siyāsatnāma* of Niẓām ul-Mulk, nothing entered into Arabic literature or the standard Islamic works on ethics. It is perhaps not difficult to explain why this was so. For the Sasanian strands which had been woven into the fabric of Muslim thought were, and remained, foreign to its native constitution. The ethical attitudes which they assumed were in open or latent opposition to the Islamic ethic, and the Sasanian tradition introduced into Islamic society a kernel of derangement, never wholly assimilated yet never wholly rejected.' Whatever one thinks of the idea that the Sāsānid elements were 'rationed' because they were foreign to the 'native constitution' of Muslim thought, the fact that Persian classics left hardly any trace in later Arabic literature is largely explained by the barrier created through the rise of Persian literature.

8 See Th. Nöldeke, 'Jakub, der Kupferschmied und seine Dynastie', *Orientalische Skizzen* (Berlin 1892) 185-217; W. Barthold, 'Zur Geschichte der Ṣaffāriden', *Festschrift Th. Nöldeke zum 70. Geburtstage gewidmet* (Giessen 1906) I, 177-91; B. Spuler, *Iran in früh-islamischer Zeit*, 69ff.

9 The name Mamshādh (not in F. Justi's *Iranisches Namensbuch*) finds its explanation when put next to Bābshādh (Justi, 55). That name is composed with *bāb*, 'father', and *shādh* (modern *shād*) 'joyful', and obviously means 'the father is joyful'–delighted by the birth of a son (rather than '[the child is] joyful because of his father [who is still alive]', as Justi has it). *Mam* seems then to be a familiar form for 'mother, mummy' (cf. *mām*), and Mamshādh = 'the mother is joyful'. (Also Dilshād, Justi, p. 84, is more likely to mean '[one who makes] the heart joyful' rather than '[one who is] joyful in his heart'.)

10 *Irshād al-arīb*, ed. Margoliouth (London 1923–6) I, 322-3.

11 I am not quite certain that I have correctly understood this phrase. I take *khayr al-nasam*, literally 'the best of those who breathe', as 'the best of people', referring to Ya'qūb's armies.

12 Cf. the English translation, 151-2.

13 *Ta'rīkh Sīstān*, 200-2.

14 See references in Spuler, *Iran in früh-islamischer Zeit*, 354. That the Ziyārids belonged to the 'royal clan' (*shāhānshāhwand*) of Gīlān we learn from fol. 3v of the extracts of al-Ṣābi's *Kitāb al-Tāj* preserved in a Ṣan'ā' MS (about which cf. M. S. Khan, in *Arabica* (1965) 267ff.)

15 In the edition the word '*alam* is vocalized–perhaps the vowels are in the MS. 'Banner of the things that are' is of course complete nonsense. '*Ilmu'l-kā'ināti*, 'knowledge of the future things' would at least make some sense–though not one fitting the context here.

16 Cf. F. Sarre, 'Die alt-orientalischen Feldzeichen', *Klio* (1903) 333ff.; A. Christensen, *Smeden Kāwäh og det gamle persiske rigsbanner* ('The smith Kāwa and the old Persian imperial banner') (Copenhagen 1919); idem, *L'Iran sous les Sassanides*, 502-4.

17 Al-Tabarī, I, 2175, 2337; al-Masʿūdī, *Murūj al-Dhahab*, IV, 200, 224; idem, *al-Tanbīh wa'l-Ishrāf*, 86. Other descriptions are reproduced by Christensen, *L'Iran.*

18 Goldziher, 164n.3, quotes examples of this feature, which also occurred in the book against the Arabs written by the Sāmānid vizier al-Jayhānī (quoted by Abu Ḥayyān al-Tawḥīdī, *al-Imtāʿ wa'l-Mu'ānasa*, I, 79).

19 See for these occasional verses M. Qazwīnī, '*Qadīmtarīn shiʿr-i Fārsī*', *Bīst Maqāla*, Teheran 1332 A.H. solar, 34-45; G. Lazard, *Les premiers poètes persans* (Teheran-Paris 1964), I, 10-11 (with further references). I find myself in agreement with Lazard that 'ces pièces, d'allure populaire, ne sont pas composées selon les principes de la métrique quantitative, sur le modèle arabe, qui sera celle de la poésie iranienne classique, mais dans le système probablement accentuel de la poésie iranienne préislamique: ce sont bien plutôt des vestiges de cette tradition ancienne que les prémices de la poésie persane proprement dite.' I would only add that (as has been already pointed out by Qazwīnī) these occasional ditties are not literature in the proper sense of the word. It cannot be said of what kind were the Persian poems composed according to al-Ṭabarī, II, 1388, by the Ādharbayjānī chief Muḥammad b. Baʿīth, who died in 235/849–50.

20 The poem composed according to ʿAwfī by a poet from Marw in 193/809 is either a fake or a later poem wrongly attributed to such an early period; see Lazard, p. 12 and the authorities quoted (to which add Barthold, in the *Bulletin of the School of Oriental Studies* (1921–3) 836-8.

21 Read: *Qad ammana'l-nāsa nakhwāhu, wa-ghurratuhū / satrun mina' llāhi* etc.

22 In Islamic writings this is a common term for Sāsānian music; see A. Christensen, *L'Iran sous les Sassanides*, 485, and my note in the *Journal of Jewish Studies* (1960) 183.

23 This is perhaps the meaning of ʿ*Arab wa-Tāziyān.*

24 Zunbīl was the title of the ruler of al-Rukhkhaj, who was defeated and killed by Ya'qūb in 250 A.H.; see the *History of Sīstān*, 205. The earlier accounts about the relations between Yaʿqūb and the Zunbīl (see the latest discussion in J. Marquart [and J. J. M. de Groot], 'Das Reich Zābul und der Gott Zūn vom 6.–9. Jahrhundert', *Festschrift Eduard Sachau* (Berlin 1915), 272-4) need drastic revision in the light of the information provided by the *History of Sīstān*; I hope to do this on another occasion.

25 ʿAmmār the Khārijite was killed in 251/895.

26 Yaʿqūb captured Herat and received letters of appointments from the Ṭāhirid Muḥammad b. Ṭāhir in 253.

27 For translations and commentaries on the poem see Ch. Rempis, 'Die ältesten Dichtungen in Neupersisch', *Zeitschrift der deutschen morgenländischen Gesellschaft* (1951), 220ff. (whose suggestions at emendation

are, however, too adventurous); G. Lazard, *Les premiers poètes persans* (Teheran-Paris 1964) I, 54.

28 This is a difficult half-line. I propose to read *chūn palang*, but have no suggestion for *blt'm*, though I assume that something like 'with a jump (or: noise)' is contained in it.

29 Allusions to the Koran, xl, 16 ('To whom belongs the kingdom on that day? To God') and ii, 250 ('How often a small party was victorious over a large one, with God's permission').

30 'Ammār's body and head were hanged on these two gates of the city of Zaranj, the capital of Sijistān.

31 See for Ḥanẓala, Lazard, 17-18, and the references given there.

32 The passage is on pp. 122-4 in the edition by H. F. al-Hamdani (Cairo 1957).

33 Ibn Fāris writes in the second half of the fourth/tenth century (*al-Ṣāḥibī* (Cairo 1910) 42-3; (Beirut 1963) 77; cf. Goldziher, *Muhammedanische Studien*, I, 214 = English trans., I, 197): 'Some people, however, whose reports must be left alone [i.e. the Shu'ūbites] believe that the philosophers also (i.e. the Greeks) possess *i'rāb* and grammatical works; but little importance can be attached to such stories. . . . They also claim that those peoples have poetry; we have read these poems ourselves and have found that they are unimportant, of little beauty, and lack a proper metre. Verily, poetry is to be found only with the Arabs who preserved their historical memories in poetical works. The Arabs have the science of prosody which distinguishes a regular poem from a defective one.' The passages of Abū Ḥātim al-Rāzī and the *History of Sīstān* provide good parallels to this text and prove that the argument that only the Arabs possessed poetry was common amongst the opponents of the Shu'ūbiyya.

34 For ancient Persian poetry cf. M. Boyce, 'The Parthian *Gōsān* and Iranian Minstrel Tradition', *Journal of the Royal Asiatic Society* (1957) 10ff. I do not wish to deny the possibility that some of the anti-Shu'ūbite authors might have based their judgement on actual knowledge of ancient Persian poems.

35 For statements by later authors about the absence of proper poetry in ancient Iran cf. Boyce, 38-9. Of special interest are the comments of Gurgānī, who in the eleventh century produced a version in classical Persian of the old poem of *Wīs u-Rāmīn*.

36 *Book of Poetry and Poets*, ed. de Goeje, 137.

37 Since the Arabic letter *bā'* can stand for both *b* and *p*, it is impossible to decide whether Ibn Qutayba pronounced the word *padh*, or in a more advanced manner *badh*; and conversely, whether Abū Ḥātim said *ba*, or in a more archaic manner *pa*. Moreover, *ba* may be due to copyists, and Abū Ḥātim may have written *badh*, i.e. *padh* or *badh*.

J. STEWART-ROBINSON

ʿAhdī and his Biography of Poets

While most of the Ottomans who composed biographies of poets known as *tez̤kere-i şuʿarā* (hereafter tezkere) are featured in relatively recent reference works, ʿAhdī is not.[1] This oversight may be explained by the fact that he is not considered important enough a literary figure to be included in up-to-date publications in constant use by students of Islamic or Ottoman culture. As a native of Baghdad, somewhat removed from the more important cultural centres of the Ottoman Empire, he may be considered by some as being a 'provincial' who is not worthy of any special consideration. Or, as may well be the case, he has escaped the attention of those who are responsible for the selection of material for inclusion in encyclopaedias and other works of reference. This article is therefore submitted with the purpose of making available to those who are interested all the details presently available on ʿAhdī. The information presented here has to be qualified as provisional until more research on the life and work of this author fills in the gaps in our knowledge and places him in proper perspective vis-à-vis the littérateurs of his age. That ʿAhdī deserves even a tentative notice in print is justified by the many references to him and to his work in books, monographs and articles devoted to the literary history of the Ottomans until the third quarter of the sixteenth century by Ottomanists especially in Turkey.

As shown elsewhere,[2] the Ottomans began to produce compilations of the biographies of the poets during the so-called golden age of the Ottoman Empire when Sehī of Edirne launched the genre among the Ottomans in 954 AH with his *Heşt Bihişt*.[3] Chronologically, ʿAhdī's contribution to this genre in Ottoman literature is the third oldest among some twenty-four similar works so far identified.

It is not inconceivable that when Süleyman the Magnificent entered Baghdad in the late autumn of the year 941, ʿAhdī was among the curious spectators who lined the streets of the city to catch a glimpse of the ruler of the Ottomans who were to have at least partial control of the province of Iraq for the next three centuries. Next to nothing is known about ʿAhdī, whose given name was Aḥmed.[4] Almost all the biographical details concerning him have to be gleaned from the introduction to his only work and from casual remarks he makes, here and there, within the biographical notices on the poets he includes in it.[5] With very few notable exceptions, the subsequent biographers of ʿAhdī made use of the same source.

There is little doubt that Aḥmed, who chose the pseudonym of ʿAhdī, was at least a resident of Baghdad if not an actual native of the city. His use of the word *vaṭan* with reference to Baghdad[6] does suggest that he had strong emotional ties with the city, but this in no way means that he was born there. His close identity with Baghdad is undoubtedly established by the fact that he is known in most of the sources as ʿAhdī-yi Bağdādī. His father was Şemsī of Baghdad, a member of the *ʿülemā* class, who is described as an ardent *şīʿī* and to whom are ascribed three unspecified *meşnevīs*. He is thought to have died in 975.[7] His son devotes a short notice to him in which he treats him in much the same way he treats the other biographees in his work. In it we are told that Şemsī, in addition to the *meşnevīs* which are here said to have been dedicated to Süleyman the Magnificent, had collected a *dīvān* containing the usual *ġazels* and *ḳaṣīdes*.[8] Other members of the family mentioned either by ʿAhdī himself in his biography of the poets or by other sources include (1) A certain ʿAbdülmelik al-Bağdādī who is identified as Şemsī's father[9]; (2) An uncle whose given name may have been Ḥüsnī but is identified by ʿAhdī as Ḥüseynī who appears to have been a wandering *dervīş* and to have died in 985[10]; (3) An elder brother of Ahdī's, Riżā'ī, who associated with poets and wits, and often left his native land for trading purposes until he died in 963[11]; (4) A younger brother, Murādī, who was still alive in 970[12]; (5) Rindī, a cousin, presumably the son of Ḥüseynī, who is credited with a *dīvān* and original *muʿammās*, and whose date of death is given, either by ʿAhdī or his copyist, as 993.[13]

Apart from the bare facts on his ancestry and a few inconsequential details concerning his sojourn in Anatolia, we have access to no other materials which allow us to reconstruct the biography of the subject of this article. There is no information on the date or place of his birth, the type of education which he must have received, the career which he pursued, his personal characteristics, or the date and place of his death. As indicated above, almost all that we know about ʿAhdī is to be found in his only known work, the *Gülşen-i Şuʿarā*. Some of the references to himself are derived by inference and, so far, are unverified. Statements such as, 'The compiler of this tezkere having acquired and completed much knowledge from him . . .' in the notice on a certain 'Ārifī of Yenişehir who was apparently not known by anyone else, could mean that 'Ārifī was one of his teachers who gave him some instruction in the sciences of the times, or simply that there was an exchange of views between the two men which proved beneficial to 'Ahdī.[14] The imprecision of similar declarations made in other instances in the work render the identification of his mentors and the nature of his studies impossible to determine. Other statements of this variety are made with references to poets and learned men whom 'Ahdī met during his extended stay in Anatolia between 960 and 971. According to his own testimony, the author of the *Gülşen-i Şu'arā* set out on his journey to Rūm in 960 accompanied by a friend described as a poet by the name of Ḫusrev.[15] The two travellers went from place to place in Rūm, we are told, along the roads fraught with danger, sometimes journeying with or calling on and meeting, the young and the old residents of the area, mendicants and sultans. After having seen new sites and thereby increased their knowledge, they finally reached Istanbul. Nowhere in the very brief account of the journey, as it is included in the *muḳaddime*, does 'Ahdī identify the towns he visited or the people whose acquaintance he made. However, in some of the biographical notices the compiler seems to make a special effort to mention the name of at least three large urban centres where he met the individuals whose biographies he is presenting. As a result, we know that he visited at least Bursa and Edirne in addition to Istanbul. Among the many biographees whom 'Ahdī claims to have met personally we may cite Pervīz Efendi (ff. 21a-22a),[16] Rıżā'ī Efendi (ff. 28a-29a),[17] Ḫātemī (ff. 73b-74a),[18] Mecdī (ff. 156a-157a),[19] and Nev'ī (ff. 168b-170a).[20] Throughout the tezkere, therefore, one tends to gain the impression that the journey into Anatolia and the long tour of the area were undertaken primarily for the purpose of study through social and intellectual intercourse with some of the literati who resided there. In 971 'Ahdī was back in Baghdad where he decided to collect, in the form of a tezkere, all the information he had acquired, through hearsay, at first hand by means of personal interviews, and by way of study, on the poets of Rūm.

Unlike his two predecessors in this branch of literary endeavour, and indeed most of his successors, 'Ahdī does not give the conventional reasons for undertaking this task. He does not seem to have been particularly concerned about serving posterity by preserving the details relating to the lives of the poets or by collecting their literary products as other tezkere writers claim.[21] It is again by reading between ʿAhdī's lines that we may infer that the compilation of the *Gülşen-i Şuʿarā* was prompted by a seemingly sincere desire to make a contribution to Ottoman literary history as a token of appreciation to the people of Anatolia and Istanbul. ʿAhdī's great admiration for Rūm and its inhabitants, and the fact that at every opportunity he refers to the kindness and hospitality shown him during the decade he spent there seems to support this suggestion. Furthermore, in addition to saying that he is dedicating the work to Prince Selīm, ʿAhdī states that he is making a present of it to the young and old of Baghdad.[22] He may, therefore, have had a dual reason for undertaking to write a tezkere: to thank the residents of Rūm and to inform the citizens of Baghdad.

There is almost no information available concerning ʿAhdī after his return home. A subsequent tezkere writer, Meḥmed Riyāżī of Istanbul who composed his own work in 1018, records that his father Birgili Muṣṭafā b. Meḥmed, while in service in Baghdad, was presented with a *ḳaṣīde* by ʿAhdī.[23] Since the appointment of Birgili Muṣṭafā as *ḳāẓī* of Baghdad occurred in 989, we know that ʿAhdī was in that city and alive at that time.[24] The next and last reasonably reliable recorded reference to ʿAhdī is given by the historian ʿAlī who states that when he arrived in Baghdad in 993/994 to take up his duties as *defterdār*, he was presented with *ḳaṣīdes*, *ġazels*, and *tā'riḫs* by some thirty local poets among whom were ʿAhdī,[25] Ṭarzī[26] and Rūḥī.[27] None of the early sources supply the date of ʿAhdī's death. Riyāżī is the only tezkere writer, once again, who says that he died towards the end of the reign of Murād III which came in 1004. Meḥmed Şüreyyā's statement that the biographer died in 1002 may be correct but the original source of this statement is not known.[28]

While ʿAhdī is well represented in anthologies, and several of his *ġazels* are featured in *mecmuʿas*, he is remembered chiefly as the compiler of a biography of poets rather than as a poet. As already indicated his tezkere bears the special title of *Gülşen-i Şuʿarā*, the sum of the numerical value of each of whose letters comes to 971, the date the work was compiled. It comprises a *muḳaddime*, three or four *ravẓas* (sections) and a *tetemme* (addendum).

The *muḳaddime* opens with the traditional eulogies to God, the Prophet and the reigning Süleyman the Magnificent. Then follows a separate eulogy to Prince Selīm who replaced Süleyman three years later and to whom the work is dedicated. The rest of the introduction is devoted to a brief account of the author's journey into Anatolia, his sojourn in Istanbul, and, finally, a note about the parts of which the tezkere is composed. This section of the work ends with another eulogy on Selīm followed by a chronogram indicating the completion of the *Gülşen-i Şuʿarā* as 971.

The contents of the tezkere are arranged into four parts in the manuscript used in the preparation of this article, but there are apparently recensions organized in three parts in which the third and fourth are merged.[29] The parts deal with the following categories: (1) *Sulṭāns*, *şehzādes* and statesmen; (2) The *ʿülemā* class; (3) The *sancāḳbeys* and *defterdārs*; (4) The poets, constituting by far the largest part of the entire work.

The addendum contains an index of personal names, the conventional method of calling attention to the fact that the work is honoured by the inclusion in it of the name of the heir-apparent Selīm and those of the members of the *ʿülemā*, and that it is further rendered distinguished by the many fine poems included in it. The work ends with the customary apologies for errors and shortcomings, and a humble request for a prayer for the author.[30]

ʿAhdī gives the impression, in the introduction and throughout the biographical notices making up the work, that all the biographical details he furnishes on the poets were acquired either directly from the poets concerned or, indirectly, from others who knew them or had heard about them. A search for internal evidence that he used material borrowed from written sources or that he made use of the two tezkeres which preceded the appearance of his, yields very little to prove the contrary.[31] However, remarks and poetic samples included in the notices on ʿIşḳī,[32] Ḳandī,[33] Ḳudsī[34] and Helākī[35] strongly suggest that ʿAhdī had before him Sehī's *Heşt Bihişt* and the *Tezkere* of Laṭīfī,[36] or perhaps a source common to all three works, while preparing the draft of the *Gülşen-i Şuʿarā*. He appears to have made greater use of the *Heşt Bihişt* which he does not mention anywhere and the author of which he does not even include in the section on the poets – at least not in the recension used here – than the *Tezkere* of Laṭīfī which he describes as unsuccessful because of its parochialism.[37]

ʿAhdī's style, throughout the work, is simple, usually to the point and devoid of the artistry, often very tiresome and obscure, displayed in some of the subsequent works of this nature. While his apparent Persian background allows him to make full use of attractive and picturesque language, the frequent repetition of words suggests a limited vocabulary.

The judgements of later critics are generally favourable. They all express surprise at his achievement despite his 'persianism'. ʿĀşıḳ Çelebi says that his tezkere is 'well-studied' and that the author is frank about the poets of Rūm.[38] Ḳınālızāde, who is copied by Beyānī finds his poetry '*rūmī*' and masterly, which he thinks is rare among Persians.[39] ʿĀlī says that he attempted to write a tezkere of the poets of Rūm forgetting that he was Persian.[40] Riyāżī, who refrains from making any personal remarks, says that, because it was not acceptable to the hard-to-please, the tezkere 'was laid in the corner of oblivion'.[41]

The *Gülşen-i Şuʿarā* numbers among the shorter of the works of this type and the biographical detail contained in it is meagre. On the other hand it may be considered as a useful Ottoman source for the poets who flourished in the Eastern fringes of the Ottoman Empire. Furthermore, the author's travels in Anatolia allowed him to hear of and meet several poets who lived there, but who never found a place in other tezkeres.

NOTES

1 He was not included in any of the versions of the first edition of the *Encyclopaedia of Islam* and has been omitted from the second edition. Curiously enough, even the *İslâm Ansiklopedisi* which makes a point of giving more thorough coverage to matters pertaining to Ottoman culture also has no article devoted to him. It should be noted that reference works dating back to the nineteenth century and to the early years of the present century do include some material on him.

A brief communication dealing with portions of this article which was completed thanks to a grant from the Center for Near Eastern and North African Studies of the University of Michigan, was read before the American Oriental Society in New York in 1958.

2 For an introduction to this literary genre among the Ottomans see, J. Stewart-Robinson, 'The Ottoman Biographies of Poets', in *Journal of Near Eastern Studies*, XXIV (January-April 1965) 57-74.

3 Edirneli Sehī, *Teẕkere-i Sehī* (Istanbul 1325) 141-4; *İslâm Ansiklopedisi*, cüz 104, 316-20.

4 Riyāżī ('Riyāż aş-Şuʿarā', Nuruosmaniye MS, 3724, f. 112a) is alone in saying that it was Mehdī.

5 The biographical details on ʿAhdī presented here come from the British Museum Manuscript Add. 7876 (hereafter, Ah). In certain cases, attempts have been made to verify these details against other manuscripts housed in various libraries in Istanbul. Until a complete check of all existing manuscripts can be made, the details given here will regrettably and inevitably have to remain tentative.

6 Ah, f. 5b.

7 Ṣādiḳī-yi Kitābdār, *Teẕkire-i Mecmaʿ al-Ḫavvāṣ* (Tabriz 1327) 281 and 295. See also, Riyāżī, op. cit. f. 89b, and ʿAbbās al-ʿAzzāwī, *Tāʾrīḫ al-Baġdād* (Baghdad 1949) IV, 117 and 263.

8 Ah, ff. 105a-b.

9 ʿAzzāwī, op. cit., 111.

10 Ah, ff. 69a-b. See also, Abdülkadir Karahan, *Fuẓūlî: Muhiti, hayatî ve şahsiyeti* (Istanbul 1949) 61-2, where he is identified as Hüsnü. This is probably the same person mentioned by ʿAzzāwī, op. cit., 136.

11 Ah, ff. 91b-92a; ʿAzzāwī, op. cit., 103-4.

12 Ah, ff. 167a-b. See also, J. von Hammer-Purgstall, *Geschichte des Osmanischen Dichtkunst* (Pesth 1836) II, 526.

13 Ah, ff. 92a-b. See also, Hammer-Purgstall, op. cit., 423.

14 Ah, f. 133b, '*Rāḳim-i teẕkere ḫākpāyindan çok maʿārif taḥṣil ü tekmil idüb* ...'.

15 Ibid., f. 4b. The name of this travelling companion is incorrectly given as Şerīfī by Charles Rieu who appears to have confused the adjective *şerīfī* as the man's name (See *Catalogue of Turkish Manuscripts in the British Museum* (London 1888), 76b). The companion's name is unmistakably identified by ʿAhdī in an enigma the answer to which is very conveniently given. The enigma (*muʿammā*) is as follows:

چشم كريانده خيال قدك اى سرو روان : سرو بتمش ارەسنده جو مثاليدر همان

The solution would appear to be: جو is like خو and in the midst of it a سرو has almost grown, i.e. the insertion of سرو in between the خ and the و results in the needed word خسرو.

16 ʿAṭā'ī, *Ẕeyl-i Şaḳā'iḳ un-Nuʿmāniye* (Istanbul 1268), 253. Was *ḳāżī* of Baghdad while ʿAhdī was still there from 955 to 957. The two men could have met later when Pervīz was *ḳāżī* of Edirne from 965 to 968.

17 ʿAṭā'ī, op. cit., 245. ʿAhdī may have met him while he was *müderris* at Bursa in 967.

18 ʿĀşıḳ Çelebi, 'Meşāʿir uş-Şuʿarā', British Museum MS, Or. 6434, f. 251b. ʿAhdī met him both in Edirne and in Istanbul.

19 ʿAṭā'ī, op. cit., 334. This is the translator of the original *Şaḳā'iḳ* with whom ʿAhdī had several meetings in Bursa, Edirne and Istanbul.

20 ʿAṭā'ī, 418. Father of ʿAṭā'ī who met ʿAhdī in Edirne and Istanbul.

21 Stewart-Robinson, op. cit., 62-3.

22 Ah,, f. 6b.

23 Riyāżī, op. cit., f. 112a where the *maṭlaʿ* of the *ḳaṣīde* in question is recorded. This presentation is also said to have led to friendship between the two men.

24 ʿAṭā'ī, 295-6, where we are told that either in the same year or early in the following Birgili Muṣṭafā was transferred to Tripoli. The fact that Riyāżī's father and ʿAhdī met in Baghdad in 989 disproves Kātib Çelebi's statement that the biographer died in 980, see *Keşf uẓ-Ẓunūn* (Istanbul 1941), I, 387.

25 'Künh ül-Aḫbār' Süleymaniye MS, Esad Efendi 2162, f. 500a. In the reference just cited the date is actually given 940. This is clearly a

mistake since ʿĀlī was not born until 948 and Baghdad did not become an Ottoman city until 941. The correct date is to be found – until other recensions can be consulted – in a variety of secondary sources such as I. H. Uzunçarşılı, *Osmanlı Tarihi* (Ankara 1954) III, Pt. 2, 534; F. E. Karatay, *Topkapı Sarayı Müzesi Kütüphanesi Türkçe Yazmalar Kataloğu* (Istanbul 1961) II, 126 where item No. 2357 – ʿĀlī's 'Cāmī al-buḥūr der mecālis-i sūr' – is given as composed in 994 while the author was *defterdār* of Baghdad. See also, Ah, ff. 39a-41b; ʿAzzāwī, op. cit., 117 and 263.

26 Ah, f. 119a.

27 Probably Rūḥī-yi Baġdādī who died in 1014. Cf. Ah, ff. 87a-b; E. J. W. Gibb, *A History of Ottoman Poetry* (London 1903) III, 186-93; Bursalı Meḥmed Ṭāhir, *ʿOṣmānlı Müʾellifleri* (Istanbul 1333) II, 182-3.

28 Gibb, op. cit. 8; Riyāżī, op. cit. f. 112a; S̱üreyyā, *Sicill-i ʿOṣmānī* (Istanbul 1311), III, 609.

29 Kātib Çelebi, op. cit., I, 387. See also, S. N. Ergun, *Türk Şairleri* (Istanbul n.d.) I, 261.

30 Ah, ff. 1b-7a (*Muḳaddime*), ff. 7a-19b (Part I), 19b-33b (Part II), 33b-43a (Part III), ff. 43a-184b (Part IV), and ff. 184b-7a (*Tetemme*).

31 For the principal sources used by the tezkere writers see, Stewart-Robinson, op. cit., 65-7.

32 Compare Ah, f. 130b with Sehī, op. cit., 136 where, in addition to similarity in language, the only two poems given by Sehī are to be found in ʿAhdī.

33 Ah, 145b, Sehī, 135, Laṭīfī 275. ʿAhdī gives five *beyts* for Ḳandī, two are the only *beyts* given by Sehī and the other three are a *tāʾrīḫ* given by Laṭīfī.

34 Ah, 146a and Sehī 134. As well as a resemblance in statement, both authors give the same one and only *beyt*.

35 Ah, 180a and Sehī, 136 where statements are rather close and the only two *beyts* given by Sehī are the only two to be found in ʿAhdī.

36 Gibb, op. cit., III, 161; *İslâm Ansiklopedisi*, VII, 19-22. See also, Laṭīfī, *Teẕkeret uş-Şuʿarā* (Istanbul 1314).

37 Ah, f. 152b.

38 ʿĀşıḳ Çelebi, op. cit., f. 176b.

39 Ḳınālızāde, 'Teẕkeret uş-Şuʿarā', British Museum MS, Add. 24957, f. 203b; Beyānī, 'Teẕkeret uş-Şuʿarā', Millet Kütüphanesi MS, Ali Emiri Efendi 757, f. 131.

40 ʿĀlī, op. cit., f. 500a.

41 Riyāżī, op. cit., f. 112b.

W. MONTGOMERY WATT

God's Caliph
Qur'ānic Interpretations and Umayyad Claims

I. The meaning of khalīfa in the Qur'ān

The semantic development of the Arabic root KH.L.F is fascinating in its width.[1] The basic meaning is presumably 'behind' (in place), but this easily passes into 'behind' (in time) or 'after'. The phrase *khalafa-hu* may mean 'he came after him', 'he seized him from behind' or 'he spoke (evil) of him behind his back' and so 'he deceived him'. Intransitively used the word can mean 'to fall behind', literally or metaphorically; thus *khalafa 'an khuluq abī-hi* is 'he was altered (for the worse) from the natural disposition of his father'. The last is not far from the meaning of 'differed' which is prominent in the eighth stem. In such a phrase as *ikhtilāf al-layl wa-n-nahār* 'the alternation of night and day', the eighth stem means 'following reciprocally', and this leads both to 'going to and fro' or 'frequenting' and 'being different'. Similarly the third stem may mean 'to oppose', as well as 'to go to a woman when her husband is absent'. The fourth stem is associated with failing to keep promises. Several different forms have meanings connected with drawing water, apparently because in a caravan those who go to draw water leave behind their goods beside the caravan. Finally the man who comes after another may act on his behalf as a substitute or deputy. This last sense is one that will receive more attention in what follows.

The singular *khalīfa* is found twice in the Qur'ān, once applied to Adam and once to David. The latter is in 38.26/5; 'O David, we have made thee a *khalīfa* in the earth; so judge between men with truth, and do not follow (personal) inclination so that it leads you astray from the way of God . . .'. The context gives no help. In the story of how Adam told the angels the names of things there occur the words (2.30/28): 'Thy Lord said to the angels, "I am making in the earth a *khalīfa*"; they said "Wilt thou make in it one (or "those") who will act corruptly and shed blood, whereas we glorify thee with thy praises and hallow thee?"' The commentators had to deal with a hard problem in discussing these verses. If they emphasized the element of succession in *khalīfa*, they had to say who was being succeeded; but if they said a *khalīfa* was a deputy, was he God's deputy? Apart from other considerations several commentators were anxious to avoid approving the Umayyad caliphs' use of the verse about Adam to enhance their own dignity (a point explained below).

In 38.26/5 Jalālayn have no objection to interpreting *khalīfa* simply as one who will direct the affairs of the people' while in 2.30/28 it is one 'who will deputize for me in executing my judgements in it (the earth)'. For 38.26/5 aṭ-Ṭabarī gives only one meaning, 'a successor of the messengers before him as an arbiter between the people'. Az-Zamakhsharī gives a meaning like this in the second place, but puts in first place one like Jalālayn though carefully phrased to express subordination: 'we made thee a deputy (*istakhlafnā-ka*) over the kingdom (*mulk*) in the earth', in the same way as a particular sultan made someone a deputy over a particular land; that is, he has only a part of the sultan's authority. With this qualification az-Zamakhsharī is prepared to accept the phrase 'God's caliphs in his earth'. Al-Bayḍāwī gives the two interpretations briefly without the qualification and without any mention of 'God's caliph'.

Aṭ-Ṭabarī has a long discussion of 2.30/28. First he mentions and rejects a view of Ibn-Is'ḥāq's that *khalīfa* means 'one who settles in or inhabits' (*sākin*, *'āmir*); he also speaks of the earth as having been previously inhabited by jinn, so that Adam is the *khalīfa* or 'successor' of the jinn. Next comes the view of al-Ḥasan al-Baṣrī that *khalīfa* means 'a posterity who will succeed one another'; this avoids the two problems mentioned and the difficulty that Adam as a prophet could not 'act corruptly and shed blood'; but the meaning of *khalīfa* can hardly be supported. The chief remaining view is the one he attributes to Ibn-'Abbās and Ibn-Mas'ūd that the *khalīfa* is 'one who will deputize for me in judgement between my creatures'. Aṭ-Ṭabarī's own definition, given at the beginning, is 'one who takes a person's position after him in respect of something'. With this definition *khalīfa* here could mean either 'a successor to the angels' or 'God's deputy'. Az-Zamakhsharī is not dissimilar. He prefers the interpretation that Adam and his progeny are to succeed the angels, but mentions as a possibility the interpretation that Adam is 'God's deputy'. He also notes a variant reading *khalīqa*. There is nothing to commend this reading; it seems to be a feeble attempt to avoid the difficulties raised by the usual text. (The reading is not among the variants listed by Arthur Jeffery in *Materials for the History of the Text of the Qur'ān*, Leiden, 1937.)

Before attempting to decide which of these meanings was conveyed to the first hearers of the Qur'ānic verses by the word *khalīfa*, there are some further points to be noticed about the use of the root in the Qur'ān. Prominent in general in the Qur'ān is the thought that contemporary communities live where other communities previously lived which have now disappeared, destroyed by God because of their disobedience. This seems to be the image behind the instances of *khalā'if* and *khulafā'*, plurals of *khalīfa*. It is seen most clearly in 10.14/15 where God, addressing the Meccans says 'We have made you *khalā'if* in the earth after them (*sc.* previous generations which have passed away) to see how you would act'. In 7.69/7 and 74/2 one community is said to have been made *khulafā'* after another. The remaining four instances of these words, however, though they could be interpreted in this way, leave the previous people or community unspecified: 'he it is who made you *khalā'if* of the earth, and raised some above others in rank' (6.165); 'we saved (Noah) and those with him in the ship and made them *khalā'if*' (10.73/4); 'he makes you *khulafā'* of the earth' (27.62/3); 'he made you *khalā'if* in the earth' (35.39/7).

All these instances may thus be referred to the image of a present-day community living where others had lived previously. The phrase 'in the earth' or 'in the land', if not in the text, is always implied. Since the people succeeded are left vague in four instances, the original meaning may not have been far from the 'inhabitants' or 'settlers' suggested by Ibn-Is'ḥāq. A similar emphasis is found in certain other forms from the same root. In 7.129/6 and 11.57/60 *istakhlafa* means 'make successors' of people who are mentioned; but in 24.55/4 it makes an excellent sense when translated 'settled', viz. 'God has promised those of you who have believed ... that he will *settle* them in the earth as he *settled* those before them, and will establish for them their religion'. The Arabic word, it may be allowed, has a connotation of 'in succession to others', but sometimes this is so slight that it may apparently be neglected in translation.

Another image associated with the root is that of one man performing some function after and as a substitute for another; e.g. where a man (or God) takes the place of a father of a family who has died. It is also used of a man going to a woman and occupying the place of an absent husband. This sense is found in the Qur'ān in 7.142/38, where Moses says to Aaron, 'Deputize for me (*ukhluf-ni*) among my people, and act well'. Along with the idea of performing a function, there is the connotation of exercising authority. The word appears to be used for 'viceroy' in a South Arabian inscription dated 543.[2]

Finally there is a verse where the root has the meaning of succession together with engaging in different activity from that of the person succeeded. After the incident of the calf Moses says to the Israelites, 'Bad is your "deputizing" for me after me' (*bi'sa-mā khalaftumū-nī ba'dī*). This appears to show that a man may be called a 'successor' or 'deputy' although his activity differs from that of his predecessor. This is in accordance with az-Zamakhsharī's insistence that the *khalīfa* appointed by a sultan had powers far inferior to those of a sultan. In the early tenth century *khalīfa* could still be applied to an assistant, and presumably inferior, teacher.[3]

This review of the usage of the root gives a basis for a conclusion about the original meaning of *khalīfa* in the two Qur'ānic passages. As applied to David, the word would appear to mean 'a person exercising authority', and to have only the slightest suggestion of succeeding someone else, or God, in this function. In the passage about Adam (2.30/28) the matter is not so clear. On the whole it would seem that the meaning is that Adam was made a settler in the earth but also exercised some authority, namely, in instructing the angels. His activity on earth might be thought of as following on the activity of God in creating animals, plants and angels; but succession is not emphasized. Neither is there any emphasis on his deputizing for God. If there is any suggestion of this it is balanced by the implication that his activity and God's are different.

There is also a further conclusion which is strongly supported by this study, though it may also be held on independent grounds. This is that the choice of the word *khalīfa* as a title for Abū-Bakr when he became head of state in succession to Muḥammad was not based on Qur'ānic usage or even influenced by it, but was derived from the use of the word in secular affairs. It has been doubted whether Abū-Bakr in fact used the title *khalīfat rasūl Allāh*, but there is no good reason for rejecting the standard view. From the present study it is seen that the title meant primarily 'successor of the Messenger of God', with a secondary connotation of exercising some authority. This was helpfully vague and permitted the development of the office. It is virtually certain that it did not connote 'deputy', though it might have suggested 'substitute' or 'replacement'. The report that Abū-Bakr was invited to take the title of *khalīfat Allāh*, but refused, cannot be genuine, since there was no question of him succeeding God or of deputizing for him. This point will become clearer in the next section.

2. The Umayyad claims to the caliphate

The difficulties in interpreting the word *khalīfa* experienced by the early Muslim scholars were partly due to the fact that the Umayyad dynasty did what it could to build up the position of caliph, and in particular used the Qur'ānic passage about Adam (2.30/28).[4] This matter will be seen in better perspective after considering how the Umayyads themselves stated their claims. For the most part scholars have accepted anti-Umayyad assertions current under the ʿAbbāsids. Virtually no use has been made, for example, of the pro-Umayyad material contained in the works of the poets Jarīr and al-Farazdaq.[5] The material has to be carefully used, for often there is excessive adulation: the mothers of Walīd I and Yazīd II are compared to the sun and the Virgin Mary respectively[6]; Sulaymān is called Mahdī[7]; the caliph in general is said to be almost a prophet.[8] Yet by considering what has a degree of realism, and what corresponds to statements of opponents, we can form some idea of the arguments used by the Umayyads to justify the monopoly of the caliphate in their family.

The main claim appears to have been that the Umayyad family, and in particular the Marwānid branch, had inherited the caliphate from ʿUthmān.

> 'They (the Umayyads) are the trustees (*awliyā'*) of ʿUthmān's heritage (*turāth*), – an apparel of *mulk* over them, not to be stripped off.'[9]

> 'The sons of Marwān inherited from him (the Caliphate), and from ʿUthmān after a momentous event.'[10]

An interesting verse addressed to Sulaymān regards this inheritance as being not simply in the family of Umayya, but in that of his grandfather (ʿAbd-) Manāf.

> 'You (pl.) have inherited the staff of *mulk*, not as distant relatives, from the two sons of Manāf, ʿAbd-Shams and Hāshim.'[11]

(ʿAbd-Shams was the father of Umayya.) This mention of Hāshim suggests an attempt to counter Shīʿite propaganda by asserting that the charisma of leadership was not restricted to the clan of Hāshim, but was transmitted in the wider clan-group of ʿAbd-Manāf. Another item of the charge against them was that they had seized the caliphate by force. To this the reply is that ʿUthmān from whom they have inherited the caliphate, gained it as a result of a decision by an official council.

> 'I saw that the *mulk* of the sons of Marwān had been firmly based by a true council of which their kinsman (*sc.* ʿUthmān) was one.'[12]

The same point is probably made in another verse addressed to Walīd I:

> 'A caliphate sprung from counsel without force.
> whose foundations the Merciful and Bountiful had firmly established.'[13]

This line of argument presumably goes back to Muʿāwiya who gave great prominence to his claim to be the avenger of blood for ʿUthmān. ʿAlī, though accepted as caliph by most of the Muslims, refused to take action against those of the murderers who were among his supporters. This probably strengthened Muʿāwiya's case at the Arbitration, and he presumably also made the most of the tendency for the heir and the avenger of blood to be one and the same.[14]

A subordinate line of argument is that the Umayyad family is worthy of the caliphate because it has many noble deeds to its credit.

'The caliphate, because of the fair deeds you have done,
is among you; its *mulk* will not be turned away (from you).'[15]

The noble acts are frequently made more specific as fighting on behalf of Islam.

'When the sons of Marwān meet (enemies), they unsheath
for God's religion angry swords
(And) sharp, by which they defend Islam;
the sword-blows fall only on the doubt-raisers.'[16]

The word *mulk* has been left untranslated because it appears to connote both 'kingship' and 'possession', with the emphasis sometimes on the one, sometimes on the other. Where *mulk* is closely associated with inheritance there is emphasis on possession; and part at least of the objection to Umayyad rule[17] seems to have been that it was something heritable, and indeed only to be inherited within the family. On the other hand, the Umayyads did not object to being called 'kings'. Yazīd II is described as

'The scion of kings (*mulūk*) in an inheritance (*mawārīth*) in which
not a king (*malik*) dies, but he bequeaths (*awratha*) a *minbar*'[18].

In the Qur'ān *mulk* has a similar double connotation. It may be that after the Umayyads had disappeared it was more tactful to emphasize the aspect of kingship, since the ʿAbbāsids also kept it as a possession within the family.

The second main line of argument is that the caliphate has been bestowed on the Umayyads by God:

'The earth is God's; he has entrusted it (*wallā-hā*) to his *khalīfa*: he who is head in it will not be overcome.'[19]

'God has garlanded you with the *khilāfa* and guidance; for what God decrees (*qaḍā*) there is no change.'[20]

This is more than a verbal compliment, for important religious functions are ascribed to the caliphs.

'We have found the sons of Marwān pillars of our religion as the earth has mountains for its pillars.'[21]

'Were it not for the caliph and the Qur'ān he recites, the people had no judgements established for them and no communal worship.'[22]

The ideas of the invincibility and unchanging character of the Umayyad caliphate lead on to the corollary of this assertion, namely, that disobedience to the caliph and his subordinate officers is a refusal to acknowledge God and so tantamount to unbelief. Al-Ḥajjāj is addressed as follows:

> 'You regard support of the Imam as a duty laid upon you; while they cover over their religion with doubt.'[23]

Al-Ḥajjāj, in dealing with the men taken prisoner in the rising of Ibn-al-Ash'ath, made them, before he would free them, confess that they were unbelievers; those who refused were executed.[24] In a poem the enemies of al-Ḥajjāj are referred to as 'opposing the religion of the Muslims'.[25] Other terms applied to the enemies of the Umayyads are *mulḥidūn*, *munāfiqūn*, *mushrikūn*, *kuffār*.[26]

In view of all this material, especially the phrase about God entrusting the earth to 'his *khalīfa*', it is not surprising to find the phrase *khalīfat Allāh* being used both by Jarīr and by a number of other persons.[27] In these cases the meaning must be 'the deputy appointed by God'. Goldziher's suggestion that 'God's caliph' meant 'the caliph or successor of the Prophet approved by God' is incompatible with the further material here presented.[28] The same scholar's earlier remarks[29] on the differing attitudes of the Umayyads and 'Abbāsids towards this title require some revision. He asserts that because of the more theocratic interpretation of the function of the ruler under the 'Abbāsids, this title and other similar ones like 'shadow of God on earth' were more frequently used; and he further maintains that, whereas for the Umayyads the title was an expression of their absolute power, for the 'Abbāsids it had a 'theocratic' (or perhaps rather 'theological') content. In view of the material quoted above and much other material from the Umayyad period in the historians, what Goldziher said about lack of theological content under the Umayyads is hardly convincing. A more serious objection to his remarks is that, while other titles with a reference to God become more frequent under the 'Abbāsids, the title of 'God's caliph' seems to be less frequently used. The evidence for this is not altogether clear, but the reduced frequency, besides being probable on the available evidence, is what might be expected in view of the points about to be made.[30]

A further point of great importance is contained in the report that al-Ḥajjāj asserted that the caliph was superior to angels and prophets and adduced in proof the Qur'ānic passage about God making Adam a *khalīfa* in the earth and enabling him to instruct the angels.[31] The story implies that by the time of al-Ḥajjāj *khalīfa* was being understood as 'deputy', and also shows that the Umayyads or their supporters produced theological reasons to justify their claims.

The familiar story that Abū-Bakr was addressed by the title *khalīfat Allāh* and objected to it, saying he was only the *khalīfa* of the Messenger of God is almost certainly an invention made to oppose the Umayyad claims (as are also some of the interpretations of the verse about Adam). We are told that the propriety of the title 'God's caliph' was discussed by scholars, and that on the whole they thought it improper.[32] The earliest version of it so far traced is that in the *Musnad* of Aḥmad ibn-Ḥanbal,[33] where the earliest source named in the *isnād* is Ibn-Abī-Mulayka. Since this man, who died in 735, was a *qāḍī* under Ibn-az-Zubayr during the latter's rebellion against the Umayyads,[34] the probability is that the story was invented in Mecca about this time.

From a modern historical standpoint the alleged absence of a theological justification for the Umayyad claim to the caliphate, cannot be regarded as a factor in the dynasty's downfall. It might perhaps be held that their theology contained an undue emphasis on pre-Islamic ideas of predestination. Yet the chief ideological failure must be that their primary claim to the caliphate was based on the Arab idea of blood-revenge, and the associated idea that the heir was the avenger of blood. The essentially Arab basis of their rule made it difficult for them to adjust the governmental institution to the needs of a vast empire.

NOTES

1 Cf. Lane, *Arabic-English Lexicon*, s.v.

2 Glaser, *Corpus Inscriptionum Himyariticarum*, no. 618, dated 543 ḍ.D. (quoted from R. Blachère, *Le Coran* (Paris 1949) II, 241n.).

3 Cf. Nöldeke-Schwally-Bergsträsser, *Geschichte des Qorans*, III, 148n.1; 210n.6; Ibn-Mujāhid had 84 assistants to whom the term *khalīfa* was applied. In Ottoman Turkish the word was applied to quite humble persons; cf. J. W. Redhouse, *Turkish-English Lexicon*, s.v.

4 See p. 571 below.

5 I am indebted for this material to a post-graduate student, Dr Awn ash-Sharif Qasim of Khartoum. The editions referred to are: Jarīr, *Dīwān* (Beirut 1960); al-Farazdaq, *Dīwān* (Beirut 1960, two vols.). These are indicated by 'J.' and 'F.' respectively.

6 F. I, 70, 144.

7 F. I, 264; cf. 262.

8 F. II, 282; I, 124.

9 F. I, 25.

10 F. I, 285.

11 F. II, 309. Banū 'Abd-Manāf are regarded as responsible for the blood of Muḥammad in Ibn-Hishām, 325.

12 F. I, 62.

13 F. II, 210.

14 In the passage from the *Musnad* mentioned in note 17, Abū-Bakr, 'Umar and 'Uthmān appear to have held a *khilāfat nubuwwa*, which was then followed by *mulk*. One wonders if this is derived from Umayyad propaganda which denied that 'Alī had ever been caliph.

15 J, 380.

16 F. I, 22.

17 Cf. Goldziher, *Muhammedanische Studien*, II, 31; also Aḥmad b. Ḥanbal, *Musnad*, v, 44, 50f., etc.

18 F. I, 348.

19 F. I, 24.

20 J, 380.

21 F. II, 76, addressing Sulaymān; the mountains are described as *awtād* in the Qur'ān.

22 J, 278.

23 J, 21.

24 Wellhausen, *Arab Kingdom*, 238; Ibn-Ḥajar, *Tahdhīb*, II, 210f.

25 J, 355.

26 F. I, 22; F. I, 47; F. II, 312; J, 195; etc. The opponents considered themselves *mu'minīn* (Ṭabarī, II, 1066).

27 Cf. J. 195, 210 f., 303; there are also phrases like *amīn Allāh* and *rā'ī Allāh*. Also Ḥassān b. Thābit, *Dīwān*, 98.15 (in elegy on 'Uthmān) or ed. H. Hirschfeld, XX, 9; *Aghānī*, XV, 6 (of 'Abd-al-Malik), XVIII, 71 (*banī khulafā' Allāh* used of Umayyads in presence of Mu'āwiya I); aṭ-Ṭabarī, II, 78.10 (used of Mu'āwiya I by the poet Ḥāritha b. Badr); al-Mas'ūdī, *Murūj*, v, 105 (of Mu'āwiya), 152 (of Yazīd I), 330 (of 'Abd-al-Malik).

28 I. Goldziher, 'Du sens propre des expressions Ombre de Dieu, Khalife de Dieu pour désigner les chefs dans l'Islam', *Revue de l'Histoire des Religions*, XXXV (1897) 331-8, esp. 337.

29 *Muhammedanische Studien*, II, 61.

30 *Aghānī*, III, 95.5; IX, 44.4; XXI, 28.5. *Al-'Iqd*, III, 30.3 (from foot), 32.14. Aṭ-Ṭabarī, III, 2177.9, in an edict of al-Mu'taḍid (regn. 892–902) the 'Abbāsids are called *khulafā' Allāh wa-a'immat al-hudā*. (The references here and in note 27, apart from J, are from *Muhammedanische Studien*, II, 61, but not all have been verified.) There are some instances of the use of the phrase for Ottoman and Indian rulers in T. W. Arnold, *The Caliphate* (Oxford 1924) 117, 157, 158. Khalīfa b. Khayyāṭ (d. 241/855) quotes the Khārijite al-Yashkurī as taunting the caliph

al-Mahdī with claiming to be 'caliph of God'. (*Ta'rīkh*, fol. 310, quoted from a London thesis by Farouk Omar; not in *GAL*.)

31 *Al-'Iqd* v, 332 f.

32 Al-Māwardī, *Statuts Gouvernementaux*, tr. Fagnan, 29 f.; cf. Ibn-Khaldūn, *Muqaddima*, tr. Rosenthal, I, 388 f.

33 I, 10.

34 Adh-Dhahabī, *Tadhkirat al-Ḥuffāẓ* (Hyderabad 1955) I, 101.